R. Edward Gosnell

The YearBook of British Columbia and Manual of provincial Information

R. Edward Gosnell

The YearBook of British Columbia and Manual of provincial Information

ISBN/EAN: 9783337186319

Printed in Europe, USA, Canada, Australia, Japan

Cover: Foto ©ninafisch / pixelio.de

More available books at **www.hansebooks.com**

ANNOUNCEMENT.

The publication of the Year Book of 1903, in its complete form, has, from one cause or another, been unavoidably much delayed. The principal chapters, dealing with Land and Agriculture, Timber, Fisheries and Mining, however, appeared some time ago in Bulletin form.

Other chapters have been brought fully up to date, and include the Election Returns, Trade and Navigation Statistics to the end of June 30th, 1903, and the Salmon Pack for the present year.

Considerable information intended for this edition, owing to limitations of space, has been left out. On account of the expense involved, another complete edition will not be published in 1904; but a brief supplement will be issued containing the Year's Statistics, and the information omitted, as referred to, and other matters of interest.

The present edition is intended mainly as a work of reference for libraries and other public institutions. The price to private individuals has been fixed at $1 per copy, including postage.

ERRATA.

"Columbia and Kootenay," first line 323, should be "Columbia and Western."

Under head of Municipal Aid, 324, an item of $40,000 by New Westminster City to Canadian Branch Line is omitted.

"Frenchbark Creek," second to last line, page 325, should be "French Bar Creek."

THE YEAR BOOK

- OF -

BRITISH COLUMBIA

- AND -

Manual of Provincial Information

- BY -

R. E. GOSNELL,

Secretary Bureau Provincial Information.

VICTORIA, B. C.
1903

PARLIAMENT BUILDINGS, VICTORIA, B. C.

INTRODUCTION.

THE Year Book of 1897 was undertaken as a private enterprise, with a view to the profits, if any, being applied to the Library of the Legislative Assembly. Owing to expense attaching to its publication and the delay occasioned in its printing, it proved a serious loss to the author. Later the unsold copies were purchased by the Government, and with an appendix added in 1901, bringing the edition up to date, they were distributed in various quarters through the Immigration Office.

As a medium of reliable information respecting the Province, the demand for copies has continued unabated; and as a consequence its regular continuance has been decided upon.

The present has been largely based on the edition of 1897, supplemented wherever possible by new information. Several entirely new chapters have been added. What has been kept in view is the kind of information that is mainly in demand.

In subsequent editions it is proposed to take up systematically the original sources of British Columbia history and devote 50 or 100 pages of the space each year to their exposition; and also to outline from time to time the political development, so as ultimately to present the unbroken record of events up to within a comparatively recent period.

Much of the information contained has also been issued in bulletin form for the use of those who are interested in special phases of the Province.

The author is under special obligation to deputy heads of various Government departments and to many others for assistance.

A special effort has been made to vary the illustrations as much as possible, and in this connection the very best photographs available were secured. The plates have been executed in the most artistic way possible, the object being to furnish views that are representative of the Province, as well as pleasing and interesting. In this respect the volume speaks for itself.

PHYSICAL CHARACTERISTICS

THE Province of British Columbia may be described as a great quadrangle of territory, 700 miles long by 400 miles wide, lying north of latitude 49 degrees and west of the central core of the Rocky Mountains, extending along the Pacific Coast as far as latitude 55 degrees, and including the islands adjacent. North of that degree of latitude it continues inland to latitude 60 degrees, but is shut off from the coast by a narrow strip of Alaskan territory, and is bounded on the east by longitude 120 degrees.

The southern half of the province lies between tolerably well defined boundaries. It forms a large and regular rhomboid of elevated land, which is supported on each side by ranges of mountains. Of these the eastern and western may be said to be double, and consist respectively of the Rockies and Selkirks on the east, and of the Coast and Island ranges on the west.

The easternmost range of the above enumerated is that of the Rocky Mountains. It is the northern extremity of the great range which forms so well-known a feature of the North American Continent. Entering the province at the 49th parallel of latitude, it constitutes the eastern boundary to latitude 54 degrees, and continues to between 56 and 57 degrees, where it loses its distinctive rampart-like character and dies down into lower hills. It has been shown to consist of the upturned edges of the strata that underlie the great northwest plain, and its massive walls are formed chiefly of Devonian and carboniferous limestone. The average height may be stated at about 8,000 feet. "Near the 49th parallel several summits occur with elevations exceeding 10,000 feet, but northwards few attain this elevation until the vicinity of the Bow River and Kicking Horse is reached. The range appears to culminate about the headwaters of the Saskatchewan, Mount Murchison being credited with an altitude of 13,500 feet." There are twelve principal passes, at elevations ranging from 7,100 feet — the south Kootenay — to 2,000 feet — the Peace River Valley.

Parallel to the Rocky Mountains proper, and frequently included under one name with them, though of distinct formation, run the Selkirks. This range, which has been shown by geologists to represent an earlier formation, and to exhibit an entirely different series of rocks, is so broken and complex as to have received several names in different parts of its course, as though composed of distinctly separate mountain systems. Such, however, is not the case.

Entering from the south in a three-fold system divided by important valleys, they are called respectively the Purcell, the Selkirk and the Gold Mountains. To the north of the great bend of the Columbia River these give place to the term Cariboo Mountains. At about latitude 54 degrees they die out, or are merged in the cross ranges which form the northern boundary of the interior plateau, and from whence spring the headwaters of the Peace River.

In average altitude these mountains are not greatly inferior to the Rockies, their loftier members rising from 8,000 to 9,000 feet above the sea. The contours are, generally speaking, more rounded and less precipitous than the latter, though in many places they are strikingly pointed with steep and continuous grades, down which snowslides sweep with resistless force. Their sides, up to several thousand feet, are clothed in dense forests, affording an unlimited supply of good timber.

The average width of the Rocky Mountain range is about 60 miles, diminishing to the north; that of the Selkirks is about 80 miles.

There is a valley of most remarkable length and regularity, extending from the southern boundary line along the western base of the Rocky Mountains as far as the northern limits of the Selkirks, a distance of over 700 miles, and dividing the two ranges.

To the west of these great ranges British Columbia extends in a wide plateau or table land, which has been originally elevated some 3,500 feet above sea level. This plateau has been, however, so deeply intersected and eroded by lake and river systems that in many places it presents an aspect hardly differing from that of mountain regions. At others, however, it opens out into wide plains and rolling ground, with comparatively low eminences, affording fine areas of agricultural and grazing land. The entire district has been subject to vast overflows of lava, of the disintegrated remains of which the present soil is mainly composed. There is a general but very gradual slope of the land from the mountainous country on the southern boundary of the province to the north, where, as has been previously stated, it is hedged in by cross ranges attaining an elevation of from 6,000 to 8,000 feet. Notwithstanding this general slope, the principal flow of water finds its way southwards through deep fissures penetrating the mountain boundaries on the southern and western sides. This plateau forms the chief agricultural area of the province. "The whole of British Columbia, south of 52 degrees and east of the Coast Range, is a grazing country up to 3,500 feet, and a farming country up to 2,500 feet, where irrigation is possible."— (Macoun, Geol. Rep., 1877.)

The interior plateau is terminated on the west by the Coast Range, a series of massive crystalline rocks of some 6,000 feet in average height. This range has a mean width of about 100 miles, descending to the shores of the Pacific, and is in turn flanked by the submerged Island Range, the tops of which form Vancouver and her adjacent islands, the Queen Charlotte Islands and those of the Alaskan peninsula.

"The most remarkable feature of the coast are the fiords and passages, which, while quite analogous to those of Scotland, Norway and Greenland, probably surpass those of any part of the world (unless it be the last-named country) in dimensions and complexity. The great height of the rugged mountain walls which border them also give them a grandeur quite their own."— (Dawson, Geol. Sur., 1884.)

The unique position of British Columbia as a watershed on the Pacific Coast of America will at once be recognized when it is seen that all the rivers of great importance on that coast, with the exception of one (the Colorado) arise from within its boundaries. The drainage from its extensive area of mountains and highlands is received into the numerous lakes which have been noticed as forming so striking a feature of the interior. Thence the surplus is discharged into the few large rivers or their many tributaries, which finally reach the sea. These rivers are the Columbia on the south (debouching through American territory into the Pacific Ocean); the Fraser (750 miles long), the Skeena (300 miles), and the Stikine, on the west; the Liard (over 300 miles in British Columbia), on the north; and the Peace River (over 300 miles in British Columbia), on the east. These rivers are of great size and volume, and the first four are sufficiently navigable to steamers to form waterways of no small value in the development of the country.

The submerged mountain range which lies to the west of the mainland is represented by an archipelago of islands, great and small, the most prominent being Vancouver and the Queen Charlotte Islands. Of the others it may be briefly stated that they produce in miniature all the physical features of the larger group.

Vancouver Island may be described geologically as a group of upturned gneissic rocks, embracing certain tertiary areas and worn down by glacial action, so that in one place extensive gravel moraines, in another beds of boulder clay, are to be found, while in a third a regular series of late sandstones alternate with the barren cliffs of trap. Upon such unpromising surface generations of fir trees have flourished, and by their decay have gradually deposited a mould of increasing thickness sufficient to provide suitable ground for other forms of vegetation, until the country has become covered with a dense growth of timber, varying according to its situation and adaptability to the wants of each particular kind. Thus upon the ridges the pines and many species of undergrowth have held their own, best suited to a moderate degree of moisture and the rocky subsoil. Upon the boulder clay, alder, poplar and willow have contended successfully against the larger trees; and where the gravel has afforded insufficient moisture for the conifers, the hardy but more slow-growing oaks, which had no chance for existence in the dense pine forests, have gained a foothold, and stud level plains clothed with native grass. Maples appear to have succeeded, in some places, the burnt-out pines; indeed, in time much the same sequence of soft and hard timber might be expected on this coast as is known to have occurred on that of the Atlantic, where firs, oaks and beaches have followed in successive order.— (British Columbia: Its Present Resources and Future Possibilities. Official Pamphlet.)

GEOLOGY OF BRITISH COLUMBIA.

THE general surface of the mainland of British Columbia seems to have been covered with glaciers at no very remote geological period, during which the principal movement of the ice was southeasterly and northwesterly in conformity with the trend of the mountains, leaving traces at several localities at an altitude of more than 6,000 feet above the sea. Superficial deposits of boulder-clay and water-worn stones occur at all heights up to 5,000 feet, and in the lower levels, especially in the northern low country, is found a fine white silt. Large moraines occur in great numbers, especially in the line of retreat of glaciers towards the mountain ranges. There are many evidences that large bodies of water existed at various heights between the present sea level and over 5,000 feet, such as shore lines and terraces, and clays which must have been deposited in water.

The Strait of Georgia must have been entirely filled with a great glacier, called by Dr. G. M. Dawson the Strait of Georgia Glacier, with a width of over 50 miles and a thickness in places near its termination of more than 600 feet. Ice groovings of remarkable depth and polish are seen in very recently exposed rock near Victoria, showing that the glacier must have swept over the Saanich peninsula in a direction mostly towards the south, with a slight westerly deviation. On the southwest coast of Vancouver Island, in the Strait of Fuca, the groovings point nearly west, showing that the ice probably escaped to the open ocean through that channel. Further north above Seymour Narrows indications prove that a second large glacier, fed from the fiords of the Mainland, pushed in a northwesterly direction. This is called by Dr. Dawson the Queen Charlotte Sound Glacier.

Tertiary rocks containing marine shells are found on the southwest coast of Vancouver Island, near Sooke; near Carmanah Point, at the entrance of the Strait of Fuca; and at various places between these two points, forming a narrow belt parallel with the coast. Tertiary leaf-bearing rocks are found in Burrard Inlet and about the estuary of the Fraser River. Further north in the Queen Charlotte Islands Dr. Dawson found the whole of the northeastern portion of Graham Island to be underlain by tertiary rocks, mainly of volcanic origin. On the mainland of British Columbia, east of the Coast Range, the tertiaries occupy large areas with lignites, and in certain places even bituminous coal occurs. In the north there has been but little disturbance of the beds, but the southern part of the interior plateau is more irregular and mountainous, and the strata, as on the Nicola, are sometimes found dipping at an angle of 30 degrees. Remains of plants, insects and a few fresh-water molluscs have been obtained from these interior regions, resembling those elsewhere considered to be miocene, and indicating a temperate climate.

Underlying the tertiary beds in many places are cretaceous rocks. These include the true coal-bearing beds of Nanaimo, Comox, and the anthracite region of the Queen Charlotte Islands. The flora of the Vancouver Island beds consists in the main of modern angiospermous and gymnospermous genera, such as oak, planes, poplar and sequoia. The Queen Charlotte Island fossils indicate a lower horizon. On the mainland cretaceous rocks have been described along the northeastern border of the Coast Range, to the south behind Boston Bar, on the Fraser, and near the headwaters of the Skagit. East of the Coast Range and well to the north the cretaceous is probably represented near the Lower Nechaco, and also about the upper part of the Skeena River and on Babine Lake. Sections measured in the Vancouver Island region give a thickness of about 5,000 feet; in the Queen Charlotte Islands, at Skidegate, about 13,000 feet; and at various places on the mainland from 5,000 to 7,000 feet.

The subdivisions of the pre-cretaceous rocks have not yet been satisfactorily made, but in the limestone interbedded in the layers of igneous rocks crinoidal remains, and poorly-preserved corals and molluscs indicate that the carboniferous formation is largely represented.

In the interior of the Mainland the older rocks are mainly massive limestones, diorites, felspathic rocks, quartzites and serpentines. The limestones often appear as coarse-grained marbles.

Characteristic forms of the Alpine Trias have been found by Dr. Dawson in a black calcareous argillite and in beds of limestone beneath the cretaceous series, and may be represented near Victoria by the slaty rocks of Leech River.

On the Mainland the coast is largelycomposed of granitic or gneissic rocks, not yet fully examined.

In the Rocky Mountains is seen the broken margin of the undisturbed sheets of strata which underlie the great plains. They project in block-like masses, and the total (exposed) thickness of their beds is reported to be very great. A section in the Rocky Mountains, on the west side of the range, according to Mr. McConnell, of the Geological Survey of Canada, shows 1,300 feet of dolomites and quartzites containing halysites; 1,500 feet of shales, blackish argillites and limestones containing graptolites; about 10,000 feet of calc-schists, shales and slates of the Castle Mountain group; and 10,000 or more feet of dark argillites and conglomerates of the Bow River series. The foregoing strata range from the Silurian downwards to the Cambrian.

In the Peace River region of the 55th and 56th parallels the conditions are somewhat changed. Massive limestones of Devonian and possibly Carboniferous age, associated with saccharoidal quartzites, form the axil mountains. Volcanic accumulations appear entirely absent from the limestone series.

Archaean rocks are believed to be found in the Shuswap series in Kootenaie and Adams Lakes, and also in the Selkirk Range where the Canadian Pacific Railway crosses it. This probably in Devonian or Carboniferous times formed a more or less continuous barrier along the line of the Gold Range, between the interior continental basin to the northeast and the carboniferous Pacific to the southwest.

In the eastern sea organic limestone with sandy and shaly beds was being deposited. In the west and southwest of the land barrier the conditions were widely different. Here, too, limestones were in process of formation; but extensive

THE OLYMPIC RANGE, FROM VICTORIA.

OAK BAY, SHEWING MOUNT BAKER.

siliceous deposits were also forming with a great chain of volcanic vents, nearly coincident with the present position of the Coast Range and that of the Vancouver and Queen Charlotte Islands. Trap and agglomerate rocks were thus added to the series.

Evidence of disturbance at the end of the carboniferous period is found in the unconformable superposition of the Nicola Triassic on these rocks in the southern portion of the interior of the province. To the west of the land barrier in the triassic and jurassic a great thickness of volcanic rock with limestones and argillites was being formed along the border of the Pacific.

A further circumstance of interest in connection with the jura-trias period is the evidence now obtained that the sea apparently spread uninterruptedly eastward across the Rocky Mountains into the Peace River country at least as far as the 55th parallel. This is proved by the lithological character of the rocks and the fossils they contain, giving us an approximate definition not only of the western but also of the northern limits of the great inland sea which extended southeastward to New Mexico. This period was closed by great disturbances along the whole Cordilerran region. In California the Sierra Nevada rose up as a mass of crumpled and compressed folds. In the northern part of British Columbia the disturbances affected the region from the Gold Range to the coast, extending the land area westward to the 121st meridian, and giving, so far as known, the first upthrust to the mountains of Vancouver and Queen Charlotte Islands, but forming no continuous range where the great belt of coast mountains now is.

In the earliest beds of the cretaceous there is evidence of a general subsidence in progress in the formation of conglomerates, and the shore line of the cretaceous Pacific can be traced a long distance southward and southwestward. In the southern parts of British Columbia it would appear that the Rocky Mountains proper were not elevated at this time, but that the cretaceous Mediterranean washed the eastern shore of the Gold Range. The cretaceous period closed with another period of folding, in which additional height was given to the Vancouver and Queen Charlotte Island ranges and the Coast ranges. At this time the Rocky Mountains attained their fullest development.

No trace of the earlier eocene tertiary has been found in British Columbia, and it is probable that the province was throughout, at that time, a land area. In the miocene the relative elevation of the sea and land was much as at present, but great inland lakes were in existence.

The miocene closed with extensive volcanic disturbances throughout the country southwest of the Gold Range, and eventually by another period of crumpling and elevation, probably coincident with that which produced the tertiary coast hills in California, and which gave to the northern part of the British Columbian coast the greater elevation it appears to have possessed during pliocene times, when the wonderful system of fiords, by which it is now dissected, were cut out.

Among the striking points of geological interest in British Columbia are: First, the repeated corrugation, parallel in the main to a single axis which has occurred in the Cordilerra region; and second, the great and widespread masses of volcanic material at at least four distinct horizons, proving the activity of an immense period of volcanic forces along this portion of the Pacific margin.

RIVERS AND LAKES.

THE principal rivers of British Columbia are the Fraser, the Columbia, the Thompson, the Kootenay, the Skeena, the Stikine, the Liard and the Peace.

The Fraser is the great watercourse of the province. It rises in the northern part of the Rocky Mountains, runs for about 200 miles in two branches in a westerly direction, and then in one stream runs due south for nearly 400 miles before turning to rush through the gorges of the Coast Range to the Straits of Georgia. Its total length is about 740 miles. On its way it receives the waters of the Thompson, the Chilcoten, the Lillooet, the Nicola, the Harrison, the Pitt and numerous other streams. For the last 80 miles of its course it flows through a wide alluvial plain, which has mainly been deposited from its own silt. It is navigable for vessels drawing 20 feet to New Westminster, about 15 miles from its mouth; and for light draught boats to Yale, a small town 110 miles from the mouth; and again for smaller craft for about 60 miles of its course through the northern interior — from Quesnel Mouth to Soda Creek, in Cariboo.

The Columbia, a large river rising in the southeastern part of the province, in the neighbourhood of the Rocky Mountains, near Kootenay Lake, runs north beyond the 52nd degree of latitude, when it takes a sudden turn and runs due south into the State of Washington. It is this loop made by the abrupt turn of the river that is known as the "Big Bend of the Columbia." The Columbia drains an area of 195,000 square miles.

The Kootenay, which rises near the headwaters of the Columbia, flows south through East Kootenay into the states of Montana and Idaho, and, returning to British Columbia, empties into Kootenay Lake, its waters again being discharged through the Lower Kootenay River into the returning branch of the Columbia some distance south of the main line of the Canadian Pacific Railway.

The Peace River rises some distance north of the north bend of the Fraser, and flows eastwardly through the Rocky Mountains, draining the plains on the other side. Gold discoveries at its headwaters have been reported in recent years; but the river more properly belongs to the district east of the mountains that bears its name.

The Thompson River has two branches, known as the North Thompson and the South Thompson. The former rises in small lakes in the Cariboo District, and the other in the Shuswap Lakes, in the Yale District. They join at Kamloops, and flow out of Kamloops Lake into the Fraser River at Lytton.

The Skeena River, 300 miles long, runs southwesterly to the coast, almost uniformly parallel with its twin sister, the Naas River, from which it is about 50 miles distant. The headwaters are in the Omineca district, near the source of the Oslinca, a tributary of the Parsnip. The Skeena is navigable for some distance beyond Hazelton, but is navigated only as far as that point, 150 miles from the mouth, and has several important tributaries, including the Zymoetz, Kispyox, Bulkley and Babine. The course of the Skeena is tortuous and is practicable for navigation only about seven months in the year. At its mouth are located a number of salmon canneries.

The Stikine flows into the Pacific Ocean through a short stretch of Alaskan territory, and forms the main artery of communication for a large portion of the province north of latitude 57 degrees, and for years has been regularly navigated. The Cassiar mining district is reached by it. It is navigable for river steamboats for about 130 miles to Glenora and Telegraph Creek.

The principal lakes are the Kootenay, Slocan, Arrow (Upper and Lower), Okanagan, Trout, Shuswap and Harrison, in Southern British Columbia; and Quesnel, in Northern.

The following tables are taken from the official census :—

Lakes.	Area in Acres.
Adams	33,280
Atlin (part)	211,680
Babine	196,000
Chilko	109,760
Harrison	78,400
Kootenay	141,120
Lower Arrow	40,960
Okanagan	86,240
Owikano	62,720
Quesnel	94,080
Shuswap	79,150
Stuart	141,120
Tacla	86,240
Tagish (part)	58,180
Teslin (part)	78,400
Upper Arrow	63,500

The area of British Columbia in lakes is 1,560,830 acres; that of Canada, 77,391,304 acres.

COMPARATIVE AREAS.

Provinces and Territories.	Land. Acres.	Lake. Acres.	Total Acres.	Total Sq. Miles.
British Columbia	236,922,177	1,560,830	238,483,007	372,630
Manitoba	41,169,098	6,019,200	47,188,298	73,732
New Brunswick	17,863,266	47,232	17,910,498	27,985
Nova Scotia	13,483,671	230,100	13,713,771	21,428
Ontario	141,125,330	25,826,306	166,951,636	260,862
Prince Edward Island	1,397,991	....	1,397,991	2,184
Quebec	218,723,687	6,474,874	225,198,561	351,873
Alberta	64,973,212	232,000	65,205,212	101,883
Assiniboia	56,498,546	384,000	56,882,546	88,879
Saskatchewan	66,460,859	2,414,500	68,875,359	107,618
Athabaska	155,622,704	5,635,120	161,257,824	251,965
Mackenzie	340,886,420	18,910,080	359,796,500	562,182
Keewatin	292,478,010	8,588,260	301,066,270	470,416
Franklin	320,000,000	....	320,000,000	500,000
Ungava	223,429,600	3,745,440	227,175,040	354,961
Yukon	125,649,500	415,280	126,064,780	196,970
Total	2,316,684,071	80,483,222	2,397,167,293	3,745,574

POLITICAL DIVISIONS.

THE area of British Columbia has been variously set down from 380,000 square miles to 394,000 square miles. From careful surface measurements of the map, the following results approximately have been obtained, according to the present main political divisions :—

	Square Miles.	Square Acres.
Kootenay	23,500	15,060,000
Yale	24,300	15,850,000
Lillooet	16,100	10,300,000
Westminster	7,660	4,900,000
Cariboo	150,550	96,350,000
Cassiar	164,300	105,150,000
Comox (Mainland)	7,100	4,550,000
Vancouver Island	16,400	10,000,000
	409,910	262,160,000

The above figures are given approximately, to approach round figures as nearly as possible, and include the territory claimed by Canada in connection with the Alaskan boundary dispute.

THE KOOTENAY DISTRICT.

The Kootenay District, which includes East and West Kootenay, comprises an area of 15,060,000 acres, and occupies a triangular space of the southeast corner of British Columbia. The apex of this district is at a point where 52 degrees north latitude crosses the Rocky Mountains; and the base extends from 118 degrees west latitude to 114 degrees west latitude. The triangle is divided into about two equal parts, called East and West Kootenay, respectively, the Purcell Range of the Selkirks constituting the dividing line. The whole territory is drained by the Columbia, which forms what it known as "the great bend," passing north through East and south through West Kootenay.

There are three main valleys — one in East Kootenay, occupying or being the drainage basin of the Columbia River, going north; the other, the valley of the Kootenay River and the Kootenay Lakes, in West Kootenay; the third lying between the Selkirk and Gold ranges, through which the Columbia River, expanding into the Arrow Lakes, flows into the three valleys in question, constituting the main routes of communication northward and southward.

East Kootenay contains a large extent of agricultural land, but requiring irrigation as a rule. West Kootenay has but little arable land, the principal part of which lies at the southern boundary along the Kootenay River, and is made up of a tract included in the Kootenay Reclamation Scheme, containing about 50,000 acres.

It is unnecessary, however, to state that the name Kootenay in British Columbia has become almost synonymous with mineral wealth, its mountains being rich with gold, silver, lead and copper, and disclosing so far indications of remarkable promise. In consequence of the development that has taken place a number of towns, several incorporated, have sprung up and are enjoying a large measure of prosperity — Revelstoke, Nelson, Kaslo, Rossland, Trail, New Denver, Sandon, Slocan City, Three Forks, Fort Steele, Cranbrook, Fernie, Moyie, Kimberley, Morrissey, Elko, Michelle, etc. (referred to elsewhere). With the present and prospective railway development there is no doubt that the population and wealth of this district will be surprisingly augmented from this time forward. In East Kootenay, as a result of the building of the Crow's Nest Railway and branches and the Crow's Nest smelter, in conjunction with the development of the coal mines in the Crow's Nest Pass, the population has doubled since the census of 1901.

YALE.

Yale occupies a large area to the west of Kootenay, extending to the 22nd degree of west longitude, and from about 49 degrees to 52 degrees north latitude. The whole occupies an area of about 15,850,000 square miles, and lies almost wholly within the dry belt of the province, although, from its extent, it has a variety of soil and climate. It includes the rich valleys of the Okanagan, the Nicola, the

Similkameen, the Kettle River country, and the valleys of the North and South Thompson, in the vicinity of Kamloops. It possesses perhaps the largest area of purely agricultural and pastoral lands of any district in the province. The valleys of the Okanagan District raise excellent wheat, which is milled at two local grist mills.

Yale contains large cattle ranges and many large herds of cattle, and in addition gives excellent promise as a fruit-growing district, the range of products including tomatoes, watermelons, grapes, peaches, almonds, etc., which are not raised to perfection anywhere in the Coast districts. Fruit-growing has made rapid strides, and though yet only in its incipiency, promises to become a very important industry. The Canadian Pacific Railway passes very nearly through the centre of the district, a little to the north; while the Shuswap & Okanagan branch, from Sicamous to Vernon, affords communication southward, which is continued to the boundary line by means of the Okanagan and other lakes, forming a system of water stretches parallel to those referred to in the Kootenays. Railways are projected from Spence's Bridge and Midway into the Similkameen, and from Midway to Vernon.

Yale, in addition to its agricultural resources, has come into prominence as a mineral district, the new Boundary country being in the southern part, besides which, in the locality of Nicola, in the Similkameen, at Cherry Creek, Hope, Kamloops and other parts, there have been numerous locations and rich discoveries of minerals, metalliferous and coal.

LILLOOET.

Lillooet contains 10,300,000 acres, lying west of the northern half of Yale District. The northern part of Lillooet forms a parallelogram, extending from 51 degrees to 52 degrees north latitude, and between 120 degrees 30 minutes and 125 degrees west longitude. The southern part forms a smaller parallelogram between 121 degrees and 124 degrees west longitude, and extends from 50 degrees 25 minutes to 51 degrees north latitude. It contains a large portion of the interior plateau previously referred to, and in a general way exhibits characteristics similar to those in Yale. It is largely a pastoral country, but in the southern portion of it fruit-growing is making good progress.

The district is bisected by the Fraser River, and the Cariboo waggon road passes through it northward from Ashcroft. The district is well adapted for dairying and cattle-raising. Irrigation is necessary in many places, owing to the dryness of the climate, and is accompanied by success wherever it has been tried.

Formerly, in the days of the Cariboo gold excitement, Lillooet supplied the miners with farm produce, and agriculturally is still more flourishing at the present time. There is a number of placer deposits which have been developed to some extent, and have for years been yielding returns. In the vicinity of Bridge River important metalliferous deposits were discovered recently, and give promise of considerable development. A number of locations were made there, also on Seaton Lake and along Bonaparte River. The Bridge River district is noted for big game, and throughout the district fishing and shooting are good.

WESTMINSTER DISTRICT.

Westminster District lies to the west of the southern half of Yale, and although by the Redistribution Act of 1894 its area was very much diminished, it is territorially still an important district, containing about 4,900,000 acres, and occupies an unique position in the province, being bounded on the west by the Gulf of Georgia, on the north by Lillooet, on the east by Yale, and on the south by United States territory. Westminster District is largely made up of the valley of the Fraser River, which, according to Dr. Dawson, is the bed of an ancient arm of the sea, which extended as far inland as Hope, and is thus to a large extent made up of alluvial deposits of the Fraser River. What is known as the Fraser River Valley is very fertile, and, with the exception of its being subject to occasional overflow in places, is agriculturally one of the most desirable locations in the province. The drawback of floods, however, has been overcome by a series of important dyking schemes, and the Dominion Government is dealing with the problem of protecting the banks of the Fraser by a system of dredging and defences. The Fraser River Valley, with the exception of the Peace River country, is the largest compact area of arable land in the province. In this district a number of improved and partially improved lands are for sale, at reasonable prices, and afford a good investment for those seeking farms. More particular reference is made to this district in the chapter on agriculture.

Lumbering is also an important resource, whilst the mineral zone along the northern boundary is regarded as of extreme promise.

Politically Westminster is divided into four ridings — Richmond, Dewdney, Chilliwack and Delta — the latter two being on the south side of the river and the former on the north side of the river. It is largely made up of municipalities, which include Richmond, Delta, Surrey, Langley, Matsqui, Chilliwack, Kent, Dewdney, Mission, Maple Ridge, Coquitlam, Burnaby, North and South Vancouver. In this respect Westminster differs largely from the rest of the province, inasmuch as it is the only district in which development on municipal lines has taken place to any extent. At the southwest corner are the cities of Vancouver (the terminus of the Canadian Pacific Railway) and Westminster, which is often referred to as the fresh water terminus, and is the centre of the salmon-canning industry.

CARIBOO.

North of Yale and Lillooet lies the great district of Cariboo, which extends from 52 degrees to 60 degrees north latitude, the latter being the northern boundary line of the province, and from the 120th to the 126th degree of west longitude, containing in the aggregate the vast area of about 96,350,000 acres. It is drained in the south by the Fraser River and its numerous tributaries, in the centre by the Parsnip and Peace Rivers and tributaries, and in the north by the Nelson and Liard and tributaries. It was in the district drained by the tributaries of the Fraser River, in the vicinity of Barkerville, that occurred the great gold excitement of British Columbia in early days. It is estimated that out of these rich creeks has been taken an amount equal to between $45,000,000 and $50,000,000 in gold.

The northern half of the district has been but very imperfectly explored, and the information regarding it is limited. The central portion was a rich fur preserve of the Hudson's Bay Company in early days, and in it are located Forts St. John, McLeod, Stuart and St. James. The Omineca gold mining district lies in the western portion near the centre between the northern and southern limits; and to the southwest lie the large pastoral and agricultural districts included in the Blackwater and Nechaco Valleys, in which are contained areas of grazing land and rich river bottoms, several million acres in extent, which, when communication has been provided, will afford homes for a large number of settlers.

In the auriferous district already referred to, where the rich placer mines exist, large hydraulicing enterprises have been inaugurated, and some half dozen companies, expending from $250,000 to $1,500,000 each, have obtained extensive leases and are operating on a very comprehensive scale. The result of these operations will no doubt bring back to Cariboo much of its old-time prosperity. Railways are projected into the mining districts from both sides — one from the main line of the Canadian Pacific Railway at Ashcroft or Kamloops, and the other by way of Bute Inlet, on the Mainland coast, either of which would materially advance the mining interests and open up a district which has long suffered from lack of communication.

In the Cariboo District, in the vicinity of Alexandria, 150-Mile House, Soda Creek and the mouth of Quesnel River, there are a number of fine ranches producing grain, vegetables and cattle. One of the finest roller mills in the province is in operation at the mouth of Quesnel, and a grist mill operates at Soda Creek.

In the northeastern corner is the famed Peace River country, which has an area, it is estimated, of at least 1,500,000 acres of good agricultural land.

CASSIAR.

Cassiar lies west of Cariboo, occupying an area considerably larger than the latter, or about 105,150,000 acres, extending from the northern boundary of Comox at 51 degrees north latitude, to the northern boundary of the province, at 60 degrees north latitude, and all the territory west of that meridian to the Pacific Ocean, including Queen Charlotte Islands, except the territory of Alaska, which extends to a little south of 55 degrees north latitude. This extensive tract of land has for many years lain practically dormant, although much attention has recently been drawn to it, and very much of it is still unexplored. It is drained to the westward by two large parallel rivers, the Skeena and the Stikine, reference to which is made elsewhere. There are also within its northern limits the sources of the Liard, known as Dease River, and the headwaters of the Yukon. In former years (from 1871 onward) Omineca and Cassiar were the scenes of mining excitement to some extent similar to that of Cariboo in the early days and Klondike in the present, only on a smaller scale. The Omineca District occupies a central part of Cassiar, while the richer gold diggings in the vicinity of Dease Lake lie at the extreme north, and are accessible by the Stikine River. Recently much attention has been attracted to Omineca and Northern Cassiar, and a revival of interest in their mines has taken place. This interest has been intensified by the Yukon rush and the discovery of gold in the Atlin country, and it is altogether probable that the whole northern interior of British Columbia, including Cariboo, will be thoroughly prospected by miners, railway promoters and others within the next few years, and it is probable that a very important industrial future is in store.

In the Skeena District, at Observatory Inlet, Kitsalas Canyon and other points, active mining development is going on, and a railway is projected from Kitimaat to Hazelton.

Agriculturally, little can be said; in fact, little is definitely known, although there are many valleys adapted for agriculture, and low ranges of hills which will afford a very considerable area of pasturage, and it is also probable that vegetables and the hardier fruits and cereals may be grown in many places.

COMOX.

Comox District may be described as a large rectangle, including the northern part of Vancouver Island and a portion of the opposite Mainland, being bounded on the north by the 51st degree of north latitude, and on the east by the 124th degree of west longitude, and comprising about 9,750,000 acres. On the Mainland side it is deeply indented with inlets, of which Jervis, Toba, Bute, Knight and Kingcombe are the principal. These inlets are the outlets for a number of rivers which flow through canyons and are fed by numerous glaciers. The country generally is very rugged, and the coast on both sides of the straits, and the many islands, large and small, which intervene are heavily timbered. Here are found the principal logging camps of the province, and a very important supply of the best merchantable timber. Although sparsely populated as yet, perhaps no other area of British Columbia of similar size contains so much and varied natural wealth, represented in timber, minerals, fish and agricultural land, the last named, though considerable in the aggregate, being, comparatively speaking, the least important. Many of the islands contain good land, and in the vicinity of Comox there are some excellent stretches; while north from Seymour Narrows to the head of the island there are considerable areas which, if drained and cultivated, would make valuable cattle ranges and meadows. Coal measures, which at Comox are extensively worked, extend almost to the end of the island. Good fishing is found everywhere, and several salmon canneries are in operation. On this coast are abundant fine building materials — stone and slate — while of minerals, iron, copper, gold and silver are largely represented. In the vicinity of Phillips Arm are promising mining camps; in fact the whole district is richly endowed and is capable of prosperous development. The west coast has been but little prospected as yet; there is comparatively little known of its resources, but there are good fisheries all along it, and recently a number of mineral discoveries, principally of copper, have been made.

VANCOUVER ISLAND.

The main physical features of Vancouver Island have already been referred to in the opening part of this chapter, and the part not heretofore described consists of the large districts of Cowichan and Alberni, lying south of Comox on the west side, extending south to Esquimalt District, and other political divisions lying eastward. The greater part of Alberni is rugged and mountainous, and has — as is, in fact, true of the whole interior of the Island of Vancouver — been only partially explored. There are some grand scenic effects and beautiful inland lakes. Along Alberni Canal, however, is a large area of fertile land and a number of settlers. Here, too, there are many promising mineral indications, with a good deal of preliminary development and one or two well developed mines. On Barkley Sound and up the coast as far as Quatsino prospecting is active, and, particularly for copper and iron, is regarded as one of the coming mining districts of the province. Owing, however, to the heavy undergrowth, prospecting is difficult. Esquimalt District occupies the southeastern corner of the Island, in which Victoria City and Esquimalt are situated. North of Esquimalt is the Cowichan District, and north of that the Nanaimo District. In Cowichan District the mines of Mount Sicker have come prominently to the front, with two smelters erected to smelt the ores. Lumbering is also an important industry. It may be stated here that the main portion of the marketable timber of British Columbia is found on Vancouver Island and adjacent islands. Victoria District, north and South, including Saanich and Salt' Spring Island, and others of a group known as The Islands, lies east of Cowichan and Esquimalt Districts, on and in the Gulf of Georgia. All the southeastern portion of Vancouver Island is, comparatively speaking, well settled, and contains a good deal of agricultural land and many well-cultivated farms. This portion of the Island is well served with good roads, and has railway communication by the Esquimalt & Nanaimo and Victoria & Sidney railways. From a sporting and residential point of view, Vancouver Island is ideal in many respects, and, apart from its great natural resources, will attract a large population.

A COAST TRIP.

IF a business man, worried by the ceaseless demands on his attention, and mentally and physically exhausted by close application to office work; if a student whose cheek has paled under the light of the midnight oil; if a man of leisure whose routine of social responsibilities and pleasurable pursuits has produced ennui ; if a lover of sport and travel, keen for adventure, and his spirit restless for fresh trophies and a new arena ; if a pupil in nature's school, eager to witness the operation of her laws in other and wider forms ; if an artist, in whose soul burns the desire for subjects of sublime beauty and massive grandeur; if a collector of rare and interesting objects ; if he belong to the literati and is thirsting for fresh fields and unhackneyed topics; if plunged in statecraft and worried for

murder of the crew of that ship, with the exception of two men — Jewitt, the armourer, and Thompson, the sailmaker — who after a two years' captivity effected their release by the arrival of a British trading vessel.

A WILD, BROKEN COAST.

Leaving Nootka, the coast is extremely broken, wild and dangerous, upon the outer rocks of which the ocean breaks unceasingly, the bugbear and terror of all navigators. However, to navigators knowing the coast and recognizing the landmarks, by shaping their course properly, in a short time they can glide from the stormy waters of the Pacific into beautiful land-locked havens, such as Esperanza, Kyuquot, Ou-Ou-Kinsh and Nasparti. Here the flotsam and jetsam of the Pacific Ocean is to be met with. After a vessel disappears, this is where the Government steamer goes to find traces of her. The outer coast along here is simply one mass of wreckage.

Rounding the tremendous promontory of Cape Cook, the traveller will notice the solitary and majestic rock, named by Captain Cook after Dr. Solander, the astronomer and naturalist of the "Endeavor," when on his first voyage to the Pacific in 1769, "Solander Island." Here it will be of interest to note that elk are found on the adjacent shores, and it will probably be their last resort on the Island of Vancouver.

QUATSINO AND CAPE SCOTT.

The largest inlet after passing Cape Cook is named Quatsino — a paradise for the sportsman. Here large flats extend for miles on the north shore of the Sound — known as Forward Inlet and Winter Harbour — which flats are crowded with water-fowl of all descriptions.

From this point westward the characteristics of the country completely change; we lose the heavily-wooded coast-line and precipitous mountain peaks, together with the Douglas fir, and the land is comparatively level and covered with spruce, hemlock and cedar.

Quatsino has a splendid harbour, which extends inland for miles, and has long been looked upon as the coming commercial entrepot, and is one of the proposed Pacific termini. Coal is found in the formation here, and the miners are also engaged in the development of metalliferous deposits. In the San Josef Valley land is being surveyed for a Danish colony, an offshoot of the settlement at Cape Scott, where some thirty or forty families are locating and developing agricultural and other resources at that point. As is well known from surveys that have been made, the northern end of the Island is comparatively level and contains considerable good land, particularly suitable for cattle-raising.

Rounding Cape Scott, we proceed due easterly along the northern end of Vancouver Island, where extensive deposits of black sand exist, containing more or less of placer gold, which is being mined by various prospectors.

Steering an easterly course, you are taken through Goletas Channel, where the placid inland waters are entered and the voyageur again meets the channel used by boats going through Seymour Narrows, northward along the protected and inland waters of British Columbia.

FROM VICTORIA TO VANCOUVER.

On the inside trip, which is the usual one, the passage from Victoria to Vancouver affords only an inkling of the scenic effects that will be obtained for the next twelve or fourteen days. Leaving the inner harbour, the boat swings out into the Straits of Fuca, and you get the first swell of the ocean, fifty miles to the westward. To the right is passed the historic island of San Juan. To the left Vancouver Island is in view. The Strait of Georgia is crossed at its greatest width. After San Juan is a succession of beautiful low-lying and timbered islands. Midway is Active Pass, always a point of great interest and beauty, and which is now a popular summer resort. Having passed Point Roberts, the mouth of the Fraser River, Point Grey, and through the narrows into Burrard Inlet, Vancouver City is reached in about five hours' easy sailing. Right under the bold, high bluff of Brockton Point promontory were visible for some years the remains of the old Beaver, the first steamer on the Pacific Ocean, which went to pieces on the rocks, and for some time before its final plunge lay the prey of teredo and relic-hunters.

UP THE GULF OF GEORGIA.

From Vancouver the steamer takes a straight cut of thirty miles across the Strait of Georgia, passing Nanaimo and Wellington, where the coal mines of Vancouver Island are located. From here for the whole length of Vancouver Island the steamer hugs its shore, and here, too, begins that maze of islands which continues in more or less bewildering profusion as far north as you go, gradually increasing in size and in character from low-lying and heavily timbered to high, bold and rocky. The Strait of Georgia continues about 75 miles. The Mainland shore to the right is indented with numerous inlets or arms of the sea — Howe Sound, Jervis Inlet, Toba Inlet, Bute Inlet, and so on — up which, were there time to go, wonderful beauties would be disclosed. There are Indian reservations and logging camps and settlers found all along. Up Jervis Inlet is a quarry of excellent slate. Texada, thirty miles long, low and timbered, with a bold, rocky shore, and traversed by a ridge of rugged trap mountains, is on the Mainland side. It contains important gold, iron, marble, lime and other mineral deposits. To the left are Hornby and Denman, picturesque islands. Over these are seen the mountain ridges of Vancouver Island, the peaks of which here are the highest of the range. Point Holmes, on the left, a bold promontory, is passed. From here to Comox the coast is low and heavily timbered inland, and here lies one of the most important coal measures of Vancouver Island, included in the Esquimalt & Nanaimo Railway belt. Opposite, in the direction of Desolation Sound, are numerous islands — Hernando, Cortez, Mary, and so on — upon some of which are settlers and logging camps. Over in the distance, on the Mainland, rise up the Cascade Mountains, range after range.

SEYMOUR NARROWS.

Now you creep closer to the Vancouver shore and presently enter the celebrated Seymour Narrows, once in which, by reason of the high bluff shores, you are shut out from the view on either side. The Narrows proper are about 800 yards wide and about a mile and a half long, though Discovery Pass, to which it is the entrance, is about 23 miles long. At flood the tide runs from six to twelve knots an hour, and at ebb from six to eight, the flood and ebb running equal intervals of about six hours each, with about ten minutes still water. Valdez Island, lying at the entrance to Bute Inlet and forming the right shore of this channel, is a finely timbered island, with a number of logging camps on it, and some well-to-do ranchers on the benches back from the shore. The Euclataw or Back Narrows, of almost equal note among navigators, on the other side of the island, are also very rapid, and dangerous as well. It was at this point where it was once proposed to bring the line of the Canadian Pacific Railway, through the Yellow Head Pass, down Bute Inlet and connecting with a line of railway to Victoria by bridging Seymour Narrows, the present proposed route of the Canadian Northern.

Just before entering the Narrows is a village of Euclataw Indians, once regarded as the worst of all the British Columbia tribes, and said to have been cannibalistic. Passing the mouth of Campbell River, you look up the fine Menzies Valley, and over westward on Vancouver Island are towering snow-clad peaks extending for miles. Sailing by Menzies Bay, you enter the Narrows, already described, which, after an exciting run, widen out into Johnston Straits. Along here, on the Vancouver shore, are some beautiful beaches and snug coves and bays, and on the other side a group of small rocky islands — Helmcken, Hardwick, etc.— on the timbered benches of which is to be found the finest Douglas fir in the province. The famous Bickley Bay logging camp is located on the back channel on Hardwick Island.

IN JOHNSTON'S STRAITS.

After having rounded Chatham Point the steamer gets in closer and closer to Vancouver Island, and the shores become more and more precipitous. Along Johnston Straits westward you pass the mouth of Salmon River, where there are rapids and overfalls, with heavy sea. The straits widen out to about three miles, and now you are directly between the shores of Vancouver Island and the Mainland, the only place where they directly approach each other. This approximation continues ten or twelve miles, both shores being thickly wooded. On the Mainland side are Blinkinsop Bay and Port Neville. The former is a good harbour, with rocky, picturesque shore. The latter is an inlet seven miles long, up which first-class building granite is found. On the Vancouver shore, which presents a bold, rocky front, is the mouth of Adams River, just opposite which commences Cracroft Island, running twenty miles parallel with our course. At the southeast end of it is Port Hartney, a fine harbour.

Myriads of islands, large and small, are to be seen all along the Mainland side as far as Cape Caution, locally known as the Broughton Archipelago. The next point of interest, on your left, is Beaver Cove, which, in addition to being a good harbour, has an excellent milling site. A marble quarry has been located here. Back of Beaver Cove, extending to the great Nimkish Lake, is an extensive valley. Nimkish River, which is the outlet of the lake into Broughton Sound, Nimkish Lake and Kammutseena River, which empties into it, all afford the finest trout fishing in the province. This district is a veritable sportsman's paradise, now much frequented for big game — elk, deer, panther, etc.— while the scenery is simply enchanting. From this point the centre of the Island is easily accessible.

ALERT BAY.

Five miles above Beaver Cove we arrive at our first stopping place, Alert Bay, on Cormorant Island, just opposite the mouth of Nimkish River. It is very prettily situated, and is a favourite calling place, both up and down. Here are an Indian village with a population of 150 or so, whites included, a salmon cannery, a sawmill and two stores, an English Church mission and an industrial school. Here the salmon canners have turned their attention to canning clams, which abound in the neighbourhood.

The first thing which strikes the tourist's eye on rounding into Alert Bay is the Indian burial ground, on the south point on the right hand entering the bay. It is fantastically decorated with streamers and flags of different colours, and a variety of grave fences and epitaphs. The next thing which particularly attracts a stranger is a fine totem pole, about thirty feet high, beautifully painted and carved, which guards the entrance to the present chief's house.

Cormorant Island possesses coal formations. Near it are several rocky islets, upon which discoveries of silver and copper have been made. Farther up is passed Haddington Island, all one quarry of the finest building stone, out of which the stone for the new Parliament Buildings was taken; and still farther on is Malcolm Island, agriculturally the best piece of land on the coast. At this point on our trip we are beginning to lose the companionship of the Douglas fir, which has been abundantly with us from the outset, finding instead forests of hemlock, spruce, red cedar, cypress, birch and alder, which prevail more or less for the rest of our journey. Opposite Malcolm Island is Port McNeill, boasting a commodious harbour. The country all along here comprises coal measures, which extend for twenty-five miles through to the west coast. Three miles beyond Broughton Straits we enter Queen Charlotte Sound, where the ocean swell is already noticeable; and, skirting the northeast coast of Vancouver Island, we put in at the historic Fort Rupert, twenty-one miles beyond Alert Bay.

FORT RUPERT.

It consists of the old Hudson's Bay fort, and a large Indian village, situated on a long open beach of shingle and shells, which gives it a white, snowy look. There are no wharf accommodations, and consequently it is only in cases of absolute necessity that steamers call here, in which case communication has to be made with the shore by boat or canoe. On two occasions this huge village has been shelled and laid in ashes by gunboats sent to demand the surrender of murderers among them.

Twenty miles beyond Fort Rupert we enter the Galiano Channel and pass Galiano Island, and into Queen Charlotte Sound; thence through Christie Passage, where for the first time we receive the full sweep of the Pacific Ocean, and sniff the salt sea breeze. In the next two hours the steamer has to buffet the long rolling sea from Queen Charlotte Sound, and, heading northwesterly in the direction of Cape Caution, we encounter a low-lying, rocky shore, where are dangerous sunken reefs. Cape Caution is appropriately named, as in its vicinity are innumerable rocks and shoals, requiring great caution on the part of the navigator. This brings us to the entrance to Fitzhugh Sound, and on the right is Rivers Inlet.

THE SCENERY ON THE WAY.

During the time since starting up the Straits of Georgia we have not omitted to note the scenery, which, though not on so magnificent a scale as that yet to come, has been nevertheless peculiarly charming. It has been one long series of subjects for the artist, in which rare and elusive effects have entered—marine sketches, land and water combinations, here depressed and there bold and broken shores, backed by recurring benches densely timbered, and away over all, far off and high up, have risen majestically the tops of the Coast Range of mountains ridging the entire length of Vancouver Island on one side, and the mighty peaks of the Cascades of the Mainland on the other, giving, on the whole sweep of vision, that indefinable charm which "magnificent distance" alone can lend. Leaving out the few tide rips, which you experience with delight, you have been gliding, not propelled, over water as smooth as glass, and at times your impressions have been dream-like — now weird and solemn, and again exhilarating. Sea fowl innumerable — gulls, ducks, geese and others — have kept you company, and occasionally, sometimes frequently, the attention of the party has been diverted to a spouting whale, or a swarm of porpoise, and even land animals, which are to be seen once in a while from the deck. To Rivers Inlet, our next objective point, we will have covered some 350 or 400 miles, and our promises so far have been more than fulfilled.

Now we have entered a distinctly new phase of our trip. We are going north, with the ocean and scattered islands on the left of us, and the Mainland on the right. Leaving Cape Caution and passing Smith's Inlet, a few miles on we enter Fitzhugh Sound, and steam up Rivers Inlet. This was named Rivers Canal by the great Vancouver. Our friends will have recognised in the names of the islands passed some time ago — Hernando, Cortez, Texada, Valdez, and so on — historic memories of early Spanish explorers, who held the coast for a time conjointly with the British, but, as usual, the christening, which remained with British ascendancy, was done by Vancouver over a hundred years ago.

RIVERS INLET.

Rivers Inlet runs up about thirty miles. At the entrance and for several miles up, the sides of the inlet, which is only 1 to 1½ miles in width, are steep and covered with dense forests of spruce and cedar. At the head of the Inlet the sides mount up abruptly for about 2,000 feet, and are almost bare of verdure through the action of landslides and avalanches. In this inlet are seven canneries, a sawmill, and a station, formerly used as a salmon saltery. One peculiarity of the salmon run here is that it never, or very rarely, fails. Rivers Inlet is a strikingly pretty place. We travel from here up Fitzhugh Sound, on the right shore of which is to be seen Namu Harbour, where Messrs. Drany and Shotbolt have a cannery, and enter Bentinck Arm, at the head of which are situated the Bella Coola Indians. There is an Indian village here. John Clayton, a trader, and family reside here, and keep a store. He has as well a large stock ranch. There is a large extent of agricultural country here, where a prosperous colony of Norwegians have settled. The Bella Coola Valley affords the easiest and best route into the Chilcotin country. From here you pass into Lama Passage, where the Bella Bella Indians reside. They have a large, beautiful village, with several stores and a resident missionary. This was the old Fort McLaughlin, of Hudson's Bay Company days. Leaving Bella Bella, we sail into Millbank Sound and enter Graham Reach, passing along the inside of Princess Royal Island, which has high, bluff, rocky shores, and thence through various passages we reach the mouth of the great Gardner Inlet.

GARDNER INLET.

The sail up this discloses the most wonderful scenery on the route. The shores are thousands of feet high, and almost perpendicular, lending a grandeur and impressiveness to the scene almost indescribable, while magnificent waterfalls and glaciers are to be seen. Perhaps there is not on the whole western coast of America scenery which quite equals it in its way. Captain Vancouver, who explored this channel over a hundred years ago, described its beauties most graphically. At its head is situated the Kitlupe tribe of Indians, after whom the inlet is sometimes called. Almost parallel with Gardner Canal is Douglas Channel, the extension of which is known as Kitimat Arm. At the head of this arm there is considerable good land, and a pass into the interior. Kitimat Arm is similar in the massiveness and beauty of its scenery to Kitlupe Inlet, but differs in the character of detail. The shores, which are wooded with hemlock, spruce and cedar, are not so abrupt, but are bounded with lofty ranges of mountains running parallel to each other.

A BEAUTIFUL LANDSCAPE.

Going out of Gardner Canal, we enter Grenville Channel, which is ninety miles long, passing along Pitt Island. Here the scenery is extremely picturesque, with adjacent bare walls of rock and high distant peaks. At Lowe Inlet, off the channel, is an Indian station and a cannery. The general effect of so many mountains rising one above the other renders Grenville Passage one of the most beautiful landscapes on the coast, and is equalled only by Klemtoo Passage.

It was omitted to state that on Gribbell Island, at the mouth of Gardner Inlet, is a very fine hot spring. Through Grenville Channel, on Pitt Island, China Hat is passed. This is an Indian village, with the usual missionary and trader.

Lowe Inlet is the residence during the fishing season of the Kitkahtla Indians, whose chief was the far-famed Sheiks. Chief Sheiks had a monopoly of the fishing here, and with a seine net in the bay often hauled in from 2,000 to 3,000 salmon a day, for which he got the highest market price. We have already passed Hartley Bay, where there is a sawmill and an Indian village. And now we are at the mouth of the Skeena River, and take Telegraph Passage, passing the well-known Standard cannery.

THE SKEENA.

The Skeena River, the mouth of which we have entered, is the largest river on the British Columbia coast except the Fraser, and takes its rise several hundreds of miles in New Caledonia, near Babine Lake. It is the route into the gold country of Omineca. The scenery up to Hazelton and beyond is not unlike that of the Fraser, and in some places quite equals it. Its rugged canyons and fierce rapids require skilful navigation. It is to the Forks of the Skeena where one of the alternative surveys for the Canadian Pacific Railway was run, and here in 1866 the Western Union Telegraph Company reached with a line which was to connect overland, by crossing Behring Straits, with a Siberian line, when the news of the Atlantic cable being laid was received, and the scheme was abandoned. We, however, only explore the mouth of the wonderful river as far as Port Essington. In it are located a number of salmon canneries and three sawmills, the timber used being red cedar, cypress, hemlock and spruce. There is an Indian village here and a church. The view from any point here is very fine, and there is a great deal to interest tourists. The shores are heavily wooded, with mountainous background, and potatoes and berries of all kinds are very plentiful.

METLAKAHTLA.

Leaving the Skeena, we pass out into Chatham Straits, and, rounding the Tsimpsean Peninsula, soon arrive at one of the most noted places on the coast — Metlakahtla, a very prettily situated Indian village, about twelve miles from the Skeena.

This at one time used to be a veritable beehive, under the management of Rev. Mr. Duncan, a missionary sent out in the early days by the Church Missionary Society of London, England. He had a sawmill, a woollen mill, a cannery, a brick-yard, a boys' home, a girls' home, an industrial school, and many other means of keeping the Indians employed. Later on the Home Society sent out Bishop Ridley (the Bishop of Caledonia) to take charge and look after the Society's interests. This caused a strife between two factions, which arose, some siding with Duncan and others with the Bishop, which ended in Duncan leaving with his adherents for a new settlement some thirty miles above Fort Simpson, called New Metlakahtla. The boys' and girls' homes are still running, and the industrial school is doing good work.

Their houses, until lately, were all built in one style — a lofty two-story building, which if divided up would contain about eight or ten rooms — and each one has a nice little garden patch laid out in fruit trees and vegetables, which have been much neglected of late; but nevertheless, gooseberries, raspberries, currants and strawberries thrive here wonderfully. The Church of England, built by Mr. Duncan, is a beautiful piece of work, and is the largest and most Anglican in appearance in the province. The Indians are very musical, and have a brass band, and in almost every other house is an organ. The church organist is an Indian. Metlakahtla is situated on the great Tsimpsean Peninsula, inhabited by the once mighty Tsimpsean nation of Indians, of whom those at Metlakahtla and Fort Simpson are notable examples.

FORT SIMPSON.

A few miles farther north, the chief of the Hudson's Bay Company's trading posts, is a populous Indian village, situated on an excellent harbour, which was once also an aspirant as a terminus of the Canadian Pacific Railway, by way of the Forks of the Skeena. Even here there was an incipient boom in town lots, looking in the direction of another railway. The Hudson's Bay Company have a large store here, where anything can be procured, from a needle to the latest pattern Winchester rifle. There is also a wharf, about a quarter of a mile long, and a warehouse at the extremity. The harbour here affords excellent anchorage at any depth up to thirty fathoms, with good mud and sand bottom. The rise and fall of the tide is from 18 to 20 feet, and on this account considerable of the shore is dry at low-water tide. The Metlakahtla Indians are first cousins to the Fort Simpsons, with whom they inter-marry. The latter, however, are Methodists. They have a church, two school-houses, a two-story fire hall with a tower, a two-story drill hall, a sash and door factory, a shingle mill worked by water-power, a boys' home, a girls' home, an excellent mission house, and a hospital. They have also an excellent brass band.

INTO ALASKA

Bidding good-bye to Fort Simpson, we sail past the mouth of the Naas River, where there are several canneries and imposing views, across Chatham Strait,

VIEW FROM BAMFIELD CREEK CABLE STATION.

THE ALBERNI CANAL.

AN ALBERNI PASTORAL SCENE.

HAYING ON VANCOUVER ISLAND.

around Cape Fox, into Dixon's Entrance, and into Alaska. On the way up we sail by Tongas Islands, the home of the Tongas Indians. In Tongas is where Mr. Duncan has established his celebrated mission, New Metlakahtla. On the way up we visit Sitka and Juneau, and circle around among numerous channels and enter several noted glacier bays. This is the land of the midnight sun, and a great attraction to American tourists. However, for diversity of scenery, for beauty and for interest, apart from icebergs and glaciers, it contains nothing which will outrival, or, some might even say, compare with the route just passed over, wholly in British Columbia waters and in Canadian territory. Here ends the journey, and the homeward trip is made.

CLIMATE.

NOTWITHSTANDING that much has been written about the climate of British Columbia, many misconceptions appear to prevail on the subject outside of the province. In some quarters, through confusion with the northwest interior of the Dominion, an impression has been formed that at least to the east of the Coast Range fearful extremes of cold are to be endured by the inhabitants; while in others, through a misapprehension of the reports of travellers, it has been imagined that the climate of the coast resembles that of the shores of the Mediterranean. In order to acquire a reasonable idea of the true state of the case, let anyone first examine upon a map of Europe that portion of land which lies between the same parallels of latitude and extends over the same area from the Atlantic coast east, and then consider how far conditions which are known to exist there will be modified by local differences on the Pacific. It will be seen that between latitudes 49 degrees and 59 degrees must be included Great Britain, the northeast corner of France, Belgium, Holland, North Germany, Prussia, Denmark, the south of Sweden, the Baltic Provinces, and the coast of Russia to the Gulf of Finland. This tract of country in area and latitude approximately represents British Columbia, and may be considered as a whole to present almost the same climatic conditions. The moderating influences upon the climate immediately on the coast are due to the presence of the Japan Current, or Gulf Stream of the Pacific, the prevalent moisture-laden winds from the ocean, and to latent heat liberated during the conversion of the moist air to rain upon the western slopes of the Coast Ranges. The higher mountain ranges also prevent to a great extent the overflow of cold northerly winds from the interior, and produces a humidity most beneficial to the vegetation of the province. The winds are arrested, in a measure, by the Coast Range, creating a dry belt to the east of these mountains; but the higher currents of air discharge their moisture against the Selkirks, causing the more copious snowfall which distinguishes that range from its neighbour, the Rockies.

Thus a series of alternate moist and dry belts are formed throughout the province, which have no parallel on the coast of Europe, where the more broken coast line and absence of lofty mountain ranges, together with the practical non-existence of an Arctic current, tend to distribute the rainfall over the whole area. It will be easily seen how these belts will be broken and modified in places by the varied elevation of the mountains and the presence of passes such as the Fraser Canyon.

Again, the decrease in elevation of the Rocky and Selkirk ranges as they approach to the north admits a free passage for the winds of the Arctic regions to sweep down over the northern portion of the province, bringing with them a corresponding reduction in temperature in winter or increase in the summer, when the long Arctic day admits an accumulation of dry hot air over these regions. Since there is open sea to the north of the European continent, these conditions exist there only in a modified form, although the Baltic Provinces, Poland and Prussia experience very similar effects from the northeast winds.

And, lastly, the elevation of the interior plateau is, of course, greatly superior to that of Northern Europe, making an average difference in barometric pressure of some two inches.

The general result of the above differences between the two regions is to accentuate the rainfall on the shores of the Pacific Coast and the extremes of temperature in the interior. Where the latter extends in areas of high elevation, these extremes of temperatures will necessarily be more felt; while in the valleys and canyons open to the coast, and well protected from the north, a more mild and equable climate will result. At the same time, there is a greater symmetry in the main features of land and water, the straight coast line and parallel mountain ranges, so the great ocean winds are probably less interfered with by local conditions, and there is a greater regularity of the seasons.

It may be said, then, that the climate of British Columbia, as a whole, presents all the features which are to be met with in European countries lying within the temperate zone, the cradle of the greatest nations of the world, and is, therefore, a climate well adapted to the development of the human race under the most favourable conditions.

The various local differences alluded to in general terms above, in relation to those causes which produce them, may now be more particularly described.

In the valley of the Columbia and throughout the Kootenay Districts, which correspond, as has been seen, with the mountain belt of the Selkirks, the high average altitude renders the air rarified and bracing, the precipitation of moisture being greater on the eastern flank of the Rockies, but falling far below that of the coast. Regular meteorological returns have not hitherto been made from stations in this section of the country, but from observations taken by Lieut.-Col. Baker during some years' residence at Cranbrook, in the Upper Columbia Valley, the following data may be depended upon as fairly accurate :

The rainfall averages from 18 to 20 inches per annum, the lesser amount being experienced in East Kootenay, and the snow attains to a depth of from 1 to 3 feet, making a total precipitation of about 20 to 24 inches of moisture, according to locality.

The winters extend from December to March, snow not falling, to lie, earlier than the last week in December, as a rule. Navigation on the Upper Columbia closes about the beginning of November; on the Arrow Lakes and Lower Columbia, not till the end of that month; it opens again about the middle of March. The Kootenay Lake does not freeze over. During the winter the thermometer falls at times considerably below zero, and in summer rises as high as 80 or 90 degrees in the shade, the nights being always comparatively cool. The extreme cold is not severely felt, and is of short duration, nor is the summer heat exhausting, as in the interior of the continent. Vegetation is rarely affected by drought, and, although summer frosts occasionally cause damage in swampy localities, their effects are modified by drainage and cultivation.

Farther west, throughout the region of the interior plateau, a drier climate prevails, culminating in the bunch-grass country immediately east of the Coast Range. Here luxuriant vegetation is entirely confined to the borders of the lakes and watercourses, while the higher benches and round-topped hills present the characteristic semi-barren appearance of this class of pasture land. The rain and snow fall is very moderate, total precipitation averaging from 7 to 12 inches according to locality. The winter is confined to 8 or 10 weeks' frost, when the thermometer falls to zero, and in severe seasons considerably below. The average is not extreme, nor are the cold spells protracted. The summers, like those of Kootenay, are warm during the day, with cool evenings. As the mean elevation is some 1,500 feet, the air of the interior plateau is clear and bracing.

South of the Shuswap Lake a climate is experienced typical of the milder and more moist conditions which prevail in the wide depressions once formed by glacial lakes, and which may be said to present a mean between the dryness of the true bunch-grass country and the humidity of the coast. The timber is here plentiful but scattered, vegetation is varied and luxuriant, the rainfall sufficient to obviate the need of irrigation, the winter and summer not appreciably differing from that of Central Europe.

In the narrow valleys which traverse the Coast Range a climate is found which once more calls for special remark as presenting features of some interest and peculiar to these situations. At Spence's Bridge, on the Fraser, a characteristic point, a meteorological station has been established for some years and accurate data of this class of climate obtained. Sheltered as these canyons are from the cold northern winds, they admit the warm breezes of the coast, and upon their sides the sun's rays are concentrated with almost tropical intensity. A temperature much warmer than would be expected is the result.

No sooner is the Coast Range crossed than an entirely new order of things becomes manifest, indicating a great change in climatic conditions. Vegetation is extraordinarily luxuriant, forests are everywhere, the undergrowth impenetrably dense. The reason of this is at once apparent when it is seen that the rainfall attains to some 70 inches, increasing as you proceed north and come more within the immediate influence of the Japan current to over 100 inches. The winters are shorter and much less severe, nor are the summers so hot as those of the interior; yet, owing to the increased amount of moisture in suspension, extremes, such as they are, make themselves more felt by the inhabitants. Still, no one can call the climate of the coast of British Columbia an unhealthy or uncomfortable one. Equable, sunny and with a singular absence of storms or tempests, the vicissitudes of life, so far as they depend upon climate, are perhaps less accentuated here than in most parts of the globe.

As was previously stated above in the general account of the climate, the driest point on the coast is seen to be the southeastern extremity of Vancouver Island, which includes Victoria, and is represented by the observations taken at Esquimalt. To speak more generally of the climate in this section, the nights, even in the height of summer, are invariably cool, more so than is ordinarily experienced in England during spells of warm summer weather. The harvest time is rarely unsettled, so that until recently many years had elapsed since damage was incurred in reaping the crops. Winters occur every now and then during which, from the absence of northerly winds, no perceptible degree of frost is experienced, and geraniums and other delicate plants can be grown in the open air. Such severe weather as is met with comes usually in short spells during the months of January and February.

Local fogs prevail over the water during the early spring and late autumn, chiefly in November, when they are sometimes a serious hindrance to navigation. The tides of the coast, between Vancouver Island and the Mainland, as they flow through narrow channels at the northern and southern extremities of the Island (Seymour Narrows and San Juan de Fuca Straits), appear to the casual observer most complicated and too eccentric to be reduced to a fixed scale. From observations obtained for several years, the Dominion Tidal Survey are now publishing tide tables a year in advance for several of the chief points here. They have proved to be very accurate and of great service to mariners. It is expected tidal predictions will shortly be published for the west coast of Vancouver Island and the more northern coast. The currents and tide-rips which prevail along the islands of the coast are somewhat perplexing, and require local study.

In the northern interior of the province the higher altitude is responsible for a correspondingly severe climate. In Cariboo and through the Chilcotin country the winters are, for instance, somewhat longer and colder than those experienced in the Okanagan and Columbia valleys. At Barkerville, in the first-named district, the mean January temperature has averaged, for the last four years, 19 degrees, that of April 34 degrees, of July 54 degrees, and October 40 degrees. This, considering the altitude and situation, which corresponds with that of Central Russia, is not extraordinarily severe, indeed is very moderate as compared with the interior of the continent of America far to the south.

NOTE.—The foregoing has been taken from the very excellent description of British Columbia climate contained in an official handbook entitled, "British Columbia, Its Present Resources and Future Possibilities."

Not the least important consideration to the individual seeking a home in a new country is the climatic conditions. Mr. James Lumsden, editorial representative of the Leeds and Yorkshire Mercury, visited Canada in 1902 with the British editorial party, at the invitation of the Dominion Government. A series of articles from his pen were published in the Mercury, from one of which the following extract on the subject of climate is made :—

"To farm in British Columbia requires capital, but here farming has many attractions superior to those of Manitoba. The winter is mild and genial. The citizens of Victoria and Vancouver City would think it a severe winter indeed if there were no roses blooming in their gardens on Christmas Day. The English farmer who acquires land in British Columbia can have all, and more than all, that he has in the finest agricultural counties in England. His house is surrounded by orchards, shrubberies and lawns; he is within easy access of a home market, and everything that he rears is equally remunerative. He obtains splendid prices for all the minor products of his farm—poultry, dairy produce and fruit—and can never rear sufficient to meet the demand. His only trouble is with the native vegetation, the persistent encroachment of which renders it difficult to farm upon a large scale English farmers with a few hundred pounds of capital, who are minded to throw up the anxieties of farming in the Old Country and make a bid for fortune in Canada, would be well advised not to settle in Manitoba or the Territories until they have paid a visit to British Columbia, where they would find an equally brilliant prospect of making money, and, to my mind, a more desirable mode of living. It is possible even for those who have little or no capital to make money by farming here, but English farmers are seldom successful in adventures of this description. Along the new lines of railway and the steamboat routes up the lakes you find Swiss and French settlers who burn out an acre or two of timber, start in with a few cows, and by selling cream, milk and butter push a lucrative trade along the lines of communication. Far in the recesses of the lakes and mountains you often strike these settlers, whose picturesque wooden houses perched on some romantic promontory, at once bring all the peripatetic photographers into action."

NICOLA RIVER.

JUNE—																	
Highest	74.0	89.2	82.5	74.0	93.4	73.4	70.0	81.0	89.0	78.0	79.1	84.0	84.0	76.0	85.0	81.0	89.0
Lowest	43.7	41.0	37.2	28.0	35.5	36.9	35.0	35.5	41.0	37.0	30.0	40.0	33.0	39.0	28.5	31.0	60.0
Mean highest	60.9	72.3	64.2	59.1	64.4	61.0	62.0	62.0	71.5	64.4	62.6	64.9	66.6	64.3	65.2	64.7	70.2
Mean lowest	48.4	40.3	47.1	35.6	47.0	45.3	45.2	44.0	46.6	45.4	39.2	47.5	41.8	47.3	46.5	40.6	41.8
Monthly mean	54.7	60.8	55.6	47.4	55.7	53.1	53.6	53.0	53.7	54.9	50.0	56.2	54.2	55.8	55.9	52.6	56.0
JULY—																	
Highest	68.0	93.0	75.5	72.0	79.9	79.4	69.5	81.0	83.0	74.0	93.1	81.0	90.0	86.0	80.0	83.0	98.0
Lowest	45.8	44.0	40.5	36.0	44.0	42.2	43.5	37.0	42.0	41.0	34.0	40.0	32.1	46.0	37.5	36.0	39.0
Mean highest	63.9	81.3	69.5	61.2	70.4	62.5	62.8	71.0	75.1	68.1	70.3	72.6	79.1	76.7	71.3	71.2	85.0
Mean lowest	50.8	53.0	49.5	39.6	51.0	49.0	49.3	48.1	45.7	47.0	45.1	50.0	44.8	53.9	49.1	43.6	44.1
Monthly mean	57.4	67.1	59.5	51.9	60.7	55.7	56.1	59.6	60.4	57.5	62.2	61.3	61.9	65.4	60.2	57.4	64.5
AUGUST—																	
Highest	79.2	98.5	84.1	82.0	83.0	78.7	71.0	88.0	91.0	84.0	90.1	90.0	95.0	84.0	88.0	87.0	102.5
Lowest	48.2	45.8	46.4	30.0	46.0	43.9	44.0	41.5	45.0	42.0	37.0	48.0	40.0	43.0	44.0	32.0	34.0
Mean highest	60.6	88.4	75.0	72.1	74.1	65.6	63.1	79.0	81.6	74.8	83.4	78.3	85.0	78.1	76.3	78.6	89.0
Mean lowest	32.4	55.7	51.6	40.4	50.9	51.0	51.3	40.6	47.7	47.3	45.3	51.6	45.3	52.6	48.8	42.4	42.0
Monthly mean	61.0	72.0	63.3	56.2	62.5	58.3	57.2	64.0	64.7	61.1	64.4	65.0	65.2	65.4	62.6	60.5	65.5
SEPTEMBER—																	
Highest	75.2	83.1	78.5	70.0	82.0	74.0	68.0	74.0	79.0	77.0	86.1	81.0	79.0	74.0	79.5	73.0	84.0
Lowest	39.3	32.0	33.5	20.0	33.9	37.5	41.5	30.0	35.0	34.0	21.0	35.0	24.0	31.0	31.0	27.0	27.0
Mean highest	62.8	69.0	65.0	55.3	65.0	61.2	50.5	61.5	72.2	66.6	61.3	67.9	67.4	60.6	65.7	60.8	67.8
Mean lowes	49.3	45.6	45.4	33.1	43.5	46.6	45.2	40.7	40.9	42.9	37.9	47.8	37.0	41.5	43.9	37.0	35.5
Monthly Mean	56.1	57.3	55.2	41.2	54.3	53.9	52.4	51.1	51.6	54.8	49.6	57.8	52.2	51.1	54.8	48.9	51.6
OCTOBER—																	
Highest	69.0	72.0	72.0	66.0	68.9	70.9	63.5	70.5	76.0	72.0	68.1	78.0	80.0	66.0	73.0	75.0	81.0
Lowest	44.2	31.0	38.5	24.0	33.0	37.1	36.5	26.0	36.0	34.0	24.0	39.0	23.0	28.0	38.5	28.0	21.0
Mean highest	60.5	62.8	61.3	52.4	60.5	56.9	55.0	61.0	69.0	59.9	61.4	63.4	66.1	58.4	63.2	60.3	68.8
Mean lowest	48.3	41.4	47.0	34.8	45.5	47.2	44.1	35.0	40.4	42.3	30.2	46.6	29.1	34.9	45.5	38.4	37.6
Monthly mean	54.4	52.1	54.2	43.6	53.0	52.0	49.6	48.0	55.2	51.1	45.8	55.0	47.9	46.6	54.3	49.4	50.2
NOVEMBER—																	
Highest	63.1	60.5	55.5	46.0	56.9	53.9	53.0	55.0	66.0	58.0	54.0	55.0	52.0	58.0	54.0	57.0	55.0
Lowest	40.0	26.0	33.8	10.0	31.0	31.1	18.0	20.0	31.0	30.0	20.0	33.0	23.0	23.0	31.0	19.0	19.0
Mean highest	51.9	47.3	48.8	36.5	49.7	46.2	46.3	45.6	53.3	50.0	44.9	49.7	42.4	43.8	49.5	42.7	43.4
Mean lowest	45.0	35.1	41.3	20.0	39.0	40.0	35.7	29.8	35.6	37.9	30.3	40.9	29.2	30.6	38.4	30.8	24.6
Monthly mean	48.5	41.2	45.0	31.2	44.4	43.1	41.0	37.2	44.4	44.2	37.6	45.3	35.8	37.1	44.0	36.7	30.0
DECEMBER—																	
Highest	53.2	50.5	50.2	40.0	52.9	46.5	62.0	50.5	48.0	56.4	49.0	54.0	44.0	43.0	51.0	47.0	34.0
Lowest	29.5	10.5	21.0	−4.0	22.0	26.1	24.0	10.0	25.0	23.0	5.0	23.0	2.0	12.0	20.0	7.0	−4.0
Mean highest	46.1	36.3	41.8	20.5	43.9	40.2	45.2	37.7	42.0	44.4	30.4	44.0	31.8	35.1	43.3	34.8	25.1
Mean lowest	39.9	26.2	33.2	18.7	32.0	33.7	34.0	22.1	32.3	31.8	21.4	34.0	17.5	12.0	31.8	22.1	15.6
Monthly mean	43.0	31.2	37.5	24.1	37.9	57.0	39.6	29.9	37.1	38.1	28.0	39.0	24.7	35.1	37.5	28.4	20.4
Annual means	49.85	48.46	48.65	36.63	48.47	46.14	45.78	43.44	48.96	47.59	43.33	49.92	43.06	45.26	48.77	41.37	43.03

Table showing for each Month the Average of the Highest, Lowest, Mean Highest, Mean Lowest, and the Mean Temperature at the Principal Stations in British Columbia derived from the whole group of years, and the Average Annual Temperature at each Station for the same period.

	Victoria.	Barkerville.	Kamloops.	New West.	French Ck.	Matsqui Pr.	Rivers Inlet.	Pt. Simpson.	Agassiz.	N. Nicomen.	Midway.	W. Kootenay.	Tobacco Pls.
	°	°	°	°	°	°	°	°	°	°	°	°	°
JANUARY—													
Highest	57.4	40.3	47.8	51.0	51.9	52.1	48.7	54.1	52.0	52.0	41.0	46.6	48.3
Lowest	21.8	—19.1	— 4.7	16.3	18.6	12.4	21.3	8.4	10.8	11.9	—14.1	— 5.8	—12.2
Mean highest	42.2	24.8	30.8	40.8	40.5	30.9	38.5	39.7	40.4	40.7	30.0	33.1	32.6
Mean lowest	33.5	11.8	17.9	32.6	30.9	28.1	31.1	27.0	29.5	30.7	12.6	18.0	19.3
Monthly mean	39.1	18.3	26.0	35.3	35.7	23.9	33.7	33.5	33.1	35.1	20.9	25.2	24.4
FEBRUARY—													
Highest	57.5	40.2	50.6	54.0	52.7	54.1	50.0	51.4	55.6	54.9	50.2	50.0	51.9
Lowest	22.4	—18.5	— 2.4	22.7	20.4	16.6	19.9	10.1	16.6	16.9	—14.4	— 1.2	— 6.2
Mean highest	44.2	26.6	33.9	44.2	43.0	42.2	40.9	40.0	44.7	42.9	34.2	37.3	35.5
Mean lowest	31.2	11.2	19.3	33.2	31.9	29.5	31.2	20.6	31.7	32.5	13.1	20.6	20.5
Monthly mean	39.7	19.0	26.1	39.3	37.8	30.0	35.1	33.7	36.7	37.7	23.3	27.5	27.3
MARCH—													
Highest	63.5	48.4	60.6	59.6	57.6	62.8	56.9	54.0	65.5	60.8	59.7	55.2	56.1
Lowest	26.7	— 6.5	8.4	25.8	23.2	22.5	23.2	17.7	23.6	24.1	3.5	6.0	1.5
Mean highest	48.9	34.4	46.1	40.7	48.1	50.2	45.2	44.8	53.1	49.3	46.0	43.8	42.0
Mean lowest	36.6	16.9	27.0	35.0	31.4	33.2	32.0	29.7	35.2	34.7	19.8	24.7	22.7
Monthly mean	42.6	25.8	36.6	42.5	40.0	41.8	37.6	38.1	41.4	42.2	32.9	35.8	33.2
APRIL—													
Highest	73.3	65.6	74.0	71.6	68.5	75.0	46.1	65.0	77.8	73.9	77.6	74.2	73.2
Lowest	31.5	8.3	27.8	30.6	27.3	25.9	29.2	25.4	31.1	31.3	20.4	25.6	16.2
Mean highest	55.1	43.9	60.5	57.7	54.9	57.2	51.4	49.5	59.3	57.5	60.1	59.8	57.9
Mean lowest	39.7	24.0	37.7	40.3	35.8	37.6	36.4	34.5	38.1	30.4	30.5	34.4	33.5
Monthly mean	47.0	34.7	49.1	48.6	46.3	47.2	43.2	42.4	46.2	48.1	45.0	47.2	45.1
MAY—													
Highest	80.2	74.9	84.1	80.4	75.8	84.5	75.4	70.5	95.8	82.6	86.0	82.8	83.6
Lowest	37.5	22.5	33.6	38.4	32.2	35.0	35.6	30.8	35.2	36.3	25.2	31.2	28.2
Mean highest	61.3	56.5	69.5	64.5	61.2	65.1	67.8	56.7	67.0	65.3	68.5	67.9	67.8
Mean lowest	44.4	33.9	45.7	44.1	41.7	44.4	41.8	39.5	43.6	44.9	36.4	43.8	37.6
Monthly mean	62.6	45.2	57.7	55.1	51.4	54.3	50.0	48.1	54.3	54.8	32.9	55.9	54.6

JUNE—													
Highest	84.6	78.6	91.2	83.8	80.4	85.3	78.1	66.9	86.8	84.9	93.0	82.3	91.7
Lowest	41.9	31.0	41.5	42.5	36.4	40.1	39.4	37.4	30.2	40.9	31.8	42.0	32.8
Mean highest	65.4	62.9	76.1	69.6	66.6	69.0	61.4	60.1	70.5	69.0	76.8	72.6	74.0
Mean lowest	48.0	38.7	51.5	50.9	46.6	49.0	44.9	43.7	47.4	44.6	42.8	51.4	45.5
Monthly mean	56.5	50.8	63.8	59.6	56.9	58.4	54.1	52.8	56.8	59.1	59.1	61.0	58.3
JULY—													
Highest	87.5	83.2	97.3	88.0	86.4	90.1	82.9	74.2	91.9	87.8	97.8	87.8	95.7
Lowest	44.7	33.8	47.6	46.5	43.6	43.2	45.1	30.0	42.7	45.5	36.2	40.4	39.0
Mean highest	69.4	68.4	81.5	74.7	73.7	74.9	66.1	62.9	77.7	76.4	84.5	78.1	80.4
Mean lowest	49.9	41.9	55.4	52.8	50.0	50.9	51.0	48.4	50.4	52.9	45.7	57.7	48.8
Monthly mean	60.0	55.0	68.7	63.7	61.7	61.9	59.5	56.2	63.4	64.3	65.0	67.5	64.2
AUGUST—													
Highest	78.8	82.8	98.3	77.9	85.7	87.4	77.8	73.1	92.4	85.9	96.0	85.2	92.4
Lowest	44.9	32.5	45.6	47.1	41.4	42.7	42.9	40.2	43.7	44.4	33.0	45.2	35.4
Mean highest	69.1	69.6	81.3	73.4	73.7	74.8	66.4	64.1	80.2	75.4	82.8	75.4	79.1
Mean lowest	50.0	42.2	54.8	54.0	50.0	51.2	51.2	40.1	49.8	53.2	45.2	53.0	46.8
Monthly mean	60.8	55.9	68.0	64.0	62.2	62.6	59.4	56.9	62.0	64.3	63.9	64.4	62.4
SEPTEMBER—													
Highest	72.8	75.5	83.6	79.2	80.3	82.1	71.1	67.9	86.5	80.7	88.6	77.0	83.5
Lowest	38.9	23.8	34.3	40.1	33.4	35.5	39.1	36.6	37.0	39.4	27.4	33.8	31.1
Mean highest	63.7	58.8	69.6	66.6	64.7	66.2	60.9	59.9	70.7	66.4	72.8	66.6	68.4
Mean lowest	46.3	35.3	46.1	47.7	44.3	45.9	47.5	45.0	45.7	47.9	37.5	41.5	37.7
Monthly mean	55.0	47.0	57.9	57.5	55.1	58.2	53.7	52.8	55.5	57.3	53.8	54.8	53.4
OCTOBER—													
Highest	64.3	62.6	70.3	68.1	64.1	69.5	62.4	62.9	72.5	67.7	70.3	66.4	70.0
Lowest	31.2	15.5	25.8	35.1	30.0	30.7	35.4	29.7	32.0	32.6	19.0	24.8	20.2
Mean highest	55.8	46.8	56.0	57.2	55.4	57.7	52.9	54.2	62.4	56.7	57.9	54.3	54.4
Mean lowest	43.1	29.5	38.7	43.9	38.9	41.0	43.1	40.2	40.5	43.0	20.6	34.1	32.4
Monthly mean	49.3	38.1	47.6	50.5	47.6	49.8	47.1	47.2	48.8	50.4	42.0	44.5	43.8
NOVEMBER—													
Highest	55.8	51.2	59.5	58.0	56.3	60.1	52.4	59.9	62.4	58.7	57.7	54.6	54.9
Lowest	28.7	6.3	7.5	25.9	22.7	20.5	29.2	18.4	20.4	21.9	—7.8	6.8	—7.5
Mean highest	48.3	31.9	30.8	46.2	45.4	46.5	42.2	45.6	45.6	47.0	38.5	41.9	38.1
Mean lowest	38.8	15.8	27.6	38.0	34.7	33.8	34.8	32.7	33.2	36.7	21.0	26.0	23.8
Monthly mean	43.2	24.3	32.2	41.5	40.5	40.8	38.9	39.0	39.8	42.2	29.9	31.5	32.0
DECEMBER—													
Highest	53.5	41.4	51.1	53.0	52.1	53.7	52.4	55.3	49.4	53.9	45.4	48.8	53.3
Lowest	27.8	—11.3	1.7	23.0	23.9	18.0	29.9	14.8	19.8	20.6	—9.4	3.8	—11.8
Mean highest	45.7	28.3	34.2	42.6	42.7	41.5	42.1	43.1	41.9	43.2	31.0	36.0	35.0
Mean lowest	37.3	14.0	24.5	34.2	33.8	31.1	34.3	30.5	31.4	34.4	14.8	23.5	22.7
Monthly mean	41.2	21.0	29.3	38.5	38.3	30.0	37.7	36.8	36.6	38.4	22.4	31.4	28.9
Annual means	48.84	36.26	46.92	49.07	47.79	48.66	46.08	44.79	47.88	49.53	42.07	45.80	43.97

Monthly and Annual Amount of Rainfall in inches at the Stations in British Columbia reporting during the year 1901, with the Average of the Stations derived from a group of years.

	January.	February.	March.	April.	May.	June.	July.	August.	September.	October.	November.	December.	Year.
	in.	in.	in.	in.	in.	in.	in.	in.	in.	in.	in.	in.	in.
Victoria average	4.40	3.31	2.45	1.97	1.15	1.15	0.43	0.57	1.79	2.93	5.15	5.97	31.27
1901	3.72	3.18	0.03	3.01	0.08	1.06	0.19	0.00	0.90	1.65	6.44	3.46	25.52
New Westminster average	7.34	6.02	3.92	3.98	3.47	4.32	1.14	1.32	2.92	4.88	9.22	6.80	55.33
1901	4.67	7.38	3.71	4.09	3.79	5.52	1.41	0.20	2.76	4.33	11.98	7.01	56.85
Agassiz average	6.02	4.97	4.73	4.52	5.00	4.52	1.92	1.86	4.55	6.49	7.84	7.97	60.39
1901	5.07	4.76	3.16	2.79	4.80	7.08	1.25	0.00	1.59	4.15	10.57	4.76	49.98
Barkerville average	0.23	0.13	0.11	0.46	2.29	3.49	3.05	2.93	2.86	1.72	0.79	0.06	18.12
1901	0.00	0.22	0.30	0.26	2.97	3.80	3.38	0.94	2.92	2.06	1.00	0.00	18.75
Port Simpson average	9.98	7.00	4.52	6.79	4.73	4.34	5.51	6.30	8.40	12.03	10.58	12.19	92.38
1901	7.10	6.08	7.14	5.03	3.13	2.30	2.04	11.66	5.85	14.48	12.92	13.12	90.85
French Creek average	3.99	2.46	2.78	1.94	2.29	1.64	0.92	0.79	2.04	2.79	5.49	5.54	32.07
1901	3.31	2.65	1.62	3.32	2.28	1.94	0.62	0.38	1.12	1.80	6.58	3.69	29.27
Rivers Inlet average	11.42	11.38	6.99	9.12	5.80	4.52	3.88	4.03	7.38	13.71	13.76	13.33	105.32
1901	10.92	8.80	10.50	6.80	7.42	3.30	6.60	3.43	4.43	18.13	20.12	20.58	121.12
North Nicomen average	6.85	8.61	5.50	6.40	5.70	5.61	2.03	1.99	4.70	6.73	11.10	9.37	74.69
1901	5.41	9.19	5.55	8.43	4.87	6.1	0.82	0.05	2.70	6.50	14.60	7.00	71.24
Matsqui average	5.46	4.86	4.81	5.05	4.52	4.12	1.34	1.43	4.49	5.35	8.58	7.83	57.84
1901	4.42	7.50	5.48	5.43	5.74	2.99	0.98	0.09	2.71	4.63	12.29	6.10	58.45
Kamloops average	0.13	0.28	0.33	0.31	1.09	1.48	1.33	0.91	0.89	0.62	0.44	0.26	8.07
1901	0.00	0.07	0.06	0.15	0.00	1.99	0.42	0.00	1.21	0.16	1.23	0.46	5.75
Midway average	0.10	0.04	0.73	1.14	2.19	1.20	0.91	1.22	1.07	0.88	0.72	0.08	10.28
1901	0.00	0.00	0.25	0.60	2.71	1.95	0.15	0.41	1.44	0.00	0.55	0.00	8.06
Carmanah average	12.70	13.35	9.09	10.67	6.39	4.0	1.97	1.04	5.01	8.76	16.74	17.55	107.87
1901	7.69	9.25	2.94	8.33	11.34	3.48	0.80	0.08	6.10	6.84	20.68	16.08	93.61
Chilliwack, 1901	5.40	7.60	3.40	7.51	5.18	4.83	1.42	0.04	2.47	4.50	13.74	5.54	61.63
Ladner, 1901	1.36	3.50	1.25	2.71	2.55	2.78	....	....	....	....	....	....	....
Bella Coola, 1901	2.70	1.00	2.83	1.58	2.43	1.00	2.78	1.74	0.50	8.99	9.10	9.75	44.49
Tobacco Plains, 1901	0.95	1.07	0.21	0.32	2.13	4.10	0.92	0.14	1.85	0.63	1.24	0.65	14.41
Kuper Island, 1901	3.37	4.56	1.18	2.46	2.67	2.45	0.45	0.16	1.92	2.35	9.76	5.87	....
Hazlemere, 1901	3.06	2.17	2.07	5.35	3.47	3.15	1.23	....	....	....	....	....	....
Nicola Lake, 1901	0.10	0.35	0.14	0.48	0.65	2.45	1.02	0.08	1.12	0.22	0.96	0.37	7.89
Reclamation Farm, 1901	0.78	0.95	0.68	1.84	3.20	3.10	1.43	0.17	1.78	0.92	1.76	0.96	17.52
Nelson, 1901	2.74	0.95	1.16	1.60	2.70	....	....	....	....	....	....	....	....
Quesnell, 1901	0.00	0.00	0.00	0.00	0.65	1.9[illegible]	2.31	....	....	....	0.15	0.00	....

Bullion, 1901	0.00	0.22	0.00	0.03	1.44	2.95	1.32	0.53	2.94	1.06	0.81	0.36	12.46
Chilcotin, 1901	0.15	0.00	0.29	0.47	....	....	....	....	....	....	....	....	....
Okanagan Mission, 1901	....	2.59	0.27	0.51	0.58	0.70	0.52	0.00	....	....	....	....	....
Port Bobs, 1901	14.66	10.45	15.09	....	....	....	5.39	2.58	3.63	12.18	24.84	20.88	....
Masset, 1901	1.60	1.75	5.30	4.15	3.65	1.35	4.30	2.75	2.60	....	....	....	....
Alberni, 1901	4.49	6.71	3.61	6.97	6.06	2.61	1.37	0.42	2.18	5.07	17.78	6.71	63.98
Enderby, 1901	0.00	0.27	0.48	0.32	0.81	2.50	....	....	....	....	....	....	....
Stuart Lake, 1901	0.00	0.00	0.30	0.60	1.35	1.65	1.45	0.15	0.40	0.20	0.50	0.32	6.92
Vancouver, 1901	6.22	6.30	3.04	5.29	4.38	5.01	0.83	0.22	2.65	5.20	14.06	8.09	61.29
Garry Point, 1901	3.10	4.18	1.54	3.13	3.50	2.01	0.90	0.05	2.40	3.35	7.00	4.08	36.20
Cape Scott, 1901	....	....	....	....	....	3.34	4.91	3.27	2.25	16.73	28.50	17.45	....
Revelstoke, 1901	3.84	10.40	2.27	1.03	3.02	....	....	....	....	....	....	....	....
Coldstream Ranch, 1901	0.00	0.00	0.00	0.42	0.55	1.41	0.50	0.12	1.27	....	....	....	....
Clayoquot, 1901	10.60	17.60	13.31	12.38	17.65	4.63	4.77	1.52	4.57	10.96	32.87	16.67	147.53
Naas Harbor, 1901	8.45	5.08	4.39	2.06	3.14	1.32	3.02	9.80	6.39	15.26	8.52	12.93	81.05
Port Essington, 1901	14.83	9.57	12.16	6.62	4.13	2.93	3.27	12.95	5.64	21.31	17.10	25.62	136.22
Royal Oak, 1901	6.20	4.88	2.54	3.37	1.46	0.87	0.45	0.00	1.16	3.28	8.55	5.10	37.86
Caulfield, 1901	5.64	7.21	3.46	4.61	3.32	4.61	0.82	0.06	3.90	4.43	8.85	6.07	52.98
Goldstream Lake, 1901	7.00	8.59	1.07	5.01	3.37	2.13	0.29	0.04	1.82	4.56	14.83	10.01	60.49
Nanaimo (City), 1901	4.41	4.27	1.83	2.36	1.81	2.54	1.02	0.20	1.05	2.49	8.32	4.79	35.69
Vancouver, 1901	5.51	6.29	6.04	5.27	4.48	5.03	0.83	0.27	2.64	5.20	....	....	....
Cranbrook, 1901	....	....	....	....	....	....	....	0.00	1.28	0.43	0.73	0.00	....
Nanaimo, 1901	....	....	1.19	2.40	1.62	2.68	0.32	0.23	1.73	2.51	7.08	4.70	....
Duncans, 1901	....	4.36	1.15	2.42	1.94	1.91	0.34	0.31	1.40	2.39	11.05	5.81	....
Saturna Island, 1901	....	....	....	0.89	2.08	1.53	0.29	0.00	1.31	2.97	5.38	4.08	....
Kaslo, 1901	....	....	....	....	....	1.52	1.69	0.56	1.40	1.46	3.67	1.22	....
Princeton, 1901	0.00	0.54	0.03	0.13	1.03	1.04	0.46	0.05	1.00	0.11	0.74	0.00	5.13
Pilot Bay, 1901	2.11	4.98	0.64	4.87	5.17	....	....	....	....	....	....	....	....
Coquitlam, 1901	....	....	....	....	....	....	1.28	0.07	3.06	5.85	12.86	10.08	....
Cumberland, 1901	1.24	....	....	....	....	....	....	....	....	....	....	....	....

Monthly and Annual Amount of Snowfall in inches at the Stations in British Columbia during the year 1901, with the Average for the Stations derived from a group of years.

	January.	February.	March.	April.	May.	June.	July.	August.	September.	October.	November.	December.	Year.
	in.	in.	in.	in.	in.	in.	in.	in.	in.	in.	in.	in.	in.
Victoria, average	6.8	5.5	1.2	....	....	....	....	....	....	0.1	1.4	1.6	16.6
1901	4.3	1.8	....	....	....	....	....	....	....	....	0.0	0.0	6.1
New Westminster, average	10.5	7.6	4.4	0.1	....	....	....	....	....	....	6.5	1.9	31.0
1901	43.0	12.4	9.8	....	....	....	....	....	....	....	....	0.8	66.0
Agassiz, average	14.0	11.4	4.7	0.5	....	....	....	....	....	....	6.1	10.0	46.7
1901	19.0	7.0	0.0	4.0	....	....	....	....	....	....	....	....	30.0
Barkerville, average	25.2	27.7	18.1	13.7	2.1	0.3	....	0.1	1.6	10.3	21.0	30.0	150.3
1901	44.0	10.0	26.0	16.0	2.0	2.0	....	....	6.0	2.0	20.0	42.0	170.0
Port Simpson, average	6.8	13.8	6.4	3.1	....	....	....	....	....	....	1.8	6.8	38.7
1901	4.0	1.8	2.5	1.0	....	....	....	....	....	....	0.8	....	10.1
French Creek, average	13.6	7.1	2.1	1.0	....	....	....	....	....	....	5.3	4.9	34.0
1901	37.0	2.0	....	....	....	....	....	....	....	....	0.0	0.0	30.0
Rivers Inlet, average	11.6	14.8	19.2	5.6	1.5	....	....	....	....	0.1	7.7	6.7	67.2
1901	2.0	5.0	....	1.9	....	....	....	....	....	....	0.0	2.0	10.0
North Nicomen, average	11.3	9.2	6.5	....	....	....	....	....	....	....	5.1	8.4	40.5
1901	28.5	14.2	....	....	....	....	....	....	....	....	....	....	42.7
Matsqui, average	6.5	7.7	3.4	....	....	....	....	....	....	....	3.2	6.6	27.4
1901	15.5	0.0	....	....	....	....	....	....	....	....	....	....	15.5
Kamloops, average	6.9	5.1	1.1	....	....	....	....	....	....	0.4	7.9	4.5	25.9
1901	9.0	4.0	0.0	0.2	....	....	....	....	....	....	....	....	13.2
Midway, average	10.0	5.3	2.1	....	....	....	....	....	....	....	7.3	9.9	34.6
1901	8.8	3.7	4.8	....	....	....	....	....	....	....	....	3.0	20.3
Carmanah, average	5.8	6.3	1.9	0.3	....	....	....	....	....	....	2.2	2.0	18.5
1901	5.0	0.0	0.0	....	....	....	....	....	....	....	0.0	....	5.0
Chilliwack, 1901	18.0	5.5	....	....	....	....	....	....	....	....	0.0	0.0	23.5
Ladner, 1901	14.1	0.3	....	....	....	....	....	....	....	....	....	....	....
Bella Coola, 1901	20.0	0.5	0.0	14.2	....	....	....	....	....	....	9.0	0.0	43.7
Tobacco Plains, 1901	19.0	5.0	0.9	2.5	....	....	....	....	....	....	1.0	....	28.4
Kuper Island, 1901	34.0	4.1	....	....	....	....	....	....	....	....	0.0	0.0	38.1
Hazlemere, 1901	12.0	3.1	....	....	....	....	....	....	....	....	....	....	....
Nicola Lake, 1901	7.0	2.4	2.5	....	....	....	....	....	....	....	0.2	....	11.9
Reclamation Farm, 1901	25.0	4.0	5.1	2.0	....	....	....	....	....	....	8.2	7.6	51.9
Nelson, 1901	25.0	5.0	0.0	3.5	....	....	....	....	....	....	....	....	....
Quesnell, 1901	11.0	0.5	....	....	....	....	....	....	....	....	1.5	7.0	20.0

Buffton, 1901	19.2	6.0	15.3	20.6	1.6	....	....	....	....	....	15.4	23.6	101.9
Chilcotin, 1901	3.0	0.7	2.0	0.6	....	....	....	....	....	....	....	....	....
Okanagan Mission, 1901	....	5.4	0.0	0.3	....	....	....	....	....	....	....	....	....
Port Bobs, 1901	0.5	6.2	....	....	....	....	....	....	....	....	....	....	6.7
Masset, 1901	9.5	10.0	1.0	7.0	....	....	....	....	....	....	....	....	....
Alberni, 1901	19.5	12.5	2.0	0.8	....	....	....	....	....	....	....	0.3	65.1
Enderby, 1901	9.2	7.0	1.0	3.0	....	....	....	....	....	....	....	....	....
Stuart Lake, 1901	12.0	2.5	4.0	6.0	....	....	....	....	....	1.0	21.0	11.0	57.5
Vancouver, 1901	50.6	0.1	....	....	....	....	....	....	....	....	....	....	50.7
Garry Point, 1901	60.3	2.0	....	....	....	....	....	....	....	....	....	....	32.3
Cape Scott, 1901	....	....	....	....	....	....	....	....	....	....	0.0	0.0	....
Revelstoke, 1901	2.0	37.0	6.0	....	....	....	....	....	....	....	....	....	....
Coldstream Ranch, 1901	7.5	5.9	1.0	5.9	....	....	....	....	....	....	....	....	....
Clayoquot, 1901	9.0	2.4	....	....	....	....	....	....	....	....	....	....	11.4
Naas Harbor, 1901	38.0	13.0	15.0	10.0	....	....	....	....	....	....	1.0	2.0	79.0
Royal Oak, 1901	7.0	1.0	....	....	....	....	....	....	....	....	0.0	0.0	8.0
Caulfields, 1901	38.5	0.0	....	....	....	....	....	....	....	....	0.0	0.0	38.5
Goldstream Lake, 1901	40.5	25.0	26.4	22.0	....	....	....	....	....	....	0.0	0.0	113.9
Nanaimo (City), 1901	40.0	4.0	0.0	0.5	....	....	....	....	....	....	0.0	0.0	44.5
Vancouver, 1901	30.3	0.0	....	....	....	....	....	....	....	....	....	....	....
Cranbrook, 1901	....	....	....	....	....	....	....	....	....	....	4.5	5.0	....
Nanaimo, 1901	....	....	....	....	....	....	....	....	....	....	....	....	....
Duncans, 1901	....	2.5	....	....	....	....	....	....	....	....	0.0	0.0	....
Saturna Island, 1901	....	....	....	....	....	....	....	....	....	....	....	....	....
Kaslo, 1901	....	....	....	....	....	....	....	....	....	....	....	16.8	....
Princeton, 1901	4.9	4.6	3.8	0.4	....	....	....	....	....	....	3.4	3.5	20.6
Pilot Bay, 1901	16.0	4.0	....	....	....	....	....	....	....	....	....	....	....
Port Essington, 1901	....	....	....	....	....	....	....	....	....	....	0.5	1.6	....

Aggregate Amount of Snowfall in the Winter of 1900-1901.

STATION.	First Snow 1900.	Last Snow 1901.	Total Amount.
			In.
Victoria	24th January (1901)	15th March	11.0
Barkerville	25th August	3rd June	174.0
Kamloops	15th November	6th April	16.0
New Westminster	14th December	5th April	27.1
Port Simpson	20th November	2nd May	16.2
Rivers Inlet	24th December	9th April	27.7
Alberni	18th November	23rd April	40.1
Agassiz	16th November	5th April	50.0
Carmanah	17th November	23rd April	9.0
Clayoquot	18th November	2nd April	16.9
Enderby	17th November	3rd April	36.2
French Creek	16th November	21st February	48.0
Garry Point	17th November	18th February	38.7
Goldstream Lake	17th November	1st April	103.1
Hazlemere	1st January (1901)	15th February	3.7
Matsqui	17th November	10th January	20.5
Massett	23rd November	11th April	24.8
Midway	16th November	31st March	27.1
Naas Harbor	22nd November	13th April	91.0
North Nicomen	22nd November	21st February	65.7
Nicola Lake	3rd October	23rd March	23.4
Nanaimo	17th November	2nd April	54.5
Port Bobs	21st November	20th February	8.7
Quesnel	21st November	26th March	15.5
Nelson	17th November	24th February	54.3
Royal Oak	16th November	1st April	14.5
Stuart Lake	20th October	22nd April	36.5
Bullion	21st October	3rd June	79.6
Tobacco Plains	4th October	15th April	39.5
West Kootenay	15th November	1st April	61.1
Vancouver	17th November	18th February	62.7

RAPIDS, KICKING HORSE RIVER.

Periodical Events at Stations in British Columbia during the year 1901.

STATION.	Last Snow.	Last Frost.	First Thunder.	Warmest Day.	Mean Tempt.	Heaviest Days Rain.	Amount in Inches.	Last Thunder.	First Frost.	First Snow.
					°		in.			
Victoria	17 Feb.	10 Apl.	3 May	31 July	66.5	12 Jan.	1.23	16 Dec.	3 Nov.	22 Oct.
Kamloops	6 Apl.	10 May	....	24 Aug.	76.0	1 June	0.18	....	30 Sep.	11 Nov.
New Westminster	5 Apl.	6 May	27 Mar.	6 Aug.	70.5	28 Feb.	3.01	3 Dec.	7 Dec.	14 Dec.
Barkerville	8 June	28 June	16 May	4 Aug.	62.0	16 May	1.00	....	2 Sep.	27 Sep.
Port Simpson	2 May	26 Apl.	14 Sep.	23 Aug.	63.3	30 Aug.	3.46	14 Sep.	9 Nov.	25 Nov.
Rivers Inlet	25 Apl.	3 May	19 June	17 June	67.4	31 Oct.	3.47	7 Dec.	24 Nov.	24 Dec.
Chilliwack	5 Apl.	26 Apl.	20 Apl.	26 May	75.1	12 Nov.	2.61	1 July	30 Sep.	24 Dec.
Carmanah	23 Apl.	27 Apl.	23 Apl.	14 Aug.	65.5	28 Feb.	4.45	22 Nov.	11 Dec.	6 Dec.
French Creek	21 Mar.	8 May	....	15 Aug.	67.5	26 Nov.	1.23	....	1 Nov.	....
Agassiz	5 Apl.	20 Apl.	....	28 May	75.5	13 Jan.	1.96	....	11 Nov.	....
Duncan	2 Apl.	19 May	....	14 Aug.	68.0	26 Nov.	1.83	....	29 Sep.	....
Bullion	3 June	5 June	16 May	25 May	66.0	21 Sep.	0.73	9 Oct.	1 Aug.	30 Oct.
Garry Point	18 Feb.	26 Apl.	....	6 Aug.	69.0	27 Nov.	1.30	....	1 Oct.	....
Princeton	7 May	15 June	11 June	15 Aug.	71.0	18 May	0.50	11 Sep.	16 Sep.	12 Nov.
West Kootenay	1 Apl.	10 May	7 May	22 July	72.5	5 Apl.	1.00	19 Aug.	29 Sep.	9 Nov.
Clayoquot	2 Apl.	9 May	21 Apl.	13 Aug.	64.5	31 May	4.93	22 Nov.	10 Nov.	....
Midway	31 Mar.	7 June	....	15 Aug.	75.2	28 May	1.50	....	4 Sep.	7 Dec.
Alberni	23 Apl.	9 May	8 May	10 Aug.	73.2	26 Nov.	2.35	8 Nov.	6 Sep.	9 Dec.
Vancouver	10 Jan.	16 Apl.	16 Apl.	23 July	69.7	28 Feb.	2.10	....	29 Sep.	....
Nicola Lake	23 Mar.	10 May	29 Apl.	16 Aug.	70.5	20 May	0.56	26 July	15 Sep.	19 Nov.
N. Nicomen	21 Feb.	26 Apl.	20 Apl.	14 Aug.	72.0	28 Feb.	3.53	5 Nov.	18 Nov.	14 Dec.
Stuart Lake	22 Apl.	23 June	17 July	30 Aug.	60.0	19 Apl.	0.60	....	24 July	31 Oct.
Quesnel	26 Feb.	29 May	....	18 June	67.2	26 June	0.38	....	9 Sep.	2 Nov.
Tobacco Plains	15 Apl.	9 June	9 May	16 Aug.	73.0	28 Feb.	0.80	4 Sep.	15 Sep.	9 Nov.
Matsqui	10 Jan.	5 May	....	26 May	69.8	11 Nov.	2.44	....	10 Nov.	....
Port Bobs	20 Feb.	20 Mar.	....	24 Aug.	65.0	3 Nov.	4.35	21 Nov.	6 Dec.	7 Nov.
Massett	24 Apl.	27 Apl.	....	23 Aug.	62.0	21 Apl.	1.75	21 Nov.	6 Dec.	7 Nov.
Kuper Island	23 Feb.	9 May	12 June	23 Aug.	62.0	27 Nov.	1.92	....	30 Sep.	7 Nov.
Nanaimo	2 Apl.	16 May	9 May	15 Aug.	80.0	7 Dec.	1.25	15 Nov.	2 Nov.	13 Dec.

Monthly and Annual Number of Days of Snowfall at Stations.

	January.	February.	March.	April.	May.	June.	July.	August.	September.	October.	November.	December.	Year.
Victoria average...	3	2	1	..	..	..	..	..	..	1	2	1	10
1901	7	3	0	..	..	..	..	..	..	..	0	0	10
Westminster, av'ge.	7	3	2	..	..	..	..	..	..	..	2	1	15
1901	10	4	3	..	..	..	..	..	..	..	0	1	18
Agassiz, average...	4	4	2	1	..	..	..	..	..	..	4	3	18
1901	6	3	0	3	..	..	..	..	..	..	0	0	12
Barkerville, av'ge...	11	8	8	7	1	1	..	..	1	4	10	11	62
1901	17	5	12	6	1	1	..	..	2	1	7	12	64
Port Simpson, av'ge	5	7	3	2	1	..	..	..	..	..	2	3	23
1901	4	3	2	2	1	..	..	..	..	..	1	1	14
French Creek, av'ge	5	3	1	..	..	..	..	..	..	..	3	2	14
1901	8	2	..	..	..	..	..	..	..	..	0	0	10
Rivers Inlet, av'ge.	4	5	5	3	..	..	..	..	..	..	3	5	25
1901	1	3	3	2	..	..	..	..	..	..	0	1	10
N. Nicomen, av'ge.	3	4	4	..	..	..	..	..	..	..	2	3	16
1901	5	3	..	..	..	..	..	..	..	..	0	1	9
Matsqui, average...	3	5	3	1	..	..	..	..	..	..	2	2	16
1901	5	0	..	..	..	..	..	..	..	..	0	0	5
Kamloops, average.	6	5	5	..	..	..	..	..	..	1	4	5	26
1901	5	4	0	1	..	..	..	..	..	..	1	1	12
Midway, average...	9	4	3	..	..	..	..	..	..	..	3	5	24
1901	7	3	3	..	..	..	..	..	..	..	0	2	15
Carmanah, average.	5	4	4	1	1	..	..	..	..	..	2	2	19
1901	10	0	..	..	..	..	..	..	..	..	0	2	12
Chilliwack, 1901...	4	2	0	..	..	..	..	..	..	..	0	0	6
Ladner, 1901	4	7	..	..	..	..	..	..	..	..	..	..	..
Bella Coola, 1901..	3	1	0	2	..	..	..	..	..	..	2	0	8
Tobacco Plains, '01.	7	2	3	3	..	..	..	..	..	..	1	1	17
Kuper Island, 1901.	8	2	..	..	..	..	..	..	..	..	0	0	10
Hazlemere, 1901...	4	3	..	..	..	..	..	..	..	..	..	..	..
Nicola Lake, 1901.	10	5	6	..	..	..	..	..	..	..	1	2	24
Reclamat'n F'm, '01	11	1	5	1	..	..	..	..	..	..	4	4	26
Nelson, 1901	12	3	0	1	..	..	..	..	..	..	..	..	..
Quesnel, 1901	3	1	..	..	..	..	..	..	..	..	2	4	10
Bullion, 1901	14	4	10	6	2	..	..	..	..	..	6	8	50
Chilcotin, 1901	5	6	4	1	..	..	..	..	..	..	..	..	..
Okanagan Mis'n, '01	..	4	0	1	..	..	..	..	..	..	..	..	..
Port Bobs, 1901...	3	5	..	..	..	..	..	..	..	..	..	..	..
Masset, 1901	4	9	2	4	..	..	..	..	..	..	..	..	..
Alberni, 1901	9	5	2	2	..	..	..	..	..	..	0	1	19
Enderby, 1901	9	5	1	2	..	..	..	..	..	..	..	..	..
Stuart Lake, 1901..	4	2	4	6	..	..	..	..	..	2	11	4	33
Vancouver, 1901 ..	9	1	..	..	..	..	..	..	..	..	..	..	..
Garry Point, 1901..	8	1	..	..	..	..	..	..	..	..	0	0	9
Cape Scott, 1901...	..	..	..	..	..	..	..	..	..	..	0	0	..
Revelstoke, 1901...	2	9	1	1	..	..	..	..	..	..	..	..	..
Coldstr'm R'nch, '01	2	6	4	4	..	..	..	..	..	..	..	..	..
Clayoquot, 1901....	9	1	..	..	..	..	..	..	..	..	0	0	10
Naas Harbour, '01.	9	5	2	3	..	..	..	..	..	..	2	1	22
Royal Oak, 1901...	4	3	..	..	..	..	..	..	..	..	0	0	7
Caulfield, 1901	7	0	..	..	..	..	..	..	..	..	0	0	7
Goldstr'm Lake, '01	12	9	9	3	..	..	..	..	..	..	0	0	33
Nanaimo City, 1901	7	4	0	1	..	..	..	..	..	..	0	0	12
Vancouver, 1901...	5	0	0	..	..	..	..	..	..	..	0	0	5
Cranbrook, 1901...	..	..	..	..	..	..	..	..	..	..	2	3	..
Nanaimo, 1901	..	..	1	1	..	..	..	..	..	..	11	0	..
Duncans, 1901	..	2	..	..	..	..	..	..	..	..	..	..	..
Saturna Island, '01.	..	..	..	..	..	..	..	..	..	..	0	0	11
Kaslo, 1901	..	..	..	..	..	..	..	..	..	..	1	6	..
Princeton, 1901 ...	11	8	1	3	2	..	..	..	..	..	2	5	32
Pilot Bay, 1901....	4	2	..	..	..	..	..	..	..	..	..	..	..
Port Essington, '01	..	..	..	..	..	..	..	..	..	..	1	2	..

Meteorological Stations in British Columbia reporting during the year 1901, with their Latitude, Longitude, and Height above Sea Level when known.

STATION.	OBSERVER.	Latitude N.		Longitude W.		Height in Feet.	Class.
Victoria	E. Baynes Reed	48	21	123	19	85	C. S.
New Westminster	Hugh Wilson	49	13	122	54	330	1
Agassiz Exp. Farm	T. A. Sharpe	49	14	121	31	52	II. S.
Barkerville	James Stone	53	2	121	35	4180	I.
Port Simpson	Miss M. W. O'Neill	54	34	130	26	26	I.
French Creek	W. H. Lee, B. A.	49	20	124	36	..	II.
Kuper Island	Rev. R. J. Roberts	48	58	123	38	..	III.
Rivers Inlet	S. Grant	51	39	127	19	20	I.
Hazlemere	H. T. Thrift	49	3	122	43	..	II.
North Nicomen	J. F. Harris	49	12	122	22	59	II.
Matsqui Prairie	W. S. Maher	49	7	122	16	..	II.
Kamloops	C. S. Stevens	50	41	120	29	1193	I.
Midway	R. Gardom	49	0	118	46	1800	II.
Carmanah	W. P. Daykin	48	38	124	47	130	I.
Chilliwack	Mrs. W. H. DeWolf.	49	10	121	57	21	I.
Ladner	A. DeR. Taylor	49	5	123	4	..	II.
Rossland	A. W. Dyer	49	6	117	40	3400	II.
Bella Coola	H. B. Christensen	52	20	126	54	150	II.
Tobacco Plains	Michael Phillipps	49	1	115	5	2300	II.
Nicola Lake	Edwin Dolley	50	9	120	39	2120	II.
Reclamation Farm	William Henderson	49	20	117	50	....	II.
Nelson	C. St. Barbe	49	29	117	21	....	II.
Quesnel	A. Bowron	52	59	122	30	1700	II.
Bullion	H. B. Ferguson	52	45	121	55	....	II.
Chilcotin	M. G. Drummond	52	2	122	40	217	II.
Okanagan Mission	F. E. R. Woolaston.	49	52	119	29	....	II.
Pilot Bay	D. H. Riddell	49	39	116	55	....	II.
Port Bobs	B. W. Leeson	50	32	128	3	....	II.
Masset	C. Harrison	53	38	132	9	30	II.
Alberni	S. R. S. Bayne	49	15	124	49	300	II.
Enderby	G. R. Lawes	50	32	119	7	1180	II.
Stuart Lake	H. A. E. Greenwood	54	28	124	12	1800	II.
Vancouver	J. T. Brown	49	17	123	5	195	II.
Garry Point	William McColl	49	21	123	17	....	II.
Cape Scott	N. C. Nelson	50	48	128	27	....	II.
Revelstoke	W.B. McKechnie, M.D	51	0	118	6	1476	II.
Coldstream Ranch	R. H. Helmer	50	14	119	15	1246	II.
Clayoquot	Rev. R. Maurus	49	11	125	47	40	II.
Naas Harbour	L. A. Chambers	54	56	129	56	..	III.
Port Essington	Rev. D. Jennings	54	9	129	55	..	III.
Langley	G. Simpson	49	5	122	32	..	III.
Royal Oak (Victoria)	D. Lehman	48	24	123	19	..	III.
Caulfields	Leonard Frolander	49	21	123	16	..	III.
Goldstream Lake	G. R. Crook	48	27	123	33	..	III.
Nanaimo (City)	M. Bray	49	10	123	57	..	III.
Vancouver	F. T. Underhill, M. D.	49	17	123	5	..	III.
Cranbrook	James Gill	49	30	115	50	..	II.
Nanaimo	Henry L. Good	49	10	123	57	..	I. S.
Duncan	E. F. Clarke	48	45	123	42	40	II.
Saturna Island	James Mair	48	47	123	12	14	II.
Spence's Bridge	J. A. Teit	50	23	121	20	770	II.

Chief Station—Observations registered continuously day and night.

First Class—Observations of pressure, temperatures, extremes, rain, snow and weather, three times daily.

Second Class—observations of temperature, extremes, rain, snow and weather daily.

Third Class—Observations of rain, snow and weather daily.

Sunshine Stations, at which the duration of bright sunshine is registered daily.

Monthly and Annual Number of Days of Rainfall at Stations.

	January.	February.	March.	April.	May.	June.	July.	August.	September.	October.	November.	December.	Year.
Victoria average	18	18	15	12	14	10	3	5	8	15	20	19	157
1901	14	15	13	12	13	12	3	0	8	10	21	20	141
New Westminster average	15	14	11	14	12	13	6	5	7	15	18	16	146
1901	14	10	17	16	14	19	7	2	9	15	26	22	171
Agassiz average	12	12	15	16	14	17	10	7	14	15	18	16	166
1901	12	13	17	12	13	21	7	0	10	11	24	14	154
Barkerville average	1	1	2	2	7	12	13	7	7	6	3	1	62
1901	0	0	1	2	14	17	21	6	9	8	0	0	87
Port Simpson average	18	11	13	19	13	14	15	13	17	22	21	19	197
1901	14	8	16	15	13	7	15	13	6	21	29	21	178
French Creek average	14	11	13	15	12	11	6	3	9	14	17	16	141
1901	9	9	12	15	11	11	7	1	9	10	18	12	124
Rivers Inlet average	17	17	15	18	18	14	12	9	13	21	21	20	195
1901	16	11	24	17	18	11	17	5	8	20	30	21	198
North Nicomen average	13	14	16	16	16	14	4	5	10	16	20	18	162
1901	12	10	21	17	13	18	6	1	11	13	25	21	108
Matsqui average	14	13	16	13	15	15	6	6	12	19	20	17	166
1901	12	14	22	13	13	19	9	1	15	16	26	16	176
Kamloops average	1	2	5	6	10	12	12	5	6	6	4	2	71
1901	0	4	1	3	0	14	7	0	12	3	5	3	52
Midway average	1	1	2	4	10	9	6	8	6	9	5	1	61
1901	0	0	2	3	10	14	1	3	5	0	3	2	43
Carmanah average	16	16	14	16	14	10	6	4	8	14	20	19	157
1901	15	9	11	13	17	11	5	2	6	12	22	21	144
Chilliwack, 1901	6	10	10	13	15	20	8	2	14	13	24	19	154
Ladner, 1901	6	11	8	11	9	9	..	..	..	..	..	..	...
Bella Coola, 1901	2	1	8	3	8	9	15	6	4	14	15	12	97
Tobacco Plains, 1901	2	2	1	5	11	18	4	2	11	7	9	5	77
Kuper Island, 1901	10	14	14	13	12	15	5	1	11	14	22	22	153
Hazlemere, 1901	11	7	16	15	16	15	8	..	..	..	..	..	...
Nicola Lake, 1901	2	3	2	6	4	13	8	1	11	6	10	5	71
Reclamation Farm, 1901	3	4	4	11	9	19	5	2	14	8	11	4	94
Nelson, 1901	2	3	13	8	12	..	..	..	..	..	..	..	...
Quesnell, 1901	0	0	0	0	4	10	13	..	..	..	2	0	...
Bullion, 1901	0	3	0	2	12	18	10	7	11	9	8	2	82
Chilcotin, 1901	1	0	2	2	..	..	..	..	..	..	..	..	...
Okanagan Mission, 1901	..	2	6	3	7	12	3	0	..	..	..	..	...
Port Robs, 1901	17	13	25	..	..	..	15	2	14	17	28	24	...

Masset, 1901	5	5	8	6	11	4	12	14	15	..	..	..	...
Alberni, 1901	12	11	21	15	16	18	11	1	9	13	25	14	160
Enderby, 1901	0	1	3	4	3	9	..	..	..	..	..	..	...
Stuart Lake, 1901	0	0	1	1	6	4	6	1	2	1	2	1	25
Vancouver, 1901	13	11	18	16	17	16	7	1	9	16	27	17	168
Garry Point, 1901	12	14	11	13	11	12	6	1	9	11	21	15	136
Cape Scott, 1901	..	..	..	..	..	10	23	14	17	26	30	27	...
Revelstoke, 1901	9	3	8	6	14	..	..	..	..	..	..	..	...
Coldstream Ranch, 1901	0	0	0	2	7	9	2	2	9	..	..	..	...
Clayoquot, 1901	18	14	28	17	18	11	6	3	9	16	29	22	191
Naas Harbor, 1901	6	4	9	14	15	10	17	12	15	21	16	11	150
Port Essington, 1901	16	12	28	21	21	17	19	16	15	26	27	21	239
Royal Oak, 1901	13	13	13	13	11	6	6	0	6	10	19	14	121
Caulfield's, 1901	15	13	18	18	11	16	8	2	9	10	23	17	160
Goldstream Lake, 1901	12	9	7	15	16	12	3	1	10	13	24	22	144
Nanaimo (City)	9	8	6	10	7	10	6	1	6	10	22	13	108
Vancouver, 1901	13	11	18	16	18	16	7	2	9	16	..	..	...
Cranbrook, 1901	..	..	..	..	..	..	..	0	5	1	1	0	...
Nanaimo, 1901	..	..	13	18	12	14	7	1	10	12	26	21	...
Duncans, 1901	..	7	5	11	7	11	2	2	7	7	19	12	...
Saturna Island, 1901	..	..	..	10	16	13	5	0	9	12	20	16	...
Kaslo, 1901	..	..	..	..	..	14	8	4	12	8	19	4	...
Princeton, 1901	0	2	2	3	5	8	7	2	9	3	13	0	54
Pilot Bay, 1901	2	4	4	7	10	..	..	..	..	..	..	..	...
Coquitlam, 1901	..	..	..	..	..	9	7	1	8	14	20	16	...

THE CANADIAN AND BRITISH COLUMBIA CLIMATE.

By R. F. Stupart, Director Meteorological Service, Dominion of Canada.

CANADIANS reading newspapers and journals published in Great Britain cannot fail to be struck with the profound misconception which appears to be fairly general regarding the climate and geographical position of Canada. Perhaps Canadians may be to a certain extent guilty of having unwittingly assisted in spreading the erroneous notions regarding their country, by annually, at Christmas time, disseminating photographs of winter scenery to friends in the Old Land. It is the Christmas pictorial papers, with their Santa Claus and reindeer, snow-banks and ice-palaces, fur-coats and snow-shoes, which find their way most frequently to England. It is at Christmas that persons wish to send home some small remembrance; what more interesting than a winter scene with people walking about dressed in furs, with snow-shoes slung over the shoulder, or pictures of people sliding down ice-covered hills in the wildly exhilarating sport of tobogganing? This, going on year after year, has constantly had a tendency to make Britishers associate Canada with the polar regions. As there is certainly fallacy in the conception of Canada as an exceedingly cold country, the writer will endeavour briefly to present certain facts regarding the Canadian climate, in the hope that at least some erroneous impressions may be removed. Vancouver Island, in the Pacific Ocean, occupies somewhat the same position in relation to the American continent that Great Britain, in the Atlantic, does to Europe; lying between nearly the same parallels of latitude. The climate, as in all other parts of British Columbia, varies much with the geographical features of the country. The annual rainfall along the exposed western coast of the island is very great, generally exceeding 100 inches, but in the more eastern districts it is less than half that amount. May to September is usually a comparatively dry period, while copious rains fall between September and March. The mean monthly and mean annual temperatures correspond very closely with those found in parts of England; the summers are quite as long, and severe frost scarcely ever occurs.

Crossing the Strait of Georgia to the Mainland and considering the country south of the Canadian Pacific Railway, we are still in latitudes corresponding to the southern half of England. We here find a warm summer, and a winter increasing in severity as we ascend the Fraser Valley and reach higher levels. At Agassiz, on the Lower Fraser, about 70 miles from Vancouver, is situated one of the Dominion experimental farms; the average mean temperature of January at this place is 33 degrees, and of July 64 degrees, with a daily range of ten degrees in the former month and 26 degrees in thelatter; the lowest temperature on record is —13 degrees, and the highest 97 degrees. Frosts seldom occur in May, and there is no record of any during the summer months. The annual rainfall is 67 inches, 66 per cent. of which falls between October 1st and March 31st. This shows very approximately the climate of the Lower Fraser Valley.

To the eastward of the Coast Range in the Yale and West Kootenay districts the climate is distinctly different; the summers are warmer and the winters are colder, and the rainfall rather scant; bright, dry weather is the rule.

The cold of winter is, however, scarcely ever severe, and the hottest days of summer are rendered pleasant from the fact that the air is dry and the nights are cool. In this region March is distinctly a spring month, and the temperature of April corresponds very closely with that of the same month in England. Grapes and peaches thrive, and tobacco is a crop which is yearly proving a greater success. In the mountainous region of East Kootenay the winters are colder again, but even here the summers are warmer and the winters not as cold as in St. Petersburg.

A few facts regarding the climate of the "Golden" Klondike may, perhaps, be acceptable to some persons. Its geographical position is as follows: Yukon Territory has nearly the shape of a right-angled triangle, of which the base is an arc of the 60th parallel, the perpendicular an arc of the 141st meridian, and the hypothenuse the Rocky Mountains. To reach the Klondike the traveller now lands at Skagway, on the Pacific Coast, crosses the Coast Range of mountains by railway, passing through superb scenery, and then has a trip of 430 miles by steamer down the Yukon River. The distance from Toronto to Dawson City is 2,700 miles as the crow flies.

A somewhat broken series of observations at Dawson and various other places in Yukon Territory between 1895 and 1898, and a continuous series at Dawson during the past three years, afford data for estimating with a fair degree of accuracy the average climatic conditions of the Klondike. The average annual mean temperature is about 22 degrees; the mean of the three summer months is about 57 degrees, July being 61 degrees; and of the three winter months, —16 degrees, with January —23 degrees. Spring may be said to open towards the end of April, the last zero temperature of the winter usually occurring about the 5th of that month. May, with an average temperature of 44 degrees, is by no means an unpleasant month, and the 27th is the average date of the last frost of spring. Daily observations during five summers indicate that, on the average, the temperature rises to 70 degrees or higher on 46 days, and to 80 degrees or higher on 14 days; 90 degrees was recorded in Dawson in June, 1899, and 95 degrees in July of the same year. These temperatures, with much bright sunshine and an absence of frost during three months, together with the long days of a latitude within a few degrees of the Arctic Circle, amply account for the success so far achieved by market gardeners near Dawson in growing a large variety of garden produce, including lettuce, radish, cabbage, cauliflower and potatoes, and warrant the belief that the hardier cereals might possibly be a successful crop, both in parts of the Yukon Territory and the far northern districts of the MacKenzie Basin. August 23rd would appear to be the average date of the first autumnal frost, the temperature rapidly declining towards the close of that month. Although night frosts are not infrequent in September, the month as a whole is mild, with a mean temperature of 42 degrees. October may be fairly termed a winter month, the mean temperature being but 22.5 degrees; and the first zero of the winter is recorded on the average about the 18th. Ice usually begins to run in the Yukon about the second week of October, but it is not until quite the end of the month, or early in November, that the river is frozen fast. The temperature on the average during a winter falls to 02 degrees below zero or lower on 72 days, to 40 degrees below or lower on 21 days, to 50 degrees below or lower on 7 days, and to 60 degrees below or lower on 2 days. In January, 1896, 65 degrees below zero was registered at Fort Constantine; and in January, 1901, —68 degrees was recorded at Dawson.

HON. J. D. PRENTICE,
Minister of Agriculture.

SEASONAL NOTES, 1901.

KUPER ISLAND—February 8th, blue grouse hooting; April 8th, apple trees in blossom; July 31st, not enough of rain for gardens; September 30th, white frost; December 11th, thin ice.

MASSETT—February 12th, heavy gale, two shocks of earthquake; February 25th, robins seen; March 1st, fruit bushes budding; 20th, daisies in bloom; April 28th, swallows seen; May 29th, two shocks of earthquake 5 a. m.; July 15th, hay-making begins.

PORT BOBS—February 11th, salmonberries in blossom; December 3rd, first light frost.

TOBACCO PLAINS—March 10th, geese seen; 11th, larks arrive; 12th, wild flowers in bloom; 14th, robins arrive; 15th, plowing begins; 16th, bluebirds; May 4th, cut rhubarb; 12th, cherries in blossom; 13th, apples; June 6th, snow low down on mountain; July 5th, grain heading out; 11th, hay harvest on; 18th, digging potatoes; August 27th, grain nearly all in; October 6th, geese going south; 31st, sweet peas and hardy flowers in bloom.

NORTH NICOMEN—January 11th, chinook, snow melting rapidly; March 13th, bats seen; 15th, bluebirds; 16th, bird cherries in bloom; 20th, salmonberries in bloom; 29th, dandelions in bloom; May 8th, apples in flower; 9th, corn planting; 10th, swallows; 11th, humming birds; 16th, white clover in flower; 25th, red clover in flower; 30th, salmonberries ripe; September 5th, swallows last seen; 22nd, first snow on mountains; November 18th, maples bare of leaves; 30th, cattle out and fields green; December 5th, first ice.

GOLDSTREAM LAKE—March 22nd to 30th, wet snow every day.

PORT ESSINGTON—January unusually mild; March 15th, most of the deciduous trees and shrubs beginning to bud.

HAZLEMERE—April 19th, plum, cherry and pear trees in bloom; 28th, apple trees in bloom.

ALBERNI—January 13th, warm chinook; 20th, robins back; March 2nd, frogs croaking; 4th, skunk cabbage in blossom; 7th, peach blossoms out; 31st, dyletra in flower; April 6th, trillium and ribas in flower; 7th, salmonberries in flower; 11th, wild plums in flower; 12th, humming birds; 13th, swallows; 14th, dogtooth violets; 19th, Oregon grapes; 25th, cherries in blossom; 27th, sowed oats; 29th, sowed barley;. May 6th, early potatoes frozen; 8th, apples and pears in blossom; 15th, wild cherries in blossom; July 13th, blackberries ripe; 13th, black cherries ripe; August 14th, cut peas and oats; 22nd, cut barley; 26th, cut wheat; September 1st, French prunes ripe; 7th, peaches ripe; 10th, tomatoes ripe; 23rd. gathered onions; October 7th, ploughing; December 7th, geese flying south.

CLAYOQUOT—January 17th, rose bushes sprout; 31st, maples budding; April 10th, geese going north; 21st, heavy hail storm; June 23rd, cutting roses.

OKANAGAN MISSION—April 1st, wild gooseberry; 2nd, robins; 6th, swallows; 28th, cherry and plum blossoms.

CHILCOTIN—March 9th, chinook; 10th, crows arrive; 12th, spring birds come; 14th, ploughing.

PRINCETON—April 9th, blackbirds; June 15th, leaves of tender plants touched by frost; July 12th, squash leaves and potatoes cut down; September 16th, every tender plant cut down.

BULLION—February 12th, chinook wind.

AGRICULTURE.

AS at the present time there are perhaps more enquiries for farm lands in British Columbia than ever before in its history, it is the intention in this chapter to give all the information available respecting not only farm lands themselves, but respecting the conditions which affect agriculture in its every phase. For this purpose the author has drawn from a variety of sources, official and otherwise, as will be seen by what follows :

The Department of Agriculture has from time to time published a valuable compendium of information, dealing more or less in detail with particular districts, and it has been deemed advisable to adapt as much as possible of this report. The information, having been supplied by correspondents of the Department, residents of, and familiar with, the respective districts and localities described, may be regarded as authentic. The latest report published was in 1901, and deals largely with returns and conditions of the year 1900, but for practical purposes these are sufficiently up to date. The year 1900, however, was in many respects exceptional, and does not fairly represent average crop yields. In the first place, there was a cutworm plague that year, which extended throughout the province. Much damage was done, particularly to vegetables. On the Mainland, too, the continued and unusually wet weather which prevailed for a long season was most unfavourable to fruit and grain. The latter was badly harvested and did not properly mature, while in the case of fruit fungus diseases were very prevalent. Owing to the cost and great labour involved, these reports have not been issued regularly, and an effort has been made in this instance to present in condensed form the substance of what is valuable contained therein.

To properly understand the report in this form, some explanations are necessary to supply a number of hiatus.

GRAIN.

In the interior, where there are no milling facilities — as is the case in most parts — wheat, though sufficiently hard for the purpose, is only grown for chicken feed, and, therefore, sale is limited to a restricted local market. Only in the Okanagan is milling carried on on a large commercial scale. On the coast, as it is too soft for milling, wheat is altogether grown for feed. Owing to the lack of malting establishments in the province, barley, although it can be grown everywhere successfully, is marketed or used for feeding exclusively. Oats is everywhere grown for market, and the home consumption is large. The quality is almost invariably high, and oats grown in British Columbia, and manufactured into oatmeal and rolled oats, produce the finest brands of these popular foods to be found on the market anywhere.

LIVE STOCK

In many instances the fact that sheep are not raised, or only to a limited extent, in the interior, is not an evidence of unsuitability of the country for such industry.

On the contrary, the country is generally well suited for sheep-raising; but several important considerations must be taken into account. In the first place, from the fact that there are no woollen factories in the province, there is no local market — in fact, no market at all — and there is, therefore, a large factor of waste. In the second place, throughout the southern interior the coyotes are very destructive, and it has been found extremely difficult to rid the country of this pest. And what is very important, too, in this connection, where cattle range cattlemen have very strong objections to sheep running; and as cattle are much the more profitable, sheep are excluded. When woollen mills are in operation, particularly as the price of mutton is always good and the quality of our mutton is the best, undoubtedly measures will be devised to overcome these disabilities. It may be stated here parenthetically that there seems to be a favourable opportunity for undertaking the manufacture of woollen goods in this province. There is a large market for woollen fabrics of all kinds, especially blankets, and by the importation of cheap Australian wools it would be possible to utilize the native product by mixing the two. On the coast of the Mainland, the lowlands, on account of the heavy rainfall in the winter season, are wet and develop foot-rot; and the higher grounds are too heavily wooded to afford suitable runs for sheep until more clearing is done. The islands between the island of Vancouver and the Mainland are best adapted for the industry, but even here the industry is not carried on to the extent which is possible, as both on the islands and the southern part of the island of Vancouver the flocks are subject to the depredations of wild beasts, although that trouble is yearly growing less. With a market for wool, increased attention would be paid to the industry.

HORSES.

For many years the raising of horses in the interior was unprofitable, owing to over-production and the great predominance of the cayuse strain in the horses. The cayuse, when properly broken, is a very hardy and useful animal, and invaluable for the uses to which he has been put; but the instinct to revert is strong, and when in bands on the range they soon degenerate to the wild horse of nature. By prolific breeding they have become a curse to the country, against which all attempts of preventive legislation have been futile. Owing, however, first to the demand created by the Klondike excitement, and later on to the scarcity in other parts, the result of the South African war, horses have materially increased in value, and the market for good serviceable animals has greatly improved. The interior especially is well adapted for their breeding.

DAIRYING, POULTRY - RAISING, ETC.

Those who are familiar with the conditions that obtain in stock-raising countries will understand how it is that dairying has not made greater progress in the Upper Country. The two are distinct, and milk and butter are usually scarce commodities in a grazing district. As pointed out by Mr. Palmer in a subsequent part of this chapter, new conditions are arising through the introduction and cultivation of alfalfa, whereby it is possible to grow feed extensively for stock; and with the demand for dairy products and the great improvements that are being made in that respect, the dairying industry will be stimulated so as to in time overshadow stock-raising for beef purposes in that country.

So, too, although there has always been a good market for eggs and poultry throughout the interior, under old conditions the poultry industry has been neglected. Farmers, with large ranches chiefly devoted to stock-raising, yielding fair profits and a comparatively easy life, despised or were disinclined to engage in those branches of the industry of farming which demand a more or less exacting attention to details to render them a success. That was a most natural condition of affairs, and is usual in stock-raising districts everywhere. Similar remarks apply to the raising of hogs, fruit-growing and other departments of farm life in which success is possible.

The tendency, as is elsewhere explained, is now to break up the large holdings, and with smaller allotments and settlers familiar with the economics of mixed farming, the latter, wherever conditions are favourable, will be carried on and yearly expanded.

Attention has been paid in some localities and at various times to the subjects of the sugar-beet, tobacco and flax growing; but economic conditions do not — at the present time at least—favour the development of these industries, even though the natural conditions are favourable. The opportunities in already established lines of production and the demand for the standard crops are so great that the necessity or incentive to engage in them does not sufficiently exist. Hop-growing must be excepted from that category. With a steady market to rely upon, no crop would be more profitable, and certainly no part of the world can grow better hops or more to the acre. Cranberry cultivation is another industry for which the province offers inducements. On the west coast of Vancouver Island some of the settlers have undertaken it in a small way, and so far are pleased with the results.

THE LARGER PROBLEMS.

Drainage and dyking are two enterprises that have received a good deal of governmental as well as individual attention, and the latter, especially in Westminster District, has been undertaken on a large and expensive scale. Two other matters which have of late been the subject of considerable discussion are the clearing of land and the irrigation of lands in the dry belts of the province. Conditions are such that, as a rule, the capital required to bring the available unoccupied land fit for cultivation into use is beyond the resources of private individuals — at least of the great majority of those who are interested in making it useful and earning a livelihood thereby. This difficulty has suggested the advisability of formulating a scheme of governmental assistance, whereby large tracts could be dealt with so as to embrace a number of smaller interests in one system, as has been done in dyking and drainage in British Columbia and elsewhere, and, with respect to irrigation, in many parts of the United States. Whether it should be undertaken on purely government lines or by combined capitalistic efforts, or by the co-operation of government and private enterprise, is a question which need not be discussed here; but the necessity of undertaking it in one of these forms obviously exists. In the Okanagan and Kamloops districts a beginning has been made on company lines with success, and it is contended that what has been and can be done by private enterprise for private profit can be more successfully undertaken in the public interests by the government as purely government work.

This one important fact stands out as the controlling factor in the situation — and that is that the rush to the West for land, and the increasing number of inquiries that are received from all parts of this continent and from Great Britain, reflect the world-wide want for homes. The climate and soil of British Columbia, added to its many natural attractions as a place of residence, as inducements to settlers are becoming widely known and understood. It is significant that very many of the inquiries come from Manitoba and the Northwest, where there are millions of acres of free land, or cheap lands, of the most fertile character. As a matter of fact, the present increase of farming population in British Columbia has largely percolated through that country, and in the Okanagan from $50 to $100 per acre for land is being paid by them. Such settlers represent a class who have sold out in the Northwest to new-comers and sought a milder climate to spend the remainder of their days. They are persons, many of them, who have, in Ontario and other parts of Canada, had previous experience in fruit-growing and other branches of agriculture for which this province is particularly well adapted. The present inrush to the Northwest will materially increase the number who will seek the Pacific Coast in the future. We will not only be enabled to secure the overflow, but a selection of the best and most successful farmers of that country, with sufficient capital to ensure their successful establishment here. This depends entirely upon their ability to secure suitable lands in the province. There is, therefore, not a question as to where we shall obtain settlers, but rather where we can place them. Under such circumstances the risk of disposing of lands that may be made amenable to settlement by a comprehensive system of betterment as the result of organized effort of some kind, is reduced to the lowest possible minimum. It, in fact, does not exist. On the other hand, the peopling of the Northwest, the opening up of markets in the Orient, and the increase of local industries arising out of our natural resources, place the possibility of disposing profitably of all the agricultural foodstuffs we can grow forever out of the question.

The topography and climatic conditions seem to lend themselves to a natural division of the province into three distinct divisions :—

The Upper Mainland — Being all that portion to the eastward of the Coast Range of Mountains, and including within its limits the large cattle ranges and what is known, owing to the small precipitation, as the Dry Belt.

The Lower Mainland — Being all that portion on the sea coast to the westward of the Coast Range, and including within its boundaries the rich delta lands of the Fraser. This part of the country is generally heavily wooded with forests of magnificent timber, and is the most humid portion of the province.

The Islands — Being all that portion including Vancouver Island and the islands adjacent thereto. This portion of the province partakes somewhat of the characteristics of the two other divisions, and resembles the first part in the distribution of the flora and its lessened precipitation.

UPPER MAINLAND.

BOUNDARY.

THE Boundary District forms the extreme southern part of the District of Yale. In it are four distinct mineral basins—that around Christina Lake on the east, that adjacent to the north fork of Kettle River, of Boundary Creek, and that of the main Kettle River, with Rock Creek and other tributaries. The whole area covers a distance of about 40 miles east and west, and extends about 50 miles northwards. The southern boundary is the international frontier.

The topography of the district, while it offers a considerable diversity, is not very different from that of all the great interior plateaux of British Columbia. Whilst mountainous, its highest points seldom exceed 5,000 feet, Kettle River being about 1,700 feet above sea level. Most of the hills are forested to their very summits with a variety of coniferous trees. The eastern, southern and western slopes are open, and afford a prolific growth of bunch-grass, and along the valleys are many ranches which are especially adapted to diversified farming, with the aid of irrigation.

The climate is an ideal one, with no extremes of heat or cold. The snowfall in the valley is light. Spring opens early. The summers are pleasant and not excessively hot, the temperature always declining at sundown. The Boundary is famous for its bracing atmosphere, and has been described by Dr. Bryce in his "Climates of Canada" as the ideal national sanitarium.

Grand Forks is situated in the centre of an extensive valley, the extreme length of which (in Canada) is not less than 20 miles, and the average width 3½ miles. This represents an area of over 45,000 acres of splendid loamy soil, admirably adapted for general farming and fruit-raising. Apples, peaches, pears, plums and prunes here attain perfection. The small fruits also thrive, strawberries bearing the first season. The apples grown in the valley captured the highest awards at the Spokane Fruit Fair. An exhibit was sent to the recent World's Fair at Paris, France. Vegetables also yield prolific crops. Small fruit and vegetable farms derive large profits, as close proximity to an increasing mining market gives the producer an advantage over outside competitors who have to pay railway rates. Of late there has been a tendency to cut up farms into tracts of 20 or 30 acres each, to be devoted to fruit and vegetable raising. The prices for cleared lands, near Grand Forks, average about $50 per acre. A good crop can be raised the first season. One general farmer had a crop this past season that yielded a total income of about $10,000. The major portion of the revenue was derived from the sale of fruits. There is an unlimited demand for all these products in the Boundary country, and this is especially so of the various mining camps.

Throughout the district there is a good supply of timber, such as pine, fir, cedar and tamarack, and this stretches all the way up to the headwaters of the North Fork, assuring an unlimited supply for years to come. In this neighbourhood are superior clay beds for the making of brick and tiles, besides lime and building stone quarries.

Only oats are produced to any extent; ruling price, $30 per ton. Potatoes are raised in considerable quantities; ruling price, $20 per ton. Timothy is grown for hay; fetches $25 per ton. Wild grasses grow luxuriantly on the hills, and give excellent pasture for animals. Labourers — Whites, $2.50 per day.

Mr. R. Sidley, Sidley, reports: This is an agricultural settlement situated on the mountain between Osoyoos Lake and Rock Creek. The altitude (3,500 feet) is too high to be an ideal farming region, but the rich soil and the high prices obtained for what is raised have made the settlers prosperous and contented. The land is fairly level, being park-like in appearance, and a horse can be ridden all through the timber. The open land has been all taken up, but there is a large quantity of timbered Government lands still vacant. The air is very dry and bracing, and sickness is unknown. There are no roads, except through the United States. The market is the various mining camps around. Average yield of oats was 40 bushels per acre last year; average price was 2 cents per pound on the ranch. Beardless and common barley is produced; average yield, 30 bushels. Potatoes produce about 200 bushels to the acre; 1½ cents per pound. Timothy does well; produces 1 ton to the acre, and the price was $20 per ton on the ranch.

SIMILKAMEEN.

In which is included White Lake, Keremeos, Princeton, Granite Creek and Otter Creek.

White Lake is situated on an elevated plateau on the road between Keremeos and Penticton. The country is open, with patches of brush along the water-courses and depressions, which are easily cleared. The land is of excellent quality, and yields all the usual crops.

Keremeos is a settlement in the valley of the Similkameen River, considerably below the altitude of White Lake; probably about 1,000 feet above the level of the sea, White Lake being possibly 500 or 600 feet higher. A good waggon road, leading to Osoyoos, the mines in the Boundary country and Penticton, is the only means of communication at the present time.

Princeton is about 40 miles higher up the Similkameen River than Keremeos, in a northwesterly direction, at the confluence of Granite Creek, into which Otter Creek empties some 12 miles above. It is reached by a trail from Keremeos and Hope, and by a waggon road from Nicola.

Owing to lack of transportation facilities, many things that can be produced at Keremeos, and in the valley of the Similkameen generally, to the greatest perfection and in large quantities, are now quite neglected.

Mr. E. Bullock-Webster says of this section: Very little grain grown in the valley; cheaper to buy flour than to raise wheat. Roots and vegetables reach perfection on the rich, black lands of the valley; carrots, onions and parsnips do well on the sandy benches. Red clover and timothy are the chief hay grasses. Indian corn grows well, but is not used for forage. The valley is, above everything, a fruit country, and will in time be the first in British Columbia. The benches are entirely free from summer frosts. Apples, pears, plums, apricots, cherries, peaches, strawberries and all small fruits — with irrigation — are a grand crop and of good flavour. Grapes are not planted as they should be; in fact, very little attention has been paid to fruit. At present the valley is entirely devoted to cattle raising in a rough and ready way; but in the future, when better methods are adopted, the valley should produce a large amount of butter. Portions of the hillsides and mountains are very steep, but the tops are covered with bunch-grass and winter grass; the bottom is rye grass, which stands up through the snow and makes good winter forage.

Hiram Inglee reports: Apples are successful; there was a good yield of good apples in the two local orchards. Plums give splendid yields of good quality. Peaches also do well. Small fruits of exceptional quality. Horned cattle is a profitable industry, the ranges being exceptionally good. Sheep would certainly pay well if it were not for coyotes. Very suitable country, however, except for winter feed, which would have to be provided in the neighbouring valleys. Irrigation must be resorted to on the bench lands to insure good crops, but there is not much easily available water for the purpose. No valuable timber. Small Douglas fir and red pine. Chiefly bunch-grass ranges. Wild horses are a pest.

Labour — Very little demand. Whites, chiefly miners, \$3.50 per day; Chinese cooks at \$30 to \$60 per month. Indians won't work if they can do without, and they all have land and cattle.

Stock-raising is at the present time the prevailing industry, but on account of the lack of irrigation and railway communication, the agricultural capabilities of the country are restricted to the narrowest limits. The whole country from Spence's Bridge and from Kamloops to Princeton and the valleys of the Similkameen and Tulameen rivers are splendidly adapted for fruit-growing, especially in the way of apples, which require a more vigorous climate than ours to produce the best texture; and, to a greater or less extent, to the growing of peaches, grapes, melons and tomatoes, which the Coast districts cannot produce successfully on account of the lack of summer heat and the cool nights.

All the land suitable for agriculture or pastoral purposes in the Nicola and Similkameen countries has been taken up and is being held for future development. Including the Kettle River country, Midway and Rock Creek, Keremeos and Osoyoos, the Nicola Valley, etc., the districts immediately tributary to a railway route amount in the aggregate to 350,000 acres. Of this amount about 250,000 is prairie and meadow land, but of the whole amount only about 15,000 acres is under cultivation.

It is scarcely necessary to refer to the character of the climate which is characteristic of the whole of the interior of Southern British Columbia — that is to say, dry and warm in summer, with light snowfall and light, clear winters, though not cold in the extreme except for about two or three weeks each year; a climate that is bracing and healthful, without the objections to be urged against the sweep of prairies in the Northwest.

It is also a country beautiful and park-like in appearance, varied by lake and river effects, with rare opportunities for sport, such a country as would be attractive and rapidly filled up with population were there a comprehensive system of irrigation carried out and railway facilities provided.

I have not referred to the extensive coal deposits that exist in the neighbourhood of Kamloops, in the Nicola country, throughout the Similkameen Valley, and, it is supposed, in the Kettle River country.

These coals would never find a market on the coast in competition with the Vancouver Island mines, but would create an immense industry in supplying the smelters of the interior and the demands of the mineral industry south of the line. There are also, of course, metalliferous deposits throughout the whole district, which, however, have not yet been exploited in the same way as they have been in the Kootenay and Boundary districts, where communication has been provided to cheapen facilities of transport and to render development possible and probable. The district, taken as a whole, I think contains the maximum of possibilities in British Columbia, apart from the Coast line.

OKANAGAN LAKE.

In which is included Okanagan Mission, Penticton, Trout Lake, Peachland and the various ranches and settlements on the shores of that fine sheet of water, some 90 miles long. The general altitude ranges from 1,130 at the lake to 1,400 at the highest points under cultivation.

Penticton is the end of navigation for the steamers plying on the lake. Trout Creek is eight miles to the northward, on the west side of the lake. Peachland is a few miles higher up the lake, and thence northward all the way up is admirably adapted for fruit-growing. The settlers are somewhat scattered, owing to the abrupt nature of the shores, which do not permit of ranching everywhere nor at a distance from the lake. Communication is maintained by steamers, which ply on the lake, there being no road on the western side except between Penticton and Trout Creek. On the east side, about half way up the lake, is Okanagan Mission, of which Kelowna is the chief place and shipping point. An excellent waggon road connects this place with Vernon, the practical terminus of the Shuswap & Okanagan Railroad; this, with the steamer service on the lake, gives it access to all points. Okanagan Mission Valley is one of the most fertile and beautiful in the province, and is capable of producing crops and fruit belonging to the temperate, as well as many of those to the sub-tropical zones. Large quantities of produce are shipped out from this section to all parts of the province, a large proportion going to the Kootenay mining region. Tobacco of an excellent quality is produced and manufactured into cigars at a factory in Kelowna.

Mr. A. H. Crichton reports : Some wheat is produced, the price of which is from $18 to $25 per ton. Oats, of which a large quantity is produced, fetch from $20 to $30 per ton. A good deal of fall rye is grown successfully for hay, on the lands where water is not available; price, about $20 per ton. All root crops are successfully grown, especially potatoes. Timothy hay is the principal crop grown for sale; averages about three tons to the acre on irrigated land; prices rule up to $12.50 per ton. Clover, especially, grows well here. Early Indian corn does well. Fruit is successfully grown. Apples yield well and fetch about 75c. per box. Plums and cherries are good. Peaches and apricots do well if flowers escape early frost. Dairying—A few private dairies are successful with local trade, but lack of facilities for shipping any distance prevents co-operative creameries. Irrigation is necessary and is carried on to a considerable extent. Lots of water for present purposes. All Government land that is any good is pre-empted; nothing but wild range land left. Improved farms sell for from $20 to $100 and $200 per acre.

Mr. W. Smythe Parker, Penticton, says: Nickel Plate Camp and Princeton will, ere long, prove to possess immense mineral wealth, and with the present opening up of waggon roads and railways will have good markets close at hand for all farming products. The soils within these districts are extremely rich where water can be obtained, and grow almost anything. Climate unsurpassed; scenery grand; and is also a health resort. There is abundance of fish and game. Fruit-growing will surpass anything in British Columbia if attention is bestowed upon it. Stock-raising is at present the principal industry. The same rewards await all industrious and enterprising settlers for mixed farming, etc. I should consider that there are upwards of 200 people engaged altogether in ranching, fruit-growing and mixed farming.

Alex. McLennan, west side of Okanagan Lake, opposite Kelowna, says: This section of the country is badly broken up. What agricultural land there is of any account is held by Indians. There are two reserves within three miles of each other, with about 20 Indians, all told, on both of them. They cultivate altogether about 20 acres, and this part of the district will never amount to much until those reserves are opened up for settlement. There are, I suppose, between 200 and 300 acres under cultivation by whites, mostly in small patches. Nearly any part of it is well adapted for fruit or grain and vegetables. There are 15 pre-emptions taken up, and the population, all told, big and small, 73 white.

The principal grasses are timothy and red clover. Timothy would go from 1½ to 2 tons per acre; clover would about double that, or from 3 to 4 tons per acre. Price in the fall was $10 per ton, delivered at C. P. R. wharf. Number of acres under hay would be about $100. Plums and prunes do well. Small fruits do well. Prices: Currants, 2 cents per pound; raspberries, from 10 to 12 cents; and strawberries, from 10 to 15 cents. The supply of horses here has been greater than the demand for some time. A fine sheep country if it were not for coyotes. Irrigation is required here everywhere, and land is of no use without it. There is quite a lot of land that could be cultivated if water could be got on to it. The principal timber trees in this section are pine and fir, with cottonwood growing on low land. Timber is very easily got, and useful for lumber. There is Government land to be had here, dry bench land. I don't know of any improved land for sale. Labour — Whites, plenty; wages from $20 to $40 per month. Chinese, plenty; wages from $15 to $25. Japanese, not many yet. Indians, plenty; wages about the same as Chinese.

OKANAGAN.

Under this is included the Commonage, White and Creighton Valleys, Mabel and Sugar Lakes, Priest Valley and Spallumcheen. This section may fairly be called the garden of the Upper Country, embracing as it does such a large and varied area of territory adapted to all conditions of husbandry and to the production of anything that can be expected to be grown in these latitudes. A branch line of the Canadian Pacific Railway runs through the district, connecting with the main line at Sicamous. The principal town is Vernon, beautifully situated at the head of Okanagan Lake, and whence good waggon roads radiate to all parts of the district. Steamers connect it also with all points on the lake. Armstrong and Enderby are two other towns on the line of railway north of Vernon — 14 and 23 miles respectively. Each of these places has flour and saw mills, the flour mill at Armstrong being a co-operative concern owned by the people of the district, and is supplied with good up-to-date machinery. That of Enderby has the largest capacity and is provided with all the latest improvements. About five miles from Vernon, on the White Valley road, is the Coldstream Ranch, owned by Lord Aberdeen. It is well situated for general farming, with good soil and an abundant supply of water for irrigation purposes. Under the able superintendence of Mr. Ricardo this farm has been greatly improved, and forms a good object lesson. Unquestionably the best apples in the province are produced in this section of the country, including all points on the lake. Hops are also produced in large quantities by irrigation. The road in this direction connects with Mabel and Sugar Lakes, the headwaters of the Spallumcheen River, also with Creighton valley, and a cattle trail with Fire Valley and Killarney, on the Lower Arrow Lake. Two good waggon roads lead from Vernon to Armstrong and Enderby, and another from the latter place to Salmon Arm, on the main line of the Canadian Pacific Railway. The Spallumcheen River flows past Enderby into the Shuswap Lake at Sicamous, and is navigable for stern-wheel steamers. A great

EXHIBITION BUILDINGS AT NEW WESTMINSTER.

VICTORIA AGRICULTURAL ASSOCIATION BUILDINGS.

CITY MARKET, NEW WESTMINSTER.

FLOUR MILL ENDERBY.

portion of the country is open, some of it lightly wooded and some of it rather heavily wooded for this part of the country; the principal trees being Douglas fir and larch on the higher parts, and yellow pine (Pinus ponderosa) on the lower levels, intermixed in all cases with a good deal of birch and poplar. The land is all highly fertile, requiring irrigation in that part in the vicinity of Vernon. The necessity for irrigation for the successful production of crops is, however, not as general as was formerly believed — this belief having been somewhat dispelled by the operations of the settlers who took up land on what is known as the Commonage, an extensive tract lying to the south of Vernon, between Okanagan and Long Lakes, and which in view of the absence of water for irrigation purposes, was not considered worth taking up by the early settlers. By judicious farming and putting in early fall crops it has been found that a great deal of the land can be successfully utilised for the production of cereals and roots. In the Spallumcheen Valley and the Salmon River Valley east — that is, in the vicinity of Armstrong and Enderby — irrigation is not necessary, the precipitation being sufficient. The lands lying contiguous to the Spallumcheen River, all the way to Mara, a station on the line of railway north of Enderby, are eminently well suited for dairying.

The general altitude runs from 1,150 feet (the lake level) to perhaps 1,500 at the highest points under cultivation.

Mr. Donald Graham, Armstrong, reports : The Spallumcheen Valley extends practically from the head of Okanagan Lake, in the south, to the Mara and Shuswap Lakes, to the north, a distance of over 40 miles, and averaging through its entire length between three and four miles in width. To the eastward the agricultural lands run right up to the foot of a high and somewhat rugged mountain, being only broken midway, near Enderby, by the entrance into the valley of the Spallumcheen River. To the westward, however, the country is more of a rolling nature, a large portion of the land being available for agricultural purposes. The whole valley is extremely fertile, the soil being a clay loam, ranging from somewhat light to clays of the heaviest kind, most of it, however, with several inches of black loam on the surface. The rolling and higher land to the westward is mostly a sandy loam, the chief area of which is the Salmon River Valley and land in the immediate vicinity. This land is very productive, and although possibly not averaging as high in wheat returns, for vegetables and small fruits particularly it is better adapted than the heavier lands adjoining.

Until now, wheat production has been the chief dependence of the farmers, the returns being very high, averaging nearly 30 bushels per acre. This has always been easily disposed of, there being three flour mills in the Okanagan — one each at Enderby, Vernon and Armstrong — the price for wheat being about 60 cents per bushel. The flour manufactured has deservedly a high reputation in British Columbia, the wheat raised being chiefly Red Fife and Fall Fife, from which the best flours are made. With the development of the Kootenay mines, however, conditions are changing very fast; potatoes, hay and vegetables of all descriptions are being produced in ever-increasing quantities, and bid fair in a very short time to force wheat-production into a secondary position. Dairying and fruit-raising are also coming to the front, so that mixed farming is likely soon to supplant the straight wheat industry. Of fruit, apples, plums, prunes and pears and all small fruits yield abundantly and of the best quality. On Okanagan Lake, peaches, apricots, cherries and grapes do well, possibly on account of the warm sub-soil, although it must also be said that the climatic conditions vary in the most unaccountable manner within a very few miles, a change from sleigh to waggon not being uncommon in a 12 or 15 mile winter journey. The climate generally may be described as a very fine one, although we sometimes have exceptionally hot days in summer and extremely cold ones in winter. The winter temperature for four months would not, however, average over ten degrees of frost, with from a foot to a foot and a half of snow. Going southward to the Okanagan Lake and along its shores, both frost and snow decrease, until the latter becomes a very uncertain quantity on the lower levels.

The cost of living, machinery, wages, transportation, etc., is high. Were it not for that, the position of the farmers would be an ideal one. However, those conditions are slowly and gradually changing. There is very little Government land of any value to be obtained throughout the Okanagan now, the lands being all settled upon and improved to a greater or less degree. There is plenty of unimproved land, which can still be bought at from $3 to $10 per acre. Improved lands are held at from $40 to as high as $100 per acre, according to quality and locality.

Game in past years has been very plentiful, and is still fairly so: grouse and prairie chicken, geese and ducks on the lakes and meadows. Deer are still fairly plentiful, although requiring more hunting to obtain than formerly. In fact, it may be called a hunter's paradise, as a ten days' hunting in the mountains can bring one in contact with caribou, mountain goat, mountain sheep, grizzly, black bear and panther, and wolves also. The latter four, however, are wary and very hard to get at

Of spring and fall wheat combined, possibly about 5,000 tons; about 6,000 acres under wheat. Average of oats, about 1,000 pounds per acre; about 1,500 acres under oats; price, $20 to $25 per ton. The acreage under root crops is increasing greatly, and will receive a good deal of attention in the future; potatoes fetch about $10 per ton. Numberless varieties of apples grown successfully; ruling price, $1 per box. Pears and plums do well, but not cherries. Small fruits do well, especially on the higher lands. There has been an over-production of horses in the past; the trade has been improving somewhat; prices higher, but only local demand. Swine production is one of our chief industries; price, 5½ cents per pound on foot, during past season. Labourers are to be had at $30 per month.

F. Appleton, Enderby, says: Wheat is largely grown, and is profitable; price is about 60 cents per bushel. Oats are grown, the average price being $20 per ton. Mixed grasses and clover do well, and make better hay and pasture for dairy stock; price for baled timothy was $12 per ton. Small fruits produce abundantly. Cattle do well; milch cows bring from $45 to $60 each; beef cattle, about 5 cents per pound. Sheep are only kept on a very limited scale. Coyotes are troublesome. Prices, 5 cents per pound live weight, 7 cents for wool. Horses are fetching a fair price. Swine production is not general; price, 5½ cents, live weight. Poultry production pays well; eggs average 25 cents per dozen, fowls 10 to 12½ cents per pound.

Some Government lands up Mabel Lake Valley; farms can be bought for from $5 per acre up to $40. Labour—Whites, $25 to $30 per month and board. Chinese, only cooks employed; Indians, during harvest, get from $1.25 to $1.50 per day.

SHUSWAP LAKE.

In which is included Craigellachie, Sicamous, Salmon Arm, Notch Hill and Tappen Siding, including all that portion of the country between Craigellachie and Shuswap, on the main line of the Canadian Pacific Railroad. This section is peculiar, in that it is all wooded more or less heavily, and that the precipitation is ample for agricultural purposes.

Craigellachie is in the valley of Eagle River, which flows into the Shuswap Lake at Sicamous, and is on the main line of the Canadian Pacific Railway. It is on the foothills of the Gold Range, sixteen miles to the east of Sicamous. The valley is fairly wide, but heavily timbered. Altitude, 1,223 feet.

Sicamous is situated at the head of the Shuswap Lake, where the Shuswap and Okanagan Railway joins the main line, sixteen miles west of Craigellachie. There is some farming done in a small way about Craigellachie, but none at Sicamous, although there is bottom land at the latter place which could be utilised if cleared.

Salmon Arm is a settlement in the valley of the Salmon River where it debouches into the Salmon Arm of Shuswap Lake, nineteen miles to the northwest of Sicamous. The Canadian Pacific Railway runs through the settlement, and a waggon road connects it with Spallumcheen. All kinds of grain, except corn, are produced. Wheat growing is profitable for home use, but not otherwise. Timothy and red clover mixed give the best result for fodder, and seem well adapted to the place and climate. The district is especially adapted for the production of fruits and for dairying, and on account of its favourable shipping facilities, both east and west, large quantities of small fruits, vegetables and milk are sent to the markets along the line. The altitude at the station, which is nearly at the level of the lake, is 1,152 feet.

Besides the railroad, this part of the country has water communication via the lake and Thompson River with all points as far as Savona in one direction, and up the Spallumcheen River as far as Enderby in the other.

Tappen Siding is seven miles west of Salmon Arm, and at about the same altitude. Notch Hill is ten miles further on, at an altitude of 1,687 feet, it being on the height of land between Tappen Siding and Shuswap. This district is quite thickly wooded.

Mr. W. F. Smith, Tappen Siding, says : Only oats and peas grown in any quantity, and cut green for hay. Potatoes do well; yield, about 6 tons per acre; ruling price in 1900, $10 to $12 per ton. Hay and grasses, ruling prices $12 per ton. Others principally for home use in feeding stock. Labour—Whites, $30 per month; Chinese, $20; Indians, $20.

THOMPSON RIVER VALLEY.

Including Shuswap, Ducks, Grand Prairie, Kamloops, Campbell Creek, Cherry Creek, North Thompson, and Tranquille.

Shuswap is westward from Notch Hill 15 miles, and is lower by 541 feet, with a drier climate and an open country. Communication east and west by rail and water.

Mr. J. P. Shaw, Shuswap, reports : Wheat has not been grown in large quantities in the past; favourable for milling wheat; price, from $20 to $25 per ton. Considerable quantity of oats produced. Potatoes are grown in considerable quantities; price, from $10 to $15 per ton. Timothy, Red and Alsike clover are grown; crop averaged 2 or 2½ tons per acre; sold in stack at $10 per ton. All common varieties of apples grow to perfection; price last fall was about 3 cents per pound. Pears do well; price, 5 cents per pound. Plums and prunes also, and small fruits successful..

Beef steers are worth $40 and cows $30; profitable and large industry. Horses here are poor property. Sheep-raising is very little engaged in, though small bands are profitable; sell from $5 to $8 dressed; wool, 8 to 12 cents. Very few hogs are raised; hogs on foot are worth 5 cents per pound. Poultry-raising is not entered into; price of fowls $6, and eggs average 25 cents per dozen.

Irrigation is necessary, and is carried on to a large extent.

Labour — Whites, $1.25 to $1.50 per day, or $30 to $35 per month, with board; Chinese, $15 to $25 per month, with board; Japanese, $15 to $20 per month, with board; Indians, $1 to $1.25 per day. Indians plentiful; Japanese and Chinese not resident, and if wanted have to be procured from the cities.

Ducks and Grand Prairie, the former being on the Thompson River and the main line of the Canadian Pacific Railway, 16 miles below Shuswap, and the latter about 14 miles to the southeast, on the waggon road to Spallumcheen. The altitude of Ducks is 1,148 feet, with a considerable rise towards Grand Prairie. The soil is generally a light sandy loam near the river, and of a heavier nature towards Grand Prairie; productive when water is available, but which is not always the case, especially near the river. Timber is fairly abundant on the hillsides. Cereals and root crops produce well. Fruit will no doubt do well in parts.

Many cattle and horses are produced, the former almost entirely for beef, little or no dairying being done. Sheep-raising is not prosecuted to any extent. Swine are produced in greater quantities than probably in any other part of the province, and are found to be very profitable. An excellent country for poultry.

Mr. V. D. Curry, Campbell Creek, writes: Wheat, principally for chicken feed at home and for the local market; average production, 30 bushels per acre. Oats are largely grown; yield, 40 bushels per acre. Root crops are all grown to great perfection. Hay and grasses are grown, and produce about 1 ton of hay per acre; price, about $12 per ton. Indian corn can be successfully grown in some parts of this district. All hardy varieties of apples very good; ruling price, 2½ cents per pound. Pears, plums and cherries attain great perfection in all parts of the district, and peaches and apricots in some parts. Small fruits very productive, and prices good. Private dairying is very profitable in this country. The production of horned cattle is successful. Prices are 3½ and 4 cents on foot for beef; good milch cows, $40 and $50 per head of ordinary stock. The district is suitable for sheep, and the industry is carried on to some extent with profit. Prices range from 12 cents to 15 cents per pound. Horses have been profitable. Horses weighing 1,500 pounds and upwards fetch $100 and upwards. Swine production is prosecuted systematically; pigs on foot sell for 6 to 7 cents. Poultry-raising is very remunerative, but not taken up systematically; prices, 30 cents per dozen for eggs, $4 per dozen for cockerels.

Irrigation is necessary, and is carried on to a considerable extent. The supply of water could be materially increased by conserving it, and many thousands of acres brought into cultivation. The cost of ordinary irrigation ditches is about $500 per mile; water has been pumped by steam, etc.

Mr. J. F. Smith, North Thompson and Louis Creek, says: That which is known as the Louis Creek section comprises an extensive area of excellent agricultural land, admirably adapted to mixed farming and stock-raising. The soil along the river front is mostly of a rich sandy loam, in certain parts a heavy clay. This section begins practically from a point known as the "Fish Trap," and includes the Adams Lake Valley, the Louis Creek Valley, and extends and includes the North Thompson Valley. The initial point of Louis Creek is at the confluence of that creek with the North Thompson River, a distance of 36 miles from Kamloops. There is a good waggon road from Kamloops to and beyond that point, and the river is navigable for a considerable distance beyond. Good fishing is had on both Louis Creek and the Barrier River, four miles beyond. The district has a promising future, in consequence of its vast resources, as it abounds in mineral. There are large deposits of excellent bituminous coal and a large area of excellent land, which will furnish homes for hundreds of families, and to which the attention of incoming settlers will surely be directed. This section is worthy of the attention of the Government.

Wheat — None of it raised for milling, but is applied chiefly to fattening hogs and for chicken feed. The average yield was about ¾ of a ton to the acre; a ready market is had in Kamloops, the ruling price being from $20 to $26 per ton. Oats — In places such as Adams Lake, and at certain points in the Louis Creek and Dixon Creek valleys, the growth is very rank, sometimes causing the grain to lodge. The yield at these points is from 1,800 to 2,000 pounds to the acre. The general average yield in the district is about 1,500 pounds to the acre. Ruling price, $20 to $30 per ton. Beans are successfully grown as a field crop. Potatoes yield from 6 to 8 tons to the acre; prices range from $10 to $15 per ton. Indian corn is successfully grown. Very little attention so far has been given to fruit-growing. Small fruits of every kind do well. Strawberries and raspberries are exceptionally luscious. Cattle-raising is practically the only paying branch connected with the agricultural industry in this section. Each settler is aiming to increase his herd; 1,500 head of cattle in the district at present.

Irrigation is carried on to some extent, but in many years crops are raised without irrigation. Nearly all the occupied land has sufficient water for present use. The principal trees in this section are fir, bull pine, jack pine, birch, cottonwood, poplar, willow, spruce, cedar, hemlock and balsam. There is over 50,000 acres of excellent arable land that is available for pre-emption in this section. It is outside of the railroad belt, and is all good bottom land on both sides of the North Thompson River, lightly timbered with some fir, poplar, cottonwood, willows and such like, extending for 80 miles up the river.

Labourers can be obtained — Whites from $25 to $35; Chinese, $35 per month; and Indians, $1.50 per day.

NICOLA,

In which is included Upper, Central and Lower Nicola, is a fine pastoral country, with extensive valleys of good land for general agriculture. A waggon road, some 110 miles in length, having its termini at Spence's Bridge and Kamloops, gives access to the Canadian Pacific Railway. The Douglas Lake Cattle Company and the British Columbia Cattle Company have extensive cattle ranges in this section, where a large number of beef cattle are produced for the Coast markets. General crops of grain, grasses and roots are successfully produced with irrigation, the soil being very productive, and available water is to be had in most parts. Large fruits are not generally successful, but are produced in some favoured spots, such as Quilchena, on Nicola Lake. The altitude of the lake is variously given at from 1,920 to 2,120 feet, that of Spence's Bridge being 996 feet, and of Kamloops 1,153 feet.

Mr. Thomas Bulman, Upper Nicola, Stump Lake, reports: Wheat is only raised for hog and chicken feed. Production is about 28 bushels per acre, first-class for milling; ruling price, $25 per ton. Potatoes are very successfully grown; ruling price, $10 per ton. Timothy, large Red Clover, Alsike and Sanfoin are the principal grasses; about two tons to the acre; prices ruling, $5 to $10 per ton. The production of beef cattle is profitable; price of beef cattle, 3½ cents per pound; milch cows, $45 per head. The horse industry is looking up, and is on a little better basis here now. Sheep-raising is carried on to a small extent, and pays very well; ruling prices are $3.50 for lambs, $5 to $7 per head for ewes and wethers. There is no land available for pre-emption suitable for farming. Improved farms can be bought at $4 to $5 per acre — good paying investments.

Labour — Whites, $25 to $30 per month; Chinese and Japanese, $20 per month. We get plenty of help of any class.

Mr. John Clapperton, Central Nicola, says: The village of Nicola Lake, at which point the Provincial Government Office is located, is about the centre of the division. It is situate by waggon road from Spence's Bridge, C. P. R. station, 50 miles; from Kamloops, 60 miles; Princeton, $70 miles. A bi-weekly mail service between Kamloops and Spence's Bridge, through the whole Nicola Valley, exists; a weekly mail service between Nicola Lake and Princeton. Telephonic communication between Lower Nicola and Kamloops is present, and much valued by the people. Railway transit through the division is expected ere long.

Wheat is now very little grown in the district. Flour of best quality can be brought into the valley and sold as cheaply as that made from local wheat; prices were $1.25 to $1.50 per 100 pounds, mostly for poultry-feeding. Oats — Crop of 1900 averaged between 40 and 50 bushels per acre. Last spring oats were worth $2 per 100 lbs.; present price, on the farm, $1.25 per 100 lbs. Potatoes are only grown for home use. From 1½ to 3 tons of cured hay per acre is about the annual yield from irrigated meadows. Plums and cherries do well in places, and small fruits of all kinds do splendidly.

Very little butter made. Stock breeding and feeding is the main industry of the division. Horse-breeding has not been a profitable pursuit of late years. Some two or three farmers breed and feed pigs for the Coast consumption.

Cultivation in this division has been so far limited. All lands under irrigation yield good returns. Everything that requires cultivation must on all plains or bench lands be irrigated. Most ranches are fairly supplied with water. Very little crown land in this division open to pre-emption; all taken up years ago that was worth locating. Mountain pasturage is $1 per acre; arable land that can be irrigated, $2.50 per acre; wild meadow, $5 per acre.

Labourers — Whites, $1.25 to $1.50 per day, with board; Chinese, $1; Japanese, $1; Indians, $1, $1.25 and $1.50.

Mr. H. S. Cleasby, Lower Nicola, writes: This district forms part of the well-known Nicola Valley, being, in fact, the lower end of that fertile trough in British Columbia's sea of mountains. The valley, as a rule, is not more than three-quarters of a mile wide, through which the Nicola River meanders with many a turn and twist. In what is locally known as the Forks, being the land at the junction of the Nicola and Coldwater rivers, is a triangle of level land, containing about 1,000 acres of very fertile land. The alluvial soil along the banks of the rivers, originally covered with a heavy growth of poplars, willows and alders, is, when cleared, very productive, producing immense crops of hay and grain. The bench lands, when sufficient water can be procured, are capable of growing almost anything which can be produced in the temperate zone. The principal industry is cattle-raising. Some cattle are winter-fed for the spring market, affording an outlet for surplus hay. There is a local market with teamsters and the neighbouring mining camps of Aspen Grove, Granite Creek and Similkameen, for a certain amount of grain and garden produce. The population is scattered. There is one school at Lower Nicola. Fish abound in the rivers and streams, and there is no lack of shooting in the proper season.

Wheat is not much grown, owing to lack of milling facilities; average yield, 1,500 pounds; prices, $30 for new and $35 for old. Oats — Average yield, 1,500 pounds per acre; price up to September 1, $45 per ton, new crop $25 per ton. Barley not much grown; yield, about 2,000 pounds per acre; price, $25 per ton. Peas yield 2,000 pounds per acre; price, $25 per ton. Potatoes yield 6 to 7 tons per acre; price, $10 to $15 per ton. Only the hardiest varieties of apples are a success here; prices low, 2½ cents. Pears, a precarious crop. Plums the same. Cherries do well. Small fruits do splendidly.

Some parties on outlying places milk several cows. In the Nicola Valley itself pasturage is too scarce and scant. The principal industry, and at present in a thriving condition, is cattle, because of high prices; fat steers, 3½ cents per pound, live weight, $40 per head; fat cows, 3 cents per pound, live weight, $30 per head. Horses profitable if good ones are bred; not an over-production of good horses. Pigs on foot are worth 5½ to 6½ cents per pound.

Irrigation is necessary in most cases; in this district there is an abundance of water. The timber trees are: Yellow pine, dry lands; fir, damp and rocky lands; poplar, semi-damp lands; cottonwood, alder, black and silver birch, damp lands; black pine, dry mountains; water spruce, wet mountains.

No Government land left worth taking up; no railway lands. Improved farms, from $10 per acre up.

Labour—Whites, $25 to $30 per monh, good men; Chinese, $15 to $25, summer months; Indians, $1 to $1.50 per day. Indians in the preponderance; supply about equal to the demand; slight scarcity sometimes for a few weeks in harvest time

LOWER THOMPSON RIVER VALLEY.

Including Ashcroft, Spence's Bridge, Lytton and Savona. This district may truly be said to be unexcelled for the production of fruit of nearly all kinds; and although peaches have not, owing to the peculiarity of the climate, been a perfect success, I have no doubt that certain kinds, and in certain locations, may yet be successfully cultivated. With cheap freight rates and its proximity to the Coast markets, this district would be able to supply all the tomatoes, grapes, melons and similar products that are consumed, to the exclusion of the California fruits. Timber is not abundant on the lower lands; there is, however, a sufficiency for farming purposes and fuel. On the hills, however, there is an ample supply. The principal timber trees are bull or yellow pine, Douglas fir and poplar.

The valleys in this district are mostly between 700 and 2,500 feet above the sea level. The tops of the surrounding mountains are mostly from 2,000 to 5,000 feet above the sea. The district may be said to consist of round or sloping mountains, intersected by numerous narrow valleys of different altitudes, and containing more or less agricultural land. Small lakes and creeks are numerous in some parts. The mountains and valleys, up to an elevation of almost 2,000 feet, are covered principally with sagebrush, greasewood, wormwood, cactus, considerable bunchgrass in some places, and scattering yellow pine trees. Above 2,000 feet the mountain sides and valleys are almost everywhere covered with grass and scattering timber, pine and fir, the latter seldom very thick. Along the water-courses there is often a little brush, and many poplar and birch trees, seldom of large size. The country is nowhere thickly timbered.

Lytton is a small town situated at the confluence of the Thompson and Fraser Rivers. The ranches are situated in the valley of the Fraser, on both sides of the river, and are reached, those on the eastern side by road and bridge across the Thompson, and those on the west by ferry. The altitude of the railway station is 687 feet, whilst the river is fully 100 feet lower.

Spence's Bridge, on the Thompson River, 22 miles above Lytton; altitude, 996 feet at the C. P. R. Station. Like the rest of this district, it is a famous section for fruit, but there is more land here for general crops and for pasture. The Nicola River empties into the Thompson at this point, and the waggon road to Nicola and Kamloops follows its valley.

Ashcroft is the point on the Canadian Pacific Railway at which the Cariboo waggon road takes its departure. It is situated on the Thompson River, about 26 miles above Spence's Bridge. The country around it, which includes Cache Creek, is generally open, with rolling hills, fairly well supplied with water for irrigation, but the channels of the large rivers are so deeply cut as to render the water unavailable. The altitude of Ashcroft is 996 feet (C. P. R.), whilst that of Ashcroft Farm (Cornwall's), three miles distant, on the other or northern side of the river, is placed at 1,508 by Captain Parsons, R. E. The latter probably represents the altitude, approximately, of most of the ranches about here.

Savonas is at the foot of Kamloops Lake, on the Thompson, 22 miles above Ashcroft. The country is open, with some scattered pine trees. The rolling hills afford good pasturage, for which purpose it is best adapted. Irrigation is necessary throughout all this region for the production of crops.

Hon. C. F. Cornwall, formerly Lieutenant-Governor of the province, says: In this neighbourhood 40 bushels of either wheat or barley per acre is, in my experience, but an average crop, where the land is properly treated. Oats may run from 60 to 100 bushels. Hay, as may be supposed, with irrigation will yield enormously, especially so the clovers, Alfalfa or Lucerne, and Sanfoin; while the ordinary fruits of all kinds, with but little practised attention in the way of treatment, are splendid alike in appearance and productiveness, and in quality. Vegetables of all sorts flourish.

and tomatoes, melons, grapes, cucumbers, etc., ripen readily. Thus the land of this neighbourhood, owing to the rich quality of its disintegrated soils and climatic influences, is richly productive where water can be brought on to it.

Amusement and relaxation from work is by no means wanting. There is splendid trout-fishing in the Thompson, extending over a long season; three-pound fish are by no means uncommon, while heavier weights are continually recorded. Bright, strong fish, they afford wonderful sport in the heavy waters of the river. Many streams and lakes in the neighbourhood are also full of trout that rise well. There are still many big mule deer in the district and some mountain sheep, but winged game is scarcer than it should be.

There is a very pleasant climate for camping out through the summer and autumn. Horse flesh is very cheap, and the animals can be cheaply kept, so what with the open country and numerous roads and trails, it is well suited to equestrian exercise. There is room for dozens of camping parties, who would be sure of a certain sufficiency of sport, and who would be captivated by the scenic beauty of the localities they would reach in the hills, mountains and higher levels of the country.

Merely a local sale for fruit, and, therefore, difficult to quote fixed prices. Cherries do well. On the low benches on the Thompson River peaches succeed very well and yield heavily, the fruit being delicious. The crop of apricots is more uncertain. Grapes are grown very successfully on the lower benches of the river. Although nowhere can better wheat be grown than in this neighbourhood, yet at the price paid by millers no one will grow it. Everybody grows some oats; average yield, 70 bushels per acre. On one farm I know the yield, and have seen of weighed grain 100 bushels per acre all around! Prices from $25 to $30 per ton. Barley only grown in small quantities; average price, $30 per ton. Chinamen alone grow beans, and they produce them in considerable quantities; at present they are worth 2½ cents per pound — higher than usual. Many different varieties of potatoes are grown; average yield in 1900, 400 bushels per acre; prices varied from $10 to $13 per ton. The potatoes grown in this neighbourhood have deservedly earned a provincial reputation. Some 65 carloads (say 3,000,000 lbs.) were shipped by C. P. R. in October; value, $17,250, or thereabouts. Good stable hay is worth $15 per ton. Small fruits of all sorts yield abundantly.

Nothing done in dairying, except for private use. The breeding of cattle is the industry of this district. The price of beef cattle has been high this year. There has been a great demand for fat stock, and the average price has been 3¼ to 3½ cents per pound, live weight. Sheep thrive well in this district, but are kept by but few people, and only in small numbers. Poultry is not taken up with much system; average price of eggs, 25 cents a dozen; of chickens for food, $5 to $6 per dozen. Bees are successfully kept in certain instances.

Labour — Whites, very scarce; wages, $25 to $40 per month. Chinese, $20 to $25 per month, or $1 per day; Japanese, $20 to $25 per month, or $1 per day; Indians, $20 to $25 per month, or $1 per day; $1.25 in hay or harvest time. Labour for temporary purposes is hard to obtain. There are now more Chinese and Indians available than of any other class.

J. A. Teit, Spence's Bridge, says: Soil is mostly a sandy loam, but in some places consists of clay sub-soil, in some places gravel and in others clay. The yield of apples was large; price, about $1 per 40-lb. box. Other fruits yielded well, and all succeed. Grapes grow well. All varieties of small fruits grown; strawberries do not do so well as the others.

Beef, about 8c. per pound; milk cows, about $35 to $40.

Timber — In the lowest parts of the district — in dry places, yellow pine; along streams, etc., maple and cottonwood. In the lower mountains — in dry places, fir and juniper; in damp places, cottonwood, alder, maple and willow. In the higher

ROUNDING UP CATTLE AT KAMLOOPS.

BRANDING CATTLE.

mountains — In dry places, black pine and nut pine; in wet places, spruce, willow, etc.

CARIBOO WAGGON ROAD.

Including all points between Ashcroft and Quesnel, the principal of which are Clinton, Bridge Creek, Lac la Hache, Williams Lake, Soda Creek and Alexandria. All of these points are connected by stage — three times a week — with Ashcroft, the point of connection with the Canadian Pacific Railway. Clinton is situated 32 miles from Ashcroft, at the point at which the Lillooet and Big Bar roads leave the main waggon road.

Mr. F. W. Foster, Clinton, writes : In Clinton Valley wheat cannot be raised as a reliable crop suitable for milling; as a general crop, only feed for horses and cattle is raised, such as oats, barley, timothy, clover, Sanfoin, red-top, beets, potatoes, carrots, and the general run of hardy vegetables. The average yield of oats is 1,500 pounds to the acre; ruling prices, $38 to $40 per ton. At 3,000 feet apples freeze out; going out of this valley to the lower ones, such as Bonaparte and Fraser, they do well, at altitudes of say 700 to 1,000 feet lower than Clinton. This may also be said of other large fruits. Small fruits yield well.

The nearest place to Clinton Valley for dairying is Lac la Hache. They have no creamery as yet; private farmers produce a good deal of butter, which is readily bought up.

We lack vegetable mould; our soils are moraine, the remnants of the glacial period; but by irrigation and average seasons we raise fair crops. Irrigation is necessary through the whole district. Land is more plentiful than the water to irrigate with, unless at immense expense.

Labour — Whites, from $25 to $35 on farms; Chinese, $25; Japanese, none; Indians, $25 to $30 per month.

Bridge Creek and Lac la Hache, the former about 85 miles from Ashcroft, and the latter 100 miles. The road, shortly after leaving Clinton, enters what is known as the green timber, an elevated plateau covered with pine trees, mostly of stunted growth, with here and there small ponds and swamps, all highly impregnated with alkali. With few exceptions, the country is indescribably dreary and generally worthless. One of these exceptions is the 70 - Mile House, kept by William Boyd, who has a good dairy farm. At Bridge Creek the road descends into the valley of that stream, and thence along Lac la Hache, and the character of the country changes, for the better.

Timber is plentiful everywhere for all purposes of the ranchers, and of water there is no lack for purposes of irrigation. Barley, oats, rye and hay give good returns, and are extensively cultivated to supply local demands. Root crops are also good, but large fruits are not grown. Cattle are produced in large numbers for beef and dairying. The latter industry, for which this part is well adapted, has some attention paid to it here, and a considerable quantity of butter is produced. A good many horses are reared, and a few sheep and pigs.

Quite an extent of good land lies in the vicinity of Williams Lake, 150-Mile House and Chimney Creek. A road leads from the 150 - Mile House, on the Cariboo waggon road, past Williams Lake to the mouth of Chimney Creek, on the Fraser River, at which point there is a good ferry, and by swimming horses access is had to Chilcotin. Another road, which branches off at Williams Lake, leads down the Fraser past the Spring House Ranch to Alkali Lake. The country along this road is very beautiful, but on account of the altitude, which is from 1,750 to 3,500 feet, practically nothing is raised with the exception of hay, stock-raising being exclusively carried on. About Williams Lake, however, all the ordinary roots and cereals are grown, and a good market is always obtained at the Cariboo mines.

Soda Creek and Alexandria lie along the Fraser River and the Cariboo waggon road. The valley of the Fraser, above Soda Creek, widens out considerably, so that the ranches are much nearer the level of the river than they are lower down. Most of the ranches are on the eastern side of the river, on the Cariboo waggon road, some of them very fine ones, where extensive and profitable operations are carried on. On the western side, above Alexandria, are also some large and fertile farms, including that of Mr. Adams, upon which very heavy crops of cereals are grown. The former is 165 miles and the latter 185 miles from Ashcroft.

Mr. P. C. Dunlevy, Soda Creek, says: The timber is mostly fir, with some cottonwood. The soil is sandy, clay loam; the ranches are mostly on the benches along the Fraser River. There is considerable fall wheat raised; the yield in 1900 was about 45 bushels per acre; the ruling price is about 2 cents per pound. Oats yield about 60 bushels to the acre; the average price was 2½ cents per pound. Potatoes succeed well, and produce about 500 bushels per acre. Onions, about 300 bushels per acre. A few apples raised, with moderate success. Small fruits are successfully raised.

There are quite a number of private dairies; all seem to do well. The cattle industry pays well; the price of cattle ranges from $30 for 2-year-olds to $50 for 4-year-olds. The raising of hogs is profitable; nearly all ranchers raise a few; price on foot, about 10c. per pound. Poultry do quite well; all farmers raise from 50 to 100; eggs sell at 50c. per dozen.

Labour — Labourers are procurable at from $25 to $35 per month for whites, and from $15 to $25 for Chinese. White labourers are scarce; plenty of Chinese and Indians, but no Japanese. Chinese preponderate over all other classes.

VALLEY OF THE UPPER FRASER.

From Lillooet to Alkali Lake, and including, besides the two places mentioned, Pavilion, Big Bar Creek, Empire Valley, Dog Creek, Gang Ranch and Chilcotin.

This part of the country, being off the main Cariboo waggon road, is devoted extensively to stock-raising, as the expense attached to the transportation of general crops is too great to admit of general production. They, however, do well, and all local demand is supplied with all kinds of produce.

Alkali Lake and Dog Creek are on the east side of the Fraser River, on the road which branches from the Cariboo road at 150-Mile House and runs along the Fraser to the vicinity of Big Bar, where it leaves the river and joins the main road at Clinton. The Canada Western Company's property, called the Gang Ranch, is on the opposite side of the Fraser River, on Gaspard Creek. Chilcotin and Empire Valley are also on the same side.

Lillooet and Pavilion are below Big Bar Creek, on the river road. Lillooet includes Pemberton Meadows and what is known as the Douglas Portage — that part between Port Douglas and Harrison Lake and Lillooet, on the original Cariboo Road. Lillooet, when the trail went that way, was a place of some commercial importance; but since the present Cariboo road was built, much of its early prosperity has been taken away from it. It is situated on the western side of the Fraser River, which is here crossed by a fine bridge, giving access to the road leading to Pavilion, and thence over Pavilion Mountain to Clinton, or through the Marble Canyon to Ashcroft, on the Canadian Pacific Railway. Another road, recently constructed, leads down the Fraser to Lytton.

Pavilion and Pavilion Mountain include all the country on the east side of the Fraser, Marble Canyon, as well as that on the mountain, which is at an elevation of some 3,000 to 3,500 feet, increasing until it reaches about 5,000 feet. Communication is maintained by good waggon roads to Clinton over the mountain 21 miles, with Lillooet 17 miles, and Ashcroft, through the Marble Canyon, about 36 miles.

Mr. R. Carson, Pavilion Mountain: There is only a limited amount of land to be had in Lillooet district fit for farming. This makes prices better for those engaged in general farming. Beef is the best paying article for sale here, good two-year-old steers bringing $30 to $35 readily during the summer. Oats sell at 2c. per lb.; wheat, 1½c. at Pavilion flour mill. There is little barley grown.

Good work horses bring from $100 to $150. There are only two dairies in operation; good butter is in demand at 30c. per lb.

Labour — Wages are extremely high, from $25 for Chinese help to $35 for Indian and white help during the summer.

Mr. J. N. J. Brown, Empire Valley: The country is chiefly a grazing section, with prairie land, well watered and well timbered. Large numbers of cattle are annually raised. Grain is also extensively grown; the ruling price for wheat is 2c. Oats are grown in quantities, and give good yields; ruling price, 2c. Apples are successfully grown at McEwen's, Empire Valley, and also at Lesser Dog Creek, Alkali Lake, Big Bar and Dog Creek. Plums and cherries are successfully grown in places. Small fruits do well. Oats, about 2,000 lbs. to the acre; ruling price, $2 per 100 lbs. There is a great quantity of potatoes successfully grown, for table use and hogs.

The horse industry has been quite profitable, and there has not been any over-production. It is the best sheep country in British Columbia; ruling prices, $6 per head for sheep and $5 for lambs. There is a great number of pigs raised; they are nearly all bought up by Chinese miners, who pay from 5 to 6 cents per pound on foot; the balance are killed and turned into bacon for home use.

Irrigation is required for the successful production of crops; there is plenty of water available; ditching costs about 75 cents per yard. There is unlimited Government land which would make good farms. It is mostly all located in the heart of the settlement, land that would raise any kind of a crop. Improved farms can be bought, but fetch good prices.

Labour — Whites, $1.50 per day, or $30 per month; Chinese, $20 per month, as cooks; Indians, $1.50 per day. There is always a scarcity of white labour.

In Chilcotin is included all that section lying on the western side of the Fraser, between Soda Creek and Chilcotin River, a distance of about forty miles, and running back about the same. It is but sparsely settled, the country being principally adapted to stock-raising; in parts, however, good crops of grain and roots are obtained, although the general altitude is unfavourable to mixed farming. According to Mr. Sanford Fleming, the average altitude of Chilcotin Valley is 2,625; of the plain, 3,411; of the Chilcotin Lake, 3,150; of the old Chilcotin Fort, 3,800; and of the foot of Risky Creek, 2,170 feet; the Fraser being in the neighbourhood of 1,400, giving some idea of the climb necessary to attain the level of the plain above. The crossing at Soda Creek is effected by a good wire-rope ferry, whence there is an excellent road through Chilcotin proper; another crosses Chimney Creek, and is effected by boat and swimming horses; the latter route is a great saving of distance, for settlers living on Chilcotin River and Valley, in reaching the Cariboo waggon road. Risky Creek, above mentioned, empties into the Fraser a few miles above Chilcotin.

Mr. Charles Crowhurst writes: The soil is bottom land and bench bunch-grass. The market is mostly Cariboo, reached by waggon road. There are neither mines nor school. There are game and fish of all kinds. It is one of the best stock countries in British Columbia. Wheat is grown for milling; about 2,000 lbs. to the acre is the average. Prices, $2 per 100 lbs. for wheat, $5 per 100 lbs. for flour.

VALLEY OF THE UPPER COLUMBIA,

In which is included Golden, Galena, Windermere and Canal Flat. This valley lies between the mountain ranges of the Selkirks and Rockies. The valley varies in width from a mile or two to probably five miles. It must not be understood, however, that the whole of it is cultivable; much of it is low-lying swamp land formed by the Columbia, which is here a sluggish stream and navigable for stern-wheel steamers to within a few miles of its source. This land is, no doubt, susceptible of being dyked, and, being alluvial deposit, is naturally very fertile. At the present time the only use it is put to is for cutting wild hay. There is also a considerable quantity of rough and wooded land which requires clearing; this, however, is not of the formidable nature of the clearing required on the lands of the coast. Lastly, there is a considerable area of land which is easily brought under cultivation and which is very fertile, producing all the usual crops and fruits. The foothills are lightly timbered and form good ranges for stock.

Golden is on the main line of the Canadian Pacific Railway, at the confluence of the Kicking Horse River with the Columbia, and at an altitude of some 2,580 feet above sea level.

Galena is about 40 miles by road from Golden; Windermere about 41 miles further, and Canal Flat about 28 miles from Windermere. A good waggon road connects all these places, and during part of the season communication is maintained also by steamer. The land in the vicinity of Galena is generally wooded. Windermere is a charming spot situated on the lake of that name, the lake being really an enlargement of the Columbia River. Canal Flat is situated at the head of the Columbia Lake, the source of the river. A bit of rough water between the outlet and a point a few miles further down, however, stops steamer navigation a few miles above Windermere.

Mr. John Bulman, Windermere: Land for agricultural purposes is very limited where irrigation is possible. Of course, the pasturage is good over the whole district, native grasses being bunch-grass, buffalo and pine-grass in abundance. This is a good sporting district; deer, goat, moose, elk and mountain sheep abound in the mountains around; fish are plentiful in the lake, char and ling principally. Char have been caught weighing 13 pounds, but the average weight of each species is about 8 pounds.

Only a little spring wheat produced, principally for chicken feed, the average being 30 bushels per acre; ruling price, 2½ cents per pound. The average yield of oats is 55 bushels per acre; ruling price, 2½ cents per pound. Potatoes yield, on an average, six tons per acre; price, 1½ to 2 cents per pound. Timothy is mostly grown for hay; average yield, 1½ tons per acre; average price, $25 per ton. There are only two small orchards in this district. Small fruits are successfully grown.

Private dairying is carried on, but on a small scale, with satisfactory results. Butter sells at 35 cents per pound. Horses — Agricultural horses are mostly imported, there being none bred of necessary size and weight. Prices range from $100 up to $125. Those bred in the valley are small, but suitable for saddle and packing; prices from $15 to $30, according to size. I have no doubt sheep would do well if carried on in a systematic way; prices from $3 up to $7. Pork sells at from 12 to 15 cents per pound. There are quite a number of fowls raised; prices, from 50 cents to $1 each for chickens, 35 to 40 cents per dozen for eggs.

Timber trees are Douglas fir, tamarack, bull pine, and a little cedar. Government land is now very limited where irrigation is possible. There are a few sections of good land belonging to the C. P. R. and Kootenay Valleys Company; prices from $1 to $8 per acre. Improved farms are increasing in value; prices from $10 to $20 per acre.

Labour — Whites, $30 to $40 per month and board; Chinese, $25 to $30 per month and board; Indians, $1 per day and board. Supply quite equal to demand.

EAST KOOTENAY.

In which is included all the country in the valley of the Kootenay River, from Canal Flat to the United States boundary at Tobacco Plains, a distance of some 113 miles, Fort Steele and Cranbrook occupying about the centre. The waggon road spoken of as running through the Upper Columbia valley continues through this district to Tobacco Plains; the river is also navigable for steamboats to the boundary; and, lastly, the Crow's Nest Railway, recently completed, gives access to Alberta, in the Northwest Territories, and to West Kootenay. Fort Steele is beautifully situated on the bank of the Kootenay River opposite to where the St. Mary's River empties. Cranbrook is a town on the line of the railroad. A considerable quantity of the land all through the valley is fit for agricultural puposes, some of it quite clear and some partly wooded. A good local market is afforded by the mining camps in the vicinity, and by rail with the places situated along its line.

Mr. R. L. T. Galbraith, Fort Steele, writes: The best land lies along the Kootenay River, bench and bottom lands. The bottom land is a rich, black loam, and on the benches the soil is not so heavy, and is well adapted for roots of all kinds and fruits. There is a good market at Kimberley, Moyie and Fernie for the products raised; these places can be reached by rail. The rivers abound with fish, and there is still a good deal of game, such as mountain sheep, goats, elk, bear and other fur-bearing animals. About fifty families can get good homes in the valley. The land is held by the C. P. R. and Kootenay Valleys Company, whose agent resides at Fort Steele; they are giving liberal terms to settlers.

Not much fall wheat sown; ruling prices, $1.75 to $2 per 100 lbs. Oats, ruling prices from $1 to $1.50 per 100 lbs. Other grains are not grown. Potatoes fetch $1 per 100 lbs., and are grown to some extent. Timothy is the principal grass grown, and yields from ½ to 3 tons of hay per acre; ruling price was $15 for loose and $25 for baled hay per ton. Apples — All the hardy varieties, both summer, fall and winter, are grown; prices, from 2 to 5 cents per lb.

Horned cattle is a successful industry; from $50 to $60 each for beef. Not many horses raised; good horses brought from $75 to $125.

Irrigation is necessary for the successful production of crops on the benches. The principal timber trees are Douglas fir, yellow pine, spruce and tamarack (larch). Not much left of Government lands. Railway land can be bought at a reasonable price. Bottom and bench lands, $2, $2.50 and $2.75 per acre, on time — say ten years for payment. Improved lands, from $5 to $10 per acre.

Labour — Whites, labourers, $2.50; miners, $3 to $3.50 per day; Chinese, $2; Indians, $1.50 per day. We have now no difficulty in getting all the supply required.

Michael Phillipps, Tobacco Plains: As fair a valley as any in British Columbia, sheltered to the north and east by the Rocky Mountain range, and open to the south and west. The climate is an exceptionally good one. The Tobacco Plains has long been celebrated as a winter range. Here, in days gone by, the Hudson's Bay Company sent their horses to winter from as far as Fort Colville, on the Columbia River.

Wheat is grown only for chicken and hog feed; spring wheat grows remarkably well; wheat grows well on much of the bench land without irrigation; the price during the year has been $1.50 per 100 lbs. All kinds of oats grow well, sometimes going as high as 80 bushels to the acre; price, $1 per 100 lbs. Barley, if planted early, grows well on the high grass lands without irrigation; yield is always good; price, $1 per 100 lbs. The potato crop is, take it all around, the main crop; price, 75c. per 100 lbs.; yield, 300 to 400 bushels per acre. Of apples, the Yellow Transparent, Duchess of Oldenberg, Ben Davis, Wealthy, Fameuse and Henry Anderson are all in fine bearing; no country could suit them better. There are also growing on the Plains the Blenheim Orange, Golden Pippin, Martha, Transcendent Crabs — bearing; price, from 3c. to 5c. per lb. Cherries do very well. Small fruits do very well indeed.

A good deal of butter is made, but not enough for the home market; there is a good opening for several dairies. Horned cattle do well and pay well. There are few sheep here; they do very well on the dry grass hills; lambs by September weigh 70 lbs; price, 10c. (6c. by the quarter); no country could possibly be better adapted for sheep. Good team horses fetch $150 a pair; riding horses, $40 to $70; ponies, $10 to $30. Only a limited number of swine are kept on each farm. A large and never-failing demand for eggs at fair prices; 20 cents per dozen in summer; 40 cents per dozen in winter.

All the best farms are irrigated. Douglas fir on the foothills, red pine on the plains, black pine in the mountains, cottonwood and spruce along the rivers. Most of the land left is railway land; about $4 per acre for grass land; improved farms of value fetch a high figure.

Labour — Whites, $2.50 per day at harvest time, $30 per month; no Chinese or Japanese; Indians, $1.50 to $2 per day for harvest work, $1.25 occasional.

WEST KOOTENAY,

Including the valley of the Columbia from the Big Bend, above Revelstoke, south to the international boundary, a distance of some 200 miles, and the valley of the Kootenay River and Lakes from the boundary line north, a distance of some 45 miles. This covers a vast extent of territory, but inasmuch as it is almost altogether a mining region, it is all lumped together. Several towns, some of considerable size, such as Nelson and Rossland, are included in this section; also others of lesser size, such as Revelstoke, Kaslo and others. The communication between these places is good, and consists of railroads, steamers and roads, and access is easy by the same means of transportation to outside places. The land fit for agricultural purposes is comparatively small, generally wooded, along the valleys of the rivers, and in places requiring dyking; and while there does not exist large bodies of land suitable, still there are patches from 50 to 1,000 acres in extent. In the Big Bend, on Goldstream, there exist large stretches of land that are covered with wild grass, at the same time the land is subject to overflow during high water. George Laforme, the packer, finds this land suitable for grazing his pack animals during the open season in the Big Bend. Between Revelstoke and Carnes Creek there are some splendid flats suitable for cultivation, but covered with heavy growth of cedar. Between Carnes Creek and Downie Creek there are some nice benches, also covered with a growth of heavy timber. The great drawback is, there is no market available for their products; everything has to be packed on mules' backs, costing on an average 7 cents per pound. In the vicinity of Revelstoke quite a large quantity of land is under cultivation. Hall's Landing is the best farming land in this district. Galena Bay has quite a good piece of land that requires clearing. In the pass between Thompson's Landing and Trout Lake quite a lot of land has been taken up during the last few years, and no doubt as soon as the mines are worked the land will be cleared and placed under cultivation. On Fish Creek there are large sections of good land which is heavily timbered. Along the Arrow and Kootenay Lakes there are small patches of alluvial bottom land at the mouths of streams, flats of small extent on the lake shores, and here and there strips of higher land, gravelly loam slopes forming the base of mountains which rise abruptly along almost the whole of the shores of the lakes, comprising the only area fit for cultivation. The rest of the district is rugged in the extreme, and were it not for the great wealth of the mines would be worthless for all purposes. As it is, the large and increasing mining populations of the cities of Rossland, Nelson, Kaslo and elsewhere are creating such a profitable market that agricultural lands of this description must soon be occupied and cultivated. Such patches of land as have been referred to are extremely productive, especially for fruits. On the ranch of Mr. Collins, on the lake shore opposite Nelson, are found apple, pear, plum, cherry and peach trees, all exceedingly healthy and free from pests. At a point on the Lower Arrow Lake called Killarney, a trail leads into White Valley to Vernon, about 72 miles, through which cattle can be driven.

Mr. J. William Cockle, Kaslo : The valley of Kootenay River, south from the end of Kootenay Lake to the international boundary, and from the northern end of the lake for a distance of over 30 miles, is particularly adapted for agriculture. The soil, a rich silt, is remarkably productive, and all kinds of fruit flourish luxuriantly. A ready market for everything grown is found at the mining centres of Kaslo and Nelson, to both of which there is daily connection by two lines of steamers, which connect with railways at either end.

Potatoes have sold for $20 per ton this fall. The dyking of the Kootenay River bottom has proved a failure. Douglas fir on all hillsides; white pine on bottoms and gulches; cedar on bottoms; hemlock, spruce and tamarack on mountain sides — all abundant.

LOWER MAINLAND.

SOUTH SIDE OF FRASER RIVER.

FROM the mouth of the Fraser River to Hope is one of the most fertile sections of the province; the land, being mostly composed of silt, is an alluvial deposit of great depth. In this section are included the municipalities of Delta, Surrey, Langley, Matsqui, Sumas and Chilliwack, and the unorganised district between the last named and Hope.

Mr. E. A. Brown, Delta, reports : The Delta of the Fraser River includes all the low land lying south of and adjacent to the Fraser River for a distance of 15 miles from its mouth, and also includes Westham Island, which is separated from the rest of the district by the Canoe Pass of the Fraser River. The district is protected from the river and from the tidal waters of the Gulf of Georgia and Boundary Bay by a system of dykes, which cost the municipality in the neighbourhood of $100,000. The soil is for the most part very rich, and produces abundant crops. It has every advantage which proximity of market affords, being in direct communication by steamboat with Victoria, Vancouver, Nanaimo, New Westminster and other important points. Shipping facilities are of the best, for it is possible to ship at almost any point of the 15 miles of river front, and also at Boundary and Mud Bays. The waggon roads are good, the principal materials used in their construction being plank and gravel. There are no railroads or mines in the district, as the ease with which produce can be shipped by water makes railroads unnecessary; and the formation of the land, being built up by deposits of the river, makes mines out of the question. The schools are good, and are so placed as to make it possible for every child in the district to attend without any hardship. There is a school situated at each of the following points in the district : At Gulfside, at Boundary Bay, at East Delta, at Trennant, at Sunbury, at Westham Island, and a department school at Ladner, presided over by three teachers, making a total of seven schools and nine teachers. The fisheries of the district are of great importance, as they embrace a large portion of the world-famous fishing ground of the Fraser River. There are twelve salmon canneries located here, including some of the largest on the river; the large number of men employed and the value of the product makes this a very important industry. The resident population of the district is about 2,000, but this is increased during fishing season to 5,000 or 6,000. Taken as a whole, the district is one of the richest and most prosperous in the province; the taxes are not high, and the financial condition is good; the people are contented and prosperous, and satisfactory and steady progress is being made in wealth and population.

Wheat is very little grown here; ruling price, $25 per ton. Oats, average yield per acre, 2,500 pounds; the ruling prices were from $20 to $25 per ton. Barley is grown successfully, and is used almost entirely for hog feed. All standard varieties are successfully grown; average price, $15 per ton. Other roots and vegetables yield largely usually. All the standard varieties of fruit are grown with fair success; ruling prices, apples, 75 cents to $1 per box, plums 2 cents per pound.

Dairying is carried on to a considerable extent, and is increasing rapidly from year to year. The horse business has been profitable; there has been no over-production of good horses; good horses have been worth from $125 to $200. A good many sheep are raised; the industry is said to be a profitable one. Swine production is being prosecuted systematically; the price has been about 6c. for pigs on foot.

There are some hundreds of miles of under-drains in this district. It has cost $100,000 to dyke this district. The work was done by steam dredgers. The dyke has been most successful, and has increased the value of the land at least $20 per acre, or about $1,000,000 for the whole district.

Labour — Whites, $25 to $30 per month, with board, or $2 per day; Chinese, $15 per month, with board, or $1 per day. The supply is generally equal to the demand.

H. T. Thrift and H. Bose, Surrey: The District of Surrey is well situated. being readily accessible from the markets of the Coast cities. It is bounded on the north by the Fraser River, through its entire length on that side; on the east by the municipal district of Langley; on the south by the international boundary line and Semiahmoo Bay; and on the west by Mud Bay and the municipal district of Delta, and contains some 120 square miles of territory. There are in the District of Surrey about 20,000 acres of rich, alluvial soil, which, when brought in, is immensely productive, as high as 120 bushels of oats having been produced to the acre. There are about 7,000 acres of peat lands, on which at present but little has been done, but which will, when properly treated, respond bountifully to the efforts of the dairyman and agriculturist. The former of these lands are located at the delta and in the valleys of the Nicomekl and Serpentine rivers, while the latter class of land is found principally a little back from the Fraser River, in North Surrey. Besides these two classes of land we have what is popularly known as alder bottom land; this is highly timbered and about 10,000 acres in extent. This land is also very productive when cleared, and readily responds to the settlers' efforts. The balance of the land, some 39,000 acres, is more or less heavily timbered, logging camps having operated for many years in the district, until now the greater part of the merchantable timber has been taken off. A large proportion of the land is, when cleaned up, of very fair quality and will produce excellent crops. Some of the land, however, is very poor, every vestige of humus having been burnt out of it. It must not on this account be despised, as a great deal of it will eventually become valuable as the best sheep-raising land in the province.

Wheat not much grown, except for hen-feed; ruling prices, $25 per ton. Prices of oats averaged from $18 to $23 per ton; this is the most important crop grown in this district. No barley grown for malting purposes; chiefly grown for fattening hogs; ruling prices were $18 to $22 per ton. The pea crop is in some parts of this district the principal crop. Generally this district produces a large crop of most excellent potatoes; prices are good; from $14 to $20 per ton have been realised. The principal grasses and clovers grown here for hay are timothy and clover, either Alsike or Broad Leaf. On the swamp lands there is a good deal of Red Top and Blue Joint grass cut for hay; for this district the yield is 2 to 4 tons per acre; price, $8 to $12 per ton, baled. Apples — Black spot on bark destroys more trees than everything else put together; price, 80 cents to $1 per box of 40 lbs. Pears — Price, 80 cents to $1.25 per box of 40 lbs. All ordinary varieties

THOROUGHBRED SHEEP, LADNER.

THOROUGHBRED CATTLE, LADNER.

HARVESTING SCENE, DELTA.

A WESTMINSTER FARM HOUSE.

of plums and prunes are grown; prices, 25 cents to 75 cents per box of 20 pounds. Cherries — Prices, 50 cents to $1 per box of 20 pounds. Small fruits do well in this district; the price varies from 3 cents to 10 cents per lb.

In the aggregate there are a great many cows in this district and a very considerable quantity of butter made and sold at the weekly market in Westminster. No open cattle ranges in this district. Price of beef is from 6 cents to 9 cents a pound, dressed, according to time of year; price of milch cows, from $30 to $60 each. Some of the lands are particularly well adapted to sheep-raising; sheep have brought from $3 to $7 each; there is no demand for wool, 6 or 7 cents per pound. Swine-raising is carried on with some system; prices are from 6 cents to 9 cents per pound. A number of farmers are beginning to give a little more attention to the poultry branch. It is the most profitable branch of agriculture, for the small amount of capital it takes. Last year the prices for eggs were 20 cents to 50 cents per dozen; my average was 26 cents a dozen; broilers, $3 per dozen, to as high as $9 for hens; an average price is $5 per dozen.

The timber in this district is plentiful, and consists principally of Douglas fir, white fir, white pine, black spruce, hemlock, cedar, yew, cottonwood, soft maple, alder, red and white birch, vine maple, several varieties of willow, and dogwood. There are about eight sections of Dominion Government land in Surrey. It is mostly timbered land, or rather stump land, the good timber having been taken off. Some of the soil is good, while some is rather light and in places gravelly. Improved land can be purchased at from $15 to $100 per acre. There are a great many most desirable places, with more or less improvements, that can be purchased at from $5 to $15 per acre, now in the hands of mortgage companies, who are prepared to deal on the most liberal terms with prospective settlers.

Labour — Whites, $1 to $1.50 a day, with board; Chinese, $1 a day and board themselves; Japanese, $5 to $25 a month and board, according to time of year. During the fishing season we have a short supply; the rest of the year the supply is equal to the demand.

A. H. P. Matthew, Langley, and Z. D. Page, Port Kells, report: Langley lies between Surrey and Matsqui, and stretches from the Fraser River to the international boundary, and comprises about 120 square miles. The total assessed acreage is 76,542 acres, of which 59,740 are occupied and 6,704 under cultivation; and 10,008 acres of wild lands held by speculators. The total assessment of the district is $1,858,250, of which $311,260 is value of improvements. There are no railway or government lands in the district. The soil is generally fertile — some alder-bottoms and some heavily timbered with fir, spruce, etc. The district is well watered, and, as a rule, easily drained. Good crops of wheat, oats, potatoes, roots and fruits are raised. Of the fruits, peaches, grapes, pears, plums, apples and small fruits do well. Cattle and hay are also raised in abundance. Markets are situated at New Westminster and Vancouver. Three boats ply daily on the Fraser River. The district is well off for roads — about 200 miles in all, of which about 120 are good and the remainder passable. The Yale road intersects from east to west, and connects with Westminster about nine miles from the boundary of the district. Game of various kinds is abundant. Port Kells, including Barnston Island, is ten miles from New Westminster. The soil is very varied; there is no government land, but improved or unimproved land can be bought very reasonably.

Timothy and clover are principally grown for hay; average price, $8 per ton.

Private dairying is very largely carried on here. Horned cattle are produced profitably; milch cows, from $35 to $60; beef, from 5 to 8 cents per pound. A large number of sheep are raised here, but all except lambs are affected badly with flukes; price, $4 to $8.

John Ball and M. W. Morrison, Matsqui: The District of Matsqui comprises Mount Lehman, Peardonville, parts of Aldergrove and Abbottsford, and extends from the Fraser River north to the international boundary line south, and bounded on its west by Langley and east by Sumas municipalities, the Yale trunk road running through its centre east and west. The land is generally level and accessible; soils good, with abundant supplies of good, pure, running streams. Roads are being made and improved very much lately.

Potatoes are, as a rule, very successfully grown on the high lands, and are equal to the Ashcroft in every respect; ruling prices net the farmer probably about $15 per ton. The ruling prices of apples are from 80 cents to $1 per box.

Butter ranges in price from 15 and 18 cents in summer to about 25 cents in winter, and often the shipping charges have to be met out of these prices. Cheese is not manufactured at all. The average price for a team of fair horses during the past year has been from $250 to $300. Our district is and will be most eminently suited for sheep ; the ruling price has been, for good sheep, from $6 to $8 per head for ewes, and from $4 to $5 for lambs, ready for the market.

In Matsqui there are large areas of land which are being reclaimed by the dyking and pumping operations now being carried out. There are both peaty and alluvial deposits, with a clay subsoil in places, while the peat deposits in others reach to a great depth. There are a few government claims still to be had for pre-emption, but they are mostly in inaccessible parts, chiefly in unsurveyed or mountainous places, and not considered of much value for agricultural purposes. The price of improved farms — I mean by that a few acres cleared and some outbuildings, such as abandoned or mortgaged lands — from $5 to $10 and $15 per acre, according to location and nature of the clearing and soils.

Labour — Whites, $1.50 per day in summer and $1 in the winter season, with board; Chinese, about $30 in summer and $20 to $25 in winter; Japanese, from $10 to $20 per month, with board; Indians, about same rate of wages as whites.

Orion Bowman, Upper Sumas : Upper Sumas is that portion of the Sumas Valley situated southwest of Sumas Lake and extending to the United States boundary line, comprising about half a township. The soil is nearly all alluvial except about one square mile in the southwest corner, where it is peaty. Nearly all is within the flooded district of the Fraser. There are, however, ridges (sand dunes) evenly distributed over the valley, so that no point is more than a mile from high ground.

Sumas creamery is near the post office; it receives both milk and cream, mostly cream. Most of the patrons have cream separators. There were 15 patrons this summer, and about 40,000 pounds of butter have been made from 250 cows.

On high land, timber comes in this order of predominance: Fir, cedar, alder, hemlock, soft maple, birch, willow, etc. On low land, flooded: Willow, birch, cottonwood, alder, hardhack (a red-flowered spirea). Unimproved land can be bought for from $5 to $10 per acre.

Mr. Horatio Webb, Chilliwack : Chilliwack is situated on the Fraser River, about 65 miles from its mouth. It is the best agricultural district in the province, has good water communication daily with New Westminster, connecting by steamers there for Victoria, Nanaimo and Vancouver. The Canadian Pacific Railway runs on the opposite side of the river, and there is daily communication with it by boat. There is a trunk road also to New Westminster, crossing by ferry at that place. A good home market for most of the produce, dealers coming up from the cities and buying from the farmers: plenty of game, pheasants getting very plentiful; fishing, especially trout, is good. About 2,500 of a population. Good exhibition grounds. Some very promising gold mines in the vicinity.

Not much wheat grown, mostly for chicken feed and Graham flour. Excepting oats, about the same conditions prevail in other grains as with wheat, viz., generally produced in limited quantites for local use in feeding stock. Oats are produced in large quantities for sale. Root crops and vegetables are all successfully grown. Grasses and clover yield 2½ tons hay to the acre; price, $8 (baled and delivered at steamboat landing). Hops are successfully produced; the crop of 1900 was short; the principal market is England; low prices do not warrant increased production, however. Apples were mostly spotted, and we are troubled with a great many pests; price, 50 cents to $1.25 per box of 40 pounds. Crab-apples do well and find a ready market at good prices, from 1½ to 3 cents per pound. Pears succeed well; price, 75 cents to $1 per box. All small fruits do well, both in yield and quality.

Private dairying is a thing of the past; only a few are engaged in it, and they brand their butter "Creamery Butter." The horse industry has been a profitable one. Horses have been in great demand and at good prices; ruling prices, from $100 to $175. Sheep are successfully, but not largely, produced; prices are $6 for ewes, $4 for lambs (weaned), 6 to 8 cents per lb. for wool. The production of pigs is entered into quite largely; pigs on foot, 4½ to 6 cents per lb. Poultry is entered into, in one or two cases, with satisfactory returns.

Quite large dyking works are going on at the present time, with every prospect of good success. Farming land, improved, from $35 to $100 per acre; unimproved, $10 to $25 per acre. Land has changed hands at these prices this year.

Labour — Whites, $15 to $25 per month, with board; Chinese, $10 to $20 per month, with board.

NORTH SIDE OF FRASER RIVER.

From the mouth of the river to Yale, including the municipalities of Richmond, South Vancouver, Burnaby, Coquitlam, Maple Ridge, Mission, Dewdney, Nicomen and Kent, and the unorganised districts adjacent to and to the eastward of the last-mentioned municipality. In this area are situated two of the principal cities of the province — Vancouver and New Westminster — and the Canadian Pacific Railway runs through its entire length. There is more high land in this section than on the south side, but also an immense area of low lands, liable, where not protected by dykes, to floods when the snows melt in the mountains, during the months of May and June. These lands are equally fertile with those on the other side of the river, and much the same conditions prevail.

W. R. Austin, Coquitlam: In the municipality of Coquitlam, especially in Pitt Meadows, are good agricultural lands open for sale. Meadow land, ready for ditching, and all clear for plowing; prices, $10 to $40 per acre. Uplands in the municipality, more or less timbered, some good land, some medium, and some light; prices, from $5 per acre to $30. A good opening for small farms and large ones, quite convenient to New Westminster City, with one of the best markets on the continent, which has to supply Vancouver largely.

Dairying is carried on in the district by private people, most of the milk being sold in the cities. Swine not produced to any extent; prices on foot, 6 to 8½ cents; poultry production is profitable; fowls fetch from $6 to $6.50 per dozen; eggs average 40 cents per dozen.

Labour — Whites, $20 and board; Chinese, about $20, without board; Japanese, $1 per day.

Hector Ferguson (Port Haney), J. M. Webster (Webster's Corners), and H. J. Percy (Wharnock): Port Haney is situated on the north side of the Fraser River and on the Canadian Pacific Railway, 27 miles from Vancouver and 16 by steamer (daily) from New Westminster. There are about 30,000 acres of good agricultural high land (clay loam) tributary to it; and Pitt Meadows, containing about 20,000 acres, is only from two miles on the north to three miles on the west from it. It contains two large brickyards, which turn out about 3,000,000 bricks of all kinds per year, and furnish a splendid market for over 2,000 cords of wood per season to the settlers in the vicinity. The Fraser River at this point is a favourite part with fishermen, and many new settlers make enough in the fishing season to materially assist them during the remainder of the year in clearing up their places. All kinds of grain and roots, as well as grasses, do well here. Fruit, stock and dairying, however, are the occupations of the future in this municipality. All kinds of small fruit, cherries, apples, pears and plums do exceptionally well here, and find a most convenient shipping place at Haney to all parts of the Dominion.

Wharnock is situated on the north side of the Fraser, also on the main line of the Canadian Pacific Railway, 34 miles from Vancouver and 9 miles below Mission Junction. The land commences to rise almost immediately on leaving the river bank to benches or flats. The soil is mostly a dark sandy loam, with a hard clay subsoil. There is a good market at Vancouver and New Westminster, which can be reached by the Canadian Pacific Railway and river steamboats; and also a market is now open in the Northwest for fruit. The game consists of grouse, geese, ducks and some deer. Good trout fishing on the Stave River and other streams. The salmon fishing industry employs a great part of the population in the summer time.

Oats are one of the standard crops. Peas are the best grain crop grown here, and yield well where the land is not too wet. Maple Ridge potatoes, being mostly grown on high land, are of extra quality; price, $15 to $20 per ton. Although this is most decidedly a fruit section, many apple trees have died during the last ten years with bark blight; ruling price, 75 cents and $1 per box. Pears are proving to be a much more valuable tree on clay land than the apple; price, from $1.50 per box for Bartlett to $1 for late varieties. Plums and prunes are perhaps the most extensively grown large fruit in this vicinity, all varieties doing well; price, about 60c. per crate of 20 lbs. A large quantity of all classes of small fruits are grown and marketed.

Dairying is not carried on to any extent; price of beef, 6½ to 8 cents; milch cows, $35 to $50. The land here is generally too wet for successful sheep-raising. Hog-raising is carried on to a considerable extent here, in connection with dairying; prices have been from 7 to 8½ cents per pound, dressed.

Dyking has been done on Pitt Meadows with marked success. The soil is black alluvial, inclined to be peaty in places. The principal timber here is fir, cedar, alder and hemlock. The bark of alder is held to be the best for tanning purposes, the wood about the best for fuel. It seems to follow and replace the other timber where cleared off. Little or no Government land; improved land can be bought at from $10 to $50 per acre, according to location.

Labour — Whites, easily procured, $2 per day, without board; Chinese, $1 per day, without board; Japanese, $5 to $15 per month, with board; Indians, about the same as whites.

A. M. Verchere and A. W. Peen, Mission : The District of Mission Farmers' Institute comprises Mission and Dewdney municipalities, thus extending from Stave River east to Nicomen Island, on the north bank of the Fraser River. This stretch of country contains areas of lands of many varieties, and which, according to location, are good for many of the various lines of agriculture. The flat lands lying adjacent to the river, and but slightly above the level of the water during the season of the high water, consist mostly of heavy clay lands of a very rich and apparently almost inexhaustible nature. The lands on the higher ridges occurring frequently throughout these flats, and which are not subject to overflow except on occasions of extremely high water, will bring in the best returns for all kinds of grain, hay and roots; and the large stretches of wild grass lands that occupy all the lower part of these flats, and which are too low and wet, are especially valuable for pasture, and large numbers of cattle are carried by all the farmers thereon. On the lands rising back from the river towards the mountains, several miles in the background, the country comprises a great variety of soil; running as it does from heavy clay, where upland marshes occur, to light gravelly and sandy hillsides. The land throughout this section is mostly heavily timbered, although large sections may be found whereon the timber is very light and readily removed; but here still may be found old dead firs and cedars of great size, of a past generation, lying fallen on the ground. The first are of little use except for firewood, and are hard to remove: but the latter are very valuable for making rails, boards and timbers for building purposes. These uplands, although thus slow to bring into cultivation, are more especially valuable for fruit-growing; at the same time, after a little cultivation, good crops of all kinds of farm produce can be raised with surety and success.

On the river, steamers ply daily between New Westminster and Chilliwack, thus giving communication by boat in either direction daily. Educational facilities are extremely good. The country is well opened up along the river front and extending back for some miles with waggon roads, which, although not good, yet afford means of traffic and communication throughout the district. The chief direction of the farmers' efforts is along the low front lands, the raising of cattle, horses, sheep and hogs forming a considerable part of the production. Large quantities of hay and many tons of oats are also yearly shipped. The majority of these farmers also carry a large number of cows, the cream from which is shipped daily by boats to the creamery at New Westminster.

On the upland holdings, fruit-growing and chicken-raising form the chief items. The fruit industry of this section is assuming yearly larger proportions, and the district is rapidly becoming the largest fruit-shipping district of the province. Many tons of strawberries, raspberries, plums and apples, besides other fruits, are shipped yearly to the Northwest, with remunerative results. The poultry business is as yet in almost an infant state, but there are already some good breeders of pure-bred stock, and what small business has been done has proved encouraging. Eggs throughout the winter bringing in the cities from 30 to 50 cents per dozen, and the demand for table fowls being always good, it can be seen that considerable expansion in this business is to be expected. Turkeys and geese prove especially profitable.

For those who have the inclination and time, shooting and fishing can be indulged in, the duck-shooting and trout-fishing being as good as can be obtained in the province, and frequently a deer or bear falls a prize to the ardent sportsman.

The Fraser River affords occupation during the season for fishermen to take the salmon and sturgeon with which its waters abound, and considerable lumbering is done on the streams emptying into the Fraser, and work can nearly always be obtained in this line, if desired by those who are experienced woodsmen.

The Government is building a trunk road from Vancouver to Agassiz, which will traverse the district from one end to the other, and will thus open up much desirable land which can be pre-empted for settlement. Much of this land, although first-class, is heavily timbered; but large tracts occur whereon the timber is but light, and can be easily removed. Lands can be purchased throughout the district, both on the low and uplands, in blocks of almost any acreage, at reasónable figures; and there is considerable land open for pre-emption, some two or three miles back from the river, and which will in the course of a few years be valuable properties.

Considerable dairying is carried on, but cream is for the most part shipped by boat to New Westminster creamery. Considerable local butter is made, but very little cheese; good profits are made. Cattle-raising is a successful industry in this district; prices good — cattle, beef, from 7 to 8 cents on foot; veal, according to quality, but generally good; milch cows, good, from $35 to $50. Sheep are very remunerative. Prices of swine, 5 cents per ℔., on foot. The poultry industry has been slightly taken up, and is a remunerative branch of agriculture; ruling prices, hens $6 per dozen, chickens $4.50 to $5 per dozen, eggs 20 cents to 40 cents per dozen, according to season.

There is quite an extent of land in this district that could be reclaimed by dyking Dewdney and Hatzic Prairies. Character of the soil is clay. There is both government land for pre-emption and railway land to be had. Generally poor, heavily timbered, and far back from the river, and the lack of roads is very detrimental to settlement. Various prices; circumstances are so extremely different in locations which may be close together, that it is hard to estimate figures of valuation.

Labour — Whites scarce in summer at $2 to $2.50 per day, plentiful in winter at $25 to $30 per month; Chinese plentiful in summer at $1 per day, winter 75c. per day or $12 to $15 per month; Japanese $5 to $15 per month in winter; Indians plentiful at good wages, but will seldom work except on contract or berry-picking. White labour in harvest time is somewhat scarce, and cannot be procured except at high wages.

George W. Beebe, Agassiz: Kent Municipality is located 62 miles east of Vancouver; Harrison River Station is located at the mouth of the Harrison River, where it empties into the Fraser. A large sawmill, a shingle mill, two general stores, etc., comprise the settlement, with an Indian reserve. Ruby Creek, the eastern boundary, is an Indian reserve, with one store and a station. Agassiz is the principal station in the municipality, and the most important along the Canadian Pacific Railway for many miles. The Dominion Government Experimental Farm is located directly opposite the C. P. R. station. Six miles northwest is the Harrison Hot Springs, hotel and pleasure resort, with Harrison Lake, nearly 30 miles long. Here is located one of the largest hotels in the province. Agassiz Valley proper is a fine farming district of very limited area, almost entirely closed in on three sides by low mountains. Six or seven miles distant and across the Fraser River is the snow-capped peak of Cheam Mountain, that rises some 7,000 or more feet from the Fraser.

Cereals, root crops and grasses as in other districts on this side of the river. Considerable quantities of hops are grown here, and averaged in 1900 about three-quarters of a ton to the acre; the crop is shipped partly directly to England, and the balance to Eastern points.

Some very high mountain land, I am told, to be had; small quantities of timber lands to be pre-empted within ten to fifteen miles, good for farming purposes, I am informed.

Labour — Whites, generally at $1.50 per day; Chinese, plentiful at $1 per day; Japanese, a few at 50 cents to $1 per day; Indians, a good many, but usually work by the job and hop-picking. Chinamen are in preponderance.

THE NORTHWEST COAST OF THE MAINLAND.

Including the various settlements at Howe Sound, Squamish, Frock, Bute Inlet, Bella Coola, etc. Communication with these settlements is maintained altogether by steamers, there being no roads, and the character of the country being of such a nature that their construction is all but impossible, and must of necessity remain in abeyance until the population is sufficient to justify it. The country is, without exception, thickly wooded, principally with Douglas fir, spruce, hemlock, red cedar, balsam fir, maple, alder, birch and other woods, and a great variety of underbrush. The coast line is indented along its whole length with deep fiords, which run many miles into the interior, and at the heads of which are large streams. The shores of these fiords are, except where rivers debouch, almost invariably precipitous. At the mouths of the streams and along their valleys are generally flats, fit for agricultural purposes after they are cleared of timber. As may be imagined from the description given, the precipitation is excessive, consisting almost entirely of rain, the snowfall, owing to the influence of the sea, being comparatively small, and the temperature, from the same cause, never very low. The markets of this part consist mostly of loggers' camps and Indians.

Howe Sound includes all that part at the entrance of the Sound, including Anvil, Gambier, Keat's and Bowen Islands, where there are a good many settlers, principally engaged in fruit culture, for which this part is well suited. Communication is maintained altogether by water, the country being too mountainous for making a road to Burrard Inlet. The distance from the Sound to Vancouver by water is 10 miles, and to Nanaimo about 23 miles; these are the nearest markets. Very fine fruit is produced in this section, which finds a good market in Vancouver.

Squamish is a settlement in the valley of the river of that name, at the head of Howe Sound, about 40 miles by water from Vancouver. It is comparatively a sparsely settled district, and as it is heavily timbered, necessitates much clearing, and cereals are not produced to any extent; fruit-raising and hop-growing are found more profitable. The hops produced here are of excellent quality, and the land is well adapted to that purpose.

Mr. A. G. Deighton and Mr. N. Frolander, Froek, which is a settlement at Malaspina Strait, about 65 miles from Vancouver: There are no roads, trails or railroads. Fish and game in abundance. Potatoes are grown in fair quantities, the price being about $25 per ton. Timothy and red clover are grown for home stock; yield, about 3 tons of hay per acre. Fruits succeed well if attended to. Labour — Whites, $2.50 to $3 per day; Chinese, 90 cents; Japanese, $1; Indians, $3 — all without board.

Bute Inlet is about 130 miles to the northward of Vancouver. The climate is described by those who have visited the district as quite equable and the soil of excellent quality, but it is timbered in some parts heavily. The Southgate and Homalko Rivers empty into the head of the Inlet, and it was the valley of the latter which was originally selected as the route of the Canadian Pacific Railway, and later for the proposed British Pacific. The settlers who have taken up land are well satisfied with their lot, and anticipate that a thriving town will spring up in the future. The land is wooded with alder, maple, cedar and a few fir trees. It costs from $30 to $40 per acre to clear and leave it ready for planting, not including the removal of stumps. There are some bottom lands up the Homalko River Valley, which would cost but $15 per acre to clear.

Bella Coola is at the head of Bentinck Arm, about 400 miles to the northwest of Victoria, with which communication is maintained by the coasting steamers, which all call there. A fine wharf has been constructed by the Government, and there is every facility for loading and discharging. Bella Coola has been established by a thriving colony of Norwegian settlers.

Mr. G. A. Gibson: The Bella Coola colony is situated inland a distance of about 60 miles from the coast line, and running eastward about 30 miles, with a gradual rise from the sea to an altitude of about 900 feet at the head of the valley. It has a climate very different from what is generally found upon the coast, the humidity, even at the mouth of the river, being much less than on the coast, and as the valley is ascended it quickly changes to a drier climate, a marked difference being found even a few miles up from the head of the inlet.

With regard to crops grown here, it has been fully demonstrated by the few settlers who were here for several years previous to the advent of the Norwegian colonists, that the various roots, vegetables and corn can be successfully raised, and of excellent quality. Wheat and oats have also been tried and proved very satisfactory.

The timber of this valley is varied, principally cedar, fir, spruce, cottonwood, alder, maple, birch and willow.

Winter sets in generally the latter part of December. The winters are not severe, although the temperature has been as low as 10 degrees below zero, but as a rule it seldom reaches lower than 12 degrees above — that is, 20 degrees of frost. Two or three feet of snow usually falls, chiefly in January. Sleighing lasts from six to nine weeks. From information gleaned, the winters are sometimes very open, with frequent rains. Spring sets in about the beginning of April, sometimes earlier.

B. Brynildson, Bella Coola: Potatoes yield 300 bushels per acre; price, $20 per ton. Timothy is mostly grown for hay; I estimate the production to be 2½ tons per acre. Red Top production, 3½ tons per acre; price, $12 per ton. The soil and weather seem to be favourable for all kinds of small fruits.

Dairying is carried on to some extent by private parties; the price of milch cattle is from $40 to $75.

Irrigation is required some years. There is some Government land for preemption. Improved farms can be bought for $1,000 and up. Labourers (white), $2 per day.

[Further reference is made to the Bella Coola route to the interior elsewhere.—Ed.]

VANCOUVER ISLAND AND ADJACENT ISLANDS.

ESQUIMALT, HIGHLAND, METCHOSIN AND SOOKE DISTRICTS.

THESE are the most southern districts in British Columbia, being at the extreme southern end of Vancouver Island, and lying very little above sea level.

The districts of Esquimalt, Goldstream and Highland adjoin Victoria District to the westward, and much the same characteristics prevail as in Metchosin, Highland being more hilly and rocky and heavily timbered.

Metchosin includes Rocky Point, Pedder Bay and Happy Valley, all accessible by water and by waggon road to Victoria, which is 15 miles from the centre of the district. A great part is covered with timber, mostly fir; some small second growth; some heavily timbered; some open oak land, and alder and maple bottoms.

Sooke includes Jordan Meadows, which lie some distance in the interior and are reached by a trail via Sooke Lake. Sooke proper is on the sea coast, with a good harbour for small vessels, but an indifferent entrance, a few miles to the northward and westward of Race Rocks, and 23 miles from Victoria by waggon road or by water. The country generally is heavily wooded, rocky in parts near the coast, with open meadows up the Jordan River.

Mr. Arthur H. Peatt, Colwood: Grain, except oats, is not grown largely; wheat, principally for feed, $30 per ton; oats, from $25 to $30 per ton; peas, $30 to $40 per ton. Potatoes produce 7 tons to the acre, and of good quality; price. $18 to $20 per ton. The principal grasses grown are rye grass, orchard grass, timothy and red clover; the yield was about 1½ tons per acre. Apples, 1½ cents to 3 cents per lb.

Dairying is carried on to a considerable extent by private dairies, and is profitable, if properly managed. Cattle-raising is a successful industry in this district; beef was worth from 7c. to 9c., milch cows from $50 to $75. Horses are profitable; ruling prices were from $50 to $250. Sheep not very profitable, on account of wild animals and dogs; ruling prices, lambs from $4 to $5, sheep from 10 to 12½c. per lb., wool 8c. per lb. The raising of pigs is prosecuted; ruling price, 6c. to 7c. per pound. Poultry-raising is being taken up with system and fairly good success; it is remunerative; broilers are worth from $4 to $6 per dozen; hens, $6 to $9; eggs, 16c. to 50c. per dozen.

Labour — Whites, $20 to $40 per month; Chinese, $10 to $30 per month; Japanese, $5 to $30 per month. Supply equal to the demand.

Mr. John Muir, Sooke: Thirty-five families in this district are engaged in farming. Wheat is produced only for feeding purposes; ruling price, 1¼ cents per pound. Average yield of oats, 40 bushels per acre. Peas, 20 bushels per acre; price, 1½ cents per pound. Average yield of potatoes in fair years, 6 tons per acre; ruling price, $18 per ton. Average yield of grasses and clovers, 2 tons per acre; ruling price in 1900, $12 per ton. Fruit of all kinds does well

HARVESTING, VERNON.

The district is suitable for the sheep industry, and is carried on to a small extent; lambs are worth $3.50, sheep $5, and wool 8 cents per pound.

No Government lands open for pre-emption; from $6 to $30 per acre, according to location and improvements, is the price for improved lands.

Labour — Whites, $1.50 per day; Chinese, $20 per month; Japanese, $10 per month; Indians, none. Supply equal to the demand.

VICTORIA, LAKE, NORTH AND SOUTH SAANICH, AND INCLUDING JAMES ISLAND.

These districts lie to the northward of the City of Victoria, and are connected with it by good waggon roads, railroad and water. The principal products are hops, roots, vegetables, hay, dairy products and fruit.

Victoria District comprises all that part between Esquimalt and Highland on one side and Lake District on the other. A large portion of the land is slightly wooded, and much of it partly open oak land.

Lake is a district north of Victoria and between it and south Saanich, the eastern boundary being Haro Straits. Most of the land is timbered, lightly in some parts and heavily in others. The district is well watered by streams and lakes. Fruit-raising and market gardening are principally followed.

South Saanich, on the Saanich Peninsula, is about 12 miles north of Victoria, with which it is connected by good waggon roads and railway. Saanich Arm separates the peninsula from the main island, so that its eastern and western boundaries are the salt water, the south being Lake District and the north North Saanich.

North Saanich adjoins South Saanich to the north, and occupies the end of the peninsula. Sidney, the terminus of the railway from Victoria, is on the east coast. Several good waggon roads also give access to Victoria. This is a beautiful district, well suited to the cultivation of hops and fruits of all kinds.

James Island lies off North Saanich, and very near to it. The settlers cross in small boats with produce for the markets. Noted for the large quantity of strawberries produced, of good quality, and usually about the first of the local product in the Victoria market.

Mr. C. E. King, Victoria: "Hills and valleys" would best describe my district, the valleys having as a rule good black loamy soil, on which large crops can be grown. The hilly ground is inclined to be gravelly, and in many places is too rocky for cultivation. The City of Victoria, three to five miles distant, affords a good market for all the produce grown in the district. There is fairly good shooting of pheasants, grouse, quail and ducks.

There is a lot of fall wheat grown; price, $25 to $30 per ton. Oats yield 42 bushels to the acre. Root crops of all kinds are produced; potatoes sell at from $18 to $20 per ton; mangolds, $6 to $10; carrots, $8 to $10; turnips, $5 to $7. Indian corn can be successfully grown. Hops are produced in the Saanich peninsula, of extra good quality. Apples yield good; price, $1 per box (40 lbs.). Pears of exceptionally good quality are grown; price, $1 per box. Plums, cherries and quinces are all grown very successfully, yielding heavily, and not troubled with pests. Small fruits, especially strawberries, are grown in large quantities, and find a ready market.

Dairying is carried on largely and profitably in the sale of milk and also in butter-making. Horses have been profitable, the demand having exceeded the production; prices, $125 to $250. This is a suitable district for sheep, and their production is carried on to a considerable extent with profit. Poultry production is being taken up with system, and is remunerative; prices of eggs range from 15 to 75 cents per dozen; spring chickens, 35 cents and upwards.

COWICHAN.

Which includes the districts of Cowichan, Comiaken, Quamichan, Somenos, Chemainus, Sahtlam, Seymour and Shawnigan, is one of the most flourishing settlements on the Island, about 40 miles north of Victoria, on the line of the Esquimalt & Nanaimo Railway, midway to Nanaimo, being centrally situated in regard to markets. The first two mentioned districts front on the water, Sansome Narrows; these, with the following two, have a fair quantity of comparatively clear land on the Cowichan River, and on Quamichan and Somenos Lakes, with good bottoms and a good deal of timber lands. The others are farther back, and are for the most part heavily wooded and sparsely settled.

Chemainus adjoins Cowichan to the north, Thetis and Kuper Islands, which lie off Chemainus, being included. The latter are fairly cleared of timber, and are well suited to sheep-raising and fruit-growing. The mainland is heavily wooded, except in the valley of the Chemainus River. There is a sawmill and quite a village at the harbour.

Cowichan Lake is centrally located between the eastern and western coasts of the Island, and about twenty miles from Duncan Station, on the Esquimalt & Nanaimo Railway, with which point it is connected by a good waggon road. The country is all heavily timbered, principally with fir and cedar, and some maple and alder in the bottoms.

Shawnigan is a district on the line of the E. & N. Railway, about 30 miles from Victoria, and includes Shawnigan Lake and Koksilah River. The country is heavily wooded, but there are some extensive low-lying lands, which with drainage can easily be brought into cultivation.

Mr. H. de M. Mellin, Somenos, says : The Cowichan District comprises the valley watered by the Cowichan River, and the adjacent country as far south as Shawnigan, and to the north as far as Chemainus. This district is particularly adapted for the pursuit of both agriculture and horticulture. It is centrally situated on the Esquimalt and Nanaimo Railway, between two excellent markets, Victoria and Nanaimo. The soils, chiefly alluvial, submit readily to cultivation, and produce large crops of all grains and plants belonging to the temperate zone. The population consists chiefly of English and Scotch settlers, many of them of exceedingly good social position. The district is traversed by some of the best roads in the Island, kept always in good order by a well-administered Municipal Council. There is also good water communication along the coast from Saanich Arm to Chemainus. At the latter place may be found the largest sawmill in British Columbia, and at Cowichan Lake extensive logging operations are carried on every year.

No wheat grown. A considerable quantity of oats grown; yield, about 60 bushels per acre; price, $25 per ton; a large quantity also cut for hay. Peas, between 30 and 40 bushels per acre; price, about $30 per ton. Potatoes yield from 400 to 600 bushels per acre; prices, from $15 to $25 per ton. Production of hay, from 2 to 3 tons per acre; price, from $12 to $18 per ton. Approximate number of apple trees, 10,000; prices, 75c. to $1 per box, rising to as high as $1.90 in the spring. Pears yield fairly good. Plums and prunes yield very good; approximate number of trees, 2,000; prices, from 2c. to 4c. per lb. for certain varieties. Cherries yield good; number of trees, about 500; prices, from 4c. to 6c. per lb. Peaches, apricots and nectarines, with care and cultivation, can all be successfully produced here. Most small fruits do very well in favourable seasons. Gooseberries yield good; price, 4c. to 5c. per pound. Currants yield good; price, 4c. to 5c. per pound. Raspberries yield good; price, $1.50 per 24-pound crate. Strawberries yield good; price, 6c. per pound.

The Cowichan Creamery now includes as patrons all the larger farmers who had a reputation for their butter. This creamery has been so successfully worked that it does not pay the average farmer to do his own churning, if he can by any means manage to send the cream into Duncan. There are 53 patrons, who have altogether about 450 cows. The number of cows available for creamery purposes within a reasonable radius will amount altogether to about 650. Cowichan District is very suitable for sheep-raising. The industry is carried on to a fairly large and increasing extent, and it is profitable; the prices paid by the butchers for the sheep raised here this year were: Wethers in good condition, from $5 to $6; good grade ewes for stock, $6; lambs, from $4.50 to $5; wool, 7c. The raising of pigs is carried on on most farms as part of the system of mixed farming. The ruling prices during the year have been: For pigs on foot, from 5 to 6 cents per pound; dressed, from 8 to 9 cents. Poultry-raising is not prosecuted with any great degree of system, or on a large scale; eggs vary throughout the year from 20 to 60 cents per dozen, and there is always a sale for them; chickens, from $3 to $6 per dozen.

Farm lands fairly well drained, as a rule. Usual price for ditching: Ditch 2 feet deep, filled in with cedar slabs, from 40 to 50 cents per rod. Trees are Douglas fir, balsam, hemlock, red cedar, yellow cedar, white pine, yew, arbutus, crab, wild cherry, alder, maple, dogwood, willow (several varieties), oak and cottonwood; all the trees are in abundance except yellow cedar, white pine and yew. There is no Government land for pre-emption in any easily accessible part of the district. Most of the railway land available for agricultural purposes has also been disposed of. Such railway land as remains unsold, in outlying parts of the district, may be bought for from $3 to $5 per acre; improved farms, usually including a considerable amount of bush land, about $50 per acre.

Labour — Whites, $1.50 per day (not easily procurable in busy season); Chinese, $10 to $20 per month; Japanese, $8 to $15 per month; Indians, $1 to $1.50 per day. Throughout the summer months white labour is scarce, and Mongolians often expensive. The Indians go to the canneries.

Grasses and clover yield about 2 to 3 tons per acre; price in 1900, about $15 per ton. Raspberries are most largely grown; yield, 4,000 to 6,000 pounds per acre. Strawberries, gooseberries, currants, etc., grown on a small scale; price, about 5 cents per pound.

Labour — Whites, very few wanted for farm work; Chinese procurable, $1 per day, without board; Japanese, procurable, $10 to $15 per month, with board; Indians, procurable, men $2 per day, women $1 per day, without board.

Mr. Charles Bayly, Cowichan Lake: Farmers on north side of the lake are going in for general farming. Cattle, sheep, roots, cereals and fruit all do well. There is a fairly good road through the settlement. Settlers are increasing, and manage to make ends meet. There is plenty of room for a good settlement on the south side of the lake.

NORTH AND SOUTH NANAIMO,

In which is included Oyster, Cedar, Bright, Cranberry, Nanaimo, Douglas, Mountain, Wellington, Nanoose and Cameron Districts, and the Islands of Gabriola, Lasqueti and Texada, is the chief coal-producing section of the province.

Mr. John Stewart, Stark's Crossing, Nanaimo: The Electoral District of North and South Nanaimo extends from Chemainus on the south to Qualicum on the north, a distance of 60 miles. The district, except what has been cleared, is all bush land, with mountainous, rocky ridges around Oyster Bay, Extension, Wellington, Nanaimo, Nanoose Bay and Englishman's River. The Esquimalt & Nanaimo Railway, which extends from the City of Victoria, at the south end of Vancouver Island, to Wellington, a distance of 78 miles, has 28 miles of track in the district. The town of Ladysmith, which is little more than three years old, is situated five miles from the south boundary of the district, on Oyster Harbour. Ladysmith is the shipping point for the Extension and South Wellington coal mines. The Extension coal mines are situated 12 miles to the north-northwest of Ladysmith, and South Wellington 9 miles to the north. Along the water front from the south boundary, between the railway and salt water, there is partially cleared land as far as Haslam Creek, and the soil is good clay loam. From Brenton Crossing, three miles to the north of Ladysmith, following the waggon road to Nanaimo, there are a number of well-cleared farms. In Cedar District, which extends from near Oyster Bay to Nanaimo River bridge, the soil is all good, and would give returns if it were further improved by tile draining and good cultivation. Dairying is carried on on a small scale, but grain, potatoes and hay are the principal products of Cedar District. Nanaimo is the principal market for this district. The roads are good. To the west and south of Nanaimo are situated the five-acre lots of the New Vancouver Coal Company, which have been mostly taken up by miners. To the west of Nanaimo, about 1½ miles, the New Vancouver Coal Company's farm is situated. This farm, of fully 500 acres, has been cleared up within the last 10 years out of the bush, some of it costing fully $200 an acre to clear. It is all drained with tile. It grows the supplies of hay, oats and roots for the company's mules and horses. Nanaimo is a city of 6,500 inhabitants, and is a good market for all farm produce. To the south of Wellington, in the Millstream Valley, the large farm belonging to R. Dunsmuir & Sons, with an area of several hundred acres of excellent land, is situated. The company raises hay on this farm for the use of the mules and horses in their employ.

There are many small farms, well cleared and with good soil, between Nanaimo and Nanoose Bay. From the point where the Comox road comes into view of Nanoose Bay and Parksville, the soil is inclined to be sandy and gravelly. Following the Comox road from Parksville, by French Creek, to Qualicum, the best farming land in the whole district is found at Qualicum. Turning off the Comox road three miles to the south of Englishman's River, near Beaver Creek wharf, the Alberni road runs through a bush country mostly. There is excellent shooting and fishing around Parksville, Nanoose Bay and Qualicum. There are three islands in the Gulf of Georgia which belong to the district, viz., Gabriola, Lasqueti and Texada. Gabriola, especially the south end, has excellent land; when cleared, it will yield large returns. Lasqueti Island is essentially adapted for sheep-raising, but the methods followed are not productive of the best results. Texada, the farthest north, in the Gulf of Georgia, is a mining centre. Copper and iron are abundant, with gold and silver in less paying quantities. These islands, with the exception of Lasqueti, have steamboat communication three or four times a week.

Timothy largely grown; selling for from $12 to $15 a ton. Pears only grown on a very small scale; prices, 75c. to $1 per box. Plums and prunes, 3c. and 4c. a pound. Cherries sold readily at 8c. to 10c. a pound. Strawberries yield 2 to 4 tons to the acre; price, 7½ to 10 cents per pound. Raspberries, about 2 tons to the acre; 4½ to 8½ cents a pound. Gooseberries yield 2 to 3 tons to the acre, on three-year-old bushes; prices, 5 to 8½ cents a pound.

Some of the Islands in the Gulf of Georgia are well adapted to sheep-raising — Lasqueti Island especially, and Gabriola. In two or three places in the district poultry-breeding has been carried on with system. R. J. Craig, Parksville, has made a profit of $2 a head. Mr. Smith, five-acre lots, made a daily profit of from $1.50 to $2 from 200 hens, all raised by the incubator in 1900, since the month of October. Eggs never sold for less than 25 cents a dozen; during November and December 65 cents was the ruling price. Bee-keeping is being carried on more largely every year, especially in the neighbourhood of the New Vancouver Coal Company's farm. One man made $250 out of $32 colonies; honey fetched 25 cents a pound this year.

Esquimalt & Nanaimo Railway land is to be had in this district. The price of railway land is $5 an acre.

Labour — Whites, very scarce, $20 to $35 a month, with board; Chinese, $8 to $15 a month, with board; Japanese, $8 to $22, without board. Chinese and Japanese labourers can usually be got, except during the fishing season.

COMOX.

Extending from the northern boundary of North Nanaimo to the northern boundary of Comox District, a distance of some 65 miles, and including the islands of Hornby and Denman and the districts of Castle, Nelson and Comox, is for the most part heavily wooded and sparsely populated, especially the two first named districts. Comox itself is one of the most beautiful and promising districts in the province. In it are situated the Union coal mines, where a fine article of coal is produced, the most of which is exported to California. These mines afford an excellent market for all the produce of the neighbouring agricultural sections. In the vicinity of the bay and extending back some distance, the country is fairly open, with a good many oaks scattered about. Further back and extending to Campbell River, a distance of some 30 miles, there is a large extent of level country, heavily timbered for the most part with fir, cedar, hemlock, spruce and maple, with some extensive swamps, which are capable of being easily drained, the land throughout being of excellent quality.

This is considered one of the best dairying districts in the province. It is well watered throughout, and the land produces fine crops of clover, corn and other fodders suitable for milch cattle. A considerable quantity of butter is manufactured, and a co-operative creamery materially adds to the output of dairy products. The means of communication are by waggon road and by steamer to Nanaimo. The projected extension of the Esquimalt & Nanaimo Railroad would, if constructed, pass through the entire district.

The timber consists principally of Douglas fir, cedar (a very fine quality), maple, alder and oak. This is the most northerly limit of the oak, the southern limit being Sooke, and none being found on the Mainland.

The soil is fertile, but draining is most essential. In the swamps it is mostly black muck, with a bluish clay subsoil, and in other parts varying from a black or sandy loam in the bottoms to a red gravelly loam on the higher parts.

There are a number of good swamps in the district that can be cleared at little cost; they run in size from 20 to 100 acres. The soil is good, being composed largely of decomposed vegetation, and generally covered with a broad-leafed grass, which keeps green all winter and grows high. The cattle are very fond of it, and it keeps them in good condition. These swamps are easily ditched, and the timber, which is principally crab-apple and willow, is light.

Denman and Hornby are about 42 miles from Nanaimo, and lie close to Vancouver Island shore, the upper end of Denman being opposite the Union Mines, the latter place affording good market for produce.

J. A. Halliday, Comox: There are three classes of soil — fir, alder and swamps. The soil is generally good, but the fir land is expensive to reclaim. The timber is good, but of no commercial value, except along the streams. It may cost from $30 to $200 an acre to prepare it for crop. Alder is easily cleared; stumps soon decay; soil friable and yields a good crop at the first; cost of clearing, from $20 to $30 an acre. The swamps are old beaver dams, where an outlet can be gotten at moderate expense; they are easily reclaimed, and yield great crops of grass from the first; as they get firmer, they raise good grain and root crops. They vary in size from a few acres to 200 and 300 acres.

Grain is produced entirely for feeding stock. Oats yield ½ ton to 1 ton on the better farms; price, 1¼ to 1⅜ cents per pound. Ensilage corn will produce 70 tons to the acre; had samples at the Agricultural Show 14 feet high, 4 to 6 ears on each stem. Excellent apples are grown. Other fruits all succeed well and are grown in small quantities.

Dairying is the chief industry of Comox. One farmer alone sold in 1900 17,000 pounds, from 22 to 33 cents per pound; 25 cents ruled. Cows are worth $50 to $70 each; beef sells freely at 7½ to 10 cents, dressed, by the carcass. Perhaps 1,000 sheep in the valley; lambs bring $5 to $6; ewes usually breed twins. The hog industry is carried on by all the dairymen; say 800 are sold young, at 8 to 9 cents, live weight. Quite a number devote their whole time to poultry, and do well; eggs vary from 25 to 60 cents per dozen.

Labour — Whites, $25 per month, yearly engagements; Chinese, 50 cents to $1 per day, as occasion requires; some pay $15 per month; Japanese, $15 to $18 per month.

Mr. George Heatherbell, Hornby Island: Oats are the main crop; price, 1½ cents. Barley does well indeed. Peas are the largest crop grown, next to oats; price, 2 cents per pound. Potatoes do well nearly always. Apples are extensively raised; there would be about 1,500 bearing trees and 400 young ones; this island will compare favourably with any place in the province for raising fruit; price, $1 a box. Pears do well; price, $1.25 a box. Plums and prunes do fine here; price, about 50 cents for a box of 20 pounds.

Cattle-raising is a successful industry on this island; beef has been from 7c. to 9c. this season. As compared with cattle, sheep are more profitable, where land is suitable; everyone has more or less sheep; prices for mutton, from 4½c. to 6c. per pound, live weight, and about $6 each for breeding ewes; wool is of no value, viz., 6c. Good heavy horses bring a good price. Swine-raising is not much prosecuted; prices have been 6c. to 8c. on foot. Properly cared for, poultry is the most remunerative thing on the farm; price for eggs has been from 20c. to 50c. per dozen at time of writing (November 8, 1900). Improved farms for sale at from $10 an acre up.

Labour — Whites, $1 per day and board; Japanese, $10 to $15 per month. White labour is not always plentiful.

NORTHERN PART OF VANCOUVER ISLAND, AND ADJACENT ISLANDS,

Including Alert Bay, Fort Rupert, Cape Scott and Quatsino on the main island, being the only spots of any consequence where there are any white settlers, and the islands of Valdez, Thurlow, Read, Cortez, Hernando, Savory, Redonda, Hardwicke, Camp and Wyatt. There are many more islands which it is not necessary to mention specifically. This portion of the province is very sparsely settled, and the means of communication is confined to steamers. A railway, now projected, connecting the two extremes of Vancouver Island, would no doubt be a great factor in settling up this portion.

Alert Bay, about 70 miles to the northwest of Valdez Island, is on the northeast coast of Vancouver. Some settlers have taken up land on the islands in the vicinity, and in the valleys of streams. The country is generally wooded and well watered, and the soil is good. On Haddington Island a fine quality of stone is found, of which the new Parliament Buildings at Victoria are constructed. Coal also exists at Port McNeil, and these, together with the salmon canning and the fishing industry, will no doubt form important factors in the development of this part of the country.

Quatsino and Cape Scott include all the country in the northernmost part of Vancouver Island. A colony of Danish and Norwegian settlers have recently been established there, and it is hoped that with the assistance of other settlers the section will become a place of importance. The soil is described as productive, well watered, timbered with fir, cedar and hemlock. The climate is well suited to the production of all the usual cereals, vegetables and fruits. Although the fisheries are, so far, wholly undeveloped, enough is known regarding them to justify the belief that they are of immense value, and will form a valuable adjunct to the resources of that section, and contribute largely to the means of livelihood.

Mr. Henry Varney, Quatsino: This is a small settlement at present, there being about 15 or 16 people occupying land here; but we have a population of about 60 souls, including children, and, as you are doubtless aware, composed chiefly of Scandinavians.

There is an immense area of land stretching from Marble Creek Valley to Alert Bay, on the east coast of the island, which does not appear to require the aid of manure, for potatoes have been grown to a prodigious size in this valley, without the use of any manure whatever. I have seen some weighing 2¾ pounds each. The land in question is at present not bought up, and is unoccupied, and would furnish farms for several hundred people. It is drained by Marble Creek, which is a large river, with a winding course of 40 or 50 miles in a northwesterly direction, and draining several large lakes. The land, I believe, will be settled upon in the near future.

Last winter the climbing roses on the house walls remained all winter luxuriant in foliage.

Mr. Nicholas Thompson, Cortez Island: There are about 16 settlers living on their places on this island at present. Each rancher has about 10 acres cleared; there may be one or two who have a little more than that, but 10 is about the average. The land is heavy clearing. Our nearest market is Vancouver, a distance of 100 miles. The steamer calls twice a week. We have very poor roads. The climate up here is good, and there are plenty of deer, grouse and fish to be had for the hunting of them. I may say the principal crops are potatoes and roots, which do well. The great drawback here is the land is so rocky — more rock than good land. The timber on the island is principally fir and cedar.

Mr. S. A. Spencer, Alert Bay: The country is generally mountainous and unfit for agriculture. In a few isolated places, small patches of land, when cleared, might be productive. The country is more likely to be productive of mineral. No roads; all communication is by water. There is a public school for white children at Alert Bay. Game, fairly plentiful, consists of deer, elk, grouse and bear. There are salmon and trout in nearly all the rivers and streams. White population, about 60.

CAPE SCOTT.

Mr. C. B. Christiansen, Secretary of the Cape Scott Colony, has supplied the following description of the Cape Scott District: This District is situated at the north end of Vancouver Island. The land rises gradually from the coast to 100 feet over sea level, as far as the lowlands extend; while the hills reach from 200 to 400 feet in height. Several streams, of which the largest is the San Josef River, run in a northerly and westerly direction. The largest lake is one mile north of San Josef River. The outlet of this lake would furnish excellent water power. The lake is two miles long and one and a half miles wide.

The district is well timbered. The lowlands are only thinly wooded and easily cleared. Along the rivers are hemlock, spruce, red and yellow cedar. San Josef River would be a very good location for a pulp mill.

The soil is very diversified. Most of the hills and part of the lowlands is made up of what is generally known as sallal soil. Along the rivers is excellent bottom land, covered with alder and raspberry brush. About 100 acres could be reclaimed from the action of the tides by a dyke, besides the grass lands already reclaimed by a dyke at the head of Goose Hardy.

The climate is very healthful. Eighty degrees is the highest temperature in summer. Frosts occur seldom before December or after April. The rainfall is about 100 inches. All vegetables and small fruits grow well. Barley and oats will ripen. Clover and grasses grown luxuriantly.

The land seems excellently adapted for cattle-raising and dairying. It is the purpose of the settlers to turn their activity in that direction chiefly. Other resources are the deep-water fisheries, halibut, and the salmon fisheries in the several streams.

There are about thirty ranches occupied at Cape Scott, well-built houses and well-cultivated gardens surrounding them.

N. T. Neilsen, Cape Scott: Cape Scott forms the north end of Vancouver Island. Three large rivers and creeks are running through the district, along which there is more or less alluvial soil, which will make splendid homes to many industrious settlers. The higher lands consist principally of sallal soil, and are about from 100 to 200 feet above the level of the sea. There are a good many hills from 300 to about 2,000 feet above sea level. Some land is only very lightly timbered. There is a public school, open all the year around. Sportsmen will find an abundance of game and fish, trout, salmon, cod, flounders and halibut, in the water; swans, geese and ducks. Grouse, deer, elk and larger game, such as wolves and bears, may also be found. The climate is very healthful; yearly rainfall, about 100 inches; highest and lowest temperature, 84 degrees and 15 degrees above zero. Population is about 70 people, but a large immigration to this district is expected.

There are about 1,000 acres which might be reclaimed by dyking. It is principally peatty, but near the rivers there is some alluvial deposit. There is not much valuable timber here, except along the larger rivers and creeks. The following kinds of trees grow here: Hemlock, red and yellow cedar, balsam, fir, alder, bull pine, yew, and some fine spruce on river bottom. There are thousands of acres of Government lands open for pre-emption in this district. The soil consists partly of what is commonly known as sallal soil, and partly of alluvial soils along the rivers and larger creeks. There is still some very good river bottom to be had.

WEST COAST OF VANCOUVER ISLAND.

Including Alberni, Clayoquot, Ucluelet and Port Renfrew.

F. H. Avery and Stanley R. S. Bayne, Alberni: The Alberni Valley is about 20 miles long and 4 miles wide, and is divided into three districts, viz., Sproat Lake to the west, Beaver Creek to the north, and Cherry Creek to the east. Of these, Beaver Creek has the most settlers. In this direction the valley extends for 12 or 14 miles, and there is much unoccupied land, which, with co-operative drainage, ought to be very valuable in time to come. In the other districts, too, there is good land lying vacant. The soil is for the most part a clayey loam, and very productive. Market mostly local. Roads good; communication twice weekly with Nanaimo by stage, and three times monthly by steamer with Victoria and the northern part of the Island. Three schools. Game is plentiful, as also trout and salmon in season. Population, about 300. It is well watered, having several large and small lakes, besides rivers and creeks.

Oats are produced for feed principally; average yield, 30 bushels per acre; prices, 1c. to 1¾c. per pound. Potatoes yield about five tons per acre; prices, $1 to $1.25 per 100 pounds. Timothy, orchard, red clover and alsike yield from 1½ to 2 tons per acre; price, $10 to $15 per ton. Apples do well; prices range from 1c. to 3c. per pound. Pears yield good; prices, 1c. to 3c. per pound. Plums and prunes yield heavily. Other fruits produce well.

Dairying is carried on by quite a number on a small scale, and is fairly remunerative. Cattle-raising is a successful industry; beef is worth from 7 to 9 cents per pound, dressed; milch cows, according to breed, $30 to $60. This district is too wet on the low lands for sheep; they, however, do well on the high lands and ridges; lambs bring about $4.50, and sheep from $3.50 to $6; wool is worthless. Not many pigs in this district; home market easily supplied; price, from 8 to 10 cents per pound, dressed. Some few have gone into poultry of late; prices rule from 20 to 40 cents per dozen for eggs. Very few bees kept so far, but increasing gradually; Italian bees are the most suitable; price of honey, 25 cents per pound; yield, 30 to 40 pounds per hive.

A red clay loam chiefly, with ridges of glacial clay on the mountains; the hollows, black clay loam, with white, yellow and blue clay subsoil; also beaver meadows. Cost of clearing land here, from $25 to $50 per acre — that is, leaving the stumps in the ground. The timber in this section is Douglas fir, spruce, hemlock, maple, dogwood, bearwood, crabapple, balsam, arbutus (very scarce), white pine, cottonwood, alder, cedar, yellow cedar (top of mountain), yew. Douglas fir is

HOME FARM, B. X. RANCH, VERNON.

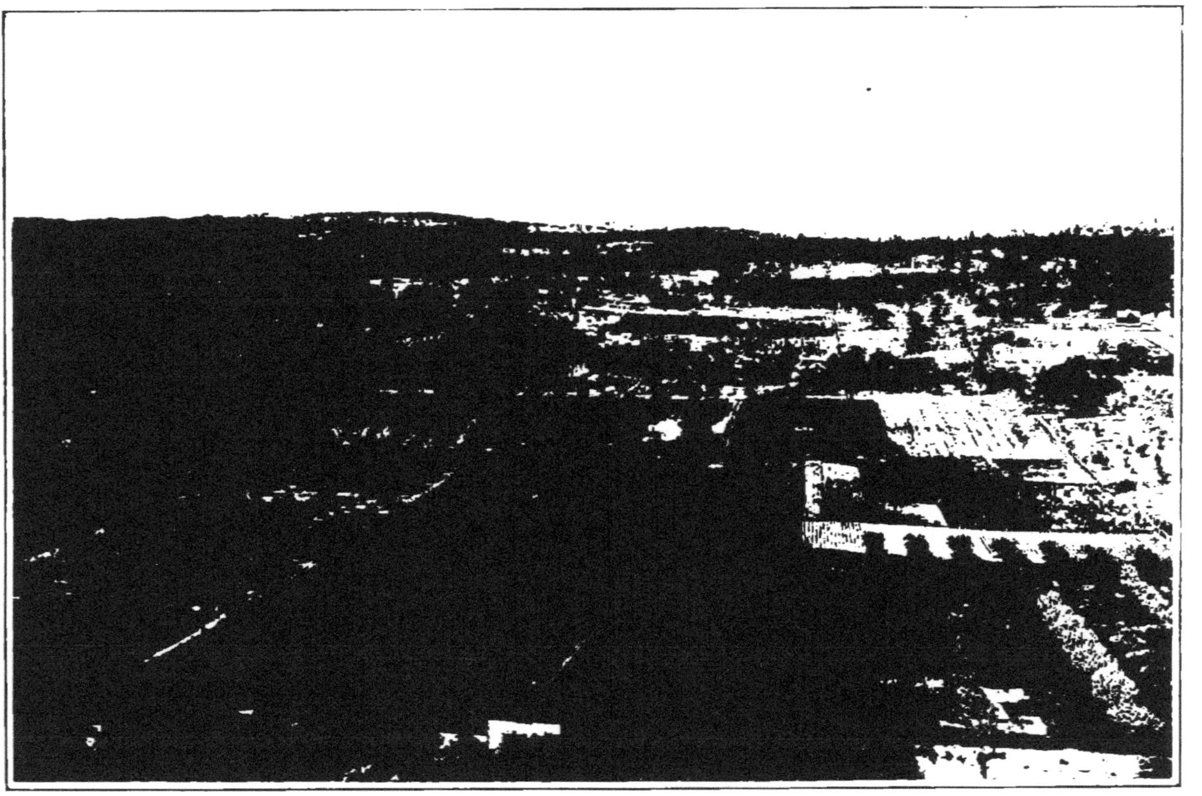

FARMING SCENE NEAR VICTORIA, B. C.

the chief timber to the mountain top; cedar, in patches, and generally swamp lands; spruce, in patches and low, gravelly lands; alder, chiefly in the bottoms, on clay; dogwood, scattered on high lands; and the same with maple. Government land for pre-emption on Alberni Canal, Taylor Arm and Road, and Sproat's and Great Central Lakes. Lots of railway land waiting to be settled on, good, bad and indifferent. The valley is not a quarter taken up. The land varies from cedar swamps and alder bottoms to ridge land. The quantity, location and prices can be seen on the E. & N. Railway maps of Alberni District; price, $3 per acre, with 6 per cent. interest on deferred payments. About 30,000 acres of vacant land located between Alberni and Comox. From $500 to $6,000 for improved farms.

Labour — Whites, $2.50 per day; Chinese, few, $1.50 per day. This year white labour has been scarce, owing to new roads being built.

Mr. John Chesterman, Clayoquot: Clayoquot is situated on the west coast of Vancouver Island, about 140 miles from Victoria. Its natural resources consist of mining, fishing and timber. Although a large quantity of mineral is found in this district, the claims are not enough developed to be shipping ore.

Fishing is carried on to some extent by the C. F. & T. Co., who own the cannery situated at the mouth of Kennedy River, which puts up about 7,000 cases annually. There is a large amount of halibut in the adjacent waters which have not yet been utilised.

The number of people engaged in agriculture in this district is about 100. As it is a recently settled district, there are only about 200 acres under cultivation and in meadow. Grasses and clovers do well. Small fruits are successful.

This district is naturally adapted for dairying purposes. Cattle raising is a success in this district.

There are thousands of acres of tide lands that could be reclaimed by dyking. The subsoil is clay. What dyking has been done demonstrates the fact that it can be carried on to a success. The principal timbers in this district are cedar, spruce, balsam and hemlock, with some fir, crab-apple, alder, yew, white pine, yellow cedar and soft maple. There is plenty of surveyed agricultural land open for pre-emption in this district.

From Port Renfrew Mr. C. Blackstaff reports: This district is commonly known as San Juan Valley. We have very rich alluvial soil, on which can be raised large quantities of hay. Then we have land suitable for fruit-growing. The valley is very healthy. There is plenty of game and fish. Our market is Victoria, and we have a weekly steamer. The valley and mountains are densely wooded, and very large quantities can easily be got to the harbour. We have spruce, Douglas fir, balsam fir, hemlock, soft maple, vine maple, red and yellow cedar, and yew.

THE ISLANDS.

In which are included Salt Spring, Galiano, Mayne, Pender, Saturna, Moresby, Sidney, Prevost and all the smaller islands lying between the southern end of Vancouver Island and the Mainland. The climate of these islands is equable in the extreme, and consequently well adapted for fruit culture, which industry is carried on to a considerable extent and with great success. On account also of their immunity from predatory animals, the raising of sheep is most successfully prosecuted.

Mr. Theo. Trage, Beaver Point, Salt Spring Island: There is no more land to be pre-empted. About one-fourth of the soil is real good land; the balance rocks. For markets we have Victoria and Nanaimo; we are connected four times per week with Victoria and twice with Nanaimo by steamer.

Cereals are not cultivated to any extent, oats excepted. Peas are also grown in fair quantities. The ruling price of potatoes is $18 per ton. Two tons per acre for hay; none grown for sale. Apples are grown; good yield; price about 2c. per pound. All the other large fruits do exceedingly well, but are not produced to any extent, there being more profit in apples. Strawberries are the only small fruit grown for the market; price, 7c. per pound.

Dairying only carried on by private dairies; pays well. Part of the district is suitable enough for sheep; good prices were paid for lambs, about $4 each; mutton has been 4½c. per pound; pays well enough. The poultry industry is systematically prosecuted, and is remunerative; price, $5 per dozen; eggs, from 20c. to 40c. per dozen.

Draining is carried on to a large extent. Timber trees are Douglas fir, cedar, balsam, hemlock, maple, alder, spruce, willow, poplar and dogwood.

Labour — Whites, $1.50 per day; Japanese, 50c. per day. Plenty of Japanese here, but white labour is scarce.

Mr. R. A. R. Purdy, Vesuvius : This district is suitable for sheep raising. It is carried on to a considerable extent, and is profitable. Ruling prices were $4.50 for early lambs, 6c. per pound for sheep, and 6c. per pound for wool.

It costs about $100 per acre to clear the high lands; the low lands can be cleared for less.

Mr. Washington Grimmer, Pender Island : North Pender Island is that portion lying north of Browning Harbour on the east side and Boat Harbour on the west side, which is the side that most of the shipping from the Mainland and east coast of Vancouver Island passes. The land is divided up into separate valleys, varying from 20 acres up to over 300 acres in extent. The soil is really good in most of the valleys, and comparatively easy to clear; but high up on the side-hills the timber is larger, the soil rather rocky, and on the summits almost solid rock, but timbered more or less, and some wild grasses and clover. Plenty of fish, deer, grouse, pheasants and Bob White quail. Mostly Old Country settlers, industrious and thrifty, with pretty, attractive homes. Population of North Pender, about 60. Markets, chiefly Victoria, but Nanaimo, Vancouver and New Westminster about equal distance away, this place being about the centre of the coast markets. Mixed farming is carried on successfully, but lamb-raising is remunerative and the chief branch of agriculture here.

Potatoes yield about six tons to the acre; quality good; ruling price, $20 per ton. Onions are produced in considerable quantities, and yield well; ruling price, 2 cents per pound. Grasses and clovers yield about 2 tons per acre; all fed on farms to the stock. Most of the leading varieties of apples do well; prices, 75c. to $1 per box in the fall. Winter pears of several varieties are grown; seem well suited to this island; ruling price, 75 cents to $1 per box. Plums and prunes do well; price, about 3 cents per pound.

Dairying is carried on in a limited way at present; rather profitable. Sheep very suitable, and industry carried on successfully wherever tried carefully; price for 1900, 4½ to 5 cents per pound for mutton; lambs, $4.50 to $3.50. The want of a woollen mill in British Columbia, which would make a price for wool, is the chief drawback to the industry. Swine-breeding is profitable, if carried on systematically; ruling price, 5½ to 7 cents per pound, live weight.

To clear the most easily cleared land here will cost about $50 per acre, and the heaviest over $100 per acre. The timber here is alder, maple, arbutus, willow, wild cherry, several varieties of pine and cedar, balsam, but no spruce, and hemlock scarce. Very little Government land open to pre-emption on this island. Improved farms can be bought from $15 per acre up to $50.

Labour—White labourers are few, $1.50 to $2 per day, without board; Japanese, $6 to $15 per month, and board. Too many Japs, and unsatisfactory as farm labourers anyhow.

GENERAL CONDITIONS.

IN the Year Book of 1897 there was a chapter on "General Conditions," which at that time was considered by those who understood the conditions of farming in this province to fairly and honestly reflect the agricultural situation as it then was. Conditions have very materially altered since then, and for the better. Much more land has been brought into cultivation, methods have greatly improved, prices have become better, and conditions generally stable and business-like. In a word, the speculative and real estate atmosphere which surrounded farm lands has largely disappeared, and farming has become a regular and legitimate industry, depending upon intelligent and systematic application of efforts to the soil and products for a dividend upon the investment of labour and capital expended. However, a good deal of the chapter in question is still pertinent and true, and it is reproduced, with necessary emendations and additions.

In a general way, the districts may be referred to as the Fraser Valley, Westminster District, in which there are about 350,000 acres of arable land, 150,000 acres being alluvial deposit; the southwestern portion of Vancouver Island, which is comparatively well settled and contains some excellent land; and the Okanagan District, in which there are numerous fertile valleys, comprising in all about 500,000 acres suitable for general agricultural purposes. In the latter, in addition to the areas referred to there are still larger areas of pastoral land, suitable and used for grazing only. The three foregoing districts have been referred to first because they are distinctly agricultural and are the localities in which the principal farming settlements are to be found. There are, however, extensive tracts of open country in the North and South Thompson River Valleys, in the Nicola Valleys, in the Similkameen, in Lillooet, Cariboo and East Kootenay, in which, though principally pastoral and requiring irrigation for crops, are to be found at intervals good farms, or, as they are usually designated, "ranches," and these detached areas constitute in the aggregate many thousands of acres, which either do produce or are capable of producing any crops within the possibilities of the temperate zone — cereals, fruits and vegetables.

OUTLYING AREAS.

And, added to these, the capabilities of which, with intelligent and intensive methods of farming, are very great, are still more extensive, though remoter, tracts to be found in the Columbia Valley, East Kootenay; in the Canoe River Valley, opening the way to the northern interior from Kootenay; in the Chilcotin country, including the Nechaco and Blackwater Valleys; in the Bulkley and Kispyox Valleys, in the Ootsa Lake and Peace River countries; on the northern end of Vancouver Island and on the islands and coast of the Mainland, which with increased facilities of communication and the demand created by the almost certain immense development about to take place and the consequent rapid augmentation of population, will provide homes for thousands of settlers. As yet these lands are mainly in the hands of the Government, and until communication is afforded and development takes place they are not recommended for settlement, because, without facilities for reaching a market, farming life in isolated communities presents many obvious obstacles to success.

IMPROVED FARMS.

Although suitable land in the already settled districts has been all taken up and is in the hands of private parties, farms partially improved, or in favourable localities, may be obtained from $10 to $50 an acre, according to situation and character of land, improvement, etc., and it may be remarked here that a small farm of from 40 to 100 acres in extent is sufficient in British Columbia for the average farmer. A good many farms in good localities may now be obtained, and the average price for 100 to 160 acres, with from 10 to 25 acres cleared, and buildings is from $15 to $50 an acre, on easy terms. However, it is difficult to give exact prices. Farms with excellent possibilities may be obtained for the latter figure. In most cases, however, a settler who has improved farming in view may count on having a good deal of extra fencing, clearing, under-draining and building to do after he has acquired any land, in order to obtain the best results. Many of the farms have young orchards, but here, too, improvements of varieties and further planting will be desirable. Plenty of good water and good timber are almost always available.

FARMING DESCRIBED.

It is difficult to give a fairly honest and average description of the conditions of agriculture in British Columbia. In the first place, farming was until recently in a somewhat primitive condition, and to understand why it was so, one must really know the history of the province, and have lived in it. Farming, like mining, suffered from lack of communication, and very little incentive to progress can exist without an easy market. In the majority of instances it was not farmers who took up and settled on the land, hence farming was not undertaken systematically; and, besides, the difficulties of clearing land are great, compared with most other places. Numbers of persons who came to the Coast without a very definite purpose in view — to take chances in mining, speculation or anything else that might happen to turn up — in the absence of any other occupation to employ their energies, took up land and, figuratively speaking, sat down on it, waiting for prospective development to make it valuable. It is easy to imagine how, under such circumstances, a general condition of farming on tentative principles came about. A few applied themselves intelligently and industriously to the task, and demonstrated locally the wider possibilities; but the rule was otherwise. On the better lands in favourable localities, by the growing of hay, fruits, etc., many were enabled, owing to local demand, to live comfortably and even grow prosperous without too great exertion.

CHANGED CONDITIONS.

With the coming of the railways, however, and the competition of outside produce conditions were altered, more especially as the first boom consequent upon the railway construction was followed by a long period of depression, which, to use a favourite Western expression, made farming on former lines a most "difficult proposition." As a result many became dissatisfied, especially as mining offered — as it does still — peculiar temptations, and either sold their farms, where that was possible, to others, or encumbered their estates with liabilities. This period was a very trying one for the agricultural industry of the province, and for many individual farmers. Fortunately, owing to a variety of causes — the principal, of course, to the return of prosperous times in Canada and the United States — agriculture in British Columbia has not only regained what was lost during the hard times, but has made very decided advances; so much so that it may be said that conditions have entirely changed for the better.

Farming is finding its level in British Columbia, as elsewhere, as a business which requires the same careful attention and intelligent application as other businesses. As a further and necessary explanation, it may be added that throughout the interior the settlers, as a rule, engaged in cattle-raising as the easiest and readiest means of utilizing their land. There has always existed a good market in the Coast cities for beef, and cattle can be driven long distances to a market or point for shipment. The life, too, of a cattle rancher is not without its attractions, and is rarely arduous.

LARGE HOLDINGS.

It being necessary under such circumstances to have plenty of pasturage, farms were, as a consequence, taken up on a large scale, and usually with a view to utilising the ranges on the side-hills, covered with bunch-grass. The favourite location was a river bottom or valley, which, once secured, commanded the hillsides and commons, and even these, if not leased or purchased, were often deliberately fenced in and occupied. In this way the pastoral and agricultural lands have been secured in large allotments and the settlers are far apart, unfortunately surrounding the question of further settlement with peculiar difficulties. In the Okanagan Valleys, however, many of the landholders are cutting up their holdings, seeing the inutility under changed conditions of endeavouring to retain unproductive property and the wisdom of parting with portions to others who will improve them and add value to what remains in their own hands. There is generally a growing inclination in a similar direction among land holders in British Columbia, but a great deal still requires to be done before the possibilities of settlement are achieved. There are several districts in the province in which this is particularly true. There is, for instance, in Enderby, Armstrong and Mara, in the Okanagan District, a large number of farms suitable for dairying, fruit on high ridges, and mixed farming generally, offering for sale. These represent the best values obtainable in the province; and the cost of clearing, which averages about $25 or $30 an acre, is comparatively light. At Armstrong a creamery has been established and is in successful operation.

CLIMATIC ZONES.

Climate is, of course, a factor which always affects the agricultural conditions of any country — is, in fact, in itself one of the main factors. Elsewhere this subject has been dealt with fully. As will have been seen, there are several distinct climatic zones in the province, and the treatment of agriculture must be divided on corresponding lines. On the coast, where the direct effect of the ocean is felt, there are : A decidedly humid atmosphere, a good deal of rain during the winter months, no extremes of heat and cold, a long growing season, cool nights, and profuse vegetation. It is scarcely necessary to explain the general effect of such conditions — tree growth is generally greatly stimulated; roots and vegetables flourish; the softer grains, such as oats and barley, yield largely and grow to great perfection; grasses are abundant; fruits, such as pears, cherries and plums and all small fruits, are practically indigenous to the soil, and yield enormously; flowers, especially roses and all the good old-fashioned varieties, are profuse bloomers; and shrubbery is dense; it is a country of great growth, and, where fertile soil deposits exist, no better results can be obtained anywhere. Unfortunately, the beneficial effect of the climate in contributing such favourable conditions is accompanied by corresponding disadvantages in the creation of dense forests and thick and heavy undergrowth, in encouraging the growth of weeds, and in the propagation of insect pests and plant diseases once they have found a foothold. Under average conditions, to clear a farm for cultivation requires much more labour than it does to keep it in a clean condition. Eternal vigilance is the price of immunity from weeds, second growth and insect pests. On the other hand, intensive farming gives wonderful results.

INSECT PESTS AND PLANT DISEASES.

Adverting to insect pests and plant diseases, which have been of recent importation, coming with nursery and fruit shipments, a quotation is made from Mr. Palmer's report to the Provincial Board of Horticulture, 1901, which has done much towards their eradication and prevention :

The dread of the total destruction of the industry on account of insect pests, which at one time prevailed, has been largely removed since the life history and habits of the common orchard pests have become more generally known, and the methods and means for checking or destroying them common knowledge. It is true, constant watchfulness and care will always be necessary in this connection, however, and no measures are too drastic which aim to prevent the introduction of the most dreaded pests of other fruit-growing countries, viz., the codlin moth (Carpocapsa pomonella) and the San Jose scale (Aspidiotus perniciosus). At present this province occupies an enviable position in its freedom from these foes of the fruit-grower.

THE COAST CONSIDERED.

Owing to the character of the Coast climate already referred to, there are other crops, which do not do so well, and as a general rule do not pay to raise. These are: Wheat, which, though yielding heavily and producing a fine-looking kernel, is too soft for milling purposes, and in limited quantities is mainly valuable for feeding chickens; fruit and vegetables requiring plenty of heat and sunshine to mature them — grapes, peaches, nectarines, almonds, tomatoes, watermelons, and the like. These all do well, but except in favoured localities are not generally well suited, and may not mature properly. Apples which are perhaps indigenous to more rigorous climates do fairly well, and, generally speaking, succeed on the Coast; but their success is subject to exceptions which materially modify the experience of growers in Ontario. In colour and size apples of all varieties excel in British Columbia. The number of varieties, however, that reach the highest point of development is limited. In fact, the apples that have been developed on the eastern side of America, as distinctively American, do not as a rule succeed best on this Coast. Experience has shown that Old Country and Continental varieties, some of them hundreds of years old, are better adapted to this climate. Most of these where tried are succeeding admirably; and this fact is in accordance with well established laws of development. It may be stated as axiomatic that, while the general principles underlying the science of horticulture obtain, the experience of fruit-growers in Ontario in matters of detail does not apply in British Columbia, and many of their methods and theories in practice demand revision. It may also be added that in this province trees bear quickly and wood rapidly, and in this exists the greatest drawback. Young orchards, if not carefully watched, over-fruit and exhaust themselves before maturity is reached.

CONDITIONS IN THE INTERIOR.

In the interior of the province, which is characterised as the Dry Belt, conditions are somewhat reversed. The Pacific Ocean still exercises its beneficent influences, but the atmosphere is stripped of its excessive moisture by the intervening mountains. In summer there is greater heat and more sunshine, and in winter a greater degree of cold, with much drier and clearer atmosphere. Given good soil and facilities for irrigation where necessary, and the conditions for production are perfect, and, within the capabilities of the temperate zone, there are no limits to what may be grown. In this zone are found all that the Coast produces, and those other crops referred to for which the environments seaward are not favourable. It must be understood, however, that local modifications are important factors, and conditions are not by any means uiform. Irrigation, for instance, is not everywhere required; local winds in exposed localities have sometimes a disastrous effect; and in winter in some places the sudden barometrical dips render orcharding precarious. Exceptions to any general statement of conditions are numerous, and an adequate knowledge of individual localities is only obtained by experience. . Stating what may be regarded as applicable in the average, wheat ripens and mills well. In many places peaches, grapes, watermelons and tomatoes mature fully and are prolific in yield and excellent in quality. The most favoured localities for these fruits are in Southern Okanagan, Similkameen, and in some portions of the Thompson and Upper Fraser valleys. Apples, if we except such localities as have been referred to, do remarkably well with careful treatment. It would be difficult to find more beautiful or better specimens in any country than those exhibited at fall fairs from the interior districts. All other fruits, subject to similar exceptions, do equally well in the interior.

FRUIT - GROWING.

Many orchards have been planted out and are bearing, some of them quite old; but the care — or, rather, lack of care — exercised in their cultivation, and the promiscuous character of the fruit trees, purchased without knowledge of local requirements from unscrupulous agents of foreign nursery stock, afford but little indication of what would have been possible under ordinary skilful management. Strangers to this province, who have for a long time heard of its fruit-growing capabilities, would undoubtedly be surprised that more has not been accomplished under conditions so favourable; but the truth is that the industry began wrong, and has practically had to be recreated in order to obtain desired results. The selection of proper varieties in due proportion, the preparation of the soil, the husbanding of the trees afterwards, the picking and — what is equally important — the marketing of the fruit, are all features of the industry requiring attention, and each is essential to ultimate success. Speaking of the fruit-growing industry in British Columbia, Mr. Palmer in the report referred to states as follows :

Reviewing the condition of the fruit-growing interests of the province, it may be stated that the commercial stage of fruit growing and marketing has now fairly been attained, and from this time forward development should progress on safe lines, in harmony with the known capabilities of the different districts concerned.

SPECIAL PRODUCTS.

Hop and flax growing are referred to elsewhere. Tobacco does well. It has been tried in the Okanagan district with good success, and an official report on the quality of the leaf grown speaks highly of it. For a time a cigar factory, manufacturing native leaf, was carried on successfully at Kelowna, but commercial and economic conditions have not been as favourable to success as was anticipated. A sugar beet, from experiments made, would undoubtedly succeed. The yield is exceptionally large, and specimens tested for saccharine qualities were favourably reported upon. This industry, however, is not recommended for consideration, as economic conditions so far are unfavourable to success. Apiculture has only been tried in a limited way, but with sufficient success to demonstrate that as the cultivated area extends, bee-keeping is well within the limits of practical and profitable husbandry.

SOILS AND SUB-SOILS.

There is a diversity of soils in the province, as there is of climate, and any, even a limited area of land, is apt to exhibit many variations. This is, indeed, so true that it is difficult to describe with any degree of accuracy what are predominant soils and what are not; sub-soils vary quite as much as surface soils. This diversity is, of course, due to the action of water and glaciers and a series of physical disturbances, the conspicuous evidences of the force of which we see in the entire Cordilleran region, and the explanation is found in the study of its geology. The most prevalent and what may be regarded as the characteristic soil of the coast is a brownish sandy and gravelly loam with gravelly sub-soil. This frequently gives place to clay-loam, clay, coarse gravel and granitic wash. The sub-soils seem to have no definite relation to the top-soil, ranging from sand and gravel to heavy clay, and not infrequently an agglomerate, often very hard. The brown soil is largely characteristic of heavily-timbered and uplands. The river bottoms and valleys are usually made up of alluvial deposits, known as "black muck," very fertile when drained. The land skirting the foothills and mountains is principally granitic wash. Of the forest land the best is what is known as "alder bottom," upon which alder, maple, willow and some cedar grow. The heavily forested land is not the richest soil, as in the case of Eastern provinces, where heavy timber is indicative of fertility. The conifers return little in the way of leaf mould to the soil, and the thin layer of vegetable deposit is usually burned off in clearing. Such land is deficient in humus, but when brought into cultivation and fertilised grows surprisingly good crops of vegetables, fruit and clover. The atmosphere, which is a humid one, contributes greatly to plant growth and grasses, and, especially leguminous plants, which assimilate nitrogen by bacterial processes from the air, do remarkably well. Clovers, which grow luxuriantly, play a most important economic part in such land. Experiments have shown that hill and mountain sides are capable of cultivation to an extent that will ultimately greatly increase the area of arable lands.

IRRIGATION.

As previously pointed out, irrigation in the interior is one of the problems to be dealt with. In many places the facilities are excellent, and in many individual instances have been successful, though, particularly for fruit, care is necessary as to the time for irrigation and the quantity of water to be brought on the land. For considerable areas, however, there are not only engineering but other difficulties in the way of inaugurating a comprehensive scheme. In some cases the question of water rights is involved; in others, the height of the land above the water level or distance from a source of supply places the accomplishment out of reach of individual enterprise, while the large allotments of lands and the distance between settlers render co-operative efforts unavailing even if the inclination existed, which in too many cases is absent. The remedy seems to be in the subdivision of lands into smaller holdings, and the union of effort on the basis of the betterment system. This condition of affairs is, in fact, being remedied. In the Okanagan and Kamloops districts large companies are purchasing large holdings of land and dividing them up for settlement. In such demand indeed is this land when subdivided that settlers from the Northwest are paying as high as $100 an acre, the company providing facilities of irrigation. Large ranches under present conditions are necessary for stock-raising, but with small holdings, cultivated and irrigated, so as to render winter feeding with ensilage or stored hay practicable, and, if necessary, ranging in common, an increased beef supply and generally better results would follow. More settlers with fewer stock each would be infinitely better for the province than few settlers and large bands of cattle, as at present.

As pointed out elsewhere, conditions are altering in this respect, and very much for the better. One of the factors in the improvement of conditions is the growing of alfalfa, now becoming more or less general where formerly wild meadow land was relied upon for hay which was used only to a very small extent. Now alfalfa, of which three crops are cut, producing from five to ten tons to the acre per season, is being largely grown upon lands that can be irrigated. The effect of this upon the economic conditions in the interior is very great, and in time will completely alter the old state of affairs.

COLD STORAGE.

Closely associated with the subject of cattle-raising is that of cold storage. It is stated on good authority that there is sufficient beef in prime condition standing on the ranges in November of each year to supply the province until the following June, by which time the pastures would have time to renew themselves. With no market except the regular consumption of the cities, cattle have either to be held over and fed at a large expense, or allowed to winter on the ranges, subject to much loss and depreciation. With public cold storage at one or two points on the railway, to which cattle could be driven and slaughtered, there would be a tremendous saving to the farmer, as well as to the province. Farmers by such a system could also draw on warehouse receipts and realize on a portion of their stock early in the season. The economy of such a system is too obvious to require further comment.

STOCK - RAISING.

The raising of horses in the interior has been carried on to an extreme, and of the large bands many have become wild, and constitute one of the greatest nuisances there are in the way of animal pests. Horses of that class, owing to their rapid multiplication on the ranges, are a drug on the market. First-class stock,

PEEPS INTO INTERIOR VANCOUVER ISLAND.

BONNINGTON FALLS, KOOTENAY RIVER.

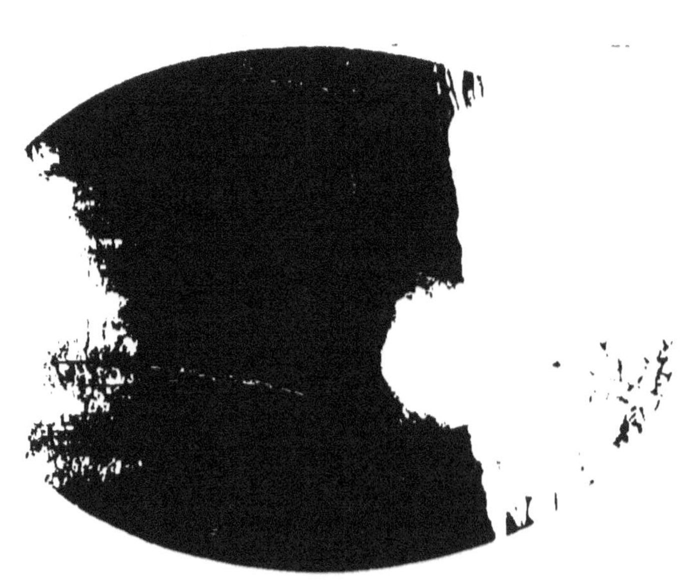

POWELL LAKE FALLS.

however, has never been too plentiful. Sheep-raising has had some attention, but so far has not proved remunerative. There are several reasons for this. In the absence of woollen mills there is a limited market for wool. In the interior the raising of sheep is discouraged by ranchers engaged in cattle-raising, as the sheep destroy the pasturage by too close cropping, and injure the grass roots with their sharp trotters. The experience has been that cattle and sheep do not do well together, and for this reason a statutory limitation has been placed on sheep-ranging. In addition the coyotes are destructive, destroying large numbers annually. On the Lower Mainland the conditions are not favourable, the lower meadows encouraging the development of foot-rot, and the heavy rains in the winter months being detrimental. On the Islands there exists probably the best opportunity for success, but so far sheep-farming has not been carried on extensively, and will not until they are more largely cleared and settled. Wherever wolves exist they will work havoc with the sheep. On Vancouver Island, in the Cowichan District, the industry has been carried on to a larger degree than elsewhere; but there panthers are numerous, and although harmless in respect to the settlers themselves, are sometimes destructive to sheep and pigs. Generally speaking, the natural conditions throughout the province are rather favourable than otherwise to sheep-raising, but its success depends upon improved methods and better breeds. With respect to sheep-farming on the Island of Vancouver and adjacent islands, a very great improvement has been effected in the breeds, largely owing to the efforts of the Flock Masters' Association, by the importation of thoroughbred rams.

POULTRY AND PIGS.

Poultry and pigs in small farming are probably the most promising of live stock: and owing to the general demand for dressed poultry, eggs, pork, bacon and hams, and the high average prices of these products, much attention has been paid to them during the past few years, and an increasing degree of system is being imported into their production. Formerly — in fact, not longer than a few years ago — notwithstanding the opportunities afforded in these lines, the industry was prosecuted indifferently, and practically without system.

CATTLE - RAISING.

Perhaps the most marked progress which has been made in the farming districts of British Columbia has been in connection with cattle-raising and dairying. The remarks which were made in the Year Book of 1897, pointing out the disabilities and disadvantages in connection with these industries, which at that time were generally true, are now wholly, or almost wholly inapplicable. The change has not only been very marked, but it has also been very rapid and substantial. Owing to the efforts of the Dairymen's Association, large numbers of thoroughbred stock have been imported from Eastern Canada and distributed throughout the grazing districts, where they were eagerly bought up by the ranchers. This work has been carried on systematically and effectively, and the results are very apparent. While it is still true that we do not wholly supply our own market with home-grown produce, such as eggs, butter, poultry, etc., at the same time the imported article has been largely substituted.

DAIRYING.

Dairying, which is a most important adjunct of cattle-raising, and which, as has been stated, was until very recently in a very unsatisfactory condition, has rapidly come to the front; and, as will be seen by the returns given elsewhere, there are a number of creameries established in various districts, all doing well and yielding satisfactory dividends. In the larger districts, where mixed farming has been carried on, nothing has done so much towards placing the farmers upon a sure and prosperous footing. It has also tended to a greater interest being taken in scientific and systematic agriculture, justifying remarks made in the previous edition that "British Columbia possesses every element necessary to constitute it a great dairying province, the products of which should include cheese and condensed milk. There are extensive areas of pastoral land in the interior, while increased cultivation in the lower country will form the necessary feeding ground. With a plentiful supply of good water and luxuriant and nutritious grasses, there is every required facility added."

FARMERS' DRAWBACKS.

The incidental obstacles and drawbacks of insect pests and plant diseases have been referred to. There are also noxious weeds in plenty; and of animal pests there are in the outlying districts wolves, panthers, coyotes and wild horses. Crows, bluejays and robins are complained of by orchardists, and owls sometimes infest the poultry yard. In the interior irrigation is a problem; and on the Lower Mainland dyking and draining are important considerations. The difficulty and expense of clearing land have not been overlooked. Indeed, the more heavily timbered lands cannot be economically dealt with for farming purposes until mechanical means can be devised to reduce the labour involved and cheapen the cost. The expense, which varies from $50 to $150 an acre, is a burden on the land, which, under the most intensive farming, cannot return interest on the investment. The financial problem is one which affects the farmer in British Columbia, as elsewhere. He has had, and still has, his share of troubles; but certainly the altered conditions of the past few years, and the season of prosperity enjoyed by him in common with the farmers of the Dominion of Canada as a whole, has greatly improved his condition. The local circumstances affecting his welfare have been and will be overcome by patient, persistent and intelligent effort, without which no avenue of industry can be smoothed; and, comparing all his present and prospective advantages with his disadvantages, the outlook for agriculture is more promising here than in perhaps any other part of the Dominion. The very physical obstacles to be overcome, considered in connection with the comparatively limited area of farming lands, will, when fully overcome, constitute a positive advantage to the tiller of the soil. In this connection, the remarks made by Mr. Palmer in the Farmers' Advocate of 10th December, 1901, are apropos :

LAND CLEARING.

Summing up the situation, there is no question but the future is most promising for agriculturists with cleared lands, who can devote their time to the production of staple crops or finished farm products. On the other hand, the problem of cheap and rapid clearing of the forest lands suitable for farming purposes still remains to be solved. Of these lands, many thousands of acres are available in the proximity of proved mining districts in the Kootenay, Boundary and Kettle River sections, where markets are near at hand and certain. The cost of land-clearing has been reduced by the more general use of stumping machinery and blasting powder, but these means are not always available, and are beyond the reach of many of the poorer settlers, with whom the pressing problem is "how to clear their farms and make a living at the same time."

A rapidly growing population and the enormous expansion of industry bound to ensue as a consequence of the development of immense natural resources, together with a contiguous great future market in the northwestern and northern territories of Canada and a remarkable vantage ground on the seaboard, will yet create a demand, local interprovincial and foreign, that will tax the agriculturist to his utmost to supply. Having contrasted all his advantages fairly with his disadvantages, it is not an over-sanguine view, taking into account his remarkable situation and the balance in his favour, conditional upon the application of scientific, practical and business methods, to predict for the farmer of this province a great and prosperous future.

LOOKING FORWARD.

The province is entering on a new agricultural era, and a large number of farmers are making earnest and diligent efforts, under many difficulties, to re-create the industry on a sound, economic and healthy basis. Progress so far is not measured by many or conspicuous mile-posts, but looking back over ten years a decided advance has been made, and in ten years hence the change will have been marvellous. The time may reasonably be anticipated when the adjacent forests will be cleared away, the valleys fertile with waving grain, the hillsides vine-clad, and the landscape dotted with farmhouses nestling among orchards and clusters of home-born trees and shrubbery, with long vistas of hedge-lines and roadways to guide the eye — a pleasing picture to which the mountain background of native grandeur and the reflection of summer skies will impart a rare charm of scenic beauty and an air of pastoral and picturesque repose.

FRUIT GROWING IN THE OKANAGAN.

IN a letter to the Secretary of the Bureau of Provincial Information, dated Kelowna, B. C., October 24, 1902, T. W. Stirling, a successful grower there, writes as follows: It is difficult to give any exact figures as to the cost of putting out an orchard, the expense of working, the profits per acre and the cost of land, because all these vary according to the location of the land, the class of land, the distance from shipping point, the kind of fruit grown, the cost of getting on water, etc., etc.

COST OF LAND AND SETTING OUT.

Land suitable for fruit-growing near Kelowna sells for $100 an acre, within a mile of the town, to $5 or $10 an acre on the benches some miles away. The land on the benches is very suitable for fruit, generally speaking, but it is usually more costly and difficult to irrigate than on the flat, also is farther away from the shipping point.

With regard to my own experience. I planted my orchard on land about a mile from Kelowna, on the flat, which cost me $60 an acre. The cost of setting out an orchard of apple trees on such land would figure out somewhat as follows: Suppose the orchard was 20 acres —

20 acres, @ $60	$1,200 00
Fencing, about	200 00
Plowing and fixing, @ $5	100 00
Trees, set 30 feet apart, 968 @ 15c	145 00
Freight on same, about	20 00
Setting out and planting, @ 4c. a tree	38 72
Total cost	$1,703 92

For the first and second year potatoes or root crops may well be grown between the trees; the third and fourth, and perhaps for longer, it is a good plan to grow red clover between the trees, leaving a strip of ground in line with each row of trees for cultivating them. After the fifth year or so it would probably be found better to plow the clover down. It is a disputed point whether later on it would not be better to seed the orchard down altogether, but this should certainly not be done until the trees had attained a considerable size.

SUBSEQUENT COST.

The trees will occupy about one-fifth of the ground the first year, about one-fourth the second and third, about one-third the fourth, etc. Leaving out the cost of working the rest of the land, because this should at least be paid for by the crops grown, the cost of working the land, etc., where the trees are will be somewhat as follows:

Cultivating, spraying, pruning, etc.—

First year, @ $10 an acre	$ 200 00
Second year, @ $10 an acre	200 00
Third year, @ $15 an acre	300 00
Fourth year, at $20 an acre	400 00
Fifth year, @ $25 an acre	500 00
Total	$1,600 00

The above figures are ample for giving thorough care to the orchard in every way. The land that was used for other crops — that is, the space between the trees — might well be worked so as to more than pay for the cost of paying for the trees. For instance, in the fourth year, if clover was grown, there would be about 14 acres which should yield in two cuttings 40 to 45 tons, worth $300 or $400; the trees would also in that year produce some fruit, perhaps $100 worth.

Leaving out, however, what might have been made on the unoccupied part of the ground, the total cost of the orchard up to the beginning of the sixth year would be $3,302.92, or $165 per acre.

THE ERA OF RETURNS.

After this the orchard should pay its expenses out of the fruit it produced; but how soon it would produce a full crop would depend on the varieties, the care it had, and other things.

About the ninth year the trees should anyway be big enough to produce a good crop, and if the season were favourable the crop should amount to somewhere around seven tons per acre, worth on the trees perhaps $150.

I should judge of what I know of the few orchards down here that have been planted long enough to get data from, that an orchard of apple trees might be expected to have an average crop of 8 to 10 tons per acre per year, if properly cared for. It is possible that this average might be considerably exceeded. Some trees in a garden near Kelowna, planted some fourteen years ago, and which have had good cultivation right along, have averaged 600 pounds over some years.

To sum up. To plant an orchard is to get into an investment that takes ten years to properly mature.

The property is improving all the time.

For about the first four or five years it will be a charge and an expense. Afterwards it should pay expenses.

The total money sunk in it might be from $150 to $200 per acre.

The returns from it after the tenth year should average $150 or so above expenses.

THE RIGHT VARIETIES.

To get the best results it is necessary to plant the right kind of trees, as some varieties are very much more profitable than others. Fruit has not been grown long enough here as a business to enable anyone to make out anything like a complete list of the varieties of apples that should be planted. Most varieties have not been planted long enough to enable one to come to a definite opinion as to their profitableness.

In summer apples the Red Astrachan fulfils all the conditions necessary to constitute a profitable variety. It is thrifty, a good bearer, and readily sold.

In fall apples, the Macintosh Red and Snow are the best at present known.

In winter apples, the Ben Davis is pre-eminently the most profitable, but it is of a poor quality, and although at present it sells readily, it might not always do so.

The Northern Spy is very profitable when it does begin to bear, but it does not bear a full crop before the tenth year.

*CATTLE RAISING.

THE cattle business is at present in a state of boom, higher prices being paid for good stock than has been the case for years. The reason for this is that the growth of population in the United States has gradually caught up with the supply of food products, especially meats, and the logical conclusion is that food-stuffs are higher. So far as can at present be seen, there is nothing to prevent meats reaching as high a figure on this continent as is usual in the European markets, the large consumers in this country earning higher wages and using more meat than is the case in Europe The general result is that on the American continent generally there is quite a raise in prices, and the farmers are going into stock-raising more extensively. Last year there were imported 248 grades and thoroughbred cattle from Ontario, and the movement still continues, as the market demands a higher quality than has been usually produced.

The parts of the province particularly adapted for cattle-raising are the interior ranges and the valley of the Fraser River. The high prices which good cattle demand justify stall feeding. This was not so several years ago, the price of beef being cheaper and fodder higher, but this is at present reversed. There is a good market for beef right in the province. The ranges are certainly capable of supporting more cattle, and especially with the development of the irrigation possibilities of the province the cattle could be increased threefold, in which case beef, instead of being marketed as three and four year olds, would be two year olds. This, of course, involves feeding the cattle, which would be done from the time they were born until they were slaughtered.

There is a possibility of re-pasturing depleted ranges, and if the land could be fenced and the cattle kept off for a time, they would almost repasture themselves. Bromus Inermis in many instances would be the best means of doing this, although the question of the best grass with which to replace the bunchgrass when destroyed is still an open one.

A system of cold storage available for the interior district would be the greatest boon that could be given to the stock interest generally. It would enable all the cattle ready for market to be slaughtered at their best and held for market until required. The question of cold storage, however, is bound up with that of abattoirs and meat-packing. Cold storage in conjunction with these would mean the saving of the wastes which are now practically lost, such as hides, horns, hoofs and all the by-products, the manufacture of glue, and the carrying on of tanneries. The packing of cheaper cuts, too, which now fetch very little, when canned would fetch a good price. Markets which draw their supply of meat from abattoirs handle almost entirely the best cuts. Only the cheaper meats are canned.

*DAIRYING.

DAIRYING in the upper country is limited to certain valleys where water is abundant or the rainfall sufficient to develop crops of clover and other forage plants. Portions of the Okanagan and Thompson River valleys are suitable.

Dairying pays better than any other branch of mixed farming. The principal difficulty where conditions are otherwise favourable is the scarcity of skilled labour

* See foot note page 108.

for milking, etc. Dairying is profitable and likely to continue profitable on account of the high prices realized for fresh butter, and the fact that the demand is constantly increasing.

Strictly first-class butter must be produced within a few days of the time of consumption. Although we get constant and uniform supplies of butter from Manitoba and the Northwest Territories, yet the qualities which command high prices are lacking. Notwithstanding the fact that the creamery output of the province is increasing all the time, the demand is increasing still faster. Creameries have been established at Ladner, Chilliwack, New Westminster and Upper Sumas, and all are doing well. Besides the co-operative creamery at Ladner, there are two private creameries — Rithet's and Guichons. There is a company formed for the purpose of starting another creamery at Armstrong. On the Island, there are creameries at Comox, Cowichan and Victoria. All these have been established within the last six years.

With regard to breeds of cattle most suitable, all breeds have been tried, but the conclusion which practical dairymen have arrived at here is the same as has been arrived at in other places — that the breed is of little importance, but it is the cow herself. If there is any preference at all at the present time, it is for Jerseys and the milking type of Shorthorns.

The creamery prospects are so good that they will interfere with the development of the condensed milk business, which is being tried, inasmuch as the price of milk will be too high. There is greater risk in the manufacture of condensed milk. The grasses, climate, etc., of the Coast are particularly well adapted for dairying — for the making of lots of good butter and raising of young stock.

The following contains particulars of the dairy output and the progress of development:

DAIRYING RETURNS.

In 1901 the Delta Creamery Company, Limited, Ladner, B. C., manufactured and sold 85,127 lbs. of butter, for $23,398. For comparison the last four years are shown, with the average selling price:

	Lbs. of Butter.	Average Selling price.	Total Sales.
1901	84,127	27 4-5c	$23,398 00
1900	75,820	28 c	21,332 46
1899	70,138	26 3-4c	18,787 91
1898	61,542	25 3-8c	15,810 00

At the annual meeting of 1901 the President stated that in the seven years the company had been in existence $113,000 worth of butter had been sold, and that the shareholders had the satisfaction of knowing that in these seven years what was an experiment, backed by their money without Government assistance, had turned out a success; that the shares were paying 10 per cent. inerest dividend for the last four years, and that the company had a surplus over all liabilities of $2,473.67. He considered the $10 shares to be worth $15.16. The capital stock of the company is $4,850, fully paid.

The Eden Bank Creamery, of Sardis, Chilliwack, did good business during 1901. A comparative statement of the past five years shows a steady increase in the output and a yearly decrease in the cost of making, as follows:

	Lbs. of Butter.	Cash to Patrons.	Cost of Making.	Average Price.
1897	53,605	$10,501 30	$4 35	$10 76
1898	81,212	16,763 04	4 02	20 64
1899	96,943	19,527 24	3 86	20 14
1900	107,615	24,174 42	2 95	22 46
1901	130,181	28,037 85	2 75	24 39

AN EFFECT IN REFLECTION, OKANAGAN LAKE.

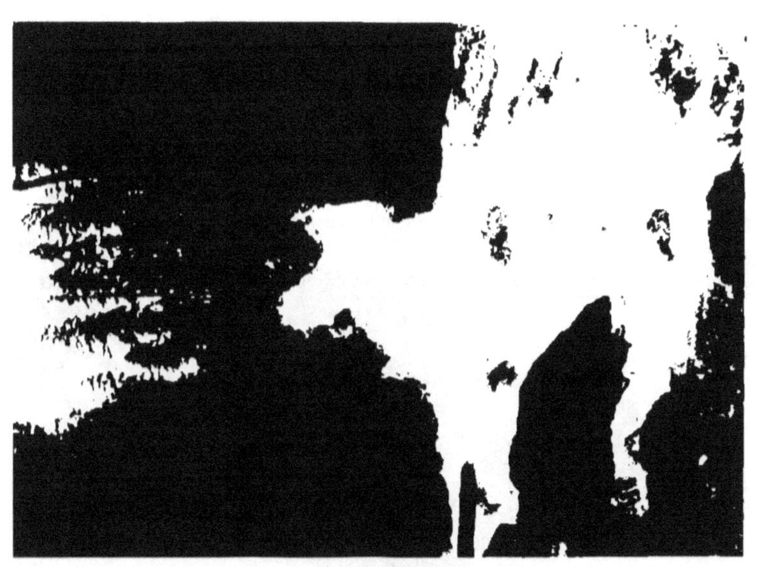

POWELL RIVER MIDDLE FALLS.

ON OKANAGAN LAKE.

SS. "ABERDEEN," OKANAGAN LAKE.

The trade account for the year ending December 31, 1901, shows a net profit of $2,033.53. Of this amount $50 was donated to the managing director, $210 was reserved for repairs and renewals, $57.50 for insurance, $574.51 for bad debts, and the balance $1,141.52, was returned to the patrons supplying cream or milk during the year. The capital stock of the company is $3,000, of which $2,100 is paid up, carrying interest at 9 per cent. per annum.

The Cowichan Creamery has a capital account of $3,000, fully paid. The output from this creamery for the year ending October 31, 1901, was 80,358 lbs., which sold at $22,375.76. The total cash paid patrons was $19,651.02, or an average of 24.2 cents per pound. The following table will show the progress this creamery has made :

	Cash to Patrons.	Total sales Butter.
1897	$7,464 92	$10,368 79
1898	8,828 57	11,375 84
*1899	9,406 54	12,864 53
1900	16,247 00	19,350 30
1901	19,651 02	22,375 76

*Eleven months only included in 1899. In addition to amount shown as paid to patrons, ½ cent per lb. bonus was paid for 1900.

The returns from the New Westminster Creamery are :

	Butter made, Lbs.	Amount paid for Cream.	Value of Product.
1897	10,867	$ 1,933 00	$ 2,475 75
1898	37,994	7,352 00	8,870 02
1899	50,800	9,392 32	12,151 01
1900	84,872	17,403 36	22,857 08
1901	74,673	15,308 67	20,841 95

The manager of the Western Condensed Milk Canning, Coffee & Creamery Company, Limited, writes as follows, under date of February 15, 1902 : "We are not a creamery in the ordinary sense, our aim being to make as little butter as possible, our purchases being whole milk. We may say that for the short time we have been running — which has only been equal to about two months' work, for we have been practically closed down for the past three months, as we cannot obtain the milk — we have paid the farmers in this vicinity to January 31st, $11,000. Our extensive plant, costing over $20,000, could use up, and we actually require something like 20 tons of milk per day; but we now discover that it is useless, under present conditions in this province, to expect anything of the kind, and we have to put a herd of cattle on for ourselves. We have, as a side line, made in a short time, to end of last month, 37,618 lbs. of butter, but we have a churn capacity of 1,500 lbs. per day.

RETURNS FOR 1902.

The following are complete returns from the different creameries of the province for the year 1902, showing a total of 750,000 pounds. In sending their returns some of the creamery companies give one class of information and some another, so that it is impossible to make the particulars uniform. The returns show a very considerable increase over the year 1901. Of the twelve creameries, returns from which are given, four are owned by private parties, and two of these have operated for only a short period of the year.

	Output	Average Selling Price	Price to Patrons	Capital Invested	Cash to Patrons	Butter Fat	Value Output
	Lbs.			$	$	Lbs.	$
*Comox Creamery Ass'n, Courtenay	....	....	....	....	....	....	....
Cowichan Creamery Ass'n, Duncans	90,616	27.15c.	23.65c.	3,304.65	....	....	....
Eden Bank Creamery Co., Sardis, Chilliwack	118,580	....	24.58c.	....	25,706.83	104,590	....
Delta Creamery Co., Ladner	198,535	26.72c.	....	4,850.00	....	....	26,334.00
‡Guichon's, Ladner (Private)	....	....	....	....	....	....	....
New Westminster Creamery Co	133,920	21-30c.	....	....	....	....	....
Bowman, O.; Sumas (Private)	33,830	25c.	....	1,000.00	7,504.00	....	....
†Okanagan Creamery Ass'n, Armstrong	2,861	25c.	20c.	5,000.00	460.61	....	....
‡Rithet, R. P. & Co., Ltd., Ladner (Private)	4,678	26c.	....	....	....	....	....
Urquhart, A., Courtenay (Private)	16,500	27c.	....	....	....	....	....
Victoria Creamery Association, Victoria	115,000	28c.	....	4,651.34	....	....	17,617.82
§Western Cond. Milk Canning, Coffee and Creamery Co., Mission	38,482	27c.	25c.	....	....	....	....

* No returns. Factory was in operation only a portion of the year.

† Operated seven weeks only as experiment.

§ The Western Condensed Milk Canning, Coffee and Creamery Co., say: "We think the returns asked for by you are more from a creamery point of view than that of a condensed milk factory, and as we make very little butter it is difficult to give you returns that would make a good showing in your report. Our principal business is the manufacture of condensed milk and evaporated cream for which we pay the farmers on an average about $1.27 per hundred-weight for milk. For the cream we pay them for their individual percentage of butter fat, at the rate of 25c. per pound. We do not skim any milk for the purpose of making butter."

‡ No returns were supplied by the Guichon Creamery, but it is estimated to have produced about equal to Rithet's. Both of these creameries now find it more profitable to ship the cream to New Westminster than to manufacture it in a small way.

*FRUIT GROWING.

THE province, for better consideration, may be divided into three zones — the Interior District, Lower Mainland, and Vancouver and other islands in the Gulf.

Conditions are eminently favourable all through the interior for the production of apples of the finest quality and appearance. The varieties grown will not be the same in all sections, but there is no question that good market varieties can be grown in all districts where ordinary farming operations are carried on. A great many varieties have been successfully grown in the interior, but the market varieties most profitable are Duchess of Oldenburg, Wealthy, Mackintosh Red, King of Tompkins, Red-Cheeked Pippin, Ben Davis and Northern Spy.

There are certain valleys where wheat-growing has been carried on which are particularly well suited for apple-growing, and no doubt a great portion of this area will be used for the purpose, as the profits from apple-growing are much greater than those obtained from wheat-growing, when the business is intelligently carried on — in the Okanagan, Thompson and Kettle River Valleys, and in the Similkameen.

Small fruits grow everywhere. Prunes do remarkably well in the Okanagan, and plums, too. The quality of prunes raised at Kelowna is superior to anything seen, even in Oregon and California. Certain varieties of pears do extremely well in the Okanagan country, the principal varieties being Bartlett, Flemish, Beauty, and Winter Nellis.

* See foot note page 108.

SEVERAL CONCLUSIONS.

The expansion and extension of the agricultural industry depend upon the clearing of land, and that depends upon how economically it can be done — how cheaply, whether it will pay or not. It also depends to what extent irrigation can take place; also to what extent land subject to overflow can be reclaimed. With these problems solved, the expansion and extension of the agricultural industry would be very great. Present prospects are excedingly good for agriculture, barring the labour question; that is, there is large demand in every line and good prices; and the prospects are that under almost any circumstances or conditions in the future, with the increase in population, this demand will be more than maintained. The difference between the consumption and production is growing larger year by year. As a matter of fact, prices in the last two years have been higher on the Sound than in British Columbia.

HOP AND FLAX GROWING.

Hop-growing is a decided success in the Okanagan, Agassiz and Chilliwack Districts. The best market heretofore has been the Old Country, and most of the hops have been shipped there; but the last two years the Eastern market has taken large shipments of hops, and the Australian market is bidding for them also. The industry is likely to grow. Hop pests are controlled by spraying and have been found to scarcely interfere with the development of the industry.

With regard to flax-growing for fibre, it is perhaps best to let this alone, because we have not the supply of cheap labour necessary for working flax when grown; and another reason is that other farm crops are more profitable which demand less labour, and sometimes more profitable than the flax crop would be with cheap labour.

SMALL HOLDINGS.

A general system of small holdings is very much wanted. A well-devised system of small holdings will do more to develop the agricultural prospects of British Columbia than any other one thing. The farmers throughout the province have been circulating a petition asking the Government to lend them money for the purpose of clearing land, but it would probably be better for the Government to clear the land and charge the land with the cost of this, on a straight business basis, making the loan at as low a rate of interest as possible. But I do not think the interests of the farmers are yet sufficiently consolidated in the province to make a co-operative plan such as is provided for in the Mutual Credits Association Act practicable. The work by the Government should be experimental and for the purpose of demonstrating what can be done, and the people will take hold of it themselves as soon as they recognize the benefits to be derived by cheaper methods and co-operative efforts.

DOMINION CENSUS RETURNS.

THE following is condensed from a recent bulletin issued by the Census Department at Ottawa, entitled "Agriculture in British Columbia." It contains the results of the census-taking in 1901 :

The Province of British Columbia has an area above tide level of 236,922,177 acres, and only 0.63 p. c. of it is occupied as farms and lots whose agricultural statistics have been compiled into the tables. The average size of lots is 1.21 acres and of farms 252 acres, and in Table I. they are grouped to show the number of holdings within specified limits of size. Of the 801 lots under 5 acres, 29.7 p. c. are less than an acre each, and 70.3 p. c. are an acre or more; and of the 5,938 farms of 5 acres and over, 9.18 p. c. are 5 to 10 acres, 12.46 p. c. are 11 to 50 acres, 13.69 p. c. are 51 to 100 acres, 36.81 p. c. are 101 to 200 acres, and 27.86 p. c. are 201 acres or more. The land owned is 86.04 p. c., and the land leased or rented 13.96 p. c. of the whole area occupied as farms; while of the small area occupied as lots, 64.78 p. c. is owned, and 35.22 p. c. leased or rented. Nearly the whole extent of the land in lots is in an improved state, with 54.89 of it in crops and pasture, and 42.22 p. c. in orchard and garden. The land in farms comprises 31.59 p. c. in an improved and 68.41 p. c. in an unimproved state. The unimproved land consists of 391,096 acres in forest and 632,640 acres in various conditions, such as rock, swamp, marsh or waste land, and land in rough or natural pasture, but not in a state fit for cultivation. Field crops, fruits and vegetables, and pasture to a large extent, occupy the improved land; about 36 p. c. is in field crops, 2 p. c. in orchard and garden, and the rest in pasture. Forest plantations cover only 471 acres, and ornamental trees have been planted on farms and lots to the number of 42,832, or an average of 6 for each farm and lot.

The area of improved land is given as 57,881 acres. This was ascertained from the areas of land in wheat, barley, oats, rye, corn, peas, potatoes and other roots, 50,126 acres, together with the areas in orchard and garden, 7,755 acres, whose aggregate, exclusive of hay and some minor crops, was taken as the area of improved land.

Table II. gives the number of acres in orchard as 7,430, of which 299 acres is on lots. This shows an increase of 993 acres in the decade. The land in vegetables and small fruits has increased from 1,288 acres to 2,840 acres, but decreases are shown for the areas of vineyards and nurseries. Compared with the former census, the crop of apples shows an increase of 213 p. c., of peaches 70 p. c., of pears, 108.6 p. c., of plums 194.38 p. c., and of grapes 96.57 p. c.; but the crop of other fruit trees shows a decrease of nearly 57 p. c. Apple, pear and plum trees yielded an average of about 1 bushel per bearing tree, peach and cherry trees about ¾ of a bushel, and grape vines about 9 pounds.

Hay, oats, wheat and roots occupied about 94 p. c. of the whole area devoted to field culture in 1900 — hay 60, oats 20.07, wheat 9.21, and potatoes 4.72 p. c. Volume IV. of the census of 1891 gave the area in hay as 64,611 acres, with a yield of 102,146 tons. The present census shows an area of 102,751 acres, and a yield of 170,187 tons. Potatoes show an increase in the ten years of 3,971 acres, or 94.25 p. c., and oats an increase of 10,218 acres or 42.3 p. c. Wheat and barley have remained almost stationary, both in area and production, while peas and beans show decreases in production. The cultivation of tobacco and hops is extending, and a substantial beginning has been made with mixed grains and forage crops. The whole area in crops in the last census year was 171,424 acres, and all save 251 acres was on farms.

As already stated, the area of land in wheat, oats, barley, rye, corn, peas, potatoes and other field roots in the census year 1891 was 50,126 acres, and in hay 64,611 acres. Beans, buckwheat, flax, tobacco and hops, computed on the basis of average yields of the present census, would give an additional area of 211 acres, or an aggregate of 114,948 acres for the field crops of the 1890 season. The increase at the end of the last decade, therefore, is 56,476 acres, or 49 p. c.

The following table shows the average yield per acre of the principal crops for the harvests of 1890 and 1900 :

	1900.	1890.
Wheat, bushels	23.07	25.62
Oats, bushels	41.94	39.05
Potatoes, bushels	116.83	102.78
Hay, tons	1.65	1.58

Compared with the former census, there are decreases in horses and sheep, but in milch cows and poultry there are increases. Milch cows show a gain of 7,031, and other horned cattle a loss of 8,948. The averages in round numbers of live stock per farm are: Horses 5, milch cows 4, other horned cattle 17, sheep 6, swine 7, and poultry of all kinds 43.

The table of animal products shows decreases in the number of cattle and sheep killed, or sold for slaughter or export, and increase in the number of swine. The wool product shows that the decrease of sheep has taken place in the coarse-wooled breeds; the quantity of fine wool is less than at the former census by only 1,000 lbs., and the coarse wool by 38,896 lbs. The product of home-made butter is nearly three times more than ten years ago, and in the interval seven factories have been put into operation. Eggs were not enumerated in 1891, but this census shows a production of 1,651,741 dozen, valued at $426,629.

Agricultural values have been taken for the first time in this census. They show for farms and lots in the province a total for land and buildings of $26,001,377, for implements and machinery $1,201,196, for live stock $6,184,313, and for the crops and animal products of the census year $6,064,369. For farms alone the value of land and buildings is $25,924,174, of implements and machinery $1,180,724, of live stock $5,360,614, and of crops and animal products $6,219,761.

The total value of farm property is $32,465,512, and of this sum land represents 64.69 p. c., buildings 15.15 p. c., implements and machinery 3.64 p. c., and the live stock 16.52 p. c.

Reduced to a farm of the average size in the province (252 acres, whereof 79.62 acres is improved and 172.38 unimproved), the value of the property is $5,467.41, made up of $4,365.81 for land and buildings, $198.84 for implements and machinery, and $902.76 for live stock.

The total gross value of farm products for the census year is $3,479,682 for crops (55.95 p. c.) and $2,740,079 for animal products (44.05 p. c.). This makes the aggregate of $6,219,761, or $1,047.45 in the year for an average farm, which is 19.16 p. c. of the investment.

In detail, the proportional value of field crops on farms is 49.62 p. c. of the year's production, fruit and vegetables and nursery stock 6.32 p. c., live stock sold 18.72 p. c., meats and products of animals slaughtered on the farm 4.77 p. c., dairy products 16.11 p. c., and wool, eggs, honey and wax 4.46 p. c.

The average value of horses on farms is 50.87, milch cows $42.59, other horned cattle $23.95, sheep $4.93, and swine 6.49; and the average value of horses per farm is $253.86, milch cows $157.43, other horned cattle $395.06, sheep $27.19, swine $42.59, and poultry and bees $26.63.

In the value of dairy products is included the milk and cream sold to butter factories, amounting to $95,804. There were seven factories in operation in the province during the census year, which produced 395,461 lbs. of butter, worth $103,497. The first of the factories began operations in 1895, and two others were added in the following year.

The extent of land rented as farms is 208,830 acres, and the rental value for the year is $213,216, being an average of $1.02 per acre, or $257 a year for an average farm. The rate of wages for hired labour on the farm, including board, is $9.04 per week, which is nearly 2½ times more than in Prince Edward Island.

On lots of less than 5 acres the value of agricultural products in the census year was $444,608, or $555.06 per lot, which is $48.25 p. c. of the $921,374 valuation of lands, buildings, implements and machinery, and live stock. The rent value of leased lots, comprising 35¼ p. c. of the land occupied, is $5.24 per acre. The value of hired labour, including board, is $7.31 per week.

FARM AND LOT HOLDINGS.

Occupiers.	1901.	1891.
Occupiers being —		
Owners	5,412	5,456
Tenants	1,031	*1,995
Owners and tenants	296	
Occupiers of —		
Under 1 acre	238	
1 to under 5 acres	563	
5 to 10 acres	545	2,811
11 to 50 acres	740	685
51 to 100 acres	813	528
101 to 200 acres	2,186	2,169
201 acres and over	1,654	1,258
Total occupiers	6,739	7,451

*Including 100 employees.

FARMS AND LOTS.

Schedule of Lands.	Farms 5 acres and over.	Lots under 5 acres.	Total. 1901.	Total. 1891.
Occupiers of land, No.	5,938	801	6,739	7,451
Land occupied, acres	1,496,411	971	1,497,382	3,329,660
Land owned, acres	1,287,581	629	1,288,210	......
Land leased or rented, acres	208,830	342	209,172	......
Land improved	472,785	861	473,646	57,881
Land unimproved	1,023,626	110	1,023,736	......
Land in forest	391,032	64	391,096	2,558,342
Land in field crops	171,173	251	171,424	50,126
Land in pasture	556,762	282	557,044	713,437
Land in orchard	7,131	299	7,430	6,437
Land in vegetables and small fruits	2,732	108	2,840	1,288
Land in vineyard	16	2	18	30
Land in nurseries	71	1	72	83
Trees planted	24,794	18,038	42,832	..
Forest plantations	428	43	471	..

FRUITS.

Schedule of Fruits.	Farms 5 acres and over.	Lots under 5 acres.	Total. 1901.	Total. 1891.
Apple trees, bearing	202,247	18,437	220,684	......
Apple trees, non-bearing	208,651	7,309	215,960	......
Apples	221,843	18,718	240,561	76,856
Peach trees, bearing	2,644	682	3,326	......
Peach trees, non-bearing	4,396	505	4,901	......
Peaches	2,237	303	2,540	1,494
Pear trees, bearing	20,065	4,883	24,948	......
Pear trees, non-bearing	20 803	1,492	22,295	......
Pears	18,407	6.951	25,358	12,156
Plum trees, bearing	53,101	6,679	59,780	......
Plum trees, non-bearing	27,022	2,141	29,163	......
Plums	50,459	7,755	58,214	19,775
Cherry trees, bearing	12,623	4,699	17,322	......
Cherry trees, non-bearing	9,743	1,147	10,890	......
Cherries	9,894	4,545	14,439	4,227
Other fruit trees, bearing	18,137	6,038	24,175	......
Other fruit trees, non-bearing	14,158	1,489	15,647	......
Other fruits	2,725	553	3,278	7,612
Grape vines, bearing	3,205	186	3,391	......
Grape vines, non-bearing	5,356	128	5,484	......
Grapes	27,392	2,790	30,182	15,354
Small fruits, quarts	600,844	83,784	684,628	......
Maple sugar and syrup	......	31	31	320

The total number of bearing and non-bearing apple trees in the province is 436,644, of peach trees 8,227, of pear trees 47,243, of plum trees 88,943, of cherry trees 28,212, of other fruit trees 39,822, and of grape vines 8,875. The yield of fruit

YALE.
Head of Navigation, Lower Fraser River.

CITY OF KASLO, KOOTENAY LAKE, B. C.

JUNCTION OF WOSS AND KLA-ANCH RIVERS, VANCOUVER ISLAND

FOOT OF WOSS LAKE, VANCOUVER ISLAND.

trees in the last census year was 344,390 bushels, and in the former census year it was 122,120 bushles.

GRAINS.

Schedule of Grains.	Farms 5 acres and over.	Lots under 5 acres.	Total. 1901.	1891.
Spring wheat, acres	12,060	4	12,064	15,156
Spring wheat, bushels	276,590	88	276,678	318,543
Fall wheat, acres	3,902	1	3,903	......
Fall wheat, bushels	91,724	17	91,741	69,847
Barley, acres	2,232	..	2,232	2,228
Barley, bushels	73,790	..	73,790	79,024
Oats, acres	34,360	6	34,366	24,148
Oats, bushels	1,441,281	285	1,441,566	943,068
Rye, acres	730	..	730	.....
Rye, bushels	17,328	..	17,328	6,141
Corn in ear, acres	51	..	51	.....
Corn in ear, bushels	1,849	..	1,849	3,938
Buckwheat, acres	57	..	57	.....
Buckwheat, bushels	1,899	..	1,899	276
Peas, acres	2,948	..	2,948	...
Peas, bushels	60,074	..	60,074	85,774
Beans, acres	56	..	56	.....
Beans, bushels	1,780	..	1,780	4,888
Mixed grains, acres	571	..	571	.....
Mixed grains, bushels	13,699	..	13,699	.....

HAY. ROOTS, ETC.

Hay, Roots, etc.	Farms 5 acres and over.	Lots under 5 acres.	Total. 1901.	1891.
Hay, acres	102,646	105	102,751	64,611
Hay, tons	169,969	218	170,187	102,146
Forage crops (summer feeding), acres	543	...	543	.....
Forage crops (winter feeding), acres	664	1	665	.....
Forage crops (winter feeding), tons	3,304	2	3,306	.....
Potatoes, acres	8,078	106	8,184	4,213
Potatoes, bushels	940,957	15,169	956,126	685.802
Other field roots, acres	1.951	28	1.979	1.443
Other field roots, bushels	631,728	4,260	635,988	516,242
Flax, acres	1	.....	1	...
Flax, bushels	4	.....	4	364
Tobacco, acres	61	.....	61	...
Tobacco, lbs.	61,830	.....	61,830	343
Hops, acres	262	.....	262	...
Hops, lbs.	299,717	.....	299,717	55,288
Grass seed, bushels	462	.....	462	.....
Clover seed, bushels	150	.....	150	1,658

LIVE STOCK.

Live Stock.	Farms 5 acres and over.	Lots under 5 acres.	Total. 1901.	1891.
Horses, 3 years and over	22.730	7,159	29.889	32,105
Horses, under 3 years	6,904	532	7,436	12,416
Milch cows	21,949	2,586	24,535	17.504
Other horned cattle	97,954	2,513	100,467	109,415
Sheep	32,723	627	33,350	49,163
Swine	38,963	2,456	41,419	30,764
Turkeys	2,564	226	2,790	4,044
Geese	3,567	219	3,786	2,914
Ducks	8,088	1,283	9,371	11,822
Hens and chickens	241,775	104,705	346,480	217,985
Other fowls	582	313	895	1,621
Hives of bees	1,992	392	2,384	515
Pure-bred Animals—				
Horses	365	74	439	...
Cattle	1,921	57	1,978	...
Sheep	549	1	550	...
Swine	1,044	14	1,058	...
Poultry	11,660	3,020	14,680	...

ANIMAL PRODUCTS.

Animal Products.	Farms 5 acres and over.	Lots under 5 acres.	Total. 1901.	Total. 1891.
Killed for slaughter or export —				
Cattle	21,910	751	22,661	33,822
Sheep	14,049	297	14,346	65,491
Swine	30,422	4,364	34,786	26,618
Poultry	93,837	8,503	102,340	......
Fine wool, lbs.	30,601	100	30,701	31,701
Coarse wool, lbs.	69,159	489	69,648	108,544
Butter, home-made, lbs.	1,065,606	26,949	1,092,555	393,089
Honey, lbs.	26,169	7,688	33,837	8,990
Eggs, dozen	1,050,816	600,925	1,651,741	.....

PURE - BRED STOCK.

Horses — Blood 2, Clydesdale 146, Coach 2, Hackney 1, Hambletonian 26, Percheron 35, Shire 10, Standard 3, Suffolk Punch 9, not specified 202.

Cattle — Ayrshire 102, Guernsey 7, Hereford 255, Holstein 212, Jersey 278, Polled Angus 31, Shorthorn 776, not specified 317.

Sheep — Cheviot 11, Cotswold 34, Dorset 7, Leicester 80, Lincoln 26, Oxford 133, Shropshire 81, Southdown 73, not specified 105.

Swine — Berkshire 465, Chester 107, Durac Jersey 3, Essex 9, Poland China 89, Suffolk 25, Tamworth 23, Yorkshire 32, not specified 305.

Hens and Chickens — Andalusian 130, Bantam 50, Black Spanish 44, Brahma 258, Buff Cochin 28, Cochin China 52, Dorking 46, Game 263, Hamburg 71, Langshan 348, Leghorn 2,997, Minorca 1,088, Plymouth Rock 3,119, Polish 11, Wyandotte 1,177, not specified 4,527.

Ducks — Pekin 380, Rouen 3, not specified 4.

Geese — Toulouse 3, White Emden 21, not specified 6.

Turkeys — Bronze 44, White 10.

VALUES.

Land	$21,004,720	$ 37,120	$21,041,840
Buildings	4,919,454	40,083	4,959,537
Rent of land and buildings leased	213,216	1,791	215,007
Farm implements and machinery	1,180,724	20,472	1,201,196
Horses	1,507,415	567,113	2,074,528
Milch cows	934,838	125,769	1,060,607
Other horned cattle	2,345,865	45,561	2,391,426
Sheep	161,447	3,232	164,679
Swine	252,885	18,442	271,327
Poultry	148,387	61,360	209,747
Bees	9,777	2,222	11,999
Pure-bred stock	*228,590	*23,582	*252,172
Field crops	3,086,552	14,025	3,100,577
Fruit and vegetables	378,769	57,025	435,794
Nursery stock sold	14,361	3,783	18,144
Live stock sold during year	1,164,566	38,051	1,202,607
Meats and products of all animals slaughtered on the farm	296,365	11,032	307,397
Dairy products	1,001,683	158,310	1,159,993
Wool	8,198	90	8,288
Eggs	265,648	169,981	426,629
Honey and wax	3,629	1,311	4,940
Hired labour on farm, weeks	134,186	1,411	135,597
Value of hired labour	1,212,916	10,314	1,223,230

*Included with the values of other animals.

LAND RETURNS.

IT is interesting to compare census returns as contained in the foregoing with the returns compiled by the Agricultural Department in 1894, so far as the comparison extends. Although considerable progress has been made since that time, and the area under cultivation has materially increased, for practical purposes the tables below represent fairly well the conditions to-day. No complete statistics have been obtained since 1894.

UPPER COUNTRY.

District.	Total acres of land owned.	Acres of cultivated land.	Acres of forest or woodland.	Acres of swamp or marsh.	Acres of prairie or pasture (including hay meadows)
Kettle River	17,000	1,300	7,000	1,200	4,500
Midway and Rock Creek	8,160	510	1,560	328	4,062
Keremeos and Osoyoos	42,418	447	1,040	580	37,638
Princeton, Granite Creek and Otter Creek	19,093	390	1,755	125	15,779
Penticton, Dog Lake and Trout Creek	14,020	410	1,540	765	9,830
West side Okanagan Lake	7,040	165	1,000	375	3,000
Okanagan Mission	92,800	6,000	5,000	3,000	70,800
Okanagan, White Valley, etc.	48,479	5,484	13,461	1,700	18,864
Spallumcheen	51,903	8,124	32,815	1,982	8,379
Craigellachie	1,740	38	1,117	368	17
Salmon Arm	4,887	541	4,052	232	17
Tappen Siding and Notch Hill	2,852	100	2,036	401	45
Shuswap	6,442	1,640	520	35	4,247
Ducks and Grand Prairie	20,556	1,154	8,049	2,365	7,540
Kamloops	40,378	3,048	6,561	391	26,868
Nicola	133,601	4,415	17,639	2,388	105,335
North Bend (Emory to Keefers)	2,477	321	1,515	..	102
Lytton to Spence's Bridge	4,077	970	1,047	30	814
Ashcroft, Savona and Cache Creek	25,652	3,256	4,062	1,100	14,953
Lillooet and Pemberton Meadows	5,382	630	729	90	3,848
Pavilion and Pavilion Mountain	5,796	1,406	436	193	3,651
Clinton	3,800	50	090	980	1,980
Bridge Creek and Lac La Hache.	9,000	500	2,000	1,000	5,500
Williams Lake	14,943	1,219	3,961	1,466	8,087
Soda Creek, Alexandria and Quesnel	15,762	2,095	9,140	943	2,774
Chilcotin	13,060	640	1,461	716	8.971
Alkali Lake, Dog Creek, Big Bar and Empire Valley	62,260	1,724	1,661	1,083	57,522
Golden and Galena	6,097	464	2,618	749	2,241
Windermere	8,585	507	3,381	.....	4,607
Fort Steele and Tobacco Plains	23,637	360	19,197	1,125	2,955
West Kootenay (no returns)	......	...	......	.....	.....
	711,897	40,008	158,243	25,710	434,910

LOWER MAINLAND.

Delta	21,107	12,391	1,428	222	7,060
Surrey	39,432	4,174	26,145	2,412	6,701
Langley	51,307	4,212	44,480	...	2,215
Matsqui	50,392	1,619	33,695	117	14.961
Sumas	16,992	579	7,693	100	8,590
Chilliwack	42,836	6,484	18,489	531	17,326
Hope and St. Elmo	1,746	223	1,106	30	216
Agassiz	11,407	1,643	8,340	64	882
Nicomen and Harrison (no returns)	.....	...	.....	..	...
Dewdney	5,289	821	3,645	40	683
Mission	5,224	655	3,918	79	572
Maple Ridge	20,039	2,108	14,557	..	3,374
Coquitlam (no returns)	.....	...	.....	...	.....
Burnaby and South Vancouver...	3,693	980	2,163	550	.....
Lulu and Sea Islands	12,897	6,907	831	509	4,650
Squamish and Howe Sound	11,752	331	9,629	5	58
	294,083	43,127	176,519	4,659	67,287

VANCOUVER ISLAND AND ADJACENT ISLANDS.

Sooke	6,803	502	4,864	250	410
Metchosin	7,776	1,164	3,477	25	1,253
Esquimalt	2,358	194	1,719	201	104
Victoria	5,018	1,800	1,738	232	617
Lake	4,833	850	3,807	46	55
South Saanich	7,932	2,032	5,573	34	293
North Saanich	7,925	2,468	4,658	16	445
Cowichan, Chemainus, Shawnigan	50,429	3,170	45,606	3,493	1,849
Salt Spring Island	28,514	1,027	17,376	96	1,448
The Islands	7,616	214	3,977	20	835
Nanaimo, Nanoose, Gabriola Island, etc.	68,226	3,736	56,142	2,295	1,958
Comox, Denman and Hornby Islands	12,365	1,817	8,326	611	1,349
Oyster Bay	2,224	50	1,714	400	60
Alberni (no returns)	.....	.....	.....	...	...
Clayoquot	3,040	3,040	1,746	900	350
Valdez Island, etc.	12,577	12,577	9,012	872	209
	232,636	19,200	169,735	9,471	11,235

GRAND TOTAL,

Upper Country	711,897	49,098	158,243	25,710	434,916
Lower Mainland	204083	43,127	176,519	4,659	67,287
Vancouver Island and adjacent Islands	232,636	19,200	169,735	9,491	11,235
	1,238,616	111,425	504,497	39,860	513,438

MARKET PRICES.

Incidentally throughout the opening division of this chapter, dealing with the districts in detail, local market prices are given. These vary, however, very much according to locality. The prices given in the following are those which have prevailed at the Coast cities during the five years mentioned, and represent mainly jobbing and wholesale rates. As the labour involved in compiling these tables is very great, the average for every item for the twelve months being given, the statement for 1902 is not included, not having been compiled in time. The average is, however, kept up, and in many items exceeds previous years. It will be seen that there has been a steady improvement, and that a high average price has been maintained. Following this there is given a statement of prices at New Westminster, where a regular farmers' market is held, and where quotations represent more accurately what is actually paid to farmers for produce.

Article.	Average for 1897.	Average for 1898.	Average for 1899.	Average for 1900.	Average for 1901.	Average for 5 yrs.
MEATS—						
Dry salt	10	10½	9¾	11½	....	10½
Rolled bacon	10	10½	11¼	12½	13⅓	11½
Breakfast bacon	13⅛	13⅓	13⅜	14	16⅙	14
Hams	13⅙	12¾	13½	14¾	15½	14
Mess pork	....	....	....	....	....	....
LARD—						
Tins	9¾	10 1/5	9¾	11⅓	13½	10⅞
Pails and tubs	9¼	9¾	9¼	10¾	13	10½
SUGAR—						
Yellow	4	4	4½	4⅝	4½	4 5/16
Granulated	4⅞	4¾	5⅛	5⅜	5¼	5 1/16
Pow'd, bar and icing	6⅜	6½	6⅝	7	6⅞	6⅝
BUTTER—						
Creamery	27 B.C.	24½ B.C.	32½	25⅔	27	27⅓
Dairy	17	19¾	18¾	20½	17½	18¾
CHEESE	11¾	11⅞	12½	14½	12 1/5	12½
FLOUR—						
Manitoba patents	5.86	6.35	4.73	5.03	4.87	5.37
Manitoba bakers	5.53	6.02	4.42	4.68	4.50	5.15
Oregon	5.67	5.25	4.52	4.46	4.50	4.88
British Columbia	5.52	5.63	4.75	4.62	4.82	5.07
POTATOES, per ton	17.25	12.18	17.85	16.00	21.50	16.96
HAY	15.25	15.21	11.36	13.83	14.18	13.97
WHEAT	35.00	29.75	25.75	26.00	28.75	29.05
OATS	27.17	27.00	25.00	25.33	28.75	26.25
SHORTS	21.33	22.83	22.50	20.84	23.25	22.15
BRAN	19.33	21.00	20.50	19.00	21.42	20.25
CHOPPED FEED	24.38	25.50	25.33	24.75	24.67	24.93
ROLLED OATS, 90 lbs	2.92	2.84	2.80	2.54	2.81	2.78
OAT MEAL, 100 lbs	3.25	3.29	3.24	3.25	3.17	3.24
ONIONS, lb	1⅞	2¼	1½	2⅓	2⅓	2 1/16
EGGS, fresh, per doz	30	25½	38	35	30½	32
EGGS, case, per doz	17	17	19	19½	19¾	18½
FRUITS—						
Apples, per box	.82 B.C.	1.14	1.18	1.13	1.20	1.09
Pears, "	....	....	....	....	....	....
Plums, "	....	....	....	....	....	....
ROOTS—						
Turnips, Carrots, Beets	9.58	11.11	12.00	11.50	....	11.05
FRESH MEATS—						
Live steers	4.08	4.00	4.60	4.10	4.90	4.34
Live cows	....	3.46	4.00	3.75	3.00	3.55
Live calves	....	....	....	....	....	....
" hogs	5.53	6.53	6.60	5.75	6.89	6.26
" sheep	4.31	4.75	5.48	5.51	5.33	5.08
Dressed beef	8.00	7⅛	8¼	8⅔	8.09	8.03
" veal	8.00	8¾	10¾	10⅔	9.67	9.57
" pork	6¼	....	8⅞	9	8.42	8.14
" mutton	9	8¼	11	11	10.82	10.01
POULTRY—						
Chickens	10¼ lb.	11½ lb.	65c. each	....	3.75 doz.	....
Ducks	12 "	12½ "	....	....	5.00 "	....
Geese	11 "	....		12 lb.	9.00 "	....
Turkeys	12 "	16¼ "	....	14 "	17 lb.	14¾

PRICES CURRENT IN NEW WESTMINSTER MARKET.

THE following is a comparison of prices realised by farmers at the market of New Westminster for the years ending June 30, 1901, and June 30, 1902, respectively. The two columns represent the average prices for the twelve months of the year, and are thus more trustworthy than prices taken in any particular month, when local conditions might have favourably or unfavourably affected the quotations.

	1901.	1902.
Beef, per lb.	$ 7¾	$ 12
Mutton, per lb.	9 1-6	10½
Pork, per lb.	8	9
Veal, per lb.	9 1-9	9½
Potatoes, per ton	20 00	1 60 per sack
Turnips, per ton	8 00	60 per sack
Carrots, per ton	10 00	66 per sack
Onions, per ton	30 62	1 50 per sack
Cabbage, per lb.	1	2
Wheat, per ton	30 00	25 00
Oats, per ton	23 75	28 06
Hay, per ton	11 00	9 80
Butter, per lb.	27½	28
Eggs, per dozen	32	32
Fowls, per dozen	6 00	6 50
Chickens, per dozen	5 38	3 87
Ducks, per dozen	6 40	6 38
Rhubarb, per lb.	6	4½
Gooseberries, per lb.	6	7
Strawberries, 24 lbs.	1 44	1 70
Cherries, 10 lbs.	75	9 per lb.
Currants, per lb.	7	6½
Raspberries, 24 lbs.	1 28	1 60
Plums, 20 lbs.	46	95
Peaches, 20 lbs.	1 37	1 50
Apples, 40 lbs.	1 18	1 23
Pears, 40 lbs.	95	60
Tomatoes, per lb.	6 2-5	8

WATER FOR AGRICULTURAL PURPOSES.

Under the provisions of the Water Clauses consolidation Act, 1897, and amending Acts, unrecorded water may be diverted from any natural sources for irrigation or agricultural purposes generally. The scale of fees is the same as for water for industrial purposes, and is calculated on a sliding scale. For a record fee of $10.75 per 100 miner's inches up to $110.75 for 500 inches; $260.75 for 1,000 inches; $560.75 for 2,000 inches; $680.75 for 5,000 inches; $880.75 for 10,000 inches, and so on. For industrial purposes there is an annual fee calculated according to the same sliding scale; but no annual fee is charged on water recorded and actually used for agricultural purposes.

FREE GOODS.

(From Canadian Customs Tariff.)

Wearing apparel, household furniture, books, implements and tools of trade, occupation or employment, musical instruments, domestic sewing machines, live stock, carts and other vehicles and agricultural implements in use by the settler for at least six months before his removal to Canada, not to include machinery or articles imported for any use in any manufacturing establishment or for sale; also books, pictures, family plate or furniture, personal effects and heirlooms left by bequest: Provided that any dutiable article entered as settlers' effects may not be so entered unless brought with the settler on his first arrival, and shall not be sold or otherwise disposed of without payment of duty until twelve months' actual use in Canada: Provided, also, that under regulations to be made by the Controller of Customs, live stock, when imported into Manitoba or the Northwest Territory by intending settlers shall be free until otherwise ordered by the Governor-in-Council.

The following is the authorised number of live stock allowed to be imported under the conditions of the excerpt above quoted: Horses, 1 to every 10 acres, 16 in all allowed; cattle, the same; sheep, 1 to each acre, 160 in all allowed; swine, the same.

LIST OF AGRICULTURAL ASSOCIATIONS, 1902.

Association and Treasurer's Address.	No. of Members.	Cash Receipts.
Chilliwack — C. B. Reeves, Chilliwack	45	$2,270 32
Comox — J. A. Halliday, Sandwick	46	477 44
Cowichan — H. de M. Mellin Duncan	74	678 50
Delta — A. W. R. Taylor, Ladner	42	467 15
Inland — H. L. Roberts, Ashcroft	43	446 60
Islands — Percy Purvis, Salt Spring Island	84	906 65
Kamloops — J. F. Robertson, Kamloops	111	1,312 65
Kent — L. A. Agassiz, Agassiz	89	398 50
Langley — W. J. McIntosh, Langley	80	450 75
Mission — A. M. Verchere, Mission City	34	237 30
Maple Ridge — E. W. Beckett, Port Haney	76	144 00
Nanaimo — E. S. Cook, Nanaimo	36	1,123 50
Okanagan Mission — D. N. Sutherland, Kelowna	149	1,555 25
Okanagan and Spallumcheen — H. F. Wilmot, Vernon	..	1,027 00
Richmond — B. W. Garratt, Eburne	54	644 15
Royal — W. H. Geary, New Westminster	..	......
Saanich (North and South) — T. Turgoose, Turgoose	56	603 95
Salmon Arm — S. M. McGuire, Salmon Arm	..	......
Surrey — H. Bose, Surrey Centre	49	608 40
Victoria — Beaumont Boggs, Victoria	..	......
Vancouver — C. H. Macaulay, Vancouver	130	648 00

DAIRYMEN'S ASSOCIATION.

The Dairymen's Association was established in 1894, and was incorporated the same year by Act of the Legislature. The objects of the Association were to promote and encourage the dairying interests of the province. Its meetings have often been of particular interest, and have without doubt assisted in bringing about the adoption of the creamery system in our province. Assistance has also been rendered to the various exhibitions by prizes, judging in the dairying class, and introducing proper scoring methods.

The three pioneer creameries of the province — the Delta, Cowichan and Eden Bank (Chilliwack) — were established about this time, 1894-95, and have steadily increased their output year by year. There are now twelve, with several more in contemplation at different points in the province. The Dairymen's Association may properly be regarded as a connecting link between the various creameries.

The adoption of the creamery system soon brought about improved methods and a demand for better stock; with the rise in price of all meats, due to various causes, it became evident to the directors of the Association that breeding stock for milk products, and also for beef, mutton and pork, would be required, and that the supply from local breeders would be quite inadequate to the demand. About 1890 the

Ontario Government was organising the export trade in pure-bred stock amongst their breeders, and made arrangements whereby their Department of Agriculture would select, purchase and ship stock to order for individuals or the Provincial Government. After a good deal of correspondence and deliberation the directors, with the consent of the Provincial Government, decided to import one carload of stock and offer the same at auction at the New Westminster Fair in 1900. A mixed carload, containing Shorthorns, Ayrshires and Jerseys, and a few swine, were sold, at a slight loss to the Association. The venture, however, was successful enough to warrant further work in this direction, and the correspondence and inquiry for more fully justified subsequent importations, which have been large and very successful.

The officers of the Association are: President, A. C. Wells, Chilliwack; Vice-President, W. P. Jaynes, Duncan; Secretary, L. W. Paisley.

FLOCKMASTERS' ASSOCIATION.

Among the important agricultural associations is the Flockmaster's Association, which was organized some years ago for the purpose of improving and introducing pure-bred sheep for the use of members. This Association has been instrumental in not only introducing better breeds of sheep, but also of improving methods generally. The usefulness of the Association has been recognised by the Provincial Government, who make an annual grant of $250. Among the features of the Society's work is the annual dinner, which is attended by the leading breeders in the province, and which is looked forward to every year with interest.

The officers for the present year are: President, Major J. M. Mutter; First Vice-President, W. H. Hayward, M. P. P.; Second Vice-President, W. R. Robertson; Secretary, G. H. Hadwen.

FARMERS' INSTITUTES.

Institute and Secretary's Address.	No. of Members.
Alberni—Henry Hills, Alberni	34
Comox—J. A. Halliday, Sandwick	50
Cowichan—H. de M. Mellin, Duncan	127
Nanaimo-Cedar—Rev. G. W. Taylor, Wellington	122
Victoria—C. E. King, Cedar Hill	170
Islands—E. Walter, Ganges Harbour	35
Surrey—H. Bose, Surrey Centre	50
Langley—J. T. Bramwell, Langley	62
Burrard—W. H. Lewis, New Westminster	21
Richmond—James Sexsmith, Eburne	37
Mission—A. M. Verchere, Mission City	40
Chilliwack—G. W. Chadsey, Chilliwack	40
Kent—R. E. McDonald, Agassiz	54
Maple Ridge—J. M. Webster, Webster's Corners	41
Matsqui—John Ball, Abbottsford	31
Spallumcheen—W. P. Horsley, Armstrong	57
Osoyoos—H. V. Chaplin, Kelowna	99
Kamloops—J. F. Smith, Kamloops	40
Okanagan—A. F. Venables, Vernon	137
Bella Coola—A. Hammer, Bella Coola	41
Metchosin—George Trenchard, Metchosin	106
Delta—E. A. Bown, Ladner	27
Total Membership	1,591

OTHER ASSOCIATIONS.

Association and Secretary's Address.	No. of Members.
Dairymen's Association—L. W. Paislay, Chilliwack	32
Vancouver Island Flockmasters' Association—G. H. Hadwen, Duncan	39
Victoria Poultry and Pet Stock Association	..
Vancouver Poultry and Pet Stock Association—J. C. Dixon, Vancouver	60
Nanaimo Poultry and Pet Stock Association	..
British Columbia Fruit Growers' Association	..

VAN ANDA SMELTER.

B. C. GOPPER CO.'S SMELTER, GREENWOOD. B. C.

SUNSET SMELTER, BOUNDARY FALLS, B. C.

LAND RETURNS.

	1870.	1871.	1872.	1873.	1874.	1875.	1876.	1877.	1878.	1879.	1880.	1881.	1882.	1883.	1884	1885.	1886.	1887.	1888.
Pre-emption Records	287	204	223	441	208	198	188	322	245	100	64	85	77	200	308	345	311	307	548
Certificates of Improvement.	67	44	30	69	72	59	42	....	....	58	54	55	29	60	77	82	60	73	157
Certificates of Purchase......	60	84	28	142	196	199	162	261	317	404	234	205	201	328	604	305	369	351	355
Crown Grants...............	100	177	81	32	125	184	128	88	172	211	132	111	129	274	406	306	274	320	322
Total Acreage deeded........	....	....	....	....	....	....	17,984⅓	9,901	31,210	46,815	24,115	23,141	23,609	54,037	146,197	128,811	50,472	73,950	94,278
Acreage leased for timber cutting	....	....	....	....	....	....	....	....	....	....	....	....	....	35,000	1,947	1,380	23,012	16,805	58,566
Acreage covered by Coal Prospecting Licenses	....	....	....	....	....	....	....	....	....	....	....	....	....	....	....	....	....	8,960	90
Letters received............	660	1301	1289	2068	3252	4110	....	....	....	....	....	1,314	1,617	2,463	3,357	3,260	3,185	3,079	3,141

	1889.	1890.	1891.	1892.	1893.	1894.	1895.	1896.	1897.	1898.	1899.	1900.	1901.	1902.
Pre-emption Records	496	616	988	869	832	700	630	486	462	467	616	728	646	655
Certificates of Improvement.	132	169	260	272	173	117	113	141	204	141	113	107	168	143
Certificates of Purchase.....	587	829	863	1,000	261	153	334	694	977	765	418	399	531	655
Crown Grants...............	481	573	685	820	393	159	215	411	766	951	868	1,101	912	1,059
Total Acreage deeded.... ...	134,169	99,331.33	143,455	309,878	124,634	47,166.86	95,456	36,821	609,597	371,394	672,148.12	104,723.91	4,632,831.87	87,906.79
Acreage leased for timber cutting	....	....	....	....	....	....	....	....	....	....	....	....	....	....
Acreage covered by Coal Prospecting Licenses	....	....	....	....	....	....	....	....	....	....	....	....	....	....
Letters received.............	3,326	4,168	5,221	5,321	4,339	4,018	5,079	6,532	8,034	9,126	10,993	12,943	13,306	13,546

LAWS AFFECTING AGRICULTURE.

THAT the Government and Legislature of British Columbia have not failed to carefully guard and assist the interests of agriculture is evident from the fact that there are on the Statute Books of British Columbia forty-two Acts, including amending Acts, dealing with subjects either directly or indirectly connected with farming. These have been passed from time to time, as the development of the agricultural industry has seemed to warrant, and the conditions affecting the agriculturist demanded attention.

AGRICULTURAL DEPARTMENT.

First in the order naturally comes the "Department of Agriculture Act," containing provisions for the regulation of the Department of Agriculture, and for defining the powers and duties of the Minister and other officers of the Department. Principal among its provisions is one for the appointment of a statistician for the collecting, abstracting and tabulating of statistics and information of public interest, a general report to be presented to the House at the end of each year. In this connection it may be stated that all persons engaged in agricultural pursuits of any kind are required to furnish replies to official enquiries, and to give such statistics and information as are in their power in regard to the industry under their particular control. Provision is also made for the interchange between the Federal and Provincial authorities of statistics and information bearing on the subject of agriculture.

AGRICULTURAL ASSOCIATIONS.

There are several statutes making provision for organisation and establishment of agricultural and horticultural and other societies, having for their object the mutual benefit and co-operation of agricultural communities. Associations and societies in respect to the following classes of subjects may be formed, namely: (a) Agricultural and horticultural; (b) benevolent and friendly; (c) co-operative; (d) industrial and provident; and (e) investment and loan. Only the first and third of these associations directly refer to agriculture as an industry, the others being of a general character. In respect to the incorporation of agricultural and horticultural societies, under Chapter 12, Consolidated Statutes, any number of persons may unite themselves into a society for the protection of agricultural, horticultural or fruit-growing industries. The provisions are of such a character as not to be briefly summarised here, but indicate the procedure for the formation of such societies, as to their officers, regulations, property, liabilities and general powers. Part II. of this Act relates to the Horticultural Society and Fruit Growers' Association of British Columbia, which was organised in 1890, and which has been in existence ever since. It has particularly for its object the advancement of the fruit-growing industry. The Act respecting the co-operative associations, passed in 1896, although it does not specifically refer to agriculture, was really intended to afford a cheap and easy method of forming co-operative societies for the purpose of carrying on any branch of agriculture, or business connected with agriculture. Its provisions are largely technical, simply dealing with the methods of procedure and functions of societies formed under its authority.

FARMERS' INSTITUTES.

One of the most important Acts passed by the Legislative Assembly affecting the interests of the farmer was the "Farmers' Institutes and Co-operation Act," enacted in 1897. This was a decided step in advance, and brought our legislation in line with that existing in Ontario, Manitoba and other provinces; and while it contained many of the provisions common to the Acts of Ontario and Manitoba, the measure went still further in the line of progress, and in several respects may be said to be an improvement on its prototypes. Farmers' Institutes, under this Act, may be organised by a petition to the Minister of Agriculture, signed by fifteen persons resident in the district in which it is proposed to organise, and have for their objects the encouragement and improvement of agriculture, horticulture, arboriculture, manufactures, the useful arts, and displays of agricultural products; holding meetings for discussion and hearing lectures; for importing and distributing seeds, plants and animals; for offering prizes for essays and scientific enquiry; for dissemination of information regarding bee-keeping; and for carrying on, by co-operation, any industry relating to agriculture. The annual fee of members is 50 cents, which is supplemented by the Government by an amount based on membership, the grant being made conditional upon all the provisions of the Act being complied with. Provision is also made for the organisation of divisional institutes, and of a Central Farmers' Institute for the whole province, and also for the amalgation with the Central Farmers' Institute of the Fruit Growers' Association or any other existing agricultural association. Authority is taken under the Act by the Lieutenant-Governor-in-Council to frame rules and regulations defining in greater detail the work of the institutes and the system under which they may operate. The officers are a Superintendent, who is appointed and paid by the Provincial Government, and Secretary-Treasurers of the local Institutes, who are paid $25 a year by the Government. It is the duty of the Secretary-Treasurer of each district to prepare a full report of each year's work and forward it to the Provincial Government.

CO-OPERATION.

Under this Act, too, the principle of co-operation is recognised. Upon application to the Minister, ten or more residents and bona fide farmers may engage in and carry on, on a co-operative basis, any of the following, viz.: (a) A Farmers' Exchange, for buying and selling farm produce; (b) a cheese factory; (c) a creamery; (d) a fruit-canning, preserving or evaporating factory; (e) a mutual credit association, for the purpose of receiving deposits and loaning money to its members; (f) or in any other enterprise that may be approved by the Lieutenant-Governor-in-Council as coming among the objects and within the meaning of the Act, and such applicants are constituted provisional directors under the Act for managing the affairs of the Association until the first annual election of officers, and possess all the powers of an incorporated company under the "Companies Act," Part I., the "Companies Act, 1862," (Imperial), to hold property, to sue and be sued, make bylaws, and do all things necessary and purtenant to the carrying on of any business for the mutual benefit and profit of the members subscribing and holding stock: Provided, among other things: (a) That a notice of incorporation containing the names of such applicants be published in the British Columbia Gazette, for which a fee of $10 shall be charged; (b) that no subscriber may hold or hereafter acquire more than one-tenth of the stock allotted by the Association; (c) that 25 per cent. of the capital stock be subscribed at the time of making application.

BOARD OF HORTICULTURE.

One more important feature of legislation is the Act providing for the creation of a Board of Horticulture, which has very comprehensive powers with respect to the inspection of orchards, imported nursery stock and fruits. The Board is composed of three members — one representing the Island of Vancouver, one the Lower Mainland, one the Interior or Upper Country, with the Secretary, who is also the Deputy Minister of Agriculture, and the Minister of Agriculture, acting ex officio.

This Board, which is purely of an official character and under the direct control of the Government, has been in existence since 1894, and has not only a strongly preventive influence in the matter of the spread of pestilential forms of disease and pests, but has exerted an educational influence which is very manifest to-day, and in connection with the farmers' Institutes has done very effective work in the province.

Another important Act, known as the "Agricultural Credit Societies Act," was passed in 1898, whereby a certain number of Farmers, by joining together and pooling their credit, may obtain advances from the Government, with the object of loaning to other members for various purposes of improvement. So far no societies have been formed under the Act, and the rules and regulations authorised thereunder have never been drafted.

RESPECTING DAIRYING.

Provision is made by the "Dairymen's Association Act" for the formation: (a) Of a Provincial Dairymen's Association, for the general advancement of dairying throughout the province; (b) the local Dairymen's Associations, known as Cheese and Butter Associations, for the purpose of carrying on the manufacture of cheese and butter; and (c) the establishment of creameries on the co-operative system, which, when so established, may, on compliance with the Act, obtain Government aid by way of loans to the extent of one-half the cost of creamery buildings, plants and fixtures, such loans to bear interest at the rate of 5 per cent. and be re-payable in eight instalments, the first of such instalments to become due at the expiration of three years from the date of the loan, and the other seven instalments annually thereafter. The Provincial Dairymen's Association is at present doing good work in the importation of thoroughbred stock from the East. By the co-operation of the Government the purchase price of the stock is guaranteed, and the cattle sold locally to purchasers.

By the "Milk Fraud Act" of 1895 provision is made for the "prevention of" adulterated milk and the furnishing of adulterated milk to dairies and creameries.

ANIMALS AND CATTLE ACTS.

The "Animals Act" contains provisions restricting the running at large of certain animals, to prevent injury by dogs, and for the arrest and sale of animals unlawfully at large. It is also enacted that in any action brought to recover damages for injury done by animals of a domestic nature, it shall not be necessary to prove that the owner of the animal knew or had means of knowing that the animal causing the injury was vicious or mischievous, or accustomed to do acts causing injury.

There are a series of Acts dealing with cattle in various ways. The "Cattle Farming Act" makes provision whereby the owners of cattle may entrust them to a farmer for the purpose of securing their care and increase. Under a registered agreement the registered cattle are protected from all claims against and liabilities of the farmer to whom they are entrusted. The "Cattle Lien Act" confers upon agisters of cattle and animals and keepers of livery stables a lien upon cattle and effects left with them, for the value and price of any food, care, attendance, etc. The "Cattle Act" contains elaborate provisions for the protection and marking of cattle, under which registries are established and a mode provided for the registration of brands and marks upon cattle. Penalties are provided for the contravention of the Act; also provision for the mode of transfer of brands and marks, for the inspection of hides, and for a record of cattle and sheep from east of the Cascades into other portions of the province, so as to guard against stealing. Under the "Breeding Stock Act," the "Cattle Ranges Act," and the "Island Pasturage Act" provision is made for the protection and preservation of cattle ranges, and for their being rendered available on an equitable basis for the use of provincial settlers.

PREVENTIVE LEGISLATION.

Under another series of Acts for the regulation of various matters : (a) There is the "Contagious Diseases Act," which provides for the appointment of inspectors for the inspection of cattle and for quarantine, and, whenever necessary, the destruction of cattle infected with disease. The provisions of the Act are especially directed towards the prevention and the eradication of tuberculosis and pleuro-pneumonia, and against the transmission of disease by milk; (b) the " Line Fences and Watercourses Act," which provides for the appointment of fence-viewers, the construction and maintenance of boundary fences and ditches, and the settlement of disputes between owners in regard to such matters; (c) the "Fence Act," in which is contained a definition of a lawful fence, and the trespass of cattle in case of land protected and unprotected by lawful fences; (d) the " Bush Fire Act," establishing fire districts and the regulation of fires in fire districts, by which, except under certain conditions, it shall not be lawful for any person to set fires between the first day of May and the first day of October, and also the equipment of locomotive engines with the most improved and effectual means to prevent the escape of fire from furnaces, ash-heaps and smoke-stacks; (e) an Act for the better regulation of traffic on highways, providing for the passing of vehicles to the left, preservation of roadways west of the Cascade range, by wide tires for loads over 2,000 pounds, and the prevention of certain unlawful practices which impede traffic or render it dangerous; (f) the "Thistle Prevention Act," and the "Noxious Weeds Prevention Act," the objects of which are sufficiently indicated by their titles; and (g) "An Act for the Extermination of Wild Horses," by which it is made lawful for any person to kill unbranded stallions running at large upon the public lands, provided that such person has first obtained a license for killing, and has made unsuccessful efforts and reasonable endeavors to capture such stallion, and reports the facts of killing to the nearest Government Agent.

LAND ACTS.

The Acts relating to settlement and taking up of land are dealt with under the general title of land laws. These include the "Homestead Act," "Land Registry and Amendments," the "Land Clauses Consolidation Act," and the amended "Land Act," and the "Water Clauses Consolidation Act" as amended in 1899 and 1900. The " Land Clauses Consolidation Act " contains complete procedure relative to the acquisition of lands required for undertakings or works of a public nature, and in this respect is allied with the "Water Clauses Consolidation Act," which makes provision for the acquirement and regulation of water rights for a number of purposes, including ordinary domestic and agricultural purposes. The provisions of these Acts are too elaborate to be even briefly summarised here.

DYKING AND DRAINAGE.

In view of the fact that there exist throughout the province large tracts of land which could be rendered available for cultivation by dyking and drainage, careful and extended provision is made for such work in the "Drainage, Dyking and Irrigation Act" for the appointment of commissioners to undertake and carry out such works. By the " Dyking Debenture Loan Act " of 1897 the Government of British Columbia is given authority to authorise the redemption of certain debentures for the construction of dyking works, and to authorise expenditure of additional moneys in strengthening, extending and repairing certain dykes By a further Act in 1898 the powers of the Government in respect to dyking matters were still further extended, whereby they assumed a liability exceeding $500,000 in respect to the dyking works in Maple Ridge, Sumas, Coquitlam, Pitt Meadows and Matsqui, and of borrowing a further sum of $225,000 with respect to further dyking works in Chilliwack, Agassiz, Hatzic, Surrey, and New Westminster District generally. These works are of an important character, and have made fit for cultivation various tracts of land, aggregating about 100,000 acres, otherwise subject to overflow.

PROVINCIAL GOVERNMENT LANDS.

Crown lands in British Columbia are classified as either surveyed or unsurveyed lands, and may be acquired by entry at the Government Lands Office, pre-emption or purchase.

The following persons may pre-empt crown lands: Any person, being the head of a family, a widow, or a single man over eighteen years of age, being a British subject, may record surveyed or unsurveyed crown lands, which are unoccupied or unreserved and unrecorded (that is, unreserved for Indians or others, or unrecorded in the name of any other applicant).

Aliens may also record such surveyed or unsurveyed land on making a declaration of intention to become a British subject.

The quantity of land that may be recorded or pre-empted is not to exceed 320 acres northward and eastward of the Cascade or Coast Mountains, or 160 acres in the rest of the province.

No person can hold more than one pre-emption claim at a time. Prior record of pre-emption of one claim and all rights under it are forfeited by subsequent record or pre-emption of another claim.

Land recorded or pre-empted cannot be transferred or conveyed until after a crown grant has been issued.

Such land, until the crown grant is issued, is held by occupation Such occupation must be a bona fide personal residence of the settler or his family.

The settler must enter into occupation of the land within thirty days after recording, and must continue to occupy it.

Continuous absence for a period longer than two months consecutively of the settler or family is deemed cessation of occupation; but leave of absence may be granted not exceeding six months in any one year, inclusive of two months' absence.

Land is considered abandoned if unoccupied for more than two months consecutively.

If so abandoned, the land becomes waste lands of the Crown.

The fee on recording is two dollars (8s.)

The settler shall have the land surveyed at his own instance (subject to the rectification of the boundaries) within five years from date of record.

After survey has been made, upon proof in declaration in writing of himself and two other persons of occupation for two years from date of pre-emption, and of having made permanent improvement on the land to the value of two dollars and fifty cents per acre, the settler on producing the pre-emption certificate obtains a certificate of improvement upon payment of a fee of $2.

After obtaining the certificate of improvement and paying for the land, the settler is entitled to a Crown grant in fee simple. He pays $5 therefor.

The price of Crown lands, pre-empted is $1 (4 shillings) per acre, which must be paid in four equal instalments, as follows: First instalment two years from date of record or pre-emption, and yearly thereafter, but the last instalment is not payable till after the survey, if the land is unsurveyed.

Two, three or four settlers may enter into partnership with pre-emptions of 160 acres each, and reside on one homestead. Improvements amounting to $2.50 per acre made on some portion thereof will secure Crown grant for the whole, conditions of payment being same as above.

The Crown-grant reserves to the Crown a royalty of five cents per ton on every ton of merchantable coal raised or gotten from the land, not including dross or fine slack, and fifty cents per M. on timber. Coal and petroleum lands do not pass under grant of lands acquired since passage of Land Act Amendment of 1899.

No Crown grant can be issued to an alien who may have recorded or pre-empted by virtue of his declaring his intention to become a British subject, unless he has become naturalised.

The heirs of devisees of the settler are entitled to the Crown grant on his decease.

Crown lands may be purchased to the extent of 640 acres. Minimum price of first-class land, $5 per acre; second-class, $2.50 per acre; third-class, $1 per acre. No settlement duties are required on such land unless a second purchase is contemplated. In such a case, the first purchase must be improved to the extent of $5 per acre for first-class; $2.50 second-class; and $1 third-class.

Leases of Crown lands in lots not exceeding 20 acres may be obtained; and if requisite improvements are made and conditions of the lease fulfilled at the expiration of lease, Crown grants are issued.

Leases are granted for hay lands for terms not exceeding ten years; and for any purpose whatsoever, except cutting hay, for a term not exceeding 21 years.

Twenty-one years' timber leases are now subject to public competition, and the highest cash bonus is accepted, subject to the 50 cents per M. royalty above mentioned, and an annual rental, in advance, of 15 cents per acre. The holder must put up a sawmill capable of cutting not less than 1,000 feet of lumber per day of 12 hours for every 400 acres of land in such lease; and such mill shall be kept running for at least six months in every year.

The farm and buildings, when registered, cannot be taken for debt incurred after registration; and it is free from seizure up to a value not greater than $2,500 (£100 English); cattle "farmed on shares" are also protected by an Exemption Act.

In reference to lands in the Dominion railway belt, the following extract from a letter received from John McKenzie, Esq., agent of Dominion lands at New Westminster, will suffice :

"I may state briefly that since July 11, 1895, the homestead regulations requiring three years' residence and cultivation were in force, being re-introduced from expiry of the old regulations of 1885 on 1st January, 1891.

"Again on 17th April, 1900, the former price of $1 per acre was cut out of the regulations, so that people obtain homesteads in the railway belt in British Columbia on the same terms as Manitoba and the Northwest Territories. And absolute sales may be made at $5 per acre.

"But as patches of timber are mixed up with our lands, we are not to give homesteads on such lands valuable for timber — only that where settlers have a little timber it now goes with the homestead to the settler when he gets a patent."

Under the present law, in the Northwest, homestead duties must be performed in one of the following ways, namely : —

(1) By at least six months' residence upon and cultivation of the land in each year during the term of three years.

(2) If the father (or the mother, if the father is deceased) of any person who is eligible to make a homestead entry resides upon a farm in the vicinity of the land entered for by such person as a homestead, the requirements of the law as to residence prior to obtaining patent may be satisfied by such person residing with the father or mother.

(3) If a settler has obtained a patent for his first homestead, or a certificate for the issue of such patent, countersigned in the manner prescribed by the Dominion Lands Act, and has obtained entry for a second homestead, the requirements of this Act as to residence prior to obtaining patent may be satisfied by residence upon the first homestead.

(4) If the settler has his permanent residence upon farming land owned by him in the vicinity of his homestead, the requirements of the law as to residence may be satisfied by residence upon the said land.

Application for patent should be made at the end of the three years, before the Local Agent, Sub-Agent or the Homestead Inspector. Before making application for patent the settler must give six months' notice in writing to the Commissioner of Dominion Lands at Ottawa of his intention to do so.

CANADIAN PACIFIC RAILWAY LANDS.

The Canadian Pacific Railway Company controls a large area of farming and ranching lands in the Kootenay and Boundary districts. The prices range from $1 (4 shillings) an acre to $5 (20 shillings) an acre, the latter being for first-class agricultural lands. These lands are now readily accessible by the Crow's Nest Pass Railway and the Columbia & Western Railway.

The Company has adopted the following terms of payment: The aggregate amount of principal and interest is divided into instalments, the first to be paid at the time of purchase, the remainder annually thereafter. If the land is paid for in full at time of purchase, a reduction from price will be allowed equal to 10 per cent. on the amount paid in excess of the usual cash instalment. Special terms and conditions govern the sale of the Company's timber lands.

Maps showing the Company's lands can be secured on application to F. T. Griffin, C. P. R. Land Commissioner, Winnipeg, Man.; J. S. Dennis, Superintendent of Irrigation and British Columbia Land Commissioner, Calgary; or to A. Taylor, District Land Agent, Nelson.

DOMINION GOVERNMENT LANDS.

All the lands in British Columbia within twenty miles on each side of the Canadian Pacific Railway main line are the property of Canada, with all the timber and minerals they contain (except precious metals). This tract of land, with its timber, hay, water-powers, coal and stone, is now administered by the Department of the Interior of Canada, practically according to the same laws and regulations as are the public lands in Manitoba and the Northwest Territories. Government agencies are established at Kamloops, in the mountains, and New Westminster, on the coast.

NATURAL HISTORY SOC'Y OF BRITISH COLUMBIA.

THE Natural History Society of British Columbia, Victoria, was founded in 1890, when a few enthusiastic naturalists and sympathisers met in the old Provincial Museum and decided to form a society which would investigate the rich local fields, collect data of a local scientific interest, and incidentally act as an adjunct to the Provincial Museum, which had then just been recently established. It existed for several years, experiencing the usual vicissitudes of a society of that nature. It was not, however, until the new Government Buildings were erected and occupied that the Society got fairly on its legs, and it has ever since enjoyed an increasing degree of prosperity, until at the present time it has over 100 members in good standing.

Since its organisation the Society has done good service in adding to the treasures of the Provincial Museum, and this work has been adequately recognised by the Government, who have taken it in a measure under their wing, and have provided the Society with commodious rooms in the new buildings, where meetings are held once every two weeks.

For some time certain members of the Society had interested themselves in local historical research and ethnological investigation. An historical branch or section of the Society, which devotes itself exclusively to local historical research, has been organised. There are also botanical and photographic sections. A fine microscope has been recently purchased. The officers for 1903 are: President, Dr. Hasell; Secretary, R. E. Gosnell; Librarian and Curator, F. Sylvester.

TWO VIEWS OF SOCIAL LIFE IN ATLIN.

VIEWS IN ATLIN IN 1901.

ATLIN GOLD DIGGINGS AND THEIR PRODUCTS.

ATLIN VIEWS.

MINING IN BRITISH COLUMBIA.

THE history of mining in British Columbia, particularly that of recent years, affords a striking instance of industrial evolution. Although coal was discovered on Vancouver Island as far back as 1835, and the first gold discoveries were made in 1851, metalliferous lode mining, which has now come to be regarded as the most important industry of the country, was not seriously engaged in until 1891, when the rich quartz discoveries in the Nelson, Slocan and Rossland districts began to attract the attention of capital. The initial developments of these new fields were carried on under almost incredible difficulties; for the regions in which the discoveries were made were mountainous, heavily timbered and inaccessible. The first mines to become productive were those of the Slocan, the circumstance being attributable to the exceptionally high-grade quality of the galena ores found in that district, which enabled, in many instances, the original discoverers to profitably work the properties without the assistance of capital. Thus, before railways were constructed through this district, a relatively large quantity of ore was mined and "packed" out on horseback a distance of 17 miles, through thick forests, to a point on Kootenay Lake, at a cost of from $40 to $45 per ton. It was then forwarded by boat and rail to smelters in the United States at a further cost of $20 a ton. Add to this the cost of mining and treatment, and it will be admitted that only remarkably high-grade ore could stand so heavy a tax and yet admit of profitable extraction. With the completion in 1894-95 of railways — the construction of which was not unattended with engineering difficulties, having regard to the high altitude and mountainous character of the country generally—an era of active mining development on a much more extensive scale was inaugurated each year thereafter until 1898, showing an increase of output of considerably more than 100 per cent. But in 1900 and 1901 conditions were less favorable. In the former year differences occurred between capital and labour, which seriously restricted operations during that season, while in 1901 the American market was practically closed to the British Columbia product, and although, notwithstanding this, the output in point of tonnage was very nearly equal to the record of 1897, the depreciation in metal prices rendered, however, a comparison of values less satisfactory. Meanwhile, a result of the action of the American Smelting and Refining Trust in refusing to bid for British Columbia lead ores, has been the stimulation of the local smelting and refining industry, and this year, for the first time in Canada, pig lead has been produced in a refinery erected at Trail and operated in connection with the Canadian Smelting Works at that place.

CHARACTERISTICS OF SLOCAN.

One of the best accounts yet published of the silver-lead deposits of the Slocan was contained in a paper read not long since before the Institute of Mining and

Metallurgy by a well-known engineer, Mr. J. D. Kendall, from which the following extracts are taken :

"The Slocan Mining District is in West Kootenay, on the eastern side of Slocan Lake. It is about 12 miles across in an east and west direction, and about 18 miles long from north to south. Part of it on the east is really in the Ainsworth Mining Division, but there is no natural line separating the Ainsworth from the Slocan Mining Division. It is merely an arbitrary line for record purposes. The entire area is mountainous, ranging in altitude from about 1,800 to about 7,500 feet. The mountains are not only high, but steep. Usually they are very uniform in outline, a result of the slight variation in the hardness of the rock out of which they have been formed, over a great part of the area.

"The solid geology is relatively simple, the greater part of the area being occupied by dark argillites or clay slates, occasionally interbedded with calcareous quartzite and dark-coloured limestone. Traversing these rocks are numerous igneous dykes and intrusive sheets, some of great thickness. Many of them are closely associated with the ore deposits, as will be seen hereafter. A number of these igneous intrusions may be seen in the neighbourhood of Three Forks, along the line of the Canadian Pacific Railway.

"The aqueous rocks are known to geologists as the Slocan slates. They seem to occupy about the same geologic horizon as the upper part of Adam's Lake series, which has been provisionally classed by the Dominion Geological Survey as Silurian or Cambro-silurian. The beds are, as a rule, highly tilted and severely faulted. Most of the faults are ordinary, but some are reversed."

The first railway built into the Slocan was the Nakusp and Slocan, commenced July, 1893, and opened for traffic as far as Three Forks (32.9 miles) in 1894. This was followed, in 1895, by the Kaslo and Slocan (31.8 miles long). In the same year the Nakusp and Slocan was extended from Three Forks to Sandon, a distance of about four miles. These lines placed the Slocan in communication with the Canadian Pacific, Northern Pacific and Great Northern railway systems, and reduced the cost of transportation $20 per ton.

COMMUNICATION WITH THE MINES.

The mines are connected with one or other of the railway systems serving the district, by either rawhide trails, waggon roads, aerial or other tramways. Rawhiding is extensively practised in the Slocan, the conditions being highly favourable for it, the steep mountain sides and the thick mantle of snow with which the ground is covered throughout the long winter making it possible to form a trail for use in this way, at a cost little exceeding that necessary to remove the underbrush and the few large trees that cannot be avoided along the selected route. In rawhiding, the ore is first sacked, each sack containing 100 to 150 lbs. of ore, according to the tenor reached in dressing, then wrapped in raw cowhides, 15 sacks being an ordinary load, and drawn by horses over the snow. A horse takes only one hide at a time, but one driver may be in charge of any number of horses up to four, the number depending upon the character of the trail. This system of haulage can only be followed in winter when a good covering of snow is on the ground. In some cases waggon roads are built to the mines. Then the haulage is done by sleighs in winter, and by four-wheeled waggons in summer, the load (depending mainly upon the grade) ranging from four to eight tons. These roads cannot be used for about four or five weeks in the spring, when the snow is melting, because part of them are then only fit for runners and part for wheels. As the melting snow disappears at the foot of the hills, runners are impossible, and wheels cannot be used until the snow has gone entirely from the higher ends of the roads. The usual time that elapses after the ground is bare in the lower valleys until the snow disappears at an altitude of about 6,000 feet, is four or five weeks, and during this time haulage by this system has to be suspended to the higher mines. Some of the mines are provided with rail, others with rope, tramways — in all cases self-acting. Both these forms of tramway, if properly arranged, are capable of continuous working throughout the year, and are, therefore, superior to either rawhiding, waggon or sleigh haulage, where the output is large enough to justify the extra cost of making them. The longest waggon road yet made is about eight miles, the longest tramway about one and a quarter miles. Most of the deposits hitherto worked are at considerable altitudes, for the simple reason that the rocks are more exposed there than at lower levels, and consequently the prospector has been more successful. The following table shows, approximately, the level at which some of the more important mines occur, disregarding the range of altitude in the several properties :

Mine.	Feet above the sea.
Payne	7,100
Idaho	6,700
Alamo	6,700
Reco	6,200
Whitewater	5,000
Slocan Star	5,000
Ruth	4,700

Nearly all the deposits known in the Slocan, and certainly those of greatest importance commercially, have the form of veins often called, here and elsewhere, "fissure veins," or "true veins," but a few are bed-like in form — that is, occur along the bed-planes of the strata.

In the early days, i. e., in 1892, when the ore had to be "packed" out to the lakes, only the best ore in a mine could stand the cost of shipping, so that then the ore had to be sorted most carefully. This will be illustrated by a few figures relating to the output of the Dardanelles mine, one of the first shippers. Three hundred and fourteen tons of ore shipped from that mine in two years ending December, 1895, gave 23.7 per cent. lead and 260.9 oz. of silver per ton; but the first 10 tons, packed out during the fall of 1892, yielded 55.6 per cent. of lead and 470.2 oz. of silver per ton.

CHARACTER OF SLOCAN ORE.

In most of the Slocan mines some very high-grade ore can be found, if only small samples be taken; but that, it need scarcely be said here, is not the way to judge of the product of a mine. The yield of large quantities shipped in the ordinary course of business is the only reliable guide. The following assay results are averages derived from smelter returns relating to the quantities standing opposite the names of the different mines named in the table :

Name of Mine.	Shipments, tons.	Silver, oz. per ton.	Lead, per ct.	Zinc, oz.	Silver-lead, lbs.
Payne	11,675	112	56	n.d.	1—10
Whitewater	5,610	113	33	18.8	1— 5.8
Ruth (galena)	1,010	105	65	n.d.	1—12.5
" (carbonates)	957	48	25	n.d.	1—10.4
Idaho	1,531	152.6	46.5	14.5	1— 6
Alamo	4,782	129	44	16.9	1— 6.8
Slocan Star	10,012	80	67	n.d.	1—16.7
Enterprise	1,054	177	22	21	1— 2.4
Reco	1,690	239	39	n.d.	1— 3.2
Washington	1,600	95	56	12.7	1—11.7
Dardanelles	255	265	26	12.5	1— 1.9
†Monitor	427	179	38	15	1— 4.24
Antoine	230	246	46	n.d.	1— 3.7
Cumberland	263	78 9	58.4	12.8	1—14.8

N. D.—Not determined.

†Also contained gold 0.35 oz. per ton.

This table shows better than many words the highly argentiferous character of the Slocan ores. It includes probably the highest and the lowest grade yet found. When we compare these results with those obtained from the ores of other important silver-lead areas, the greater richness of the Slocan ores is at once evident. A considerable part of the silver found in these ores is in the galena, which occurs in three principal forms — cubic, wavy and granular (coarse and fine). From a number of assays of ores of different mines, made with the object of learning in which of these forms the silver was most abundant, the following results were obtained :

	Silver, oz. per ton.	
Wavy..........................	165.1	...... average of 11 assays.
Cubic..........................	117.4	..... " 16 "
Granular (fine)	109.8	...... " 7 "

The facilities for mining in the Slocan are great — a good climate, abundance of timber, the contour of the ground such that the deposits can be reached and worked by tunnels without the necessity for shafts and their accompanying costly machinery, a moderately hard country rock, and abundance of surface water for dressing purposes, in addition to numerous fine veins of high-grade mineral, forming a combination of circumstances that could not easily be excelled in any part of the world.

When the ore reaches the surface it is concentrated either by hand or by means of machinery. The hand-sorted ore is usually referred to in the smelter returns as "crude ore," that which has been machine-sorted as "concentrates." The machinery employed in dressing is of the usual kind. There is often considerable loss of silver with the tailings, which is avoidable, and can only be saved by treatment in other ways. So long as the silver-bearing minerals thrown off from a mill have a value less than the cost of freight and treatment, etc., they are recovered by other methods and in a concentrated form that can be shipped at a profit.

OTHER SILVER-LEAD DISTRICTS.

Other localities in which silver-lead ores are mined are the Ainsworth and Trout Lake districts and sections of East Kootenay.

In the Ainsworth district the ores are of somewhat lower grade than those found in the vicinity of Sandon, and consequently the mines have been less considerably developed. The exposures are, however, in many instances remarkably large, and under favourable conditions will undoubtedly be made to yield profitably. It is only this summer (1902) that railway transportation facilities have been afforded mine-owners in the Trout Lake districts, but this, notwithstanding the mines from that section of the province have during the past three years produced a relatively large quantity of silver-lead ores of exceptionally high-grade character, the average value per ton of ore shipped from one mine being $18 in gold, 400 oz. silver, and 50 per cent. lead. Now that improved means for transporting the mine products have been secured, this district will unquestionably become in future a very important contributor to the annual silver-lead output of British Columbia. The developed silver-lead mines in East Kootenay are limited to three or four; but these are operated on a very extensive scale, and have distributed among their shareholders larger profits than the silver-lead mines in other sections of the country.

THE ROSSLAND ORES.

Although a small shipment of copper ore was made from the Hall Mines at Nelson in 1888-89, and from Rossland in 1891, production of this metal on any considerable scale did not commence until 1893, when consignments aggregating 700 tons were sent to American smelters from the Rossland mines. It is interesting to note in connection with this first shipment from Rossland that the exceptionally high smelter returns of $84 per ton, or 3 oz. silver, 5.21 per cent. copper, and about 4 oz. of gold, practically established that camp. The consignment, packed over 12 miles of rough trail to the Columbia River, was sent from the Le Roi mine by a small syndicate of Spokane (Washington) speculators, to whom the property was under bond, and who subsequently made a very large fortune as a result of their investment. Until the spring of 1895, however, the progress of mining in this district was comparatively slow, and it is said that no less than 42 "experts" had, in the interim, condemned the camp as worthless. In 1895, on the strength of a contract from the Le Roi Company to supply 75,000 tons of ore (on one-half of which a fixed charge of $11 a ton for freight and treatment was arranged), a land grant from the Provincial Government and a bonus from the Dominion Government of $1 on each ton of ore smelted, a smelter was erected on the Columbia River at Trail, and a narrow-gauge railway built between the mine and the works. As the crow flies, this distance is only four or five miles, but to overcome the difference in elevation of about 2,100 feet between Trail and Rossland, the switchback arrangement was employed, thus lengthening the line to over 11 miles. After the erection of the smelter, the cost of freight and treatment for nearly two years remained unchanged at $10 to $14 per ton, 95 per cent. of the assay value of the gold and silver being paid for and a deduction made of 1.3 from the percentage of copper present, to allow for the difference between wet and dry assay value; the price paid for copper being 5 cents below the New York market quotations. With the completion of their contract with the Trail smelter, the owners of the Le Roi mine erected works of their own immediately across the boundary at Northport (Washington), and succeeded in reducing their smelter costs to some extent. But with the acquisition of the Trail smelter by the Canadian Pacific Railway Company, freight and treatment charges were immediately cut down to $7 per ton. The chief cause of this reduction in costs was the great cheapening of fuel following the development of the Crow's Nest Pass coal fields. This year (1902) the Trail smelter has made still further reductions in treatment charges, while Le Roi ores are hauled to and treated at Northport at a total cost of under $5 a ton. This cost, however, is capable of considerable reduction, as with the completion recently of the new branch of the Great Northern Railway, connecting that system with the Fernie collieries, great economies will be effected in the price of coke as supplied to the Northport works. The mineral-bearing veins in the Rossland district are characteristic fissure veins, and some of the larger are known as "shear zone" fissures. Instead of being an indefinite amount of parallel fissures extending into the country an undiscoverable distance, it is always a zone of a discoverable and limited collection. The mineral deposit may lie on one plane, or they may eat up the rock between the planes and deposit another in its place, or they may occupy the whole zone, or mineralise one particular fissure and travel on that, and so on. The exterior boundary is assignable if you crosscut. These veins are of enormous extent in some places, such as 100 or 200 feet in width in the shattered mineralised zone.

The ores consist principally of sulphides of various metals. Of these pyrrhotite is by far the most abundant. It is found, as a rule, in a massive condition, ranging in texture from a fine to medium grain, but is also disseminated through the country rock. The massive variety usually holds blebs of quartz, and grains and irregular patches of other sulphides. The pyrrhotite contains gold and silver in varying quantities, a small percentage of nickel, and traces of cobalt. The gold contents are exceedingly irregular, ranging from traces up to several ounces to the ton, and the silver from traces to four or five ounces to the ton.

The pyrrhotite is usually accompanied by a certain amount of copper pyrites, intimately commingled with it. The copper pyrites is extremely irregular in its distribution, in some places constituting a considerable portion of the ore body, and in others occurring only as isolated and occasional grains and patches. It is nowhere seen in large masses. It is auriferous, and holds apparently about the same percentage of gold as the enclosing pyrrhotite.

The mines have been developed by running inclines along the dip of the vein, and from these inclines driving horizontal drifts at 100 feet intervals along the strike and usually within the walls of the vein. These drifts are afterwards enlarged, sill floors put in, timbered, and the ore in this way worked out to the next higher level.

From the reports issued by the several important mining companies operating in this territory it is gathered that the total cost of mining per ton of ore stoped is between $4 and $4.50, or a total cost for mining, smelting and marketing the ore from $10 to $11 per ton. Lately these costs, it is stated, have been reduced by about $2 per ton.

THE BOUNDARY ORES.

Another, and what is now the most important, copper-producing area in British Columbia is that known as the Boundary district. The first discoveries were made here so long ago as 1891, but the low-grade nature of the ores, their refractory character, and the extreme inaccessibility of the district effectually prohibited productive effort until nearly ten years later, when conditions were entirely changed by the completed construction of the Columbia and Western Railway from Robson to Midway. Thus while between 1891 and 1900 ore shipments from the district aggregated but slightly over 4,000 tons, the tonnage during the second half of the last-mentioned year was increased to 97,837 tons, and in 1901 the shipments were 386,675. From the figures obtainable showing production during the first six months of the present year (1902), it appears reasonably certain that the output from the Boundary district for the full twelve months will considerably exceed half a million tons of ore. The rapid manner in which these developments has taken place is partly attributable to the business-like and aggressive methods adopted by the principal mine operators in the field, and partly to the natural facilities and advantages for economic mining and reduction of ores, due to the immense size and extent of the deposits themselves and to the self-fluxing character of their mineral contents. In discussing the ore deposits of the Boundary District, Mr. R. W. Brock, of the Canadian Geological Survey, for the sake of convenience, roughly divides them into three classes — (1) the large low-grade copper-bearing sulphide deposits; (2) the oxidized copper veins; and (3) the small gold and silver-bearing quartz veins.

Undoubtedly the most striking characteristic of the deposits of the first class is their enormous size. In structure these deposits belong to the composite-vein type, formed by mineralizing solutions traversing the country rock, principally along fissures or zones of fissures in which they deposit the economic minerals, and from which they replace with their mineral contents, particle by particle, sometimes only partially, sometimes completely, the original material of the country rock. According to the most prominent mineral content, this class of deposits may be subdivided into a pyritic type, in which pyrrhotite, chalcopyrite, with some pyrite, are the chief minerals. Excepting that the pyrrhotite of the ore is represented by magnetite and the pyrrhotite replaces the constituents of the country rock in the same way, both seemed to have been formed, on the whole, a little prior to the other vein minerals, holding them in little veins, or as points scattered through, yet sometimes interbanded with them; they are both accompanied by the same accessory and gangue minerals, and the country rocks show the same alterations in both cases. Rarely do both the pyrrhotite and magnetite occur in the same deposit. Besides the metallic minerals already mentioned, some marcasite appears to occasionally be present, and sometimes arsenopyrite, galena, zinc-blende and molybdenite; but these are in all cases subordinate in quantity. Tetrahedrite has been found on the City of Paris. Specular iron is found somewhat sparingly, and bismuthinite occurs on one claim.

Porphyry dikes are usually to be found in close proximity to the ores; the ore lies parallel to the dike along its contact or in the immediate neighbourhood. The dikes, while containing traces of metallic minerals, show no signs of mineralisation. In age they are about the same or a little younger than the ore deposits, showing the deposits to have been formed during or before the close of the cooling of the eruptive magmas. While the deposition of the mineral contents of the veins is evidently largely hydrothermal, many of the minerals formed are characteristic of contact zones, and there seem to be strong reasons for supposing the deposits to be connected with eruptive after-actions. The values in the ores are principally in copper and gold, sometimes with accessory silver.

A striking feature in the deposits is the lack of surface oxidation or alteration. At most, a few feet below the surface of the ground, the ore exhibits the same characters as are found in depth. In Copper Camp oxidised copper-bearing veins occur, forming at first sight a totally different type of deposit. One deposit is found at a contact between a dike of porphyry and crystalline limestone. In the limestone, and to a less extent in the fractures in the porphyry, along the contact, are deposited various oxidation minerals of iron and copper, including native copper. The main fissures are filled with the iron and copper minerals, the smaller principally with the copper. In the porphyry it is only the fractures near the contact which contain a thin film of copper ore, the rock itself remaining fresh and unaltered, so that this type of deposits is probably an oxidized and secondarily enriched form of a sulphide deposit similar to the first type of Boundary deposits, and produced by the action of surface waters. The iron of the sulphides has been removed or re-deposited as hematite and limonite; the copper has been more or less concentrated in the form of various oxidised minerals. At greater depth the unaltered iron and copper sulphides will presumably be found, although between the oxidised minerals and the unaltered sulphides it is quite possible that a zone of enriched sulphides will be found. The quartz veins constituting the third type of deposit are found in the neighborhood of the first type, but seem more abundant on the outskirts of areas of chief mineralisation. They are sometimes parallel to the large sulphide bodies, but do not as a rule show the same regularity in their strike. In form they are more regular, and they are usually enclosed between well-defined walls. Chalcopyrite, pyrite, arsenopyrite, galena and zinc-blende are the chief metallic minerals. Tetrahedrite and some rich silver minerals are said to have been found in some of these veins. The principal values are in silver and gold.

Up to the present time the ores principally mined come under the head of Mr. Brock's first classification. As has already been stated, these ores are of low-grade character, the average constituents being as follows: Silica, 38 per cent.; oxide of iron, 16 per cent.; lime, 15 per cent.; sulphur, 4½ per cent.; copper, 1.60 to 1.80 per cent.; gold, $1.50 to $2.40; and silver, 25 cents to 50 cents. The ore now available, and of which there are several millions of tons in sight, may be conservatively estimated to contain from 25 to 35 pounds of copper per ton of 2,000 pounds, with from 25 cents to 40 cents of silver per ton, and from $1.50 to $2.50 per ton in gold, or total values of $4.75 to $7.05 per ton, considering copper as being worth 12 cents per pound. Only under the most favourable circumstances could ores of so low a value be profitably mined, but it has now been demonstrated beyond doubt that in the Boundary district the undertaking is a feasible one. The cost of mining the large deposits has varied from $1.66 to $2.10 per ton, the first-mentioned figure being the recent, while the methods introduced this year of quarrying on and handling it with steam shovels, and also by the introduction of the caving system for the lower workings, it is altogether likely that these costs will be still further considerably reduced. But if the cost of mining, having regard to the high wages paid miners, is low, the subsequent smelter treatment is still more economically conducted.

The Boundary ore being self-fluxing, indeed rather basic in character, allows the admixture of a certain quantity of silicious ores from the Republic camp or other districts, whose ores carry gold and silver; and the sulphur being low, permits of smelting without preliminary roasting. With the advent of railways from the south, the Boundary smelters can procure more dry silicious ores at profitable rates. It may also be stated at this point that the freedom of the ores from bismuth, arsenic and antimony renders it easy to obtain a ready market for the copper product.

In considering the cost of smelting, it is also necessary to take into account the losses in slag and otherwise. Before the establishment of bessemerising, the slag loss of the Boundary smelters averaged: Copper, 0.46 per cent.; gold, 12 cents per ton; and silver, 3 cents per ton. With a consumption of about 11 per cent. of coke, and with freight charges as they exist to-day, the cost of smelting at the most favourable location in the Boundary District, after charging against the smelter the cost of marketing the product, is rather under $2 per ton; and adding the present cost of mining, the total outlay for mining and smelting is less than $3 per ton. But this year the actual cost of smelting has been reduced to the extraordinary low figure of under $1.50 per ton, while mining by the quarrying system is carried on at a cost of between 30 cents and 60 cents per ton at the larger mines.

COPPER CAMPS OF VANCOUVER ISLAND.

Copper ore has also been mined in the Nelson district, but production from this section has of late fallen off considerably. Vancouver Island and the adjacent islands and Mainland coast territory is, however, rapidly coming into great prominence as a centre of copper-gold mining activity, Texada Island and the Mount Sicker district of Vancouver Island being at present the chief productive fields. The mines in the last-mentioned district have now been sufficiently developed to warrant the erection, one at Crofton and the other at Ladysmith, of two smelting works. At the Crofton smelter the ore bins have a capacity of 1,600 tons, and a trestle railway has been laid over the top of these, for convenience in unloading the ore cars. From the bins the ore goes to the crusher and sampling buildings and is thence discharged into the furnace ore bins, from which it is taken to the furnace on hand-cars. The plant consists briefly of: Three 200 h. p. boilers, one 500 h. p. Corliss engine, one 450-ton water-jacketed furnace, one 65-ton water-jacketed furnace, one Bessemer converter. The main flue is 200 feet long and 12 feet wide, communicating with a large expansion chamber where the dust settles, and from which the gases enter the brick smokestack, 12 feet in diameter and 125 feet high. The initial capacity of the smelter is between 400 and 500 tons per day, but the plant is built with a view to allow of the treatment of 1,250 tons per day. A wharf has been built, extending 750 feet into the bay. At the Tyee Copper Company's smelter at Ladysmith, on Oyster Harbour, smelting operations were commenced towards the end of December. The works were built to treat the ore from the Tyee mine and other properties. The plant consists, briefly, of a 150-ton water-jacketed furnace, a complete sampling plant, the bins having a storage capacity of 1,600 tons, an 80 h. p. Corliss engine and an 80 h. p. tubular boiler. The smelting shed is 80 by 60 feet, and the engine room 50 by 70 feet, with ample space for further extension. The ore from the sampler goes direct to the roast piles and, after burning, to the bins at the rear of the smelter. The slag is shotted with water and flumed into the lagoon. Grading has been done for considerable extension. The converter plant will not be installed at present, but arrangements are such that this may be done at any time. In the Mount Sicker district there is a belt of quartzose schists having an average strike of N. 60 degrees E., tilted up at an angle of 80 degrees and dipping S. E. The ore occurs as bedded lenticular veins, and occupying fissures and bulges in them. Therefore the strike and dip of the ore bodies and country correspond. The lode matter consists of a quartz gangue, usually dark-blue in colour, carrying chalcopyrite (copper pyrites), and ordinary iron pyrites (FeS) with some value in gold. They are thoroughly typical copper ores of their class, and not likely to present any difficulties in treatment by ordinary methods.

THE COKE WORKS AT COMOX.

THE HALL SMELTER AT NELSON.

TYEE SMELTER, LADYSMITH, B. C.

NORTHWESTERN SMELTING & REFINING CO., CROFTON, V. I. B. C.

As will be seen from the tables published elsewhere, the lode mines of the province produced in 1901 gold to the value of $4,348,603. Approximately this gold was divided as follows :

Direct smelting of copper-gold ores	$3,474,738
Combined amalgamation and concentration	873,865
	$4,348,603

It may be said that no absolutely "free-milling" gold property is working in the province; they all carry sufficient values in sulphides to necessitate the saving of such.

In addition to gold, silver, copper and gold mining, operations are being conducted in several sections of the province having to do with the development of iron, platinum, cinnabar, asbestos and other mineral deposits. Thus on the West Coast of Vancouver Island, on Texada Island, at Kitchener (near Nelson), and at Bull River (in East Kootenay), the large surface exposures of valuable iron ores, both hematite and magnetite, have of late been developed with most gratifying results, having regard to a future establishment of the iron and steel industries in Western Canada. It may, in fact, be said in conclusion that the prospects of metalliferous mining in British Columbia were never brighter than they are to-day. The industry is at length firmly established on a firm and business-like footing; production is steadily and in some instances rapidly increasing; the management of the mines and allied undertakings is generally in competent hands, and modern methods of economical operation have in consequence been applied and adopted; the relationship between capital and labour is harmonious throughout the country, and questions of common dispute, such as wages or hours of work, having already been made issues and settled on terms acceptable to both employers and employees, there is little likelihood of further friction in this direction.

Another pleasing feature of the situation is the practical cessation of "wild-catting," while on the other hand capital in a considerable degree is being invested, chiefly by Americans, in legitimate mining undertakings in this field.

The following tables show the progress of the lode mining industry in British Columbia, from its inception in 1887 to 1901. The information as to production in the earlier years is obtained from the "Mineral Statistics and Mines" for 1886, Geological Survey of Canada :

STATISTICS OF LODE MINING.

Year	Gold.		Silver.		Lead.		Copper.		Total Values.
	Oz.	Value.	Oz.	Value.	Pounds.	Value.	Pounds.	Value.	
		$		$		$		$	$
1887 ..	......	....	17,690	17,331	204,800	9,216	....	....	26,547
1888 ..	......	....	79,780	75,000	674,500	29,813	....	....	104,813
1889 ..	......	....	53,192	47,873	165,100	6,498	....	....	54,371
1890 ..	......	....	70,427	73,948	*Nil.*	*Nil.*	....	....	73,948
1891 ..	......	....	4,500	4,000	*Nil.*	*Nil.*	....	....	4,000
1892 ..	......	....	77,160	66,935	808,420	33,064	....	....	99,999
1893 ..	1,170	23,404	227,000	195,000	2,135,023	78,996	....	....	297,400
1894 ..	6,252	125,014	746,379	470,219	5,662,523	169,875	324,680	16,234	781,342
1895 ..	39,264	785,271	1,496,522	977,229	16,475,464	532,255	952,840	47,642	2,342,397
1896 ..	62,259	1,244,180	3,135,343	2,100,689	24,199,977	721,384	3,818,556	190,926	4,257,179
1897 ..	106,141	2,122,820	5,472,971	3,272,836	38,841,135	1,390,517	5,325,180	266,258	7,052,431
1898 ..	110,061	2,201,217	4,292,401	2,375,841	31,693,559	1,077,581	7,271,678	874,781	6,529,420
1899 ..	138,315	2,857,573	2,939,413	1,663,708	21,862,436	878,870	7,722,591	1,351,453	6,751,604
1900 ..	167,153	3,453,381	4,958,175	2,309,200	63,358,621	2,691,887	9,997,080	1,615,289	10,069,757
1901 ..	210,384	4,348,603	5,151,333	2,884,745	51,582,906	2,002,733	27,603,746	4,446,963	13,683,044
Total	840,990	$17,161,463	27,722,286	$16,534,554	257,664,464	$9,062,689	63,016,351	$8,886,527	$52,128,252

TOTAL METALLIFEROUS PRODUCTION FOR ALL YEARS UP TO AND INCLUDING 1901.

Gold (placer)	$ 63,554,543
Gold (lode)	17,161,463
Silver	16,534,554
Lead	9,622,689
Copper	8,809,546
Coal and coke	54,157,315
Building stone, bricks, etc.	2,350,000
Other metals	51,878
Total	$172,241,988

PRODUCTION FOR EACH YEAR FROM 1890 TO 1901 (INCLUSIVE).

1852 to 1889 (inclusive)	$ 71,981,634
1890	2,608,803
1891	3,521,102
1892	2,978,530
1893	3,588,413
1894	4,225,717
1895	5,643,042
1896	7,507,956
1897	10,455,268
1898	10,906,861
1899	12,393,131
1900	16,344,751
1901	20,086,780
Total	$172,241,988

The following comparative table states in detail the amount and value of the different mineral products for the years 1899, 1900 and 1901. As it has been impossible as yet to collect accurate statistics regarding building stone, lime, bricks, tiles, etc., these are estimated :

A TABLE BY PRODUCTS.

	Customary Measure.	1899.		1900.		1901.	
		Quantity	Value.	Quantity	Value.	Quantity	Value.
Gold, placer	Ounces	67,245	$ 1,344,900	63,936	$ 1,278,724	48,505	$ 970,100
" lode	"	138,315	2,857,573	167,153	3,453,381	210,384	4,348,603
Silver	"	2,939,413	1,663,708	3,958,175	2,309,200	5,151,333	2,884,745
Copper	Pounds	7,722,591	1,351,453	9,997,080	1,615,289	27,603,746	4,446,963
Lead	"	21,862,436	878,870	63,358,621	2,691,887	51,582,906	2,002,733
Coal	Tons, 2,240 lbs.	1,306,324	3,918,972	1,439,595	4,318,785	1,460,331	4,380,993
Coke	" "	34,251	171,252	85,149	425,745	127,081	635,405
Other materials	....	....	206,400	....	251,740	....	417,832
			$12,393,131		$16,344,751		$20,086,780

PLACER MINING.

The following table shows the yearly production of placer gold to date, as determined by the returns, sent in by the banks and express companies, of gold transmitted by them to the mints, and from returns sent in by the Gold Commissioners and Mining Recorders. To these yearly amounts one-third was added up to the year 1878; from then to 1895 and for 1897 and 1899, one-fifth; which proportions are considered to represent, approximately, the amount of gold sold of which there is no record. This placer gold contains from 10 to 25 per cent. silver, but the silver value has not been separated from the totals, as it would be insignificant :

1858	$ 705,000	1880	$1,013,827
1859	1,615,070	1881	1,046,737
1860	2,228,543	1882	954,085
1861	2,666,118	1883	794,252
1862	2,656,903	1884	736,165
1863	3,913,563	1885	713,738
1864	3,735,850	1886	903,651
1865	3,491,205	1887	693,709
1866	2,662,106	1888	616,731
1867	2,480,868	1889	588,923
1868	3,372,972	1890	490,435
1869	1,774,978	1891	429,811
1870	1,336,956	1892	399,526
1871	1,799,440	1893	356,131
1872	1,610,972	1894	405,516
1873	1,305,749	1895	481,683
1874	1,844,618	1896	544,026
1875	2,474,004	1897	513,520
1876	1,786,648	1898	643,346
1877	1,608,182	1899	1,344,900
1878	1,275,204	1900	1,278,724
1879	1,290,058	1901	970,100
		Total	$63,554,543

The decrease in output during 1901 and 1902 is attributable largely to unfavourable weather conditions, which caused a shortage in water supply. The primitive methods employed by miners in British Columbia ten and twenty years ago are now being rapidly superseded by the application of scientific systems of hydraulic and deep level mining in the placer fields.

OUTPUT FOR 1902.

By Districts.		Amount and Value of Mineral Products.		
			Quantity.	Value.
Cariboo	$ 540,395	Gold, placer, ounces	53,657	$ 1,073,140
Cassiar	426,636	" lode, "	236,491	4,888,269
Kootenay, East	1,477,466	Silver "	3,917,917	1,941,328
Kootenay, West	7,806,399	Copper, pounds	29,636,057	3,446,673
Lillooet	31,429	Lead, "	22,536,381	824,832
Yale	2,843,537	Coal, tons, 2,240 lbs.	1,397,394	4,192,182
Coast Districts	4,360,688	Coke, " "	128,015	640,075
		Other Materials	....	480,051
	$17,486,550			$17,486,550

COAL AND COKE PRODUCTION IN B. C.

NOTWITHSTANDING the less favourable conditions of market in San Francisco for British Columbia coal, consequent upon the discovery of mineral oil in California and its use for fuel purposes in competition with our product, the output of coal from British Columbia collieries during 1901 was the greatest on record. This was, however, due to increased production from the Crow's Nest collieries, the market for the output from these collieries being practically unlimited, as not only is there a very considerable American demand, but the rapid growth of the metallurgical industries in the Kootenays requires a constantly increasing supply of coke. Of the Fernie product last year, 60 per cent. of the coal and 70 per cent. of the coke was consumed in Canada, the remainder being exported to the United States.

COAL.

Years.	Tons (2,240 lbs.)	Value.
1836-52	10,000	$ 40,000
1852-59	25,396	101,592
1859 (two months)	1,989	7,956
1860	14,246	56,988
1861	13,774	55,096
1862	18,118	72,472
1863	21,345	85,380
1864	28,632	115,528
1865	32,819	131,276
1866	25,115	100,460
1867	31,239	124,956
1868	44,005	176,020
1869	35,802	143,208
1870	29,843	119,372
1871-2-3	148,549	493,836
1874	81,547	244,641
1875	110,145	330,435
1876	139,192	417,576
1877	154,052	462,156
1878	170,846	512,538
1879	241,301	723,903
1880	267,595	802,785
1881	228,357	685,071
1882	282,139	846,417
1883	213,299	639,897
1884	394,070	1,182,210
1885	265,596	796,788
1886	326,636	979,908
1887	413,360	1,248,080
1888	489,301	1,467,903
1889	578,830	1,739,490
1890	678,140	2,034,420
1891	1,029,097	3,087,291
1892	826,335	2,479,005
1893	978,294	2,934,882
1894	1,012,953	3,038,859
1895	939,654	2,818,962
1896	896,222	2,688,666
1897	882,854	2,648,562
1898	1,135,865	3,407,595
1899	1,306,324	3,918,972
1900	1,439,595	4,318,785
1901	1,460,331	4,380,993
Total	17,423,802	$52,632,930

COKE.

Years.	Tons (2,240 lbs.)	Value.
1895-6	1,565	$ 7,825
1897	17,831	89,155
1898 (estimated)	35,000	175,000
1899	34,251	171,255
1900	85,149	425,745
1901	127,081	635,405
Total	300,877	$ 1,504,385

PLACER AND HYDRAULIC MINING.

THE first discovery in British Columbia of placer gold was made in 1857, on the Thompson River, and in the following year rich finds were reported at Hill Bar, near Yale, on the Fraser. This was the beginning of the great Fraser River excitement. In 1858 between 15,000 and 20,000 persons embarked from San Francisco for the new El Dorado; but while this was the inauguration of gold mining in British Columbia, the actual returns of $543,000 for the season of 1858, from June to October, inclusive, were considered disappointing, and so great were the natural difficulties of the country — unprovided, too, as it was then, with means to support a large population — that a great number of the immigrants returned to California early in the following year. In 1859-60 good diggings were discovered at Fountain, above Lillooet, on the Fraser River, on the Thompson River, the Similkameen River, and at Antler Creek, in the Cariboo District. But it was not until 1861 that the two most noteworthy discoveries of Williams and Lightning Creeks, in the Cariboo District, occurred, and created a second considerable migration of miners to the province, increasing in volume until 1864. The average value of gold obtained per lineal foot of channel of certain claims on Williams Creek is given in the report of the Provincial Minister of Mines for 1875 as $1,075. The production of Lightning Creek, while less in the aggregate than Williams, was greater while it lasted, and from this creek alone gold to the value of $2,179,272 was extracted. From available statistics it appears that the maximum production of placer gold was reached in 1863, when the output, almost entirely from the Cariboo District, and from Wild Horse Creek, in Southeast Kootenay, was $3,913,563, and the average annual earnings per man $890. Until 1867 the production gradually but steadily decreased, although previous to that year fresh discoveries of alluvial gold were made at Leech River, on Vancouver Island, and at the bend of the Columbia River, in North Kootenay. The increased production in 1868-69 and in 1874-75-76 was doubtless due to respectively the discoveries in the Omineca District, near Latitude 56 degrees, and in Cassiar, still further north. From this latter district gold to the value of $1,000,000 was taken out in 1874, this being more than 50 per cent. of the total production of the country for that year. In 1888 the value of the production of placer gold had fallen to not much above half a million dollars. Whereas in 1875 the number of miners employed was 2,024, and the average annual earnings per man $1,222, in 1888 the average individual earning was but $307 for 2,007 men employed. The early miners worked the bars, the outcrops of the coarser wash in the terraces, and the creeks and bench deposits with no other appliances than picks and shovels, rockers and sluices. In the deeper ground in the Cariboo District sinking and drifting were resorted to, but here too only apparatus of the crudest hand-manufactured type was in use. Early in the 70's hydraulicing was attempted with cotton hose, and with perhaps a two-inch nozzle and rarely more than a hundred feet of pressure. Within the last six or seven years, however, the old — and, so far as the individual miner is concerned, worked out — diggings of Cariboo, Omineca and Cassiar have become re-vitalised. In these districts some very important enterprises, involving large capital expenditures, are being conducted under the supervision of highly trained and skilled engineers. As yet, in no instance has the success of these several undertakings been quite reached, although several are within a measurable distance of that consummation.

Although the opportunities for the remunerative investment of capital in alluvial mining in Cariboo are good, some time must elapse before the field is thoroughly exploited; and while there is abundant evidence of quartz leads, values are too low to permit of profitable mining under existing conditions of labour and transport. In the early 60's the cost of transportation of supplies from the seaboard to the mines was a dollar per pound. The present rate is from six to seven cents, and thus the freight charges on mining machinery and supplies are still not infrequently greater than the first cost of the articles themselves.

Some attempts are now being made to dredge the bottoms and bars of the Fraser, Thompson and other rivers, and recent effort in this direction, which has been conducted on carefully considered scientific lines, appears to promise success. Early in the year 1898 gold in paying quantities was discovered on Pine Creek, in the Atlin District. The field has since become largely productive, and is being worked both by hydraulic and ground-sluicing methods.

TRAIL CREEK DISTRICT.

THE mining division of Trail Creek occupies a large geographical area lying between the eastern boundary of South Yale and the Columbia River. Apart, however, from the mineral belt known as the Rossland camp, no productive mines have as yet been developed in the division. The mineral zone containing the mines at Rossland is indifferently called "The Rossland Camp," "The Trail Creek District," and "The Trail Creek Mines."

The mineral belt lies on the headwaters of Trail Creek, a small tributary of the Columbia River. The mountains here form a horseshoe-like divide between the waters of Trail Creek and of Little Sheep Creek, of which the former falls into the Columbia River north of the international boundary at Trail, and the other south of the international boundary at a point opposite Northport, in the State of Washington. There are thus two outlets to the main water-course from the Rossland mines. The mines themselves are, in an air line, about six miles north of the international boundary.

ROSSLAND.

The present site of the town of Rossland was at one time the crater of a volcano, from which lava and ashes deluged the surrounding country. The variety of igneous material which covers the district seems to indicate that the eruptions were intermittent, and that the volcano itself was of great age. The occasional presence of quartzite or metamorphosed sandstone seems also to indicate that a shallow sea existed here previous to volcanic outbreak. The district may be roughly described as an area of gabbro, surrounded by quartz diorite so highly metamorphosed that the contacts are very indistinctly defined. The gabbro area, though only about one and a half miles wide by four or five miles in length, is one of great importance to the district, for it is in the gabbro, or closely bordering it, that the best mines have been discovered.

The veins are true fissure veins, the metal in them being the result of metalliferous liquids flowing through them, attacking the country rock on each side, dissolving the rock and naturally replacing it with metallic sulphides. Such being the case, the shoots of ore often fade away into the surrounding country rock, and, there being no well-defined walls, the ore is frequently lost. This, with the very irregular width of the veins and their complex faulting, renders Rossland geology an exceedingly difficult problem to mining engineers.

LABOUR CONDITIONS.

The scale of wages for the leading positions is :

Shift boss	$5 00	Machinists	$4 00
Shaftmen	4 00	Blacksmiths	4 00
Machine men	3 50	Blacksmith's helpers	3 00
Timber men.........3 00 to	3 50	Hoisting engineers . .3 00 to	4 00
Shovellers and car men	2 50	Powder and tool boys	2 50
Carpenters	3 50	Surface labourers	2 50

The surface men work ten-hour shifts, except carpenters, who work nine. On May 1, 1899, the Provincial Eight-Hour Law went into effect; its effect is to limit underground work to eight hours. At first, at the War Eagle mines, this was applied by putting on three shifts in 24 hours, which reduced the actual working time of the men to 7½ hours, as half an hour was allowed for lunch. This was a wasteful arrangement, as in spite of the power-blowers for forcing out the smoke after blasting, such huge charges as were used to break the rock sometimes rendered a stope unapproachable thereafter for several hours. An air drill was necessarily often idle also, to permit the machine men to load, blast and then clear the muck away sufficiently to set up again.

In the spring of 1900 the three-shift system was abandoned in favor of the two-shift, arranged thus: The first shift started at 7 a. m. and worked, with an hour's intermission, till 4 p. m.; the second shift started at 4 p. m. and, with an hour for supper at 6 p. m., finished at 1 a. m. From 1 a. m. to 7 a. m. a special blasting gang loaded and fired all the ground drilled for breaking. By this method the working faces were freed from smoke before the machine men started work at 7 a. m.

As the ore bodies of Rossland are wide and homogeneous, and the rock in general offers an equal resistance to drilling, it was found practical and desirable to put the machine men on the contract system, to stimulate them to use the air drills to the best advantage during the short eight-hour shift. As the companies did not wish to allow sub-contracting, and it was expected that the machine men's time would be utilised entirely for drilling, the contracts were let on the basis of a price per foot of hole drilled, instead of by the foot of drift or shaft advanced, or by the cubic yard of stope excavated, as is customary in other camps where the contract system of mining prevails.

The contract system was inaugurated by the companies after a shut-down of several weeks, and the miners' union at first declared against the change. After a conference of several days between the mine managers and representatives of the miners, in which the Dominion Labour Commissioner and two Provincial officials assisted, a mutually satisfactory agreement was reached, and the contract system has been in successful operation ever since.

HISTORY OF THE ROSSLAND CAMP.

The name Trail Creek is derived from the Dewdney trail, which follows the course of this stream to the Columbia River, and traverses the mineral zone. The first claim located was located on the Dewdney trail. Afterwards the productive portion of the district was located about half a mile to the north of the Dewdney trail, on the southern slope of the now well-known Red Mountain. Intermittent development work was maintained on the Le Roi, War Eagle, Centre Star and Josie for some years prior to 1894, and a few tons of ore shipped from the Le Roi for experimental purposes. In 1894 the main pay chute of the War Eagle was discovered, and shipments of ore were begun during the winter of 1894-95. These were made by waggon over both routes to the Columbia River, and at Northport the ore was transferred to the cars on the Spokane & Northern Railway and transported to East Helena, Great Falls, or Everett, in the State of Washington, for treatment. The greater part of the ore went to Great Falls and East Helena. The rate of freight and treatment was in the neighborhood of $14 per ton, and it cost from $2.50 a ton up to transport the ore to the Columbia River, according to the condition of the roads. The average value of the ore shipped from the War Eagle mine was $40, and the average value of that from the Le Roi was $35. Only picked portions of the veins were mined. No official record has been kept of the amount or value of the ore mined and shipped up to the end of 1895. The following table gives the tonnage and value of the ore extracted since :

Year.	Tons.	Gold, oz.	Silver, oz.	Copper, lbs.	Total.
1896	38,075	55,275	80,285	1,580,635	$1,243,360
1897	68,804	97,024	110,068	1,819,580	2,097,280
1898	111,282	87,343	170,804	5,232,011	2,470,811
1899	172,665	102,976	185,818	5,693,889	3,229,086
1900	217,636	111,625	167,378	2,071,865	2,739,300
1901	283,360	132,333	970,460	8,333,446	4,621,299
1902	*336,860	....	....	....	*4,500,000

*Estimated.

MINING AND TREATMENT.

The ores of the Rossland camp are reduced by smelting to an auriferous copper matte, which is shipped for treatment. The first reduction in the scale of costs was made in 1896 by the construction of a smelter at Trail, and a narrow-gauge railway from Trail to Rossland. A rate of freight and treatment from the mines of $11 a ton was then secured. In 1898 the Northport smelter, served by the Red Mountain Railway, built from Northport to Rossland, was completed by the Le Roi Company. The smelter afforded a rate of freight and treatment of $8 a ton, since reduced to $4.50 a ton, while the rate at Trail is $6 a ton, subject, however, to special arrangements, as in the case of low-grade silicious ore purchased by the Trail smelter from the Le Roi mine for use in its treatment of silver-lead ores. The rate for freight and treatment does not include the cost of transporting and refining the resultant copper matte, which is met by a deduction of five cents per pound on the current market price of the copper in the ore.

Very large sums of money have been spent in the development and equipment of the principal mines in Rossland, in order to secure the greatest possible economy in the extraction of the ore. The number of men employed in and about the mines of the camp is from 1,200 to 1,500.

PRINCIPAL MINES OF THE CAMP.

Le Roi mine, owned by the Le Roi Mining Company, of London, England; address, 43 Lothbury, London, E. C., Eng.; capital, £1,000,000, divided into 200,000 shares of £5 each. Since its acquisition by the company now owning the mine, one dividend of £50,000 has been paid. The profits earned by the mine have been sunk in purchasing a quarter interest in the Northport smelter, in addition to the three-quarters already owned; sinking a vertical shaft and equipping it with hoisting machinery; doubling the capacity of the smelter, and in otherwise developing and equipping the mine. Prior to its purchase by the present company, profits amounting to $1,055,000 were distributed.

THE LE ROI NO. 2.

Owned by the Le Roi No. 2 Mines, Limited, of London; address, 43 Lothbury, London, E. C., England. Under the same general management as the Le Roi. Capital, £600,000, divided into 120,000 shares of £5 each; registered 1900. This property is a consolidation of certain claims lying to the west of the Le Roi and War Eagle, of which the most important are the Josie and the No. 1. The group

ATLIN

FREIGHTING INTO CARIBOO.

H. B. Co's POST, FORT St. JAMES, STUART LAKE.

H. B. Co.'s POST FORT McLEOD, McLEOD LAKE.

THIBERT CREEK MINING CO.'S PITS.

MOUTH OF CANYON CREEK, KETTLE RIVER.

has been undergoing careful and adequate development. During 1901, 53,600 tons were shipped. The average value in gold and particularly in copper from this property is higher than in the case of the Le Roi. The company declared a dividend of $144,000 in 1901.

THE ROSSLAND GREAT WESTERN.

Owned by the Rossland Great Western Mines, Limited, of London, England; address, 43 Lothbury, London, E. C., England; under the same general management as the Le Roi. Capital, £500,000, divided into 100,000 shares of £5 each. Registered 1900. This property is a consolidation of the Nickel Plate, Golden Chariot and Great Western claims, lying to the east of the Le Roi.

THE COLUMBIA - KOOTENAY.

Owned by the Columbia-Kootenay Mining Company, Limited, of London, England; address, 43 Lothbury, London, E. C., England. Under the same general management as the Le Roi. Capital £500,000, divided into 500,000 shares of £1 each. Registered 1898. This property is situated on the eastern boundary of the Rossland mineral belt. It has been extensively developed. No ore has as yet been shipped under its present management.

The four groups mentioned above include all the property of the Rossland camp purchased and developed by the British America Corporation, Limited, now liquidated.

THE WAR EAGLE.

Owned by the War Eagle Consolidated Mining & Development Company, Limited, of Toronto, Ontario. Capital, $2,000,000, divided into 2,000,000 shares of $1 each. The total output of this mine to 31st January, 1900, was 131,976 tons of ore, of a gross assay value of $2,646,612. The sum of $545,000 has been distributed as profits.

THE CENTRE STAR.

Owned by the Centre Star Mining Company, Limited, of Toronto, Ontario. Capital, $3,500,000, divided into 3,500,000 shares of $1 each. The Centre Star is the eastern extension of the Le Roi, and the workings in the two mines are connected. The mine has been very extensively developed to a depth of 431 feet. The amount of ore shipped during 1901 was 53,600 tons, active shipments having been resumed during the last quarter of the year. During the year the company distributed $105,000 in dividends and considerably reduced the amount of the former liability. The mine is under the same general management as the War Eagle.

THE VELVET

Owned by the Velvet (Rossland) Mine, Limited. Registered in London, June 24, 1898. Authorized capital, £200,000, in 200,000 shares of £1 each, all of which have been subscribed and £175,000 called. Head office, 23 Leadenhall Street, London, E. C. The mine has been extensively developed, and new and richer ore bodies were discovered last year.

In addition to the properties mentioned, others of promise and importance are the Giant, acquired in 1902 by an English company; the Iron Mask, Spitzee, Evening Star, I. X. L., Portland, Homestake, Monte Cristo, Cascade and White Bear.

PROGRESS OF THE YEAR.

Very important developments took place in the Rossland district during 1902; and notwithstanding the fact that neither the War Eagle nor Centre Star—heretofore two of the largest shippers of ore — were productive until late in the summer, the output from the district again shows a gratifying increase. This is, however, largely attributable to the production from one mine, the Le Roi, whose output of over 200,000 tons is considerably more than 50 per cent. of the aggregate tonnage yield. In the course of development during the period under review, several new bodies of high-grade ore have been discovered at the Le Roi, and this, together with the fact that both the cost of transporting the ore to the smelter at Northport and the cost of coke have been considerably reduced, has enabled the mine to be operated to very much greater advantage. The Le Roi No. 2 was steadily productive until the end of October, when shipping operations were suspended at the instance of the Board of Directors. Early in September the War Eagle and Centre Star mines, in consequence of a more satisfactory treatment rate having been secured from the Trail smelter, commenced heavy shipments, the Centre Star ore averaging $13 and the War Eagle $19 per ton. The Giant mine has been developed during the year with satisfactory results; and work was resumed on the Homestake and White Bear. At the Velvet mine, development operations have been in progress, and recently some very rich new ore bodies were discovered.

This year, for the first time since the inception of mining in the district, the industry has been placed on a business-like footing. For the first time, the facts as regards the position and condition of the mines have been made public, and their capabilities are consequently better understood. The mines are now on a better productive basis than at any previous period. Costs of production and treatment have been further reduced, and any likelihood of friction between the employers and the men is no longer to be apprehended. Experiments have been conducted during the year with a view to discovering a method of profitably treating the lower-grade mine products, and it is authoritatively stated that the results of these tests are such that the problem is within measurable distance of solution.

The ore shipments for the year are reported as follows :

	Tonnage.	Estimated gross value
Le Roi	217,500	$2,600,000
Le Roi No. 2	52,475	800,000
Centre Star	37,500	437,004
War Eagle	22,000	334,048
Rossland Great Western	2,400	36,000
Giant	3,000	42,000
Velvet	1,500	25,000
Cascade	300	4,000
Columbia-Kootenay	50	500
White Bear	25	500
Spitzee	20	400
Totals for 1902 (wet tons)	336,860	$4,274,952

The following table shows the amounts paid by the respective companies in wages to employees during the year.

Le Roi	$ 463,150
Le Roi No. 2	214,500
Centre Star	168,397
War Eagle	123,913
Rossland Great Western	50,000
White Bear	18,000
Kootenay	15,000
Giant	5,000
Velvet	50,000
Spitzee	3,000
Cascade and Bonanza	5,000
Other mines	5,000
	$1,120,960

The following tables from the last annual report of the Centre Star Mining Company are interesting as affording information of mining costs in the Rossland district :

Comparative Statement of Work Done and Its Cost, General Expenses Included, per foot or ton, to September 30, 1902.

	Oct. 1, '98, to Sept. 30, '99			Oct. 1, '99, to Sept. 30, '00			Oct. 1, '00, to Sept. 30, '01			Oct. 1, '01, to Sept. 30, '02		
	Work done. Feet or Tons	Total Cost.	Cost per Foot or Ton	Work done. Foot or Ton	Total Cost	Cost per Foot or Ton	Work done. Feet or Tons	Total Cost	Cost per Foot or Ton	Work done. Feet or Tons	Total Cost	Cost per Foot or Ton
DEVELOPMENT WORK—												
General work, stations, retimbering, machinery and equipment repairs, etc.	......	$ 12,223.38	......	......	$ 15,216.59	......	......	$ 15,663.36	......	......	$ 13,517.06	......
Sinking main shaft	344.	34,941.19	101.57	228.5	28,250.81	123.63	337.	33,415.68	99.16	362.	34,445.82	95.15
Sink'g small shafts or winzes	319.5	16,075.95	50.31	103.5	6,107.39	59.01	50.5	2,268.93	44.93	50.5	2,283 67	45.22
Raising	371.5	15,275.81	41.17	903.5	50,606.61	56 01	324.5	10,099.31	31.12	153.	5,081.80	33 21
Drifting	2,375.5	56,663.59	23.85	2,421.	64,942.85	26.82	2,107.	42,927.22	20.37	3,997.5	87,664.29	21 93
Total development work	3,410.5	$135,179 92	......	3,656.5	$165,124.25	......	2,819.0	$104,374.50	......	4,563.0	$142,992.64	......
ORE PRODUCTION—												
Ore from development work sold—tons	63.5	....	......	4,034.94	....	......	4,522.	....	......	1,018.166	....	......
Ore from dumps, storage, etc.—tons	......	....	......	......	....	......	7,774.	2,291.80	0.29	......	....	......
Stoped ore sold	6,533.0	19,051.59	2.91	20,489.95	73,581.37	3.39	68,123.0	151,682.93	2.23	10,069.479	29,559.82	2.93
Total ore sold	6,596.5	$ 19,054.59	2.89	24,524.89	$ 73,591.37	3.00	80,419.0	$153,974.73	1.91	11,087.645	$ 29,559.82	2.67
SUMMARY—												
Expense of development, per ton of ore sold	6,596.5	135,179.92	20.49	24,524.89	165,124 25	6.73	80,419.0	104,374.50	1.30	11,087.645	142,992.64	12.89
Expense of production, per ton of ore sold	6,596.5	19,054.59	2.89	24,524.89	73,591.37	3.00	80,419.0	153,974.73	1.91	11,087.645	29,559 82	2.67
Total expenditure, per ton of ore sold	6,596.5	$154,234.51	23.38	24,524.89	$238,715.52	9.73	80,419 0	$258,349.23	3.21	11,087.645	$172,552.46	15.56

Statement showing Values and Smelting Charges, per annum, to September 30, 1902.

For Fiscal Year Ending	Real or full assay value. Total metallic contents at full N. Y. quotations.	Indirect smelting charge. Difference between N. Y. quotations and smelter's price for the metals.	Direct smelting charge including freight from the mine.	Total smelting charge direct and indirect.	Smelter's gross assay value after deducting indirect charges only.	Smelter's net value after deducting both the indirect and direct charges from the real assay value (i. e. net value of ore F.O.B. cars at mine.)
Prior to October 1, 1898	......	......	......	$ 9.93	$ 18.91	$ 12.91
September 30th, 1899	$ 22.84	$ 3 93	$ 6.00	9 33	18.91	12.91
September 30th, 1900	20.14	3.57	6.00	9.57	16.57	10.57
September 30th, 1901	18.12	3.48	6.00	9.48	14.64	8.64
September 30th, 1902	16.24	2.93	5.22	8.15	13.31	8.09

BOUNDARY CREEK DISTRICT.

THAT portion of the province of British Columbia generally known as the Boundary District comprises an area extending approximately from the summit of the divide between the Columbia River and Christina Lake on the east to the divide between the Okanagan and Kettle River valleys on the west. Within these boundaries are the valleys of Christina Lake, the North Fork of Kettle River, and other tributary streams, the total area being between two and three thousand square miles. Gold quartz was first discovered in Camp McKinney in 1884, and two years later mineral outcroppings were found and located near Boundary Falls. In 1893-94 shipments of rich ore, carrying gold and silver values, were made from a number of claims in the vicinity of what is now the town of Greenwood. This ore was taken out on the backs of horses over a rough trail to Marcus, the cost of carriage and subsequent treatment being, therefore, exceptionally heavy. Nevertheless, it is said that very considerable profits were realized in these initial shipments. The veins from which this rich ore was taken were, however, very narrow, and also uncertain in their occurrence, and after a period work on them was discontinued, the prospectors in the district turning their attention to the opening up of the large low-grade deposits of copper-gold ore which had been meanwhile discovered. Thus in 1896 development work was commenced on the Mother Lode in Deadwood Camp, and the Old Ironsides and Knob Hill claims, in Greenwood, or, as it is called to-day, Phoenix Camp, while capital in large amounts began to be invested in the mines of the district. Since the completion of the Columbia & Western Railway, by which the mines were enabled to market their product, the industrial advancement in the district has been remarkable, and to-day this section of the province occupies the premier position in point of tonnage output. During the two and a half years over which ore shipments have extended nearly a million tons of ore have been produced and shipped to the smelters, of which there are three in the district, having a combined tonnage capacity of about 2,000 tons daily. Of this large quantity of ore, more than one-half was the production of last year. The tonnage for the years 1900, 1901 and 1902, respectively, was as follows:

	Tons.
1900 (six months)	97,837
1901	386,675
1902 (estimated)	519,962
Total	994,474

The tonnage shipped during 1902 by no means represents the full shipping capacity of the mines now in operation, for at least 100,000 tons more would have been added to last year's tonnage had it not been that owing to shortage of coke (consequent upon a disastrous explosion wrecking one of the coal mines from which the greater part of the fuel supply had been coming), and of power (low water restricting the generation of electric power), the larger mines were compelled to keep their output of ore down to the reduced treatment capacity of the smelters, the ordinary capacity of which, with seven furnaces running, is 2,200 to 2,300 tons per diem. Taking 2,250 tons as the daily average capacity and allowing all the furnaces to be idle three days in every month, or 36 days in the year, there still remains a total treatment capacity of 740,000 tons available under favourable conditions, and that quantity of ore could be supplied by the mines now working in the district, leaving out of account others already opened up to a stage admitting of their maintaining an appreciably large steady output. Shipments of individual mines were as follows:

	Tons.
Granby Con. M. S. & P. Co.'s Old Ironsides and Knob Hill group	310,601
B. C. Copper Co.'s Mother Lode mine	137,577
Snowshoe Gold & Copper Mines' (Limited) Snowshoe mine	20,800
Cariboo-McKinney M. & M. Co.'s Cariboo mine, Camp McKinney (estimated)	16,000
B. C. Chartered Co.'s B. C. mine	14,627
Montreal & Boston Copper Co.'s Sunset mine	8,010
Dominion Copper Co.'s Emma mine	7,900
Jewel Gold Mines' (Limited) Jewel mine	2,175
Winnipeg Mines' (Limited) Winnipeg mine	785
Golden Crown Mines' (Limited) Golden Crown mine	625
No. 7 Mining Co.'s No. 7 mine	532
Providence Mining Co.'s Providence Mine	172
Sundry small shipments	158
Total	519,962

For purposes of comparison the following figures, showing the tonnage of the mines that shipped more than 1,000 tons each during 1901, are given:

	1900. Tons.	1901. Tons.	1902. Tons.	Total. Tons.
Granby Mines	64,531	231,762	310,601	606,894
Mother Lode	5,564	99,548	137,577	242,689
B. C.	19,618	47,517	14,627	81,762
Snowshoe	297	1,731	20,800	22,828
Sunset	...	800	8,010	8,810
Emma	...	...	7,900	7,900
Jewel	160	325	2,175	2,660

The B. C. did not ship any ore during the first half of 1902. The Snowshoe and Emma did practically all their shipping during the latter half of the year. The Sunset's output has been restricted to making up the difference between the quantity of custom ore received at the owners' smelter and the total requirements of the smelter. The Jewel did not send out any ore during the latter half of the year.

PRINCIPAL MINES OF THE DISTRICT.

Granby Consolidated Mining, Smelting & Power Company, Limited—Authorised capital, $15,000,000, in shares of a par value of $10 each; head office, Montreal. This company is a reconstruction and consolidation of the following mining and smelting companies: The Knob Hill Gold Mining Company, Limited, incorporated in 1897; the Old Ironsides Mining Company, Limited; the Granby Consolidated Mining & Smelting Company, Limited, incorporated in 1899; and the Grey Eagle Mining Company, Limited, incorporated in 1900.

British Columbia Copper Company, Limited — Registered in 1898; authorised capital, $1,000,000, in shares of $5; head office, New York. Runs and operates a smelting plant at Greenwood, and the Mother Lode group of mines, in Deadwood Camp.

Montreal & Boston—Own the Sunset group of mines, in Deadwood Camp, and purchased this year the smelting plant at Boundary Falls, formerly owned by the Standard Company. Head office, New York.

Jewel Gold Mines, Limited — Registered in 1899; authorised capital, £80,000, in shares of £1 each. Owns and operates the Jewel mine, in Long Lake camp. Head office, London, England.

Dominion Copper Company, Limited — Incorporated 1899; authorised capital, $5,000,000, in shares of $1 each The company was formed to acquire and work the Brooklyn, Stemwinder, Montezuma, Rawhide, Standard and Idaho mines, in the Phoenix mining camp. Head office, Toronto.

Snowshoe Gold & Copper Company, Limited — Registered in 1902, to acquire and operate the Snowshoe mine group, near Phoenix. Head office, London.

A number of other mines in the district owned by joint stock companies and by individuals have also been extensively developed. Of these the most important are the Emma, Golden Crown, Winnipeg, Gold Drop, Providence, B. C., King, No. 7, and Carnie.

Mr. E. Jacobs, in an article in the Mining Record reviewing the year's work, says : —

Turning now to the development and equipment of some of the larger mines, the following summary will in a measure indicate their relative importance.

GRANBY COMPANY'S MINES.

As having, so far as yet known, the largest ore bodies, truly described as enormous, and as having done more development work and shipped more ore than any other mine or group of mines in the district, the Granby Company's mines come first. The group consists of the Old Ironsides, Knob Hill, Victoria, Fourth of July, Phoenix, Ætna, Grey Eagle, Banner, Tip Top and Triangle Fraction, all adjoining claims in or adjacent to the town of Phoenix. These claims were acquired from the four companies which were consolidated into the present Granby Consolidated Mining, Smelting & Power Company, Limited, viz., the Old Ironsides Mining Company, Knob Hill Gold Mining Company, Granby Consolidated Mining & Smelting Co., and the Grey Eagle Mining Company. The Old Ironsides and Knob Hill claims were both located on July 25, 1891, and they are the oldest mineral locations in Greenwood Camp. But little underground work was done on the Old Ironsides prior to 1897, but in that year development was actively entered upon, and a steam hoisting engine, which much facilitated mining operations, was installed. From that time on the opening up of the enormous ore bodies occurring on this group of claims has steadily proceeded, until to-day the showing of ore exposed in the extensive workings of these mines is simply marvellous. It is a literal fact that "acres of ore" have been blocked out in the Old Ironsides and Victoria, as the writer can testify from personal observation, having, when underground in these mines in 1900, walked around three blocks of ore each not less than an acre in area. Nothing short of seeing for themselves suffices to overcome the incredulity of most people as to the immense proportions of the ore bodies occurring here, and exposed both in the underground workings and in the big open quarries. So large are these that no difficulty is experienced in maintaining a daily minimum output of 1,500 tons of ore for treatment at the company's smelter, whilst additions to plant and equipment are being made to provide for an output up to 5,000 tons per diem whenever the available treatment capacity shall have reached that tonnage.

The aggregate footage of development work done on the Granby mines to the end of 1902 was 16,359 lineal feet — more than three miles — of which 3,013 feet was in sinking and raising and 13,346 feet in crosscutting and drifting. These figures show the number of feet done in underground development work proper, but leave entirely out of account the numerous large drifts and raises in the huge ore bodies preparatory to opening out the big stopes characteristic of these mines, which are being worked down to the 300-foot level. One shaft on the property is 400 feet in depth, but no levels have yet been run below 300 feet depth. Rising ground on the Knob Hill makes the 300-foot level of the Old Ironsides about 550 feet, vertical depth, below the apex or outcrop of ore on the Knob Hill, with the ore body proved to be continuous from the summit of the mountain on the Knob Hill through the Old Ironsides to other claims beyond, also owned by the Granby Company. The use of the diamond drill has shown that the ore continues down to a depth of at least 1,000 feet.

The system of ore-quarrying followed here constitutes one of the most remarkable features of mining seen in the district. On the north side of the hill on which the mines are situate workings have been opened at half a dozen points along a distance of about 1,000 feet in a body of ore known to have a length of fully 3,000 feet on the company's ground. The removal of the surface debris has exposed ore for a width of about 400 feet. Three big open quarries are being worked at different levels. The top one was the first opened, and its output of ore consequently has been by far the largest. It has an ore face about 80 feet high, and large raises from the Knob Hill main tunnel below serve as chutes down which the ore is thrown, to be trammed thence to ore bins above the main shipping track of this mine. The middle quarry is on the same level as the main tunnel, 84 feet, vertical depth, below the floor of the top one. The lowest quarry is about 50 feet lower down still, so that when it shall have been carried back far enough to be immediately under the apex of the ore body it will have an ore breast, as proved by tunnel and raise, of more than 200 feet vertical depth. Railway tracks run into the two lower quarries, so that the ore broken down in them can be loaded direct on to the railway cars and thus obviate further handling until it reaches the smelter. No. 2 tunnel connects with the 100-foot level — that is, 100 feet below the main tunnel — of the Knob Hill, and this provides another outlet for ore from the lowest quarry, by means of chutes, whence it is trammed to ore bins placed above the main shipping tracks of the Old Ironsides. A third tunnel, starting still lower down the hillside, will eventually be extended to connect with the 100-foot level of the Old Ironsides and the 200-foot level of the Knob Hill.

The machinery and plant installed at these mines some time ago includes two 80 h. p. steam boilers, 10-drill duplex Rand air-compressor, air-receivers, etc., on the Knob Hill, and a similar plant on the Old Ironsides. Each of three shafts on the Old Ironsides and Victoria is provided with a steam hoisting engine. A timber-framing machine driven by a 45 h. p. steam engine, an electric light engine and dynamo, steam pumps and much other plant and machinery are also included in the power equipment of these mines. An ore-crusher with jaws opening 42 inches by 32 inches to crush rock to not larger than 7 inches or 8 inches, at a rate of 150 tons per hour, and a 100 h. p. electric induction motor to drive same, also a 2,000-foot gravity tramway from the top quarry to crusher, with 3-wheel brake system headworks, were recently put in and are now in operation. Two tandem compound Rand air-compressors together rated at 60, three ¼-inch machine drills, and two 700 h. p. electric induction motors for motive power, are being installed. The equipment of the machine shop on the mines is also being largely added to, so as to provide it with modern improved appliances.

Prominent among the mine buildings are large bunk and boarding houses for the accommodation of employees, with a number of comfortable cottages for men having their families with them. The several buildings for housing plant and machinery, are roomy and substantially built. Ore bins give storage capacity for a large quantity of ore, and railway trackage about the mines is comparatively extensive. From the time ore-shipping was commenced in July, 1900, to the close of 1902, the output of ore aggregated 606,151 tons, of which about 310,000 tons were produced in 1902. All this ore was treated at the company's smelter at Grand Forks. When shipping 1,500 tons a day these mines employ about 425 men. The mine superintendent, Mr. William Yolen Williams, has been in charge for nearly six years, during which period he has developed the property from mere prospects into the most important and productive group of mines in the Boundary District and one of the largest copper-producers in Canada.

THE MOTHER LODE.

The Mother Lode, situate in Deadwood Camp, about three miles west of the town of Greenwood, was located on May 28, 1891. In 1896 it was bonded by Col. John Weir for himself and several other New York mining men, who in that year formed the Boundary Mines Company to develop the claim. About March, 1898, the British Columbia Copper Company, Limited, was organised in New York, to acquire and work the Mother Lode and several adjoining claims. The group now owned by the company consists of the Mother Lode, Offspring, Primrose, Ten Broeck and Don Julio and Sunflower mineral claims.

When Mr. Frederic Keffer, M. E., took charge of the Mother Lode in 1896 there was not a prospect shaft or a tunnel 25 feet in depth or length on the claim. To-day the development work totals between 7,000 and 8,000 lineal feet, besides which big stopes underground and quarries at the surface represent much productive work. The lode occurring here is large, its surface width varying from 80 to 160 feet. It has been cut in trenches along a distance of about 1,100 feet north from the main shaft to where it disappears under heavy drift, while a big surface exposure on the Primrose, about 700 feet in an opposite direction, indicates its continuity south as well. The main shaft is down 325 feet, and long levels have been run at both 200 and 300 feet depth. The ore body as opened at the 200-foot level has a width varying from 80 to 100 feet, and crosscuts show it to be continuous at this level for at least 350 feet. At the 300-foot level the workings are not yet so large, but as far as they have gone they have proved the ore body to maintain its large proportions. A second chute of ore, 18 to 20 feet in width, was met with at the 300-foot level and followed for 200 feet without its dipping out of the level. The "pillar and stope" system of mining the ore underground, as here adopted in 1901, was fully described and illustrated in the April, 1902, issue of the "Mining Record." Most of the exploratory work done underground has been done north of the main shaft, which is situate about the centre of the claim, so that little is known of the conditions as regards the occurrence of ore south of the shaft. Underground work was suspended last spring, the opening up of big surface quarries in ore having made it practicable to maintain a sufficiently large production to supply the company's smelter at Greenwood with plenty of ore to keep its two furnaces running continuously.

The main quarry is well up the side of the Mother Lode hill. Two other openings were made at lower levels, big tunnels having been driven under No. 1 quarry and connections made by means of wide raises, these serving as chutes down which the ore is thrown to No. 3, from which a double-track tramway, with three-ton ore cars drawn by mules, conveys the ore to a Farrel rock-crusher. During recent months two quarries were opened higher up the hill in ore containing more sulphur, and the ore from these is either shot down more than 200 feet to the mule tunnel, or run down a gravity tramway to another crusher above a different set of ore bins. All the ore is crushed at the mine before being shipped to the smelter, a saving being thereby effected, the ore going direct into the smelter mixture bins, instead of having to be first passed through the smelter sample mill crusher, with the attendant expense of this further handling. The mine shipped 5,564 tons of ore in the latter part of 1900; 99,548 tons in 1901, and 136,657 tons in 1902, making an aggregate of 241,769 tons. When there is no shortage of coke or other difficulty in the way of both furnaces being kept in blast at the smelter, the daily output of the mine is about 800 tons. The Mother Lode was the first mine in the district to have a power plant equal to doing much underground work. In 1898 a 10-drill straight line air-compressor, two 60 h. p. boilers, hoisting engines, etc., and electric light plant were hauled in from Marcus, then the nearest railway point, at a cost for hauling alone of about $3,000. In 1901 a 40-drill cross-compound condensing Ingersoll-Sergeant air-compressor, with two 100 h. p. boilers; a big double-cylinder first motion Jenckes hoisting engine, with two 80 h. p. boilers; a Robins ore-sorting and conveying plant; a No. 5 Gates rock-crusher, with a 70 h. p. steam engine to run it; a full equipment of tools for a machine shop, and other plant were added. Last year a 24x36-inch Farrel improved crusher, to crush 65 to 80 tons of rock per hour to a size not exceeding five inches; a Jeffrey elevating machine, with a chain of 20x12x9-inch buckets, to lift the crushed ore to ore bins over the railway track; a plain slide-valve engine, to run crusher and elevator; a 250-light Westinghouse dynamo, with 25 h. p. engine, and other machinery to bring mine equipment up to the requirements of an increased ore output, were installed. The mine buildings are commodious, and those for the accommodation of the men are comfortable. The ore bins have a total holding capacity of about 3,000 tons, and the railway facilities are sufficient for handling much larger quantities of ore than are at present produced. During construction work periods and when underground mining was in progress, up to 150 men were on the payroll, but not more than half that number are now regularly employed in getting out ore and incidental work. Mr. Keffer is still in charge of the mine, being the company's general manager.

THE SNOWSHOE.

The Snowshoe group, owned by the Snowshoe Gold & Copper Mines, Limited, of London, England, and situate in Greenwood Camp, comprises the Snowshoe mine and the Pheasant, Alma Fraction and Fairplay Fraction mineral claims. The Snowshoe was purchased by the British Columbia (Rossland and Slocan) Syndicate, Limited, in 1899; and after that company had spent about $130,000 in development work and in machinery, plant and buildings, the Snowshoe Company was organised in London in June of 1901 to acquire and operate the group. Development work done to the end of 1902 totals 6,440 lineal feet, nearly 2,000 being sinking and raising, and the remainder crosscutting and drifting. The earlier work was done in the eastern part of the Snowshoe. It consisted of an incline shaft, sunk 200 feet, with levels at 100 and 200 feet depth, respectively. On the former level some 520 feet and on the latter about 740 feet of crosscutting and drifting were done, and two raises were made from the 100-foot level to the surface. Much of this work was in ore, which dips easterly into the other claims owned by the company.

Later workings, in the western part of the claim, have opened up a big body of ore, which is being mined by quarrying as at the mines above described. The Phoenix branch of the Canadian Pacific Railway Company's Columbia & Western Railway crosses the Snowshoe. Below the railway, in the southern part of the claim, a tunnel, known as No. 1 level, has been run westward 677 feet into the hill, which rises rapidly to the western boundary of the property. For about 300 feet, excepting where a 25-foot dyke of waste crossed it, the tunnel was continuously in ore, apparently a parallel body to that in which the old shaft was sunk. Beyond this the tunnel was run about 477 feet, exploring for other ore bodies. Some 730 feet of crosscuts and drifts, mostly in ore, were run on this level. A raise 150 feet to the surface was also in ore most of the way; and a winze sunk 100 feet was in ore for 40 feet, and the ore chute was again encountered in a 250-foot crosscut from the bottom of the winze, which was in ore for 170 feet before the wall was met with. Altogether 660 feet of crosscutting and drifting have been done on this No. 2 level,

LYTTON, LOOKING SOUTH.

LILLOOET, ON THE FRASER RIVER.

KAMLOOPS.

PRINCETON, SIMILKAMEEN.

and a raise in ore 140 feet on the incline makes a second connection with No. 1 level. The ground has been explored below No. 2 level with a diamond drill, with satisfactory results. During 1902 a large main working shaft was sunk 300 feet, connecting with levels Nos. 1 and 2.

After removal of the surface debris from a comparatively large area of ground above No. 1 level, quarries were opened and drifts were run under them. Chutes were made at convenient intervals, and through these the ore is drawn and trammed direct to ore bins above the railway. It is calculated that these big open cuts will go back about 120 feet before reaching the western limit of the ore, and that a maximum face of about 60 feet in depth to floor of quarries will be obtained. A railway spur lately put in below the mouth of tunnel on No. 1 level gives shipping facilities that will admit of a much deeper face of ore being cut when quarrying operations shall have been carried down to that depth. Prior to 1902 only 2,028 tons of ore were shipped, but towards the close of that year the output was materially increased, so that the total tonnage for the year was 20,800 tons, making the aggregate 22,828 tons.

The power plant installed at the mine in 1900-01 included two steam boilers, two air-compressors together rated at about 12 drills, machine drills, hoisting engine at the shaft and an auxiliary engine in No. 1 tunnel, steam pumps, etc. Last year the high-pressure half of a 30-drill Rand-Corliss air-compressor, two 80 h. p. high-pressure boilers and an electric lighting plant were added, and a 150 h. p. electric hoist was ordered. This hoist will shortly be in operation. Meanwhile headworks over the main shaft are in course of construction. The mine buildings include bunk and boarding houses, offices, residences for superintendent and foreman, new compressor and boiler buildings, hoist house, etc., and ore bine with a holding capacity of 2,500 tons are about completed. Some 2,000 feet of railway tracks afford accommodation for shipping. The transmission lines of the Cascade Power Company cross the property, so that when electric power for operating the air-compressor hoist shall be required it will be right at hand. The average number of men employed is 44, but at times nearly double this number have been on the payroll. Mr. J. W. Astley, C. E., is the company's superintendent resident on the mine. The Snowshoe has been brought to its present stage of development under his direction. Mr. Anthony J. McMillan is managing director, and Mr. George S. Waterlow, another director, is one of the best friends the district has in England, since he loses no opportunity to express his confidence in the eventual profitableness of legitimate mining in the Boundary.

SUNSET AND CROWN SILVER.

The Sunset group is owned by the Montreal & Boston Copper Company, Limited, of Montreal, Quebec, which was organised in 1901 to acquire the mining properties and other assets of the Montreal-Boundary Creek Mining Company, Limited. The group consists of the Sunset, Crown Silver, C. O. D., and the Florence fractional claim, all adjoining and situate in Deadwood Camp, about three miles west of Greenwood. The Sunset and Crown Silver were both located on June 2, 1891. They were bonded in 1897 by Mr. W. L. Hogg, of Montreal, who with his associates did a lot of development work on them, and organised the Montreal-Boundary Creek Mining Company to further develop them. The other two claims were acquired later. In the summer of 1899 Captain Harry Johns, who had previously been superintendent at the adjoining Mother Lode mine, assumed charge at the Sunset, and ever since has directed operations on the group. The number of lineal feet of work done in development on the Sunset and Crown silver totals 7,155 feet, of which 1,070 feet represent sinking and raising done on the properties, and the remaining 6,085 feet crosscutting and drifting. The main shaft of the Sunset is 412 feet in depth, and levels have been run at 100, 176 and 300 feet depth respectively. The Crown silver shaft is 205 feet in depth, and from this about 880 feet of crosscutting and drifting have been done. The 300-foot level of the Sunset is a long tunnel driven to cut an ore-chute of higher grade than the main ore body, and with the ultimate object of connecting with the Crown Silver workings. Owing to the rise in the hill the 300-foot level in the Sunset will be about 400 feet below the surface by the time it shall be under the Crown Silver shaft. A feature on the Sunset is a knoll of rock, the weathered exterior of which was much copper-stained. A tunnel driven through this knoll disclosed the occurrence here of a big body of low-grade ore, approximately 300 feet in length by 150 feet in width, and estimated to contain above the 100-foot level about 250,000 tons of ore. The method of mining this is by opening underground a large stope or "glory hole" connecting with the 100-foot level by a series of chutes down which the broken ore is shot, to be trammed to the main shaft and hoisted thence to the surface above the ore shipping bins. The power plant installed at the Sunset includes two 80 h. p. boilers, half of a 20-drill duplex Ingersoll-Sergeant air-compressor, two air-receivers, ten Ingersoll-Sergeant 3¼ machine drills, Jenckes double hoisting engine with 14 x 20-inch cylinders, two mine safety platform cages, dynamo of 125 volts run by a 12 h. p. engine for electric lighting, well-found tool and repair shop, etc. The building improvements consist of ore bins with a capacity of 2,000 tons, comfortable bunk and boarding houses to accommodate about 60 men, men's cottages, villa residence for superintendent, assay office, boiler aud engine houses, substantial headworks, etc. A double spur from the Deadwood branch of the Columbia & Western Railway affords facilities for shipment of ore, which is sent to the Montreal & Boston Copper Company's smelter at Boundary Falls, distant about eight miles, and to which between 7,000 and 8,000 tons of ore were shipped from the Sunset during the latter part of last year.

EMMA.

Six or seven years ago a shaft was sunk 100 feet on the Emma claim, in Summit Camp, then owned chiefly by Farrell and Midgeon, well-known mining men of Butte, Montana. A big outcrop of copper ore occurs on the property, but the grade is not high, though the constituents of this ore make it very useful for fluxing purposes. After a crown grant was obtained for the claim no work of importance was done until the Hall Mining & Smelting Company, of Nelson, B. C., a few months since made an arrangement with the present owners (the Dominion Copper Company, Limited, of Toronto, Ontario) to mine and ship ore from it. Two years ago a quarry was opened alongside the railway, which crosses the claim, and some ore shipped thence to Boundary Falls; but as the smelter did not start work this was dumped alongside the railway, and lies there still. The Hall Company has expended about $4,500 in plant and buildings, and shipped 8,530 tons of ore, chiefly to Nelson. This ore was taken from a big cut made in the side of the hill just above the railway, this admitting of mining and shipping costs being very low. There appears to be a large quantity of ore available here, so that a much-increased output is anticipated for the current year. Later underground work will probably be done to determine the extent and value of the ore at depth. The opening up of the Emma claim has encouraged an attempt being made to do similar work on the neighbouring Oro Denoro, owned by the King Mining Company, of Rossland, and on which chutes of ore of a grade that under present smelting conditions can be mined and treated at a small margin of profit, have been encountered.

THE B. C. MINE.

The B. C. mine, situate in Summit Camp, within a couple of miles of Eholt, the Boundary divisional point on the Canadian Pacific Railway Company's Columbia & Western Railway, is one of a group of mineral claims owned by the B. C. Chartered Company, Limited, of Montreal, Quebec. The claims comprising the group are the B. C., Truckee, Reveille, Hilda, Vashti, Falcon, J. W., London, Daisy Fraction, B. C. Fraction and Novelty Fraction, together containing an area of 268 acres. The B. C., upon which most of the development has been done, was located in the fall of 1896, and the following summer the work of opening up the mine was commenced. To the end of 1901 the footage of work done in underground development of the mine totalled 5,876 lineal feet, 1,106 feet being sinking and raising and 4,770 feet crosscutting and drifting. The deepest shaft is down 400 feet. This mine was the first in the district to ship ore in quantity to a smelter. Commencing in January, 1900, its shipments during the first half of that year totalled 3,950 tons, and by the end of the year the output had been increased to 19,618 tons. Its production during 1901 was 47,517 tons, making an aggregate of 67,135 tons, having an average assay value of .015 oz. gold, 2.45 oz. silver, and 5.8 per cent. copper, wet assay. About four-tenths of this ore was treated at the Canadian Smelting Works, Trail, and practically the whole of the remaining six-tenths at the British Columbia Copper Company's smelter, Greenwood. The price of copper having fallen, the mine was closed down during eight months of 1902, but underground work was resumed in September, and by the end of that year 14,443 tons of ore were added to the total output of the mine. A considerable reduction having been made in freight and treatment charges, the "run of the mine" was sent to the smelter, with the result that the average value of the ore shipped fell to 1.75 oz. silver and 4.1 per cent. copper for the 1902 product. A lot of surface trenching to bedrock was done last summer, resulting in some fair showings of copper ore being met with. The power plant at the B. C. includes four boilers, together about 225 h. p.; a straight-line four-drill Rand air-compressor; half a Class G Ingersoll-Sergeant air-compressor, rated at 10 drills; one large and two small hoisting engines, two sinking pumps, an electric light engine and dynamo, and a full complement of accessories. A spur from the Phoenix branch of the Columbia & Western Railway gives the mine railway connection. Mr. S. F. Parrish, M. E., who was recently appointed general manager of the Le Roi mine at Rossland and the smelter at Northport, Washington, has been in charge of the B. C. mine since the beginning of 1900.

WINNIPEG AND GOLDEN CROWN.

The Winnipeg and Golden Crown are adjoining mines situate in Wellington Camp, about eight miles from Greenwood. Both were among the shipping mines of the Boundary during part of 1902, though their production, respectively, was comparatively small, and both are inoperative at the present time. The Winnipeg was located in the summer of 1895, and in 1897 a company named the Winnipeg Mining & Smelting Company was incorporated to acquire and develop the claim. This company did a great deal of work, and shipped some of the ore to the smelters. Towards the end of 1900 the Winnipeg Mines, Limited, was incorporated to acquire the assets of the old company. During 1901 this company shipped 1,040 tons of ore, and whilst operating in 1902 added 785 tons to the total production of the mine, which, including the output of 1900 is 2,001 tons, much of it ore running $13 per ton gross, and consequently of a generally higher grade than the average ore produced by Boundary mines. High assay values could be got from hand samples, but the best returns from carload lots were $48 per ton from one car, and $27 per ton from 57 tons, these being the gold returns from two lots from one vein. Silver varies from 1 oz. to 6 oz. per ton, and copper runs about 1½ per cent. About 4,500 lineal feet of work have been done in underground development, two-thirds in sinking and raising, and the remainder in crosscutting and drifting. The deepest workings are 400 feet depth. The ore veins are numerous, but most of the work has been done on three of them, these yielding practically all the ore produced. The Winnipeg has an area of about 27 acres. A half-mile spur from Hartford Junction connects the mine with the Phoenix branch of the Columbia & Western Railway. The power plant installed included two steam boilers, two hoisting engines, a 14x22 Rand straight-line air-compressor, air-receiver, steam pumps, machine drills, etc.; but fire last summer rendered useless some of this machinery, and the mine has not since been worked. Fortunately most of the mine buildings escaped destruction. Efforts are being made to arrange for a resumption of work.

The Golden Crown has had a somewhat similar experience to that of the Winnipeg, in that it was worked from 1897 to 1900 by one company and in 1901 passed into the possession of a re-organised company. The Brandon and Golden Crown Mining Company, Limited, did nearly 2,500 feet of underground work, and shipped 2,241 tons of ore of an average good grade; and then it gave place to the Golden Crown Mines, Limited, which has its head office in Brandon, Manitoba. The new company worked only a few months, during which its output of ore was 625 tons, making the aggregate of ore produced 2,866 tons. No. 1 shaft is 322 feet in depth, and levels have been run at 50, 100, 150 and 300 feet, the last-mentioned being about 900 feet in length. Work has been done on only three veins, the others crossing the property not yet having been opened up. The mine has railway connection similar to that giving the Winnipeg ore-shipping facilities. The power equipment includes two boilers together 100 h. p., a 12x18 Rand straight-line air-compressor, air-receiver, hoisting engine, steam pumps, machine drills, etc. This mine was the first in the district to put a mine-cage in its shaft.

OTHER COPPER-GOLD MINES.

The mines already dealt with are those that produced and shipped more or less copper-gold ore in 1902. Besides these there are some properties, on which copper ores occur, that were either inactive last year or did not ship any ore. The best known of these will have mention before the quartz mines of the district have notice. In Greenwood Camp there are the Brooklyn and Stemwinder group, owned by the Dominion Copper Company, Limited, of Toronto (above mentioned as owning the Emma mine); and the Gold Drop, belonging to the Gold Drop Mining Company, Limited, of Montreal, Quebec. The Dominion Copper Company's claims include the Brooklyn, Stemwinder, Idaho, Montezuma and Standard, all in or near the town of Phoenix; and the Rawhide, distant about half a mile to the southward.

Brooklyn and Stemwinder.— The Brooklyn and Stemwinder are among the oldest locations in Greenwood Camp, the latter by James Attwood and J. Scholefield on August 3, 1891; and the former by S. Mangott and J. M. Taylor on the following day. There is little official information available relative to these properties. From other reliable sources, though, it has been ascertained that development work approximating between 3,000 and 4,000 lineal feet has been done on the Brooklyn, which has a shaft 208 feet in depth, from which levels have been run at 150 and 250 feet respectively; whilst the adjoining Stemwinder has a shaft 344 feet in depth, but only a comparatively small footage of drifting and crosscutting. It is stated on what is believed to be good authority that one chute of ore in the Brooklyn mine has been proved to be at least 1,000 feet in length and 20 feet in width at the 250-foot level. This mine has a considerable quantity of ore on the dump, but has made only one shipment of about 150 tons, sent to the smelter in 1900 for a bulk test. The average value of the ore is understood to be about $5 in all values, but this statement has not been confirmed by anyone connected with the company. The Stemwinder has ore somewhat similar in character to that occurring on the Brooklyn, but as yet it has not been found in such great quantity on the former. The Idaho, which adjoins the Brooklyn on the south, has had a shaft sunk on it, and a crosscut has been run from this towards the Brooklyn workings, but development here is not yet extensive. The Rawhide shaft connects at 184 feet with a crosscut tunnel run about 450 feet into a high hill. This shaft passed through a chute of nice-looking ore which has not yet been opened out.

The Gold Drop.— The Gold Drop adjoins the Snowshoe, on the west of the latter. No work has been done on this property since the summer of 1900. Up to then some 1,905 lineal feet of work had been done in underground development, 1,510 feet being crosscutting and drifting, and 395 feet winzes and raises. These workings disclosed the presence in the mine of large bodies of ore, but so far as known only a single test carload was shipped to the smelter. It is understood that the owners are not disposed to work the mine at present, waiting rather for lower freight and treatment rates before resuming operations. The small power plant installed here includes a four-drill air-compressor, air-receiver, 40 h. p. locomotive boiler, steam pump, machine drills, etc.

Oro Denoro.— In Summit Camp, near Eholt, the Oro Denoro, R. Bell and Blue Bell each had attention at one time or another between 1897 and 1901. The Oro Denoro was owned until recently by the King Mining Company, Limited, of Rossland, B. C. Last December the Denoro Mines, Limited, was incorporated to acquire from the King Mining Company this and other mineral claims. More than 1,100 lineal feet of work have been done on the Oro Denoro, including a shaft 185 feet in depth and three crosscut tunnels. The showings of ore on the property are promising, whether outcroppings at the surface or encountered in the tunnels; and it is confidently believed that when work shall be resumed, which it is intended shall be at an early date, the output of ore will, at the lower freight and treatment rates now obtainable, bring in returns more than sufficient to pay operating expenses. There is on the property a small plant consisting of a 40 h. p. locomotive boiler, a 10x12 air-compressor, air-receiver, hoisting engine, steam pump, machine drills, etc. The R. Bell shipped 480 tons of ore in 1901, but no work has since been done on this claim. More than 1,000 feet of work have been done, including a vertical shaft 215 feet in depth, with levels at 80 and 200 feet, respectively.

R. Bell.— The grade of the ore obtained was satisfactory, but no permanent chute of pay ore was met with — only bunches here and there — so that there was not sufficient encouragement to continue prospecting under the conditions then existing. The claim will likely receive renewed attention later. A 25 h. p. boiler, 6x8 Bacon hoist, and a 3¼ Little Giant machine drill, operated by steam, were in use whilst work was being done underground.

The Blue Bell.— The Blue Bell, situate in the neighbourhood of the B. C. mine, was for some months under bond to a company formed in Illinois, but the option to purchase was not availed of. Whilst the agreement was in force a shaft was sunk 133 feet, but at that depth it was in a sheet of porphyry which cut off the ore. As similar conditions were found to exist in the B. C., it is probable the ore occurs below the porphyry, as it does in that mine. However, the owners declined to extend the time for a substantial payment under the bond, so the Eastern men threw it up. Short drifts were run in ore at 50 and 100 feet depth, respectively, whilst work was in progress. The Mountain View, situate between the R. Bell and the Blue Bell; Maple Leaf, one of the Rathmullen group; and the Rambler, prospected by shaft, crosscuts and diamond drilling by the Everett & Spokane Mining Company, are other mineral claims within a couple of miles of Eholt that have been prospected considerably.

The Morrison.— The Morrison, in Deadwood Camp, is a property that will probably ere long be placed on the list of regular shippers, but for some months this mine has been closed down. For several years the Morrison was operated by the Morrison Gold Mining Company, of Spokane, Washington, until January, 1900, when the Morrison Mines, Limited, was organised to take over all the assets of the old company. There are three veins of ore opened on the property, but only one has been explored to any extent. The ore bodies in the main vein upon which work has been done are from 10 to 40 feet in width. Altogether about 3,000 lineal feet of work have been done underground, some 450 feet being sinking and raising, and 2,550 feet crosscutting and drifting. The diamond drill bored 1,011 feet of holes (all on the 300-foot level), and this crosscut several large ore bodies, which have not yet been opened up, though trial shipments of ore — 433 tons in all — were made to the Greenwood, Grand Forks and Trail smelters for test purposes, but the mineral content was not published. An announcement was made recently that a contract had been arranged with the Montreal & Boston Copper Company's smelter to take ore, and that consequently operations would be resumed at the mine at an early date. The mine is equipped with two boilers, together 110 h. p.; a 16x24 straight-line Rand air-compressor, rated at 5 drills; machine drills; air-receiver; No. 7 Cameron sinking pump; and, at the 200-foot level station, a 7x9 Lidgerwood hoisting engine. With the plant and equipment now at the mine a daily output of 100 tons of ore is stated to be practicable. There are about 5,000 tons of ore on the dump. The mine buildings include boiler and engine house, boarding and bunk houses, and all other requisite accommodation. The mine is on Copper Creek, about three miles northwest of Greenwood, with which it has waggon road connection. The Deadwood Camp branch of the Columbia & Western Railway, from Greenwood to the Mother Lode and Sunset mines, passes within a mile of the Morrison, to which a survey has been made for a spur, giving about a 3 per cent. grade on a direct route.

King Solomon and Copper Mine.— In Copper Camp oxidised copper-bearing veins are met with on the King Solomon and Copper Mine (the latter known locally as the Big Copper) mineral claims. It is not unlikely that these also occur on other claims in this camp, but the two properties named are the only ones opened up in that locality. Some interesting observations by Mr. R. W. Brock, geologist of the Dominion Geological Survey, on these veins were quoted in the first of this series of papers. (See "Mining Record" for January, 1903, page 455.) On the King Solomon the oxide zone is found, and on the Copper Mine the richest sulphide zone. A prospect shaft was sunk on the King Solomon several years ago; but the work done last year was the making of a deep open cut into the side of the hill, taking out rich iron and copper oxide. Some 850 tons of this ore were sent to district smelters, but as it had to be hauled by horse teams about four miles to the railway at Deadwood, for shipment thence to the reduction works, freight costs took too large a proportion of the returns to induce the owner of the claim to continue shipping. Work done last year on the Copper Mine claim exposed an ore body 174 feet in length and 82 feet in width. An open cut, averaging 15 feet in width and 26 feet 6 inches in height, was run 93 feet in the ore, of which there is a considerable on the dump, ready for shipment whenever market conditions shall be deemed favourable enough. The opening up of this property directed attention anew to Copper Camp, and it is likely that it will lead to the claim being sold ere long to a strong company. The Copper Mine is owned by Mr. George B. McAulay, of Spokane, Washington, managing director of the Cariboo-McKinney Mining & Milling Company, Limited, and Mr. John Morand, of Greenwood. Mr. D. C. Corbin, the well-known builder of the Spokane Northern Railway, also of Spokane, owns the King Sclomon.

Ruby and Golconda.— There are several promising copper claims in Smith's Camp, near Boundary Falls, among them the Ruby and the Golconda. In 1901 the Ruby was under bond to men resident in Detroit, Michigan, who did a lot of surface work, uncovering several chutes of copper-gold ore of good grade, of which they sent to the smelter 85 tons. They installed a 45 h. p. boiler and worked two machine drills by steam, these facilitating the driving of two tunnels, one about 165 feet and the other of shorter length. Financial difficulties eventually necessitated a cessation of operations, and the bond lapsed. The Ruby, which is owned by Messrs. W. G. McMynn and George Cook, is situate within a quarter of a mile of the Boundary Falls smelter; but the Golconda group is in the hills to the west of Boundary Creek, and about a couple of miles away. No work was done on the Golconda last year, but men are now doing some further prospecting on the property. A shaft was sunk four or five years ago, and later a crosscut tunnel was driven 280 feet, the calculation being that the ledge would be encountered at 450 feet in, and would there give a vertical depth of 275 feet, but there remains 175 feet of tunnel to be driven before this expectation can be realised. The group comprises the Golconda, Cleveland, Laocoon, York, Wild Rose and Gold Bed. Hon. George E. Foster is one of the owners; and another, J. C. Haas, now of Spokane, has directed the prospecting work done on the claims. There are numerous other promising copper claims in the several camps of the Boundary.

CAMP M'KINNEY.

Work at Camp McKinney during 1902 was almost restricted to the Cariboo-McKinney Mining & Milling Company's Cariboo mine. Lately some activity has, however, been shown in connection with the further development of the Waterloo, but difficulties, first in connection with the organization of a new company to acquire the property from the old Waterloo company, and later from insecurity of title to the mineral claim, prevented much progress being made. These obstacles appear to have been overcome, and more energy is being displayed in opening up the chute of rich ore met with at the 160-foot level than has heretofore marked the development of this promising mine. A more powerful hoisting engine has been purchased and shipped from Spokane to the mine, and it has been decided to sink another 100 feet before the surface water becomes troublesome in the spring.

The Waterloo has no tonnage of consequence to add to the year's output from this camp. Prospecting has been done on several other properties in the camp, but no important developments have been reported. Three miles southeast of Camp

McKinney are the Dayton, Dewey, Jim Crow, Night Hawk and other claims on the divide between the main Rock Creek and the south fork of that stream, upon which surface prospecting has disclosed the presence of big bodies of mineral that give promise of being well worth opening up.

The Cariboo has maintained the creditable record of the several previous years. The following statistics for the year ended November 30, 1902, are official: Ore crushed, 15,616 tons; bullion produced, 8,400 ounces; concentrates produced 550 tons; value of bullion, $112,300; value of concentrates, $17,381; drifting done. 1,005 feet; raising done, 100 feet; average number of men employed, 50; dividend paid, 4 per cent. The tonnage of ore mined and milled the previous year, as shown in the Company's last annual report, was 16,862 tons, yielding 9,439 ounces of gold and 428 tons of concentrates.

THE SLOCAN DISTRICT.

THE Slocan District embraces a ruggedly mountainous area west and north of Kootenay Lake and south of a line extending east from the north end of the latter. The chief productive areas are those in the vicinity of Sandon, Three Forks, McGuigan and Whitewater. Many of the mines here are situated at very high altitudes, frequently as much as 5,000 to 6,000 feet above sea level, where erosion has cleared away the debris or waste from the veins; but locations have also been made at lesser elevations and in the valleys. The first discoveries were reported in the autumn of 1891, the Payne mine being located on the 9th of September of that year, and the Noble Five group about the same time. In the following summer a number of other discoveries were made in the districts adjoining these properties, and in 1892 the first mines began to ship ore. The Whitewater sent out a trial consignment, and shortly after the Bess and Dardanelles claims entered the productive class, and in the winter of 1892 and 1893 ore was packed out from the Washington, Freddie Lee, Idaho and Mountain Chief. Since that time the history and development in the Slocan has been a record of great activity and of almost continuous success up to 1897. In 1899, labour trouble intervening, the production somewhat fell off, but 1900 was a year of record achievement in the matter of production, this being valued at about $3,028,000. The conditions during the past two years have not been favourable to silver-lead mining, and in consequence production has fallen off considerably. The official returns for 1901 place the value of the yield at $1,865,752, and that of the Ainsworth division at $331,011, the combined tonnage from these two districts being 31,431 tons. The value of the production in 1902 is estimated to be worth approximately $1,425,000, the following mines having shipped during this period:

Mine	Tons	Mine	Tons
Payne	2,638	Ivanhoe	717
Sunset (Jackson Basin)	827	Reco	511
American Boy	1,197	Arlington	3,580
Hewett	805	Bosun	2,110
Last Chance	168	Wonderful	181
Enterprise	2,300	Lavina	85
Bismarck	62	Queen Bess	180
Silver Glance	257	Whitewater	2,962
Ottawa	68	Capella	60
Florence	1	Trade Dollar	20
Slocan Boy	158	Neepawa	123
Hartney	25	Marion	80
May	5	Paystreak	7
Surprise	22	Monitor	1,306
Slocan Star	815	Duplex	7
Emily Edith	20	Wakefield	220

Prescott	4	Rambler	4,187
Molly Gibson	2,100	Washington	187
Folliott	2	C. O. D.	2
London Hill	115	Ruth	888
Antoine	207	R. E. Lee	144
Spectator	4	Red Fox	63
Hampton	13	Mercury	21
Dardanelles	21	Porcupine	2
Charleston	11	Pinto	13
Noble Five	21	Soho	64
Fisher Maiden	20	Republic	22
		Total	28,428

In a paper recently read before the Canadian Mining Institute, the author, Mr. S. S. Fowler, thus briefly describes the general geology of the district:

"In the northern part of the district there is about 100 square miles of slate formation, from which the major part of the silver-lead output has been derived. The veins which cut across the slates are from a few inches to many feet in width, and are probably related genetically to a series of dikes of felsite and other intrusive rocks. The larger veins contain many inclusions of the country rock. The gangue minerals are chiefly spathic iron and quartz. South of the slate formation there is a large area of coarse granite, in which there are many veins of value, though they are narrower than those in the slate. They are more sharply defined and contain fewer inclusions of country rock. The ores are harder and tougher, contain a larger proportion of spathic iron and quartz, besides a greater variety of other gangue minerals, and important quantities of the richer silver-bearing minerals, finely disseminated. As in the slates, an important part—frequently the chief part—of the values is highly concentrated and is mined and shipped with but little sorting as clean ore. East of the slates and granite, along the west shore of Kootenay Lake, there is a narrow fringe of very old schists and slates, which in the vicinity of Ainsworth present valuable ore deposits of good size and appearance of considerable permanency; but the ores are of low grade in silver, and, except some which lie near the granite area, cannot be worked at much, if any, profit under present conditions.

"The ores shipped from the district comprise: (1) Silicious oxidised ore from near the surface of the veins occurring in the slates. This was formerly important in quantity, but is so no longer, the superficial ore bodies having been worked out in most cases. It assayed 20 to 30 per cent. in lead, and was often high-grade in silver. (2) Galena ore, which now forms the bulk of the output, either as lump ore (hand sorted) or fine concentrates. It averages about 40 per cent. lead, 12 per cent. zinc, and the remainder quartz and siderite, besides the sulphur combined with lead and zinc, and carries 80 to 100 ounces silver per ton. (3) Silicious lead ore, silver-bearing but very low in lead; obtained chiefly from the granite area and not amenable to the ordinary process of mechanical concentration. (4) Blende, obtained as lump ore (hand-sorted) or as a middling product from some mills. It is silver-bearing and often is of high grade. It is shipped to European zinc smelters, or is mixed to some extent with the galena concentrate. The Slocan ore is affording a gradually increasing quantity of this rich zinc ore, and a satisfactory solution of the problem of realizing on all the values in it is at present one of the greatest troubles in the district."

During the past year none of the larger mines were operated to the full extent, work being chiefly restricted to development. On the Ruth, Whitewater, Last Chance and Noble Five operations were suspended for a greater portion of the year. Three mines, however — the Rambler-Cariboo, Sunset and Monitor — paid handsome profits, and this despite the fact that metal prices were exceptionally low, silver indeed having reached the lowest point on record.

The principal silver-lead producing mines are the Payne, Slocan Star, Last Chance, Ruth, Ivanhoe, American Boy, Whitewater, Rambler-Cariboo, Idaho, Monitor and Reco. At the Payne the large concentrator, formerly part of the equipment of the Lanark mine, was placed in position and has been steadily operated. The mine has also recently sent out several carloads of zinc concentrates to a smelter at Iola, Kansas. At the Monitor large reserves of ore have been blocked out, over 3,000 feet of work having been done on the property since September. 1900. A force of 40 men have been employed on the Rambler-Cariboo, in the McGuigan Basin, and a mill was installed on the property in the spring of the year. The Ivanhoe, American Boy and Antoine have all opened up extensive bodies of ore; while a new shipping mine has been added to the list, in the Silver Glance, profits from one carload of ore being $3,200.

THE DRY ORE BELT.

The largest producing mine last year was the Arlington, in the Slocan City division. Experiments are being made at this property with a view to ascertaining the best method of concentrating the lower-grade products. This section of country comprises an area of approximately 100 square miles to the east of Slocan River and Lake. The country is extremely mountainous in character, and the difficulties in mining are increased by the frequent occurrence of faults and irregularity of the ore deposits. The characteristic ores of the district, found in the granite, contain argentite, native silver and gold in a quartz gangue, values in many instances being remarkably high. This class of material, which is known as a "dry ore," has been in great demand by local smelters, as contributing to the economical reduction of the heavy galenas or "wet ores" of the Sandon and immediately adjacent mining territory. The principal mines of the district are: The Enterprise, owned and operated by the Enterprise Mines, Limited, of London; the Iron Horse; the V. & M. Mines; the Champion Group; the Myrtle Group; the Arlington; the Speculator Group; the Mabon Group; the Hampton; the Bondholder; the Ottawa; the Tamarac; the Morning Star; the Exchange; the Phoenix-Viking; the Transfer; the Black Prince; the Fourth of July, and others.

NELSON DISTRICT.

WITH the exception of the early discoveries located on the shores of Kootenay Lake, the Nelson District is the oldest in British Columbia in which lode mining for the precious metals has been carried on. It is of irregular area, and has been defined by including that portion of the territory lying east of the Columbia not contained in the Slocan District. It embraces three known mineral belts of wide and distinct characters, namely, the copper-silver deposits of Toad Mountain, the free-gold belt to the immediate south of Kootenay River, and the mineral zone known as the Ymir and Erie camps.

The earliest discovery was the famous Silver King mine, on Toad Mountain, accidentally discovered in 1886 and located in the following year. This mine was incorporated in 1893 as the Hall Mines, Limited, and afterwards reconstructed as the Hall Mining & Smelting Company, Limited. Early in 1902 the directors of this company decided that it was advisable to suspend operations at the Silver King mine. The property was, however, leased, and work has been continued on a small scale. At the smelter during the year the total tonnage received amounted to 33,125 tons; 4,136 tons of lead bullion were shipped, and 578 tons of copper matte.

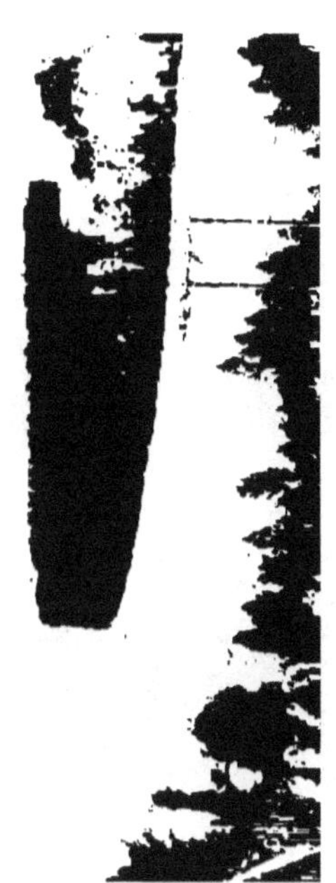

GLENORA, ON THE STIKINE RIVER.

TELEGRAPH CREEK, ON THE STIKINE.

Relatively little was accomplished in what is known as the free-gold belt during the year. An amalgamation was effected of the Athabasca and Venus companies' interests, and a tramway installed connecting the Venus mine with the Athabasca mill, and towards the end of the year shipments were commenced. Operations have also been prosecuted at the Poorman mine by the Duncans United Mines—a London company—with encouraging results. The Fern mine, at Hall Creek, has been acquired under bond, and the ten-stamp mill having been thoroughly overhauled, preparations have been made for the extensive development ot the property. At the Blue Bird mine, owned by the Montana Gold Mining Company, a 20-ton concentrator and an air-compressor plant are being installed.

THE YMIR SECTION.

The Ymir division of the Nelson district occupies a very important position as a mining area. Geologically, the rocks of the district may be divided into four main groups — (1) the granites; (2) the dark eruptives and associated fragmental rocks; (3) the schistose series, including schists, slates, crystalline limestones, dolomites and quartzites; and (4) the basal Shuswap series. Traversing the country are numerous dikes, which are often found at right angles to the veins. The natural position of and economic conditions prevailing in the district are extremely advantageous. The mines have direct railway communication with the Northport, Trail and Nelson smelters; excellent wagon roads have been built to all the producing mines; there is an abundance of timber for mining purposes, and water-power is in nearly every case available. The most important mine in this section is the Ymir, owned by the Ymir Gold Mine, Limited, of London. The production of this property during the year is placed at 50,000 tons, having a gross value of $340,000. About 8,500 tons of concentrates were shipped to the Trail and Nelson smelters, the average value of which was from $28 to $30 per ton. The 1902 returns, however, are disappointing as compared with previous output, and this is explained partly on the grounds that early in the year operations were curtailed in consequence of the quantity of water in the lower workings, and also that payable ore was not encountered at the 1,000-foot level. The tunnel on this level reached the vein at a distance of 1,000 feet from the point of entrance, in April, 1902; but, the values proving unsatisfactory, drifting was continued in an easterly direction. Mr. Edward Hooper, an English consulting mining engineer, who was sent up by the directors of the company to report on the property last summer, expressed the opinion that the ore chute had a trend towards the east, and further stated that at the easternmost face of the drift on the 1,000-foot level the average value of the ore was $7.50 a ton, or equal to the values of the mine product previously profitably milled. Developments since have been directed towards making a connection with the upper workings. As a result of Mr. Hooper's report, the company was reconstructed, in order to obtain necessary additional working capital. By the completion of the long adit tunnel, natural drainage for the mine has been secured, and a costly pumping service avoided. Another advantage is that hoisting has been rendered unnecessary, and in future the ore will be taken out through the tunnel. It is estimated that there are now 100,000 tons of ore blocked out in the mine. Stoping is in progress in the fourth, fifth and sixth levels, but the eighth and ninth levels have not as yet been mined. During the year a cyanide plant of large capacity was installed and operated with satisfactory results. The cost of mill operations approximates 75 cents a ton; and the cost of mining, including repairs and development, about $2.15.

At the Wilcox mine, owned by the Broken Hill Mining & Development Company, a stamp mill was installed in 1902, and the property extensively developed. The ore is brought down by means of an aerial tramway.

Other mines in this section are the Foghorn, owned by the Golden Monarch Mining & Milling Company, of Spokane (Washington), at which mine a large concentrator is to be shortly erected; the Union Jack, on Porcupine Creek, operated by the Active Gold Mining Company, of Cincinnati; the Hunter V., recently acquired by the Standard Development Syndicate, of Nelson; and the Queen. Of these, the Wilcox has become regularly productive, and the other properties mentioned are likely also to ship largely in the near future.

In the Erie section, the Arlington and Second Relief mines have been operated, the former having produced some 8,000 tons of ore, at a profit of $25,000. Placer gold discoveries were reported to have been made on the North Fork of Salmon River during the year, and two companies have been organized to carry on hydraulic operations there in 1903.

The ore shipments from the Nelson Division in 1902 are estimated at 70,000 tons, and the value at rather under $600,000.

EAST KOOTENAY.

THE District of East Kootenay, which includes the Golden, Windermere and Fort Steele Mining Divisions, comprises an extensive area, embracing the eastern slopes of the Selkirk and Purcell Mountains, the upper portion of the Columbia and Kootenay Valley, and the western slope of the Rocky Mountain Range. The productive area is at present chiefly confined to sections of the Fort Steele Division, or in the drainage area of the Upper Kootenay River and its tributaries south of Findlay Creek — which is itself of very considerable extent, aggregating approximately 7,000 square miles. In the Fort Steele District are situated the Crow's Nest coal fields and the four important silver-lead producing mines, namely, the St. Eugene, the North Star, the Sullivan Group and the Estelle; while both in this Division and in those of Golden and Windermere are numerous partially developed prospects of unquestionable promise. In this connection special reference may be made to the Paradise and Delphine groups, in the latter division, both of which properties are on a productive footing, despite unfavourable conditions in the matter of inadequate transportation facilities.

EARLY HISTORY OF MINING.

The commencement of operations in the East Kootenay District dates back from 1864, when rich discoveries of alluvial deposits were made on Wild Horse Creek, which joins the Kootenay River at Fort Steele. It is officially estimated that ordinary claims on two miles of this creek yielded from $20 to $30 to the hand per day, and that from 1864 to 1866 five thousand persons were engaged in placer mining in East Kootenay. By the close of 1866 the locality was largely abandoned, except by Chinese; but of late years the old workings have been operated by hydraulic methods. Meanwhile in 1888 attention was first directed to quartz mining, 102 claims being located that year in the Golden and Windermere divisions; but practically no important discoveries were made until 1892, when the North Star mine was located by a prospector named Joseph Bourgeois, who was also the discoverer of the principal Rossland mines. Many years previous to this, however, in the late seventies, the outcrops of coal in the Crow's Nest Pass valley had been noted, and the value of the measures subsequently computed by Dr. Selwyn, in a report published by the Canadian Geological Survey in 1891. Active mining operations were inaugurated at the North Star mine in 1895, and in September of that year two carloads of ore were shipped to the Everett smelter, via Jennings, the gross smelter returns being $68.70 per ton. Operations were first systematically commenced also during this year at the Sullivan and St. Eugene mines. Contemporaneously with the construction in 1897 of the Crow's Nest Pass Railway from Fort McLeod, in the Northwest Territories, through the Crow's Nest Pass and along the valleys of the Kootenay, Moyie and Goat rivers, to Kootenay Lake, the work of opening up the vast coal fields of the Crow's Nest area was started, and by the time the railway reached the mines 10,000 tons of coal had been banked out, and more than 4,000 feet of heading had been driven. The building of the railway exerted a most stimulating effect on the mining industry generally in East Kootenay, reviving the interest in the resources of the northern portions of the district, which has since been the scene of much prospecting activity, while the silver-lead production in 1900 from the Fort Steele division has since eclipsed that of the Slocan.

LABOUR CONDITIONS.

The labour conditions of the metalliferous districts are similar to those obtaining in West Kootenay. The cost of sinking a 5x8 shaft in hard diorite at the North Star mine is estimated at $28.26 per foot. At the Crow's Nest collieries the average wages earned by the miners is $3 to $4 per day; general mine labour costs $2 to $2.75 per shift; general surface labour, $1.75 to $2; boys receive $1 to $1.75. The duration of shift underground is eight hours, "from pit's mouth to pit's mouth." Miners are charged for oil, powder, squibs, and lost or broken tools, but not for tools and repairs. Not more than four pounds of powder are allowed to a pair at one time. The prices paid for work in 1900 were as follows: Per ton, in rooms with lights, 60 cents; with closed lights, 80 cents. In narrow work the usual tonnage is paid, also yardage, and $1 per set for timbers. The allowance for branching a stall is $1.25; other "considerations" are settled as they arise.

PRINCIPAL MINES.

The North Star group is owned by the North Star Mining Company, Limited; authorised capital, $1,500,000, in shares of a par value of $1; head office, Board of Trade Building, Montreal. The property comprises the North Star, O. K., Dreadnaught, Rowan, Daffodil, Notre Dame, Dorae, Maverick, Good Luck, Canton, Full House, Brandon, Stemwinder and Ontario mineral locations, situated 16 miles west of the Kootenay River as it flows from its source southwards. A branch line of railway was built from the brook in February of last year to Kimberley, to which point — a distance of four miles — the ore is transported by means of an aerial tramway having an hourly capacity of 10 tons. Shipments during the year covered the expenses of development. The company paid out of reserve capital $58,000 in dividends. The ores are clean, and consist of silver-lead sulphides and carbonates, requiring no concentration or sorting. The ore bodies occur in the form of more or less parallel depressions or channels, several hundred feet in length, with a maximum width of 75 feet and a maximum depth of 40 feet. The ore is extracted in large chambers, timbered with square sets.

The Sullivan group of mineral claims, situated on the northeast side of Mark Creek, about one and a half miles north of the North Star mine, is owned by the Sullivan Group Mining Company, Limited; authorised capital, $2,500,000, in $1 shares; head office, Spokane, Washington. The mine has been under development for several years. The ore body has been proved to be of considerable extent. The ore is a fine-grained galena, having an average value of 40 per cent. lead and 20 ounces silver per ton. Operations for the greater part of last year were suspended at the mine. The ore averages from 16 to 17 ounces silver and 33 to 35 per cent. lead per ton. The company have commenced the erection of a smelter.

The St. Eugene group of mines, comprising the St. Eugene, Peter, Moyie, Queen of the Hills, Lake Shore and other properties, situated to the east of the town of Moyie, on Moyie Lake, is owned by the St. Eugene Consolidated Mining Company.

Limited; capital, $3,500,000, upon which a dividend of $210,000 was paid in 1901. Some development work was performed during the year, but owing to unsatisfactory market conditions, no shipments were made. Under ordinarily favourable circumstances the mine is capable of producing very heavily, the ore bodies being of great size. The concentrates carry from 65 to 70 per cent. lead. The silver contents vary from 1-2 to 2-3 ounce to the per cent. lead. The ore is conveyed to the concentrator, which was built in 1900 and is the largest of its kind in the province, by means of an aerial tramway, at a cost of seven cents per ton.

CROW'S NEST COAL COMPANY.

The property of the Crow's Nest Coal Company, Limited (authorised capital $4,500,000) comprises 11,169 acres of coal lands situated near Marten Creek, Coal Creek, and Morrissey Creek. On the eastern portion of the property, near Marten Creek, containing 3,969 acres, there are fifteen seams of coal, four of which are cannel or gas coal. The remaining seams are bituminous, and admirably adapted for coking. In the western section, 12 miles distant, are 12 superimposed seams of coal outcripping from the mountain slopes, varying from 2 to 30 feet in thickness. The method of working is by the pillar and stall system. The present output is about 2,000 tons a day. The number of coke ovens now in operation is 600, but others are in course of building. The ovens are of the ordinary bee-hive shape, 12 feet in diameter, placed in double rows. The average charge of coal is 6.5 metric tons; the production of coke per charge averages 4.50 percentage, in coke 68 per cent. Time of burning, 72 hours; average output for each oven per day, 1.5. The annual product from the collieries since 1898 has been as follows: 1898, 8,996 tons; 1899, 116,200 tons; 1900, 232,245 tons; 1901, 425,350 tons. There are at present 400 ovens in operation at Fernie, producing about 700 tons of coke daily, while 200 other ovens have been built at Michel and 200 more are to be immediately erected there, and 100 are to be erected at Morrissey.

GEOLOGICAL FORMATION.

The cretaceous rocks in which the coal is found have assumed in general the form of a flat-bottomed basin, though there are many places where local faults destroy the symmetry of this arrangement. Some of these faults are of considerable dimensions, and will form an important factor to be reckoned with in the problem of systematically mining the coal. In order to furnish an idea of the character and thickness of the cretaceous rocks, Mr. McEvoy includes in his report the measurement of a section of the escarpment on the Elk River, about three miles north of the Morrissey Siding, which, it will be remembered, is a few miles west of Fernie. This particular spot is the place where years ago Mr. Fernie had made excavations on the outcrops of the coal seams. The crest of the spur in which the measured section is included has an average slope of nearly 30 degrees, and afforded the exceptional opportunity of getting an unbroken section of almost 5,000 feet. This measurement shows a total of 4,736 feet, of which 216 feet consist in coal seams of thicknesses varying from 1 foot to 46 feet. Of the total coal, by far the greater part — 198 feet — occurs in a thickness of measures of 1,847 feet. Besides the portions of coal measured as impure in the above list, there are some irregular layers of shaly material and nodular limestone in the larger seams. Making allowance for these and deducting some of the smaller seams that could not be profitably mined, say less than three feet, it may be safely concluded that there is a total thickness of workable coal of at least 100 feet.

Mr. McEvoy, continuing, points out that there is a development of 4,000 to 5,000 feet of measures above the top of the measured section, in which black shales are rarely found, brown colours prevailing throughout. The total thickness of cretaceous rocks deposited in the area, according to this estimate, is from 12,000 to

13,000 feet. It is not at all probable, says Mr. McEvoy, that a section could be found in any other part of the area corresponding exactly, or even closely, to the one given. A comparison of a part of the section with the beds at the mines on Coal Creek shows a great difference in thickness between the measures at the two places :

	Near Morrissey.	On Coal Creek.
Coal	10 feet	10 feet
Intervening beds	140 "	60 "
Coal	36 "	30 "
Intervening beds	197 "	42 "
Coal	6 "	6 "

It will be seen that while there is a great diminution of the intervening beds, the coal seams are fairly persistent. This may not be the case throughout the whole of the area, but whatever change may take place is as likely to be favourable as otherwise. Mr. McEvoy adds on this point: "The openings at Michel, 16 miles north of the mines on Coal Creek, expose three seams of coal, 15 to 17 feet in thickness, but there is not yet sufficient evidence to connect them with the seams at Coal Creek. What there is, however, tends to show that some of the seams at least have a greater thickness here than they have to the south." Since Mr. McEvoy wrote this, several other seams have been opened up, seven in all having been clearly demonstrated, in three of which development is proceeding on an extensive scale. While technical proof of the co-relation of these seams with those at Coal Creek and Morrissey is still lacking, there is a general conviction among the practical men on the spot that they are the same seams.

Mr. McEvoy concludes his valuable and interesting report with the following estimate of the ultimate yield of the mines : "Although the extent of the coal lands in the area can as yet be only somewhat roughly estimated, the estimate (230 square miles) should be near enough to the truth to be used as an argument for the calculation of the total available coal supply. The thickness used in the calculation is the minimum already given of 100 feet of workable coal:

"Total area of coal lands, 230 square miles, equalling 147,200 acres. One acre with 100 feet of coal would yield 153,480 tons of 2,240 pounds; 50,000 acres would yield 7,674,000,000 tons of 2,240 pounds; 147,200 acres would yield 22,595,200,000 tons of 2,240 pounds."

Estimated production in 1902 places the output of coal at 441,000 tons, and of coke at 112,000 tons. The output was somewhat restricted as a result of a serious explosion in the Fernie colliery in May, followed by a strike of the miners. A sum approximating a million dollars has been expended by the company in the period under review in equipment and development work. The monthly payroll at the collieries amounts to $100,000, 1,000 men being employed at Coal Creek, 600 at Michel, and 400 at Morrissey.

Extra prospecting was engaged in during the year in this section of the country, and some important discoveries of coal lands are reported to have been made in the Findley Valley and elsewhere. The government records show that no less than 252 applications were entered for coal and petroleum licences.

In the southern portion of the district the occurrence of petroleum is suspected, the indications being exceptionally promising.

Placer mining operations have been prosecuted on Perry and Wild Horse creeks, the yield from the latter locality being in the neighbourhood of $20,000, while on Perry Creek hydraulic machinery has been installed. A number of new discoveries of copper properties are reported to have been made in the St. Mary's and Elk River sections, and extensive surface showings of high-grade hematite iron ore have been partially exploited in the Bull River district and on Baker Mountain.

CARIBOO DISTRICT.

WHAT is commonly described as the Cariboo District includes the two mining divisions of Quesnel and Cariboo, and comprises a considerable area extending in a westerly direction from the summit of the Rocky Mountains coastward, for a distance of, approximately, about 360 miles, and north about 170 miles; total area being, approximately, 60,000 square miles. Through the centre of the district extends a wide and well-defined trough or valley of park-like country, through which the Cariboo waggon road, with its branches to the mining centres, passes. There is here much valuable arable and grazing land, while here are also found the extensive alluvial deposits and systems of ancient channels of buried rivers, which from their auriferous character render mining in the district an important industry. As is well known, the rich placer discoveries in the early fifties in this district were the means of first calling attention to the mineral possibilities of British Columbia. After, however, the shallow diggings had been profitably worked for a number of years by individual miners, the potentialities in the direction of hydraulic and deep-level mining presented themselves to capital, and of late years operations of a most extensive character have been carried on under company auspices in the district. With but few exceptions, however, the stage of profit-earning has hardly yet arrived, for in the equipment and exploitation of these extensive gravel beds not only large expenditures are necessary, but the time required to complete the work is considerable.

THE NEW ERA.

The new era of mining development began to manifest itself when Sir William Van Horne, then president of the Canadian Pacific Railway, and others associated with him, acquired the control of large auriferous areas on the South Fork of the Quesnel River, about four miles above the town of Quesnel Forks. Since that time other companies have begun to operate, and some of them on a very large scale. Immense dams have been constructed, and miles of fluming, tunnelling and other modern methods employed for the extraction of gold. The district has for two successive seasons suffered from a scarcity of water, consequent upon light snowfalls, and the gold yield, therefore, has fallen off very considerably. The most important mining centres of the Cariboo District are Barkerville, Quesnel Forks, Keithley Creek, Snowshoe Creek and Horsefly, and in each of these sections mining operations on a large scale are being conducted. At Quesnel Forks, however, an undertaking known as the Cariboo Consolidated Mining Co. is probably not only the most considerable hydraulic enterprise carried on in British Columbia, but also in the world. The mine is situated on the south Fork of the Quesnel River, four miles above the town of the same name, and includes a number of hydraulic leases, consisting of immense deposits of high-grade auriferous gravel, the average yield being from 20 to 92 cents per cubic yard. Under an extensive system of fluming, ditching and canals, covering an aggregate distance of 33 miles, a water supply is brought from Polley, Bootjack and Morehead lakes, having a delivering capacity of 5,000 miner's inches under a head of 400 feet. It is conservatively estimated that under normal conditions the mine is capable of producing, with a water supply at present available, from $300,000 to $400,000 per annum. Last season, on account of the adverse circumstances already referred to, the value of the gold recovered amounted to $61,000 only, actual washing operations being carried on for but a brief period. The rest of the season, however, was occupied in further opening up the mine. Up to the present time all profits from operations have been re-invested in the equipment of the property, which is now very complete; but it is confidently expected that hereafter the company will be in a position to pay handsome dividends to shareholders. The mine looks remarkably well, and the company has uncovered about half a mile of pay gravel. In this same vicinity are a number of other small enterprises, of which generally good reports have been received.

The National Hydraulic Mining Company, operating on Quesnel River, opened some promising ground during the season, and satisfactory results were obtained from the employment of a small prospecting dredge in the same locality. A considerable amount of prospecting was also done last summer on the creeks flowing into Quesnel Lake. Operations were continuously prosecuted during the season at the property of the Ward Horsefly Hydraulic Mining Company. The company were fortunate in having an abundant supply of water under a pressure of about 350 feet. The gravel is raised by means of an hydraulic elevator. The season's work is reported to have been very satisfactory.

BARKERVILLE DISTRICT.

In the Barkerville districts the conditions were somewhat more favourable as regards water supply, this being explained on the ground that the mines are at a higher elevation than are those in the Quesnel section. There is generally sufficient water to enable operations to be conducted for a period of three months, and the customary yield varies from $4,000 to $20,000 in the case of hydraulic mines, and considerably more in the case of drift mines. The principal mines here are those on Williams Creek owned by the Cariboo Gold Fields, Limited, the Mount claim, the Butts and Wintrip claims; the properties of the Cariboo Consolidated, Limited, operating on Lowhee Creek; the properties of the Dragon Creek Company, on Dragon Creek; the properties of the Cariboo Exploration Company, on Binns Creek; the Thistle Company's claims, on Eight-Mile Creek; and the Waverley Hydraulic, on Grouse Creek. Many of these mines paid large profits last year. Perhaps the most noteworthy developments of the season of 1902 were the discovery of pay gravel at depth at the Slough Creek, Limited, mine. A shaft was sunk here 362½ feet in rock, and a tunnel driven therefrom a distance of 1,100 feet. The importance of this discovery can hardly be over-estimated, for the success of the Slough Creek company means the beginning of deep-level mining on a large scale in Cariboo. The discovery of the hill channel of Keithley Creek on the Onward Creek was also a matter of much importance. The channel was tapped about 500 feet back from the present creek by running a tunnel. It is thought the gravel will average about 50 ounces or more to the set. On Lightning Creek some remarkably rich ground was also encountered on the Montgomery and Point claims, the former yielding 78 ounces of gold to the set 8-foot cap, while from the latter 162 ounces were taken out in six days, and 85 ounces from one set of timbers 8-foot cap. The output from the Barkerville district in 1901 was valued at $279,600: last year's yield is probably considerably greater.

Quartz mining in the Cariboo District is beginning to attract attention, and on Snowshoe Mountain in particular very promising properties have been opened up. There are meanwhile signs of a general revival and of increased activity in this historic section of the province, and as already the snowfall this winter has been exceptionally heavy, the season of 1903 promises to be a most successful one.

KAMLOOPS.

KAMLOOPS District, so far as mining is concerned, is yet in the prospect stage, though recent developments and explorations clearly indicate the extent of the mineralised area and point to future possibilities in the direction of important mining developments in this district. While up to the present time the principal centre of mining activity has been the Coal Hill section, situated three miles to the south of the town, there can be no doubt that the region tributary to the North Thompson River offers exceptional opportunities both to the prospector and the capitalist. The whole country north of Kamloops, for a distance of 100 miles, according to geological surveys, is rich in gold and silver ores. The territory is at present easily accessible both by trails and steamboat navigation, though, at the same time, prospecting is somewhat difficult on account of the worn-down character of the mountains and the superficial encumbrance of wash and timber. The principal mines of the Coal Hill camp lie in a belt of basic granite rocks traversing the country in a northwesterly direction. This belt extends for a distance of about six miles, and its extreme width is three miles. The granite rocks are in contact with the Nicola formation to the south, and overlaid by a bed of tertiary formation on the north. The elevation of the area, which is for the most part covered with glacial drift, is between 2,000 and 3,500 feet above sea level. The outcrops of the igneous rocks are scattered over the area, and consequently considerable surface exploration is necessary in tracing mineral exposures. The ore is primarily chalcopyrite, in some cases associated with magnetite, in others with pyrites, while calcite occurs in nearly all the veins, quartz, however, being sparingly distributed. At one mine bornite is found with chalcopyrite and some bands of grey copper in a felsite gangue.

COAL AND MICA.

In the valley of the North Thompson a number of seams of good coal have been discovered, and the analysis of the material made by the Geological Survey Department is as follows :

Hygroscopic water	2.22
Volatile combustible matter	38.10
Fixed carbon	46.76
Ash	15.92
Coke	59.68

At the headwaters of the Thompson and Canoe rivers, commercially valuable deposits of mica have also been found, the vein material or matrix of the deposits being a coarsely crystalline mixture of quartz or feldspar, in which frequently other minerals occur as crystals. The rocks from Kamloops northward are first of the Cache Creek series, which are later followed by rocks of the Adams Lake and Nisconlith series, which are sometimes massive diabases, but more frequently slate-like or schistose.

PRINCIPAL MINES.

These are the Iron Mask, Python group, Homestake group, Chieftain group, Pothook, Copper King, O. K. group, the Glen iron mines, and the Hardie cinnabar mines.

During 1902 the development work on the Iron Mask was continued. The shaft was sunk to a depth of 520 feet, and the mine opened up with levels 100 feet apart. In all, over 2,100 feet of development work has been done on the property. The

TULAMEEN VALLEY.

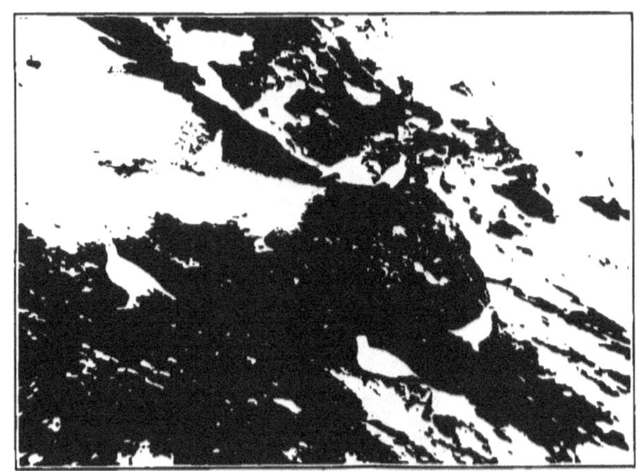

PTARMIGAN.

MARBLE CANYON, INTERIOR VANCOUVER ISLAND.

property is equipped with a Northey duplex station pump, three 50 h. p. boilers, a four-drill compressor, and a gasoline engine. A few carloads of ore were shipped during the year to the Granby smelter, the copper contents being 12 per cent.

The output from the Glen Iron mine in 1902 was 3,500 tons of magnetite, which was shipped to the Trail and Nelson smelters for fluxing purposes. The vein from which this ore was obtained is over 20 feet wide.

A company was formed early in 1902 to acquire the Python and Homestake groups. A tract of 760 acres was also purchased, on which it is proposed to erect a smelter in the near future. Another new organization is the Cherry Creek Copper King Mines, Limited, which recently purchased the O. K. group.

On the Hardie cinnabar mines over 1,000 feet of work has been done in four crosscut tunnels. A company was formed in London during the year to acquire these properties. On the Toonkwa claim, twelve miles south of Savonas, a shaft has been sunk to a depth of 20 feet, the ore, which occurs in the form of a dyke 40 feet wide, averaging in the shaft from 2½ to 3 per cent. of mercury.

Gold dredging operations on the Thompson River failed to return profitable results last season, but the dredge has been moved to Tranquille Creek, where the prospects are decidedly better, $1,000 worth of gold having been recovered in a preliminary run extending over a fortnight.

A beginning is to be made in the development of the coal areas lying to the west of the town of Kamloops, the Empire Development Company having acquired recently several leases in this vicinity, and exploratory work is to be commenced with boring machines shortly.

VANCOUVER ISLAND.

DURING the past year Vancouver Island has come very largely to the front as a mineral-producing area, and development of its resources is now rapidly proceeding. These resources include the coal occurrences on the east at Ladysmith, Nanaimo, Comox and Hardy Bay, and on the north at Quatsino Sound, the deposits of copper ores carrying gold and silver values, at Sooke, in the Cowichan district, on the east coast; in the San Juan, Alberni, Clayoquot and other districts of the west coast; and at Quatsino on the north, and immense deposits of magnetic iron ore which occur throughout the western and southeastern portions of the Island. Geologically, Vancouver Island may be divided as follows: In the southern portion the rocks are igneous in character, a belt of semi-crystalline slates traversing the Island from Saanich peninsula, on the southeast coast, to San Juan Harbour, on the southwest coast; while the northern portion is again subdivisable, the rocks forming the eastern section being sandstones, conglomerates and other sedimentary rocks; and on the west crystalline limestones and intrusive dykes of igneous rocks are characteristic.

THE VICTORIA MINING DIVISION.

Gold was first discovered in this division in 1860, when the gravels of the Leech and Sooke rivers were found to be auriferous. Leechtown, a typical mining camp, was built, and the population is reported as at one time having reached several hundreds. The yield of placer gold was satisfactory for some years, but when worked out, as no gold-bearing quartz of sufficient grade and extent was discovered, prospecting was abandoned; and it was not until about 1896 or 1897 that prospectors re-visited this section of the Island and resumed their explorations. The discovery of a heavy iron capping, below which was found high-grade chalcopyrite ore, on Skirt Mountain, at Goldstream, about ten miles from Victoria, gave the incentive to the prospector, and was followed by the location of a large number of mineral claims in that immediate neighbourhood, as well as in the Sooke Mountains, and on Mount Sicker, some 30 miles north from Goldstream.

The Sooke Mountains are formed from the uplifting of the semi-crystalline slates. These slates have much the appearance of metamorphosed Cambrian shales, and carry quite an appreciable percentage of graphite. The strata have been tilted from their horizontal position to nearly vertical, either from lateral pressure or from the upheaval of the intrusive igneous dykes, or both. The strike of these slates is northwesterly. Interfoliated comfortably with line of strike are numerous lenses of quartz; usually narrow and quite limited in strength. This quartz is generally gold-bearing, and evidently was the source of the placer gold of Leech and Sooke rivers, the waters of which have cut channels through the mountains, and crosscut the formation.

Owing to the auriferous character of the quartz lenses a number of mineral claims were located some years back, but none of them have developed into mines, although on some much work has been done.

MOUNT SKIRT.

Mount Skirt is situated on the southern flank of the belt of slate, and apparently belongs to the same formation; but the rocks, which are schistose, have been very much more metamorphosed. Some $25,000 have been expended in development of the Phair group of claims in this section, and some shipments of ore have been made. The ore, which is a chalcopyrite of good grade, averages three feet in width.

MOUNT SICKER.

The Mount Sicker District may be considered to occupy a position almost at the line of demarcation between the sedimentary rocks and the crystalline area. A zone of schist occurs extending from Maple Bay, on the east coast, through Mounts Sicker and Brenton towards the west coast, an undetermined distance. The line of strike is nearly due east and west. The widest of the mineralised zone, so far as at present known, is about 1,200 feet, and if it maintains its continuity to the west coast it should cross the Alberni Canal near its entrance to Barkley Sound. But instead of doing this the zone apparently wedges out near Cowichan Lake; while another zone of schistose rocks, very similar to those of the Mount Sicker region, occurs on China Creek, about 12 miles from the head of Alberni Canal.

The most important mines are the Lenora, Tyee, Richard III., Key City and Copper Canyon. The altitude of the summit of Mount Sicker above sea level is about 2,000 feet. The country rock is principally schist, and would probably be cast as a sericite if microscopically examined. It apparently contains considerable chlorite and feldspar. The line of strike of this belt of schist is nearly due magnetic east, and the strike of the ore bodies conforms with that of the schist.

The structure of the ore bodies in this vicinity is similar to that of the large majority on Vancouver Island, which have come under the writer's observation, and should be classed as lenticular. The ore apparently fills fissures produced when the rocks were folded and contorted. The present cleavage planes of the schists on Mount Sicker are not the original cleavage planes of the formation. At points along the line of strike of the schists the fissuring process has been so violent that the lenses of ore sometimes reach a thickness of 30 feet or more, as at the Lenora; but at others are narrow and of limited extent longitudinally. On Mount Sicker there is one feature connected with the mineralised zone which deserves attention. It is that on the northern boundary of the schist a well-defined, persistent ledge of hungry-looking quartz occurs. This has up to the present time marked the northern limit of the local occurrences of ore, the southern limit being as equally well defined and marked by a dike of porphyritic rock, which at the contact between it and schist has a peculiar appearance, and resembles a body of dirty brown, melted gutta percha with white nodules as impregnations through it. When struck with a pick or drill this material is found to be soft, but spongy, like india rubber. Its thickness varies from a few inches up to two feet, and when exposed to the air it slacks and breaks up like shale.

Mining in this district last year was very actively prosecuted, and considerable instalments of machinery were made at the principal mines. During the year construction of two large smelting works — one at Crofton, Osborne Bay, and the other at Ladysmith — was completed, and connection established therefrom to the mines — in the one case by a narrow-gauge railway, and in the other by means of an aerial tram system, over which the ore from the Tyee mine is brought down to a point on the Esquimalt & Nanaimo Railway. The Crofton smelter is equipped with three furnaces, the smallest being a cupola for re-melting matte whenever desirable, and the two larger furnaces being of the water-jacket and Garretson types respectively, the former having a capacity of 350 tons a day. In the converter building are two converters, each having a daily capacity to treat 50 tons of matte. Actual smelting operations were commenced at the Ladysmith works in December last. The plant is a very complete one, and is capable of treating 200 tons of ore daily.

In 1902 the Lenora mine shipped to the Tacoma smelter 1,943 tons of No. 1 ore, and to the Crofton smelter 643 tons of first-class and 11,915 tons of second-class ore. The property was further considerably developed, the principal work including the sinking of a double-compartment shaft to a depth of 180 feet, from the floor of No. 2 level to a point about 100 feet below No. 3 level. At the present time there are two chutes of ore that have not been stoped, between tunnels No. 2 and 3. The machinery installed during the year included a five-drill compressor and a sorting table with crusher and elevators.

At the Tyee mine the main shaft was continued to a depth of 400 feet, and cross-cutting started to intersect the lead. The main ore body was opened up a distance extending over 800 feet in ore, and stoping is being prosecuted at the rate of 150 tons daily. The following machinery is installed at the mine: Four boilers, a double-drum Hendy hoist and one smaller hoist, two Ingersoll-Sargeant compressors, a Gates crusher, an engine and belt conveyor.

On the Richard III. claim a shaft has been sunk to a depth of 150 feet, the indications being extremely promising.

On the Key City sinking has been continued to a depth of 300 feet, and development work has also been actively prosecuted on the Copper Canyon claim.

The other work done on a large number of claims scattered over Mount Sicker and Mount Brenton amounts to very little, being just sufficient assessment work to hold the claims. Various reports of strikes, etc., have been made from time to time, but the work done has not been of such a character as to prove continuity and values, and the owners of these claims are evidently waiting for "something to turn up" in increased values for properties, resulting from the successful working of the very few mines really operating on a large scale.

At Cowichan Lake and the upper waters of the Chemainus River fairly heavy development work has been done, but in neither case has the presence of ore bodies of commercial value been proved to exist.

On Malahat Mountain, near Shawnigan Lake, the usual development work has been done on some twenty claims. The surface showings on this mountain consist of pyrrhotite and magnetite, and are very large. They occur in a lime contact, and, carrying as they do some values in copper and occasionally very good gold, they are well worthy of exploitation on a large scale. The work up to the present time is scattered all over the mountain side, which is a pity, as if concentrated it might possibly have opened up a really good mining camp, as the whole country along the line of contact contains large outcrops of ore.

Some good samples of iron ore, also quartz and copper pyrites, have been brought in by prospectors from the new trail at Ladysmith. No work, however, has as yet been done on these claims.

SAN JUAN.

The western portion of the Victoria Mining Division has not been as thoroughly prospected as has the eastern. The San Juan and Gordon rivers have been explored for considerable distances above their mouths, and several mineral claims located. Most of the ore bodies so far discovered are composed of mineral deposits of high-grade magnetite, while others are bodies of pyrrhotite carrying some copper and gold values.

In addition to the ore bodies found on the west coast in this mining division, several deposits of auriferous black sands have been discovered and worked. Operations in this district are being extensively carried on by a syndicate of British capitalists.

THE ALBERNI MINING DIVISION.

Lode mining was commenced in this division at an earlier date than anywhere else on Vancouver Island. Prospectors took advantage of the Alberni Canal, which enabled them to explore the mountains contiguous to the shore line. China and Granite creeks, which empty into the canal, had been prospected some years previous to lode mining prospecting, and placer gold mined from the beds and banks. This fact led to the installation of hydraulic plants, and a more systematic exploration for gold-bearing quartz. The former are idle to-day — in fact appear to have been failures from the start — but as a result of the latter a large number of claims were located on Mineral Hill, at the head of China Creek, and the adjoining mountains, as well as on the mountains near the head of Granite Creek.

Outcroppings of gold-bearing quartz veins indicated the occurrence of free milling gold ore, and led to the building of small stamp mills and the expenditure of considerable money in an attempt to develop mines. Owing to various causes, except at the Golden Eagle, situated at the head of China Creek, but little activity has been shown in this section of the camp of late, although many promising prospects occur.

On Copper Island, in Barkley Sound, occur very extensive deposits of magnetite; while on the opposite side of the sound, or southeast from Copper Island, occur the ore bodies on the Sarita River, composed of magnetite and pyrrhotite. Northwesterly from Copper Island, a few miles distant, occur vast bodies of magnetite, known as the Sechart group.

During the year a small shipment of 150 tons of ore was made from the Monitor mine, on the Alberni Canal; and the Hayes mine, at which, however, operations were suspended for the greater part of 1902, shipped 2,000 tons. Exploratory work on the Golden Eagle was steadily prosecuted; and important developments are reported to have been made in the Kennedy Lake camp, where fissure veins of gold-bearing quartz were first discovered in 1898. The iron deposits on Barkley Sound have been extensively opened up, with the most satisfactory results.

QUATSINO SOUND.

In the north of the Island, at Quatsino Sound, some remarkably large and rich deposits of copper ore have been developed, on the Comstock and other groups. At the Comstock mine an aerial tramway was installed, and during the summer two shipments of ore were made — the one to Tacoma and the other to the Ladysmith smelter. Coal was discovered in the same neighbourhood a few years ago, and the district is likely in the near future to prove a very important mining area.

NANAIMO MINING DIVISION.

This district covers a larger area than any other on Vancouver Island, as it includes within its boundaries the islands in the Straits of Georgia, as well as an extensive territory on the Mainland.

The Vancouver Island collieries being located within this district, places it as the most important from points of development and production of any of the Island districts, though the actual operations are carried on over a comparatively small area, being confined to the neighbourhood of the following towns on the east coast of the Island: Ladysmith, at Oyster Bay; Nanaimo, at Nanaimo Harbour; Wellington, six miles northwesterly from Nanaimo; Comox, Union and Cumberland, near Union Harbour.

The collieries are operated by the following companies: Western Fuel Company, operating the Nanaimo colliery, consisting of the No. 1 shaft, Esplanade, in the City of Nanaimo; Protection Island shaft, Southfield, near Nanaimo River. The Union Colliery Company of British Columbia, Limited, operating the Union colliery, consisting of No. 4 slope and Nos. 5 and 6 shafts, in the Comox district; Wellington colliery, in Douglas district, known as the Extension mine, consisting of Nos. 1, 2 and 3 slopes, and Tunnel mine; the Alexandria colliery, in the Cranberry district, at Union Bay, where coke, fire and ordinary brick are manufactured by the same company.

The output from these collieries last year was divided as follows: New Vancouver Coal Company (Nanaimo), 490,000 tons; Wellington Colliery Co., 800,000 tons of coal and 15,800 tons of coke. The most important occurrences in connection with the coal mining industry on Vancouver Island during the year were the sale of the New Vancouver Coal Company's property to the Western Fuel Company, of San Francisco; and the discovery of a four-foot seam of high-grade anthracite coal near Brown's River, in the Comox district.

TEXADA ISLAND.

On Texada Island the Van Anda mines have passed under the control of an English syndicate. The Cornell mine has been satisfactorily developed by means of a shaft which was continued down to the 360-foot level. The Marble Bay mines have been steadily operated, a gravity tramway having been built from the mine to wharf, and the ore which has been accumulating since the property was first opened, shipped. Development operations were continued on the Golden Slipper claim — a gold-bearing quartz ore — and on the Volunteer group. The iron mines of Texada Island were in continuous operation during the year, and the ore shipped to the Irondale furnace, near Port Townsend, Washington. The pig iron here produced has found a ready market in San Francisco and other manufacturing centres on the Pacific Coast.

MINING ON THE MAINLAND COAST.

THE mineral belt of the Coast may be said to commence about ten miles north from Vancouver on Seymour Creek, where for the past two or three years parties of prospectors have been engaged in developing mineral claims, on which occur copper-gold ores. These are said to be quite extensive in body and of a fairly good grade, so far as work has progressed. The locations are reached by a waggon road from North Vancouver.

Pitt Lake may also be considered to belong to the Coast District. This is located at the head of Pitt River, which empties into the Fraser. Mineral claims in this region were located several years back, and several on which occur copper-gold ores have been partially developed. A discovery of molybdenite was reported in this vicinity during 1901.

Travelling up the coast from Burrard Inlet, there have not been so far discovered any occurrences of mineral immediately adjacent to the shore-line, until a point on Howe Sound, about ten miles above its entrance, is reached. Several mineral claims have been staked in that vicinity on outcroppings of iron capping, impregnated with chalcopyrite. The country rock is of a schistose character, and apparently this same class of rock occupies quite an extensive area, maintaining its continuity towards the north for several hundred yards, when it gives place, however, to granite, which, judging from observations from boats, is the predominating country rock along the shore-line towards the head of the Sound for several miles, or until a point is reached known as the Goldsmith and Britannia Landing. There the schistose rock again occurs, occupying a wide belt and extending in an easterly direction towards the head of the North Arm of Burrard Inlet. It is in this belt of rock that the Goldsmith and Britannia groups of mineral claims are located. These have attained a very widespread notoriety because of the enormous bluffs of iron and copper pyrites which occur as outcroppings. One of these in particular is about 600 feet long and nearly 300 feet high. A tunnel crosscutting the formation nearly diagonally for about 100 feet is in ore all the way, with ore still in the breast. The grade of this is reported to average from 3 to 5 per cent. in copper, with low gold and silver values. About 800 feet of development work has been done on this group of claims; and as the control of them passed into the hands of a wealthy Montana syndicate during 1901, it is expected that ere long active mining operations will be commenced.

The extent of the ore bodies, of which there are several in addition to the enormous bluff referred to, is so great, while the ore is of low grade, that in order to render operations successful they must be carried on on a very large scale. These ore bodies apparently occupy fissures in the schist of lenticular structure, but of very great extent. The gangue of the ore is principally quartz, but very often the iron and copper pyrites are quite massive, with but comparatively little impurities associated.

This mineral-bearing zone has been prospected towards the east along its strike for a distance in an air line of eight or nine miles, and from the discoveries reported already, Howe Sound will undoubtedly prove to be one of the most important copper-producing camps in the province. Some of the outcroppings easterly from the Britannia are high-grade bornite ore. This section of the Coast has merely been scratched over up to the present time; the first discovery of copper-gold ore was only made late in the fall of 1898; and since then, although a good deal of prospecting has been done, the actual development work done has not been as extensive as would have been expected. Whether this mineral-bearing zone maintains its continuity on the west side of Howe Sound is a question which has not yet been sufficiently investigated.

Proceeding up the Coast, the next stretch of inland water on which any discoveries of mineral have been made is Jervis Inlet. In the vicinity of one of the arms of this inlet is located the old Howe mine, which was developed to some extent about thirty years ago, but has since not been operated.

Recently the only operations which have been carried on in the vicinity are those by the British Columbia Exploring Syndicate, on an occurrence of copper-gold ore. The development work has been quite extensive, and the property promises to become a large producer in the future. Up to the present time no shipping facilities have been installed, because the policy of the owners of the property has been to develop and block out ore in sight and establish the value as a mine.

The coast-line and adjacent islands between the last-mentioned inlet and the boundary of the province are practically unexplored. Some little prospecting has been done on the Bella Coola, Skeena and Naas Rivers, Observatory Inlet and the Stikine River, as well as on Princess Royal, Gribbel and Banks Islands. Exploratory work on prospects in all of these sections was pushed during 1901, and it is expected that during the summer of the present year it will be definitely determined how great is the value of many of the discoveries already made.

THE ATLIN DISTRICT.

THE Atlin Mining Division is situated in the extreme north of the province of British Columbia. It occupies a wedge-shaped position between the Teslin Mining Division on the east and the Bennett Division on the west; its northern boundary is the 60th parallel of latitude, and it extends as far south as Alaska. The length of the district exceeds 60 miles, and its average width is about 30 miles. Lying in the middle of the division, in a north and south direction, is Atlin Lake, into which all the principal creeks flow, and of which the outlet is the Atlinto River, which empties into Taku, an arm of Lake Tagish — thus it is that the Atlin Division drains north, and eventually into the Yukon River. The country is mountainous, with many peaks above the snow-line. Some of the mountains are of volcanic origin and still preserve a cone-like appearance. All the creeks are bordered by hills, which are wooded upward for a considerable distance with Banksian pine, jack spruce and poplar. Though these trees are in many instances small—about six inches in diameter — large trees also abound. There are tracts of land which appear well suited for agriculture, for the soil is fertile and might be drained without difficulty; but as yet the population has been insufficient and the permanency of the camp too uncertain to offer inducements to the agriculturist. Excellent fish are obtainable from the lake — trout, whitefish and grayling being the ordinary varieties. Some of the trout are very large, weighing as many as 23 pounds. The chief wealth of the district, however, is in its minerals. Gold is the principal metal found, with platinum sometimes in association; but copper also is said to occur in paying quantities.

HISTORY AND POPULATION.

Russian influence did not extend as far inland as Atlin. Indeed, the district seems to have been quite uninhabited prior to the coming of the prospector, for the few Tagish Indians who are now in Atlin have come within the last four years; but old and rotten sluice-boxes have been found, which indicate that the region was visited in early days by men who probably drifted north from Cariboo and Cassiar. Authentic history begins in the summer of 1898, when Fritz Miller, guided by a sketch map in his possession, and which he had received from his brother, who obtained it in some unknown manner, crossed Atlin Lake and proceeded to Pine Creek and staked discovery claim. Miller's discovery soon became known, and occasioned a stampede from the Klondike and other places, so that before winter claims were staked on all the principal creeks and the most promising ground secured. A rush came in the spring of 1899, when 5,000 people pitched their tents on Atlin townsite. These people found that all the good ground had been staked; but the Alien Act, which had come into force in January, 1899, afforded a pretext to some for jumping claims. The fact that the early-comers were uncertain whether the district was in British Columbia or the Northwest Territories, and staked accordingly, added to the confusion, because at that time the British Columbia placer claim was 100 feet, while that of the Northwest was 250 feet. As supplies began to give out and there was no prospect of work, the population rapidly diminished. In 1900 it still further diminished, only those remaining who had found employment; while in the summer of 1901, according to the government census, there were but 1,389 people in the whole district.

ACCESSIBILITY.

In summer there is no difficulty whatever attending the trip into Atlin. The point of departure from the White Pass & Yukon Railway is Cariboo Crossing, 68 miles from Skagway. At Cariboo connection is made twice a week with the sternwheel steamer Gleaner, which runs on Taku Arm and Inlet as far as Taku City. Two miles of railway connect Taku City and Scotia Bay, and from the latter place the little steamer Scotia crosses Lake Atlin in 20 minutes. The whole journey from Skagway to Atlin takes only 24 hours. When navigation closes, Log Cabin becomes the divisional point, and Atlin is reached by the Fantail route. Travelling within the district itself is easy; the lake and creeks are the natural highways; excellent roads have been made to the principal camps, and good trails lead to the less frequented portions of the district.

ATLIN AND PINE CITY.

The town of Atlin is the focus of the district. It is beautifully situated on rising ground at the eastern side of the lake, one mile and a half north of the mouth of Pine Creek. Facing it from the opposite side of the lake are the snow-capped Atlin Mountains. About seven miles from Atlin is Pine City, or Discovery, where most of the miners working on Pine and Willow creeks reside. In population it equals Atlin, but it lacks the substantial appearance of the latter town. The two places are connected by stage.

CLIMATE.

As far as a correct estimate can be arrived at in four years, the climate of Atlin is good. The altitude is 2,200 feet, so the air is bracing. In summer, in the middle of the day it is hot, but about 4 o'clock in the afternoon it becomes cool, and at 2 in the morning quite cold. Many of the evenings are sufficiently warm to make boating on the lake very enjoyable. In winter the cold is not insupportable. Skating and snowshoeing are enjoyed, even by women. In February, 1901, the highest temperature was 29 degrees above; the lowest, 50 degrees below. In March the highest was 39 degrees above, the lowest 17 degrees below. In April the highest 42 degrees above, the lowest 10 degrees below.

GEOLOGY.

The auriferous belt to which attention has thus far been confined lies to the east of Atlin Lake, and covers about 150 square miles. It is drained by Pine Creek with its tributaries, and McKee Creek. The underlying formation consists of metamorphic rocks, of which magnesium is the predominating constituent, and these are intruded by igneous rock of volcanic type, chiefly diabase. The magnesium rocks are black, and weather-stain a rusty brown; sometimes they are fibrous and become true serpentines, and they generally contain numerous intercalations of quartz, which is peculiar on account of its apple-green colouration, due to a chromiferous mica, and probably to nickel. This gold-bearing series is cut off on the north by granite, and on the east and south by slates and quartzites. The slates may prove productive, in which case the gold area would be greatly extended. The Canadian Geological Survey had J. C. Gwillim, B. A. Sc., in the Atlin field during the summers of 1899 and 1900. Mr. Gwillim made a log and compass survey of the district, and his valuable observations and conclusions are incorporated in the reports of the Geological Survey for the two years mentioned. A geological map accompanies these reports and greatly adds to their value.

Mt. SELWYN, PEACE RIVER, FROM PARSNIP RIVER.

Gold is found on bedrock, which is sometimes three, but more often thirty, feet from the surface, and it generally occurs in paying quantities in the eight feet of gravel above bedrock. It ranges in value from $15 to $17 per ounce, and is usually coarse in character. Large nuggets are sometimes found. The largest on record is the quartz nugget of 1899, which came from Spruce Creek and which weighed 83 ounces. In June, 1901, one was obtained from McKee Creek weighing 28¾ ounces and worth $460; and in July, from Blue Canyon, on Spruce Creek, a $600 nugget was obtained — weight, 36½ ounces. Fine gold also occurs, but is ordinarily lost, because the individual miners make no attempt to separate it from the black sand.

MINING.

Placer mining and hydraulicing are the modes of mining principally adopted; lode mining has been attempted, but without very satisfactory results. In 1901 practically all work was confined to Pine, Spruce, Willow, Birch, Boulder and McKee creeks. Pine Creek, being discovery creek, is of special interest. The valley through which it flows is wide, and was apparently cut out in pre-glacial times by a stream of large proportions, and of which Surprise lake was a part. The stream would then bear the same relation to Atlin Lake that Taku Inlet now bears to Taku Arm. The present creek is about 14 miles long. For the first seven miles — from Surprise Lake to Nugget Point — the gravels are 30 to 60 feet deep and the grade of the creek is slight, so no mining has been possible; for, although the gravels might pay for working, operations could not be carried on without injury to the miners lower down the stream. From Nugget Point to a few hundred feet below Discovery the depth of gravel is comparatively shallow, and it is from this vicinity that the bulk of the gold has been derived, for the benches have proved rich, as well as the creek. Below these shallow diggings, from Spruce Junction to Atlin Lake, the creek becomes canyon-like, its bed is broken at Pine Falls, and it carries no gold. Pine Creek was the centre of interest in 1899 and 1900, and Chinese pumps, water-wheels, wing-dams, ditches and flumes attest the activity of that period. In 1901 fewer miners were at work, and these were engaged chiefly on the benches, for most of the creek claims had been worked out. The number of individual miners on the other creeks has also been decreasing. In 1901 the best paying creek placer claims were 34 below, Boulder Creek, and 27 and 28 above, McKee Creek. There bedrock was being worked upon, and the yield per day per man was about 1½ ounces. Drifting on the benches at Pine, Spruce, Boulder and McKee creeks continues during the winter as well as the summer.

HYDRAULIC MINING.

In 1899 the first hydraulic plant was installed by the Atlin Lake Mining Company on Birch Creek. Since that date plants, more or less complete, have been put in by Societe Miniere de la Colombia Britannique, Boulder Creek; by the Pendugwig Company, Wright Creek; by the Willow Creek Hydraulic Company, Willow Creek; by the Surprise Company, Pine Creek; by the Columbia Mining Company and the Blue Canyon Company, Spruce Creek; and by the Atlin Mining Company, McKee Creek. Each gold-producing creek is gradually coming under the control of a hydraulic company. This may be regretted by the individual miners, but appears necessary, for from the nature of the deposits it is only by consolidation of claims that the difficulties of successfully working the ground can be overcome. The success of the hydraulic companies is fraught with peculiar interest, for now that so much dead work has been completed and the period of profit should begin, if, contrary to expectations, the returns are insignificant and hydraulicing is pronounced a failure, the camp will be all but deserted.

LODE MINING.

Development work has been done on several veins with encouraging results, notably on the Imperial and Engineer mines.

RECENT OPERATIONS.

The season of 1902 was a very successful one, the production being over half a million dollars in coarse gold. The number of miners employed on the several creeks was approximately 800. Increased production this year was due to the satisfactory working of the hydraulic mines on Boulder, Pine and McKee Creeks, and mining on a large scale in this district is gradually taking the place of individual effort. Operations during the year were conducted by the Societe Miniere de la Colombie Britannique, on Boulder Creek; Pine Creek Power Co., on Pine Creek; Nimrod Syndicate, on McKee Creek; Columbia Hydraulic Mining Company and the Consolidated Spruce Creek Placers, Limited, on Spruce Creek. Steam hoists and centrifugal pumps are now being successfully used in the district, and operations will be prosecuted next season on a still more extensive scale.

THE GOLDEN MINING DIVISION OF E. KOOTENAY.

THIS mining division comprises the northern portion of the district of East Kootenay, and includes the country on either side of the Columbia River from the summit of the Rocky Mountains on the northeast to the summit of the Selkirk Range in the southwest, and extends in a northwesterly direction from Galena, above Spallumcheen, to about seven miles north of the Big Bend of the Columbia — a distance of about 140 miles.

The Canadian Pacific Railway traverses the district in an easterly and westerly direction; the stations within the division being Bear Creek, Beaver, Donald, Golden, Palliser, Otter Tail, Field, Hector and Stephen.

The predominating rock formation on the Rocky Mountain side of the Columbia is carboniferous limestone, overlying argillaceous slates and shales, which are exposed in some of the deeper canyons, and along the banks of the larger streams.

On the southwestern or Selkirk side, igneous granular rocks such as diorites, syenites, granites, dolerites, etc., (frequently porphyritic) form the higher mountains and ridges; while on the flanks and in the depressions or basins metamorphic slates and schists, with occasional bands of limestone, form the country rock, and in many places are traversed by porphyritic and other eruptive dikes, and metalliferous quartz lodes.

On the northeastern side more or less development work has been done at different times on the Monarch, near Field (argentiferous galena and blende), and on some silver-lead claims along the Otter Tail, also on Beaver Foot Creek and Ice River, and in the Blue Water country, north of Donald.

On the Selkirk or southwest side the mining camps are much more numerous, and are generally found near where the slates and schists have been broken through by the eruptive rocks.

The Spillimacheen and Jubilee Mountain camps, about 40 miles above Golden and on the southwest side of the Columbia, are, however, exceptions, as at these points and for some distance southeast the carboniferous limestone extends across the Columbia, and the lodes, argentiferous, galena and copper ores, are found either in the schists or limestone near the contact.

The other mining localities on this side are situated as follows:

On Bugaboo Creek (copper, gold and silver-lead), from 8 to 25 miles west of Spillimacheen Landing.

Vermont Creek (copper, gold, silver-lead and bismuth), about 21 miles southwest of Carbonate Landing.

Copper Creek (copper, gold and silver-lead), west-southwest from Carbonate.

Spruce Tree Creek, on north side of Middle Fork of Spillimacheen River (copper ores and gold quartz), 22 miles from Carbonate Landing.

Carbonate Creek and Carbonate Mountain (silver-lead, copper ore and gold quartz), on the south side of the North Fork of the Spillimacheen River, about 25 miles from Carbonate Landing.

Caribou Creek, on the opposite side of the Middle Fork and about the same distance from Carbonate Landing (gold quartz, galena and copper).

Robbie Burns Basin (gold quartz), on the north side of the Middle Fork, 27 miles from Carbonate Landing.

International Basin (gold quartz, silver-lead and copper), on the headwaters of the Middle Fork of Spillimacheen River, 30 miles from Carbonate Landing.

Boston and Bennison, across the divide from the International Basin (gold quartz, silver, lead and copper ores), 31 miles by trail from Carbonate and about the same distance from Bear Creek Station, on the Canadian Pacific Railway.

McMurdo Creek (gold quartz, silver-lead and copper ores), about 30 miles from Carbonate, and west of Robbie Burns Basin.

Prairie Mountain (gold quartz, galena and copper ores), about 10 miles east of Bear Creek Station, on the Canadian Pacific Railway.

Fifteen-Mile Creek (copper and gold), from 7 to 10 miles from the landing on the Columbia River.

Canyon Creek (copper ores and gold quartz), from 8 to 10 miles from Golden.

There are strong, well-defined lodes and very encouraging prospects in many of the above camps, and in some of them the surface showings are unusually good; but, except in one of two camps, very little work of importance in determining the extent of the ore bodies or the prospective value of the lodes has been done.

Most of the claims are at a standstill for want of capital, and there seems to be a good opening here at present for one or more development companies to take hold of properties on a stock basis or on working bonds, and do a safe and profitable mining business.

There are government trails to all the camps, and the cost of visiting and examining the most promising claims would not be great.

In almost every locality where lodes are found there are streams in the immediate vicinity capable of furnishing all the power required to generate electricity for operating mills, concentrators, trams, hoisting works, compressors, etc.

Timber is plentiful and in many places so abundant that charcoal for smelting purposes can be supplied in large quantities and at a moderate price for a number of years. This is an important consideration, as a large portion of the ores of this district might be smelted or reduced to a matte on the ground, thus saving on an average probably 75 per cent. of the cost of shipping crude ore to a market. Iron and limestone can be obtained in or near most of the camps.

LILLOOET DISTRICT.

THE creeks and streams in this district have been extensively worked for gold by placer miners for the past forty years, the benches of the Fraser River, Cayuse Creek and Bridge River having proved highly auriferous. Quartz mining operations were first commenced in 1894, when rich free-milling gold was discovered on Cayuse Creek; and later, in 1897, such promising properties as the Forty Thieves, Lorne, Ida May and Bend d'Or were discovered and worked. A stamp mill was erected at the Ben d'Or and gold to the value of $85,000 extracted during the time the mine was in operation. From the Lorne and Woodchuck claims $25,000 was recovered by the employment of an arrastra. In addition to the free-milling gold ores, large deposits of copper and other ores have been discovered in this district. The country is park-like in character, and there is an abundance of timber and water for mining purposes.

THE BIG BEND DISTRICT.

THIS section of Northwest Kootenay has produced in the aggregate a large placer gold yield, but is now being exploited for quartz. The district takes its name from a curious sinuosity of the Columbia River, which at Beaver Mouth, on the main line of the Canadian Pacific Railway, flows northward for approximately 100 miles and thereafter changes to a southerly course, again crossing the C. P. R. line at Revelstoke, the commercial centre of the district. The area comprises some 2,000 square miles, a large proportion of which is mineral-bearing. The chief drawback to mining is the inaccessibility of the region, but this has recently been to some extent overcome by the placing of a steamboat on the Columbia River, which makes regular trips between Revelstoke and Laporte. This year (1903) it is hoped that the river will be navigated for 150 miles. In some cases quartz mining development has been well advanced. Thus in the Standard Basin some 1,200 feet of work has been done on the Standard group, and large bodies of high-grade copper ore exposed. The Rosebery group, in the same vicinity, also gives great promise, an expenditure of $20,000 having been made in development. The ore here is arsenical iron, carrying values in gold. Good prospects are found on Laforme and Downie creeks and in Ground Hog Basin. On the north side of Downie Creek a remarkable showing of copper ore has been exposed by landslides, the vein being distinctly traceable over a length of 6,000 feet. On Smith, French, McCullough and Camp creeks, situated about 60 miles north of Revelstoke, placer mining operations are still successfully carried on.

THE LARDEAU DISTRICT.

THE Lardeau District comprises two mining divisions, those of Trout Lake and Lardeau and part of Ainsworth Division. The country here is extremely mountainous, although there are numerous extensive valleys and occasional stretches of open, level land, which have been utilised for agricultural purposes. Generally speaking, the country has been cut up into a series of deep and narrow valleys by numerous small creeks, and in these cases the growth of timber is heavy. The mountainous character of the country, however, is an advantage rather than otherwise, so far as mining is concerned, for in a great majority of cases it is possible to develop and open up properties by the economical method of tunnelling into the hillsides.

The area in the vicinity of Trout Lake is mainly composed of semi-crystalline slates and schists, with occasional beds of altered limestone, locally described as "dikes." The general strike of the formation is northwesterly, and the beds generally dip at a high angle to the northeast. The mineral veins or lodes, as a general rule, vary in width from one to five feet, though larger occurrences are occasionally met with; while fissure veins cutting across the formation are of occasional occurrence. The mineral characteristics of this vicinity are galena, tetrahedrite, zinc blende, and iron and copper pyrites, in gangues of quartz or calcite, siderite, etc. The high values are generally associated with the grey copper ores; though a fine grain zinc blende also as a rule carries exceptional values.

MINING OPERATIONS IN 1902.

Probably no district in British Columbia has attracted the attention of investors and capitalists to a greater degree during the past year than the Lardeau. The reason for this may probably be attributed first to the fact of the exceptionally high-grade character of the ore deposits; and secondly, to the completion of the branch line of railway, by which it has become possible to work the mines to proper advantage. Thus soon after the completion of the railway the Nettie L. mine was suitably equipped with machinery; and other properties in the same neighbourhood are also preparing to instal plants. Tramways to facilitate the handling of the ores are being constructed from the Nettie L., Silver Cup and Triune mines. These three properties have produced a considerable amount of ore in the past year, the Nettie L.'s output being 800 tons, and that of the Silver Cup 300 tons. Small shipments have also been made from a number of claims now undergoing development. A section of the district of very undoubted promise is the Fish Creek camp, which has been extensively exploited in the past few months.

AN IMPORTANT AREA.

The area, which is some 25 miles long by 20 miles wide, is divided into two parts by the Fish river, and extends from the mouth of that stream, at the head of navigation on the Arrow Lakes, to the summit of the watersheds of either side. The most important tributary creeks on the north are the Battle, Glacier, Kettle, Boyd, Ruby, Silver, Lexington and Pool; those on the west, McDougal, Bullar, McRae, Sable, Scott and Menhinick. The waters of the opposite slopes fall, those on the east into Duncan River and so into Kootenay Lake; and those on the west into the Columbia River. The country is mountainous and rugged, the scenery being particularly impressive. Communication is afforded to the mines by two good waggon roads, constructed into the camp from the head of navigation on the Upper Arrow Lake;

while the town of Camborne, the chief centre of the locality, will undoubtedly in the near future be reached by rail, a survey having also been made for the extension of the line connecting Trout Lake and Arrowhead.

The most highly developed mine in this section is the Eva, on Lexington Mountain, where over 2,000 feet of underground work has been done. The ore bodies here vary from 1 to 15 feet in width, and carry values of from $6 to $30. Excellent showings of ore have also been exposed on the Oyster-Criterion group, the Olalla group, the Erie and Sir Wilfrid groups, and on other claims in the same neighbourhood. On Menhinick Creek, the Camborne group of nine claims is being actively developed, as are also claims on Scott, Ruby, Silver and Boyd creeks. Between Pool and Lexington creeks are a number of properties having most promising showings of free-gold quartz.

The natural advantages enjoyed by this district are exceptional. There is an abundance of timber and water-power, large bodies of ore capable of being mined and treated at a minimum expense; the climate is excellent, and the valleys most fertile.

SIMILKAMEEN DISTRICT.

THE area known as the Similkameen District extends from Nicola Lake and Trout Creek on the north to the international boundary line on the south, and is bounded on the east by the Okanagan and the Similkameen Rivers, and on the west by the Hope Range of Mountains.

The territory first attracted the attention of prospectors so long ago as 1859, and more recently rich placer diggings have been discovered on Granite Creek and other streams in that neighbourhood. Associated with the gold in the gravel was a certain amount of platinum, which at first was thrown aside by the miners, who were not aware of its value. Subsequently, however, an effort was made to save this valuable product.

After the first excitement the district was more or less abandoned until 1897, when interest was first taken in the quartz deposits distributed throughout the region. In that year the Nickel Plate mine, at Hedley, and the Sunset mine, on Copper Mountain, were acquired by capitalists, and on a number of other properties development operations were started. The former property has been systematically developed during the past year by means of tunnels driven into the face of the hill, and is now regarded as being one of the richest and most promising mines in British Columbia. The deposit is not only an extensive one, but carries exceptionally high values in gold. A large stamp mill has been recently installed on the property. Other high-grade bodies of arsenical pyrites are also found on Fifteen-Mile, Sixteen-Mile, Sterling and Henry creeks.

NATURE OF DEPOSITS.

The copper deposits are found in the Lower Similkameen as chalcopyrite, while on one property the ore contains molybdenite in varying quantities. In the Middle Similkameen a promising copper property is being opened up on Twenty-Mile Creek, the ore here being pyrites. The characteristic ore of the Upper Similkameen, however, is bornite, although bodies of copper pyrites are found in this locality. Occurrences of bornite of considerable extent have been developed, with encouraging results, on Copper and Mackenzie Mountains and on Friday Creek. At the headwaters of One-Mile Creek ore has been found with copper in the form of copper glance, and a number of claims in this vicinity have recently been bonded.

Bornite also occurs above Nicola, on Ten-Mile Creek, in a talcose formation, and from one property a number of tons of high-grade ore has been taken out and sacked in readiness for transportation to smelters.

The characteristic occurrences in the Aspen Grove district are copper glance deposits, some of which carry very high values. Much attention has been attracted to this locality of late, and a number of properties have been acquired under bond by capitalists at high valuations.

COAL.

Important coal areas have been discovered and are being developed near Princeton and in the Nicola Valley. The coal basin in the former locality is clearly defined, extending in one direction from three to five miles, and in the other from ten to twelve miles. It is not yet determined whether the character of this coal admits of coking, but analyses show that it is of very fair quality. The seams vary in thickness from 6 to 20 feet.

The Similkameen District is at present reached by waggon roads and trails, viz., from the north, from Spence's Bridge, on the main line of the C. P. R., via Nicola and Princeton; or from Sicamous Junction by rail to Okanagan Landing, by steamer to Penticton, thence by stage to Princeton, Keremeos and Hedley City. An excellent trail leads also from Hope to Princeton, a distance of 60 miles; whilst the district may be approached from Wenatchee, on the Great Northern Railway, on the south, via Anneville. Surveys have meanwhile been made through the Similkameen district by different railway companies, and it is hoped that in the very near future this section, which is undoubtedly one of the richest in British Columbia, will enjoy the advantages of adequate transportation facilities.

FAIRVIEW CAMP.

The Fairview Camp, which for the sake of convenience may be considered as a part of the Similkameen District, has been actively exploited with varying success for a number of years past. The mineral veins here are free-milling quartz, ranging in value from $5 to $10. The principal mine, the Stemwinder, owned by the New Fairview Corporation, has been extensively developed, and is equipped with a large stamp mill, compressor plant and cyaniding plant. Recent arrangements have been effected to operate other properties in this locality.

OMINECA DISTRICT.

THE Omineca District comprises such portions of the drainage area of the Peace River and its tributaries as may lie within this province, the drainage area of the Stuart and Nechaco Rivers above their junction, and the drainage area of the Salmon river above its junction with the Fraser River.

The principal creeks being worked at the present time are Manson, Germansen, Slate, Lost, Kildare, Black Jack, Tom and Vital Creeks. There is a vast amount of country north of the Peace River and northwest of the Findlay that has not yet been prospected. A few white men have passed over a small portion of it, and report gold in most of the creeks, but little or nothing is known of it. Routes to the district are: By, first, the Skeena River, by steamer from Essington to Hazelton (175 miles), by trail from Hazelton to Manson (190 miles); second, from Ashcroft to Quesnel by stage, from Quesnel to Manson by trail. The Omineca District has only been prospected to any extent along the creeks above mentioned, and along the Omineca and its tributaries. Several quartz claims have been recorded on and about Mount Selwyn, at the junction of the Peace and Parsnip Rivers. This quartz is free-milling and reported to be rich. The district was first worked by white men in the early seventies, when Vital Creek was discovered, and after Vital, Germansen, Manson and Lost Creeks were discovered and worked.

The country has not been, in any sense, thoroughly prospected; in fact there still remain hundreds of square miles still untrodden by white men, which, when prospected and opened up, should surely prove as rich in gold as the developed sections of the district. The climate during the summer months, from the beginning of May until the middle of October, is delightful; the snowfall in winter is not heavy — two feet, or three feet at the most — and the cold not more intense than at Montreal or Ottawa. Fuel is plentiful; vegetables grow wherever planted; fish abound in every stream and lake, so that living is not nearly so hard as one might be led to believe.

GENERAL CHARACTERISTICS.

Gold was first found in this neighbourhood in 1861 on the Parsnip, about 20 miles from the mouth, and was successively found on Toy's Bar, on Findlay River, below the Omineca, on Silver Creek, Vital Creek, Germansen, Slate, Manson and Lost Creeks; and on Tom Creek in 1889.

The gold in the Omineca region has been obtained principally from the gravels overlying the older rocks in the beds of the present streams. The gravels, as a rule, have little depth, and the productive portions of the different streams seldom exceed three miles in length. The auriferous gravels underlying the boulder clay on Germansen, Manson and other creeks in the district have a wide distribution, and promise favourable results if worked on a sufficiently large scale. Water can be obtained almost anywhere from lakes and mountain streams within a reasonable distance; and the only drawback to successful hydraulicing is the great expanse attendant on the carriage of material and supplies from the coast. At the present time the greater part of the supplies are brought in by pack animals from Hazelton, at the forks of the Skeena, the rate to Manson Creek amounting to 17 cents per pound.

Some prospecting has been done in the Omineca region every season since its auriferous character became known, but the district has by no means been thoroughly explored. The discovery of pay gravels on Tom Creek, close to Vital Creek, twenty years after the latter was found, shows how loose the examination has been. That further discoveries of auriferous creeks will be made admits of little doubt.

The same remarks apply, with perhaps greater force, to the Findlay system. Fine gold has been found in small quantities all along the river and at the mouths of its chief branches, the Ingenica, Quadacha and Tocheica; but on Paul's branch, or the neighbouring streams from the Rockies, none of these creeks have been thoroughly prospected.

RECENT OPERATIONS.

Operations during the season of 1902 were conducted on a very small scale, and the results were far from satisfactory. The two principal companies operating in this field are the Forty-third Mining & Milling Company, of Ottawa, and the Arctic Slope Hydraulic Mining Company, of Victoria. The latter company succeeded in winning gold to the value of some $5,000, which was sufficient to pay all expenses. The run was, however, unfortunately cut short by supplies failing; and consequently, after only a few weeks of actual work, it was necessary to discharge the miners employed. Prospecting work and placer mining on a small scale was carried on at Slate, Lost, Vital and other creeks. Arrangements are now being made to secure additional working capital for the Arctic Slope Company. Under normally favourable conditions there can be no doubt that this field, which offers exceptional opportunities for successful hydraulic mining effort, can be most profitably exploited.

LAKE LOUISE.

INTERIOR ISLAND SCENERY.

ESTERO BASIN, BREDERICK ARM--(Nanaimo M. D.)

SKEENA DISTRICT.

THE Skeena Mining Division comprises territory which, though it has not so far contributed to any great extent to the productive wealth of the province, yet possesses great potential resources; and it will not now be long before capital, which has already begun to recognise the opportunities here afforded, will be largely employed in exploiting the territory, which before many years will be opened up by railways. The word "Skeena" is derived from an Indian word which means "the river," the whole district taking its name from the notable stream, navigable for nearly 200 miles, which up to the present has been utilised as the chief highway into the territory. The watershed of the Skeena contains, approximately, 20,000 square miles, or of almost equal extent and possessing much the same physical characteristics as that section of British Columbia south of the main line of the Canadian Pacific Railway to the 49th parallel, and situated between Vancouver and Arrow Lakes. From information supplied, both by early explorers employed by the Western Union Telegraph Company and by that afforded more recently by surveyors, prospectors and others, it is ascertained that the district is capable of supporting a large population, the agricultural possibilities having special regard to cattle-raising. The chief obstacle to promoting settlement of the territory heretofore has been its inaccessibility; and even to-day flour is worth $12 per sack of 50 lbs. in a locality which is directly on the line of a proposed railway. Under these circumstances it will be readily understood that but little prospecting for minerals has been here attempted; but, notwithstanding, rich deposits of gold and copper ores have been discovered on both sides of the Skeena River, while large coal areas are known to exist on the Kispyox and Telkwa, and good coal and also iron occurrences have been found in the Bulkley Valley. Mining development, however, has been restricted entirely to localities near the coast, or within easy access of deep water; but in these cases the results achieved have been of a decidedly encouraging nature. At Hocsall a large deposit of pyrites is being exploited by a Victoria syndicate, with a view to disposing of the product to chemical works engaged in the manufacture of sulphuric acid. About 90 miles up the Skeena River from Hocsall, a number of quartz claims — mostly copper ores — have been staked out on Kitsilas Mountain. Of these, the Ptarmigan Group has been perhaps the most considerably developed, on the vein which carries a high-grade silver ore. This group of properties is operated by a New York syndicate, headed by Mr. Howard Gould. The mines are situated on the top of the mountain, at an elevation of nearly 5,000 feet, and are reached from the canyon below by a recently built waggon road and horse trail. The mine has been opened up by a 100-foot perpendicular shaft, in addition to cross-cutting and drifting on the vein. At present, naturally, the cost of mining is excessive, as for example, the timber limit in this latitude being exceptionally low, it is necessary to transport the lumber required for shaft-timbering, etc., up hill for nearly a quarter of a mile. Freight and passenger charges, too, are at present costly; while another drawback is the irregularity and infrequency of steamboat travel. The recent establishment of telegraphic communication with the coast cities has, however, done a great deal towards ameliorating conditions, in enabling mine operators a quicker delivery of supplies, etc. In addition to the Ptarmigan mines, other properties in this locality are the Ormond and Four Ace groups of copper claims, both of which show promising indications of mineral; and the Bootjack, I. X. L. and Emma, these latter being almost immediately on the river bank. The Emma and I. X. L. claims have been considerably developed, but during the last two years operations have been suspended, probably in anticipation of improved transportation facilities. Free-gold quartz has also been discovered in the valleys of Tsimnawess and Kaleanza, tributary to the Skeena River, on both sides of the Kitsilas Mountain. Originally this locality was worked by placer miners.

COAL MINING IN THE PROVINCE.

(Report of Minister of Mines.)

WHILE coal mining as a practical commercial operation has as yet been confined to the various collieries operating on the east coast of Vancouver Island and to the Crow's Nest collieries on the western slope of the Rockies, workable coal has already been discovered, and has received more or less development, in various other sections of the province, its occurrence being widely distributed.

In most instances these isolated discoveries have been made at points so far removed from railway accommodation — present or prospective — that little encouragement has been offered for serious development, and they are here referred to simply to demonstrate the possibilities of the various sections of the country when opened up by lines of transportation.

ROCKY MOUNTAINS.

Starting at the Rocky Mountains, the eastern boundary of the province. This range, from the United States boundary northward, has been for miles proven to be coal-bearing, and enormous areas of the known coal fields have already been sufficiently developed to establish their value. While a large part of the known and more accessible portions of this area are now held by the Crow's Nest Pass Coal Company, there remain portions of it still unclaimed, and there is every reason to believe that future prospecting will prove the possibly productive area to be practically of unlimited extent.

An account of this coal field was given by Dr. Selwyn in the report of the Dominion Geological Survey for 1891, written at a time when little more than prospecting and no development had been done. A somewhat detailed account of that portion of the field operated by the Crow's Nest Collieries will have been found in previous pages of this report.

That the coal in the Rockies extends still further northward, for a considerable distance, is evidenced by the now producing mines near Banff, on the Canadian Pacific Railway, though these are on the eastern slope, and consequently not in this province.

NORTHERN INTERIOR.

Seams of "good bright coal," varying in thickness from 6 inches to 2 feet, were observed by Dr. Selwyn at various points in the Peace River basin, near the eastern boundary of Cariboo District, more especially at the head of the canyon on Peace River, Hudson's Hope, and on Pine River, near Table Mountain. Concerning these observations Dr. Selwyn says: "Only one of these can be considered of any economic value, but it is quite likely that there are others in the region which were not observed by us."

Continuing still further northward, and to the west, coal is again met with in the Omineca District, but so far from a market as to be at present of little commercial value. I am informed by Mr. F. W. Valleau, the Gold Commissioner of this district, that coal has been recently found some eight or ten miles south of the

Omineca River where it flows into the Peace River, and, to quote from his description, "it breaks with a conchoidal fracture; I have lit pieces of it in the flame of a candle, and it continues to burn with a smoky flame, leaving little ash."

This would indicate a cannel coal or some other of the hydro-carbons high in volatile matter.

Mr. Valleau also informs me that seams of workable coal occur in the Bulkley and Babine River valleys and intervening country, several of which seams he has personally seen. Some practical coal miners prospecting in this region took some of the coal found there down to Nanaimo, where it was reported as having good coking properties.

Proceeding westward, coal has been found in the valley of the Skeena River in various places, and is said to have been found in workable seams. But little development has been done, and the accounts are not very definite as to the results obtained.

QUEEN CHARLOTTE ISLANDS.

Again proceeding westward from the mouth of the Skeena River to Graham Island, one of the Queen Charlotte group. Here anthracite, as well as bituminous coal, has been known for many years to occur in considerable quantity, which deposits have been the subject of reports by the Geological Survey in 1872-3 by Mr. Richardson, and again in 1878-9 by Dr. G. M. Dawson.

The Queen Charlotte Coal Mining Company, Limited, spent a large sum of money in the development of their property near Skidegate Inlet, but abandoned the enterprise in 1872.

According to the best information obtainable, the coal when first opened up was from 2 to 3 feet thick, of good clean anthracite, and as the tunnel progressed the seam widened to 6 feet, but further in decreased again until it was 1 foot 6 inches at the face, at which point work was stopped.

In 1892 Mr. H. E. Parrish, C. E. and M. E., late of the staff of the Geological Survey of the State of Pennsylvania, acting on behalf of Messrs. W. A. Robertson, William Wilson and others of Victoria, made an examination of certain coal areas on this island, held by these gentlemen, and situated to the westward over the mountain range from the property of the previously mentioned company. From Mr. Parrish's report of his season's work I have taken the following information :—

Camp Robertson — Section 20, township 5, on a creek off the Yakoun River. Bed No. 1, Yakoun, 19 feet thick, bed dips vertically at surface; shaft sunk 23 feet; at foot of shaft dip was only about 5 degrees to E., strike N. and S. This coal is, in my opinion, as fine a coking coal as the Connelsville bed in Pennsylvania. About 60 feet east of No. 1, and overlaying it, is the outcropping of seam No. 2; shaft sunk 14 feet; drift to N., 9 feet; thickness of bed, 14 feet 8 inches. No. 3 seam, overlaying No. 2; 7½ feet clean coal, more bituminous than the two preceding seams.

Camp Anthracite — Section 17, township 5. Shaft sunk 39 feet; thickness at bottom of shaft, 10 feet; strike regular; dip vertical at surface, changing to 45 degrees to E. at bottom of shaft.

Camp Wilson — Section 36, township 9; about 9 miles from Camp Robertson. Dip of bed at surface is vertical, but changes in depth attained to 60 degrees to E. Shaft down 17 feet, with drift 23 feet to S. At the face the bed is 17 feet 8 inches thick, with one bench of 14 feet clean coal. This coal is of a later formation than that found at Camp Robertson. It is a very free burning bituminous coal, leaving little ash.

Mr. Parrish mentions other seams and their development, but these I have noted are quite sufficient to show the importance of the deposits in question. I shall further quote a portion of his remarks as to the condition of the measures and coal outcrops :—

"From exposures and working it is evident that once we get below the surface the formation is regular and broken at no point. It flattens off with depth and takes a moderate dip to the east and northeast.

"Your property is well to the east of the volcanic eruptions which have broken up the measures on the southwest shore of Skidegate Inlet and the west coast of the island.

"One of the strongest indications I could find of the measures flattening as we get under cover is on the creek about one mile south of Camp Robertson, and one-half mile east of the trail. At this point there is a waterfall with a drop of about 80 feet over a fine-grained blue sandstone formation, lying in seams about two feet in thickness. The upper seams have a heavy dip, which gradually lightens off until at the bottom the dip is very slight towards the east. This is the largest exposure I could find on the property. Another strong indication is the tunnel I drove at Camp Robertson. You will notice on the plan that this starts on a level with the Yakoun River, and is driven towards the east into the hill a distance of 80 feet. The face is underneath the plateau upon which Camp Robertson is situated. The measures cut dip about 5 degrees E., and at all the openings that were made show the dip to be heavy at the surface, and gradually flattening as they got under cover. All the exposures I could find show there are no serious eruptions east of the mountains of the west coast, and certainly none on the property I explored.

* * * * * *

"Conclusion.— With the knowledge I have of the coal regions of Pennsylvania, acquired there as a mining engineer, and on the geological staff of that state, it must gratify you to know that in my judgment you have the best coal field I have seen. Until I visited it I had no conception such a valuable field existed on the Pacific Coast. You possess a number of beds of unusual thickness, containing coals of superior quality, suitable for all requirements. You have anthracite, first-class steam, gas and coking coals, and a bed over 15 feet thick, excellent for domestic purposes."

VANCOUVER ISLAND.

The east coast of the Island has so many producing collieries, having a joint yearly output of over a million tons, that mention of the district here is scarcely necessary, further than to refer the reader to the report by the Inspector of Coal Mines on the working collieries which follows.

On the northwest coast, near Quatsino Sound, coal has for years been known to exist, this area having been reported on by the Geological Survey in 1868, and again by Dr. G. M. Dawson in the Survey Report for 1886. Seams of coal four feet thick were then reported and some little development work done, but this was later discontinued. In 1897 the West Vancouver Commercial Company began development of certain areas in this district, and is reported as having met with considerable success, and to be now sinking a shaft on a five-foot seam, with some hundreds of tons of coal on the dump. Some 12 men are employed in this development work, and a steam hoist and other machinery have been erected.

The coal measures also occur and have been somewhat prospected at Alert Bay, on the northeast coast; at Sooke, on the southern end of the Island; and at several points on the west coast of the Mainland opposite the Island, but so far none of the discoveries have received development sufficient to show their value.

At Sahquash, between Port McNeill and Alert Bay, some boring has been done, and a five-foot seam is reported as having been struck. The property is now under bond to an English company.

ELSEWHERE ON THE MAINLAND.

Discoveries of coal have been made in the valley of the Fraser River. The seams so far reported have been too small for profitable working, but sufficient to stimulate prospecting of a serious character.

Coal also occurs in the valley of the Nicola River, a tributary of the Thompson, and seams up to two feet thick have been exposed. At Vermillion Cliff lignite has been found in seams of from two to four feet, and a few tons of the surface coal taken out. (See Report of Geological Survey, 1887-8, by Dr. G. M. Dawson.)

Still further to the south coal has been exposed and somewhat developed in the valley of the Kettle River, seams of 4 feet of good coal being reported; an account of which measures, by S. S. Fowler, A. B. and E. M., was included in the report of this department for 1896.

CROW'S NEST FIELDS.

The following notes are taken from the Minister of Mines' report :

The coal seams so far known have, for practical purposes, been divided, in ascending series, into : (1) The Elk River Basin, bituminous, 12 seams; (2) Michel Creek, bituminous, 7 seams; (3) Michel Creek, cannel coal, 15 seams. Actual work has been confined to the Elk River Basin seams, and these are the only ones I personally inspected. This series outcrops along the mountains on the east side of Elk River, from Morrissey Creek to above Coal Creek, at a height of from 1,600 to 2,500 feet above the valley of Elk River. The beds dip to the east into the mountain at a flat angle. The other edge of the basin is said to outcrop some ten miles to the eastward and near the summit of the mountains. The measurements, etc., of this series of beds, as given to me by Mr. Smith, are as follows :

ELK RIVER SERIES OF COAL SEAMS.

Designation of Seam.	Thickness in Feet.	Work Done on Seam.	Elevation above Elk River.	
12	4		2,500 feet	900 ft. sandstones, conglomerates and shales.
11	7			
10	5			
9	6			
8	4			
7	7	No. 2 tunnel, south side of valley, also exposed in gulch and face stripped.		
6	30	No. 1 tunnel, north side of valley.		
5	6			
4	3			
3	15			
2	30			
1	30		1,600 feet	
12 Seams	147 Feet—Total thickness of coal in 900 ft. vertical coal measure.			

"The outcrop of this series of beds has been traced and found to cut both banks of Coal Creek, some four or five miles up from Elk River.

* * * * *

"The cannel coals mentioned as occurring on Michel Creek, as their characterisation would imply, contain a much larger proportion of volatile combustible matter, and a smaller proportion of fixed carbon. These will have their use principally for gas manufacture and for the somewhat ornamental open grate fires, as they light easily and burn with much flame. The volatile matter is said to be about 57 per cent. in these coals.

* * * * *

"The amount of coal available in the Coal Creek mines is so great that it will be more than sufficient for a long time to come. I have made no personal estimate of the quantity, but quote from Mr. Smith's report, in which he estimates that the Elk River basin alone has an available tonnage of 10,443,900,000 tons in the twelve seams."

Anthracite coal has been found on the Queen Charlotte Islands and on other islands off the coast, and on Vancouver Island near Comox, but has not been worked as yet, although the prospects are promising.

OTHER MINERALS.

Large deposits of gypsum, said to be of good quality, are reported in the immediate neighbourhood of Kamloops, but no attempt has so far been made to work them.

Asbestos is also reported from several localities, but the Department of Mines has been unable to get any authentic information as to values.

Several finds of plumbago have been made, samples from which indicate good quality.

Mica occurs in various parts of the province. From the neighbourhood of Tete Jeune Cache large blocks have been obtained, some as large as 16 x 28 inches, but as yet the transportation facilities are lacking to make it of commercial value.

Platinum has for years been known to exist in the Tulameen River, in the Similkameen District. It exists both as placers and in ore formation. This metal has been again noted in the neighbourhood of Dease Lake and on the Thompson River in the placer workings, but no record has been obtainable of any quantity having been saved.

Petroleum fields are known to exist in the southeast portion of East Kootenay, where large areas have recently been staked.

BUILDING MATERIALS.

No reliable returns are available as to the production of the various building materials, including lime, brick, fire-clay, building stone, cement and tile pipes, and the amount credited to these materials in the statistics has been estimated — the estimate erring on the conservative side.

Lime and brick are produced locally in almost every district for home consumption; while on the coast an excellent lime, which has considerable sale abroad, is made from a marble. On the coast, too, a cement of very good quality is made, and supplies much of the local market. On Kootenay Lake a coarsely crystalline marble quarry is being worked for building purposes. There are on the coast several first-class granite and sandstone quarries opened and doing a local trade. These quarries are so admirably situated as regards water transportation that there is a fair prospect of their becoming an important export industry. Fire-brick, drain-pipes and tile are manufactured on Vancouver Island for home consumption.

IRON ORES OF BRITISH COLUMBIA.

THE Engineering Magazine of New York and London contained some time ago an article by H. Mortimer Lamb, editor of the British Columbia Mining Record, in which is epitomised the most available information on the subject of iron deposits in British Columbia, and from which are here extracted the points of principal value and interest.

The editors of the Engineering Magazine, as a foot-note, make the following comments, which are of interest in this connection :—

"A NEW MINING CENTRE.

"Conditions on the Pacific Coast of America afford one of the most interesting studies now open in the economies of industry. Immediately at hand are vast stores of fuel and iron — the prime elements of all manufacture. Across the Pacific are the enormous new markets of the East, which water transport is bringing nearer every week. Wherever such conditions exist, foci of industry have been created. The dawning century seems likely to witness the birth of new Clevelands, Pittsburgs, Manchesters, in the neighbourhood of Puget Sound. Mr. Lamb's article is essentially a review of some of the material of this new world of wealth."

SOURCES OF SUPPLY.

Although discoveries of large bodies of iron-bearing ores have been made in various localities of the province at intervals since 1872, no annual production has much exceeded 2,000 tons, and on only one or two occasions has the aggregate output of one year reached that figure. The productive sources have been practically limited to three, or, more properly speaking, two mines — one, the Glen Iron mine, on the line of the Canadian Pacific Railway at Cherry Bluff, near Kamloops, and the other the Puget Sound Iron Company's properties at Texada Island. In the case of the former the product has been exclusively used for fluxing purposes by the smelters at Tacoma, Revelstoke and Nelson: while the Texada ore has been shipped to Irondale, Washington, and there smelted with a mixture of from one-ninth to three-tenths of bog ore, making an excellent foundry pig, which was subsequently marketed in San Francisco and utilised by the Union Iron Works in the construction of the United States warships Olympia, Monterey, Charleston and Oregon. In addition to the two mines mentioned, more or less extensive bodies of iron-bearing ores have been discovered at Sooke, Chemainus and Barkley Sound, on Vancouver Island; at Rivers and Knight Inlets, on the Mainland coast; on the Queen Charlotte Islands, and also in several localities of the inland districts of Similkameen and Cariboo.

TEXADA ISLAND.

The Puget Sound Iron Company's property of 2,700 acres is situated on the southwest side of Texada Island. The ore-mass, which on the surface varies in width from 20 to 25 feet, is an irregular contact deposit between limestone and granite, traceable northward for nearly four miles along a ridge following the coastline, and distant from it a quarter to three-quarters of a mile. Sufficient development work has been done to expose an ore-body estimated by experts as representing 5,000,000 tons of commercially valuable iron in sight. In the course of development, at one point, copper in the form of solid pyrites was found in irregular bunches and stringers in the magnetite, but with increased depth this disappeared. Analyses of the ore have been made on several occasions in the laboratory of the Canadian Geological Survey, one result showing 68.40 per cent. of iron, with only .003 per cent. of phosphorus; but a more detailed test gave :

Iron	69.85
Manganese	trace
Siliceous matter	2.75
Sulphur	.6
Phosphoric acid	trace
Moisture	trace

INDUSTRIAL CONDITIONS.

The formation containing the iron ore of Texada Island is believed to be the same as that constituting the greater part of Vancouver and adjacent islands.

The profitable local manufacture on a large scale of iron from these ores is not altogether a remote contingency, for, as I have previously stated, in a limited way the ore has been already turned to commercial uses on the Pacific Coast. Labour provided, an abundant supply of excellent fuel is available in the immediate vicinity, and a permanent market for the product would be assured in the industrial centres of the Pacific seaboard. A further incentive is the bounty granted by the Dominion Government on pig iron manufactured in the country from Canadian ores. On the other hand, supposing that local manufacture is not at present practicable, the coast iron deposits being, without exception, situated within easy access of deep water, transportation costs on the shipment of the crude ore to Puget Sound points would be very light, not exceeding 50 or 60 cents per ton. In addition to this charge, however, the duty of 40 cents per ton on ore imported into the United States must be considered.

QUEEN CHARLOTTE ISLANDS.

On Queen Charlotte Islands, clay iron-stones, the nodules varying in weight from a pound to many tons, are of frequent occurrence in the coal rocks, and might be profitably worked in conjunction with the coal seams. Magnetic iron ores of excellent grade also occur in considerable mass on these islands, to the east side of the entrance to Harriet Harbour; while remarkably pure specimens of magnetite, containing 71.57 per cent. of metallic iron, have been brought from an island in the Walker group.

THE COAST DEPOSITS.

On the Mainland, at Rivers Inlet, near the mouth of the Kildella River, an extensive deposit of ore is found outcropping on a contact of granite and limestone, the average of several analyses being 69.5 per cent. of metallic iron and .01 of phosphorus. A deposit, described as a vein 25 feet wide, also occurs on the north shore of West Redonda Island, in the Gulf of Georgia. The ore is a highly magnetic, somewhat finely crystalline granular, massive magnetite, an analysis affording the following results: Metallic iron, 65.896; phosphorus, none; sulphur, .015. A small shipment of ore was made from this island some years ago, the iron being smelted in the neighbouring state of Washington and converted into car wheels. Much attention has meanwhile been directed to the iron deposits of Vancouver Island. Of these the most important are the deposits at Barkley Sound, in the Alberni Division, on the west coast; and the deposits in the hills to the east of Sooke Harbour, on the south coast, in the Victoria Mining Division.

BARKLEY SOUND.

The first exposure of iron-bearing ore in the Barkley Sound locality is met with on the mainland about a mile up the Sarita River. Here there is a considerable showing of magnetite in a contact of coarsely crystalline limestone and diabase. The ore body, which is said to be 80 feet wide, extends back in an easterly direction a considerable distance, the exposure having been prospected by the sinking of shallow pits and with crosscuts along its length for 800 feet. The deposit has also been partially explored by means of a tunnel, and solid ore has been encountered at a depth of about 90 feet, 60 feet from the mouth of the tunnel. In a direct line northwest by west a continuation apparently of the same deposit is exposed both on Copper Island, some two and a half miles distant, and again at Sechart, on the mainland eight miles to the northwest. Mr. Carlyle, formerly provincial mineralogist of British Columbia, examined these deposits in 1897, and described them in his annual report of that year as a ledge of magnetite lying in what appeared to be diorite, and next to a very extensive area of limestone, which at the point of contact with the eruptive rock is completely crystallised into large, coarse crystals. Both on Copper Island and at Sechart the ore body, which has the appearance of being a primary deposit, has been traced for a distance of several thousand yards, the exposures in some places having been scraped clear, giving a width of over 100

feet of magnetite of good quality. Analyses of ore from these localities have been made in England, Pittsburg and Vancouver, the results being as follows :—

	1	2	3	4	5	6
Iron	64.00	64.01	66.62	66.00	67.98	69.100
Silica	7.35	.....	2.00	.....	2.67	1.500
Alumini	0.52	.....	....	0.14	....	.....
Sulphur	0.0054	0.008	0.02	0.006	trace	trace
Phosphorus	0.0071	0.01	0.01	0.003	0.008	0.007
Lime	3.76	....	4.00	.....	3.000	0.250
Manganese	trace	....	....	.....	0.250	0.160
Magnesia	....	....	....	.....	1.150	0.120

In passing, it may prove interesting to state that the rare mineral ilvaite has been discovered at the head of Barkley Sound, occurring in large irregular masses in a vein about 20 feet wide, an analysis affording the following results :—

Silica	29.81
Alumina	0.16
Ferric oxide	18.89
Ferrous oxide	32.50
Manganous oxide	2.22
Lime	13.82
Magnesia	0.30
Water	1.62
	99.32

Up to the present time the iron areas have been held by men unable, through lack of necessary means, to develop them; but recently the properties in all three localities were acquired under option by capitalists of Pennsylvania, who have commenced systematic exploration and development. If these result satisfactorily, the ores can be quarried out, it is stated, at a cost of about 20 cents per ton, and delivered on board steel scows for an additional 30 cents or less.

SOOKE HARBOUR.

The magnetic ores at Sooke Harbour are somewhat similar in character to those of Texada Island. The deposit, which, according to Dr. Dawson, partakes more of the nature of a stock-work than a true vein, can be distinctly traced in a north-easterly direction for over half a mile, and varies from 15 to 20 feet in width. The country rock is a coarsely-crystalline diorite, containing much hornblende. Analysis of the ore made by Dr. Wallace, city analyst of Glasgow, Scotland, shows it to be of fine quality, averaging over 60 per cent. of metallic iron practically free from all impurities. As in the case of the Barkley Sound properties, comparatively little even preliminary work has been done to prove the permanency or extent of the Sooke exposures; but it is stated by an engineer who examined the deposit that the promise of an almost unlimited supply of ore is undoubted, and that with the favourable facilities for working, the ore could be mined and placed on board scows at a maximum cost of $1 per ton. In the same neighbourhood occurs an exposure of hematite, but the deposit is apparently not extensive.

IRON AT KAMLOOPS.

Of the more notable occurrences of iron-bearing ore in the interior of the province, the most important is the deposit of magnetic iron, known as the Glen Iron Mine, near Kamloops. The mass of the dioritic rock in this locality is much shattered, the cracks and interspaces being filled with the ore, which forms veins of varying degrees of thickness. The ore, which is of excellent quality, containing 66.83 per cent. of metallic iron, with very little phosphorus or sulphur, is in some few places mixed to a slight degree with calcite and feldspar, but not sufficiently to affect its smelting qualities. The veins, four in number and running in an easterly and westerly direction, being nearly vertical or dipping north at wide angles, vary from 10 to 20 feet in width, and are traceable on the surface for several hundred feet. Since 1891 the annual production from this mine has been from 500 to 2,000 tons, the ore being mined and conveyed by an aerial tramway to the railway.

KOOTENAY RIVER.

In 1888 Dr. Dawson reported a remarkable occurrence of magnetic iron ore about half a mile below the lower falls of the Kootenay River. The ore was found in large loose masses, weighing several tons, but owing to the want of good exposure its actual relations to the rocks adjacent were not ascertained. The place of this occurrence is near, if not in, the line of junction of the granites with the here highly altered rocks of the stratified series. It appeared to be associated with a dyke of green-grey augite-porphyrite, and it is probable that the iron ore, when in situ, may form irregular masses along the borders of this dyke. Another noteworthy discovery was made in 1896 by a German geologist, a Mr. Ludloff, in the Cariboo District, of red hematite in a deposit measuring, so he asserts, 500 feet thick. At present, however, little if any commercial value attaches to discoveries of iron in regions so far remote from the railway or other means of communication as that of Fort George, on the Fraser River, the locality in which this occurrence of soft red hematite was discovered by Mr. Ludloff.

GREAT POTENTIALITIES.

At present the extent of information available in respect to the iron deposits of British Columbia has more of a scientific than of a practically commercial interest. As exploration, however, is usually governed by practical considerations, it is probable that those deposits of which anything is known bear but a meagre relation to those of which nothing is as yet definitely ascertainable. It is not too much to say that British Columbia possesses enormous potential resources in her iron deposits, but that these resources must wait for commercial development upon the development of those industries which stimulate a demand for iron. Sooner or later the political conditions which led to the construction of United States battleships on the Pacific Coast, for which, as we have seen, British Columbia iron was partially utilised, will give place to commercial reasons connected with the development of trade on the Pacific necessitating the building of a large mercantile marine. Sooner or later manufacturing industries, with the constant demand for the iron which is their base, will be brought into being to supply the ever-increasing market of the Orient. When these things happen, British Columbia, with its abundant coal and lumber in direct connection with its iron, must become the seat of a great iron industry. Meanwhile these resources are chiefly attractive to those who combine in a very rare degree the gift of foresight and indomitable patience.

IRON DEPOSITS AT KITCHENER.

THERE can be no question that the most important development in mining in this province during the past season has been the discovery and preliminary work upon the hematite iron ore deposits at Kitchener. These deposits occur in a mountain range running almost due north and south, starting at a point near Goat River Canyon and extending northerly about ten miles.

The formation of this mountain range is peculiar, presenting the appearance of an inverted boat, commencing with a gradual ascent from the level of Goat River, and rising in the course of three miles to an altitude of 6,000 feet, continuing at this elevation with slight undulations for a distance of seven miles, and then gradually sloping down to the former level. It will thus be seen that Iron Range is practically an isolated mountain. Along the eastern side it slopes down to Goat River, and on the west to Arrow Creek. Twenty miles away clearly can be seen the lofty snow-capped peaks of White Grouse Mountain. Along the northern side of Iron Range is an easy pass from Goat River to Arrow Creek, and as this route was originally thought of for the Crow's Nest line, it is not impossible that it may yet serve in connection with the future development of the iron mines. The nearest point to the Crow's Nest line and to the town of Kitchener at which the iron has been located is about two miles, but it is not impossible that further explorations, which are contemplated next season, may result in proving a ledge down to the level of Goat River; the only difficulty in the way of this seems to be in the exceptionally heavy drift which covers the formation at the southern end of the range.

LOCATION AND FORMATION.

From the most southerly point at which iron has been discovered it has been traced in a series of continuous and parallel ledges for a distance of seven miles; at the south end of the property only two of such ledges have been uncovered, in consequence of the difficult nature of the prospecting work, but at the north end of the property there are at least five distinct veins of iron, varying from 6 to 20 feet in thickness; in stating this as the width of the veins it is intended to convey the idea that this measurement represents the actual thickness of pure iron, no account being taken of iron-bearing rocks contiguous to the veins, which are more or less charged with iron varying from 10 to 30 per cent. One of the most striking features of the formation is the regularity and straightness of the veins, which are persistent with the slightest possible variation in direction throughout the whole course. All the veins dip to the east at an angle of 60 to 70 degrees. The country rock is gabbro-diorite, and this rock forms the western wall of the iron veins; between the different veins, and extending eastward to an extent which has not yet been definitely determined, the rock is quartzite, largely impregnated with iron. In some of the veins the iron and quartzite are mixed to such an extent that the latter carries a very high percentage, but this does not interfere with the purity and persistency of the true veins of iron.

HISTORY OF THE PROPERTIES.

The property was first introduced to the notice of Mr. W. Blakemore, mining engineer, of Montreal, in April last, and he was so favourably impressed with the reports made and samples submitted that, on his advice, an influential Montreal syndicate took a bond which allowed them practically the whole of that season in which to prove the property, on making a moderate deposit. Three months sufficed to justify Mr. Blakemore's opinion, and his associates decided to make an out-and-out purchase, without waiting for the bond to expire; this was effected in August, for a sum which is authoritatively stated as $80,000 cash; since then development has been pushed to the fullest extent possible, and from the 1st of May until the end of November something like $30,000 has been spent upon the property. Although most of this has been primary work in the shape of trails and bridges and general prospecting, time has been found to exploit the veins and determine the general character of the property; more than fifty open cuts and excavations have been made upon the iron, several tunnels driven, and three shafts started. The principal one was upon an 18-foot vein at the north end of the property, and was carried down nearly 60 feet from the surface; at this point the vein was found to continue exactly the same as at the point of exposure, maintaining its thickness and quality. As we were privileged to publish the result of numerous assays in a recent issue, it is not necessary to recapitulate them; but it may be broadly stated that at the north end of the property, where the work has been chiefly concentrated, the average assays have given from 55 to 65 per cent. of metallic iron, and from 5 to 10 per cent. of silica, with sulphur and phosphorus in negligible quantities. It is not necessary for us to say that this analysis compares favourably with any upon the Continent, being as high as Newfoundland or Michigan ores in iron, much lower than the former in sulphur and phosphorus, and at least equal to the Michigan ores in the same respect. So far as proving the property is concerned, there is still one important point to determine, and that is the depth to which these high-grade deposits continue. Whilst 60 feet is the greatest depth of actual working, there are exposures of the veins in some of the deep gulches on the mountain side at 600 to 800 feet lower than the extreme elevation, and in these gulches the quality of iron is the same. There is nothing in the geological formation to forbid the continuance of these regular veins of ore to a considerable depth, and in the opinion of the most eminent expert who has examined the property — a gentleman at the head of his profession in the Michigan iron districts — the probability is that they will continue to a depth of at least several thousand feet. Without wishing to in any way exaggerate the extent or value of these important deposits, it is clear that sufficient has been done to justify the conclusion that there is at Kitchener an enormous deposit of the highest grade of hematite ore, which cannot fail to play a most important part in the future development of the province.

MARKETS AND OTHER CONDITIONS.

The market in the first instance will be for fluxing purposes, and as these deposits are within reach of a number of smelters, both on the Canadian and American side, which are at present purchasers of iron ore for this purpose, there should be an assured market for at any rate a moderate tonnage; the exceptionally high percentage of iron makes this a valuable ore for that purpose, and renders transportation correspondingly easy. It has already been intimated that the next season may see the commencement of shipping, as nothing stands in the way but the construction of a short branch railway. However this may be, we are more than concerned to witness the fuller exploration and final development of the property upon such a scale as to justify the establishment of iron and steel works. This is the one thing which the province lacks to enable it to compete upon successful lines with any other mining district on the Continent. We already have in the magnificent coal of the Crow's Nest Pass the highest type of cheap fuel. The metalliferous mines are producing ores which are not inferior to any in the West, and it only remains to establish a permanent iron and steel industry in order, not merely to supply the province with an article which is so essential in all industrial developments, but, as we believe, to establish a large export trade in which the Pacific Coast would vie with the Atlantic. After making due allowance for the high rate of wages prevailing at present, and likely perhaps for some years to be prevalent in the West, it is certain that with an assured market, even for a moderate tonnage of steel, it would be possible to produce this commodity and market it within the province at a much lower rate than it is possible to import it from the present points of production. A high authority on this subject has stated that pig-iron could be produced from Kitchener ore at a maximum cost of $10 a ton, which is about half the cost of imported pig-iron in the centre of the province to-day. There would be a corresponding reduction in the cost of rails, machinery, tools and the other thousand and one appliances manufactured from iron and steel, the cost of prosecuting our great mining industries would be reduced, and the further prosperity of the province assured. It is not a little singular that Mr. Blakemore, who was the pioneer of the Crow's Nest coal and coke mining in this province, should also be the first to take up and develop an iron property, and if (and there seems no reason to doubt it) the latter is destined to become as valuable an asset to the province of British Columbia as the former has already proved itself to be, he cannot but be highly gratified at the results of his labours.—[Special Correspondence of the British Columbia Mining Record.]

IRON DEPOSITS OF THE COAST.

MR. W. M. BREWER, M. E., in June, 1902, at the request of the Bureau of Provincial Information, submitted the following description of iron ore deposits on Texada and Vancouver Islands :

Extensive deposits of iron ore occur on Texada and Vancouver Islands. The character of the ore is magnetite, and although the grade is somewhat variable, nearly every deposit produces ore which carries from 60 to 70 per cent. iron, from .01 to .05 per cent. phosphorus, from 3 to 10 per cent. silica, with no traces of titanium, and the sulphur contents variable, but seldom exceeding 3 per cent. So far as exploration has gone at present, the locations of the known deposits are on the west coast of Texada Island, near Gillis Bay; on the eastern side of the same island, on a portion of the Van Anda Mining Company's crown grant; on the eastern side of Vancouver Island, near Chemainus; on the west coast of Vancouver Island, on the Gordon River; on the Sarita River; Copper Island; near Sechart; and some deposits of much more limited extent near the head of Tofino Inlet.

So far as development on these various deposits is concerned, such was neglected until within the past two or three years, except on the deposits on the west coast of Texada Island. From that place iron ore was mined some eighteen years ago by quarrying from the surface, and the product was shipped to Irondale, near Port Townsend, where it was manufactured into pig iron in a charcoal furnace by the Puget Sound Iron Company, the stockholders of which are also stockholders in the Union Iron Works in San Francisco. This pig iron was shipped to San Francisco, and is reported by the Union Iron Works to have been of fine grade; in fact, some of the plates on the United States battleship Oregon were rolled from this pig. A low percentage of copper which was associated with the iron ore proved sufficiently detrimental to compel the miners to sort the ore carefully. Partly for this reason and partly because during the depressed state of the iron market for several years it was possible to ship pig iron from Alabama at a lower cost than it could be manufactured in the local charcoal furnace, which only had a capacity of thirty tons per day, the plant was closed down and remained idle until 1901, when the iron market improved. The prices went up in 1898 so that No. 1 foundry iron in Alabama was selling for $18.50 per ton, f. o. b., instead of $7.50 per ton, f. o. b., as had been the case during the years of depression. The owners of the deposits near Gillis Bay commenced a systematic development at depth. By sinking and cross-cutting the deposit was proven to a depth of about 400 feet below the outcrop, and at that depth no copper was found associated with the iron ore, and the ore itself was shown by analysis to be within the Bessemer limit.

During 1899 a good deal of attention was directed towards the iron ore deposits on the west coast of Vancouver Island, and all the known occurrences of extent were acquired, either by purchase or bond, by a syndicate from the United States. Since then this syndicate has been working a force of men at the deposits at the Sarita River, at Copper Island, and near Sechart, in order to thoroughly exploit the ground and determine the approximate tonnage in each of these deposits. This work is still being carried on at the present time, but no shipments have been made, although regular shipments are being made from the ore deposit on the west coast of Texada Island to the same furnace in which the pig iron was manufactured some years back. This furnace during 1901 was purchased from the Puget Sound Iron Mining Company by the syndicate which had bonded the iron ore deposits on the west coast of Vancouver Island, and which leased the deposits near Gillis Bay, on Texada Island, for a term of years, on a royalty basis.

In addition to the three occurrences of iron ore mentioned on the west coast of Vancouver Island, some of the deposits on Gordon River are being exploited by an English syndicate, and others are at present under bond, and it is expected that very shortly prospecting work will be commenced upon them.

All the occurrences of iron ore referred to in the foregoing occur either at the contact of basic igneous rocks and crystalline limestone or occupy fissures in the igneous rocks. The contact deposits are very much more extensive than the others, and, roughly speaking, there is usually sufficient showing to warrant the statement that any of these contact deposits will produce a remarkably large tonnage of ore. Some have been estimated to probably yield from 2,000,000 to 6,000,000 tons; but in no case has there been sufficient development work done to date to warrant other than approximate measurements.

The deposits of non-cupreous iron ore occur in a zone on Vancouver Island which lies westerly and southerly from the zone of copper-gold-bearing ore, and is apparently the extreme southwesterly mineralised belt on Vancouver Island; but in the latter there are several occurrences of magnetite outcroppings of considerable extent which, were it not for the fact that the chalcopyrite and pyrrhotite associated with the magnetite is of such grade as to make the entire ore body valuable for its copper-gold contents, would possess value as iron ore mines, but because of these contents the iron ore itself is rendered practically useless for the manufacture of pig iron.

As a matter of fact, attention has only been drawn to the iron ore deposits on the Island for such a short time, so far as concerns their value for the manufacture of pig iron, and incidentally steel, that prospectors who are searching for metalliferous lode mines have given very little attention to locating occurrences of iron ore unless such holds sufficient copper and gold value to make the ore important in their eyes.

BUGABOO CREEK IRON DEPOSITS.

The following information is extracted from the report of I. B. Atkinson, M. E., on the Conqueror group of claims, situate on Bugaboo Creek, a tributary of the Gordon River, which empties into San Juan Harbour, Renfrew District, Vancouver Island: The ore is a contact vein or deposit of magnetite, and where it shows clearly in the creek it is 230 feet in width and practically clean ore. The outcrop of magnetite has been proved by test pits and open cuts to extend throughout the main portion of the Conqueror claim, and rich float is found on two other claims. Mr. Atkinson examined several large outcrops of ore in seven extension claims lying east of the Conqueror group, practically proving a continuation of the ore body for nearly three miles. It is a contact deposit lying between a wide belt of highly crystalline limestone on the hanging wall side, and altered igneous rocks on the footwall. Since Mr. Atkinson's inspection the owners report that work on the David claim has proved high-grade ore to a width of 522 feet, and the footwall not yet reached. Samples of ore taken from the sides, roof, sole and forebreast of the tunnel, assayed by J. O'Sullivan, F. C. S., gave an average assay as follows:

	Per Cent.
*Ferric oxide	81.42
*Ferrous oxide	15.68
Silica	1.40
Sulphur	.30
Phosphorus	.06
Titanium	nil
Lime	trace
Alumina	trace
Water, very little / Chromium and loss	1.14
	100.00

*69.06 per cent. Metallic Iron.

An average analysis of the ore by Mr. O'Sullivan is as follows :

	Per Cent.
Metallic iron	68.79
Silica	1.75
Sulphur	.35
Phosphorus	.056

An average analysis made by the Provincial Government Assay Office is as follows :

	Per Cent.
Metallic iron	69.2
Sulphur	.5
Silica	2.7

The ore body is well situated for economical mining. San Juan Harbour is 60 miles from Victoria, and the mine is six miles from the harbour, at an elevation of 1,000 feet above sea-level. The position of the ore is such that it can be mined by quarrying. There is an abundance of timber and an ample supply of water on the claims. Mr. Atkinson estimates that the ore can be mined and transported to the coast at a cost of $1 per ton. The development work on the several properties and the exposure of ore by Bugaboo Creek cutting through the deposit prove that there are several millions of tons of ore in sight.

THE FUTURE COAL AND COKE SUPPLY OF THE INTERIOR OF BRITISH COLUMBIA.

(By W. Blakemore, M. E., Fernie, B. C.)

THE future prosperity of this province depends on an abundant supply of the best quality of fuel at a low price. This controlling factor is determined by two conditions — the general low-grade value of our ores, and the fact that the geological formation forbids the existence of coal in proximity to the metalliferous deposits, and so involves more or less costly transportation. This governs the conduct of our mining industry absolutely, and, as I shall be able to show further on, is of equal force as applied to other important industries that may be established, the only important consumers of fuel not likely to be handicapped in this respect being the railways, and that because the matter of quality is not so important as in the case of smelting and manufacturing.

Steam Fuel.— As there can be no considerable development without railway transportation, it may be well to consider first how our coal deposits will first serve existing and prospective railways in British Columbia. The natural surface conditions will probably limit railway construction from east to west to three lines — in the north, the Canadian Northern, from the Yellowhead Pass to the Coast; in the centre, the Canadian Pacific, from the Kicking Horse Pass to Vancouver; and in the south, the Crow's Nest Pass, with some continuation of the same by way of the Similkameen Valley to Vancouver. The difficulties and the cost of building across the mountain ranges of this province are sure to militate against more than these. The natural method of serving the interior will be by means of branch lines running north and south, between the mountain ranges. In order that transportation may be as cheap as possible, it is necessary that these main lines should pass through or near to large coal deposits of suitable quality for steaming; at any rate, this is a present necessity, and will remain so until some day, in the possibly not very distant future, when our magnificent water powers are harnessed to electric locomotion.

The main line of the Canadian Pacific Railway has hitherto been well served with fuel by the Canmore mines, and it is likely that for at least ten years these will continue to furnish all that may be required. The unworked area, however, is not large, and already it is time to look further afield. On the eastern slope of the Rockies, eight miles west of Calgary, we have exposures of coal seams running north and south which are probably continuations of the large bituminous coal field lying to the south. Little or no development work has been done at this point, but the exposures are consistent with the theory named, and I have little doubt that a season's work would show up a series of seams of good quality. A line can be gotten as to this by examining the coal at Sheep Creek, which, though inferior to that at Canmore, is still of fair quality and such as could well be used in the absence of a higher grade. Recent investigations convince me that the coals found in the Blairmore district, and as far south as the entrance to North Kootenay Pass, continue northwards parallel to the Rockies far beyond the Yellowhead Pass, and, if so, although they are on the Alberta side, they are in an ideal position to furnish steam fuel for the main lines at least half way across the province of British Columbia.

As far as the Canadian Northern is concerned, no portion of this system has yet been constructed, but the route has been surveyed from the Yellowhead Pass to the Coast; and at three points at least good steam coal has been located in large quantities. Two hundred miles east of the Pass, upon the Saskatchewan River, a high-class lignitic coal has been discovered, yielding on analysis—

Fixed carbon	52 per cent.
Volatile combustible matter	35 per cent.
Ash	12 per cent.

This is about the same grade as the Lethbridge coal, of which more than 1,000 tons a day is mined in the season for steam and domestic purposes, and which is a far superior coal to that used by the Great Northern south of the international line.

At a point 200 miles west of the Yellowhead Pass, outcroppings have been met with by the surveyors, and at the moment these are being traced. They no doubt represent the northern continuation of the cretaceous measures, and, if so, the quality will be that of a high-grade bituminous coal, and the only question will be as to the extent.

On the Pacific Coast, 400 miles north of Vancouver, there are extensive coal seams near the route of the proposed railway. The measures run north and south, and the average of several samples recently taken by a reliable expert shows:

Fixed carbon	54 per cent.
Volatile combustible matter	37 per cent.
Ash	14 per cent.

This coal, although high in ash, compares favourably with the fuel recently used on American lines in the West.

Coming to the Crow's Nest line and the prospective continuation to the Coast, we have the highest grade of steam coal known on this continent in the Crow's Nest Pass and its extensions, and it is not necessary that I should say anything about it except that its only limitation as a railway fuel is one of distance. It will always control the market for this purpose as far west as the Arrow Lakes; but recent discoveries farther west tend to show that, as the Columbia and Kootenay extension is built, it will open up new coal fields, which, by reason of their shorter haul, will secure this trade.

On the north fork of Kettle River outcroppings of high-class bituminous coal have been found and are being traced. My own analysis of a sample taken from a four-foot seam gives:—

Fixed carbon	62.6 per cent.
Volatile combustible matter	29.6 per cent.
Ash	7.8 per cent.

STIKINE GLACIER.

HISTORIC INDIAN VILLAGE, NOOTKA.

MOUTH OF NIMKISH RIVER, V. I.

If any considerable quantity of such a fuel as this can be found, it will dominate the steam coal trade from the Okanagan Lakes east to the Arrow Lakes; but it lies nearly 100 miles north of the Boundary District and out of the route of the proposed railway, although it can only be a question of time until a branch is constructed up the Kettle River. Farther west we have two well-defined coal fields near Princeton and Nicola. The former, with Ashnola as its centre, is undoubtedly upon the route of any railway from the Boundary District to the Coast, as such a railway must pass up the Similkameen Valley at least as far as Princeton, whatever route it may take thence westwards. Here we have a well-defined coal basin, 8 miles from east to west and 10 or 12 miles from north to south. Many seams of lignitic coal outcrop, of which a fair average analysis gives :—

Fixed carbon	42.0 per cent.
Volatile combustible matter	42.7 per cent.
Ash	3.0 per cent.

In the absence of a better fuel this would be used by the railway from the Boundary District to the Hope Mountains. Only a month ago, however, a nine-foot seam of good coal was bored through at a depth of 625 feet, which yielded :—

Fixed carbon	54 per cent.
Volatile combustible matter	23 per cent.
Ash	8 per cent.

This is full of promise for the future, and there are, doubtless, other seams of equal, if not superior, quality. Thus the supply of an excellent steam coal for the Columbia and Kootenay is assured.

At Nicola (near which the projected railway will pass if it joins the main line of the Canadian Pacific Railway at Spence's Bridge) there is an extensive coal field, probably of the same character as the Princeton basin, which would be easily available.

If in connection with these various sources of supply it be borne in mind that we have extensive coal mines in full operation on Vancouver Island, you will see that every part of the province is well furnished with good steam fuel, and that the first essential for cheap transportation abounds wherever an important railway is likely to be constructed. I estimate that on the Canadian Northern the maximum haul of steam fuel within the province will not exceed 250 miles; on the main line of the Canadian Pacific Railway, 200; and on the Crow's Nest line, 150. This should give fuel at an actual cost ranging from $2 to $3 a ton, a figure which would certainly be favourable for the development of the province on the lines of cheap transportation. These figures take no account of other discoveries which will be made in the near future, as there are abundant evidences that there is a continuity in the coal seams of the Rockies, from Mexico to the Yukon; and there are few valleys of British Columbia in which some trace of these does not exist.

Smelting Fuel.— We now have to consider the subject of smelting fuel, and probably this will appeal more directly to our members, because it "comes home." Without cheap and good smelting fuel the mining industry of British Columbia would come to a standstill. The men who were reviled in 1895 for pronouncing our ores "low grade" have had ample revenge, and it is now not merely proven, but an acknowledged fact. Transportation and treatment on Rossland ores have been reduced from $13 to less than $5 a ton, and shipping values from $25 or $30 to $8 or $10. To this result the Crow's Nest coal and coke have contributed not a little, having brought the delivered price of the former down from $12 to $4, and the latter from $17 to $6. During this period we have learnt many things, and some remain yet to be learnt. It must now be admitted that our ores are so low grade that every cent in cost tells, and that to develop the industry will require the cheapest fuel that can be obtained. Take for example the great self-fluxing copper district, the Boundary. Is it taking too low an estimate to say that with the exception of a few rich chutes, which may run to $7 or even $8, the vast bodies of ore in that camp will not exceed $4 ? If this is so, and if, as Dr. Ledoux says, fuel represents 05 per cent. of a total smelting cost of $2, then every dollar saved in fuel would mean about 25 cents on the ton of ore treated, a sum which probably represents the difference between profit and loss, since it is admitted on all hands, and confirmed by the highest experts, that everything has been done in the way of appliances and economic management to reduce the cost of treatment to the lowest possible figure.

Let us enquire, then, how the future of smelting in British Columbia is likely to be affected by the fuel question. This practically resolves itself into the enquiry—how can smelting fuel be still further cheapened ? There is only one way — by competition. This involves the development of other coal fields and the liberation of some portion of the Government coal lands in the Crow's Nest Pass.

First, as to the opening up of other coal fields. At the moment of writing there is, so far as I know, only one place in the interior of British Columbia (outside the Crow's Nest Pass) where coal of a suitable quality for making a first-class smelting coke has been found, viz., on the north fork of the Kettle River. The analysis was given under the heading of "Steam Fuel." If this deposit should be large enough the quality is all right, and the location being only about 100 miles from the Boundary District, would give it an advantage of at least $1.50 in cost of transportation, and would save 40 cents a ton in treating the ore.

The same coal would serve any smelters that might be erected further west, in the event of no coking coal being found in the Similkameen or Nicola Valleys, where it is certain there are valuable copper ores and at least three promising camps — Twenty-Mile Creek, Copper Mountain and Aspen Grove.

For any relief in the cost of fuel in East Kootenay and the eastern camps of West Kootenay we have to look to the Crow's Nest Pass coal field. Leaving for later consideration the Blairmore section of this (because it is in Alberta), we are confined to three sections, viz., the coal areas owned and operated by the Crow's Nest Pass Coal Company; those lying to the south beyond the British Columbia Southern reserve, in the neighbourhood of Lodgepole Creek, Greenhills and Wigwam River; and the 50,000 acres recently selected by the Dominion Government. The former are being developed slowly, and, having regard to the statement made by the managing director that in addition to the home market the Great Northern Company require 10,000 tons a day, it is not likely that this demand will be overcome for many years. In addition, the liability to accidents, like the recent deplorable disaster, and to strikes, renders it extremely undesirable that the fuel supply, upon which every industry in the Kootenays depends, should be in the hands of any one firm, however competent and well-meaning. Then there is the impossibility of getting the lowest possible price from a monopoly. At the moment the charge for coal is $2, and for coke $4 a ton at the ovens. As I shall show, effective competition would reduce these figures to $1.50 and $3 at the ovens, and possibly a little lower. The actual cost of shipping one ton of coal need not exceed $1, and will almost certainly be less after allowing for every item of charge. This would give coke at a cost of $2.25 to $2.50, and leave a margin of 50 cents profit on coal and 75 cents on coke, which is at least double the average rate of profit on coal and coke in the Eastern States or in England over the last twenty years. The present British Columbia consumption of Crow's Nest coal is 1,000 tons a day and of coke 300 tons a day, and a reduction such as the above would mean a saving to the industries of the Kootenays (and mainly to the mining industry) of about $1,000 a day or $300,000 a year. As the country is growing so rapidly this tonnage would be largely increased in the near future. From what areas could fuel be produced at these figures ? Possibly from the sections south and east of the British Columbia Southern reserve already referred to. That, however, is at present a matter of speculation, because nothing has been done beyond locating the coals; and until development work has been carried to a much more advanced stage it cannot be stated with certainty whether the measures are sufficiently contiguous and regular to yield a large working area. In any case it will take two years to prove this, and will involve the building of a branch railway nearly thirty miles up Lodgepole Creek.

If, however, the Government would liberate say 5,000 acres of their selection adjoining and on the south side of Morrissey, all the conditions exist to bring about the result I have foreshadowed. At this point the coal seams of the basin are exposed and are most accessible. The measures are regular and dip under uniform strata to the east for several miles until they meet the eastern upthrow which terminates the basin. From exploratory workings conducted here last season I got samples yielding the following analyses: —

No. 1 — 18-foot Seam.

Fixed carbon	78.7 per cent.
Volatile matter	17.0 per cent.
Ash	4.3 per cent.

No. 2 — 4-foot Seam.

Fixed carbon	77.3 per cent.
Volatile matter	18.4 per cent.
Ash	2.8 per cent.

These figures show that the celebrated coals of the Crow's Nest Pass are at their best on Morrissey Creek, as a comparison with the following samples taken from two other points in the Pass indicates: —

Fernie — 6-foot Seam.

Fixed carbon	69.14 per cent.
Volatile matter	25.45 per cent.
Ash	3.62 per cent.

Michel — 14-foot Seam.

Fixed carbon	62.40 per cent.
Volatile matter	24.10 per cent.
Ash	12.05 per cent.

This is the only point where coal of equal quality to the best Fernie coal has been discovered and explored sufficiently to enable me to speak with certainty of its extent, and in this view I am confirmed by Mr. J. McEvoy, former Government geologist. In the interests of the province, and especially of the mining and smelting industry, no effort should be spared to induce the Government to place this area on the market. There is no legal impediment and obligation in the way, and I have little doubt that an unanimous request would attain a result so important to the future of the Kootenays in particular.

This brings me to consider another source from which relief may come in any case through the ordinary healthy channels of competition. I refer to the Blairmore coal field. Having done most of the prospecting work that has been done here this year, I am able to give you the latest information. Here we have what I believe to be the same series of coal measures as are found in the Pass, only instead of having been uplifted in the form of an elongated basin or trough, they are uplifted and fractured in longitudinal lines and exposed in ridges running north and south, or nearly so, parallel with the Rockies. The result is much folding and duplication, but at the same time many more exposures of the same seam, and increased facility of access.

These conditions have been proved in extensive properties owned and controlled by Mr. Leslie Hill, Mr. T. G. Proctor, Messrs. McVittie and Leitch, Messrs. Davenport and Paine, and others. The coal seams, which correspond in thickness and occurrence with those of Fernie and Morrissey, have been traced from the entrance to the North Kootenay Pass, where Mr. J. J. Hill has secured 10,000 acres, to a point 20 miles north of Blairmore. Messrs. Frank and Geho have developed a successful mine on the east side of Turtle Mountain, which has already attained an output of 800 tons a day, the coal being excellent for steam purposes. My own object in taking up certain bonds in this important coal field was to determine its character for coking purposes and to ascertain how it compared with Fernie coal. The result you can best judge from the following analyses taken by me from comparatively shallow workings; the ash is certain to be less at greater depth :—

	Fixed Car.	Volatile.	Ash.
No. 1	63.4	29.1	7.4
No. 2	64.5	26.5	9.0
No. 3	67.7	25.5	6.8
No. 4 (20 miles north of Blairmore)....	58.9	28.5	11.8
No. 5	60.3	31.3	7.4

Samples Nos. 1, 2, and 3 are all first-class coking coals; Nos. 4 and 5 good steam.

This coal field is so near to the province of British Columbia that it will seek its natural market there for coal and coke, especially the latter; and the mode of occurrence of the seams being more favourable for cheap working than in the Pass, there is no reason why the cost of production may not offset the extra transportation, a matter of 30 to 50 miles. At any rate, I am convinced that in less than two years from date we shall see coal and coke of satisfactory quality being produced in this district at the figures I have already named, to the enormous benefit of the various industries of Southern British Columbia.

SYNOPSIS OF MINING LAWS.

THE mining laws of British Columbia are very liberal in their nature, and compare favourably with those of any other part of the world. The terms under which both lode and placer claims are held are such that a prospector is greatly encouraged in his work, and the titles, especially for mineral claims and hydraulic leases, are absolutely perfect. The fees required to be paid are as small as possible, consistent with a proper administration of the mining industry, and are much lower than those of the other provinces of Canada or the mineral lands under Dominion control. Provision is also made for the formation of mining partnerships practically without expense, and a party of miners is enabled to take advantage of these parts of the Acts and work their claims together, without the trouble or expense of forming a joint stock company.

Considering the great success that has characterised alluvial mining on a large scale in British Columbia, the rentals for hydraulic leases are particularly low. It will be found, on reference to most of the Australian colonies and Natal, that the rentals are in most instances eight times as much as in this province, while the areas permitted are generally much smaller. The period for which leases are granted is practically the same. On a lode mine of 51 acres the expenditure of $500, which may be spread over five years, is required to obtain a Crown grant; and surface rights are obtainable at a small figure, in no case exceeding $5 per acre. The following is a synopsis of the mining laws, which will be found sufficient to enable the miner or intending investor to obtain a general knowledge of their scope and requirements.

FREE MINERS' CERTIFICATES.

Any person over the age of 18, and any joint stock company, may obtain a free miner's certificate on payment of the required fee.

The fee to an individual for a free miner's certificate is $5 for one year. To a joint stock company having a capital of $100,000 or less, the fee for a year is $50; if capitalised beyond this, $100.

All these certificates expire at midnight on the 31st of May in each year. Certificates may be obtained for any part of a year, terminating on the 31st of May, for a proportionally less fee.

The possession of this certificate entitles the holder to enter on all lands of the Crown, or other lands on which the right to so enter is reserved, and prospect for minerals, locate claims and mine.

A free miner can only hold, by location, one mineral claim on the same vein or lode, but may acquire others by purchase. In the case of placer claims, only one can be held by location on each creek, ravine or hill, and not more than two in the same locality, only one of which shall be a "creek" claim.

In the event of a free miner allowing his certificate to lapse, his mining property (if not Crown-granted) reverts to the Crown; but where other free miners are interested as partners or co-owners, the interest of the defaulter becomes vested in the company continuing co-owners or partners, pro rata, according to their interests.

It is not necessary for a shareholder, as such, in an incorporated mining company to be the holder of a certificate.

MINERAL CLAIMS.

Mineral claims are located and held under the provisions of the Mineral Act.

A mineral claim is a rectangular piece of ground, not exceeding 1,500 feet square. The angles must all be right angles unless the boundaries, or one of them, are the same as those of a previously surveyed claim.

A mineral claim is located by erecting three legal posts, which are stakes having a height of not less than four feet above ground, and squared for four inches at least on each face for not less than a foot from the top. A tree stump so cut and squared also constitutes a legal post.

The "discovery post" is placed at the point where the mineral in place is discovered.

Nos. 1 and 2 posts are placed as near as possible on the line of the ledge or vein, shown by the discovery post, and mark the boundaries of the claim. Upon each of these three posts must be written the name of the claim, the name of the locator, and the date of location. On No. 1 post, in addition, the following must be written: "Initial post. Direction of post No. 2 [giving approximate compass bearing]; —— feet of this claim lie on the right, and —— feet on the left of the line from No. 1 to No. 2 posts."

The location line, between Nos. 1 and 2 posts, must be distinctly marked — in a timbered locality by blazing trees and cutting underbrush, and in bare country by monuments of earth or rock not less than two feet in diameter at the base, and at least two feet high — so that the line can be distinctly seen.

Mineral claims must be recorded in the Mining Recorder's office for the mining division in which they are situated, within fifteen days from the date of location, one day extra being allowed for each ten miles of distance from the recording office after the first ten miles. If a claim is not recorded in time it is deemed abandoned and open for re-location; but if the original locator wishes to re-locate, he can only do so by permission of the Gold Commissioner of the district, and upon payment of a fee of $10. This applies also to a claim abandoned for any reason whatever.

Mineral claims are, until the Crown grant is issued, held practically on a yearly lease, the condition of which is that assessment work be performed on the same during each year to the value of at least $100, or payment of such sum be made to the Mining Recorder. Such assessments must be recorded before the expiration of the year, or the claim is deemed abandoned. If, however, such record is omitted, a free miner may, before the expiration of thirty days thereafter, record such assessment upon payment of a fee of $10. This, however, will not hold the claim if it has been re-located by another free miner in the meantime. The actual cost of the survey of a mineral claim, to an amount not exceeding $100, may also be recorded as assessment work. If during any year work is done to a greater extent than the required $100, any further sums of $100 — but not less — may be recorded and counted as further assessments. As soon as assessment work to the extent of $500 is recorded, the owner of a mineral claim is entitled to a Crown grant on payment of a fee of $25 and giving the necessary notices required by the Act. Liberal provisions are also made in the Act for obtaining mill-sites and other facilities in the way of tunnels and drains for the better working of claims.

PLACER CLAIMS.

Placer Mining is governed by the Placer Mining Act, and by the interpretation clause its scope is defined as "the mining of any natural stratum or bed of earth, gravel or cement mined for gold or other precious minerals or stones." Placer claims are of four classes, as follows:

Creek Diggings — Any mine in the bed of any stream or ravine.

Bar Diggings — Any mine between high and low water marks on a river, lake or other large body of water.

Dry Diggings — Any mine over which water never extends.

Precious Stone Diggings — Any deposit of precious stones, whether in veins, beds or gravel deposits.

The following provisions as to extent of the various classes of claims are made by the Act:

In creek diggings a claim shall be 250 feet square; provided, always, that the side lines of each claim shall be measured in a general direction of the water course or stream.

In bar diggings a claim shall be: (a) A piece of land not exceeding 250 feet square on any bar which is covered at high water; or (b) a strip of land 250 feet long at high-water mark, and in width extending from high-water mark to extreme low-water mark.

In dry diggings a claim shall be 250 feet square.

Every placer claim shall be as nearly as possible rectangular in form, and marked by four legal posts at the corners thereof, firmly fixed in the ground. On each of such posts shall be written the name of the locator, the number and date of issue of his free miner's certificate, the date of the location and the name given to the claim. In timbered localities all boundary lines of a placer claim shall be blazed so that the posts can be distinctly seen, underbrush cut, and the locator shall also erect legal posts not more than 125 feet apart on all boundary lines. In localities where there is no timber or underbrush, monuments of earth or rock, not less than two feet high and two feet in diameter at base, may be erected in lieu of the said last-mentioned legal posts, but not in the case of the four legal posts marking the corners of the claim.

A placer claim must be recorded in the office of the Mining Recorder for the mining division within which the same is situate, within fifteen days after the location thereof, if located within ten miles of the office of the Mining Recorder by the most direct means of travel. One additional day shall be allowed for every ten miles additional or fraction thereof. The number of days shall be counted inclusive of the day upon which such location was made, but exclusive of the day of application for record. The application for such record shall be under oath, and in the form set out in the schedule to the Act. A claim which shall not have been recorded within the prescribed period shall be deemed to have been abandoned.

To hold a placer claim for more than one year, it must be re-recorded before the expiration of the record or re-record.

A placer claim must be worked by the owner or someone on his behalf, continuously, as far as practicable, during working hours. If work is discontinued for a period of 72 hours, except during the close season, lay-over, leave of absence, sickness, or for some other reason to the satisfaction of the Gold Commissioner, the claim is deemed abandoned.

Lay-overs are declared by the Gold Commissioner upon proof being given to him that the supply of water is insufficient to work the claim. Under similar circumstances he has also the power to declare a close season, by a notice in writing and published in the Gazette, for all or any claims in his district. Tunnel and drain licenses are also granted by him on the person applying giving security for any damage that may arise. Grants of right-of-way for the construction of tunnels or drains across other claims are also granted on payment of a fee of $25, the owner of the claim crossed having the right for tolls, etc., on the tunnel or drain which may be constructed. These tolls, however, are, so far as the amount goes, under the discretion of the Gold Commissioner.

DISCOVERY CLAIMS.

The following provision is made for new discoveries of placer mining ground :—

If any free miner, or party of free miners, discover a new locality for the prosecution of placer mining, and such discovery be established to the satisfaction of the Gold Commissioner, placer claims of the following sizes shall be allowed to such discoverers : To one discoverer, one claim 600 feet in length; to a party of two discoverers, two claims, amounting together to 1,000 feet in length; to each member of a party beyond two in number, a claim of the ordinary size only : Provided, that where a discovery claim has been established in any locality, no further discovery shall be allowed within five miles therefrom, measured along the water-courses. The width of such claims shall be the same as ordinary placer claims of the same class.

No special privileges are allowed for discovery of new mineral claims.

CO-OWNERS AND PARTNERSHIPS.

In both the Mineral and Placer Mining Acts provision is made for the formation of mining partnerships, both of a general and limited liability character. These are extensively taken advantage of, and have proved very satisfactory in their working. By an amendment to the Mineral Act, passed in 1901, provision is made for collection of the proportion of assessment work that may be due from any co-owner in a mineral claim. It should not be forgotten that if any co-owner permits his free miner's certificate to lapse, the title of his associates is not prejudiced, but his interest reverts to the remaining co-owners.

HYDRAULIC AND DREDGING LEASES.

Leases of unoccupied Crown lands may be granted by the Lieutenant-Governor-in-Council, upon recommendation of the Gold Commissioner of the district, after location by placing a legal post at each corner of the ground applied for. On the post nearest the placer ground then being worked the locator must post a notice stating the name of the applicant, the location of the ground to be acquired, the quantity of ground, and the term for which the lease is to be applied for. Within 30 days application must be made in writing to the Gold Commissioner, in duplicate, with the plan of the ground on the back, and the application must contain the name of each applicant, the number of each applicant's free miner's certificate, the locality of the ground, the quantity of ground, the term of the lease desired, and the rent proposed to be paid. A sum of $20 must accompany the application, which is returned if the application is not granted. The term of leases must not exceed twenty years. The extent of ground covered by leases is not in excess of the following : Creek, ½ mile; hydraulic diggings, 80 acres; dredging leases, 5 miles; precious stone diggings, 10 acres. Under order-in-council the minimum rental for a creek lease is $75 per annum and for a hydraulic lease $50 per annum, with a condition that at least $1,000 per annum shall be spent in development. For dredging leases the usual rental is $50 per mile per annum, development work worth

$1,000 per mile per annum must be done, and 50 cents royalty per ounce paid on the gold mined.

TAXATION OF MINES.

Mineral or placer claims, when crown-granted, are subject to a yearly tax of 25 cents per acre; but if $200 is spent in work in a year, this tax is not levied. A tax of 2 per cent. is levied quarterly on all ores and other mineral substances mined in the province, but where ore-producing mines produce under $5,000 in a year, half the tax is refunded; while placer or dredging mines that do not produce a gross value of $2,000 in a year are entitled to a refund of the whole tax. These taxes are in substitution for all taxes on the land, and for the personal property tax in respect of sums so produced, so long as the land is only used for mining purposes. By the Land Act a royalty of 50 cents per M., board measure, is levied on timber suitable for mining props, a cord of props being considered as 1,000 feet, board measure.

COAL AND PETROLEUM PROSPECTING.

Coal or petroleum prospecting licenses may be procured after a thirty days' notice has been placed on the land and in the Government Office of the district, as well as published in the Gazette and in a local paper for the same length of time. Application must be made in writing to the Gold Commissioner, in duplicate, accompanied by plans of the land and a fee of $50. A license may be issued for not more than 640 acres of land for one year, the said $50 covering the first year's rental. All lands must be in a square block and run due north, south, east and west. At the expiration of the first year an extension may be granted for a second and third year. Land for which a license has been granted may be leased, upon proof being given of the discovery of coal, for five years at a rental of 10 cents per annum per acre; the lease also contains provision for a royalty of 5 cents per ton of coal and 1 cent per barrel of petroleum. If the lessee is able to prove that he has worked the land continuously, he may, within three months of the expiration of his lease, purchase the land at $5 per acre.

MINING RECORDERS IN OUTLYING DISTRICTS.

Where mineral is discovered in a part of the province remote from mining recorders' offices, so that the provisions of the Act cannot be justly enforced, the miners themselves may, by a two-thirds vote at a meeting for that purpose, appoint a mining recorder from among themselves. Such recorder can issue free miners' certificates, records of mining property, etc., and such entries will be valid notwithstanding any informality. Under the Act such mining recorder shall, as soon as possible, forward a list of the free miners' certificates issued by him, and of records made, to the nearest gold commissioner or mining recorder, together with the fees required by law therefor.

TABLE OF FEES.

Individual Free Miners' Certificate	$ 5 00
Company Free Miner's Certificate (capital $100,000 or less)	50 00
Company Free Miner's Certificate (capital over $100,000)	100 00
Recording Mineral or Placer Claim	2 50
Recording Certificate of Work, Mineral Claim	2 50
Re-record of Placer Claim	2 50
Recording Lay-over	2 50
Recording Abandonment, Mineral Claim	10 00
Recording Abandonment, Placer Claim	2 50
Recording any Affidavit under three folios	2 50
Per folio over three, in addition	30
Records in "Record of Conveyances," same as Affidavits	
Filing Documents	1 00
For Crown Grant under Mineral Act	25 00
For every lease under Placer Mining Act	5 00

PRESENT CHIEF MAQUINNA, OF NOOTKA.

MOUNT BURGESS, EMERALD LAKE,
3 Miles from Field, B. C.

SALMON FLEET, MOUTH OF FRASER RIVER.
(Waiting for the Signal.)

THOMPSON RIVER, OPPOSITE KAMLOOPS.

GOLD COMMISSIONERS AND MINING RECORDERS.

Mining Districts and Divisions.	Location of Office.	Gold Commissioner.	Mining Recorder.	Sub-Recorder.
CASSIAR DISTRICT	Telegraph Creek	James Porter		
Stickine	"		James Porter	
Liard	"		"	
Teslin Lake	Telegraph Creek		"	
Sub-office	Atlin			E. J. Thain
ATLIN DISTRICT	Atlin	J A. Fraser		
Atlin Lake	"		E. J. Thain	
Bennet Lake	Bennett		W. Dalby	
Chilkat	Wells		W. J. Rant	
SKEENA DISTRICT	Victoria	W. S. Gore		
Skeena River	Fort Simpson		John Flewin	
Sub-office	Masset			C. Harrison
"	Kitsilas			S. A. Singlehurst
"	Kitimat			James Steele
"	Essington			Chas. Berryman
Bella Coola	Victoria		C. V. Cuppage	
Queen Charlotte Islands	Skidegate			W. H. Dempster
				John Conway
OMINECA DISTRICT	Manson Creek	F. W. Valleau		
Omineca District	"		F. W. Valleau	
Sub-office	Tom Creek			Jos. Lyon
Omineca	Fort St. John			F. T. H. Bedson
Sub-office	Hazelton			James Kirby
CARIBOO DISTRICT	Barkerville	John Bowron		
Cariboo	"		John McKen	
Quesnel	Quesnel Fork		W. Stephenson	
Sub-office	Harper's Camp			J. Mackay
LILLOOET DISTRICT				
Clinton	Clinton	F. Soues	F. Soues	
Lillooet	Lillooet	C. Phair	C. Phair	

Gold Commissioners and Mining Recorders.

Mining Districts and Divisions.	Location of Office.	Gold Commissioner.	Mining Recorder.	Sub-Recorder.
KAMLOOPS DISTRICT	Kamloops	G. C. Tunstall		
Kamloops	"		E. T. W. Pearse	
Sub-office	Nicola			Geo. Murray
Ashcroft	Ashcroft		J. W. Burr	
Similkameen	Princeton		H. Hunter	
Sub-office	Nicola			Geo. Murray
Yale	Yale		Wm. Dodd	
Sub-office	Hedley			F. M. Gillespie
VERNON DISTRICT	Vernon	L. Norris		
Vernon	"		J. C. Tunstall	
BOUNDARY DISTRICT				
Osoyoos	Fairview	C. A. Lambly	J. R. Brown	
Sub-office	Olalla			D. Black
Greenwood	Greenwood	W. G. McMynn	Geo. Cunningham	
Sub-office	Vernon			J. C. Tunstall
"	Camp McKinney			H. Nicholson
Grand Forks	Grand Forks	S. R. Almond	S. R. Almond	
Sub-office	Beaverdell			A. Megraw
GOLDEN DISTRICT	Golden	J. E. Griffith		
Golden	"		F. C. Lang	Chas. E. Hamilton
Windermere	Windermere		John Bulman	
FORT STEELE DISTRICT	Fort Steele	J. F. Armstrong		
Fort Steele	"		L. W. Patmore	
Sub-office	Tobacco Plains			M. Phillipps
"	Fernie			Lestock Forbes
"	Cranbrook			F. L. Morris
"	Kimberley			M. Elwell
"	Moyie			F. D. Hope
REVELSTOKE DISTRICT	Revelstoke	Frederick Fraser		
Revelstoke	"		W. E. McLauchlin	

Gold Commissioners and Mining Recorders.

Mining Districts and Divisions.	Location of Office.	Gold Commissioner.	Mining Recorder.	Sub-Recorder.
Illecillewaet				
Lardeau	Camborne		Geo. Sumner	
Trout Lake	Trout Lake		F. C. Campbell	
Slocan District	Kaslo	E. E. Chipman		
Nelson	New Denver		Angus McInnes	
Sub-office	Sandon			Thos. Brown
Slocan City	Slocan City		H. P. Christie	
Ainsworth	Kaslo		A. Lucas	
Sub-office	Howser			Wm. Simpson
Nelson District	Nelson	John A. Turner		
Nelson	"		Harry Wright	
Sub-office	Ymir			A. R. Buckworth
Goat River	Creston		W. N. Rolfe	
Arrow Lake	Nakusp		Walter Scott	
Sub-office	Vernon			J. C. Tunstall
Rossland District	Rossland	John Kirkup		
Trail Creek	"		J. A. Hooson	
Nanaimo District	Nanaimo	Marshal Bray		
Nanaimo District	"		Marshal Bray	
Sub-office	Alert Bay			Walter Woollacott
Alberni Districts	Alberni	A. L. Smith		
Alberni	"		A. L. Smith	
West Coast, V. I.	Clayoquot		W. T. Dawley	
Quatsino	Quatsino		C. E. Potts	
Victoria District	Victoria	W. S. Gore		
Victoria	"		W. S. Gore	
New Westminster	New Westminster		D. Robson	
Sub-office	Harrison Lake			L. A. Agassiz
"	Vancouver			R. J. Skinner
"	Chilliwack			J. Pelly

HON. ROBERT F. GREEN,
Minister of Mines.

THE FISHERIES.

THE British Columbia coast of the Pacific Ocean, extending from the 49th parallel to Alaska, is extensive and deeply indented. Vancouver Island and Queen Charlotte Islands, standing out seaward, are separated from the Mainland by numerous channels and thousands of islands grouped in minor archipelagoes. Stretching inland are many long inlets, the whole configuration being irregular, but exceedingly picturesque, and the waters rich in food fishes. From the time the Strait of San Juan de Fuca is entered until the farthest north point is reached, with the exception of Queen Charlotte Sound, where the ocean swell is felt, and a few tide rips, it is one continuous glassy reach of water, which offers no obstacles to navigation, and renders coasting delightfully easy and pleasant. The conditions, on the whole, are most favourable to conducting the fishing industry.

It is for the purpose of portraying the wealth of these waters that this chapter is penned. From time prehistoric the Indians of the coast in their primitive way pursued the almost sole means of livelihood, fishing, and with a temperate clime and an abundant supply of this food at all seasons, existence was, except in so far as tribal warfare endangered it, in no sense precarious.

Says Mr. Ashdown Green, a local authority in piscatorial science: "Unlike the Indians of the plains, whose lives depended on their exertions, and who had to roam over a vast extent of country to obtain meat enough to put up for winter use, the fish-eating Indians could count securely upon their winter supplies coming to their very doors." Those on the Mainland had immense supplies of salmonidae in their seasons, which for winter use they dried, smoked or otherwise preserved in unlimited quantities. Those on the western coast depended upon the halibut and cod, which, too, were without limit as to numbers, and within easy reach. These were cut into strips and dried, and were edible to even more cultivated palates than those of the natives.

THE SALMON.

Writing of the Pacific salmon, Mr. J. P. Babcock, Commissioner of Fisheries, says: "We have in our waters the five known species of the genus oncorhynchus, termed the Pacific salmon. They are distinct from the salmon of the Atlantic, which are the genus salmo. Indeed, the word salmon does not by right belong to any fish found in the Pacific, it having first been applied to a genus found in Europe. The settlement of the Atlantic coast of America was made by a people familiar with the European form, who at once recognized this fish as running in the rivers of their newly acquired territory. They naturally and by right gave it the name salmon, for it is identical with the European form. With the advent of people from the Atlantic States to the Pacific Coast, they found running in all the main rivers a fish similar in form and colour, and of apparently similar habits, and they naturally called them salmon. Structurally these fish are but slightly different, but their life history is totally dissimilar, and they are distinctly and positively placed. The greatest difference is presented in the fact that all the species found in Pacific waters die shortly after spawning once. This is true of both sexes. This remarkable characteristic, when first brought to the attention of some Atlantic and European authorities, was discredited, as they did not then generally know that the Pacific salmon was different from and not identical with the salmo salar, which does not die after spawning, and generally returns to salt water after depositing its ova. While our Pacific fish are not salmon in a scientific sense, they are now the salmon of the world, because of their abundance and their fine canning qualities, which permit them to be offered in the markets of the civilized world.

"We have in our waters the five species of salmon known to the Pacific. Taken in the order of their commercial importance in the province, they are known as : — (1) The Sockeye or Blueback (Oncorhynchus nerka); (2) the Spring or Quinnat (O. tschawytscha); (3) the Coho or Silver (O. kisutch); (4) the Dog (O. keta); (5) the Humpback (O. gorbuscha).

THE SOCKEYE.

"(1) The Sockeye weighs from 3 to 10 pounds, though specimens of 17 pounds in weight are recorded. The anal fin is long, and has about 14 developed rays. There are 14 branchiostegals. The gill-rakers are more numerous than in any other salmon, 32 to 40. The young fry of this species can always be distinguished by the great number of the gill-rakers. The scales of the adult usually average 130 to 140 in the lateral line. The tail is narrow and widely forked. The adults in salt water are free from spots; the backs are a clear blue, and below the lateral line they are immaculate. They are in form and colour considered the most beautiful of their family.

"The bluish backs and silvery sides, which so distinguish them in salt water, give place in the head waters, at spawning time, to a deep carmen, while the heads and tails become a deep olive green, the male and female being equally highly coloured in the specimens found in the extreme head waters of the province. The head of the male undergoes less distortion in our waters than any of this genus. Specimens which enter the rivers towards the last of the season's run, and which do not ascend to the head waters of the main streams, but which spawn in the lower reaches nearer the sea, do not become nearly so highly coloured at the spawning period, many of the females not showing much if any red. The flesh of the sockeye is of a deep and unfailing red. They enter the Fraser River as early as April. They are not taken until July 1st, as their capture is, by regulation, confined to nets of 5⅞-inch mesh, which are not used until that time. The main run in the Fraser is looked for toward the latter part of July. The run is at its height during the first ten days of August. The following table gives by weeks the catch of the past season, and may be taken as an average of a season's movements : —

Week ending.	Number of boats manned by			Boats nationality of fishermen not given.	Total number of boats.	Number of Sockeyes caught.
	White men.	Indians.	Japanese.			
July 19th........	246	103	79	66	494	26,267
July 26th........	695	412	560	128	1,795	133,526
August 2nd.....	796	534	919	178	2,427	404,075
August 9th	819	551	922	169	2,461	1,556,984
August 16th	912	597	923	169	2,601	524,561
August 25th	569	387	689	148	1,793	292,920
Total number of Sockeyes delivered to Canners.						2,918,333

"The sockeye run in all our Mainland rivers and in some of the rivers of the west coast of Vancouver Island, and in the Nimkish River, near the head of the east coast of that Island. In the rivers of the northwest Mainland coast they run a month earlier than in the Fraser.

"The abundance of sockeye in the Fraser varies greatly with given years; there are years known as "the big years" and as "the poor years." Their movement appears to be greatest every fourth year, and the run is the poorest in the year immediately following. The causes which may have led up to this most remarkable feature have given rise to much speculation, and many theories have been advanced to account for them, but none are sufficiently satisfactory to be generally accepted. This periodicity in the run of sockeye which is so pronounced in the Fraser has no marked counterpart in any other river in the province or on the coast.

"The spawning period of the sockeye extends from August, in the headwaters, to as late as October and November in the waters nearest the sea. They usually spawn in lake-fed or in lake-feeding streams, the first of their run seeking the extreme head waters. Very little is known of the life of the young or the length of time they live in fresh waters before seeking salt water. Nothing is known of their feeding grounds in salt water, as they are never found in the bays and inlets which distinguish our coast, and where the spring and coho are so common. It is thought that their feeding ground must be in the open sea. There is a smaller specimen of the sockeye found in many of our interior waters that appears to be a permanently small form, which is known to writers as "The Little Red Fish," "Kennerly's Salmon," or "The Evermann form of the Sockeye," and which in some lakes of the province can be shown not to be anadromous. This form of the sockeye is often mistaken by observers as a trout. It has no commercial value, and does not "take a fly" or any other device commonly used by anglers for taking trout. The Indians of Seton and Anderson Lakes cure great numbers of these small salmon by smoking them. They give them the name of "Oneesh."

THE SPRING SALMON.

"(2) The Spring or Quinnat Salmon (O. tschawytscha) ranks second in importance in the waters of the province. This species is known in Alaska as the King or Tyee salmon, in British Columbia as the Chinook, the King or Quinnat, in California as the Sacramento or Quinnat Salmon. It was the first and for many years the only salmon used for canning. The spring salmon attains in our waters an average weight of from 18 to 30 pounds. Specimens weighing from 60 to 100 pounds have been reported. It has 16 rays in the anal fin, from 15 to 19 branchiostegals, and 23 gill-rakers. The number of scales in the lateral line run from 135 to 155. The tail is forked, and, like the back and dorsal fin, is commonly covered with round black spots. The head is rather pointed and of a metallic lustre. The back is of a dark green or bluish colour; below the lateral line it is silvery. At spawning it becomes almost black, with little or no red. On the spawning grounds of the province they are often spoken of as 'black salmon.' In this respect these fish in our waters are different to those in the waters to the south, where the spawning fish are of a dull red. The spring salmon are the most powerful swimmers which seek our rivers, usually going to the extreme head of the watershed which they enter. They seem to prefer the most rapid moving streams, and apparently avoid the lake-fed tributaries. The colour of their flesh in our waters is from deep red to a very light pink, at times almost white. Owing to the uncertainty of its colour, it is less generally used for canning, and all specimens are examined by the canners before accepting them from fishermen. It is stated that the 'early run' fish are the most reliable in colour. It has also been stated that these pale pink or white-meated salmon are not any less rich in flavour or oil than the red-meated ones; but as the English market demands a red-meated salmon and refuses to accept anything else, they are rejected by the packers

"The spring fish enters the Fraser early in the spring, and the run continues more or less intermittent until July. There is no pronounced run in the fall.

COHOES.

"(3) The Coho (O. kisutch), or Silver or Fall Salmon, is found in all of the waters of the province, and of late years has become a considerable factor in the canned product. This species on an average weighs from 3 to 8 pounds. Heavier specimens are not uncommon. It has 13 or 14 developed rays in the anal fin, 13 branchiostegals, 23 gill-rakers, and there are about 127 scales in the lateral line, the scales being larger than any other of the genera. In colour these fish are very silvery, greenish above, with a few black spots on the head and fins. These fish run in August and September in the rivers on the northwest coast, and in September and October in the Fraser. Like the sockeye, they travel in compact schools. They do not seek the extreme head waters, and frequent both the streams and lakes to spawn.

DOG SALMON.

"(4) The Dog Salmon (O. keta) run in most of the rivers and coast streams late in the fall. They average from 10 to 12 pounds in weight; much larger specimens are not unusual in most of our waters. They have 14 anal rays, 14 branchiostegals, 24 gill-rakers and about 150 scales in lateral line. In provincial waters they spawn close to the sea, ascending almost every one of even the minor coast streams. In the sea they are dark silvery in colour, the fins being black. At the spawning period they become dusky, with lateral lines of black, with more or less grey and red colouring along the sides. The heads of the males undergo the most marked distortion, and the teeth in front become large and dog-like, hence the popular name. Until within the last four years these fish have not been considered of any value. Now they are captured in great numbers by the Japanese, who dry salt them for export to the Orient, many thousands of tons being exported the past season. They are never canned in the province.

THE HUMPBACK.

"(5) The Humpback Salmon (O. gorbuscha) is the smallest of the species found in our waters, averaging from 3 to 6 pounds. It has 15 rays in the anal fin, 28 gill-rakers, and 12 branchiostegals. The scales are much smaller than in any other salmon, there being 180 to 240 in the lateral line. In colour it is bluish above and silvery below. The back and tail are covered with oblong black spots. In the fall the males of this species are so greatly distorted as to give them their popular name. These fish run in abundance only every other year, coming in with the last of the sockeye run. They are but little valued, though a considerable use has sprung up during the last few years. With the development of the markets for cheap fishery products, a demand has come for all of our salmon products, with the result that the fishing season is being extended to cover the runs of all five of the salmon species found in our waters. This lengthening of the season is of marked benefit to our regular salmon fishermen, and with the development of our other fisheries, it is confidently believed that these hardy men may find ready employment during the entire year."

LOCAL CONDITIONS.

Concerning the habits of the salmon in British Columbia waters, there is a wide field for investigation, and not much is confidently known.

The facts as to the conditions governing and affecting spawning, the time of their going to sea, the effects injurious or otherwise of dumping the offal of the canneries into the river, the economic results of the hatchery and the methods of incubation and disposal of the fry, the degree of protection necessary and the proper limits of a close season are not to be determined

FISHING FLEET AT THE MOUTH OF THE FRASER RIVER.

wholly by experience elsewhere, but by local observation and systematic investigation extending over a series of years. This the Provincial Government, by the establishment of a Fisheries Department and the appointment of a Fisheries Commissioner, has undertaken to determine, and with every promise of success. The efforts of Mr. Babcock in the direction of acquiring useful data are demonstrated in a report recently published bearing on many matters of practical interest, and in the erection of a hatchery most modern in its equipment and of great capacity, near Seton Lake, in the Lillooet District.

COMMISSIONER BABCOCK'S REPORT.

Some of the problems of salmon fishing and the salmon industry are discussed by Mr. Babcock in the report in question, as follows : —

If the size of the run of fish in the Fraser River for a given year is dependent upon the abundance of fish upon the spawning grounds during the spawning period four years previous, as the canners and fishermen claim, and as the records manifestly demonstrate, and as I believe, the run in 1905 will be large and the run in 1906 small. Certainly, propagation was at its maximum in 1901 and at its minimum in 1902. * * * I am now strongly led to conclude that the seasons and regulations for the catching of sockeye, that proved so effective in allowing them to reach the spawning grounds in 1901, were altogether inadequate to produce the same result in 1902. Anyone who witnessed the great number of fish on the spawning grounds of the Fraser and Thompson Rivers in 1901, and their scarcity in 1902, cannot help being impressed with this conclusion.

The placing of restrictions upon salmon fishing is justifiable only upon the ground that they are necessary in order to allow enough fish each year to reach the spawning grounds to insure their perpetuation. To be effective in this regard, regulations governing fishing on a river should be framed so as to conform to the conditions which exist upon that particular stream.

It has been demonstrated that every fourth year there is an abundant run of sockeye salmon (O. nerka) in the Fraser River, and that in the year immediately following there is a poor run. No regulations that cover every season alike can be made that will adequately meet the remarkably varying conditions known to exist on the Fraser. There should be seasons and regulations provided for the river applicable to the years that are known as those of abundance, and other and more restrictive ones provided for the years of the poor runs. Our fishermen should be permitted to take only that portion of the run which is in excess of the number necessary to the perpetuation of their species. The present regulations for the Fraser do not accomplish the object of their enactment. Those in force in 1901 were shown to be sufficiently effective, and no further restrictions should be placed upon fishing in that stream in the known years of abundance. It was demonstrated in 1902 that these regulations did not produce the desired result, so it is evident that more stringent restrictions should be enforced during the years of poor runs.

* * * * * *

Unfortunately there is a divided jurisdiction on the fishing grounds of the Fraser River. The American fishing grounds on Puget Sound must be considered a part of the Fraser River district, as the sockeye captured there were bred in and are endeavouring to return to that river. This divided authority prevents, at least for the present time, the making of suitable protective laws which justly affect the fishery interests on both sides of the line. There are almost no restrictions placed upon fishing on the American side of the inland sea, while we have a 36-hour weekly close season in the gulf and in the river channels, do not permit fishing until July 1st, and confine our fishermen to the use of gill nets alone. The Americans have no close season for the salt waters of the Sound, and permit the use of all kinds of fixed contrivances for taking fish, including drag and purse nets. The Americans have certain restrictions within defined limits of the mouths of rivers, and in the rivers themselves, but none of these regulations give any protection whatever to the salmon seeking the Fraser.

* * * * * * *

It is not clear how regulations that will equally protect the fish in both the British and American waters can be brought about. There is certainly a great necessity for equalising the regulations affecting the sockeye salmon. A weekly close season applicable to the American waters of the Sound is much to be desired. If a 36-hour weekly close season, beginning on Thursday at 6 p.m., and extending to Saturday, 6 a.m., were adopted on that side of the line, the fish that passed through their waters during that time would be protected in our waters by the present 36-hour weekly close season which begins at 6 a. m. on Saturday and extends to 6 p. m. on Sunday, and would solve the question and insure an increase of fish on the spawning grounds. The benefits to be derived from such joint action are so great that the wisdom of their adoption should appeal to the great interests on both sides of the Sound. During the last four years there has been a general consolidation of the canning interests in both Washington and British Columbia. The American interests are now very largely centered in two or three big companies, and there is considerable unity of action between the companies operating in British Columbia. These interests are controlled and managed by men of commercial prominence, to whom the wisdom of joint action to preserve this great fishery should strongly appeal.

* * * * * *

MOVEMENTS OF SOCKEYE SALMON FROM SEA TOWARDS FRASER.

All of the sockeye which enter the Fraser come in from the sea through San Juan de Fuca Strait. There seems to be no evidence that any portion of the sockeye run comes from the north through Johnstone Strait. If any do come from that direction their presence would be clearly indicated in the narrow channel by their habit of travelling in more or less compact schools close to the surface, and their advance being marked by leaping from the water. The sockeye which come in through Juan de Fuca Strait strike the southwest corner of Vancouver Island, between Port San Juan and Sherringham Point, and appear to come from the open sea to the north-west. An examination of some of the sockeye which have been captured in the Straits discloses the fact that their stomachs are contracted and devoid of food, which indicates that they have come a considerable distance from their feeding ground, which place is unknown. The run which comes in through the strait appears to have no relation to the runs of the smaller species of fish which enter the small streams of the west coast of Vancouver Island and the State of Washington, from May to October. Nor does there seem to be any movement of fish along the American shore of Juan de Fuca Strait, which would also seem to indicate that their ocean feeding ground lies to the north of the strait.

The first fish of this annual movement of sockeye are usually reported from Sherringham or Otter Points. After the season advances their presence is, at times, disclosed as far west as Port San Juan. From Sherringham Point, along the Vancouver side of the strait east, their movement is clearly defined as they pass close in shore. They come in rapidly with the flood tides, at times close to the surface, and break water frequently. On the ebbing of the tide they disappear. Occasionally, in years of abundance, they may be seen on the ebb, circling in the eddies at Sherringham and Otter Points, and at Beachy Head. Their presence at any of these points on an ebb tide was not noticed this year. With the change from ebb to flood they return, at times in vast successive schools, and the run continues for days at a time. During the last days of July and the first two weeks of August, in years of large runs, they show themselves plainly, a racing, leaping, bluish-silver mass in the clear and rapid-moving waters. Passing Beachy Head they hold close to Race Rocks, and pass to the northeast as far as Discovery Island, and thence east towards Rosario Strait. Men who have studied their movements at these places state that the first of the run, after passing Race Rocks, move to the east, heading for Rosario, and that many of these runs pass to the south of the traps at the salmon banks on the southern end of San Juan Island, while the later runs are freely taken at these banks, and in the purse nets and traps to the north of them.

The state of the tides and weather conditions have a marked effect upon their movements. With strong westerly winds and flood tides they pass more directly towards Rosario. On bright windless days they strike the shores of San Juan Island further to the north, and many continue through the Strait of Haro to the Gulf. Such appeared to be their routes during the days of my observations in last July and August. On July 29 I located a school in the vicinity of Race Rocks, which turned to the north and made for Discovery Island, beyond which place I could not follow them. On the same day Mr. Schultz, the manager of the great lime kiln at Roach Harbour on San Juan Island, noticed a vast school, possibly a mile in length, passing outside the traps at Mosquito Pass towards the shores of Sidney Island. None were taken in the traps at Mosquito Point on that tide. The school was not traced further. It may have entered the Gulf of Georgia by the channels to the south of Saturna Island, or may have continued to the north and entered the Gulf by way of Active Pass, or Plumper's Pass, as it is locally misnamed.

It is impossible at this time to determine what proportion of the runs passes through Haro and what proportion through Rosario Straits. Unquestionably the movements of the fish in these channels vary with different years, being influenced by their number, and by the winds and tides. In the years of small runs the fish usually follow these two channels, while in the years of the big runs they are found not only in Haro and Rosario Straits, but in all the lesser passage-ways between the islands. It is generally believed the greater movement is through Rosario Strait every year, which belief appears to be well-founded by reason of the numbers captured there. It is my opinion that the greatest movement is through Rosario, for the reason that the largest proportion of the fresh water from the Fraser River flows towards the sea through that channel. With the ebbing of the tide, the waters from Howe Sound and the eastern part of the Gulf are directed south, and sweep with them the discoloured fresh water from the mouth of the Fraser, past Point Roberts, and on between Lummi and Orcas Islands, through Rosario. As the waters rush from Rosario they are turned northwestward and are driven towards Vancouver Island by the strong ebb tide which comes from the extensive inland sea to the south.

That the movements of the fish are influenced by the presence of this body of fresh water in this Strait seems to be warranted by the known effect such water has upon their movements in other sections.

The schools which pass into the Gulf either through Rosario or Haro Straits do not appear to make directly for the mouth of the Fraser. They rather seem to circle around the outer edge of the waters of the Gulf, which are discoloured by the silt brought down by the Fraser. At flood tide this discoloured area extends to Valdes Island on the west, and to Bowen's Island, at the outlet of Howe Sound. Passing around and through the edge of this silt-coloured area, the sockeye strike towards the shore of the Mainland near Point Atkinson, and then turning south past Point Grey, enter the river through two of its various channels. This route is traced by the movements of the first schools. As the run progresses, and school follows school, the fish are found throughout this area of discoloured water, and are taken by means of gill nets. Many experienced fishermen assert that by taking advantage of this early movement they make better catches at the first of the season off Point Atkinson and Point Grey than can be made off the sand-heads. This circling of the salmon in the Gulf, and the fact of their being caught to the north of the mouth of the Fraser, is probably the only foundation for the existing belief that a portion of the run enters the Gulf through Johnstone Straits.

FISHING METHODS IN BRITISH COLUMBIA AND AMERICAN WATERS.

The seasons and the methods in use for the capture of salmon in the Provincial and American waters through which they pass to reach the Fraser River are entirely dissimilar. In the former they are closely restricted; in the latter they are virtually unlimited.

In Provincial waters the Dominion regulations provide that "no nets other than drift (gill) nets shall be used for the catching of salmon," and their use is confined to "tidal waters." "Nets for the catching of 'quinnat' or 'spring' salmon shall only be used from the first day of March to the thirty-first day of October * * * and the meshes of such nets shall not be less than seven inches in extension measure."

"The meshes of nets for catching salmon, other than quinnat or spring salmon, in tidal waters shall not be less than 5¾ inches, and shall only be used between the 1st day of July in each year and the 31st day of January following." It is further provided that "no one shall fish for salmon from Saturday morning at 6 o'clock until the following Sunday afternoon at 6 o'clock, except in the rivers and waters of the Province of British Columbia north of 54th parallel of latitude" (where a different weekly closed season exists). "No nets shall exceed in length 300 yards." The licence fee for each net is $10.

In the American waters of Puget Sound, which is defined by the laws of the State of Washington as being "all that portion of the tidal waters emptying into the Straits of Fuca and the bays, inlets, streams and estuaries thereof," the restrictions placed upon the catching of salmon apply only to the distances between traps or pound nets, and the depth of water in which they may be placed. Every known appliance in the way of traps, pounds, purse, drag, drift and set nets may be used. There are no close seasons which affect the run of fish seeking the Fraser.

The scale of licence fees in the State of Washington applies to all fishermen and fishing apparatus, which fees are collected annually. Drag nets pay from $2.50 to $30 each, according to length. First-class purse nets pay $50, and second-class $25. Traps pay $50 each; those "that fish at both ends" (i. e., have pots at each end) pay $100, and in addition $1 per 1,000 for all salmon taken therein. During the past season there were 305 trap, 84 purse net, 353 gill net, 361 set net, and 92 drag net licences issued by the Fish Commissioner of the State of Washington for use in Puget Sound.

It will be seen, therefore, that while the American methods for catching salmon in the Sound, so far as those running to the Fraser River are concerned, are unrestricted, the fishermen of the province are confined to gill nets only, which cannot be successfully used outside the discoloured waters of the Gulf of Georgia, because the fish can easily see them in the clear waters of the Straits, and either pass under or around them. The provincial fishermen are also restricted to a limited open season, and by a weekly closed period of 36 hours.

Under such conditions it is not surprising that the fishery interests of the province should protest against regulations which place them at such manifest disadvantage with their American neighbours, and seek the adoption of the trap-net methods of the Americans.

USE OF TRAPS AND PURSE NETS JUSTIFIABLE AND NECESSARY.

Ever since the establishment of traps for the capture of salmon in the American waters of the Sound there has been more or less discussion upon the advisability of permitting their use in the waters of the province. With the increase in the number and effectiveness of these fixed contrivances in American waters, the movement in favour of their use on this side of the line has grown in strength. Ever since 1895 it has been demonstrated that by this improved and scientific method the Americans catch the greater portion of the fish en route to the Fraser River, and, therefore, great pressure is being brought to bear upon the authorities to amend the regulations so as to permit the use of traps in the waters of the province.

In the discussion of this question it has been pointed out on the one hand that the use of traps is a destructive method of catching fish; that too great a portion of the run is taken; that their use will exterminate the fish, and will deprive the fishermen of employment, because the cost of traps is so great that only men of means could own and operate them. On the other hand, it is said that the use of traps is more scientific, more economical, and the more easily regulated method of catching fish; that by no other method can they be taken in clear waters; that in the clear waters of the straits and sounds the fish are in better condition for use; that the fish taken are not killed until removed from the traps; that they can be held for a week or ten days without injury to their canning qualities; that when the packing capacity of the canneries has been reached the traps can be closed; that fish taken in gill nets are killed or fatally injured in being removed from them; that their catch cannot be regulated, and at times is in excess of the capacity of the canneries; that there is an ever-increasing scarcity of labourers in the packing establishments; that the men who are now engaged in the hazardous and laborious business of fishing would find ready and equally remunerative employment in the canneries and in connection with the trap fishing.

Clearly, there is much to be said on both sides of this pressing question. Independent, however, of the many arguments pro and con, I believe that the use of traps, purse and drag nets for the capture of salmon on the southwest coast of Vancouver Island is justifiable, because the main portion of the Fraser River run of sockeye salmon which comes in from the sea strikes the coast of the island east of Port San Juan, and advances close in shore through the Straits to Race Rocks, thence easterly into American waters, and the fish are there captured in vast numbers by means of traps, purse and drag nets. I also believe that by the use of traps and purse nets on the southwest coast of Vancouver Island a good portion of this run, which now passes from our waters into American waters, could be captured. I believe, from personal observation and investigation, in a season like the past, that the greater part, if not all, of the fish that strike the southeast end of San Juan Island and the waters to the south, and which direct their course for the Fraser River through Rosario Strait, are captured by the American traps and purse nets, and consequently never regain British Columbia waters. To me it is not a question as to whether the capture of these fish in provincial waters by means of traps will endanger the perpetuation of them. In my opinion the question as to whether trap-fishing is or is not a destructive method of catching fish is not one that confronts the Government at this time. It is not a theory, but a condition, that must be met. During the past season, as has been shown, the State of Washington issued 305 trap, 84 purse net and 92 drag net licences for the capture of these salmon, while under the Dominion regulations our fishermen were confined to the use of gill nets, which are not suited to successful use in the clear waters through which the fish pass before entering the American waters. If the use of traps endangers the perpetuation of our Fraser River salmon fishery, then the Americans will soon have accomplished the extinction of these fish, and will have reaped the benefit. For the above reasons I believe that the use of traps in San Juan de Fuca Strait, and south of Discovery Island, is justifiable.

If traps are permitted to be used in the waters south of Discovery Island, the use of purse nets should also be sanctioned, as very few of our fishermen are financially able to place traps. Purse nets, the use of which has become quite general and very successful on the American side, are not nearly so expensive as traps. It takes ten men to operate the kind of purse net in general use, so that our fishermen could, by combining, enter the business and compete with the Americans who use the traps.

I am not, however, at this time prepared to advocate the use of traps in any of the waters of the province that are unaffected by the use of American traps.

GENERAL REMARKS.

The active canning season extends over a period of about six weeks, during which time operations are very brisk, and a great many men and women are employed. In 1901, a large year, over 23,000 persons were engaged in fishing boats and vessels alone. The employees consist of Indians, Japanese, Chinese and licensed white fishermen. The Indian women (or klootchmen) and the Chinese are engaged on the inside; while the "siwashes," as the male Indians are termed, and the Japanese fish in boats. The fishermen, though required to be British subjects, are of various nationalities. Licenses, of which a certain number are issued and controlled by each cannery, to fish and pull boats are necessary. For some years the number of licenses issued was confined to a certain number; but as this proved to be practically a monopoly for those who were fortunate enough to obtain them, the limit was taken off, and the only restrictions now imposed are those of being a British subject and paying for a license. The salmon canning industry is one of the largest and most remarkable industries of the British Columbia coast. It has developed rapidly, and has been, on the whole, remunerative, though during the past several years canners have complained bitterly of the undue competition met with on account of the American canners just across the line, who by the use of traps and purse nets are enabled to secure their fish very much cheaper than under the regulations imposed in British Columbia.

The tendency in British Columbia, as on the other side, is towards the concentration of effort and capital in one or two large companies. One large aggregation of interests has already been effected, and other combinations are anticipated.

At one time the disposal of the offal from the canneries on the Fraser River was the subject of a great deal of controversy, and was for a period a serious question. In the Year Book of 1897 it was suggested as a practical solution of the difficulty that the waste products of the canneries should be utilized for the purpose of making fertilizers. This has to a large extent been done. Careful sanitary supervision is maintained by the provincial health authorities, and the complaints on account of offal have practically ceased, and it is no longer a "vexed question."

THE SALMON PACK OF 1901.

In his report for 1901, Mr. C. B. Sword, Dominion Inspector of Fisheries, said : "This year's pack has been the largest known in the province, amounting to 1,247,215 cases, against 1,026,545 cases in 1897, the next largest year; 1,154,717 cases were sockeye salmon (O. nerka), exceeding the total pack of 1897 of all kinds of salmon. On the Fraser River the pack of sockeyes in 1901 was 974,911 cases, as against 879,115 cases of all kinds in 1897. The pack of all kinds of salmon was as follows : —

On Fraser River.		On Puget Sound.	
Sockeye (O. nerka)	984,911	Sockeye	1,106,643
Spring (O. tschawytscha)	885	Spring	3,239
Humpback (O. gorbuscha)	3,992	Humpback	41,865
Cohoes (O. kisutch)	17,043	Cohoes	152,281
Dog (Q'ualo (O. keta)	2,082	Dog (Q'ualo)	58,748
Total	998,913	Total	1,362,776

"From this it will be seen that the Puget Sound pack of sockeyes (practically all from fish on their way to their spawning grounds on the Fraser River) exceeds by 131,732 cases the provincial pack of these fish on the Fraser River, and that the total pack of Fraser River sockeye for this year reaches a total of 2,081,554 cases. * * * The total pack for the province in 1901, 1,247,212 cases, is made up as follows:

Sockeyes	1,154,717
Spring	29,221
Cohoes	28,476
Humpbacks	31,392
Dog	3,406

SALTED SALMON.

"The returns of salmon salted in barrels show a very large increase, being 7,931 barrels, against 4,950 in 1900, 3,450 in 1899, and 2,000 in 1898.

"Dry salted salmon show an increase of 6,476,207 lbs., against 5,700,000 lbs. in 1900. This item represents almost wholly the dog salmon, or q'ualo, put up for the Japanese market; and the smallness of the increase is, to some extent at least, to be accounted for by the packers having had a difficulty in securing a sufficient supply of salt. The market for these fish, too, is largely affected by the Japanese local catch, and the price obtainable for the product has been somewhat fluctuating.

FRESH SALMON.

"There is an increase of 400,000 lbs. in this item, representing the increased business done by the cold storage plants.

THE HALIBUT.

"I have dealt with the salmon, at present the most important economic food fish on the Coast, somewhat in detail. The next in order is the halibut (Hippoglossus Vulgarus), which has already become a rival of the salmon in commerce. It is the largest and most useful member of a large family known as Pleuronectidae. It is in great abundance all along the coast of British Columbia, being principally found around and extending north of the Queen Charlotte Islands, where it attains to a size in some instances of over 200 lbs., and a length of from 5 to 6 feet. The average size is, however, about 60 pounds, and it is caught in great quantities by deep-sea fishing, which has during the past few years developed to important proportions. Not until recently, however, except a limited local consumption, has the halibut assumed any importance commercially. At the time the Year Book of 1897 was published the halibut industry was in an experimental stage, and several companies met with financial loss in endeavouring to establish a market in the East. As is usual in such matters, loss of money in experimenting and the better knowledge gained thereby of commercial conditions and the market have opened the way to success.

"As is well known, the fish trade in the Eastern States is practically controlled by a combine of Eastern fish dealers, and outside of this it is practically impossible for Western enterprise to operate. The result of this was the formation of the New England Fish Company, the members of which are included in the Eastern combine. The company has been eminently successful, and now carries on a very extensive trade. They have four steamers employed, which bring the catch regularly to Vancouver, where it is shipped in car and train loads by express service to Boston. One hundred thousand pounds is not an uncommon cargo for one of these ships to obtain in a few days' catch. The trips occupy from eight to ten days. Duration of trip and success of catch depend upon the weather. A supply of ice is taken with the steamer, and when she arrives back the fish are immediately packed in boxes with snow or broken ice, and, as stated, shipped by fast train.

"The New England Fish Company, although of foreign origin, is permitted by special license to land its fish and ship them at Vancouver in bond. This, though a modification of the regulations and has been objected to in some quarters, is really desirable, because otherwise the fish would be shipped from Seattle or Tacoma and the local benefit to the City of Vancouver and the Province lost.

"In addition to the New England Fish Company there are several other American companies operating in the Pacific, Queen Charlotte Sound and more northern waters. The vessels of these companies go direct to Seattle or Tacoma, transhipping from these latter points.

"Belonging to the same family are a number of flounders, some of them very abundant and good food fishes. The market is local."

BLACK COD, OR "SKIL."

Referring to deep-sea fishing, the skil (Anoplopoma fimbria) is perhaps one of the most delicious of table fish. It is found in great abundance off the coast of Queen Charlotte Islands, but is too delicate of fibre to stand shipment. This is often referred to as "black cod" commercially, and somewhat resembles the mackerel. I will quote what Mr. Ashdown Green, President of the Victoria Natural History Society, in a paper read in 1891, says regarding it. Speaking of their habitat on the west coast of Queen Charlotte Islands, where there were until recently several stations established for the purpose of curing them, he remarks: "The mode generally adopted was that of pickling, the fish being too fat to dry and salt, and turning rancid when kept a short time. I am sorry to learn that as a commercial venture this fishery has been abandoned; the labour and expense involved being disproportionate to the returns when compared with other fisheries. Opinion varies regarding the quality of the fish on the table. Those brought to Victoria are dry and very inferior. I have never had an opportunity of tasting one from Queen Charlotte Islands, but I can well believe that they are excellent. As I remarked before, there is no comparison between fish of all kinds in Queen Charlotte Sound and those taken near Victoria. The skil undoubtedly ranks very high in quality when taken fresh and eaten, or after being properly cured; but ordinary methods of curing fail in preserving it for use and shipment. There is, it might be remarked, a wide field on this coast for the study of the methods of preservation of these and many other fish for market; one difficulty to be overcome is the superabundance of oil as compared with Eastern fish. Some experiments tried last year at Port Essington in a small way, by bottling and canning, after special preparation, were said to have achieved excellent results. Whether an industry on these lines could be made to pay or find a market remains to be determined."

THE OOLACHAN.

Another fish belonging to the salmonidae group, oolachan (Thaleichthys pacificus), spelled in a variety of ways and also locally known as the "candle fish," should be of considerable economic value. It runs in enormous quantities up the rivers and inlets of the coast, coming into the Naas about the middle or latter part of March, and reaching the Fraser about the middle of April, deteriorating somewhat in quality as it comes southward. This is a delicious pan fish and is greatly in favour in its season. It, however, like the skil, is too tender for carriage, and has, therefore, only a local market. It is about nine inches in length, and so plentiful at times when running as to be scooped up in bucketfuls. A good many are put up in pickle in small kits and cured like bloaters, but not much progress has been made in these directions, remarks applying similarly to those in regard to the skil.

The Indians catch them in immense quantities and extract the "oolachan grease," which they use much as we do butter. Oolachan oil, properly refined, might become of commercial value, there being practically no limit to their numbers. Experiments have been made with oolachan by bottling and canning, it is said, with success. The oolachans have many enemies besides the Indians. The seal, sturgeon, salmon and porpoise follow them in their run, and even bears and pigs gorge themselves on them when the opportunity offers. If they could be preserved as indicated for export, so as to retain their flavour and body, they would undoubtedly demand a sale co-extensive with sardines.

OTHER FISH.

The anchovy (Stalephorus ringens) is also abundant, of large size and excellent quality. At times they are seen in the harbour of Victoria in phenomenal numbers. Nothing has been done so far in utilizing this most valuable fish.

There are two varieties of smelts common in the markets (the Osmerus thaleichthys and the Hypomesus pretiosus), and are in brisk local demand.

There are no true soles in our waters, what is sold as such being the Pleuronectes vetulus, a species of flounder. They are, however, a choice table article. It is a small fish, seldom exceeding a pound in weight.

The herring (Clupea mirabilis), which Mr. Ashdown Green regards as equal in flavour to the English herring, though not so large in size, are also very abundant, and are consumed locally both fresh and as bloaters. A factory was established at Burrard Inlet some time ago to cure them, and also for the extraction of oil and the manufacture of fish guano, but was burnt down and not rebuilt.

The capelin (Mallotus villosus) is common in Alaskan waters, so Mr. Green says, but only an occasional visitor to the British Columbia coast. It is sometimes exposed for sale.

COD AND BASS.

Although plentiful in northern waters, the Gadidae, of which there are several species, is not common farther south. Mr. Green says the common cod (Gadus Macrocephalus) appears in several of our harbours to spawn, but is not more than sufficient for local demand. Its principal habitat is on the banks of the northwest coast.

There are two other species of fish sold locally as cod—one the Ophiodon elongatus or "cultus cod," and the red rock cod (Sebastodes pinniger). The former is one of the best food fishes of the Pacific Coast waters and is in season almost the whole year round, generally hiding in eel grass or kelp. It takes a spoon or other bait freely. The Indians secure this fish by sinking a wooden bait shaped like a shuttlecock at the end of their spear and releasing it at the bottom. The fish follows the shuttlecock to the surface and is speared. It spawns about the end of February, and ranges in weight from 2 to 40 pounds. Another of the same family, Hexagrammus decagrammus, the kelp trout of the market, seems to be in considerable demand, to judge by the quantity exposed for sale, but Mr. Green regards it as worthless. It is sometimes dried and smoked.

The A. pinniger belongs to the bass family (Scorpaenidae), of which there are several varieties—Sebastodes ruberrimus, the red bass, A. pinniger and S. Melanops, or black bass. "As food fishes they are unsurpassed by any in our waters," says Mr. Green, "though rather expensive fish to buy, considering the amount of head and offal you have to pay for." These fish are ovoviparous.

THE STURGEON.

Another important fish, though not utilised to any large extent, is the sturgeon, the roe of which when salted forms caviar, and the bladders are manufactured into isinglass. The Pacific Coast sturgeon (Acipenser transmontanus) enters the Fraser about the end of April, following up the oolachans, and spawn, although little or nothing is known about the period. They are taken by spearing or by night-lights, baited with salmon, and very often they are caught in the nets of the salmon fishers. They grow to enormous sizes, some of them weighing from 700 to 900 pounds, and it is said that the largest caught weighed over 1,000 pounds, although it is not authenticated. There is a small local market for sturgeon. A company was formed several years ago at New Westminster for the purpose of catching and export, which was done in a limited way. Mr. C. B. Sword, Inspector of Fisheries for the Dominion in British Columbia, in his report for 1901 says regarding them :—

"This fishery shows a very small return, 65,000 lbs., against 105,000 in 1900, 278,050 lbs. in 1899, 750,000 in 1898, and 1,137,696 lbs. in 1897. It would not appear that we are ever likely again to see this fishery of any commercial importance. The cold storage companies take all they can get, but the supply, especially of the larger fish, is very limited. Several illegal lines have been seized and destroyed, but the scarcity of the fish makes the employment of this method no longer so profitable as it once was, and comparatively few of these are now used.

"There is no lack of small sturgeon in the river, so that the only reason for the failure of this fishery would seem to be the number of years that this fish takes

INDIANS FISHING IN THE FRASER CANYON.

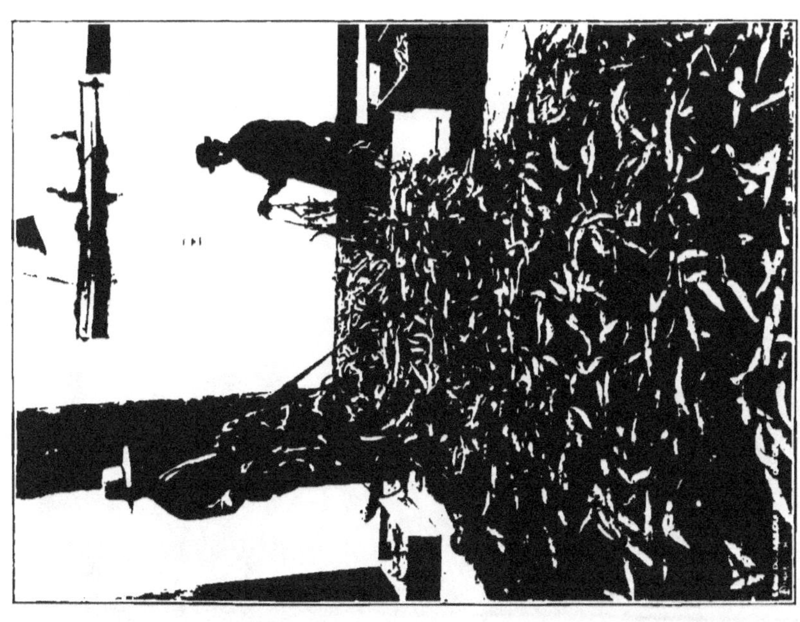

7,500 OOLACHANS IN A NET.

TRAP FISHING.

SCOW-LOAD OF SALMON.

to obtain its full growth. Until a market was found abroad for them, the local consumption was too small to affect their numbers, and many were taken of a size now rarely met with."

Sturgeon have also been taken in the interior lakes.

The most abundant skate is raja Cooperii. As a food fish it is not much in demand, probably on account of its repulsive appearance. It grows to a large size, and sometimes is over six feet in length.

SHAD.

The catch of shad this year is estimated at 10,000 lbs. This fish is now becoming quite a common feature on the fishmonger's counters, and the annual take seems likely to increase. At present those caught are taken during the season of the salmon run, mainly in the sockeye nets. In the course of a few years they may be sufficiently numerous to justify the prosecution of the fishery for itself.—[Report of Inspector of Fisheries, British Columbia, 1901.]

OIL FISH.

From an economic point of view, the dogfish, of which two varieties exist, namely Squalus acanthias, the spike dogfish, and Geleorhinus galeus, the tope shark, though not a food fish, is one of the most valuable. They are found in abundance all up the coast to Alaska, and several factories have been established for the reduction of oil from these fish, in which they are very rich. The liver contains a very superior oil, which for lubricating and machine purposes is of the very highest quality. A large amount of oil is also taken from the bodies, which are steamed in large retorts. This oil is of inferior quality and not used for machines, but undoubtedly, if subjected to a proper refining process, would become a useful and cheap product. Both the liver oil and the body oil are largely used in the province, and were formerly quite profitable as an industry, but latterly competition with Eastern oils has very materially reduced the profits.

In addition to the dogfish there are several other oil-bearing fishes, the principal of which is the Hydralagus collioei, or "rat-fish." It is found in great abundance in places, and the oil procured from its liver is used for the very finest work in watches, gun-locks, sewing machines, etc. It is a very prolific oil-bearer, and should prove to be valuable as the basis of an industry.

The Cetorhinus maximus, or basking shark, is also plentiful in Queen Charlotte Sound during the summer months. It attains to a great size, is perfectly harmless, and so tame that while basking it may be touched by the hand. In England, 150 gallons of oil is the average yield of the liver, which alone is treated.

The foregoing are the principal of the economic food and other fishes of the British Columbia coast, although the complete list, taking the representatives of the various families and their varieties, is a very long one.

In addition to these, whelks, cockles, clams and crabs are found in large quantities, both in winter and summer months, and are largely used locally and by Indian fishermen as bait. The coast is especially rich in edible crabs and clams, and incipient industries looking to their utilisation have been established.

GAME FISH.

So far the fishes of British Columbia have been treated from an economic point of view, but from a sportsman's standpoint the field is not a less interesting one. The whole interior of the province, island and Mainland, possesses a wonderful system of water communication, lakes and rivers. These, as well as the lesser streams, are abundantly stocked with fish, principally salmon or trout, the several varieties of which have already been enumerated. There are also whitefish in the northern waters. While the best known and favourite resorts are on Vancouver Island, there is no locality where a fisherman may not prosecute with zest this time-honoured sport; and even on the sea-coast, during the salmon run, with trolling line he will meet with gratifying success. The waters of Kootenay and Southern Yale are already becoming locally noted as fishing resorts, and when lines of communication are opened up, the rivers and lakes of the whole interior will attract numerous fishermen, affording as they do fish of uncommon size and number. The scenery, too, everywhere is on a grand and picturesque scale, and all natural conditions are healthful and invigorating.

BRITISH COLUMBIA TROUT.

The waters of the province are rich in trout. No other section of the Dominion offers better fishing than can be found here. Of the varieties of trout found in the rivers, streams and lakes of the province, the steelhead trout (Salmo gairdneri) is the best known and most highly considered, because of its abundance, great size, and "game" and commercial qualities. From its being more or less anadromous in its habits, it is locally and in many Coast sections classified with the Pacific salmon. The steelhead more closely resembles in form, colour of flesh and habit the Atlantic salmon than any other form found on the Pacific Coast. It, like our salmon, spawns in fresh water only, but, unlike our salmon, it survives after spawning and returns to the sea. It feeds at all times freely in fresh and salt waters. Commercially the steelhead is of importance. It is commonly found in our markets from early fall until late spring. A considerable quantity is shipped East in cold storage. It finds ready sale in all local and Eastern markets; and because of the demand for it in a fresh state, the entire catch is marketed in that way. In our waters it averages about 12 lbs. in weight, though specimens weighing from 20 to 24 lbs. are not uncommon. As a "game fish" the steelhead is considered by many fishermen to have no equal in fresh water. It readily takes a fly or spoon-bait, and "puts up a stiff fight, taxing the skill of the angler and the strength of his tackle to bring it to net or gaff."

There are numerous forms of trout to be found in the Upper Fraser and Thompson Rivers, and in many of their tributary lakes, that cannot be distinguished by any technical character from the steelhead, but which, because of the many differences in habit, form and colour, have been given many different names. Of these, perhaps the best known to anglers is the very game fish which abounds in the Kamloops, Shuswap, Okanagan and Kootenay Lake regions, to which Dr. Jordan gave the name of Kamloops trout (Salmo kamloops). The smaller specimens of this trout readily take a fly, but the largest specimens are seldom secured except by means of trolling.

In addition to the salmon and trout which abound in our waters, we have the Great Lake trout (Christicomer namaycush) and the Dolly Varden trout (salvelunis parkei), which are easily distinguished from the true trout by their red or orange spots. These last two—which should be called charr—while abundant in most of our interior waters, are not considered of great importance to the angler, because only the young ones are taken by means of a fly. Both these fish attain a large size, the Great Lake trout not uncommonly weighing as high as 30 pounds, while the Dolly Varden not uncommonly attain a weight of from 15 to 20 pounds.

FISH COMPANIES.

Several companies have been formed recently with the purpose of dealing with fish in a variety of ways—exporting them fresh, drying, salting, curing, etc. The exportation of preserved fish, however, is yet in an experimental stage, but so far the results indicate the possibility of success.

The Pack by Canneries of British Columbia Salmon, Season of 1902, and a description of the Pack. Furnished the Department by the Fraser River Canners Association.

FRASER RIVER.

	Sockeyes.	Spring and Fall.	Totals.	Grand Totals.
British Columbia Packers' Association—				
Albion Cannery	9,389	......	9,389	
Atlas Cannery	5,028	......	5,028	
Anglo-American Cannery	6,088	1,658	7,746	
Alliance Cannery	3,636	......	3,636	
Acme Cannery	4,006	......	4,006	
Brunswick No. 1 Cannery	10,057	13,994	24,051	
Brunswick No. 2 Cannery	7,830	......	7,830	
Canadian Pacific Cannery	8,117	9	8,126	
Currie & McWilliams	9,428	1,286	10,714	
Colonial Cannery	4,281	......	4,281	
Celtic Cannery	3,947	......	3,947	
Cleeve Cannery	8,208	232	8,440	
Delta Cannery	7,863	......	7,863	
Dinsmore Island Cannery	5,446	17	5,463	
Ewen's Cannery	14,301	......	14,301	
Greenwood Cannery	4,527	......	4,527	
Hume Cannery	4,496	......	4,496	
Imperial Cannery	4,756	......	4,756	
Pacific Coast Cannery	6,815	2	6,817	
Provincial Cannery	3,407	......	3,407	
Terra Nova Cannery	8,405	1,257	9,662	
Westminster Packing Company	8,382	......	8,382	
				166,868
Anglo-British Columbia Packing Company, Limited—				
Britannia Cannery	6,030	......	6,030	
British America Cannery	5,515	2,871	8,386	
British Columbia Packing Company	2,680	......	2,680	
Canoe Pass Cannery	3,420	......	3,420	
Phoenix Cannery	6,658	......	6,658	
Wadhams' Cannery	5,408	......	5,408	
				32,582
United Canneries of British Columbia, Limited—				
English Bay Cannery	7,500	......	7,500	
Gulf of Georgia Cannery	15,537	......	15,537	
Scottish-Canadian Cannery	14,520	......	14,520	
				37,557
Canadian Canning Company, Limited—				
Fraser River Cannery	7,228	1,398	8,626	
Star Cannery	11,421	......	11,421	
Vancouver Cannery	6,266	......	6,266	
				26,313
J. H. Todd & Sons—				
Beaver Cannery	7,269	1,428	8,697	
Richmond Cannery	5,990	......	5,990	
				14,687
British Columbia Canning Co., Ltd.—				
Deas Island Cannery	7,236	325	......	7,561
National Packing Co., Ltd.—				
Eagle Harbour Cannery	4,801	2,525	......	7,326
Great Northern Cannery—				
Great Northern Cannery	7,194	417		7,611
Federation Brand Salmon Canning Co., Ltd.—				
Lighthouse Cannery	4,241	3,562		7,803
St. Mungo Canning Co., Ltd.—				
St. Mungo Cannery	11,127	2,347	......	13,474
C. S. Windsor—				
Industrial Cannery	5,023	290	......	5,313
	293,477	33,618		327,095

SKEENA RIVER.

	Sockeyes.	Spring and Fall.	Totals.	Grand Totals.
British Columbia Packers' Association—				
Balmoral Cannery	5,885	1,604		
Cunningham's Cannery	12,309	5,427		
Standard Cannery	8,286	3,691	37,292	
Anglo-British Columbia Packing Co., Ltd.—				
B. A. & N. Pacific Cannery	33,385	5,778	39,163	
J. H. Todd & Sons—				
Inverness Cannery	13,227	3,855	17,082	
British Columbia Canning Co., Ltd.—				
Aberdeen Cannery	11,990	5,580	17,570	
Carlisle Canning Co., Ltd.—				
Carlisle Cannery	10,380	1,182	11,562	
Wallace Bros., Limited—				
Claxton Cannery	12,158	5,408	17,566	
P. Hermon—				
Hermon's Cannery	7,500	3,230	10,730	
J. Turnbull—				
Turnbull's Cannery	2,467	1,443	3,910	
				154,875
RIVERS INLET.				
British Columbia Packers' Association—				
Brunswick Cannery	14,223	179	14,402	
Wadhams Cannery	18,595	127	18,722	
Wannuck Cannery	9,062	618	9,680	
				42,804
Anglo-British Columbia Packing Co., Ltd.—				
Good Hope Cannery	12,000	382	12,382	
British Columbia Canning Co., Ltd.—				
Rivers Inlet and Victoria Canneries	14,939	173	15,112	
				70,298
NAAS RIVER.				
Federation Brand S. Canning Co., Ltd.—				
Mill Bay Cannery	11,519	819	12,338	
Naas Harbour Cannery	9,434	1,446	10,880	
LOWE INLET.				
British Columbia Packers' Association—				
Lowe Inlet Cannery	5,701	1,837	......	7,538
CHINA HAT.				
British Columbia Packers' Association—				
Princess Royal Cannery	2,642	966		3,608
DEAN CHANNEL.				
R. Draney—				
Kimsquit Cannery	6,491	1,416	......	7,907
NAMU HARBOUR.				
R. Draney—				
Namu Cannery	2,019	2,947		4,966
BELLA COOLA.				
British Columbia Packers' Association—				
Bella Coola Cannery	2,685	2,182		4,867
SMITH'S INLET.				
William Hickey Canning Co.—				
Hickey Cannery	5,200	.....	......	5,200
ALERT BAY.				
British Columbia Packers' Association—				
Alert Bay Cannery	1,772	9,034		10,806

WEST COAST OF VANCOUVER ISLAND.

Clayoquot Sound Fishing & Trading Co., Ltd.—	Sockeyes.	Spring and Fall.	Totals.	Grand Totals.
Clayoquot Cannery	4,000	1,604	......	5,604
	237,959	60,928		298,887

SUMMARY.

	Sockeyes.	Spring and Fall.	Grand Totals.
Total Fraser River pack	293,477	33,618	327,095
Total Northern pack	237,959	60,928	298,887
	531,436	94,546	625,982

DESCRIPTION OF PACK—Sockeyes and Spring and Fall Fish.

	1-lb. Talls.	½-lb. Talls.	1-lb. Flats.	½-lb. Flats.	1-lb. Ovals.	½ lb. Ovals.	Squats.	Totals.	Grand Totals.
Fraser River—									
Sockeyes	56,484	2,754	80,397	110,008	4,062	13,404	17,308	293,477	
Spring and Fall	29,770	.....	3,458	52	106	......	232	33,618	327,095
Skeena River—									
Sockeyes	54,890	.....	34,692	23,955	4,040	......	......	117,677	
Spring and Fall	33,243	.....	3,504	....	451	......	......	37,198	154,875
Rivers Inlet—									
Sockeyes	60,311	1,845	1,257	5,406	......	......	......	68,819	
Spring and Fall	1,442	37	....	....	......	......	......	1,479	70,298
Naas River—									
Sockeyes	10,033	.....	9,315	....	1,605	......	......	20,953	
Spring and Fall	1,788	.....	....	....	477	......	......	2,265	23,218
Lowe Inlet—									
Sockeyes	5,701	.....	....	....	......	......	......	5,701	
Spring and Fall	1,837	.....	....	....	......	......	......	1,837	7,538
China Hat—									
Sockeyes	2,642	.....	....	....	......	......	......	2,642	
Spring and Fall	966	.....	....	....	......	......	......	966	3,608
Dean Channel—									
Sockeyes	6,491	.....	....	....	......	......	......	6,491	
Spring and Fall	1,416	.....	....	....	......	......	......	1,416	7,907
Namu Harbour—									
Sockeyes	2,019	.....	....	....	......	......	......	2,019	
Spring and Fall	2,947	.....	....	....	......	......	......	2,947	4,966
Bella Coola—									
Sockeyes	2,685	.....	....	....	......	......	......	2,685	
Spring and Fall	2,182	.....	....	....	......	......	......	2,182	4,867
Smith's Inlet—									
Sockeyes	5,200	.....	....	....	......	......	......	5,200	
Spring and Fall	.....	.....	....	....	......	......	......	.....	5,200
Alert Bay—									
Sockeyes	1,772	.....	....	....	......	......	......	1,772	
Spring and Fall	9,034	.....	....	....	......	......	......	9,034	10,806
West Coast V. I.—									
Sockeyes	4,000	.....	....	....	......	......	......	4,000	
Spring and Fall	1,604	.....	....	....	......	......	......	1,604	5,604
	298,557	4,636	132,623	148,481	10,741	13,404	17,540	625,982	

PACK BY DISTRICTS, PREVIOUS YEARS.

	1901 (Cases).	1900 (Cases).	1899 (Cases).	1898 (Cases).	1897 (Cases).	1896 (Cases).	1895 (Cases).
Fraser River	990,252	316,522	510,383	256,101	860,459	356,984	400,368
Skeena River	126,092	128,529	108,026	81,234	65,905	100,140	67,707
Naas River	14,790	18,238	19,443	18,953	20,847	14,649	19,550
Lowe Inlet	6,451	10,834	10,142	10,312	10,666	10,395	8,681
China Hat	5,500	4,318	......	......	......	......	......
Rivers Inlet	66,840	75,413	71,079	104,711	40,207	107,468	58,579
Bella Coola	4,158	4,849	......	......	......	......	......
Namu and Kimsquit	11,460	10,106	7,200	......	4,357	3,987	3,000
Alert Bay	4,629	9,182	3,470	8,500	8,602	2,840	5,100
West Coast V. I..	5,984	7,602	2,694	4,350	4,434	5,107	3,320
	1,236,156	585,413	732,437	484,161	1,015,477	601,570	506,393

SHIPMENTS IN DETAIL, PREVIOUS YEARS.

	1901	1900	1899	1898	1897	1896	1895
England—							
London, direct..	206,344	51,095	150,670	79,598	325,966	182,253	96,459
London, overland	19,236	10,143	5,733	5,687	4,957	9,076	......
Liverpool, direct.	576,065	257,848	365,151	242,437	407,738	322,364	256,301
Liverpool, overl'd	46,831	60,090	26,128	8,050	38,373	11,405	......
Overl'd, prev. yrs.	......	......	......	......	......	......	65,047
Via other ports..	3,350	3,802	......	19,862	......	......	29,590
Eastern Canada...	131,875	79,171	114,736	87,881	130,815	51,041	79,289
Australia	38,022	25,903	41,518	9,644	28,579	11,609	8,832
Other destinations.	13,538	56,237	4,246	439	226	2,128	......
Local sales	19,956	20,309	11,945	1,183	4,823	3,844	4,326
Stock on hand....	180,939	20,815	12,079	29,380	74,000	7,850	25,952
Lost	......	......	231	......	......	......	......
	1,236,156	585,413	732,437	484,161	1,015,477	601,570	566,395

RECAPITULATION

Of the Yield of Fisheries of British Columbia for the Year 1901.

Kind of Fish—	Quantity.	Price.	Value.
Salmon, Canned, 48-lb. cases	1,247,212	$ 4 80	$5,986,617 60
Salmon, Salted, bbls.	7,931	10 00	79,310 00
Salmon, Dry Salted, lbs.	6,476,207	04	259,048 28
Salmon, Smoked, lbs.	301,000	10	30,100 00
Salmon, Fresh, lbs.	2,128,805	10	212,880 50
Sturgeon, lbs.	65,000	05	3,250 00
Halibut, lbs.	5,701,000	05	285,050 00
Herring, Fresh and Salted, lbs.	960,000	03	28,800 00
Herring, Smoked, lbs.	182,500	10	18,250 00
Oolachans, Fresh, lbs.	820,000	05	41,000 00
Oolachans, Salted, bbls.	2,210	10 00	22,100 00
Oolachans, Smoked, lbs.	28,500	10	2,850 00
Smelts, lbs.	101,500	05	5,075 00
Trout, lbs.	323,300	10	32,330 00
Cod, lbs.	492,000	05	24,600 00
Skil, lbs.	4,000	05	200 00
Shad, lbs.	10,000	05	500 00
Mixed Fish, lbs.	485,500	05	24,275 00
Hair Seals, skins	4,100	75	3,075 00
Fur Seals, skins	24,422	15 00	366,330 00
Sea Otter, skins	10	500 00	5,000 00
Fish Oil, gallons	152,100	30	35,630 00
Fish Guano, tons	300	30 00	9,000 00
Glue, gallons	5,000	2 50	12,500 00
Canned Clams, cases	3,000	4 00	12,000 00
Oysters, sacks	5,000	3 00	15,000 00
Caviare, lbs.	800	50	400 00
Fresh Clams and Mussels			11,000 00
Fresh Crabs and Abelonies			30,000 00
Shrimps and Prawns			6,000 00
Estimate of fish not included in above			370,000 00
Total			$7,942,771 38

HATCHERY—DISTRIBUTION OF FRY.

Year	Fry	Year	Fry
1885	1,800,000	1894	7,800,000
1886	2,625,000	1895	6,390,000
1887	4,414,000	1896	10,393,000
1888	5,857,000	1897	5,928,000
1889	4,419,000	1898	5,850,000
1890	6,640,000	1899	4,742,000
1891	3,603,800	1900	6,200,000
1892	6,000,000	1901	16,000,000
1893	5,764,000	1902	9,214,000

Note — There are now four Dominion hatcheries in operation in the province—at Fraser River, Granite Creek, Shuswap Lake, Skeena River and Nimpkish River, Vancouver Island. The Provincial Government is erecting a hatchery at Seton Lake.

BRITISH COLUMBIA SALMON PACK, 1901.

FRASER RIVER DISTRICT.

Name.	Total.	Name.	Total.
Albion	22,827	Fishermen's	14,275
Atlas	14,700	Gulf of Georgia	44,723
Anglo-American	12,830	Great Northern	18,046
Alliance	11,025	Greenwood	15,160
Acme	12,002	Harlock	26,608
Britannia	24,638	Hume's	15,630
Brunswick No. 1	25,418	Industrial	19,500
Brunswick No. 2	26,218	Imperial	14,208
Beaver	26,610	London	18,335
British-American	16,500	National	14,000
Birrell's	11,200	Phoenix	26,202
Boutillier's	11,350	Pacific Coast	20,000
Canadian Pacific	24,650	Provincial	16,200
Currie & McWilliams	32,600	Premier	11,629
Colonial	28,200	Richmond	15,090
Celtic	19,143	Scottish-Canadian	48,433
Canoe Pass	12,723	Star	19,763
Cleeve	22,734	St. Mungo (2)	24,000
Deas Island	21,562	Terra Nova	20,650
Delta	17,346	Vancouver	22,000
Dinsmore Island	24,700	Wadhams'	20,305
Ewen's	29,029	Westminster Packing Co.	16,510
English Bay	19,315	Westham Island	15,134
Federation	23,376	Wellington	14,925
Fraser River	16,891		

RIVERS INLET DISTRICT.

Name.	Total.	Name.	Total.
Wannuck	9,876	Wadhams	14,192
Brunswick No. 3	10,706	Vancouver	7,050
Rivers Inlet	7,500	Good Hope	10,663
Victoria	6,807		

NORTH COAST DISTRICT.

Name.	Total.	Name.	Total.
Bella Bella	4,000	Princess Royal	7,600
Namu	6,074	Lowe Inlet	6,451
Kemsquit	5,525		

SKEENA RIVER DISTRICT.

Name.	Total.	Name.	Total.
Carlisle	7,000	Windsor	13,133
Inverness	10,500	Balmoral	9,130
British-American	18,745	Claxton	11,958
Ladysmith	3,700	Hermann's	10,230
North Pacific	19,049	Standard	7,700
Skeena	14,700		

NAAS RIVER DISTRICT.

Name.	Total.	Name.	Total.
Naas Harbour	7,220	Mill Bay	7,784

QUEEN CHARLOTTE ISLAND DISTRICT.

Skidegate	400

ALERT BAY DISTRICT.

Alert Bay	4,620

WEST COAST VANCOUVER ISLAND.

Clayoquot	5,985

STATISTICS FOR 1902.

Through the kindness of Mr. Sword, Inspector of Fisheries, the following particulars have been received:

THE SALMON PACK

For the Province, 1902, was as follows:

Sockeye	534,161	cases (48 lbs.)
Cohoe	47,234	"
Springs	19,042	"
Humps	26,097	"
Quals	628	"
Total	627,162	"

Of the above 327,198 cases are for the Fraser River, and the balance northern waters (Skeena 155,936.)

FISHERIES PRODUCT.

	Values.
Salmon (all kinds and methods)	$3,753,874
Halibut	420,850
Herring	127,329
Oolachans	83,650
Trout	35,135
Cod	27,000
Fish Oil	56,682
Canned Clams	15,840
Miscellaneous	422,804
Fur Seals	337,660
	$5,280,824

CAPITAL INVESTED.

Fisheries	$2,681,433
Fur sealing	479,250
	$3,160,683

NUMBER OF EMPLOYEES.

Fishermen and cannery workers	17,098	
Employed on vessels	607	
		17,705
Sealers and hunters, fur sealing:		
White men	421	
Indians	437	
		858
		18,563

FRASER RIVER SALMON.

STEAM LOGGING IN VICTORIA LUMBER & MANUFACTURING CO.'S LIMITS, CHEMAINUS.

THE ANNUAL PACK SINCE THE BEGINNING OF THE INDUSTRY.

Year.	Cases.
1876	9,847
1877	67,387
1878	113,601
1879	61,093
1880	61,849
1881	117,276
1882	225,061
1883	196,292
1884	141,242
1885	108,517
1886	161,264
1887	204,083
1888	181,040
1889	414,294
1890	409,464
1891	314,893
1892	228,470
1893	590,229
1894	494,371
1895	566,395
1896	601,570
1897	1,027,204
1898	492,657
1899	765,517
1900	606,530
1901	1,236,156
1902	625,982

PACIFIC COAST SALMON PACK.

For purposes of comparison, the statistics of the various canning districts of the Pacific Coast for 1902 are here given. The figures are taken from a special edition of the San Francisco Trade Journal, December 19, 1902.

ALASKA PACK — 1902.

Canneries—	Kings. Talls.	Reds. Talls.	Cohoes. Talls.	Pinks. Talls.	Chums. Talls.	Total.
✤Alaska Packers' Assoc'n..	24,641	1,007,197	28,533	162,824	......	1,223,195
Alaska Fisheries Union..	......	23,413	3,066	....	2,848	29,327
Alaska Fish & Lumber Co.	......	2,361	1,102	19,866	10,618	33,947
Alaska-Portland P. Ass'n.	2,969	26,254	......	5,415	......	34,638
Alaska Fishermen's P. Co.	......	28,800	......	7,200	......	36,000
Bristol Packing Co......	......	22,000	......	....	......	22,000
Columbia River P. Assoc.	......	29,000	......	....	......	29,000
Chinta Cannery	3,637	11,458	2,449	5,368	......	22,912
Columbian Canning Co...	......	11,000	......	....	......	11,000
F. C. Barnes Cannery...	......	1,500	1,000	8,300	2,000	12,800
•Kasaan Bay Cannery....	......	3,432	169	16,746	6,788	27,135
Ketchikan Cannery	......	4,000	......	26,000	5,000	35,000
Metlakahtla Industrial Co.	......	5,000	......	7,000	4,000	16,000
North Alaska Salmon Co.	......	69,250	......	750	......	70,000
N. Pac. Trading & Pkg Co.	......	7,111	1,824	26,853	6,559	42,347
Naknek Packing Co.....	......	42,000	......	....	......	42,000
N. Pac. & Norway P. Co.	......	5,000	......	27,000	......	32,000
Pacific Pkg. & Nav. Co..	16,000	341,000	20,000	170,000	85,000	632,000
*Pacific Cold Storage Co..	798	10,418	4,880	23,001	2,416	41,513
Pillar Bay Packing Co...	......	7,000	......	14,000	......	21,000
✪Red Salmon Canning Co..	......	28,100	......	......	......	28,100
San Juan Fish & Pkg. Co.	......	6,000	......	14,000	......	20,000
Thlinket Pkg. & Trad'g Co.	......	3,000	3,000	26,000	......	32,000
Union Packing Co.	......	3,300	950	18,575	4,200	27,025
Wales Island	......	2,500	......	15,000	......	17,500
						2,538,439

*Pickled—Kings, 13 bbls.; pinks, 163 bbls., 350 half-bbls.; chums, 162 halfs.
✤Pickled—Sockeyes, 5,693 bbls.
✪Pickled—Sockeyes, 300 bbls.
•Pickled—Pinks, 562 bbls.; also pink bellies, 66 bbls., 208 half-bbls.

PUGET SOUND PACK—1902.

CANNERIES—	SPRINGS			SOCKEYES			COHOES			CHUMS			
	Talls	Flats	½ Flats	Talls	Flats	½ Flats	Talls	Flats	½ Flats	Talls	Flats	½ Flats	Total.
Alaska Pkrs.' Ass'n	1,590	442	...	59,659	12,169	6,703	3,277	......	......	......	....	....	83,840
Apex Packing Co...	169	.....	...	2,147	116	694	3,520	85	......	14,032	....	....	20,763
Astoria & P.S.P. Co.	.....	541	65	.....	5,067	3,258	3,759	940	5,072	2,600	....	....	21,302
*Carlisle Packing Co.	.....	.....	...	4,560	......	.....	2,400	......	......	5,305	....	....	12,265
Fidalgo Isl'd C. Co.	393	2,026	...	7,208	12,247	8,588	2,270	1,116	400	4,640	....	....	38,888
J.W. & V. Cook Co.	336	.....	38	4,713	4,122	2,460	1,102	85	524	226	....	....	13,606
Manhattan Pkg. Co.	.....	.....	...	2,052	257	842	3,058	3,003	2,950	262	126	202	13,202
*N. Amer. Fish Co..	.....	.....	...	21,409	......	.....	6,031	......	......	4,791	....	....	32,231
Pac. Northw't P. Co.	.....	.....	...	7,144	......	.....	3,489	......	......	364	....	....	10,997
*Pac. P. & Nav. Co..	.....	.....	...	129,500	......	.....	31,000	......	......	27,500	....	....	188,000
*Rosaria Straits Co..	.....	.....	...	7,500	......	.....	8,500	......	......	2,000	....	....	18,000
Sehome Canning Co..	.....	21	13	1,916	......	954	1,794	......	3,897	2,441	284	....	11,320
*George & Barker Co.	.....	.....	...	14,800	......	.....	2,400	......	......	1,200	....	....	18,400
*United Fish & P. Co.	.....	.....	...	9,400	......	.....	6,500	......	......	14,740	....	....	30,640
Washington P. Co..	.....	.....	...	582	7,258	1,527	712	892	590	27	50	....	11,638
*White Crest C. Co.	.....	.....	...	295	......	.....	1,610	......	......	12,000	....	....	13,905
													538,997

The Manhattan Packing Company also packed of pink salmon the following: Talls, 106; flats, 105; half flats, 149.
All half flats are figured at eight dozen per case.
*No reports received, so we give Kelley-Clarke Co.'s estimates. The spring's salmon are counted with sockeyes. No segregation as to size and style of cans is made, therefore all styles are placed in the "talls" column.

TOTAL PACIFIC COAST PACK.

	1900.	1901.	1902.
Alaska	1,534,740	2,032,838	2,5[illegible]8,4[illegible]9
British Columbia	527,281	1,206,473	625,982
Puget Sound	478,742	1,414,990	538,997
Columbia River	313,417	251,265	382,704
Oregon outside pack	56,500	71,366	64,085
Willapa and Gray's Harbour	47,600	51,966	58,000
Sacramento River	34,000	17,500	14,043
Klamath River (Cal.)	2,200	2,375	2,500
Total	2,994,548	5,048,773	4,224,750

Humpbacks.			Cohoes.					Grand Total.
1 lb. Talls.	1 lb. Flats.	Total.	1 lb. Talls.	1 lb. Flats.	½ lb. Flats.	Squats.	Total.	
								6,688
								3,705
								3,474
								3,769
								7,530
			9,503		30		9,533	15,745
			150	3,850			4,000	11,340
			2,973				2,973	9,350
								5,234
								4,461
								8,912
								3,440
								3,551
						13	13	4,738
				1,373	4		1,377	8,502
			1,677				1,677	5,305
				103			103	7,040
								3,197
235	2,372	2,607	586	130			716	6,867
								4,526
								5,031
			150				150	11,846
								2,309
	1,087	1,087		461			461	4,740
			165		30		195	15,847
								6,547
								5,484
								4,495
								10,463
810		810	3,283	1,044			4,327	11,175
			200				200	7,881
								7,716
								4,617
								5,396
								5,341
,045	3,459	4,504	18,687	6,961	64	13	25,725	237,162
,231		21,231	27,419	426			27,845	236,385
,276	3,450	25,735	46,106	7,387	64	13	53,570	473,547

Vicinity of Copper Island 3,397
Behring Sea catch 10,362

Total 24,442

Humpbacks.			Cohoes.					Grand Total.
b. lls.	1 lb. Flats.	Total.	1 lb. Talls.	1 lb. Flats.	½ lb. Flats.	Squats.	Total.	
			1,994				1,994	10,874
236		236	2,015				2,015	8,458
88		88	306				206	3,510
956		1,956	1,829	49			1,878	20,646
163		3,163	650				650	9,687
593		4,593	1,390				1,390	13,941
164		1,164		342			342	6,483
798		3,798	1,141				1,141	12,473
366		2,366	650				650	9,135
034		1,034	926				926	3,481
25		25						18,704
93		93						20,978
62		62	185				185	12,515
			34				34	17,192
			1,008				1,008	5,973
			1,144	35			1,179	6,127
			3,200				3,200	10,196
			1,010				1,010	6,205
835		835	1,508				1,508	5,168
			4,430				4,430	9,741
								5,950
818		1,818	219				219	3,542
			487				487	4,950
			353				353	3,868
			2,940				2,940	5,994
231		21,231	27,419	426			27,845	236,385

Car
Alas
Apex
Asto
*Carli
Fida
J. W.
Manl
*N. A
Pac.
*Pac.
*Rosa
Seho
*Geor
*Unit
Was
*Whi

T
A
*N
gation

COLUMBIA RIVER PACK.

Canneries—	Chinooks. Talls.	Flats.	½ Flats.	Ovals.	Cohoes. Talls.	Total.
Pillar Rock Packing Co.	23,000	......	......	......	......	23,000
McGowen	31,500	......	......	......	......	31,500
* U. F. Coop. Packing Co.	11,717	9,876	4,100	650	......	26,343
Seufert Bros.	16,000	......	......	......	......	16,000
Magler	4,090	7,600	5,000	1,335	1,200	21,575
Sanborn-Cutting Co.	11,502	12,562	13,708	......	......	37,772
A. Booth & Co.	15,100	5,000	8,006	550	......	28,656
Columbia River Pkrs.' Assoc'n.	136,000	......	......	......	......	❖147,000
Warren Packing Co.	29,896	7,117	7,759	......	......	✪58,858
						382,704

* Pickled—Chinooks, 200 bbls.
❖Fall—11,000 cases.
✪Steelheads—Talls, 4,971; flats, 205; half flats, 910.

OREGON COAST.

Canneries—	Chinooks. Talls.	Flats.	½ Flats.	Cohoes. Talls.	Chums. Talls.	Total.
Coos Bay Packing Co.	525	......	......	3,625	......	4,150
O. W. Hurd Packing Co.	2,135	......	......	3,300	......	5,435
Elmore Packing Co.	12,000	4,500	2,600	......	14,000	33,100
R. D. Hume	3,000	1,000	......	7,000	......	11,000
Other packs	.....	......	......	......	......	10,400
Total	......	......	......	......	......	64,085

WEST COAST OF WASHINGTON.

Canneries—	Chinooks. Talls.	Cohoes. Talls.	Pinks. Talls.	Chums. Talls.	Total.
Barnes—(Nasel River)	2,000	.....	1,000	7,000	10,000
Barnes—(South Bend)	4,000	3,000	.....	8,000	15,000
N. River Packing Co.	.....	.....	.....	.....	15,500
Other packs	.....	.....	.....	.....	17,500
Total	.....	.....	.....	.....	58,000

CALIFORNIA.

Canneries—	Chinooks. Talls.	Flats.	Total.
Klamath Packing & Trading Co.	.....	2,500	2,500
Carquinez Packing Co.	6,550	.....	6,550
Sacramento River Packers' Association	7,493	.....	7,493
Total	.....	.....	16,543

SEALING CATCH OF BRITISH COLUMBIA.

Year.	Skins.	Year.	Skins.
1889	35,310	1896	55,677
1890	43,325	1897	30,410
1891	52,365	1898	28,522
1892	49,743	1899	35,346
1893	70,592	1900	35,548
1894	97,474	1901	24,422
1895	74,124	1902	16,301

During 1901 the catch was:—

British Columbia Coast	8,533
Japan	2,130
Vicinity of Copper Island	3,397
Behring Sea catch	10,362
Total	24,442

HON. A. E. McPHILLIPS,
Attorney-General,
To whose department belongs the administration of Fisheries.

FOREST WEALTH.

NATURALLY in the consideration of the economic products of British Columbia comes the timber wealth. Apart from minerals it represents the most important and most readily available results. British Columbia may now be said to possess the greatest compact area of merchantable timber on the North American continent, and if it had not been for the great forest fires that have raged in the interior in the years gone by, during which a very large portion of the surface has been denuded of its forest, the available supply would have been much greater than it is. This was an exigency which, in the unsettled state of the country, could hardly have been provided against, if at all. However, as the coast possesses the major portion of the choice timber and that which is most accessible, the ravages of fire have not had, by reason of the dense growth and the humidity of the climate, any appreciable effect on that source of supply.

As far north as Alaska the coast is heavily timbered, the forest line following the indents and river valleys and fringing the mountain sides. Logging operations so far have extended to Knight's Inlet, a point on the coast of the Mainland opposite the north end of Vancouver Island. Here the Douglas fir, the most important and widely dispersed of the valuable trees, disappears altogether, and the cypress, or yellow cedar, takes its place. North of this, cedar, hemlock and spruce are the principal timber trees. It will be of interest to know that Douglas fir (Pseudotsuga Douglasii) was named after David Douglas, a noted botanist who explored New Caledonia in the early twenties of this century. It is a very widely distributed tree, being found from the coast to the summit of the Rocky Mountains, and as far east as Calgary and as far north as Fort McLeod. On the coast it attains immense proportions, is very high and clear of imperfections, sometimes towering three hundred feet in the air and having a base circumference of from thirty to fifty feet. The best averages, however, are one hundred and fifty feet clear of limbs and five to six feet in diameter. This is the staple timber of commerce, often classed by the trade as Oregon pine. It has about the same specific gravity as oak, with great strength, and has a wide range of usefulness, being especially adapted for construction work. It is scientifically described as standing midway between the spruce and the balsam, and in the opinion of Prof. Macoun, the Dominion naturalist, is a valuable pulp-making tree.

Mr. James M. Macoun, in his little work, "The Forests of Canada," from which a good deal of what follows is taken, says in regard to the Douglas fir:

"This is the most abundant, as it is the most valuable, tree in British Columbia. Its range on the Mainland is from the international boundary north to the Skeena River, in Latitude 54 degrees, on the coast, and in the Rocky Mountains from the international boundary north to Latitude 55 degrees, though its northern and northeastern limits are not well defined. It is not found in the Queen Charlotte Islands. It attains its greatest size on Vancouver Island, or along the shores and in river valleys near the coast on the Mainland. There, trees 300 feet in height are not rare, the average height of those felled for lumber being over 150 feet. Trees of a greater diameter than seven feet are rarely cut, though those of eight, ten or even eleven feet in diameter are not rare.

"The fact that the largest trees are found near the coast greatly facilitates the transport of the logs from the woods to the mill, and as the majority of the mills are so situated that the largest ships may load within a few yards of the saws, the cost per 1,000 feet of handling Douglas fir and other and other west coast lumber is small.

"Douglas fir is chiefly valuable for structural purposes, being largely employed in ship-building, bridge-work and the construction of wharves. It is exported as dimension timber, lumber, spars, masts and piles. Locally it is used for construction work of all kinds, fencing and railway ties, and in the manufacture of furniture. Its durability, when excluded from the air, adds greatly to its value for pile-work in the construction of bridges and wharves. The bark of the Douglas fir is largely employed in tanning."

GIANT ARBOR VITAE, RED CEDAR.

(Thuya gigantea, Nutt.)

The Giant Arbor Vitae is next to the Douglas fir in importance in British Columbia, where it attains its greatest size on Vancouver Island, along the coast and in the lower parts of the rivers of the Coast Range. It is rarely found in the dry interior of British Columbia, but is abundant in the river valleys on the slopes of the Selkirk and Coast ranges. Though seldom found more than 150 feet in height, in circumference it rivals the Douglas fir, trees of from 8 to 10 feet in diameter not being rare, and they are occasionally found much larger.

It is chiefly used in the manufacture of shingles, for which purpose it is unequalled by any other wood. Formerly the shingles were made by hand, the wood splitting easily, but improved machinery has so lowered the cost of production that comparatively few hand-made shingles are now used, though they are still in demand when a shingle of superior quality is desired. The wood of this tree takes a very brilliant polish, and is well adapted for interior finishing of all kinds. So great is the variety of shading in the color of the wood that a large house may be finished in it without two rooms being alike. It is not only largely exported, but is now being shipped in increasing quantities to Eastern Canada. In British Columbia it enters largely into the manufacture of doors and cabinet work of all kinds. Like all the cedars, it lasts well underground, and on this account is much used in the form of telegraph poles and fence posts. The immense canoes made by west coast Indians are, with very few exceptions, made of this wood.

In addition to its value commercially for shingles and interior finishings, it is the friend of the settler, inasmuch as out of its straight-grained logs he can build his house, make his furniture and fence his farm, and that solely with the use of the most primitive of tools—an axe, a saw and a froe. Owing to increasing demand for shingles in Eastern Canada and the rapid filling up of the Northwest, cedar limits are now becoming very valuable, and the shingle industry especially is assuming large proportions.

YELLOW CEDAR, YELLOW CYPRESS.

(Thuya excelsa, Bong.)

The Yellow Cypress is not nearly so abundant in British Columbia as the Arbor Vitae, nor is its circumference so great. Its height is about the same as the Arbor Vitae—150 feet—and its average diameter is about 4 feet, though occasional trees attain 5 feet. The yellow cypress is confined to the coast and the adjacent islands.

In the southern parts of British Columbia it is not found at sea-level, the finest trees growing at altitudes of from 1,000 to 2,500 feet. Though valuable for many purposes, the wood of the yellow cypress is not extensively used at present, the cost of transportation to the seaboard being too great. On the Queen Charlotte Islands it descends to the coast. When lower levels have been cleared of other trees the yellow cypress will be utilized. This wood is very durable, and on account of its pungent odour it is credited with resisting the teredo. Its grain is very close, and as the wood takes a very high polish, it is greatly valued for interior finishing and for the manufacture of furniture. It commands a higher price than either Douglas fir or arbor vitae. The natives along the northern coast of British Columbia make many articles for domestic use from this wood. It is specially valuable for its lasting qualities, and has been known to last as sills for over sixty years without being impaired. In a wet climate, such as is prevalent at Port Simpson, where it was found in old Hudson Bay Company foundations, this is remarkable. Mr. J. R. Anderson, in his paper for the Forestry Association, says that on account of its liability to shrink, lengthwise as well as laterally, it requires to be well seasoned before use. The long and slender pendulous fruits which hang from the branches give the tree a very graceful appearance; and the strong pungent odour which it emits when freshly cut, and which it never loses, renders it very easy of identification.

WESTERN WHITE PINE.

(Pinus monticola, Dougl.)

None of the Western pines are found in quantity near the coast, and so far they have been used for Western purposes only. The best of these is pinus monticola, which is little inferior to the white pine of the East. It is found in the interior of Vancouver Island and is abundant in the southern parts of the Coast Range, where there is heavy rainfall. In the Selkirk Mountains it is not very common, but attains a considerable size on the mountain slopes. The wood is used for the same purposes as the Eastern white pine. Mr. Anderson says: "It is the most useful wood for window-sashes, doors, powder barrels and similar work. Being a white and very light wood, it is unsuitable for outside uses, and has a tendency to absorb moisture when in contact with the ground, and is, therefore, liable to decay." It has not heretofore been used to a very great extent. It is a splendid looking tree, having bluish-green fronds and cones from 8 to 12 inches long.

BLACK PINE.

(Pinus Murrayana, Balfour.)

The Black Pine replaces the Pinus banksiana, or jack pine, on the eastern slopes of the Rocky Mountains. It is abundant in the northern part of the interior plateau of British Columbia, where it covers great areas. In the southern part of the province it is most abundant at altitudes ranging between 3,000 and 4,000 feet. Though esteemed of little value where other conifers grow, except for railway ties and firewood, it is much used for mine props and other construction work in the mining districts of British Columbia. It is admirably suited for this purpose, as the wood is very tough, and when not exposed to the weather does not easily decay. It is said to make excellent charcoal.

ENGELMANN SPRUCE.

(Picea Engelmanni, Engel.)

This characteristic spruce of the Rocky and Selkirk Mountains is the most useful tree growing in the interior of British Columbia, and is there largely used in bridge and trestle work and for heavy construction work generally. In the valley of the Columbia it is often more than 150 feet in height and 4 in diameter. The wood is very like that of the black and white spruces, and may be used for the same purposes. This was the chief wood used in the construction of the Canadian Pacific Railway from the Rocky Mountains westward.

MENZIES SPRUCE—SITKA SPRUCE.

(Picea Sitchensis, Carr.)

This spruce grows chiefly in the immediate vicinity of the coast, ranging in British Columbia from the international boundary north to Alaska. In the southern part of the province it grows scattered among other trees, but in the north it is relatively much more abundant, growing sometimes in large clumps. Though averaging less in diameter than the Douglas fir, occasional trees of great size are found. Those cut for lumber are, however, seldom more than five or six feet in diameter. No other tree on the west coast is used for such varied purposes, and as it is easily worked-up by machinery there is a great demand for it in the manufacture of doors, window-sashes, boxes, shelving and interior finishing. The wood is very white, is elastic, and bends with the grain without splitting, so that it is much used in boat-building, the making of light oars, staves, woodenware, etc. It resists decay for a long time, and, like the Douglas fir, is not attacked by insects. The chief value of the Sitka spruce will in the near future be in the manufacture of pulp, for which purpose it is not excelled by any other tree. As soon as pulp mills are established in the vicinity of the large sawmills, the immense waste entailed by the present method of sawing dimension lumber in British Columbia will be obviated. As the shrinkage is usually very great, it is generally kiln-dried before using, or kept stored away until it is thoroughly seasoned. On account of the sharp-pointed, short fronds, it is quite impossible to grasp them with the naked hand, and this renders this tree easily distinguished from the other British Columbia coniferae.

WESTERN HEMLOCK.

(Tsuga mertonsiana, Carr.)

The hemlock is abundant along the whole coast of British Columbia and in the interior of the province, wherever there is sufficient rainfall. Along the line of the Canadian Pacific Railway, in the Selkirk Mountains, it is very abundant, but seldom over 150 feet in height and three in diameter. The abundance of other wood of better quality has prevented the hemlock from coming into general use, and the same prejudice exists in British Columbia against the Western tree that prevailed until very recently against hemlock in Eastern Canada. Though its grain is coarse, Western hemlock is for many purposes just as serviceable as other woods which cost more. Its bark is rich in tannin, but it is too thin to be extensively used while there is such an abundance of Douglas fir in the same region. As its habitat is generally at no great distance from the sea, it is a wood which could be transported to shipping points without great expense. When young or growing singly, the tree is decidedly pretty, and the yew-like fronds which enshroud the trunk form a most welcome and soft bed for the weary prospector or trapper.

WESTERN WHITE OAK.

(Quercus Garryana, Douglas.)

Though a few trees of this species (according to Macoun) grow on the Mainland of British Columbia, it is practically confined to the southern part of Vancouver Island, the finest trees growing in the vicinity of Victoria, where trees 3 or 4 feet in diameter, from which logs 10 to 20 feet long can be obtained, are not uncommon. The wood resembles that of English oak, and is very beautiful when made up into furniture and cabinet work. It is not largely used, for two reasons—first, because the supply is limited; and second, because there are other woods more easily and cheaply obtainable. It is principally useful, and will always remain so, as an orna-

THE PIONEER STEAMSHIP "BEAVER."

SCHOOLS AND CHURCHES, VICTORIA.

EDUCATIONAL.

THE present free school system of British Columbia, which has been in operation since 1872, is, in its most salient features, a copy of the Ontario Act of 1846. The immense extent of the province, however, and the sparseness of the population have rendered it necessary to modify in many important particulars the provisions of that Act. Chief among these modifications is the method of paying the rural school teachers directly from the provincial treasury.

In 1855 the Hon. the Hudson's Bay Company established free public schools on Vancouver Island. For several years these schools supplied the educational needs of the community, which, it is needless to say, at that period were limited. In 1865 a free school system was established by the Vancouver House of Assembly, and the sum of $10,000 set apart as a school fund for that year. When the union of the colonies of Vancouver Island and British Columbia was effected in 1868, the free school system first referred to was virtually dead, and school matters throughout the province generally continued in a most crude and unsatisfactory condition until 1872.

The educational system in this province, as established by the Public School Act, 1872, was administered by a Board of Education, composed of "six fit and proper persons" appointed by the Lieutenant-Governor-in-Council, and presided over by the Superintendent of Education.

After the abolition of this Board by the Public School Act, 1879, its chief powers and duties were transferred to the Lieutenant-Governor-in-Council; more complete control over local school matters was given the Boards of Trustees, notably the power of appointment and dismissal of teachers, formerly held by the Board of Education; and a system of monthly reports of the attendance, etc., for each school was instituted, the teacher being required to supply the Minister of Education and the Trustees with monthly information in all matters pertaining to his school. By the Public School Act of 1891, which involved a somewhat radical departure, the members of the Executive Council are created a Council of Public Instruction, with power to create school districts; provided, as amended in 1896, that no school district shall be created wherein there shall not be at least twenty children of school age (between 6 and 16 years); to grant such sum or sums of money as may be required to pay the salary of the teacher in such district; in rural districts to defray the cost of erecting school houses; to appoint a Board of Examiners to examine teachers and grant certificates; to appoint Inspectors of Public Schools; to make rules and regulations for the conduct of public schools; to prescribe the duties of teachers; to determine the subjects and percentage required for teachers' certificates; to prescribe a uniform system of text books, as well as the courses and standard of study for schools; to establish a Normal School and make regulations for its conduct and management; to establish High Schools, where the higher branches may be taught; and to cancel or suspend for cause the certificate of any teacher. The chief executive officer of the Education Department is the Minister of Education, who is assisted by the Superintendent of Education. To the latter official are committed, subject to the approval of the Council of Public Instruction, the supervision and direction of the inspectors and schools; enforcing the provisions of the School Act and the regulations and decisions of the Council of Public Instruction; the organising of Teachers' Institutes; the granting of temporary certificates, countersigned by the Provincial Secretary; the preparation of an annual report of the condition of the public schools; the closing of schools when the average attendance falls below ten; and the preparation of suitable forms for making all reports required under the Act.

From the introduction of the public school system in 1872 until the passing of the amendment of 1888, the whole cost of maintaining the schools was paid directly by the Provincial Treasury. By the amendment of 1888 the City Councils of Victoria, Vancouver, New Westminster and Nanaimo were required to refund one-third of the amount of the salaries of the teachers employed in the schools of these cities. Since that time the municipal corporations of the various cities and towns throughout the province have been required to bear more and more the cost of education within their respective limits. By an Act passed during the session of 1901, all city school districts are divided into three classes, and a per capita allowance of $13, $15 and $20, respectively, based on the average actual daily attendance of public school pupils, is now the full amount of pecuniary assistance granted these cities by the Provincial Government. The salaries of all the rural school teachers are fixed and voted each year by the Legislature.

The liberality with which education is provided for is evident from the fact that, wherever outside the limits of the cities there are twenty children of school age within a radius of a few miles, known as a school district, a school house is built, the salary of the teacher paid, and the incidental expenditure borne by the province. For all purposes during the year 1900-01 the cost of education to the province was $350,532.31, and to the cities $182,160.18; or $532,692.49 in all.

The various schools embraced in the system are spoken of as common, graded and high schools. These schools are free and are conducted on strictly secular and non-sectarian principles. It is enjoined on all teachers that the highest morality shall be inculcated, but that no religious dogma or creed shall be taught. The Lord's Prayer may be used at the opening and closing of schools.

There are at present in operation 10 high schools, with a staff of 28 teachers; 55 graded schools, with 270 teachers; and 258 common schools, in which are employed 258 teachers.

The course of study in rural and graded schools embraces reading, spelling, writing, drawing, arithmetic and book-keeping, grammar, composition, literature, history (English and Canadian), geography and nature study (physiology, form, color, plants, animals, etc.) In addition to the above the following subjects may be taught: Geometry, agriculture, temperance, music, needlework and calisthenics.

The management of schools in rural districts is entrusted to a Board of three Trustees, elected by the duly qualified voters of the district. In city school districts the School Board consists of seven, five or three members. In cities of the first class there are seven trustees; in cities of the second class, five trustees; and in cities of the third class, three trustees. These are elected by the votes of the electors who are duly qualified to vote for mayor, and they act without emolument, except the Secretary of the Board. Women, the wives of qualified freeholders or leaseholders (except the latter be trustees), are eligible for the position of school trustee, and in several cities act in that capacity, with satisfactory results.

The question of providing for higher education very early occupied the attention of the Legislature, and as soon as warranted a high school was established. The City of Victoria was the seat of the first institution of this kind. The Victoria High School was opened in August, 1876, and continued to be the only free institution of that rank until the establishment of a similar one in New Westminster in 1884.

During 1886 a high school was opened in Nanaimo; and in January, 1890, one was established in Vancouver. Since 1890 six other high schools have been opened, as follows: Nelson, Rossland, Cumberland, Vernon, Chilliwack, and Grand Forks. The high schools are under the control of the local Boards of Trustees in the districts in which such high schools are situated, and no such school can be established in any school district in which there are fewer than twenty persons duly qualified and available to be admitted as high school pupils. For admission to high schools pupils are required to pass satisfactory examination in the subjects prescribed for graded and common schools. The curriculum of the high schools is as follows:

JUNIOR GRADE.

A.—ENGLISH :—

1. Reading and Orthoepy.—Oral reading, with special attention to expression and pronunciation.

2. Writing and Spelling.— In these subjects, an award will be made on each paper handed in by the candidates, but no formal paper on either subject will be demanded.

3. English Grammar.— Etymology and Syntax, as in West's (Advanced) English Grammar (The Copp, Clark Co.), Chapters VII.-XXVI. Exercises in Analysis and Parsing.

4. Composition.— Letter-writing; themes based on extracts in Composition from Models, pages 1-283 (The Copp, Clark Co.)

5. English Literature.— (a) Prose — Composition from Models, pages 1-283, with Appendix. (b) Poetry — Goldsmith's "The Traveller," Wordsworth's "The Green Linnet," "To the Cuckoo," "Thought of a Briton on the Subjugation of Switzerland"; Scott's "The Outlaw," "The Rover"; Keats' "On First Looking Into Chapman's Homer" (select poems ed. Alexander, published by The Copp, Clark Co.)

B.— HISTORY AND GEOGRAPHY :—

1. British History.— Buckley and Robertson's High School History of England (The Copp, Clark Co.); or Gardiner's Outline of English History (Longmans, Green & Co.)

2. Canadian History.— Clement's History of Canada.

3. Geography.— The general geography of the world, with special attention to that of Canada and the British Empire. (Gage's New Canadian Geography, B. C. Edition; also, Dawson and Sutherland's Geography of the British Colonies, MacMillan & Co)

C.— MATHEMATICS :—

1. Arithmetic.— Pure and commercial arithmetic, as in Hamblin Smith's Arithmetic, revised edition.

2. Algebra.— The first ten chapters of Hall and Knight's Elementary Algebra may be taken as indicating the amount required.

3. Geometry.— Euclid, Book I., Propositions I. to XXVI., with deductions (Hall and Stevens).

4. Bookkeeping.— The keeping of accounts.

D.— SCIENCE :—

1. Physiology.— Martin's Human Body (Holt & Co.), Chapters I.-XIV.

E.— CLASSICS :—

1. Latin.— Henderson and Fletcher's First Latin Book and Reader, including Nepos' "Themistocles, Aristides, and Hannibal" (The Copp, Clark Co.); or Collar and Daniell's First Latin Book (Ginn & Co.), with an equivalent from Nepos.

Note.— With the view of securing uniformity of pronunciation, it is recommended that the Roman pronunciation be used.

F.— DRAWING :—

Drawing Series, in preparation.

INTERMEDIATE GRADE.

A.—ENGLISH :—

1. Reading and Orthoepy.—As for Junior Grade.

2. Writing and Spelling.—As in Junior Grade.

3. English Grammar.—West's English Grammar, with special reference to Chapters I. - VI.

4. Composition and Rhetoric.—(a) A critical reading of the extracts in Composition from Models, pages 1-284, with a view to illustrating the principles contained in Genung's Practical Elements of Rhetoric (Ginn & Co.) (b) The writing of an essay on one of three subjects selected by the examiner.

5. English Literature.—(a) Prose—Composition from Models; Macaulay's "Essay on Milton" (The Riverside Literature Series). (b) Poetry—Goldsmith's "The Deserted Village"; Wordsworth's "Upon Westminster Bridge," "She was a Phantom of Delight," "The Inner Vision"; Scott's "Rosabelle," "Jock of Hazeldean"; Byron's "Childe Harold's Pilgrimage," Canto IV.; Shelley's "Oxymandias of Egypt," "To a Skylark," "The Recollection": Keats' "The Terror of Death," "Ode to a Nightingale," "Ode to Autumn," "The Human Seasons" (select poems ed. Alexander, published by The Copp, Clark Co.) A critical reading of the Introductory Chapter will also be exacted.

B.—HISTORY AND GEOGRAPHY :—

1. British History.—Green's "History of the English people," Chapter VI., Section IV., to Chapter VIII., Section VIII., inclusive, will be read; or Gardiner's "Student's History of England," Chapter's XXIV. - XXXV., inclusive.

2. Canadian History.—Clement's History of Canada, with special reference to the History of British Columbia.

3. Roman History.—Creighton's History Primer, Rome. (The Copp, Clark Co.)

4. Geography.—The general geography of the world, with special reference to that of the United States and Europe; Tarr's Physical Geography, Parts I. and II. (MacMillan & Co.)

C.—MATHEMATICS :—

1. Arithmetic.—Hamblin Smith's Arithmetic, revised edition.

2. Algebra.—The first thirty-one chapters of Hall and Knight's Elementary Algebra may be taken as indicating the amount required.

3. Geometry.—Euclid, Books I., II. and III., with deductions. (Hall & Stevens).

4. Bookkeeping.—The keeping of accounts by single and by double entry.

D.—SCIENCE :—

1. Physiology.—Martin's Human Body, complete.

2. Botany.—The first 90 pages of Groom and Penhallow's Elementary Botany (The Copp, Clark Co.); or the first 155 pages of Spotton's Elements of Botany (Gage & Co.)

E.—CLASSICS :—

1. Latin.—Henderson and Fletcher's First Latin Book and Reader, including Caesar's "De Bello Gallico," Book IV. and Book V., Chapters 1-23; also Vergil's "Eneid," Book I. (MacMillan's Elementary Classics, Copp, Clark Edition.)

2. Greek.—White's First Greek Book. (Ginn & Co.); or,

2. French.—Fraser and Squair's French Grammar and Reader, pages 1-336 (The Copp, Clark Co.); or Bertenshaw's French Grammar (Longmans, Green & Co.); or,

2. German.—Vandersmissen's High School German Grammar, Part I. (The Copp, Clark Co.)

F.—DRAWING :—

Drawing series in preparation.

SENIOR GRADE.

A. — ENGLISH : —

1. Reading and Orthoepy. — As for Junior Grade.
2. Writing and Spelling. — As for Junior Grade.
3. English Grammar. — West's English Grammar.
4. Composition and Rhetoric. — (a) Critical reading of the extracts in Composition from Models, pages 285-458, with a view to illustrating the principles contained in Genung's Practical Elements of Rhetoric. (b) The writing of an essay on one of three subjects selected by the examiner.
5. English Literature. — (a) Prose — Composition from Models; Macaulay's "Essay on Milton"; Addison's "The Sir Roger De Coverley Papers," Parts I. and II. (Riverside Literature Series.) (b) Poetry — The Selections for "Sight" Reading, found in the Appendix of Alexander's Select Poems (The Copp, Clark Co.); also Shakespeare's "Julius Caesar" (Riverside Literature Series). (c) History of English Literature — Stopford A. Brooke's English Literature, Chapters IV - VIII.

B. — HISTORY AND GEOGRAPHY : —

1. British History. — Green's "History of the English People," Chapter VIII., Section IX., to the end of the book will be read; or Gardiner, Chapters XXXVI.-LIV., inclusive.
2. Canadian History. — Bourinot's "How Canada is Governed."
3. Roman History. — Creighton's History Primer, Rome.
4. Grecian History. — Fyffe's History Primer, Greece.
5. Geography. — Tarr's Physical Geography, complete.

C. — MATHEMATICS :—

1. Arithmetic. — Hamblin Smith's Arithmetic, with special attention to the Metric System.
2. Algebra. — Hall & Knight's Elementary Algebra.
3. Geometry. — Books I., II., III., IV., V. (definitions), and VI., with deductions.
4. Trigonometry. — Hall & Knight's Elementary Trigonometry, or Murray's Plane Trigonometry (Longmans, Green & Co.)

D. — SCIENCE : —

1. Groom and Penhallow's Elementary Botany, complete; or Spotton's Elements of Botany, complete.
2. Chemistry. — Waddel's School Chemistry (MacMillan & Co.); or Remsen's Elements of Chemistry, Chapters I. to XVII. (MacMillan & Co.)
3. Physical Science. — Gage's Introduction to Physical Science, omitting Chapters VII. and VIII. (Ginn & Co.)

E. — CLASSICS : —

1. Vergil's "Eneid," Book II.; Horace "Odes," Book I.; also Fletcher and Henderson's Latin Prose Compositions.
2. Greek. — Xenophon's "Anabasis," Books I. and II. (MacMillan's Elementary Classics, The Copp, Clark Edition); or,
2. French. — Fraser and Squair's French Grammar and Reader, complete, with special attention to pages 395-438; or Bertenshaw's French Grammar and Daudet's "Trois Contes Choisis" (Heath & Co.); or,
2. German. — Vandersmissen's High School German Grammar, complete; Leander, "Traumereien."

F. — DRAWING : —

Drawing Series in preparation.

SENIOR ACADEMIC GRADE.

The History and Geography, Mathematics, Science and Drawing in this Grade will cover the same amount as in the Senior Grade. Students who have already passed the Senior Grade examination will be examined on the following additional English and Classics :

A. — ENGLISH : —

5. English Literature. — (a) Prose — Scott's "Ivanhoe" (Riverside Literature Series); Thackeray's "Henry Esmond" (Riverside Literature Series); Eliot's "Silas Marner," ed. Davidson (Riverside Literature Series); Ruskin's "Sesame and Lilies." (b) Poetry — Chaucer's "Prologue to the Canterbury Tales," ed. Mather (Riverside Literature Series); Milton's "L'Allegro," "Il Penseroso,' and "Lycidas" ; Gray's "Elegy Written in a Country Churchyard," and "The Progress of Poesy" ; Burns' "Cotter's Saturday Night" ; Cowper's "On the Receipt of My Mother's Picture" ; Keats' "Eve of St. Agnes (Hales' Longer English Poems, MacMillan & Co.) (c) History of English Literature — Brooke's English Literature, complete.

E — CLASSICS : —

1. Latin. — Horace, "Odes," Books II. and III.; Cicero, "Pro Lege Manilia" ; Latin Prose Composition.

2. Greek. — Lucian's "Vera Historia" (Jerram, Clarendon Press); Homer, "Iliad," Book I.; Greek Prose Composition ; or,

2. French. — Voltaire's "Histoire de Charles XII.," ed, Fasnacht (MacMillan & Co.); Victor Hugo's "Les Miserables (abridged by Sumichrast, published by Heath & Co.); Moliere's "L'Avare" (MacMillan & Co.) ; or,

2. German.— Baumbach's "Schwiegersohn" (Heath & Co.); Wachenhusen's "Vom Ersten Bis Zum Letzten Schuss" (MacMillan & Co.); Mosen's "Der Bibliothekar" (Heath & Co.)

GENERAL REMARKS.

In 1896 authority was granted the Boards of Trustees of the various high schools in the province to enter into affiliation with the leading Canadian universities ; and shortly after the passing of this Act the Board of Trustees of the Vancouver High School secured affiliation with McGill University. University classes are now carried on in the Vancouver High School, and the results so far have been eminently satisfactory.

The standard of qualification for teachers is as high as in any other province of the Dominion. Examinations take place in July of each year in those cities in which high schools are established. Certificates are of four classes — third class, second class, first class and academic. All certificates are rated for life or during good behaviour, except third-class certificates, which are rated for three years, but no person is allowed to renew a third-class certificate. All applicants for second-class, first-class and academic certificates must be graduates of the Provincial Normal School or of other Normal Schools approved of by the Council of Public Instruction; except that a period of ten years of active service in the public schools of the province is deemed equivalent to graduation from the Normal School. To secure a third-class non-professional certificate a candidate must pass the examination set for Junior Grade candidates in the High School ; while second-class, first-class and academic certificates are granted to those that successfully pass the intermediate, senior and senior academic examinations, respectively, of such high schools. The Provincial Normal School was established in 1901, and is located in the City of Vancouver.

As has been stated, the educational system of British Columbia is entirely free, undenominational and non-sectarian, and the disposition on the part of the great majority is in favour of its continuance in that form. There are, however, numerous private and denominational academies, where those who desire may have their children educated on lines agreeable to their own religious beliefs. The Roman Catholics have colleges for boys at Victoria and New Westminster, and mission schools at Victoria, Mission City, Kamloops and elsewhere ; while the Sisters of that denomination have successful academies at Victoria, Vancouver, New Westminster, Nanaimo and Mission.

The Methodist denomination carries on a well equipped college at New Westminster, which is affiliated with similar educational schools in Eastern Canada.

Mission schools for Indians are also conducted under its auspices at Port Simpson, Chilliwack and elsewhere. With the exception of the Roman Catholic body, the Church of England was the first to establish denominational schools on the Coast. There are several boys' and girls' academies in Vancouver, New Westminster, Victoria and Nanaimo, under its control, and a number of Mission stations along the coast. The kindergarten has not yet been officially incorporated in the public school system, but there are private kindergartens in several of the cities.

Recently manual training has been introduced into the schools, under an arrangement voluntarily entered upon by Sir William McDonald, Montreal.

The gradual growth of the schools, as well as the cost of maintenance, are fully shown by the record of attendance and expenditure given in the following tabular statement taken from the Annual School Report of 1901-2 :—

COMPARATIVE STATEMENT OF ATTENDANCE AND COST OF PUBLIC SCHOOLS FROM 1872-3 TO 1901-02.

Year.	Number of School Districts.	Aggregate Enrolment.	Average daily Attendance.	Percentage of Attendance	Expenditure for Education Proper.
1872-73	25	1,028	575	55.93	$ 37,763 77
1873-74	37	1,245	767	61.60	35,287 59
1874-75	41	1,403	863	61.51	34,822 28
1875-76	41	1,685	984	58.39	44,506 11
1876-77	42	1,998	1,260	63.06	47,129 63
1877-78	45	2,198	1,395.50	63.49	43,334 01
1878-79	45	2,301	1,315.90	57.19	*22,110 70
1879-80	47	2,462	1,293.93	52.56	47,006 10
1880-81	48	2,571	1,366.86	53.16	46,960 69
1881-82	50	2,653	1,358.68	51.21	49,268 63
1882-83	59	2,693	1,383.00	51.36	50,850 63
1883-84	67	3,420	1,808.60	55.88	66,655 15
1884-85	76	4,027	2,089.74	51.89	71,151 52
1885-86	86	4,471	2,481.48	65.50	79,527 56
1886-87	95	5,345	2,873.38	53.75	88,521 08
1887-88	104	6,372	3,093.46	48.54	99,902 04
1888-89	109	6,796	3,681.14	54.16	108,190 59
1889-90	123	8,042	4,333.90	53.89	122,984 83
1890-91	141	9,260	5,134.91	55.45	136,901 73
1891-92	154	10,773	6,227.10	57.80	160,627 80
1892-93	169	11,496	7,111.40	61.85	190.558 33
1893-94	178	12,613	7,785.50	61.72	169,050 18
1894-95	183	13,482	8,610.31	63.86	189,037 25
1895-96	193	14,460	9,254.25	64.00	204,930 32
1896-97	199	15,798	9,999.61	63.29	220,810 38
1897-98	213	17,648	11,055.65	62.64	247,756 37
1898-99	224	19,185	12,304.32	64.13	268,653 46
1899-00	231	21,531	13,438.41	62.41	284,909 10
1900-01	245	23,615	15,098.28	63.93	312,187 17
1901-02	257	23,903	15,564.25	65.11	365,492.15
					$3,846,887 15

*Half-year.

The expenditure for education proper during 1900-01 and 1901-02 was:—

	1900-01.	1901-02.
Teachers' Salaries	$213,088 23	$216,125 80
Incidental Expenses	20,428 07	20,602 32
Per Capita Grant to City Districts	65,840 76	103,225 20
Grant to High Schools, in addition to Per Capita Grant...	....	2,950 00
Education Office	12,205 81	6,888 24
Inspection of Schools	....	7,374 30
Normal School	1,944 30	5,547 79
Education of Deaf and Dumb	....	3,208 50
	$313,507 17	$365,922 15
Less Fees for Teachers' Examination	1,320 00	430 00
	$312,187 17	$365,492 15
Expenditure for construction of new school houses, furniture, repairs and improvements to school property..	38,345 14	....
	$350,532 31	$365,492 15

In addition to the above, the municipalities of the cities of Nanaimo, New Westminster, Vancouver and Victoria expended, in addition to the per capita grants received from the Provincial Government, the following sums:—

	1900-01.
Nanaimo	$ 7,450 17
New Westminster	22,445 61
Vancouver	117,556 20
Victoria	34,708 20
	$182,160 18
Amount expended by Provincial Government	350,532 31
Grand total cost of Education	$532,692 49

In 1901-02 the amounts were:—

Cities of the First Class—	
Vancouver	$ 44,379 73
Victoria	64,334 27
Cities of the Second Class—	
Nanaimo	5,354 84
Nelson	4,120 30
New Westminster	11,374 53
Rossland	3,287 78
Cities of the Third Class—	
Columbia	215 20
Cumberland	53 50
Grand Forks	12,852 71
Greenwood	201 45
Kamloops	458 70
Kaslo	550 84
Phoenix	367 05
Revelstoke	751 88
Sandon	479 45
Slocan	195 87
Trail	368 25
Vernon	1,045 17
	$150,481 52
Amount expended by Provincial Government	438,086 20
Grand total cost of Education	$588,567 72

HAULING OUT LOGS.

LOGGING WITH OX TEAMS.

HARRISON, SHEWING SAW-MILL.

BRUNETTE SAW-MILL, NEW WESTMINSTER.

The following table shows the cost of each pupil on enrolment and on average daily attendance during the past ten years :—

Year.	Cost of each pupil on enrolment.	Cost of each pupil on average daily attendance.
1891-92	$14 91	$25 79
1892-93	16 57	26 79
1893-94	13 40	21 71
1894-95	14 02	22 95
1895-96	14 17	22 14
1896-97	13 97	22 08
1897-98	14 03	22 40
1898-99	14 00	21 83
1899-1900	13 29	21 29
1900-01	13 20	20 67
1901-02	15 29	23 48

Average monthly salary in city districts for principals and teachers..........$59 26
Average monthly salary in rural districts for teachers and monitors.......... 52 66

VALUE OF SCHOOL PROPERTY.

	1900-01	1901-02.
Rural Districts, 224 schools	$ 287,095	*$ 256,585
Victoria City	189,000	229,000
Vancouver City	452,650	402,550
New Westminster	76,500	76,750
Nanaimo City	37,825	38.000
Nelson		36,500
Rossland		38,150
Columbia		1,900
Cumberland		11,650
Grand Forks		22,000
Greenwood		150
Kamloops		9,500
Kaslo		4.850
Phoenix		4,500
Revelstoke		7,000
Sandon		5,725
Slocan		2,900
Trail		4,250
Vernon		5,930
	$1,041.070	$1,217,890

*The decrease is accounted for by the taking out of the rural list of a number of incorporated towns.

COST OF EDUCATION TO CITIES.

	1896-97.	1898.	1899.	1900.	1901.	1902.
Nanaimo	$16,163 90	$13,102 13	$16,328 37	$15,188 25	$15,903 27	$16,625 96
New Westminster	18,217 76	18,255 36	18,202 42	19,381 17	30,596 75	21,509 09
Victoria	48,213 67	49,718 83	46,811 52	50 195 31	55,924 08	90 847 69
Vancouver	60,480 73	106,946 16	56,284 15	58,911 12	145,000 94	81,097 97
	$143,076 06	$188,022 48	$137,626 46	$143,675 85	$248,000 94	
Nelson (six months)						6,055 22
Rossland "						6,903 82
Columbia "						577 50
Cumberland						2,132 20
Grand Forks						13,828 21
Greenwood						981 55
Kamloops						2,268 60
Kaslo						1,591 54
Phoenix						1,068 25
Revelstoke						2,830 68
Sandon						788 55
Slocan						905 17
Trail						1,322 65
Vernon						2,372 07
						$281,938 72
Total for six years						1,142,310 51

PER CAPITA GRANT TO CITIES.

Nanaimo	$ 6,506 34	$ 7,575 78	$ 8,023 14	$ 7,391 38	$ 8,453 10	$11,571 12
New Westminster	6,714 54	6,424 44	8 141 74	6,936 90	8,151 14	10,534 56
Victoria	18,744 24	19,094 78	20,622 54	20,353 64	21,215 88	27,203 42
Vancouver	17,722 68	19,827 64	25,000 04	22,010 20	28,020 64	37,918 29
	$49,687 80	$52,922 64	$61,787 46	$56,692 12	$65,840 76	
Columbia (six months)						302 30
Cumberland "						2,078 70
Grand Forks "						975 60
Greenwood "						690 10
Kamloops "						1,809 90
Kaslo "						1,040 70
Nelson						2,084 92
Phoenix						701 20
Revelstoke						2,078 80
Rossland						3,766 04
Sandon						309 10
Slocan						709 30
Trail						954 40
						$111,948 30
Total six years						510,827 33

COST OF CONSTRUCTION AND REPAIRS.

		Education proper.
1896-97	$15,870 94	$220,810 38
1897-98	42,498 89	247,756 37
1898-99	67,362 84	268,053 46
1899-1900	22,569 90	284,909 10
1900-1901	38,345 14	312,187 17
1901-1902	72,594 05	365,492 15

TOTAL EXPENDITURE TO DATE.

	Government.	Cities.	Total.
Education proper	$3,846,924	$1,248,780	$5,095,704
Construction, repairs, etc.	661,722	565,309	1,227,031
			$6,322,735
Less Government grant to cities since 1891			623,889
			$5,698,846

The following table gives the names of the several High Schools, the number of divisions in each, the total enrolment, the total actual daily attendance, and the percentage of regular attendance:—

High Schools.	No. of Divisions.	Total Enrolment.	Actual Daily Attendance.	Percentage of Regular Attendance.
Nanaimo	2	74	38.96	52.65
Nelson	1	34	19.99	58.79
New Westminster	3	95	70.82	74.55
Rossland	1	29	16.62	57.31
*Vancouver	8	312	245.42	78.66
Vernon	1	20	18.61	93.05
‖Victoria	5	220	144.70	65.77

*Note.—Is affiliated to McGill University, in so far as regards the work of the first and second years in arts.

‖Is affiliated to McGill University, in so far as regards the work of the first year in arts.

STANDING AND NUMBER OF TEACHERS.

At the present time the number of persons in the province holding certificates of qualification is as follows, according to standing and sex :—

	Male.	Female.	Total.
Academic	110	30	140
First Class	105	98	203
Second Class	20	96	116
Third Class	21	98	119
Old Line Certificates.			
Second A	54	106	160
Second B	30	68	98
Third A	3	3	6
Temporary Certificates	8	15	23
Renewals	2	2	4
Graduated from Normal School	28	184	212

INDIAN SCHOOLS.

The following is a list of the schools for the training of Indians under the control of the Indian Department, but conducted on denominational lines :—

SCHOOL.	LOCATION.	DENOMINATION.
Ahousaht	Cowichan	Presbyterian
Aiyaush	Northwest Coast	Church of England
Alberni Home	West Coast	Presbyterian
Alert Bay Industrial	Alert Bay	Church of England
Alert Bay Girls' Home	Alert Bay	Church of England
Alert Bay Day	Nimkish	Church of England
Bella Bella	Bella Bella	Methodist
Cape Mudge	Cape Mudge	Methodist
Coqualeetza Home	Chilliwack	Methodist
Gwayasdums	Kwawhewlth	Church of England
Hazelton	Hazelton	Church of England
Kamloops Industrial	Kamloops	Roman Catholic
Kincolith	Kincolith	Church of England
Kishfiax	Babine Lake	Methodist
Kootenay Industrial	Northwest Coast	Church of England
Kitkahtla	Kootenay	Roman Catholic
Kuper Island Industrial	Kuper Island	Roman Catholic
Lakalsap	Northwest Coast	Methodist
Massett	Massett, Q. C. I.	Church of England
Metlakatla Industrial	Metlakatla	Church of England
Metlakatla Day	Metlakatla	Church of England
Nanaimo	Nanaimo	Methodist
Nitinat	West Coast	Methodist
Oiaht	Haines Island	Roman Catholic
Port Essington	Skeena	Methodist
Port Simpson Girls' Home	Port Simpson	Methodist
Port Simpson Day	Simpson's	Methodist
Skidegate	Queen Charlotte Islands	Methodist
Somenos	Somenos	Methodist
Songhees	Victoria	Roman Catholic
St. Mary's Boarding	St. Mary's Mission	Roman Catholic
Ucluelet	West Coast	Presbyterian
William's Lake Industrial	William's Lake	Roman Catholic
Yale Boarding	Yale	Church of England

PROVINCIAL HEALTH LAWS.

ON the 23rd of February, 1869, the "Health Ordinance, 1869," was passed, the preamble reciting: "Whereas it is necessary to adopt measures with the object of preventing or guarding against the origin, rise or progress of endemic, epidemic or contagious diseases, and to protect the health of the inhabitants of this colony, and for the purpose to grant to the Governor-in-Council extraordinary powers to be used when urgent occasion demands." This Act remained in force at the time of the consolidation of the Provincial Statutes in 1888, and, with the exception of the preamble, was incorporated into that consolidation as Chap. 55. Its provisions were found to be inadequate when put to the test at the time of the smallpox epidemic in 1892.

The development of health legislation in British Columbia has followed the same course that such legislation has usually followed in the several provinces, states of the Union, and other countries. The incentive of every improvement in the laws concerning the health of the people has been a visitation, or threatened visitation, of some dread disease.

The need of a better Health Act was made apparent by the occurrence of an epidemic of smallpox in Victoria in 1892. Over 150 cases occurred, which cost the City of Victoria alone some $60,000. In consequence, at the next session of the Legislature the then Attorney-General and Premier, Hon. Theodore Davie, introduced an Act modelled on the Ontario Public Health Act, which was very much more comprehensive and complete. An important feature of the new Act was the establishment of a Provincial Board of Health, consisting of five members.

The Health Act was again amended in 1899, constituting the Lieutenant-Governor-in-Council the "Provincial Board of Health," and providing for the appointment of a qualified medical practitioner as Secretary.

In accordance with the above, Charles J. Fagan, M. D., was appointed Secretary in November, 1899.

*TIMBER ON DOMINION LANDS.

A LICENSE to cut timber can be acquired at public competition. A rental of $5 per square mile is charged for all timber berths excepting those situated west of Yale in the Province of British Columbia, for which the rental is at the rate of 5 cents per acre per annum. In addition to the rental, dues at the following rates are charged: Sawn lumber, 50 cents per thousand feet, B. M.; railway ties, eight and nine feet long, 1½ and 1¾ cents each; shingle bolts, 25 cents a cord; all other products, 5 per cent. on the sales.

A license is issued as soon as a berth is granted, but in unsurveyed territory no timber can be cut on the berth until the licensee has made a survey thereof.

Permits to cut timber are also granted at public competition, except in the case of actual settlers who require the timber for their own use. Settlers and others may also obtain permits to cut up to 100 cords of wood for sale, without competition. The dues payable under a permit are $1.50 per thousand feet, B. M., for square timber and sawlogs of any wood except oak; from ½ to 1½ cents per lineal foot for building logs; from 12½ to 25 cents per cord for wood; 1 cent for fence-posts; 3 cents for railway ties; and 20 cents per thousand for shingles.

Homesteaders having no timber of their own are entitled to a permit, free of dues, to cut the following quantities: Three thousand feet of building logs, not to exceed 12 inches at the butt end (if the timber is cut from dry trees, 3,000 lineal feet of any diameter may be taken); 400 roof poles; 500 fence posts; 2,000 fence rails.

Homesteaders and all bona fide settlers whose farms may not have thereon a supply of timber, or who are not in possession of wood lots or other timbered lands, will be granted a free permit to take and cut dry timber for their own use on their farms, for fuel and fencing. A permit fee of 25 cents in each case is charged.

*Omitted from the chapter on "Timber."

TRAVELLING LIBRARIES.

IN 1897 the Government, recognizing the special needs of outlying communities, especially of farmers, for literature of an interesting and instructive character, decided, upon the recommendation of the then librarian of the Legislative Assembly, to establish a system of travelling libraries, which is practically an extension of the Provincial Library.

The system adopted is very simple indeed, and the details easily worked out. A certain number of persons in a community send an application, asking for a library to be sent. Upon security being given by responsible persons that the library will be cared for and duly returned, it is forwarded to its destination. Each locality is entitled to retain the library for a period of six months, when it is exchanged for a library from another locality, and thus the various libraries are kept in circulation. In making up the libraries, the needs of each district are kept in mind — that is to say, in farming districts particular attention is paid to farming books, and the latest and most authoritative works on agriculture are bought and supplied. There is a sprinkling of history, fiction, works of travel, philosophy, etc., making up, in 100 or 150 volumes, as the case may be, a very comprehensive, up-to-date assortment. As books are worn out or destroyed, they are replaced with others. Mining camps have special books of mining interest substituted for agricultural works, and so on according to the character of the readers.

The system so far has met with gratifying success, and the demand for libraries is rapidly increasing. Up to the present time thirty-nine library stations have been created and supplied with libraries, among which are the following: —

New Westminster District — Mount Lehman, Port Moody, Cloverdale, Haney, Coquitlam, Tynehead, Chilliwack, Port Kells, Langley, Hazelmere, Hall's Prairie, Abbotsford, Shortreed, Eburne, Upper Sumas, Huntingdon, Langley Prairie.

Cariboo District — 150-Mile House, Quesnel.

Vancouver Island — Comox, Gordon Head, Cape Scott, Metchosin, Ucluelet, Saanich, East Sooke, Cumberland.

Salt Spring Island — Ganges Harbour, Beaver Point.

Yale District — Savonas, Falkland, Ashcroft, Lower Nicola.

West Kootenay — Camborne, Slocan City, Trout Lake, Trail.

Coast — Bella Coola, Port Simpson.

Each library is composed of at least 100 volumes, divided into the following classes: Ethics, Social Science, Natural Science, Useful Arts, Literature, Description and Travel, Fiction, Juvenile Works, Biography, History, and Reference.

The libraries at present in use are scattered over an immense area — from 150-Mile House, in Cariboo, to Port Simpson, on the northern coast — among communities widely divergent in interests and tastes. Many of them are stationed in agricultural districts more or less thickly settled and organised; others in recently formed mining communities; and others again in the Scandinavian settlements at Cape Scott and Bella Coola.

At meetings of the Central Farmers' Institute held at Victoria, resolutions favouring the continuance and extension of the travelling library system have been unanimously passed.

It is gratifying to know that the example thus set by British Columbia, which is one of the pioneers in adopting the travelling library system, has been followed in many other parts of the world, and the Librarian is constantly in receipt of enquiries as to the working and success of the system. Moreover, the work is sincerely appreciated by those among whom the libraries circulate.

TAXATION AND ASSESSMENT.

TAXES are paid on the assessed value of all property. The assessed value is the actual cash value as the property would be appraised in payment of a just debt from a solvent debtor. The rate of taxation is as follows: On real estate, four-fifths of one per cent.; on wild land, 3 per cent.; on personal property, three-fourths of one per cent. On income exceeding $1,000: Class A, upon excess not above $10,000, 1½ per cent. up to $5,000, and 2½ per cent. on remainder; Class B, on $10,000 and not exceeding $20,000, 2 per cent. up to $10,000 and 3 per cent. on remainder; Class C, on $20,000 and not exceeding $40,000, 3 per cent. up to $20,000, and 3½ per cent. on the remainder; Class D, on all others in excess of $40,000, 3½ per cent. up to $40,000, and 4 per cent. on the remainder.

Taxes are due and payable on the 2nd of January in each year, but if paid on or before the 30th June, the rate is as follows: On real estate, three-fifths of 1 per cent.; on wild land, 2½ per cent.; on personal property, one-half of 1 per cent.; on income upon excess of $1,000, under Class A, on $1,000 and not exceeding $10,000, 1 per cent. up to $5,000 and 2 per cent. on the remainder; Class B, on $10,000 and not exceeding $20,000, 1½ per cent. up to $10,000 and 2½ per cent. on the remainder; Class C, on $20,000 and not exceeding $40,000, 2½ per cent. up to $20,000 and 3 per cent. on the remainder; Class D, on all others in excess of $40,000 3½ per cent. up to $40,000 and 3½ per cent. on the remainder.

Banks and other corporations transacting business in the province are taxed the same as individuals. All have to make returns, on forms provided, to the assessor, and these returns must be full and complete of all personal property and of the gross income. Certain deductions are allowed from personal property and from income under rules laid down by the Lieutenant-Governor-in-Council, which are printed on the returns. The tax is calculated on both personal property and on income, and if tax on either is greater, the tax on the greater is taken; if equal, the tax on income is taken.

Cattle and sheep depastured on Crown lands are taxed 25 per cent. per head on all cattle, and 5 per cent. per head on sheep. This tax entitles owners to depasture for six months. If tax is not paid on demand, it may be collected by distress and sale.

There is also a tax at 25 cents per acre and fractional part of an acre on all unworked Crown granted mineral or placer claims, due and payable annually on the 30th day of June following the date of issue of the Crown grant. An affidavit may be lodged with the Assessor before 30th June annually that mining development work has been done on the claim, to the value of $200 during the year to entitle the owner exemption from the tax. The work may be done upon any one or more adjoining claims not exceeding eight, to the full value at the rate of $200 per claim, to entitle all of such claims to exemption in lieu of the tax.

Taxes not paid when due and on demand may be recovered by distress and sale of goods and chattels, and may be levied against lands. Lands may be sold for arrears of taxes at any time after publication for four weeks, and may be redeemed at any time within two years upon paying costs and interest at 12 per cent. per annum.

All taxes become delinquent at 31st December after they become legally due, and interest at 12 per cent. per annum is added from that date. Lands on which the taxes are delinquent must be exposed for sale if not paid, annually, between 15th June and 15th September, and if no sale is effected, the lands are absolutely forfeited to the Crown. Lands pre-empted, upon which there may be delinquent taxes, are not exposed for sale, but the Record of Pre-emption is cancelled after notice is given. Mineral or placer claims upon which taxes become delinquent are exposed for sale on the first Monday in November annually after the legal due date, and if not sold revert to the Crown. If sold, one year from date of sale is allowed for redemption.

Mines and minerals are regarded as a separate class of property for taxation purposes. Two per cent. tax on the assessed value of all ore or mineral-bearing substances, the assessed value to be based on the market value of the ore at the mine, deducting from the gross output the cost of transportation to smelter and cost of smelting or reduction only. Ore not sold or removed from the mine is not taxed. Placer or dredging mines not producing in any one year a gross value of $2,000 are exempt; other mines not producing in any one year a market value of $5,000 are entitled to a refund of one-half of the tax. The 2 per cent. tax is in substitution for all taxes upon the land, and for taxes on personal property used in the workings of the mines, and for the income from the mine. Mine-owners must notify assessor of any mine being in active production, and no ore can be shipped until such notification has been made. All mineral taxes are payable quarterly. Mine-owners must make returns to assessor, verified on oath, within seven days from end of quarter, under penalty for non-compliance.

All male residents of the Province above the age of 18 years are taxed annually $3 per head for revenue tax and the tax is due after the 2nd January in each year. All male persons over the age of 60 years are exempt, if their incomes are less than $700. Employers of labor are responsible for the tax on employees, and may deduct tax from wages. Employers must furnish assessor with list of employees on demand.

There is the usual list of exemptions, which include all incomes up to $1,000; capital invested in government or municipal bonds or debentures; income of a farmer from his farm; income of merchants; income of mechanics or other persons derived from capital liable to assessment; all property, real or personal, situate out of land, if the fee is still in taxpayer; so much of the personal property equal to just debt owing on account of the purchase price of the said personal property to the vendor thereof; the net personal property over $300; ministers' salaries; household effects, books, etc. (except furniture rented from which a revenue is derived); homesteads to the value of $500; dividends or interest from companies when the personal property or income of such companies is assessed or taxed.

Railway companies are assessed under the Railway Assessment Act, at the rate of $3,000 per mile, and the tax levied at the rate mentioned above on real estate. This tax includes personal property used for railway purposes.

Every owner of a coal mine shall pay a tax of five cents per ton upon all coal (except shipments to coke ovens in the province) since 1st July, 1900; and every owner of coke ovens shall pay a tax of nine cents per ton upon all coke since that date shipped, exported or delivered from said coke ovens; provided, however, that no tax has been paid upon the coal from which the coke has been produced.

For rate of municipal taxation see Municipal Statistics.

Gross premium incomes from all insurance companies doing business in British Columbia (except life insurance companies), namely: fire, marine, accident, plate glass, guarantee, etc., for the year ended 31st December, 1902, and the taxes paid thereon for the assessment year of 1903:

Gross premiums	$1,134,243 89
Losses and expenses	797,742 81
Taxable income	$336,501 08
Taxes thereon at lower rate	$5,065 19

Gross premium income from life insurance companies, doing business in British Columbia for the year ended 21st December, 1902, and the taxes paid on their taxable income for the assessment year 1903:

Gross Premiums	$861,579 75
Taxable income, being 12.7 of gross premiums	$109,420 56
Taxes thereon at lower rate	$1,497 61

Total gross premiums:

All insurance companies (except life)	$1,134,243 89
Life companies	869,579 75
Total gross premiums paid in British Columbia	$2,003,823 64

Taxes paid:

All insurance companies (except life)	$5,065 19
Life companies	1,497 61
Total taxes	$6,562 80

PROVINCIAL ASSESSMENT, 1903.

DISTRICT	REAL PROPERTY		WILD LAND		PERSONAL PROPERTY		INCOME	
	Assessed Value	Tax Lower Rate	Assessed Value	Tax Lower Rate	Assessed Value	Tax Lower Rate	Assessed Value	Tax at Lower Rate
Victoria	$4,983,499	$29,900 99	$297,970	$ 7,449 24	$5,172,579	$25,863 14	$757,610	$11,344 18
Nanaimo City and North Nanaimo	801,502	4,809 02	34,036	850 90	571,500	2,857 50	54,255	890 55
South Nanaimo	869,050	5,214 50	125,916	3,147 90	92,900	464 50	9,920	99 20
Cowichan	365,365	2,192 19	189,544	4,738 59	266,200	1,331 00	8,300	83 00
Alberni	379,791	2,278 78	193,473	4,836 88	38,000	190 00	140	1 40
Comox	721,235	4,327 43	683,366	17,084 00	182,090	910 45	8,300	83 00
Pender Island	33,400	200 40	3,100	77 50	2,200	11 00	....	....
Galiano Island	28,450	170 70	17,490	437 25	....	....	....	....
Mayne Island	45,380	272 28	....	....	2,400	12 00	....	....
Salt Spring Island	194,200	1,163 80	11,505	287 65	56,520	282 75	2,000	20 00
Vancouver	531,804	3,195 65	226,719	5,669 30	4,417,530	22,090 10	743,004	12,281 20
New Westminster	626,000	3,756 00	36,700	917 50	1,400,000	7,000 00	51,200	512 00
Rossland	1,965,569	11,793 37	23,245	581 12	824,775	4,123 87	107,645	2,153 45
Slocan	949,991	5,689 53	34,657	866 50	266,900	1,334 50	25,949	259 49
Nelson	797,199	4,783 20	50,189	1,254 75	760,325	3,801 63	147,470	1,874 70
Kettle River	753,191	4,519 14	12,560	313 50	170,450	825 25	4,000	40 00
Princeton	228,530	1,371 18	13,360	330 00	39,708	198 54	1,080	10 80
Revelstoke	566,955	3,402 35	220,075	5,501 95	262,000	1,310 00	30,480	304 80
Ashcroft	380,102	2,280 57	17,274	431 85	295,350	1,476 75	780	12 80
Nicola	1,163,000	6,967 60	9,300	232 00	457,576	2,287 90	200	2 00
Lillooet	949,175	5,695 05	58,370	1,459 25	485,552	2,427 76	2,850	28 50
Kamloops	990,225	5,941 35	38,005	950 12	646,865	3,234 34	24,357	243 57
Vernon	1,730,485	10,382 91	15,910	397 75	422,700	2,113 50	1,780	17 80
Golden	518,723	3,112 35	54,797	1,369 92	189,860	949 29	16,877	168 77
Fort Steele	1,247,493	7,491 95	209,754	5,243 60	577,878	2,889 40	35,195	371 95
Quesnel Forks	220,080	1,320 48	....	....	103,300	516 50	5,820	58 20
Barkerville	122,250	733 50	3,362	84 05	273,018	1,365 11	9,126	91 26
Telegraph Creek	2,135	12 81	....	....	20,950	104 75	800	8 00
Omineca	14,075	84 45	....	....	11,500	57 50	....	....
Atlin	266,665	1,597 90	....	....	66,300	343 75	....	....
	22,460,069	134,664 43	2,580,677	64,513 07	18,076,926	90,372 78	2,049,138	30,930 62
Railways Victoria District	2,343,000	14,058 00	....	....	....	....	....	....
Insurance Cos., 1902	....	....	....	....	....	....	511,985	9,199 98
	24,789,069	148,722 43	2,580,677	64,513 07	18,076,926	90,372 78	2,561,123	40,130 60

CHURCHES, VANCOUVER.

PUBLIC SCHOOLS, VANCOUVER.

DISTRICT SCHOOL, KETTLE RIVER, B. C.

PUBLIC SCHOOL, NANAIMO, B. C.

ALL HALLOW'S SCHOOL, YALE.

PUBLIC SCHOOL, ROSSLAND, B. C.

MUNICIPAL.

THE policy concerning municipal legislation continuously followed by the Legislature of this Province has been to give as large as possible a measure of local and self-government to municipal corporations, and to facilitate the incorporation of municipalities wherever warranted by population and property. This general legislation at present in force respecting municipalities is contained in three Statutes passed during the session of 1896, known as the Municipal Incorporation Act, the Municipal Elections Act, and the Municipal Clauses Act and amendments to the two last-mentioned Acts, passed in 1897, dealing respectively with municipal incorporations, elections, government and internal management and amendments thereto in the years 1898, 1900, 1901, and 1902. Adequate provisions in these Acts conserve the corporate rights, powers and liabilities of existing municipalities.

Under the first mentioned Act a city municipality, to include a tract of land of not more than 2,000 acres in area, may be incorporated by Letters Patent upon petition signed by the owners of more than one-half in value of the lands within the proposed boundaries, if within such boundaries there are resident and have been so resident for six months immediately previous to the signing of the petition, not less than one hundred male British subjects of full age; and a township or district municipality upon petition by the like proportion of owners (including pre-emption of at least one year's standing), if there be so resident at least thirty male British subjects of full age. The Act also contains elaborate provisions for securing an extension or reduction of corporate limits, and for securing the dissolution of a municipal corporation upon petition of the ratepayers, should circumstances render such a course necessary.

The Election Act codifies the provisions relating to this branch of law; the qualifications of electors, the methods of their registration and the time and method of holding the annual elections being all fixed by Statute, it being left to the Municipal Councils to fix by by-law the places for holding the nominations and polls and to appoint returning officers and their deputies. For the annual elections the nominations are held on the second Monday in January, and the polling, if any, on the Thursday following. The voting is by ballot. By an amendment in 1900 a provision is made for the use of voting machines in all municipalities. The provisions regulating the mode of voting, the counting of ballots and announcing the results, and for the prevention of intimidation and corrupt practices being substantially to the same effect as those regulating elections for the Legislative Assembly; there are also provisions providing for the filling of vacancies in Councils and provisions empowering the Supreme and County Courts to try upon petition the validity of contested elections. In order to be qualified for nomination and election in a city municipality as Mayor, the candidate must be a British subject and must have been registered as the owner of the property to the extent of $1,000 in assessed value above any registered encumbrance or judgment, and as Alderman must be a British subject, with a similar real property qualification of $500. In Nanaimo, the qualification is $500 for Mayor and $350 for Alderman. The qualifications of Reeve and Councillors in district municipalities are similar, with the exception that the real property qualifications are $500 and $250 respectively. All civic officers and employees are elected by ballot or appointed by resolution and hold office at the pleasure of the Council. Every municipality is divided into wards so as to allow equal representation as near as may be on the basis of assessed values, and a re-division on this basis is necessary when the amount of assessed pr. p rty in any ward exceeds in proportion to its representation in the Council more than 40 per cent. of the assessed property in any other ward.

Any male or female being a British subject of the full age of twenty-one years who in city municipalities has paid on or before the 1st of November, and in district municipalities before the 30th day of November prior to the date of nomination all rates, taxes, fees, imposts, etc., is qualified to vote at the municipal elections, (a) who is a land owner; (b) who is the holder of a trade license, the annual fee for which is not less than $5, or (c) who is a householder, (d) authorized representatives of corporations owning assessed real property within the municipality.

The Municipal Clauses Act, continuing and elaborating the policy of the former Municipal Acts, has for its object the creation of a comprehensive system of municipal government and management, altogether self-supporting, that is to say, dependent for municipal expenditures entirely upon municipal revenue; the Municipal Councils being for the more effectual accomplishment of this object invested with powers to raise a revenue by taxation, and also with legislative and executive powers, the scope and limits of these powers and the methods of their exercise being fully and carefully defined.

In city municipalities the Mayor, and in district municipalities the Reeve, is the chief executive officer of the corporation, his duties and powers being defined by the Act, and including unrestricted powers and authority to order the conduct of all municipal officers, to direct the method and management of corporate business, and to return for re-consideration any by-law or resolution of the Council, this power of veto being subject to the right of the Council to re-consider and again pass the by-law or resolution over the veto of the Mayor or Reeve. The Council exercise the corporate powers of the municipalities and in cities consist of a Mayor and not less than five and not more than nine Aldermen, and in districts of a Reeve and not less than four and not more than seven Councillors.

Real property ownership, as before mentioned, is a necessary qualification for holding elective office in a municipality. Civic officers may be elected by ballot or appointed by resolution and hold office at the pleasure of the Council.

The Council of every municipality has power to make, alter and repeal by-laws in relation to upwards of 150 classes of subjects, the general effect of the elaborate statutory enumeration of their legislative powers being to invest them with authority by by-law to assist the establishment of various enterprises within the corporation limits; to construct and acquire water works, lighting, sewerage, and tramway systems; to aid educational and charitable institutions and objects; to raise municipal revenue by means of taxation and by the issue of trades licenses; to prevent fires and accidents, and to regulate the carrying on of all trades which have in them elements of danger to life or health; to prevent practices injurious to public morals or tending to disturb the peace; to maintain, repair and regulate streets, bridges and wharves; and to enable permanent works to be carried out on the local improvement principle.

The general power of a Municipal Council to incur liabilities on behalf of the corporation is restricted to the extent of the municipal revenue for the current year. The carrying out of municipal works involving expenditure which cannot be met out of the current revenue, loans by the issue of debentures upon the security of rateable lands or improvements (either or both) of the municipality may be obtained upon by-laws passed by the Council and assented to by the ratepayers assessed for property within the municipality up to an aggregate amount (exclusive of loans for works to be performed on the local improvement principle or a debt created under the "Corporation of Victoria Water Works Act, 1873,) not to exceed twenty per cent. of the assessed value of the lands and improvements of the municipality. For the purpose of carrying out works to be performed on the local improvement principal by local assessment loans may be obtained upon by-laws in like manner, except that the by-law must expressly show that the debt is created on the special rate settled by the by-law and on that security only. A by-law passed illegally may be quashed upon application of any ratepayer made to the Supreme Court within thirty days after the by-law has been finally passed by the Council

By-laws for contracting debts for other than ordinary expenditure can only be introduced on a petition of at least one-half of the value of the land in township or district municipalities, and no such by-law after having been passed can be altered or repealed except by consent of the Lieutenant-Governor-in-Council.

Only those who are the assessed owners of land or real property may vote on money by-laws. In city municipalities a three-fifths majority is necessary to carry a by-law requiring the assent of the electors.

The Council of every city municipality may invest its sinking fund in Dominion or Provincial Government securities or deposit it in an incorporated bank, or may invest it in other securities.

District municipalities may from time to time invest in Dominion or Provincial Government securities or in first mortgages of real property held and used for farming purposes and being the first lien on such property, but no sum invested in mortgages shall exceed one-half of the value of the real property on which it is secured.

IN every municipality the Assessment Roll, as annually prepared and returned by the Assessor on the date fixed for such return by resolution of the Council, is revised by the Council sitting as a Court of Revision to hear and determine all complaints made by ratepayers of having been wrongfully inserted in or omitted from the Assessment Roll, or of having been therein undercharged or overcharged. The sittings of the Court are advertised for one month in the "Official Gazette" and in the local press; and the Court is composed of five members of the Council, of whom three form a quorum. An appeal lies from the Court of Revision to a County Court Judge or to a Judge of the Supreme Court and again to the Court of Appeal. The Council may, after the final revision of the Assessment Roll, levy a rate of one mill for health purposes and two mills for school purposes. The Court of Revision is also empowered to act as, and its members are constituted a Board for the equalization of the assessed value of land and improvements which are, under the Act, assessed separately; improvements, in many instances, being exempted.

All arrears of taxes bearing interest at six per cent., are by the Act made a first charge on the property affected, and payment may be enforced by action and judgment, or by the sale at public auction of the lands in respect of which taxes are in arrear. Owners of real property which has been sold for taxes have the right to redeem within one year, by paying or tendering to the Clerk of the municipality the sum paid by the purchaser with legal interest thereon.

In district municipalities every male person between twenty-one and fifty years of age inclusive, not otherwise assessed, is liable to perform two days' statute labor annually. Any property holder not assessed over $500, and whether resident or non-resident, is also charged with two days; over $500 and not exceeding $1,000, three days; and for every additional $1,000, one day. Statute labour may be commuted in cash, at the amount fixed by by-law, not in any case to exceed $2 per day.

Municipalities in addition to powers of taxation by statute labour and assessment may levy and collect license fees in respect of some twenty-nine trades, occupations and privileges at various rates, the limits of which are defined.

Cities are also empowered to construct certain works such as sewers, drains, sidewalks, pavements, etc., under the local improvement system, for which the property specially benefitted may be taxed. No such local improvements, however, except branch sewers and connections, may be undertaken if a majority of the owners of the property affected (holding at least one-half in value of such property) petition against it. Provision is also made for the carrying out of the works on the local improvement principle in district municipalities. Drainage and dyking under the supervision of the Commissioners on the local improvement plan are also fully provided for, and in respect of all works of local improvement, the ratepayers are empowered to proceed against the proposed by-law for illegality or to appeal, in regard to any errors in the assessment, to a Court of Revision in the same way as provided for in the general assessment.

The following property is exempt from taxation: Churches, burying-grounds and cemeteries, hospitals (and grounds not exceeding twenty acres for public and three acres for private hospitals); orphanages (and grounds not exceeding five acres); and property vested in or held by His Majesty in an official capacity; Indian lands; and lands and improvements belonging to the municipality (except where chargeable in respect of local improvement).

POLICE Magistrates in city municipalities are appointed by the Lieutenant-Governor-in-Council, who also fixes the salaries, but they are paid by the municipality. A Police Magistrate is also ex officio a Stipendiary Magistrate, and is not allowed, directly or indirectly, to act as a barrister or solicitor in criminal matters. Mayors and Reeves are ex officio Justices of the Peace. The Act expressly imposes upon all municipalities the duty of maintaining a sufficient force of police and providing a gaol and also of enforcing not only the municipal by-laws, but the criminal law, and the general laws of the Province. In township or district municipalities the police are appointed and paid by, and hold office at the pleasure of the Council. In city municipalities the police are appointed by and are under the control of the Police Commissioners. The Commissioners fix the remuneration of the police, and the Council is obliged, subject to the right of appeal to the Lieutenant-Governor-in-Council, to pay such remuneration, and to provide clothing, accoutrements and accommodation for the police.

The Board of Police Commissioners consists of the Mayor and two persons appointed by the Lieutenant-Governor-in-Council, one of whom must be a member of the Council. Provision is made for the filling of vacancies. The Commissioners have full power as to summoning and examining witnesses and the making of police regulations. In all cities and towns there are required to be a Chief of Police and such number of officers and assistants as may be deemed necessary by the Council, but not less than is reported as absolutely necessary by the Police Commissioners.

All fines, fees and forfeitures imposed under by-laws, and in cases where a municipality pays $250 or over for a Police Magistrate, those collected under the authority of the Provincial Laws are paid into the Municipal Treasury and used as a part of its revenue.

Board of Licensing Commissioners are constituted in each city or district municipality who have exclusive powers in the granting, transfer, renewal and cancellation of licenses for the sale of liquor. In cities the Mayor, and in district municipalities, the Reeve, two Councillors elected annually for that purpose by the Council, and two Justices of the Peace with jurisdiction in the municipality and being the registered owners of property of the value of $500 or over. The Mayor or Reeve as the case may be is the presiding officer. The Board does not make regulations, but simply administers the law. The Council of every municipality has power to pass by-laws regulating the conditions under which the Commissioners may act, and limiting, prescribing and otherwise regulating the issuance of licenses. Retail liquor licenses are granted in respect to premises only, and all applications for transfer or new licenses must be duly advertised in a local newspaper. An important feature of the licensing system in regard to new applications is that it recognizes the local option principle. No retail liquor license can be granted in a city unless the application therefor be supported by a petition of two-thirds of the lot owners and resident house-holders and two-thirds of their wives as well within the lot in which the premises are situated, or in the block opposite; and if the premises be situated on a street corner, then of two-thirds of all the lot owners and resident house-holders and their wives. In city or town municipalities of less than 1,000 inhabitants and in township and district municipalities no retail licenses may issue without a similar petition in its favour with respect to the whole of the municipality; and in order to obtain a license in any rural settlement a like petition must be presented signed by two-thirds in number of the house-holders, and the wives of such house-holders, residing within five miles of the premises for which the license is sought.

ASSISTANCE to public schools is dealt with under the head of Education. Local Boards of Health are also dealt with in a special chapter. It is the duty of every city municipality to make suitable provision for its poor and destitute.

It is also the duty of all municipalities to publish periodically statements of its financial affairs in pamphlet form; and no municipality can grant special privileges or give exemptions of any kind unless assented to by a vote of the people. Councils may, however, by resolution, grant aid to Hospitals, Agricultural Societies, Mechanics' Institutes and charitable institutions, give bounties for the destruction of wild beasts, provide buildings for municipal purposes, acquire land for sanitary purposes, regulate the meeting of the Council and pay the expenses of delegates so far as these relate to their own municipality.

Provisions is made with the assent of the electors for the establishment of a free library, and any municipality may by resolution grant aid in celebrating Victoria Day or in any gathering for public sports and amusements; or in establishing an institution for persons afflicted with contagious or infectious diseases. The city municipalities of Vancouver and New Westminster are incorporated under Statutes granting special charters, which have been from time to time amended by the Legislature. The general Acts, of which an outline has been given above, do not apply except where especially provided, brought into force by, or where no special enactments in that behalf is contained in the special Act. In the charters of the two cities in question, while the methods of organization and administration differ in many details, the principal of government is in general effect the same as that in cities governed by the general Act. In Vancouver the local improvement system has been extensively adopted, while this has not been the case in other cities. In Vancouver also the ratepayers elect representatives to the Licensing and Police Boards and the Boards of Park and Water Commissioners.

The municipal system of British Columbia is largely founded on the experience of other Provinces, modified to suit local conditions, but more especially is it based on that of Ontario, where the development of municipal institutions received its earliest and most successful exemplification. In this Province, unlike Ontario, with its extensive and compact rural population, the conditions of municipal growth have been mainly urban in character. In the outlying districts, owing to extent of territory, sparseness of population, and magnitude and costliness of municipal undertakings, the development of municipal organizations has been limited and of slow growth, and attended with difficulties which it is anticipated will be to a great extent removed by the growth of population and consequent development of the natural resources of the Province.

As in all new countries, perfection has not been attained at the outset, and the law has been subject to numerous alterations from time to time to suit conditions which are necessarily more or less transitory. As the Province develops in wealth and population we may look for a more rapid expansion of the municipal system, more particularly in the interior mining districts; and although our municipal code has at last been fairly well established and worked out, it must continue for some time to be the subject of periodical revision and grave consideration on the part of the Legislative Assembly.

A.—MUNICIPAL

	Assessed value of real estate (actually taxed).	Assessed value of improvm'ts (actually taxed).	Total value of exemptions (nearly as possible).	Total value of Municipal buildings.	No. acres assessed as improved.	No. acres assessed as wild.	T'l acreage within Munici-pality.	Total taxes on imprv'd land.	Total taxes on wild land.	Total taxes on real estate.
RURAL.	$	$	$	$				$	$	$
Burnaby	685,462	...	67,134	148	...	...	23,000	2,826	6,519	...
Chilliwack	805,671	...	...	2,000	43,593	...	43,593	7,251	...	...
Coquitlam	245,446	...	...	1,000	9,000	6,700	25,000	1,358	2,760	...
Cowichan, North	310,627	358,543	10,000	800	29,117	7,897	...	2,963	890	...
Delta	1,677,482	276,705	17,500	2,390	...	...	...	11,955	1,937	...
Kent	304,439	...	...	793	10,855	172	11,027	1,315	71	...
Langley	702,995	157,070	...	1,300	60,855	10,292	71,147	3,943	1,735	...
Maple Ridge	226,302	20,655	211,145	1,750	3,649	4,321	24,527	3,081	755	...
Matsqui	580,000	130,500	...	1,900	42,500	7,480	49,980	2,500	1,600	...
Mission	121,706	42,107	...	300	17,799	1,086	18,885	1,779	271	...
Richmond	1,193,194	377,040	6,000	...	29,411	787	30,204	...	24,380	...
Spallumcheen	437,400	83,109	...	...	8,440	3,061	58,930	2,871	251	...
Sumas	101,992	...	...	1,924	16,267	1,623	...	522	36	...
Surrey	917,935	...	...	860	55,595	10,415	73,680	5,012	2,066	...
Vancouver, North	853,356	...	4,350	2,801	41,589	...	63,964	13,624	...	...
Vancouver, South	1,049,720	98,135	14,325	4,032	8,721	4,166	12,920	8,367	6,223	...
	19,661,207	1,543,864	330,454	21,998	377,391	58,000	506,857	69,367	49,497	
URBAN.										
Columbia	277,925	17,452	75,000	3,000	...	...	960	...	...	4,169
Cumberland	62,550	119,150	7,000	600	...	...	45	...	...	375
Grand Forks	730,140	168,875	205,370	27,000	...	...	756	...	...	14,603
Greenwood	853,690	128,759	16,900	6,095	...	...	640	...	...	20,470
Kamloops	223,310	223,370	76,360	78,034	...	...	764	...	...	4,446
Kaslo	291,921	329,260	76,211	12,412	...	...	600	...	...	8,142
Nanaimo	1,385,380	...	34,650	162,524	...	...	600	...	...	33,481
Nelson	1,250,360	540,305	120,000	220,000	...	...	483	...	...	18,130
New Westminster	2,504,075	809,450	1,345,030	881,471	...	...	3,700	...	...	60,098
Phoenix	183,825	20,225	...	2,158	...	...	...	...	...	2,206
Revelstoke	314,851	338,420	30,000	4,500	...	...	595	...	...	8,650
Rossland	1,378,250	267,500	415,975	177,250	...	...	800	...	...	27,565
Sandon	107,120	131,140	30,850	6,000	...	...	103	...	...	2,383
Slocan	111,675	...	4,000	29	...	...	150	...	...	568
Trail	179,810	...	4,000	6,750	...	...	343	...	...	1,079
Vancouver	12,792,530	2,720,300	3,000,000	1,824,000	...	...	6,000	...	...	255,851
Vernon	223,287	111,413	25,000	...	...	...	1,700	...	...	4,019
Victoria	10,814,280	6,552,420	3,381,415	866,860	...	...	5,400	...	...	238,034
	33,684,979	13,478,039	8,847,761	4,278,681			23,639			704,289

STATISTICS.

Total taxes on improvm'ts.	Total rate imposed.	Rate on improved land.	Rate on wild land.	Amt. of road tax collected.	Amt. of poll tax collected.	Total taxes imposed, 1901.	Taxes specially imposed for drainage, pavements and other local imp'ts.	Population last enumeration.	No. of ratepayers on roll.	No. entitled to vote.	No. who voted at last gen. election	Number of absentee ratepayers
$				$	$		$					
....	....	8 mills	20 mills	......	......	9,345	....	....	.....	....	......	.....
....	....	9 mills	not given	......	.....	9,577	2,326	2,670	562	610	365	.....
....	....	9 mills	2½%	......	....	4,118	....	200	147	91	61	120
....	....	7-16 of 1%	2½%	782	.....	5,443	761	1,000	314	314	......	52
....	....	7 mills	10 mills	2,206	....	16,098	....	2,137	373	388	....	112
....	....	½ of 1%	2½%	.....	.....	2,229	....	400	122	83	73	29
....	....	½ of 1%	2½%	.....	.....	9,998	....	....	533	346	215	.....
....	....	1¼%	2½%	.....	.....	4,253	....	....	249	215	.....	98
....	....	6-10 of 1%	2½%	......	.....	4,502	....	450	320	299	....	183
....	....	10 mills	25 mills	......	......	2,884	....	600	210	210	60	100
....	....	10 mills	25 mills	.....	......	33,582	....	....	......	442	206	.....
....	....	6-10 of 1%	2½%	......	......	3,904	782	......	195	210	120	37
....	......	....	....	......	.....	558	....	....	146	140	......	......
....	....	6 mills	2½%	......	.....	9,026	....	....	995	476	218	......
....	....	16 mills	16 mills	.....	.....	13,624	....	450	1,110	503	139	199
....	....	1%	2%	......	932	15,522	....	450	692	517	174	139
				2,988	932	144,663	3,869	8,357	5,968	4,844	1,631	1,069
262	....	....	....	.....	......	4,43:	....	475	160	172	......	......
715	3-5 of 1%	....	....	270	.....	3,751	36	800	150	130	101	19
3,377	20 mills	....	....	374	......	30,000	7,500	1,455	343	438	276	85
3,120	24 mills	....	....	318	......	23,590	....	1,500	464	550	......	159
4,467	20 mills	....	....	574	.....	8,934	....	1,596	409	409	306	52
3,356	....	....	....	232	....	11,849	....	1,680	398	495	223	194
....	24 3-20 ms.	....	....	2,098	4,872	41,217	....	6,000	740	740	...	40
1,351	{ 14½ m. 2½%	....	....	1,276	......	21,073	....	5,273	855	855	608	155
19,427	24 mills	....	....	1,258	5,919	87,157	....	6,950	1,550	1,444	667	.....
243	12 mills	....	....	416	......	2,954	....	1,050	178	175	......	48
....	17⅖ to 20 m	....	....	248	......	8,898	....	1,600	320	335	275	53
5,350	20 mills	....	....	3,212	......	33,369	....	6,500	1,125	900	861	200
1,459	22¼ mills	....	....	......	......	3,880	....	541	177	74	.....	39
....	8 mills	....	....	......	......	2,355	....	....	149	183	89	.....
....	3-5 of 1%	....	....	....	......	1,145	....	1,535	189	166	.....	142
74,406	2%	....	....	......	14,082	395,099	17,289	26,133	5,000	9,100	3,190	1,000
2,005	....	....	....	......	.....	7,328	....	800	265	202	90	127
72,085	22 mills	....	....	3,188	10,180	327,338	3,851	20,821	3,113	3,948	.....	400
191,623				13,464	35,053	1,014,368	28,676	84,709	15,585	20,316	6,686	2,713

B. 1. URBAN—RECEIPTS

	Columbia	Cumberland	Grand Forks	Greenwood	Kamloops	Kaslo	Nanaimo
	$	$	$	$	$	$	$
Balance, 1901	946 03	39 66	449 66	829 01	3,786 71	1,777 25	17 83
Taxes	4,700 00	1,303 50	18,911 62	12,815 50	9,652 19	16,116 75	42,958 31
Licenses—							
1 Hotel and liquor	1,560 00	1,100 00	9,012 50	6,976 00	1,600 00	5,050 00	6,850 00
2 All other	125 00	501 25	1,912 04	1,285 50	1,755 00	1,137 50	2,663 50
Fees, fines, tolls, etc	39 00	22 75	2,550 50	2,797 62	1,425 55	884 50	1,232 30
Water rates	166 20		6,632 49	3,806 20	7,527 10	5,351 70	8,516 33
Electric light			6,632 50		9,056 44		
Interest and dividends— On Bank deposits							
" Sinking funds			410 96	203 90	489 63		1,026 50
" Taxes in arrears				165 71		1,249 88	667 57
Subsidies and refunds from Government on account of— 1 Schools			6,000 00				8,586 70
2 Administration of justice							
3 Any other grants (except loans)							511 11
Refunds of money loaned, etc					1,400 00 †	13 55	
Receipts from loans— Borrowed for current expenses	1,500 00			10,000 00			2,574 15
Borrowed from Sinking Fund							
Advanced by Treasurer							
Borrowed on Debentures (face value)— 1 Street and sidewalks			1,650 00				
2 Drainage							
Waterworks					38,610 00	116,250 00	
Electric light					10,395 00		
Other municipal works							
6 Aid to railways							
7 School purposes			9,000 00				
8 Other purposes			6,000 00				
Miscellaneous— Money from Sinking Fund to pay Debentures			1,312 53				
Premiums on Debentures sold							122 54
Poll tax							
Unpaid warrants							
Sale of lots and real estate						‡ 225 78	
All other sources		823 25		* 5,000 00		971 53	800 81
Total	9,036 23	3,790 41	70,474 80	43,879 44	85,697 62	149,028 44	76,527 65

* Forfeited by G. & P. Tramway Co. † Duty on water meters. ‡ Amount bid over and above taxes

PENITENTIARY, NEW WESTMINSTER.

ASYLUM FOR THE INSANE, NEW WESTMINSTER.

A THOMPSON RIVER INDIAN SPEARING FISH.

DOUGLAS LAKE INDIANS WASHING GOLD.

ENDING DECEMBER 31st, 1901.

Nelson	New Westm'r	Phoenix	Revel-stoke	Rossland	Sandon	Slocan	Trail	Vancouv'r	Vernon	Victoria
$	$	$	$	$	$	$	$	$	$	$
....	950 74	644 16	118 37	1,080 90	58 59	....	....	....	976 91	9,490 02
16,197 19	79,524 60	3,007 59	7,089 79	25,563 75	1,350 41	672 53	429 69	414,114 84	5,552 49	278,300 34
7,500 00	3,597 50	6,521 05	1,700 00	16,601 00	6,150 00	1,233 87	2,281 61	22,615 00	950 00	17,420 00
5,340 00	4,824 75	....	817 50	2,707 50	585 00	445 16	437 42	10,510 25	353 00	14,189 70
15,053 28	6,278 52	1,998 00	726 25	13,036 00	1,003 75	3 50	328 00	21,378 12	3 00	42,491 95
17,920 96	18,653 96	....	....	18,049 26	....	....	....	82,734 18	1,854 15	55,979 25
23,747 19	18,501 23	....	....	....	....	....	....	....	....	....
....	....	....	....	....	....	....	....	86 27	....	747 40
640 00	....	....	....	437 01	....	....	....	11,117 97	....	9,058 82
99 29	449 54	....	....	....	5 52	....	....	13,428 78	44 14	4,423 25
....	8,234 74	....	....	9,999 25	....	....	....	30,490 74	....	22,214 68
....	....	....	....	....	....	....	....	....	101 25	....
....	11,563 72	....	....	387 39	1,067 90	....	....	9,762 50	....	....
....	....	....	....	....	....	....	....	....	300 00	520 70
....	39,000 00	500 00	3,000 00	17,438 94	2,500 00	....	....	....	....	....
....	....	....	....	....	....	....	....	53,724 15	....	....
....	....	....	....	....	....	....	....	....	....	....
20,000 00	....	10,000 00	....	....	....	....	....	4,850 00	....	238,500 00
20,000 00	....	....	....	....	....	....	....	25,000 00	....	....
15,000 00	....	1,000 00	....	8,000 00	....	....	....	52,000 00	679 00	....
15,000 00	....	....	....	....	....	....	....	....	....	....
6,000 00	....	....	....	20,000 00	....	....	....	....	....	....
....	....	....	....	....	....	....	....	....	....	....
....	....	....	....	....	....	....	....	20,000 00	....	30,000 00
24,000 00	....	....	....	....	....	....	....	20,000 00	42 15	....
....	....	....	....	....	....	....	....	....	....	....
3,781 25	....	....	....	....	....	....	....	....	....	16 25
....	....	....	....	....	....	....	....	14,081 75	....	....
....	....	....	....	....	....	....	....	14,772 36	....	....
....	....	....	....	....	....	....	....	6,000 00	....	....
3,611 50	23,559 97	....	....	294 00	944 50	673 47	....	....	114 35	1,470 96
193,890 66	215,139 27	23,670 80	13,451 91	133,595 00	13,665 67	3,028 53	3,476 72	826,702 71	10,970 44	724,823 32

and costs at tax sale, and held in trust.

B. 2. URBAN—EXPENDITURE

	Columbia	Cumberland	Grand Forks	Greenwood	Kamloops	Kaslo	Nanaimo
	$	$	$	$	$	$	$
Municipal Government—							
1 Elections	46 90	22 50	60 00	....	74 40	91 20	138 25
2 Salaries, commissions, etc.	825 00	256 00	2,065 00	7,251 00	1,890 00	2,378 87	2,953 31
3 Printing, advertising, etc.	153 75	108 65	670 15	418 65	664 15	585 47	543 24
4 Insurance, heat, light, etc.	34 50	....	389 30	185 78	120 00	691 64	171 95
5 Water supply (maintenance)	281 87	....	....	339 94	4,587 60	2,122 12	3,261 56
6 Lighting streets	45 15	1,510 75	* 8,630 61	1,115 00	6,684 00	1,199 63	5,913 01
7 Fire protection	75 00	19 35	515 01	1,763 91	232 15	1,104 69	1,898 36
8 Police Protection	194 00	....	....	224 55	1,864 30	1,506 10	3,684 97
9 Law costs	120 00	25 00	2,623 19	40 00	140 60	....	113 10
10 Other expenditures of governm't.	88 89	....	736 23	988 20	627 60	376 79	2,763 11
Public Works—(Construction)							
Streets, bridges and parks	3,013 87	266 31	2,485 00	2,950 18	3,739 00	1,851 50	7,419 26
Sewers and drains	....	675 27	....	....	....	....	....
Water works	2,474 15	31 80	....	607 30	17,701 26	161 00	117,792 08
Electric lights	....	....	6,808 32	....	8,005 65	....	....
Building and other works	....	488 39	1,650 05	....	....	80 60	461 71
Schools	....	....	12,472 61	2,308 45	....	....	....
Board of Health (including salaries)	30 00	85 00	995 75	943 25	400 00	362 25	1,194 60
All charities	188 50	250 00	996 75	117 20	282 92	351 90	571 30
Administration of justice	....	....	† 3,376 10	....	....	524 98	500 00
School Board	....	....	....	....	....	510 00	16,642 18
Investments and Deposits—							
Sinking funds	302 25	....	5,901 45	6,288 92	4,150 00	....	15,000 00
Others	....	....	....	....	....	....	....
Bonded Debt—							
Debentures redeemed	....	....	....	....	....	....	....
1 Principal	....	....	7,063 67	....	....	9,733 34	....
2 Interest	240 00	....	....	4,416 00	3,087 50	2,131 94	4,434 44
Refund of money	....	36 25	....	....	....	....	8,113 49
Interest on loans	....	....	10,862 60	1,790 84	....	178 59	421 20
Miscellaneous	732 53	....	1,514 01	13,896 42	....	5,445 10	14,572 12
	8,846 36	3,775 27	69,815 65	45,645 59	54,251 13	31,387 71	208,563 24

* Including water supply maintenance. † Including police. ‡ Including sewers and drains.

ENDING DECEMBER 31st, 1901.

Nelson	New Westm'r	Phoenix	Revel-stoke	Ross-land	Sandon	Slocan	Trail	Vancouv'r	Vernon	Victoria
$	$	$	$	$	$	$	$	$	$	$
....	103 40	....	46 50	313 05	35 15	60 00	21 00	852 07	....	1,703 15
6,106 60	11,401 28	1,114 30	1,519 21	10,491 75	1,775 00	872 50	265 00	19,099 32	2,176 35	26,876 75
3,094 13	675 33	503 50	405 90	787 69	160 55	261 17	372 10	1,986 57	158 30	9,509 44
189 90	1,576 56	....	194 50	2,827 20	174 35	....	....	1,130 83	95 24	1,525 50
2,872 63	3,177 95	....	328 95	7,973 30	....	....	....	20,903 38	287 81	24,083 69
1,100 00	20,192 53	....	1,279 00	....	....	....	....	29,669 70	....	16,674 62
8,488 62	8,713 47	1,579 41	810 30	12,932 61	701 40	75 65	86 19	33,197 71	113 84	23,475 54
5,101 99	4,232 55	1,415 70	....	6,883 18	1,315 00	2 00	718 20	30,161 20	....	25,546 76
1,312 35	430 55	360 00	....	2,445 58	225 00	9 45	....	2,492 72	....	9,613 10
5,753 20	....	1,512 82	421 92	2,518 61	951 50	461 40	104 34	31,752 31	....	4,679 67
19,743 30	18,447 92	12,443 73	121 10	5,846 66	....	585 74	161 93	103,131 16	1,815 23	75,341 58
5,752 12	....	....	....	406 68	....	....	....	44,395 41	....	5,930 20
5,557 36	1,117 37	1,000 00	....	3,420 23	....	....	......	54,619 50	1,043 21	15,136 29
12,862 04	3,080 84	....	....	....	....	....	....	....	....	....
1,201 00	20,792 00	360 00	18 50	10,753 48	2,701 20	29 28	....	18,646 83	168 00	4,714 98
920 08	5,340 13	....	....	9,999 25	....	....	....	14,544 90	....	15,545 00
4,227 15	1,491 91	1,997 87	2,498 22	3,164 89	594 00	....	......	34,849 26	488 00	15,656 98
4,530 08	53 50	250 00	179 16	963 20	125 00	......	2000	2,789 13	180 00	6,555 95
900 00	914 90	300 00	2,173 26	1,500 00	350 00	....	26 50	2,119 83	132 25	2,520 00
....	19,522 76	....	....	....	....	....	462 40	93,406 18	....	57,188 00
6,939 75	100 00	....	527 99	9,002 63	....	....	....	53,724 15	425 62	38,866 79
....	1,089 26	....	....	....	....	....	....	11,117 97	....	....
....	100 00	....	....	....	....	....	....	....	....	....
....	....	....	....	....	....	....	......	32,459 02	....	....
....	14,562 30	....	1,075 00	....	900 00	....	....	103,549 92	2,150 00	95,352 52
76,672 87	38,000 00	....	....	....	2,500 00	....	....	2,590 61	....	....
14,772 93	647 30	....	198 92	2,393 61	52 50	20 16	35 67	....	109 90	....
5,892 56	38,689 31	....	841 07	....	398 11	229 74	....	2,205 52	1,139 35	18,361 00
193,990 66	214,653 12	22,837 33	12,657 50	94,623 60	12,958 76	2,607 09	2,273 33	745,395 20	10,483 10	494,857 51

C. 1. URBAN—Assets,

	Columbia	Cumberland	Grand Forks	Greenwood.	Kamloops	Kaslo	Nanaimo
	$	$	$	$	$	$	$
Cash in treasury	189 87	15 14	1,514 01	3,023 69	32,406 20	1,833 31	36 65
Taxes in arrears	566 40	120 40	14,331 62	23,031 07	1,994 80	8,137 50	11,020 64
Sinking funds	302 25		11,453 00	6,288 92	1,502 33		11,811 63
Other investments					7,400 00		18,000 00
Land (excluding parks, roads or other non-realizable assets)	300 00		3,000 00			2,428 00	5,550 98
Buildings, furniture, etc	250 00	677 00	5,100 00	10,955 86		9,984 38	3,966 80
School property (lands, buildings, etc)	2,000 00		17,500 00				6,600 00
Water Works	3,900 00		52,000 00	25,926 60	† 76,316 63	28,132 50	125,755 69
Fire Hall (and appliances)	400 00	1,100 00	12,000 00	5,216 39	1,000 00	3,631 45	13,895 65
Electric light (building and plant)			30,000 00				
Cemetery				3,966 19	1,717 28		
Any other assets			35,765 52	1,227 64	1,745 50	4,042 33	6,753 88
Total	7,908 52	1,912 54	182,664 15	79,636 36	124,082 74	58,189 47	203,592 52

C. 2. URBAN—Liabilities,

	Columbia	Cumberland	Grand Forks	Greenwood.	Kamloops	Kaslo	Nanaimo
Debentures, for							
1 Local improvements			28,479 78	39,000 00			
2 Water works		12 50		19,100 00	66,500 00	14,600 00	125,000 00
3 Electric light		38 65	* 80,000 00		25,500 00		
4 Municipal works	4,000 00	111 00	15,000 00	11,900 00		12,000 00	65,500 00
5 Aid to railways			‡ 41,000 00				
6 Schools			9,000 00				500 00
7 Other objects	5,000 00		25,000 00	3,600 00			4,500 00
School rates							
Interest coupons on debentures				2,352 35	1,489 60		
Due Sinking Funds				9,663 16		4,212 83	
Loans for current expenses	1,500 00			15,000 00			2,574 15
Interest due on loans				2,871 31			
Balance due Treasurer							
Other liabilities				19,767 97		1,678 81	80 00
Total	10,500 00	162 15	198,479 78	126,504 79	93,489 60	32,491 64	198,154 15

* Including water works. † Including electric light plant. ‡ Including subsidy to smelter, $30,000.

DECEMBER 31st, 1901.

Nelson	New Westm'r	Phoenix	Revel-stoke	Ross-land	Sandon	Slocan	Trail	Vancouver	Vernon	Victoria
$	$	$	$	$	$	$	$	$	$	$
1,983 07	585 72	193 44	925 07	650 65	706 91	...	1,203 39	41,286 19	381 52	230,065 18
17,101 02	91,964 93	579 85	3,764 06	11,022 94	4,973 49	419 92	20 00	123,081 06	664 21	59,675 84
20,299 25	31,858 21	...	527 99	21,900 04	...	...	...	285,562 76	1,562 22	258,792 15
2,111 70	80,784 47	1,000 00	...	...	332 50	...	...	...	682 83	...
5,000 00	103,507 29	...	1,000 00	6,000 00	...	...	...	...	1,264 56	...
4,009 47	27,847 47	525 00	...	7,243 56	4,897 64	126 49	90 00	‖ 196,400 00	353 00	‖ 418,875 00
920 08	68,572 58	...	...	...	...	...	...	393,800 00	...	178,950 00
85,299 85	472,159 42	...	...	104,381 95	...	...	...	1,060,000 00	37,662 07	822,815 69
9,186 05	24,353 35	1,566 91	4,961 50	34,267 27	2,423 45	75 65	1,861 00	76,600 00	2,557 88	35,860 00
617,260 06	133,536 31	...	...	...	...	...	...	...	233 78	81,000 00
...	...	...	...	4,948 46	...	...	...	15,000 00	171 00	47,410 00
6,154 47	7,160 39	...	...	1,329 95	12,440 24	...	125 00	5,500 00	40 00	...
213,791 02	1,042,330 14	3,865 20	11,578 62	191,744 82	25,774 23	622 06	3,299 39	2,197,230 01	45,573 07	2,133,443 86

DECEMBER 31st, 1901.

Nelson	New Westm'r	Phoenix	Revel-stoke	Ross-land	Sandon	Slocan	Trail	Vancouver	Vernon	Victoria
50,000 00	...	...	...	...	...	...	...	349,624 55	...	30,438 43
55,000 00	455,000 00	...	...	90,000 00	...	...	...	976,633 94	37,000 00	265,000 00
70,000 00	116,000 00	...	...	...	...	...	...	...	...	71,000 00
65,000 00	382,000 00	...	21,500 00	137,030 00	15,000 00	...	...	994,370 79	...	1,173,500 00
9,000 00	...	...	§3,000 00	...	...	...	...	...	...	...
...	...	...	...	...	...	...	...	302,292 63	...	115,000 00
21,000 00	94,200 00	...	...	...	...	...	...	66,045 60	5,000 00	493,000 00
...	2,978 64	...	...	...	...	...	...	...	...	...
...	...	...	...	...	450 00	...	...	...	...	1,982 50
1,800 00	...	...	839 99	...	...	...	...	...	...	...
...	5,000 00	500 00	3,000 00	46,533 71	...	...	...	...	...	...
...	...	...	...	...	...	...	...	...	...	...
...	...	...	...	...	...		...	...	...	...
21,444 90	14,006 89	11,000 00	...	...	2,347 93	673 47	581 15	14,772 36	682 83	10,310 29
298,244 90	1,069,185 53	11,500 00	28,339 99	273,533 71	17,797 93	673 47	581 15	2,703,739 87	42,682 83	2,160,231 22

§ Steamboat. ‖ Including lands.

C.—3. RURAL—Assets,

	Burnaby	Chilliwack	Coquitlam	Cowichan (North)	Delta	Kent	Langley
	$	$	$	$	$	$	$
Cash in Treasury..	3,994 59	667 92	901 03	130 73	4,055 20	804 19	981 95
Taxes in arrears....	11,153 30	3,433 86	6,574 60	611 33	12,983 43	1,358 93	7,670 79
Sinking Funds.....	5,032 00	9,000 00	1,309 70	....	6,566 23	....	....
Other investments..	....	476 56	455 00	....	10,300 00	....	....
Lands, exclusive of parks, roads, etc..	1,809 17	2,000 00	....	....	673 76	....	267 75
Bld'gs, furniture, etc.	1,752 35	1,539 30	1,000 00	800 00	3,123 00	802 25	1,170 00
Other assets	162 35	3,533 00	11 56	....	4,090 00	12 50	3,301 10
Total assets....	23,903 76	20,650 64	10,251 89	1,542 06	41,791 62	2,977 87	13,391 59

C.—4. RURAL—Liabilities

Debentures (princip'l only) Outstanding (face value) for							
1 Railways	....	....	....	....	....	....	....
2 Drainage & Dyk'g	....	13,000 00	....	....	102,924 79	....	....
3 All other objects..	3,500 00	6,000 00	20,000 00	....	....	....	....
Interest coupons on debentures due...	225 00	1,142 90	500 00	....	....	....	....
Due Sinking Funds.	....	1,789 82	....	....	....	....	....
Loans for current expenses (princp'l)	117 04	1,836 67	....	....	....	....	....
Interest due on current loans	....	....	....	....	....	....	....
Other liabilities.....	45 75	....	595 19	....	....	157 85	655 75
Total liabilities	3,887 79	23,769 39	21,095 19	....	102,924 79	157 85	655 75

DECEMBER 31st, 1901.

Maple Ridge	Matsqui	Mission	Richmond	Spallumcheen	Sumas	Surrey	Vancouv'r (North)	Vancouv'r (South)
$	$	$	$	$	$	$	$	$
37 25	1,384 72	174 99	5,732 24	31 08	10 01	1,514 79	2,007 32	628 92
2,372 21	6,823 58	2,765 39	42,281 80	514 29	986 27	7,209 39	15,758 40	4,717 80
....	....	....	35,398 20	....	....	10,049 94	4,176 47	8,046 25
....	1,197 44	....	....	277 00	....	....	11,844 48	....
750 00	....	....	1,200 00	100 00	847 05	6,720 33	2,637 20	4,032 30
1,000 00	1,908 23	....	2,980 00	25 00	56 00	860 00	164 00	....
95 00	45 00	200 50	1,628 00	64,082 64	388 83	4,785 26	4,666 25	....
4,254 46	11,358 97	3,140 88	89,220 24	65,030 01	2,288 16	31,139 71	41,254 12	17,425 27

DECEMBER 31st, 1901.

....	....	....	....	....	....	........*	60,000 00	....
....	....	....	8,000 00	....	....	2,500 00	....	....
....	1,110 52	....	100,000 00	....	....	....	12,000 00	35,000 00
....	....	....	....	....	....	750 00	2,413 35	875 00
....	....	....	....	....	....	....	....	....
....	....	....	....	....	....	....	....	....
....	....	....	....	....	....	....	....	....
36 56	....	250 00	1,400 00	64,000 00	79 68	1,450 05	1,951 62	405 00
36 56	1,110 52	250 00	109,400 00	64,000 00	79 68	4,700 05	76,364 97	36,280 00

* Roads and bridges.

RURAL MUNICIPALITIES.

RECEIPTS—Ending December 31st, 1901.	
Balance 31st December, 1900	$ 12,595 22
GROSS REVENUE TAXES	137,735 41
LICENSES—	
Liquor	4,945 00
Others	1,742 00
FEES, RENTS, FINES, &c.	10,653 41
INTEREST AND DIVIDENDS—	
1 Bank Deposits	53 55
2 Sinking Funds	3,443 73
3 Taxes in arrears	2,725 08
SUBSIDIES AND REFUNDS—	
Government	3,143 15
Money loaned or invested	90 30
RECEIPTS FROM LOANS—	
Current expense	19,933 71
Borrowed from Sinking Fund	4 351 40
BORROWED ON DEBENTURES—	
1 Drainage or dyking	
2 Aid to Railways	
3 Roads and Bridges	
4 Other purposes	12,000 00
MISCELLANEOUS—	
Money from Sinking Fund to pay Debentures	11,362 04
Premiums on Debentures sold	
All other sources	5,042 31
	$229,816 31

D–1	D–2	
$ 16,627 36	Burnaby	$ 12,632 77
16,165 56	Chilliwack	15,497 64
8,048 00	Coquitlam	7,153 66
5,049 65	Cowichan (North)	4,918 72
33,492 27	Delta	33,692 27
2,663 86	Kent	1,859 27
10,166 25	Langley	9,184 30
4,467 03	Maple Ridge	4,429 78
5,989 81	Matsqui	4,605 09
1,812 56	Mission	1,637 57
41,851 78	Richmond	36,119 54
5,006 75	Spallumcheen	4,975 67
3,482 05	Sumas	2,245 38
20,784 61	Surrey	16,722 82
32,721 05	Vancouver (N'th)	30,713 73
21,487 72	Vancouver (S'th)	20,858 80
$229,816 31		$207,247 01

EXPENDITURE ending December 31st, 1901.	
MUNICIPAL GOVERNMENT—	
1 Elections	$ 417 40
2 Salaries, etc.	15,034 15
3 Printing, etc.	2,373 97
4 Insurance, heat, light, etc.	694 18
5 Law Costs	4,692 63
6 Other expenditures of Gov't.	1,710 24
PUBLIC WORKS—Construction—	
1 Roads and Bridges	$ 15,798 82
2 Drainage and Dyking	40 00
3 Building and other works	548 24
PUBLIC WORKS—Maintenance—	
1 Roads and bridges	$ 48,882 62
2 Drainage and dyking	4,359 79
3 Building and other works	13,686 98
HEALTH	733 75
CHARITIES	1,473 67
INVESTMENTS AND DEPOSITS	5,653 95
SINKING FUND AND OTHER INVESTMENTS—	
1 Mortgages	7,800 00
2 Debentures	5,464 34
3 Loans and deposits	8,166 00
4 Other investments	7,231 50
BONDED AND TEMPORARY DEBT— Debentures redeemed—	
1 Principal	1,000 00
2 Interest	20,735 07
Refund of money borrowed	25,756 47
Interest or discount on loans	1,990 12
MISCELLANEOUS—	
Discount on debentures sold	1,500 00
Allowance on taxes	2,229 35
All other disbursements	9,273 77
	$207,247 01

THE CAMP, NEW WESTMINSTER, IN 1864.

NEW WESTMINSTER CITY TO-DAY.

BRIDAL VEIL FALLS, KAMLOOPS.

STAVE RIVER FALLS.

KICKING HORSE RIVER.

YALE CREEK FALLS.

LIST OF MUNICIPALITIES.

Name of Municipality	Date of Incorporation		Clerk	Address
	Month	Year		
(Rural)				
Burnaby.	Sept. 22	1892	W. J. Walker	New Westminster
*Chilliwack.	April 26	1873	S. A. Cawley	Chilliwack
Coquitlam	July 30	1891	John Smith	Westminster Junct.
*Delta	Nov. 10	1879	N. A. McDiarmid	Ladner
Dewdney	April 7	1892	Edwin Davies	Hatzic
Kent	Sept. 27	1894	Harry Fooks.	Agassiz
Langley	April 26	1873	R. J. Wark	Langley Prairie
*Maple Ridge	Sept. 12	1874	Ernest Wm. Beckett	Maple Ridge
Matsqui.	Dec. 1	1892	John Ball	Abbotsford
Mission	June 14	1892	Anthony M. Verchere	Mission City
North Cowichan	June 18	1873	James Norcross	Somenos
North Vancouver	Aug. 13	1891	Alex. Philip	Vancouver
*Richmond	Nov. 10	1879	Alfred B. Dixon	Terra Nova
South Vancouver.	April 13	1892	W. G. Walker	Vancouver
Spallumcheen	July 21	1892	Rich'd Stuart Pelly	Armstrong
Sumas	Jan. 7	1892	F. York	Upper Sumas
*Surrey.	Nov. 10	1879	E. M. Carncross	Cloverdale
Columbia	May 4	1899	J. A. McCallum	Columbia
Cumberland	Jan. 1	1898	L. W. Nunns	Cumberland
(Urban)				
Grand Forks	April 5	1897	W. B. Bower	Grand Forks
Greenwood	Aug. 12	1897	A. B. Taylor	Greenwood
Kamloops	July 1	1893	John J. Carment	Kamloops
Kaslo	Sept. 14	1893	A. W. Allen	Kaslo
Nanaimo	Dec. 24	1874	S. Gough	Nanaimo
Nelson	Mar. 18	1897	J. K. Strachan	Nelson
†New Westminster	July 16	1860	W. A. Duncan	New Westminster
Phoenix	Oct. 11	1900	D. McMillan	Phoenix
Rossland	Mar. 18	1897	W. McQueen	Rossland
Sandon	Jan. 1	1898	C. E. Lyons	Sandon
Slocan	June 1	1901	J. A. Foley	Slocan
Trail	June 14	1901	W. J. Devitt	Trail
‡Vancouver	May —	1886	Thos. F. McGuigan	Vancouver
§Victoria	Aug. 2	1862	W. J. Dowler	Victoria

*Letters patent of Chilliwack were surrendered and new letters patent issued in 1881 and again in 1883; those of Maple Ridge and Surrey in 1882; Richmond 1885, reincorporated 1892; Delta 1888.

†New Westminster was created a municipality by proclamation of Sir James Douglas July 16, 1860. Its limits were extended October 22, 1861, and made subject to the provisions of the Municipality Act of 1872. Letters patent were surrendered and new letters issued in 1881. A special charter of incorporation was obtained in 1887, which was amended in 1895.

‡Vancouver was incorporated by special act in 1886. The first by-law appointing officers (not dated) appeared in the B. C. Gazette, May 27, 1886. The act of incorporation was amended by the Legislature in 1887, 1889, 1890, 1891, 1892, 1893 and 1895.

§Victoria was created a municipality by ordinance, dated April 2, 1867, which repealed the original act of incorporation of 1862, and subsequently came under the provisions of the Municipality Act of 1872 on the 25th of June, 1873. The General Municipal Act, under which it is governed, has been amended from time to time.

Rossland, Nelson, Greenwood and Grand Forks were incorporated under a special act passed in 1897, entitled the "Speedy Incorporation Act."

Nicomen, Salt Spring Island and Wellington were municipalities which ceased to exist. Squamish was incorporated in 1892, but did not organize.

OUR INDIANS.

THE Indian of British Columbia is sui generis. He resembles the Plain Indian in nothing except the colour of the skin. The Coast tribes are the most diverse in this respect. These are heavy, thick-set, with broad face and large bodies and short legs. Their home is the canoe, and thus after ages have become physically adapted to their peculiar looking crafts, in the management of which they are exceedingly expert. Fish, in which the waters of the Coast abound, is their staple diet. As the tribes distribute themselves farther inland they more nearly reach the type of the tall, lithe, sinewy and aquiline-featured red man of the novel. Ethnologists are of the opinion that they are physically more nearly allied with the Mongoloids than with the latter, who may not even be their cousins many times removed. Their mental, moral and physical characteristics are quite distinct from the Sioux or the Blackfeet. The same is true of their language, their cult and their traditions. They are not the same in any respect.

The Indians of British Columbia are not Treaty Indians, and receive no annuities or assistance of any kind from the Dominion Government. In other words, they are self-sustaining; and while not models of domestic life or industry are, nevertheless, possessed of a superior civilization. Though not so picturesque, perhaps, as the Plain Indians they are, nevertheless, much more useful. They live on reserves, selected from the Crown lands of the Province. For a number of years, after their first contact with the white man, their numbers were seriously reduced, especially the tribes immediately on the Coast. The sudden change from old conditions, the contact with the whites, who introduced epidemic diseases, and other causes, produced the inevitable result; but now that the transition stage has almost been lived through and the "Siwash," as he is more familiarly termed, has become habituated to a new and modern life a healthy reaction has set in and he is actually showing a slight increase in numbers. While not under treaty regulations in this Province, the Indian is still a ward of the nation, he does not possess the right to vote, and while remaining in a tribal relationship is subject to certain disabilities of citizenship contained in the Indian Act. As to his present status, it is well described in the admirable report of Mr. Vowell, Superintendent of Indian Affairs of British Columbia, in his last Annual Report to the Department, from which the following extracts have been made :—

"RESOURCES AND OCCUPATIONS.—Coming under the scope of the above may be mentioned farming, gardening and working as farm-hands on the ranches of their white neighbours; stock-raising and employment as cowboys on many of the cattle ranges; logging on their own account and working in saw-mills; employment as trimmers on ships loading coal, for which they are paid from $3 to $5 a day; loading lumber on ships for export, at which they earn equally high wages; as fishermen, and at other employments around the canneries; fur-sealing on their own account, and as hunters on schooners owned by white men; curing salmon, halibut and other fish products for sale and for home consumption; as sectionmen on railways and labourers on Provincial roads; as deck-hands on steamers plying between different ports; as boatmen, packers, freighters, guides to hunters, miners and others; mining on their own account and for hire; hop-picking; dairying on their reserves; catching fish and procuring game in season, which they sell at different cities and towns; fruit-culture; poultry raising; making curios (mostly during the winter season), copied from ancient native models, for which they find a ready sale to tourists; building fishing boats and other kinds, also canoes for their own requirements and for sale; manufacturing dogfish and oulachon oil; working as carpenters, and in various capacities, chiefly in new towns springing up all over the province; cutting cordwood for sale to canneries and to steamboat owners on Crown lands; acting as interpreters; as lighthouse-keepers, and engaging from time to time in all such other desultory occupations wherefrom they expect to derive sufficient remuneration to recompense them for their labour. The Indian women, it may be remarked, are also money-earners to no inconsiderable extent, during the canning season and at the hop fields they find profitable employment; they engage extensively in the manufacture of baskets, which they dispose of profitably to tourists and others; they cure and dress deer and cariboo skins, out of which are made gloves and moccasins, and they frequently find a market for the dressed skins intact, they being useful for many purposes; mats from the inner bark of the cedar and of rags are also made, some of which are of an attractive and superior quality; they make their own and their children's clothing, being much assisted in the latter by sewing and knitting machines; they also gather large quantities of berries, which in some cases they sell among the white people, a major portion is, however, dried for winter use; in doing chores and laundry work for their white neighbours they also find considerable employment.

* * *

"Stock.—Where grazing lands and hay meadows are available, the cattle and horses owned by the Indians are steadily increasing, large sums being paid from time to time for imported stock of a superior breed. In many localities the native ponies are being sold off and cattle purchased in their stead. Sheep and pigs are also becoming more general among them, and, on account of their being easily managed and producing good returns, will be extensively raised in the future.

* * *

"In the Northwest Coast Agency the Indians own saw-mills and dogfish oil manufactories; they also have many stores, and have commenced in a small way to can salmon and clams; nearly all the trades are there carried on, such as carpenters, blacksmiths, painters, etc., etc., as well as many other different enterprises which are being started, and wholly managed by the advanced natives, with every reasonable prospect of an average measure of success. In other portions of this extensive superintendency may also be noticed many undertakings in the way of substantial progress by the wards of the Government who are steadily working their way towards independence and beginning to think that they are not only above the assistance of the Department, but altogether superior to advice or control, except, perhaps, when they get into difficulties."

CENSUS RETURNS OF RESIDENT AND NOMADIC INDIANS OF BRITISH COLUMBIA.

DENOMINATIONS TO WHICH THEY BELONG.

INDIANS	Census Returns	RELIGION						Under 6 years		From 6 to 15 years inclusive		From 16 to 20 yrs. inclusive		From 21 to 65 years inclusive		From 65 years upwards		No. Tribes.
		Anglican	Presbyterian	Methodist	Roman Catholic	Other Christian Beliefs	Pagan	Male	Female	Male	Female	Male	Female	Male	Female	Male	Female	
West Coast Agency........	2,414	.....	287	150	631	....	1,346	165	157	213	202	57	69	649	725	97	80	18
Fraser River Agency.......	2,865	73	....	158	2,582	....	52	283	284	240	241	105	101	697	697	117	100	46
Babine and Upper Skeena River Agency	2,898	592	....	288	1,792	129	97	169	169	253	276	155	155	794	808	65	54	27
Williams Lake Agency.....	1,985	19	....	......	1,966	....	.....	213	201	91	85	160	170	456	456	80	73	25
Northwest Coast Agency...	4,149	1,202	....	2,309	....	....	638	332	323	331	321	246	232	1,096	1,075	92	101	23
Kootenay Agency..........	562	.....	...	......	562	....	.....	57	56	52	44	22	25	130	138	21	17	5
Cowichan Agency	1,934	......	57	347	1,465	....	65	189	179	196	180	41	38	528	570	4	9	31
Kamloops-Okanagan Agc'y.	3,834	1,396	....	......	2,437	....	1	296	298	317	312	167	163	1,049	1,039	93	100	26
Kwawkewlth Agency......	1,359	662	....	96	......	....	601	111	92	65	77	38	14	471	401	29	61	16
Nomadic Indians (about)...	3,500	......	....	......	.....	....	.....	.....	... ..	.....	.....	....	....	.....	....	....	....	....
Grand total........	25,500	3,944	344	3,348	11,435	129	2,800	1,815	1,759	1,758	1,738	991	967	5,870	5,909	598	595	217

TOWNS AND CITIES.

IN the main the information contained in the following, which has been obtained from a variety of local sources, was prepared in 1902; but has been revised as far as possible to date. The object of this chapter, also contained in the edition of 1897, apart from general information, is to preserve a record of the various new places in British Columbia, many of which rise and fall as conditions in a new country change within a few years. Not a few of these enumerated and described are now mere memories of a former temporary activity.

AGASSIZ.

Agassiz, on the main line of the C. P. R., 71 miles east of Vancouver, is the site of the Dominion Government Experimental Farm. Besides all kinds of cereals, roots, fodder and plants that are under test, very many varieties of apples, pears, plums, cherries, peaches, apricots, grapes and all varieties of smaller fruits are under cultivation. Almonds, walnuts, filberts and chestnuts are also grown. Attention is paid to the raising of live stock at the farm, and in the district hop-growing is extensively carried on. Agassiz is a starting point for Harrison Hot Springs, which is reached by stage.

AINSWORTH.

Ainsworth is the oldest mining town in Kootenay, and is situated on Kootenay Lake. It has seen a great many ups and downs. In the mountain back of it are a number of silver-lead properties, which with either an advance in the cost of lead or a sufficiently reduced price of smelting would make it one of the busiest towns in Kootenay.

ALBERNI.

Alberni is at the head of Alberni Canal, some 52 miles from Nanaimo and 140 miles from Victoria, the boats from which arrive once a week. There are two sawmills located here, a shingle mill, two churches and three schools. The mines at Alberni, which for some time were in statu quo, have recently been more actively developed, and two or three have shipped ore. The principal quartz mines are the Golden Eagle, 18 miles from Alberni, yielding gold and copper; the Hayes mine, principally copper, 12 miles southwest of Alberni on the canal; and the Monitor, close to the Hayes. There are also important iron deposits on the canal, and several properties are being worked by the Pacific Steel Company. Alberni is divided into two parts—New Alberni and Old Alberni—which are about 2½ miles apart.

ALLISON.

Allison is a prospective town on the Similkameen River. From Hedley to about three miles below Allison the Valley of the Similkameen is from one to two miles wide, with fine stretches of bottom land and some splendid ranch property. The valley is well timbered, and there is good grazing ground on the benches.

ARGENTA.

Argenta is a stopping-place at the head of Kootenay Lake, from which a number of trails radiate to different mining properties.

ARMSTRONG.

Armstrong is situated 15 miles from Vernon on the Shuswap & Okanagan Railway, and has a population of about 350. It is the centre of the Spallumcheen municipality, and is surrounded by fertile, prosperous and a well-populated country. There is a large co-operative flour mill owned and successfully operated by the farmers. It is equipped in the most modern way. A creamery has been erected and is being operated, capable of handling the milk of 1,000 cows. There are also a sawmill, a fine new public school, a number of large business houses, town hall, and churches of the leading denominations. In the surrounding country farming generally is carried on, but principally grain-growing.

ASHCROFT.

Ashcroft is a town on the Canadian Pacific Railway, 205 miles east of Vancouver, in the Yale District. Its importance consists in its being the forwarding point to Cariboo, Clinton and Lillooet, via the Cariboo wagon road. The British Columbia Express Company have their headquarters there. The Ashcroft Journal, a mining and general newspaper, is published. It is the centre of the best grazing sections in the interior, and the cattle-shipping point of the Chilcotin, Cariboo and Lillooet grazing districts. It has electric light and water systems, owned by the Ashcroft Water & Electric Light Company. Population 500. It is also surrounded by large areas of agricultural land particularly adapted for fruit-growing.

ATLIN.

Atlin is situated on the east side of Atlin Lake, 140 miles from Skagway, and is reached via the White Pass Railway and lake steamer. It came into existence in 1898 as the result of the discovery of gold in Pine Creek, which has its rise in Surprise Lake and flows into Atlin Lake. It is prettily situated and an ideal location for a town, being on a rise gently sloping towards the lake and towards the meadows behind.

Atlin was the scene of great activity in 1899 and 1900, during which time there were, it is estimated, 10,000 people in the district, the present population of which is about 3,000.

The mineral characteristics and mining development are described elsewhere. The output for 1901 and 1902 increased considerably over previous years, and the outlook is most encouraging.

Hydraulic, placer and quartz mining are carried on. Valuable copper deposits are being developed on Copper Island, across the lake from Atlin, and also on the mainland just opposite Copper Island. Several free-milling properties have been partly developed, showing excellent results so far.

There are three large companies operating on McKee Creek, three on Spruce Creek, two on Pine Creek, one on Birch Creek, one on Boulder Creek, and one on Wright Creek.

Atlin is the official centre of the district, with three hundred houses, Government post office and telegraph office, a hospital, two churches and a school, three sawmills, a brewery, and several good hotels and business blocks.

BARKERVILLE.

Barkerville is situated on Williams Creek, 180 miles from Ashcroft, at the terminus of the Cariboo wagon road, being reached by the Express Company's stage once a week. Barkerville is an important mining town, and is the centre of a mineral district which is again rapidly coming into prominence. There is a population of about 300. There are several large companies operating on Williams Creek—the Cariboo Gold Fields, which has already expended over half a million dollars, and the First of May Mining Company. Large companies are also at work on Lowhee Creek and Stout's Gulch, within a short distance of the town. Barkerville has a fire department, a theatre and two churches.

BEAVERDELL.

Beaverdell is a new mining town, the centre of the new West Fork mining district. Its growth now depends upon railway communication to render available the rich mineral deposits of gold, copper, lead and silver existing there.

BENNETT.

Bennett is situated on Bennett Lake, on the route of the White Pass Railway, about 85 miles from Atlin. For a time it enjoyed considerable prosperity, but the extension of the railway to White Horse practically gave it a quietus. There is a good railway station and several hotels.

CAMP McKINNEY.

Camp McKinney lies about midway between Penticton and Greenwood, and is the oldest quartz mining camp in Southern British Columbia. The properties here are principally free gold producers, and several years ago there was a large amount of activity, a number of properties being developed on a large scale. Recently, however, very little has been done. The Cariboo Amelia group, which has been one of the large and steady dividend-payers from the first, is the principal property at present being operated.

CARIBOO CROSSING.

Cariboo Crossing is the point on the White Pass Railway where the steamers connect for and from Atlin. It is the point where the scows are built for the river trade, and M. King's large sawmills were located there. In summer 300 men have been employed in boat-building and in the sawmill.

CASCADE CITY.

Cascade City is situated near the international boundary, and occupies an attractive and advantageously-located town site. It has hotels, stores and several saw-mills. It is the natural market for the new mining country around Christina Lake, from whose waters it is but a mile distant. The Cascade Water Power & Light Company has its plant here, generating power for Boundary mines and smelters. During the construction of the Columbia & Western, Cascade City was an important point.

CHEMAINUS.

Chemainus, six miles from Ladysmith, is situated on the harbour of Chemainus, one of the best on the Coast. Here the Victoria Lumber and Manufacturing Co. has the largest saw-mills in the Province, doing solely an export business. It is also the terminus of a short line of railway built into the logging camps. Several miles from Chemainus are situated the Mount Sicker and Mount Brenton mines. The country in the immediate district, however, is very heavily timbered and here are found some of the finest trees in the Province.

CHILLIWACK.

Chilliwack is a thriving little town situated in the centre of the famous Fraser Valley, on the banks of the Fraser River, and is 50 miles east of New Westminster and about 30 miles west of Hope. The district of Chilliwack is distinctly a farming community, and all kinds of fruit, cereals and farm produce grow abundantly. It is also noted for stock-raising and dairying. A great many of the best and most successful farmers and fruit-growers of British Columbia have large, well-cleared farms and comfortable houses here. Fish and game abound, and it is a desirable resort for summer tourists.

Among other enterprises carried on here are two finely equipped and modern creameries and several hop-yards, both of which have been successful and remunerative. There are good trunk roads. Chilliwack is the supply point for the Mount Baker mining district, recently opened up.

CLINTON.

Clinton is a small village situated at the junction of the Cariboo wagon road from Ashcroft and the road from Lytton, Lillooet and Pavilion Mountain. Branch roads lead to the Fraser River from this point. It is the chief town of Lillooet District, containing the Government offices. It is surrounded by considerable farming and grazing lands, and from its altitude and scenery would make an ideal spot for health-seekers. There are a number of fishing lakes and trout streams contiguous to the village. In the fall it is headquarters for sportsmen in quest of feathered game and deer.

COMAPLIX.

Comaplix is a lumbering town, situated at the Northeast Arm of the Arrow Lakes. The principal sawmilling industry is operated by the Fred Robinson Lumber Company. There are very extensive timber areas in the vicinity. Population, about 200 in 1902. Comaplix is a supply point for the miners on Fish Creek.

CRANBROOK.

Outside of Fernie, Cranbrook is the principal town on the line of the Crow's Nest Pass Railway. It is most delightfully located on a fertile stretch of prairie in the valley between the Rocky and Selkirk Mountains, and has already become a centre of great importance. It is the chief divisional point on the Crow's Nest Pass Road, and has, besides the shops of the railway, a number of well-stocked stores, chartered banks, hotels, churches, schools, etc. It is the principal lumber manufacturing point in East Kootenay, having four saw-mills operating within its limits. A branch line of railway connects the North Star Mines and Kimberley with Cranbrook.

CRESTON.

Creston, on the Crow's Nest line of the C. P. R., 10 miles from Kootenay Landing, is in the midst of a good farming and grazing district, where fruit growing is being prosecuted with excellent results.

CROFTON.

Crofton is a new town beautifully situated on Osborne Bay, V. I., about 40 miles north of Victoria, on the east coast. It is named after Mr. Henry Croft, who founded it and who arranged that the Northwestern Smelting & Refining Co. should there erect a 400-ton smelter to treat ores from the Lenora-Mount Sicker mine, with the Mount Sicker district as a base of supply. A narrow-gauge railway connects the town with Mount Sicker and Westholme, on the Esquimalt & Nanaimo Railway, and a stage runs from the latter place. Telephonic communication can be made with Victoria. Owing to the closing down of the smelter and the Lenora mine, Crofton suffered a period of depression for a time, but the smelter and mines are again fully in operation.

DEADWOOD.

Deadwood is two miles west of Greenwood. It has two hotels, store, saw-mill, public school, etc., and is in proximity to the Mother Lode, Sunset, Morrison, King Solomon, Big Copper and other mines.

DISCOVERY.

Discovery is a mining town on Pine Creek, seven miles east of Atlin, built on the site of discovery claim. It has a population of about 300 and has a post office, a church and school, and several hotels and business buildings.

DUNCAN.

Duncan, on the E. & N. Railway, 50 miles north of Victoria, is a substantial business place, which is gradually assuming the importance of a county town, deriving its business from the neighbouring farming community and the mines of Mount Sicker and Brenton. The Cowichan creamery at Duncan is famed for the quality of its product. Duncan is a rendezvous for sportsmen, being the centre of a fine fishing and hunting district. Duncan is also the centre of a community, the population of which is largely drawn from Great Britain, and particularly from England.

EHOLT.

Eholt is a small town on the Columbia & Western Railway extension of the C. P. R. at Eholt Summit, about nine miles east of Greenwood. It was started in 1899 as the result of the construction of the Columbia & Western, and is the point of shipment for the Summit and Phoenix camps, which are reached from this point by a spur line of railway. There are two sawmills near Eholt.

ELKO.

Elko is situated at Elk River Falls, at the junction of the two railways, 18 miles north of Fernie. There is a fine water-power here, suitable for carrying on large industries, and there is also considerable agricultural land in the vicinity.

ENDERBY.

Enderby is situated about 23 miles from Sicamous Junction, and has a population of about 250. At this point is located one of the most modern roller flour mills in Canada, owned by R. P. Rithet & Co., Limited. It has a capacity of 250 barrels per day, and does an extensive business.

The same general remarks made with regard to Armstrong apply equally—almost identically—to Enderby, with the exception that there is no creamery here. Hogs, hay and grain are the principal products of the farming community here, as throughout the Okanagan District as a whole. Spallumcheen River intersects the town.

CHIEF JOHN AND HIS SON—HAIDAS.

A CHILLIWHACK CHIEFTIAN
(A Fine Type).

TAL-TAN (NORTHERN INTERIOR) INDIANS IN CEREMONIAL DRESS.

TWO TAL-TAN CHIEFS IN FULL DRESS.

ESQUIMALT.

Esquimalt, three miles from Victoria, is the naval station for His Majesty's ships on the Pacific Coast, where a dry dock and marine railway have been built and extensive fortifications erected. It is rather a quaint old village, and is one of the points for sight-seers visiting Victoria. The harbour is one of the finest on the Coast.

FAIRVIEW.

Fairview is a mining camp a few miles from Penticton, which has had its ups and downs of recent years, but which is now once more on the up grade, with prospects of a good future. A large amount of capital has been invested in the mines in the vicinity by the Fairview Corporation, the properties of which embrace coal lands, townsites and quartz mines. A 48-stamp mill is at work on the Stemwinder, the principal property of the district, the showings of ore in which are said to be enormous. Population, about 300.

FERGUSON.

Ferguson is situated on the Lardeau River, four miles from Trout Lake, 26 miles from Arrowhead and 54 miles from Revelstoke. It is the centre of the rich mining district of Trout Lake, commonly known as the Lardeau. A numb r of important shipping mines are tributary to this town. Among these are the Silver Cup, sold for $150,000 cash; the Nettie L. and the Triune, sold for $600,000. These are exceptionally rich in silver and lead. A branch line of railway from Kootenay Lake to Trout Lake, 35 miles in length, has recently been completed. This gives the district the necessary transportation facilities so long required. The population is about 400. The Lardeau Eagle is published. Five hotels serve the public. A 30-ton vulcan smelter has been erected to treat local ores.

FIELD.

At Field is a charming chalet hotel managed by the railway company—the Mt. Stephen House—not far from the base of Mt. Stephen, which rises 10,450 feet above the sea level and facing Mt. Burgess. This is a favorite stopping place for tourists, and has been recently enlarged to meet the wants of increased travel. Field is the portal to the wonderful Yoho Valley, whose Takakkaw Falls, with a sheer drop of 1.200 feet, and the Twin and Laughing Falls are but three of a number of glacier-fed cataracts. There are immense glaciers rivalling the Illecillewaet of the Selkirks in vastness, and a remarkable canyon whose vertical walls are from 200 to 300 feet high. Trails head along the mountains' sides and through the valley, and shelters are being erected for the convenience of visitors to this new wonderland. North of Yoho Valley are some of the highest peaks of the Rockies, rising 12,000 to 13,000 feet above the sea level. En route to the valley there is a natural bridge, and Emerald Lake, 7 miles from Field, is one of the most charming of the mountain waters. Here a comfortable chalet has been erected by the railway company. On the shoulder of Mount Stephen, is a fossil bed, rich in rare specimens of trilobite. During the summer Swiss guides are also stationed here to accompany tourists and mountain climbers. Looking down the valley from the hotel, the Van Horne range is seen on the right.—Annotated Time-table C. P. R.

FORT STEELE.

Fort Steele is the present judicial centre of East Kootenay. It is situated on the Kootenay River, 180 miles from Golden, 12 miles from Cranbrook, and 8 miles from Fort Steele Junction. It is about 90 miles from the Crow's Nest Pass. The Fort Steele Prospector, the pioneer newspaper of the district, is published. A steamer also runs daily from Tobacco Plains, where connection is made with the Crow's Nest Southern. It is in the centre of a mining district of considerab'e prominence; and the North Star mine, one of the principal properties of East Kootenay, is in the vicinity. A smelter has been built at Marysville, on the North Star branch, 16 miles from Cranbrook, to smelt lead ores.

GERRARD.

Gerrard, at the south end of Trout Lake, is a distributing point for the Trout Lake mining division, and the present northern terminus of the Kootenay & Arrowhead Railway.

GLACIER HOUSE.

Glacier House, on the C. P. R., is within thirty minutes' walk of the Great Glacier, from which, at the left, Sir Donald rises a naked and abrupt pyramid, to a height of a mile and a quarter above the railway. This stately monolith was named after Sir Donald Smith (now Lord Strathcona and Mount Royal), one of the chief promoters of the Canadian Pacific Railway. Farther to the left, looking from the hotel, are two or three sharp peaks, second only to Sir Donald. Roger's Pass and the snowy mountain beyond (a member of the Hermit range, which is called Grizzly, from the frequency with which bears are met upon its berry-bearing slopes) are in full view. Again to the left comes Cheops, and in the foreground, and far down among the trees, the Illecillewaet glistens. Somewhat at the left of Cheops the shoulders of Ross Peak are visible over the wooded slope of the mountain behind the hotel. The hotel is a handsome structure resembling a Swiss chalet, which serves not only as a dining station for passing trains, but affords a most delightful stopping place for tourists who wish to hunt, or explore the surrounding mountains or glaciers. The Great Glacier is exactly a mile and a half away, and its slowly receding forefoot is only a few hundred feet above the level of the hotel. Swiss guides are stationed here during the summer months, this being a favorite resort of mountaineers. Game is very abundant throughout these lofty ranges. Their summits are the home of the mountain goat, which are seldom found southward of Canada. Bears can also be obtained.—Annotated Time-table C.P.R.

GLENORA.

Glenora, on the Stikine River, at the head of navigation, was a point of prominence while the Cassiar Central and Mackenzie & Mann's Yukon Railway were in prospect, but is now practically deserted. There is a Hudson's Bay Company's store, and several small buildings are still there.

GOLDEN.

Golden is situated in the valley of the Upper Columbia River, at its junction with the Kicking Horse River. The town derives its importance from the fact that it is the headquarters of navigation on the Upper Columbia River, and also the supply point for the country extending along the Columbia and Kootenay valleys.

A great deal of lumber is exported annually from Golden, Beaver and Palliser, at which places sawmills are established.

Mining is assuming extensive proportions, and great activity was for a time displayed in the development of the ore deposits in the McMurdo District, Cariboo, Bugaboo Basin, and at Ottertail, in the Kicking Horse Canyon. The recorder's office for the Golden Mining District is located in the town, and contains a large and fine collection of specimens of the mineral ores of the district.

Agriculture is carried on along the Columbia Valley. The breeding of horses and cattle-raising are pursuits followed by a large number of settlers. Fishing, shooting and boating are available pastimes, the large sloughs on the Columbia River north of this town affording excellent facilities for canoeing and boating. The present population of Golden is 500.

GRAND FORKS.

Grand Forks is a city of which the Province and Canada have heard much during the past few years in connection with the development and progress of the Boundary country. It is situated at the junction of the North and South Forks of the Kettle River, two miles from the international boundary line, in a beautifully picturesque valley, 22 miles east of Greenwood. The valley of the Kettle River at this point is over 20 miles long, with an average width of three miles, representing an area of over 40,000 acres, a large portion of which is fertile and eminently adapted for the production of grain, fruit and vegetables and cattle-raising. Much attention has been attracted to it recently for residential and farming purposes. The city owns its waterworks and electric light plant, and has several fine hotels. One of the important adjuncts of the city is the smelter of the Granby Consolidated Company, which owns and operates extensive mining properties in the Boundary District, notably the Knob Hill and Old Ironsides mines. This smelter has a present capacity of 2,000 tons of ore per day, and its success has done much to establish the reputation of the Boundary country as a mining district, and contributed largely to its prosperity. There are at present three lines of railway leading to and through Grand Forks, viz.: The Columbia & Western, from Robson to Midway, being part of the C. P. R. line; the Kettle River Valley lines, from Republic to Grand Forks; and the Victoria, Vancouver & Eastern, being an extension of the Great Northern system from Marcus via Grand Forks to Republic. Grand Forks is a port of entry, and has a mining recorder's office, three large sawmills, two breweries, churches, public schools, etc. Population, 1,500.

GREENWOOD.

Greenwood is one of the many prominent towns which have sprung up in the midst of newly-discovered mining camps, situated on Boundary Creek where Twin

Creek joins it, some nine miles from its mouth. Its growth during the years 1897, 1898, 1899 and 1900 was very rapid and substantial. The Boundary Creek Times is published at Greenwood. The success of the town is dependent upon the development of rich and varied mineral resources of Central, Wellington, Skylark, Providence, Summit, Long Lake, Kimberley, Pass Creek, Deadwood, Copper, Smith's and Graham Camps, which encircle the town and none of which are at a greater distance than nine miles. All the camps are at a higher altitude than Greenwood, so that the ores can be hauled down hill on an easy grade. An ample supply of water and water-power for smelting and other purposes can be secured from Boundary Creek or any of its numerous tributaries. Two smelters have been erected and are in operation—one at Greenwood and the other at Boundary Falls, a short distance below it on Boundary Creek. The route for the Columbia & Western is through the Boundary Creek valley, and the road is constructed through it as far as Midway, nine miles further. Greenwood is reached from the west by tri-weekly stages from Penticton, a distance of 83 miles. Greenwood is pleasantly situated between hills; stands about 2,400 feet above the sea-level, and in summer is, climatically, a delightful spot to live in, while the winters are not sufficiently severe to prevent mining operations being carried on at all seasons of the year.

HALCYON HOT SPRINGS.

Halcyon Hot Springs, on Upper Arrow Lake, twelve miles from Arrowhead, is a favorite health resort, the waters of the springs having peculiar curative properties. A fine hotel and cottages for visitors are erected here.

HARPER'S CAMP.

Forty-five miles from Quesnel Forks is what is known as Harper's Camp, on the Horsefly River, where are located Senator Campbell's Miocene claim and the Ward Company's claim, operated by a hydraulic lift. At the headwaters of the Horsefly were the new discoveries made in the fall of 1901, the value and extent of which were never definitely ascertained.

HARRISON HOT SPRINGS.

Harrison Hot Springs, a health resort, is situated on Harrison Lake, five miles from Agassiz, on the main line of the Canadian Pacific Railway. It obtains its name from the mineral springs existing there, to which a large number of persons go for treatment. The Harrison Hot Springs Hotel is located on the lake. The situation altogether is picturesque as well as healthful, and good fishing is available. A new mineral district is being opened up north of this lake.

HEDLEY.

Hedley City, on Twenty-Mile Creek, near Similkameen River, is another mining camp which has recently sprung into existence owing to the promising character of the mines in the vicinity. It is situated on the proposed line of the Victoria, Vancouver & Eastern Railway.

KAMLOOPS.

Kamloops is the oldest city of any commercial importance in the interior of the province. It is charmingly situated at the junction of the North and South Thompson Rivers, on the line of the Canadian Pacific Railway, in the district of Yale, 250 miles from the Pacific seaboard at Vancouver. More than 80 years ago the Hudson's Bay Company established a trading post here, and around this gradually clustered a population which carried on a very widespread commerce throughout the interior. Kamloops (which is the Indian word signifying "the meeting of the waters") was the outfitting place for the adventurous miner and trapper; and the splendid pasturage afforded by the table lands and valleys for many miles around early attracted people to the business of cattle-raising. Ranching, mining, trading and trapping were the industries which first gave Kamloops its start, and it is the progress being made in these industries, but chiefly in that of mining, which is now advancing the prosperity of Kamloops.

The completion through the mountains to Eastern Canada in 1886 of the Canadian Pacific Railway ushered in a new era in the progress of this thriving city, and its growth from that time has continued steadily. In 1896 gold-copper ores were discovered on Coal Hill, about four miles south of the city, and development of one of the principal claims has demonstrated the existence of prominent ore bodies and a promising mine.

The cattle ranges adjacent and tributary to Kamloops are very extensive, and give pasturage from year to year to about 40,000 head of cattle. About 10,000 head are sent to market each year. Agriculture in the vicinity of the city is carried on by irrigation, and wherever water can be obtained, fine crops of fruit, grain, hops, vegetables, etc., are raised, for which good prices are obtained.

Ten years ago the city of Kamloops was incorporated. The city has put in a system of electric lighting and waterworks, assuring at all times a wholesome and copious supply of water for domestic purposes and an efficient protection from fire.

One of the most delightful features of this city is the fine climate with which it is blessed. Sunshine is the prevailing condition the year around; there is very little wet weather; the winters are mild and not of long duration, and the spring, summer and fall seasons charming. The remarkable salubrity of the climate has made Kamloops a favorite health resort.

Kamloops is well supplied with stores of general merchandise, lumber mills, schools and churches of nearly all denominations; and very many of the citizens have supplied themselves with residences of comfortable and pretty design. At Kamloops the Inland Sentinel and Standard are published. The population of Kamloops is about 1,600. The city is the seat of government for the great Yale District. The Court House and Jail are located here, as well as the land and registry offices of both Dominion and Provincial Governments. There are steamboats plying on the waters of the North and South Thompson Rivers, and in these waters also is to be found as good trout-fishing as is to be had in British Columbia. In season, grouse, duck, chicken and deer are plentiful, so that the angler and hunter are here favored with good sport in a good climate.

KASLO.

The city of Kaslo is situated on the west side of Lake Kootenay, 60 miles north from the international boundary line, and 78 miles southeast from Revelstoke, on the main line of the Canadian Pacific Railway, and has been incorporated about ten years; population, 1,680. It has a splendid water supply by gravitation from Kaslo Creek, and good fire protection. The waterworks cost $28,000. Kaslo is the central distributing point for the Slocan mines, a large number of shipping mines being tributary to it. These may be worked all the year round, and at very little expense. The development work is very considerable, and still increasing. Splendidly equipped steamers run on the lake, making connection with the through trains on the C. P. R., N. P. R. and Great Northern. The Kaslo & Slocan Railway (Robert Irving, general traffic manager) runs daily trains between Kaslo and Sandon, distance 29 miles, where connection is made with the C. P. R. system to Nakusp. The International Trading & Navigation Company's steamers International and Alberta and the Kaslo run daily between Kaslo and Nelson, and make connection with Five-Mile Point and the various transcontinental railways to the United States, calling at way ports such as Balfour, Ainsworth, Pilot Bay and Proctor. The steamer Kokanee, of the C. P. R., also makes daily trips to and from Nelson. Other steamers ply on the lake to Bonner's Ferry, Lardeau, Argenta and Duncan River districts.

Kaslo has a beautiful situation on a flat plateau on the lake front. There are numerous fine buildings (chiefly wooden frame), churches, school-house, public offices, sawmill (capacity 40,000 feet per day), planing mill, sash and door factory, ore sampling works, brewery and bottling works, a bank, electric light works, and numerous stores for miners' supplies, etc. Kaslo has one newspaper, the Kootenaian. It is conceded that Kaslo is a good point for the smelting of Slocan and Duncan River lead ores, and the city is offering $50,000 bonus for the erection of a plant of 200 tons daily capacity.

KELOWNA.

Kelowna is situated on the east side of Okanagan Lake, 35 miles from the terminus of the Shuswap & Okanagan Railway, and has a daily service with the fine C. P. R. boats running alternately from north to south as far as Penticton. Kelowna has a sawmill, sash and door factory, a cigar factory in which are manufactured cigars from local-grown tobacco, and a pork-packing establishment. The business of the place is largely carried on by the Kelowna Shippers' Union, which includes among other things evaporated fruits. Kelowna is the centre of the fertile Mission Valley, which is essentially a fruit-growing district, although mixed farming is carried on as well. It may be remarked here that the products of the whole Okanagan Valley find a market principally in the Kootenays and in the Northwest; fruit only, however, is shipped to the latter.

KEREMEOS.

Keremeos is situated about 35 miles southwesterly of Penticton. It is purely a mining camp. The Ollalla Mining Company is operating here, and the Nickel Plate, a large and rich mining property, in which the late Marcus Daly was interested, is situated near it, between Keremeos and Penticton.

KIMBERLEY.

Kimberley is the terminus of the North Star branch of the Crow's Nest Railway, and is 20 miles from Cranbrook. Near Kimberley are located the celebrated North Star and Sullivan mines, two of the largest silver properties in British Columbia, to smelt the ores of which a large plant was erected at Marysville, a few miles away.

KITCHENER.

Kitchener, on the Crow's Nest line of the C. P. R., 27 miles from Kootenay Landing, near which iron ore deposits are being developed, is on account of the prospective iron industry there likely to be a place of some importance in the future.

LADNER.

Ladner's Landing, a town on the south bank of the Fraser River, four miles from its mouth, is the business centre of Delta Municipality, one of the best agricultural districts of the province. It is largely prairie land and extremely fertile. There are also a number of salmon canneries in the vicinity, and steamers from Victoria and Vancouver to New Westminster and up-river points call regularly.

LADYSMITH.

Ladysmith is a small but thriving seaport at the entrance of Oyster Harbor, 14 miles south of Nanaimo and five miles north of Chemainus. The place took its name from the famous town in Natal, which had been relieved after the memorable siege just about the time that its western namesake was taking shape. The streets in the British Columbia Ladysmith are all named after the celebrated generals who took part in the war, and an eminence at the northwest of the town is called Spion Kop; on the summit has been built a handsome public school. Ladysmith was called into existence by the need of the Wellington Colliery Company for a port from which to export their coal, and upon the site selected stands the busy and progressive seaport of Ladysmith. The company erected a first-class system of coal bunkers and coal-shipping wharves. The facilities at those wharves for giving quick despatch to the largest vessels are unrivalled in this country. It is the point, too, at which the C. P. R. cars are received from the Mainland ferry and sent north and south. Amongst the industries may be mentioned the Tyee Copper Company's large smelter, completed in September last; an iron foundry; the Ladysmith Lumber Company's extensive yards. Ladysmith is the centre of Newcastle distrct, and County and Licensing Courts are held there at regular intervals. The Recorder, a weekly newspaper, is published in the place. With the increased development of the great coal areas at Wellington, Extension and nearer, and of the metalliferous deposits in the adjacent mountains, Ladysmith has fair prospects of attaining to considerable importance.

LARDEAU.

Lardeau is situated at the mouth of Duncan River, and is the Kootenay Lake terminus of the Arrowhead and Kootenay Railway, which has been completed to Trout Lake, a distance of 35 miles. Population, about 100. The C. P. R. lime quarries, which supply the Trail and Hall Mines smelters, are situated here.

LILLOOET.

Lillooet is situated 49 miles from the C. P. R. at the town of Lytton, near the junction of Cayoose Creek and the Fraser River, on the west bank. It is the supply depot for the quartz mining district of Bridge River, and the outfitting point for big game parties in pursuit of grizzly, deer and bighorn. The Mining Recorder's office is located at Lillooet, and considerable business is done in the purchase of placer gold, mined from the adjacent creeks.

LUMBY.

Lumby is a thriving little town 16 miles east of Vernon, the centre of a prosperous agricultural district. It has a population of about 100. A sawmill is located here, and steps are being taken to put in an electric tram line from Vernon. A number of French-Canadians reside in this vicinity, and are among the most thriving and industrious of the population.

MARYSVILLE.

Marysville is the site of a smelter, built in connection with the Sullivan group of mines, and is 14 miles from Cranbrook, from which it is reached by railway.

MICHEL.

Michel is a coal mining camp, the proposed terminus of the Crow's Nest Southern Railway. One of the largest mines of the Crow's Nest Coal Company is being operated here, and a number of coke ovens have been built. The population is 700.

MIDWAY.

Midway is a town near the international boundary, in Yale, 28 miles distant from Osoyoos. It is beautifully situated in one of the most picturesque valleys of the southern interior, on the Kettle River, and is in the centre of a farming and mining district. It is the present terminus of the Columbia & Western Railway, and is connected by stage with the points west and north of it.

MISSION CITY.

Mission City is a C. P. R. junction point with its Mission branch connecting with the American system. It is 43 miles from Vancouver, on the north side of the Fraser, and has a large area of farming lands tributary to it, which are also well adapted for fruit-growing. The Pitt Meadows, which include 40,000 acres of bottom lands being reclaimed by dyking, are contiguous to the town. Near Mission City is located a convent conducted by Sisters of St. Ann.

MORRISSEY.

Morrissey is a mining town about nine miles south of Fernie, on Morrissey Creek. It is a coal mining camp, the operations here being a branch of the Crow's Nest Coal Company's general works. At this point is located one of the finest outcroppings in the whole Crow's Nest coal fields; and the Dominion Government have selected in this district their coal areas. The Crow's Nest Coal Company are building a large number of coke ovens here for the supply of the smelters. The population is between 300 and 400.

MOUNT SICKER.

Mount Sicker, situated near the summit of the mountain of that name, and about 53 miles from Victoria, and several miles from Chemainus, is a flourishing mining camp. It has a good school-house, an hotel and several general stores. It is the headquarters of the Lenora, Tyee, Copper Canyon, Richard III., and other mines. The Mount Sicker Railway connects the town with Westholme and Crofton, and there is a daily stage service to Duncan, the county town of Cowichan district.

MOYIE.

Moyie is a mining town on Moyie Lake, where the largest silver mine in North America is situated. Population, 500. Concentrator; mine fully developed.

NAKUSP.

Nakusp, near the foot of Upper Arrow Lake, is the initial point of the Nakusp & Slocan branch of the Canadian Pacific Railway. It is prettily situated, and has a shipyard, at which the fine steamers plying on the Columbia River and Arrow Lakes are constructed. A large saw-mill is in operation.

NANAIMO.

Coal was discovered at this point in the year 1850, and two years later the Hudson's Bay Company transferred their workmen from Fort Rupert to Nanaimo. At that time the old "Bastion" was erected, which is yet a prominent landmark, and is about the first item of interest to attract the eye of the visitor. From the start Nanaimo assumed an importance peculiarly its own as the centre and chief point of the coal mining industry of British Columbia. Mining operations are carried on by the New Vancouver Coal Mining & Land Company, recently bought out by the Western Fuel Company, and a large number of men are employed; in these mines Asiatic labor is not utilized. This Company was the successor of the Vancouver Coal Company, which purchased its property from the Hudson's Bay Company.

The Nanaimo Sawmill and Factory, owned by Mr. A. Haslam, is modern in all its appointments, and gives employment to quite a large number of men. The city possesses a shoe factory, water works (now owned by the municipality), electric light, telephone system, gas works, etc.

Nanaimo was incorporated as a municipality in the year 1874, since which time it has gradually increased in importance and population until at the last census the population was given at 6,130, besides a large number of people who reside in the Five Acre Lots, just outside the corporate limits. The city is well supplied with graded and high schools, with an efficient staff of teachers. The Episcopal, Methodist, Presbyterian, Baptist and Roman Catholic churches are represented with commodious edifices. Communication is had with Victoria, 72 miles distant, by the Esquimalt & Nanaimo Railway, and by steamer with Vancouver, 35 miles distant, the service being daily in both instances. It is also connected by steamer with Comox on the one side and Sidney on the other, and the various points intermediate. It is favourably situated for the growing of fruits, and farming is carried on to a considerable extent in the city and vicinity.

NELSON.

Nelson became a trading point in 1887 through the discovery of the Hall mines in the fall of 1886. Its growth was continuous, if not rapid, and it became an incorporated city in April, 1897. It has a population of 5,500, and is the third city in the province in commercial importance.

It is situated on the West Arm of Kootenay Lake, 20 miles southwest of Kootenay Lake, and is connected by railways and steamboats with Rossland, Trail, Grand Forks, Phoenix, Greenwood, Kaslo, Sandon, Cranbrook, Fernie and all the important towns and mining camps in the southeastern portion of the province. The main line of the Canadian Pacific, at Revelstoke, is reached by travelling 56 miles on railways and 130 miles on steamboats; the Crow's Nest branch of the Canadian Pacific is reached by travelling 55 miles on steamboats; the Great Northern, the Northern Pacific and the Union Pacific Railway systems are reached, within 200 miles, at Spokane, Washington, over the Nelson & Fort Sheppard Railway and connecting roads.

The Land Registry Office for both East and West Kootenay is at Nelson; the office of the Inspector of all Government Offices in the province is at Nelson, as are the offices of the District Chief of Provincial Constables, Timber Inspector, Mines Inspector, Steam Boiler Inspector, and Public Schools Inspector. Four chartered banks have branches in Nelson, and a number of wholesale houses and manufacturing industries do a prosperous business. The city owns it own electric lighting and water works, has graded and macadamized streets, and several miles of sewers. The British Electric Traction Company, of London, England, operate an electric street car system; and the Hall Mines Company operate lead and copper smelting works.

The Daily News, Weekly Tribune and Weekly Economist are the newspaper publications. The Presbyterians, Methodists, Baptists, Congregationalists, Episcopalians, Roman Catholics and Salvation Army have churches.

There are a number of military and athletic organizations, and last year (1902) the annual regatta of the North Pacific Coast Amateur Rowing Association took place at Nelson, over the finest and longest straight-away course in British Columbia.

Among other mines in the immediate vicinity of Nelson is the famous Ymir mine, which paid regular dividends at the rate of 25 per cent. per annum on a capital of $1,000,000.

NEW DENVER.

New Denver is an important town on the east side of Slocan Lake, at the mouth of Carpenter Creek. It is nine miles from Sandon and about 40 miles west of Kaslo, and 22 miles north of Slocan City. Steamer accommodation is had daily to Roseberry, Silverton and Slocan City. There are a number of mining properties in the vicinity. The New Denver Ledge, a characteristic mining paper, is its journalistic exponent. The Canadian Pacific Railway branch from Nakusp passes close to the city. New Denver is beautifully situated on the lake, and is a residential centre and local watering place.

NEW WESTMINSTER.

The particulars regarding the founding and early growth of the City of New Westminster are familiar to B.C. readers, and it will not be necessary to refer at length to its history and development. It was founded in 1859. Its commanding situation on the north bank of the Fraser was the reason for its being selected as the capital of the colony of British Columbia. The city is 16 miles from the Gulf of Georgia, 75 miles from Victoria, and 12 miles in a direct line from Vancouver City, on Burrard Inlet. By the census of 1901 it possessed a population of 6,500 inhabitants, and for practical purposes that may be taken as the population at the present time. In addition to the regular steamer communication from Victoria, Vancouver and river points, the city is connected with the main line of the Canadian Pacific Railway by a branch from Westminster Junction, and hourly communication by electric tram line from Vancouver, 12 miles distant, is had. The Royal City, as it is sometimes called, is the centre of the salmon-canning industry of the Fraser River, on which there are located about 44 salmon canneries. Sailing vessels from England and other parts of the world come up the Fraser as far as New Westminster to load lumber and salmon. The city, prior to the great fire of 1898, had a large number of splendid business blocks of brick and stone, which have been rebuilt, but not on so elaborate, though more practical scale. In many respects the city has been greatly improved as the result of the conflagration.

Here are located the Dominion Penitentiary, the Provincial Asylum for the Insane, and the Provincial Gaol. The city owns its electric light system, and was the first in the province to recognize the principle of municipal ownership in this. It also has a splendid system of waterworks. There are several large sawmills, iron foundries, carriage and furniture factories, a city market which is very successfully carried on, cold storage, creameries and other industries. The Great Northern Railway, via Blaine, has its terminus on the opposite bank of the river, and a bridge is under contract to connect the two shores at this point, and permit railways to enter from the south. There is one daily newspaper, the Columbian; a number of churches, a Methodist college, and good schools. New Westminster City is the centre and chief market town of New Westminster District, which, in respect to farming development, is foremost in the province, and upon the agricultural wealth of the district and the salmon canneries of the Fraser River its future must largely depend.

PEACHLAND.

Peachland is a new settlement, largely made up of retired settlers from the Northwest, who have come here for residential purposes or to engage in fruit farming. Peachland is beautifully situated on Okanagan Lake, and as a residential point, especially from the standpoint of climate and scenery, has everything to recommend it. Two hundred is about the present limit of the population.

PENTICTON.

Penticton is a stopping place at the foot of Okanagan Lake, where connection is made with the steamers from the north and the stages to the south to the Boundary and Similkameen countries.

PHOENIX.

Phoenix is one of the towns of the mining district of Boundary, which had a remarkable growth as a result of the development of such mines as the Knob Hill and Old Ironsides and other phenomenal properties there and in the vicinity. It came into existence in 1899 and 1900, and now has a population of 1,200, with a branch line of railway, incorporation, a live newspaper and other adjuncts of a city.

PILOT BAY.

Pilot Bay is the site of a smelter, which is not now in operation. It is an outfitting point for prospectors for the St. Mary's country. The Davies-Sayward sawmill at this point is operating with a large force of men.

PORT MOODY.

Port Moody, at the head of Burrard Inlet, was the former terminus of the Canadian Pacific Railway, from which place the line was subsequently extended to Vancouver. At the time the C. P. R. was completed to that point there was considerable activity in real estate, and Port Moody promised to become what Vancouver is to-day, but the change of terminus suspended all building operations. With the growth of industries around the shores of Burrard Inlet, it will undoubtedly yet assume a considerable degree of importance. The sawmill industry is already assuming large proportions, which will react on the future of the place.

PORT SIMPSON.

Port Simpson is a Hudson's Bay Company post on the northwest coast of British Columbia, near Alaska, 640 miles north of Victoria. A large village of Tsimpshean Indians is located here, and in connection with this there is a Methodist mission and several industries. The harbour at Port Simpson is a good one, and for this reason it was at one time regarded as a possible terminus of the Canadian Pacific Railway, and it is considered as a probable terminus of the Canadian Northern, under construction east of the Rockies, or of the Grand Trunk Pacific; much attention has been attracted to it recently for that reason.

PRINCETON.

Princeton is situated at the forks of the Similkameen and Tulameen Rivers. It is the centre of a large mining and ranching district. Here are several hotels and stores, and a local newspaper. The more important mining camps are those on

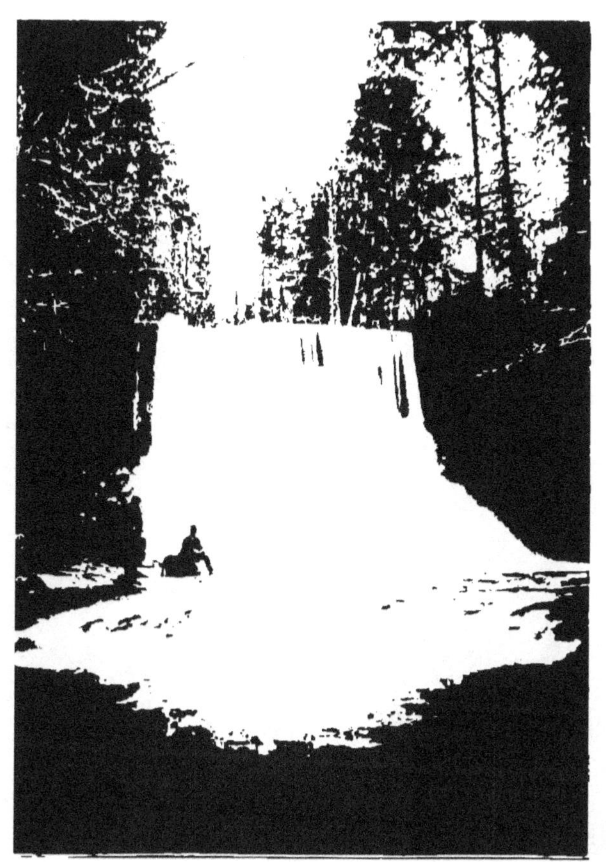

FALLS, KANAKA CREEK, MAPLE RIDGE.

FALLS ON BOULDER CREEK.

LOOKING DOWN PEACE RIVER CANYON.

H. B. Co.'s POST, FORT St. JOHN, PEACE RIVER.

THE SKEENA RIVER.

prettily situated town and an ideal spot for tourists and summer residents. It is kept clean and neat, and is an attractive resort.

SLOCAN.

Slocan is a mining town at the south end of Slocan Lake, 18 miles from Denver and 30 miles from Rosebery, at which latter place there is daily steamer connection with the trains of the Nakusp & Slocan Railway. Slocan was incorporated as a town in 1901, and has a population of nearly a thousand. It is situated at the mouth of Springer Creek at the head of Slocan River. Slocan is the distributing point for the rich groups of mines up Springer and Lemon Creeks. On Springer Creek, quite near the town, there is a good water power. The Slocan Drill is the newspaper of the place. Daily connection with Nelson is afforded by railway to Slocan Crossing.

SLOCAN JUNCTION.

Slocan Junction is a station on the Columbia & Kootenay Railway, 13 miles from Nelson, where the branch of the Columbia & Kootenay leaves for Slocan City, 32 miles distant.

SODA CREEK.

Soda Creek is situated on the lower bank of the Fraser River, 56 miles below Quesnel, at the lower end of navigation on the Upper Fraser River. It is surrounded by a prosperous ranching district, in which stock-raising and general agriculture are carried on.

SPENCE'S BRIDGE.

Spence's Bridge, on the main line of the C. P. R., is 178 miles east of Vancouver and is bisected by the Thompson River. It is the point from which the Nicola Valley and Similkameen country is reached, 45 miles to Nicola Lake, and 110 miles to Princeton. The district here is well adapted for fruit-growing, including among its products peaches, melons, grapes, etc, though these are only grown in a limited way as yet.

STEVESTON.

Steveston is a fishing village at the mouth of the South Arm of the Fraser River, and is the chief town of Richmond municipality. It is surrounded by numerous salmon canneries, to which it owes its existence. There is regular communication by steamers from Victoria, Vancouver, New Westminster and river points. The Vancouver & Lulu Island Railway, projected by the C. P. R., which has its terminus here, was completed last year. A railway bridge across the North Arm of the Fraser, connecting the Lulu Island, has been constructed. The agricultural interests of Richmond municipality, which is principally alluvial in character, are steadily improving, and with the advent of the railway values have been materially enhanced.

SUMMIT CITY.

Summit City is a townsite between Eholt and Phoenix on the Phoenix branch of the Canadian Pacific Railway.

TELEGRAPH CREEK.

Telegraph Creek is the point where the old telegraph line was to have crossed the Stikine, and where as a matter of fact the new telegraph line crosses the river. It is a divisional point and the headquarters of the inspector; it is the supply point for the Dease Lake Mining Division. Several hotels and stores are located here. The population consists of about 50 whites and several hundred Indians.

THREE FORKS.

Three Forks is a mining town on the Nakusp & Slocan Railway, 33 miles from Nakusp and two miles from Sandon. Alamo is one mile west of Three Forks, where a concentrator is located.

TRAIL.

Trail, situated on the Columbia River, six miles north of the international boundary line, seven miles in a direct line from Rossland—14 miles by railway—is the site of a smelter of the Canadian Smelting & Refining Company, with a capacity of 1,500 tons of ore per day. To the smelting plant there has recently been added a refinery plant for the purpose of treating the silver-lead ores of Slocan. It is the terminus of the C. P. R. line of steamers plying between that point and Arrowhead, at the mouth of the Arrow Lakes. Besides the business incidental to the demands of the large staff of men employed at the smelter and in the mining properties of the vicinity, an excellent supply trade is done with mining camps along the Columbia River. There are excellent hotels, and religious services are regularly held by Roman Catholic, Episcopal, Presbyterian and Methodist denominations.

TROUT LAKE.

Trout Lake is a town of 500 inhabitants, situated at the head of Trout Lake, and is connected by steamer with the Arrowhead and Kootenay Railway terminus at the foot of the lake, Gerrard townsite. In addition to the mines referred to as tributary to Ferguson, Trout Lake has three mining camps tributary to and surrounding the lake. The location is picturesque and residentially charming.

VANCOUVER.

Vancouver is called the Terminal City because it is the terminus of the Canadian Pacific Railway in British Columbia, and on account of that fact and its situation on Burrard Inlet, one of the finest natural harbours in the world, it has acquired the importance it has during the last decade, within which period it was created and has grown to its present proportions. Early in its existence it was swept by fire, but the loss it then sustained only tended as a further stimulus to the exertions of the citizens. Vancouver, from its position, has always been regarded as a city with a future.

As the terminus of the C. P. R., with its multifarious connections, and as a natural seaport, it has every prospect of, and is surrounded by the proper conditions for becoming one of the great shipping marts of the Pacific Coast. At present Burrard Inlet is the centre of the lumber trade of British Columbia, and the shipping port of the Australian and Oriental steamers running in connection with the Canadian Pacific Railway. The city itself was laid out on a comprehensive scale and made rapid growth. The authorities early applied themselves to the problems of water supply, sewerage, street paving, electric light and tramways, etc., and succeeded in completing satisfactory and substantial systems. Its paved streets and fine water supply are two things of which its citizens are especially proud. Vancouver is the only city in Canada, and among the very few in America, which has adopted the septic tank system of disposing of sewage. Results have been highly satisfactory, and as a consequence the city has become a point of special interest in connection with this system.

It possesses many churches, good schools, several social clubs, a fine theatre, fraternal and benevolent orders in abundance, athletic associations, etc. Conspicuous among the last-named is the Brockton Point Association, which has done much in the direction of encouraging athletic sports in British Columbia and on the Coast.

Industrially it has made good progress. Its principal industries are lumbering, sugar refining, jute and cooperage works, iron works (including the C. P. R. shops), fruit-preserving, furniture and candy factories. One of the largest shingle factories in the world is located here.

At English Bay, near the city limits, is good bathing, where very modern facilities have been provided for the convenience of bathers; and with Stanley Park, a very large reserve of 950 acres, form the principal pleasure resorts. The beach at English Bay is one of the best natural bathing points on the Coast, and will eventually become a noted bathing place.

A number of large wholesale firms have established themselves in Vancouver and are competing successfully for a share of the business of the province. As a distributing point for the province it is attracting increased attention.

The population at the last general census (1901) was 26,000.

Vancouver is surrounded by the very finest scenery, having on all sides the elements which go to make up the picturesque. Burrard Inlet lies to the north, with a broad expanse of two or three miles. Beyond, the slopes rise gradually to the foot of the Coast Range of mountains, which then attain a height of about 4,000 feet; their lofty broken crests form a most impressive view.

The business portion of the city is located on a peninsula, False Creek to the south, and Burrard Inlet, as mentioned, to the north. The surface rises gradually from the water's edge on both sides to a central elevation of about 100 feet, affording an ideal site for a city from a commercial, sanitary and scenic point of view.

The city was incorporated in 1886. What at that time was primeval forest of Douglas fir is now a well laid out centre of population and business, with its business streets paved with bituminous rock or wood block pavement, and lined with handsome stone and brick buildings. It has 160 miles of streets graded, 95 miles of sidewalks, 39 miles of sewers, 51 miles of water-main, and 282 hydrants. A fine electrical tramway service is in operation, and the streets are well lighted by arc lights. The waterworks, which cost the city $1,000,000, is a gravity system, the water being brought by submerged mains across the Narrows of Burrard Inlet from Capilano Creek, which is fed by the glaciers and snows of the Coast Range of mountains, giving the inhabitants a supply of the coldest and purest of water. The receipts for water rates for 1901 were $82,076. The assessed valuation of the city for the same year was $16,512,830. The News-Advertiser, World, Province and Ledger are published.

VERNON.

Vernon is the centre and chief supply point for the Okanagan District, which contains several large agricultural valleys of peculiar promise. It is the terminus of the Shuswap & Okanagan Railway, 46 miles from Sicamous Junction, and has, in addition to the Government Offices, a branch of the Bank of Montreal, and a newspaper—the News—which has creditably reflected the enterprise of the district. There is daily communication via the Canadian Pacific Railway with the southern country, and as far as the Boundary by means of steamers on Okanagan and Dog Lakes, and by stages with various points of the district. Some attention has been directed to mineral development in the vicinity, but up to the present development has been limited. The city is beautifully situated and the climate is healthful and exhilarating, and will undoubtedly attract a large population of farmers and small holders from other points in Canada, seeking for such conditions as exist there. Already the large estates are being divided up, and settlers from the Northwest are coming in. A movement is on foot also to connect Vernon with the valleys by short lines of light railway. The surrounding country affords good facilities for fishing and shooting. The whole Okanagan country is very picturesque.

VICTORIA.

Victoria is the Capital and oldest city of British Columbia, and its history from the outset up until about 15 years ago is practically the history of the Province. Its nucleus of growth was the old Hudson's Bay Company's fort erected in 1843. The city was laid out in 1851 and incorporated in 1862. The fact to which, however, it owes its greatest stimulus in the way of development, was the gold rush in 1858, when it suddenly grew into a city of tents with from 20,000 to 30,000 inhabitants. This population was, however, of a very temporary character and it subsequently dwindled down to much smaller proportions. The city after 1858 experienced many ups and downs, its fortunes varying with those of mining development. Between the years of 1881 and 1891 the population increased very rapidly. At the latter date it was 16,800 according to the official census. Its growth since has been steady and substantial. The population in 1901 was, officially, 21,000. Victoria is very beautifully situated on the southeastern part of Vancouver Island, overlooking the waters of Juan de Fuca Strait with the Olympian Mountains in the background. The view from all sides is very picturesque, and its many attractions from a scenic and other points of view have made it a great tourist resort. Latterly much has been done in the way of block pavement and macadamizing, and in the planting of trees and shrubs to render the city beautiful, and work in this direction is still going on. The James Bay mud flats are being filled in, a handsome retaining wall has been erected and an hotel, built by the C. P. R., will occupy part of the reclaimed area. Owing to the attractions of Victoria, already enumerated, the favorable climatic and residential conditions generally promise a future peculiarly its own. Its numerous home-like residences, and profusion of flowers by which it is surrounded, are always favourably commented upon by visitors, and added to these are the different pleasure resorts easy of access, including Beacon Hill Park, the Gorge, Oak Bay, Esquimalt, where the Naval Station of the North Pacific Squadron is located. The city owns its own waterworks and electric lighting and has a very complete system of electric tram lines and lighting, owned by a private company. Its shipping trade is a large one, and its industries, of which there are a number, include oatmeal mills, iron foundries, machine shops, furniture and biscuit factories, chemical works, fruit preserving, pickling and spice factories, soap factories, and powder works. The Government Buildings and the new Government House are interesting and attractive structures. It is well supplied with schools, churches, and social and athletic associations. It is a port of call for all the trans-Pacific steamship lines to the Orient and Australia, and has communication with San Francisco, the Sound points, and all ports as far north as Alaska. The Victoria Colonist and Times are the morning and evening papers, respectively.

WELLINGTON.

Wellington is the terminus of the E. & N. Railway, five miles from Nanaimo by the railway, on Departure Bay. It was formerly a place of very considerable importance and an incorporated town. Since the closing down of the mines there the greater part of the population has left. It still retains the machine shops of the E. & N. Railway Company.

WHITEWATER.

Whitewater is a mining town in the Slocan District, 17 miles from Kaslo, on the Kaslo & Slocan Railway. It is the shipping point for the Whitewater, Jackson and other mines in the vicinity. Population, about 100.

WINDERMERE.

Windermere is the site of the mining record office for the Windermere division, and is situated on Windermere Lake, which is an expansion of the Kootenay, about midway between Golden on the main line of the C.P.R. and Fort Steele in East Kootenay. It is the centre of a promising mining district.

YALE.

Yale was formerly the site of a Hudson's Bay Company post, and in early days and also during the construction of the C. P. R., was a town of very considerable importance, being at the head of navigation and the gateway into the interior. It is 102 miles from Vancouver. It possesses a first-class ladies' school, conducted by the Anglican Sisters.

ADDENDA.

In the following list is a number of places that have been inadvertantly omitted in the regular order in the foregoing, and are given here alphabetically :—

Alert Bay, on Cormorant Island, is one of the calling points of the steamers going north. It is 231 miles from Victoria and five miles above Beaver Cove. There is a large Indian village here, with an Indian burying ground and a large totem pole which are conspicuous from the steamer and always attract attention. There are a salmon cannery and a saw-mill located at this place. Nimkish River, the mouth of which is opposite Cormorant Island, is a famous fishing stream.

Bamfield is the Canadian terminus of the new Pacific cable. It is situated at the mouth of Bamfield Creek on the east side of Barkley Sound north of Cape Beale. The cable station, with a staff of operators, and officials is located here.

Bella Coola is a settlement on the Bella Coola River at the head of Bentinck Arm, an extension of Burke Channel, 325 miles from Nanaimo. At this point has been located a colony of Norwegians. There is considerable farming land in the valley and conditions are favorable to agricultural development. This is the point where Sir Alexander Mackenzie reached the Pacific Coast on his memorable overland journey in 1793. From here into the interior is one of the best available routes for a trans-continental railway, being the most direct to and through the Rocky Mountains and possessing the easiest gradients.

Bullion is a new mining town in Cariboo, four miles north of Quesnel Forks. It is the direct result of the extensive operations of the Cariboo Consolidated Mining Company.

Camborne, a new mining camp with sudden and remarkable growth, is situated at the mouth of Bull River, Fish River Basin. It is seven miles northeast of Comaplix, in the heart of a new district very rich in minerals.

Canterbury is a new mining camp three miles south of Wilmer at the northwest end of Windermere Lake, near the mouth of the Columbia River.

Cape Scott is the site of the Danish settlement at the extreme northwest corner of Vancouver Island, 300 miles from Victoria, with a steamer connection with the latter once a month.

Central Park is a residential suburb of Vancouver, six miles east of Carroll Street, and is connected with Vancouver and New Westminster by the B.C. Electric Railway. Is is surrounded by a number of residences built on small holdings purchased from the Government.

Clayoquot is situated on Meares Island, Clayoquot Sound, 150 miles from Victoria and is the principal settlement between that city and Quatsino. There are a large Indian population and a number of whites. Mining and saw-milling are the principal industries carried on.

Cobble Hill is on the E. & N. Railway, 31 miles from Victoria, and is the centre of an agricultural settlement.

Courtney is a village in Comox District, six miles from Cumberland, on the Courtney River. Population about 100.

Denoro is a townsite in Summit mining camp, two miles from Eholt, and is so named from an adjacent mine.

Erie is a mining camp on the Nelson & Fort Sheppard Railway on the north fork of the Salmon River. It is 32 miles from Nelson and 28 miles from the American boundary.

Extension, near the Extension Coal Mines, the largest on Vancouver Island, depends upon the mining industry entirely. Coal is shipped from here to Ladysmith, a distance of 12 miles. Large numbers of men are employed here by the Wellington collieries.

FERNIE.

Fernie is 146 miles from Kootenay Landing, on the Crow's Nest Pass Railway, and is the most important town in East Kootenay. It sprang into life as the consequence of the extensive operations of the Crow's Nest Pass Coal Company in coal mining and the manufacture of coke at that point. It is situated at the junction of Coal Creek and the Elk River and has a population of over 3,000 persons. About 500 coke ovens are in operation and from these are supplied all the smelters of the interior with coke.

Fort Graham is a Hudson's Bay Company's post on Findlay River, 50 miles north of the junction of Parsnip and Peace Rivers.

Fort McLeod is a Hudson's Bay Company's trading post at the north end of McLeod Lake, 85 miles northeast of Fort St. James.

Fort Rupert is a trading post on Hardy Bay near the north end of Vancouver Island. It was here the first coal mining on Vancouver Island was carried on by the Hudson's Bay Company, who had a fort and trading post at this point. The mining plant was subsequently removed to Nanaimo.

Fort St. George is a Hudson's Bay Company's trading post on the Fraser River, 90 miles from Quesnel.

Fort St. James is a Hudson's Bay Company trading post on the south end of Stuart's Lake, 160 miles southeast of Hazelton. There is a large Indian Reserve in the vicinity.

Fraser's Lake is a trading post on Fraser Lake, the headwaters of the Fraser River, about 150 miles from the mouth of the Quesnel River.

Fredericton is a townsite on Toad Mountain, near the Hall Mines, eight miles from Nelson.

Galena is a mining camp on the Columbia River, 42 miles from Golden in the East Kootenay District.

Granite Creek is a mining camp situated on the forks of the Tulameen River, 60 miles from Lower Nicola. Placer mining for gold and platinum is carried on, also cattle raising. It is 77 miles from Hope and 110 miles from Spence's Bridge.

Hanceville, in the Chilcoten country, is situated on the Chilcoten River, 40 miles above its mouth. It may be regarded as the outpost of settlement in the Cariboo District.

Hazelton is a village situated 153 miles from the mouth of the Skeena River at the point where the Kispyox River on the north and the Bulkley River on the south join the Skeena. It is the point of entrance into the northern interior, both north and south. The Hudson's Bay Company and another line of steamers ply as far as Hazelton from Port Essington during the season navigation is open.

Hope, an old town on the south side of the Fraser River about 90 miles from the mouth. Hope Station is on the opposite side of the river. It is from this point that entrance is made into the Similkameen country over Hope Mountain.

Huntingdon is situated at the International Boundary line at the point where the Mission branch of the C. P. R. connects with the Bellingham Bay & British Columbia Railway. It has a population of about 170.

Illecillewaet, a mining camp and station of the C. P. R., 28 miles east of Revelstoke.

Inverness is a fishing and trading station near the mouth of the Skeena River, where there is an Indian Mission and a large salmon cannery.

Keithley Creek is a mining camp in Cariboo, distant 210 miles from Ashcroft and 18 miles northeast of Quesnel. It was an important gold mining section in the palmy days of Cariboo.

Kimberley is a mining town which has grown up in East Kootenay as a result of extensive mining developments and is in proximity to the North Star and Sullivan mines. A branch of the Canadian Pacific Railway has been built to Kimberley, a distance of 18 miles.

Kincolith is a settlement at the mouth of the Naas River, where a saw-mill and an English Church Mission station are situated.

Kootenay Landing is the western terminus of the Crow's Nest Pass Railway, from which point cars are ferried to Nelson, 55 miles distant.

Kuskanook, a town situated at the south end of the Kootenay Lake. During the construction of the Crow's Nest Pass Railway it enjoyed somewhat of a boom. It is the present terminus of the Nelson & Bedlington Railway, 52 miles distant from Nelson.

Laggan is a station on the main line of the C. P. R. which marks the boundary line between British Columbia and the Northwest Territories. In the vicinity of Laggan are many objects of scenic interest which attract the tourist.

Laketon is a trading post in the Cassiar District on Dease Lake, 80 miles from the Stikine. It is the official centre of the North Cassiar District.

Langley, 15 miles from New Westminster on the south side of the Fraser River, is a landing point for a large and prosperous agricultural district, including Langley Prairie.

Liverpool, otherwise known as South Westminster, was laid out as a new town some years ago. It is situated on the Fraser River opposite New Westminster City.

Manson Town is a mining camp on Manson River, in the Omineca District. where the Arctic Slope Mining Company, the Forty-Third Mining & Milling Company and other companies are in operation.

Metlakahtla is a celebrated Indian Mission Station on Timpshean Peninsula, between Port Essington and Port Simpson. It was here that Mr. Duncan carried on his missionary work before he left for New Metlakahtla, taking with him a large number of his Indian adherents. It is still an important mission station.

McGuigan, on the Kaslo & Slocan Railway line, 23 miles from Kaslo, is an important point for a group of silver-lead mines. Has a population of about 200.

North Bend is a divisional town on the main line of the C. P. R., 129 miles east of Vancouver. It is very prettily situated and the C. P. R. hotel and beautiful grounds surrounding them are very picturesque and attractive.

Northfield, two and a-half miles from Nanaimo on the main road to Wellington, is where the New Wellington coal was mined by the New Vancouver Coal Company. The shaft there is not now in operation.

North Vancouver is practically a suburb of the City of Vancouver, on the north side of Burrard Inlet, communication being maintained by ferry.

Okanagan Falls was laid out as a townsite in 1900, at the foot of Dog Lake, 74 miles from Okanagan Landing.

Ollalla is a new townsite laid out on Keremeos Creek near Keremeos by the Ollalla Copper Refining and Smelting Company.

One Hundred and Fifty Mile House is one of the important stage stations on the Cariboo road, 135 miles from Ashcroft, and is a distributing point for a number of hydraulic mines.

Port Kells is a settlement on the South Fraser River, near New Westminster. It was laid out as a townsite in 1890.

Rivers Inlet is an important stopping place and fishing village at the head of Rivers Inlet, 326 miles from Vancouver.

BRUNETTE RIVER—AN IDEAL TROUT STREAM.

A PROSPECTING EXPEDITION STARTING OUT.

LAKE LOUISE.

A GREAT GLACIER.

CENSUS OF BRITISH COLUMBIA.

THE decennial census-taking of Canada occurred in 1901. The first volume of census returns has recently been issued by the Census Commissioner. From it there have been extracted the following tables respecting British Columbia. There have also been added some particulars that appeared in previous bulletins; and the particulars of the first census taken in British Columbia in 1871, prior to entering Confederation. It is unnecessary in view of the complete details given to make comment, except to note the steady and remarkable expansion shown in the population of the Province, especially during the past two decades.

CENSUS RETURNS, 1901.

Districts and S. Districts.	Area in acres.	Houses.	Families.	Population.	Male.	Female.
CANADA	2,316,681,071	1,028,892	1,070,747	5,371,315	2,751,708	2,619,607
BRITISH COLUMBIA	236,922,177	36,938	38,445	178,657	114,160	64,497
BURRARD	119,794,762	7,209	7,942	42,060	26,060	16,000
Bennett and Atlin		524	525	2,042	1,826	216
Cassiar (Stikine)	119,789,671	161	161	770	479	291
Cassiar (Skeena)		931	1,443	12,238	7,777	4,461
Vancouver, City	5 091	5,593	5,813	27,010	15,978	11,032
NEW WESTMINSTER	4,421,687	5,128	5,191	23,822	15,017	8,805
Chilliwack	206,592	838	842	3,680	2,106	1,574
Delta	195,895	1,108	1,119	5,074	3,288	1,786
Dewdney	1,971,200	891	906	3,767	2,203	1,564
New Westminster, City	3,700	1,206	1,234	6,499	3,960	2,539
Richmond	2,044,300	1,085	1,090	4,802	3,460	1,342
VANCOUVER	7,793,049	5,638	5,917	27,198	16,968	10,230
Alberni	3,451,392	870	1,098	4,181	2,286	1,895
Comox	2,539,008	705	708	3,493	2,494	999
Cowichan	640,000	677	682	3,613	2,471	1,142
Esquimalt (part)	435,200	116	128	504	308	196
Nanaimo, City	630	1,279	1,291	6,130	3,488	2,642
Nanaimo, North	111,513	326	327	1,439	788	651
Nanaimo, South	469,386	1,116	1,131	5,146	3,427	1,719
Victoria, North	89,600	323	326	1,056	1,083	573
Victoria, South	56,320	226	226	1,036	623	413
VICTORIA	43,251	4,669	4,752	23,688	14,275	9,413
Esquimalt (part)	12,077	291	296	1,191	702	489
Metchosin	15,162	34	34	160	105	55
Victoria	14,118	283	284	1,418	850	568
Victoria, City	1,894	4,061	4,138	20,919	12,618	8,301
YALE AND CARIBOO	104,809,428	14,294	14,643	61,889	41,840	20,049
Cariboo	59,715,688	708	757	3,507	2,462	1,045
Lillooet, East	3,829,760	150	155	789	553	236
Lillooet, West	6,528,000	741	746	3,196	1,870	1,326
Kootenay, E., North R.	4.428,800	451	452	1,938	1,382	556
Kootenay, E., South R.	5,145,600	1,264	1,406	6.508	4,653	1,855
Kootenay, W.—O., Nelson R.	1,418,240	1,650	1,697	7,102	4,885	2,217
Kootenay, W.—O., Revelstoke R.	3,389,690	766	776	3,003	2,038	965
Kootenay, W.—O., Rossland R.	1,546,240	3,481	3,540	14,603	10,214	4,389
Kootenay. W.—O., Slocan R.	2.688,000	1,212	1,216	5,321	3,962	1,359
Yale, East	4,224,000	1,160	1,179	4,930	3,097	1,833
Yale, North	7,270,610	856	860	3,837	2,519	1,318
Yale, West	4,684,800	1,855	1,859	7,155	4,205	2,950

CENSUS RETURNS, 1901.

Districts.	Single.		Married.		Widowed.		Divorced.	
	Male.	Female.	Male.	Female.	Male.	Female.	M.	F.
CANADA	1,748,582	1,564,011	928,952	904,091	73,837	151,181	337	324
BRITISH COLUMBIA	75,093	35,274	36,429	26,000	2,586	3,096	52	37
Burrard	17,220	8.844	8,228	6,323	610	832	2	1
New Westminster	9,419	4,847	5,260	3,565	331	387	7	6
Vancouver	10,330	5,329	6,161	4,307	467	587	7	7
Victoria	9.014	5,159	4,941	3,616	313	629	7	9
Yale and Cariboo	29,110	11,095	11,836	8,278	865	061	29	14

ORIGINS OF THE PEOPLE.

English 52,863
Irish 20,658
Scotch 31,068
Others 1,814
French 4,600
German 5,807
Dutch 437
Scandinavian 4,880
Russian 1,143
Austro-Hungarian 1,377
Italian 1,976
Jewish 543
Swiss 240
Belgian 410
Half-Breeds 3,461
Indian 25,488
Chinese and Japanese 19,482
Negro 532
Various origins 479
Unspecified 1,390

NATIONALITIES.

American (U.S.) 10,088
Austro-Hungarian 871
Belgian 161
Canadian 144,989
Chinese 14,201
Dutch 23
Danish 271
French 178
German 602
Grecian 31
Italian 1,010
Japanese 3,516
Norwegian 365
Rumanian 1
Russian 601
Spanish 28
Swedish 850
Swiss 83
Turkish 20
Various 57
Unspecified 711

BIRTHPLACE OF THE PEOPLE.

BRITISH BORN 132,085
CANADA 99,612
British Columbia 59,589
Manitoba 2,203
New Brunswick 2,839
Nova Scotia 4,003
Ontario 23,642
Prince Edward Island 1,180
Quebec 4,329
The Territories 091
Unorganized Territories ......
Canada, not given 236
BRITISH ISLANDS 30,030
England 19,385
Ireland 3,957
Scotland 6,457
Wales 710
Lesser Isles 121
BRITISH POSSESSIONS 1,843
Australia 378
India 196
Newfoundland 953
New Zealand 203
South Africa 14
Other Possessions 99

Foreign Born	46,110	Rumania	5
Austria-Hungary	1,151	Russia	1,007
Belgium	321	Spain and Portugal	59
China	14,576	Switzerland	168
Denmark	351	Syria	28
East Indies	40	Turkey	6
France	433	United States	17,164
Germany	1,478	West Indies	78
Greece	59	Other countries	303
Holland	49	At sea	38
Iceland	116	Not given	424
Italy	1,470		
Japan	4,515	Total	178,657
Norway and Sweden	2,742		

RELIGIONS OF THE PEOPLE.

Adventists	254	Lutherans	5,335
Agnostics	1,069	Mennonites	11
Anglicans	40,689	Methodists	25,047
Baptists	6,471	Mohammedans	6
Baptist, Free	29	New Church (Swedenborgians)	21
Brethren	164	Non-Sectarian	2
Buddhists	10,027	No Religion	1,605
Catholic Apostolic (Irvingites)	21	Pagans	5,139
Christadelphians	117	Plymouth Brethren	68
Christians	351	Presbyterians	34,081
Christian Scientists	94	Protestants	844
Church of Christ	25	Reformed Episcopalians	307
Church of God		Roman Catholics	33,639
Confucians	4,859	Salvation Army	570
Congregationalists	1,198	Spiritualists	143
Deists	29	Theosophists	34
Disciples	99	Tunkers	6
Doukhobors		Unitarians	133
Evangelicals	28	United Brethren	18
Friends (Quakers)	130	Universalists	48
Greek Church	101	Unspecified	5,003
Holiness Movement (Hornerites)		Various sects	132
Jews	554	Zionites	31
Latter Day Saints (Mormons)	125		

INFIRMITIES.

Blind	115	Unsound mind	299
Deaf and dumb	92	Totally infirm	506

AGES.

Year.		Year.	
0-1	2,564	15-19	11,862
1-2	3,317	20-24	16,618
2-3	3,163	25-29	19,103
3-4	3,066	30-34	18,730
4-5	3,211	35-39	16,586
5-9	14,939	40-44	12,690
10-14	11,959	45-49	8,241

Year.		Year.	
50-54	6,278	80-89	61
55-59	3,847	90-94	19
60-64	3,266	95-00	18
65-69	1,909	Not given	15,203
70-74	1,177		
75-79	563	Total	178,657
80-84	270		

IMMIGRANTS.

When immigrated:	
Before 1851	618
1851-1855	440
1856-1860	1,028
1861-1865	1,312
1866-1870	1,423
1871-1875	2,198
1876-1880	3,467
1881-1885	7,351
1886-1890	12,885
1891-1895	14 280
1896-1900	27,273
1901, 31st March	1,845
Not given	4.551
Total	78,621
Number of males	57,238
Number of females	21,303

Whence immigrated:	
England	19,388
Ireland	3,957
Scotland	6,457
Wales	710
Lesser Isles	12)
Australasia	578
India	199
Newfoundland	953
New Zealand	203
Other possessions	92
Austria-Hungary	1,153
Belgium	312
China	14,516
Denmark	351
France	429
Germany	1,478
Italy	1,470
Japan	4,515
Norway and Sweden	2,742
Russia	1,007
Spain and Portugal	59
Switzerland	168
United States	17,164
Iceland	116
All other countries	1,687

Summary.

British Islands	30,629
British possessions	1,825
Foreign countries	46,167
	78,621

POPULATION TOWNS AND VILLAGES.

Alberni	502	Greenwood	1,359
Port Moody	539	Kamloops	1,594
Vancouver	26,103	Kaslo	1,680
New Westminster	6,499	Moyie	582
Cumberland	1,149	Nelson	5,273
Rossland	6,159	Phoenix	866
Sandon	551	Revelstoke	1,600
Slocan	950	Ashcroft	475
Trail	1,369	Fairview	282
Vernon	802	Princeton	316
Nanaimo	6,130	Duncan	465
Victoria	20,816	Esquimalt	946
Cranbrook	1,196	Extension	2,160
Columbia	350	Atlin	486
Fernie	1,640	Fort Steele	590
Golden	705	Ymir	256
Grand Forks	1,012	Kimberley	262

Comaplix	100	Lumby	284
Nakusp	223	Hope	263
New Denver	725	Yale	174
Armstrong	221	North Bend	276
Enderby	270		

RURAL AND URBAN.

The population under these heads is given as follows:

	Population 1901.			Population 1891.		
	Total.	Rural.	Urban.	Total.	Rural.	Urban.
Burrard	41,407	14,233	27,174	24,360	10,651	13,709
New Westminster	23,822	17,323	6,499	17,866	11,188	6,678
Vancouver	26,391	19,112	7,279	18,229	18,229	.....
Victoria	23,763	2,947	20,810	18,538	1,697	16,841
Yale and Cariboo	61,889	34,201	27,679	19,180	19,180	.....
Totals	177,272	87,825	89,447	98,173	60,945	37,228

The census returns for areas, etc., are given in the chapter entitled "Physical Characteristics" and the census of agriculture under heading of "Agriculture" beginning at page 123.

So far only one volume of the Census Report has appeared, so that it is impossible, except in a limited degree, to institute comparisons with former decades:

COMPARISON BY POPULATION.

	1901.	1891.	1881.	1871.
Burrard	42,060	24,360	8,417	
New Westminster	23,822	17,866	7,000	
Vancouver	27,198	18,229	9,991	36,247
Victoria	23,688	18,538	7,301	
Yale and Cariboo	61,889	19,180	16,750	
Totals	178,657	98,173	49,459	36,247

	Houses.			Families.			Population.		
	1901.	1891.	1881.	1901.	1891.	1881.	1901.	1891.	1881.
Burrard	7,209	4,796	.....	7,942	4,870	.....	42,060	24,360	.....
N. West.	5,128	3,542	3,151	5,191	3,649	3,190	23,822	17,866	15,417
Vancouver.	5,638	3,039	1,406	5,917	3,712	1,591	27,198	18,229	9 991
Victoria	4,669	3,537	1,919	4,752	3,650	1,940	23,688	18,538	7,301
Yale and Cariboo	14,294	4,502	3,257	14,643	4,837	3,718	61,889	19,180	16,750
Totals	36,938	20,016	9,793	38,445	20.718	10,439	178,657	98,173	49,459

COMPARISON OF POPULATION BY ORIGIN.

	1871.	1881.	1891.	1891.
Whites	7,612	19,448	65,527	133,075
Chinese	1,243	4,350	9,386	14,869
(1) Japanese	.....	.....	.....	4,597
Colored	439	274	(2)	523
(3) Indian	35,000	25,661	23,257	25,593

(1) The number of Japanese specifically is not given in any census returns prior to 1901.

(2) The population was not enumerated by "origin" in the census of 1891. The number of whites, Chinese and Indians was ascertained by a special revision of the schedules for British Columbia.

(3) The number of Indians in 1871 was largely a guess. In 1881 their number was arrived at fairly accurately. In 1891 several hundreds in the northern interior were not enumerated. The census of Indians in 1901 corresponds with very careful enumeration on the part of the Indian Department.

*CENSUS OF 1871.

District.	Whites.	Colored.	Chinese.	Natives.	Total.
Victoria City	2,842	217	211	360	3,600
District adjacent to Victoria	1,512	56	60	553	2,181
Cowichan, Chemainus, Salt Spring Island, estimated at 1,400 to					2,000
Nanaimo and District	601	92	35	850	1,579
Comox	102	....	....	1,100	1,202
New Westminster and District	1,292	37	27	(est) 300	1,656
Yale-Lytton (estimated)	....	....	....	....	1,000
Lillooet-Clinton	235	3	80	906	1,224
Cariboo	920	32	685	570	2,207
Columbia and Kootenay	108	2	145	543	798
Omineca (as now estimated)					1,800
Total estimated population from settled districts					19,277

*The census of British Columbia was not taken in 1871 by the Dominion authorities. The above enumeration, which as will be seen is not very complete, and did not include the Indians except in the settled districts, was made by the Government of the Province of that day.

PASSENGER AND FREIGHT TRAFFIC AND EARNINGS

	Passengers carried.	Tons moved.	Passenger traffic.	Freight traffic.	Total earnings.	Net earnings.
Bedlington & Nelson	5,401	31,293	$ 4,027	$ 10,272	$ 14,543	$* - 12,632
British Yukon	18,033	38,208	113,022	708,532	846,321	562,790
†C. P. R. lines	....	....	....	....	....	....
Esquimalt & Nanaimo	130,562	158,595	99,920	115,886	234,194	18,028
Kaslo and Slocan	14,853	18,597	15,289	50,329	67,427	26,962
Lenora and Mt. Sicker	....	7,775	...	1,127	1,127	* - 7,877
New Westminster and Southern	6,964	8,652	5,348	2,064	9,053	* - 24,771
Nelson and Ft. Sheppard	17,309	24,285	34,077	48,739	86,315	21,364
Red Mountain	11,901	275,881	13,900	87,645	103,680	45,595
Victoria and Sidney	22,761	18,726	9,703	10,281	20,386	154

* These are represented by minus signs, indicating losses.

† As the C. P. R. lines are all bunched in the returns for the general system no details as to the main or branch lines in B. C. can be given.

RAILWAY ENTERPRISE.

IN the Year Book of 1897 a chapter of some length was devoted to railways then present and prospective. Substantial advance has been made since that time in the construction and operation of steam highways. All that was anticipated has not, however, been realized. The short table of statistics appended hereto is a history in itself of what has been accomplished up to the present time, and little is to be added to complete the information. It is mainly official, and has been abstracted from the Dominion Government Report on Railways and Canals.

Brief reference may be made to projected railways. Readers are familiar with the details of the new proposed transcontinental line of the Grand Trunk Pacific from Monckton, in New Brunswick, to some point on the Pacific Ocean, at or near Port Simpson. So far as the Province is concerned, it will enter British Columbia either through the Pine River Pass, in the Peace River country, or through the Yellowhead Pass, and be carried along one of the routes surveyed for the Canadian Pacific Railway in the early seventies. The actual route has not yet been fixed, that being a matter for determination as soon as the engineers can take the field. As the project is authorized and liberally assisted by the Dominion Government, and is being undertaken by the Grand Trunk Railway of Canada, its construction in the near future may be regarded as a certainty. The length of line will be about 3,500 miles and its cost roughly estimated at $100,-000,000. It will open up an entirely new district with considerable agricultural possibilities and mineral resources of great potentiality. The Peace River District, containing possibly the largest agricultural area in the Province; the Canoe River Valley, with an area of 75,000 acres of tillable land contiguous to the Yellowhead Pass; Nechaco Valley, lying north of Quesnel Forks, available for pastoral, if not agricultural, purposes; the Bulkley Valley, south of the Skeena River on the Bulkley River; the Ootsa Lake District in the vicinity of Ootsa Lake, said to be considerable in extent and very fertile; the Kispyox Valley, along the Kispyox River, a northern tributary of the Skeena, known to be rich pasture land; and not inconsiderable grazing tracts between the Naas and the Kispyox Rivers, will all, if not directly tapped, be rendered tributary to this line of railway, and no doubt will in time be reached by branch lines of railway or public highways. There are extensive coal formations; but enough is not known concerning their value to speak definitely, as they have never been carefully prospected. The same is true to some extent of the metalliferous deposits of gold, copper, iron and silver. That the whole country, however, is mineralized is certain; and the discoveries in former years of placer gold in the Omineca, in Cassiar and on the Skeena are sufficient upon which to base flattering hopes of the future. The Coast line has abundant timber. The adjacent waters of the Pacific have abundance of salmon, halibut, cod and other merchantable fishes; and the geographical position in relation to the trade of the Orient, being the shortest of all the ocean routes by many miles, and possessing good harbors render the outlook from a commercial point of view, both locally and internationally, very promising indeed. It is a route pregnant with many possibilities for the Province and the Dominion of Canada. To this section of the Northwest will be directed for the next few years the energies and capital of many Americans and of the people of Great Britain.

Another enterprise of a similar character was projected in advance of the Grand Trunk Pacific. The Canada Northern Railway Company, having in view the completion of a transcontinental railway, entered into negotiations with the Government of British Columbia to continue their line by way of Edmonton, N. W. T., through the Yellowhead Pass. After following the natural passes to a point near the Coast it was intended to divert the line down along the Homalthco Valley to the mouth of Bute Inlet, and from there by ferry cross to the Island and proceed along the east coast of the Island to Victoria. This line would have had one, at least, of its terminii at the latter place. A provisional arrangement was entered into for a cash bonus of $4,000 per mile and 20,000 acres of land per mile, with numerous conditions attached. This, it was found, would not receive the support of the Legislature, and was changed to a straight land subsidy of $5,000 per mile for 480 miles, which, however, was not effectual in bringing about construction. Whether or not it is the intention of the Canadian Northern Railway Company to renew the negotiations at a later date has not transpired. Much of the benefits ascribed to the building of the Grand Trunk Pacific Railway would have accrued in this instance. One of these not yet referred to was the bringing of the Northwest and British Columbia markets into more direct contact with each other.

Another railway enterprise that has been long talked of and has undergone many mutations as the result of political conditions is what is popularly known as the Coast-Kootenay line from a point at or near Midway, the terminus of the Columbia & Western Railway, to Vancouver City, passing through the Similkameen Valley, over Hope Mountain, and through the Westminster District. The object of this railway, for which there was a great deal of agitation at one time, was a more direct connection between the cities of the Coast and the mining regions of the Southern Interior, and as well to open up a new and rich district known generally as Similkameen. It received various forms of assistance from the Provincial Government, none of which have so far resulted in a scheme being matured for its construction. At the session of Parliament of 1902 it was placed on practically the same basis as the Canadian Northern, except that the cash subsidy was $4,500 per mile, not exceeding 330 miles. These subsidies expired on the 1st of September of this year. An application was before the Dominion Parliament for assistance, with what success at the time of writing was not known. It is said that what is known as the V. V. & E., which has been built into the Boundary by the Great Northern, will be extended to the Coast without the assistance of governments. This road, which begins at Marcus on the Columbia River and extends to Republic, in Washington State, is now under construction.

Another railway was projected to join Midway with the Okanagan Valley, and to afford communication to the mining properties in course of development in the West Fork country. It is known as the Midway & Vernon. It is proposed to be 152 miles in length. It was before the Provincial Legislature in 1901 and also in 1902, and received a subsidy of $5,000 per mile, which was not considered sufficent for the purpose. Assistance was also asked for this line at Ottawa during the recent session. The Okanagan Valley at its southern extreme is connected with the Boundary country by stage, the distance by time from Vernon being 48 hours. It is claimed for the Midway & Vernon, if built, that it will reduce the time between Boundary and Vernon to six hours, and the time to the Coast by one day.

On the Island of Vancouver two projects have been particularly in view, one is the extension of the Esquimalt & Nanaimo Railway to the north end of the

A FAMOUS BIG GAME HUNTER AND GUIDE.

A GRIZZLY ASLEEP.

BRUIN TAKING A NAP.

ELK HUNTERS, VANCOUVER ISLAND.

Island, a distance of about 240 miles; and another, a line of railway from Nanaimo, or Duncan, to Alberni. For the first of these, in 1901, provision was made in the Public Works Loan Act for assistance to the extent of $4,000 per mile. An application has also been before the Dominion Government for assistance for the Cape Scott & Comox Railway, which is the extension of the Island Railway referred to. The latter has been strongly agitated and the Government had a preliminary survey and report made in respect to it.

In 1902 an Act was passed to incorporate the Victoria & Seymour Narrows Railway Company to run from Victoria by way of Nanaimo City and Alberni to Seymour Narrows. This was proposed in connection with the construction of the Canadian Northern Railway.

During the present year a charter was obtained to build a line of railway from Hardy Bay to Rupert Arm, on Quatsino Sound. Another incorporation was that of the Adams River Railway Company, proposing to run a line from the Adams River to the valley of the Klaanch River, and from there to a point at or near Hecate Channel, via the mouth of Gold River on the West Coast.

The Kootenay Central Railway Company, which has also had an application before the Dominion Government, at Ottawa, during the present year, was incorporated during a recent session of the Legislature. It proposes to run a line of railway from Fort Steele to Elko, and thence to the International Boundary on the south, and from Fort Steele to Golden, on the C. P. R., via Windermere, following the valley of the Kootenay River about 150 miles. Provision was made in 1902 for a cash subsidy of $4,000 a mile for 150 miles.

The Public Works Loan Act of 1901 also subsidized a line of railway from the Coast at Kitimaat to Hazelton, a distance of approximately 100 miles. Another Act was passed in 1902 increasing the subsidy to $5,000 a mile.

A very large number of charters for railways have been obtained since 1897, which indicate the possibilities of development in various sections of the Province rather than the probabilities of all of them being constructed. Many of these were purely speculative in character. Regarding some others, there is a fair probability of realization, provided aid is obtained from the Dominion Government in addition to what has already been done by the Provincial Government.

Among the lines of railway which have been constructed without assistance of any kind are: The Grand Forks & Kettle River Railway from Republic, Washington, to Grand Forks to connect the mining camp of Republic with the Granby Smelter; the Vancouver & Lulu Island Railway from Vancouver to Steveston; the Crow's Nest Southern Railway from Michel to the International Boundary, built by the Crow's Nest Pass Coal Company to form part of the Montana & Great Northern Railway system, extending from the International Boundary to Jennings, Montana, a distance of fifty-one miles; the branch line of the C. P. R. from Lardo to Gerrard, in the Lardeau country; the line from Revelstoke to Arrowhead on Arrow Lake; the C. P. R. branch line from Cranbrook to Kimberley; the Bedlington & Nelson, owned by the Great Northern; the V. V. & E. from Marcus, on the Columbia River, to Republic via Grand Forks, now under construction; the Lenora & Mount Sicker Railway, from Lenora Mine to Crofton and Osborne Bay; the Red Mountain Railway, from Rossland to Northport; and the line from Vancouver to New Westminster to connect the Great Northern system on the opposite side of the Fraser River, now under construction.

Prior to 1903 the principal charters obtained were: The Canadian Yukon, from Douglas Channel to the end of Teslin Lake. This was to form part of the all-Canadian railway to the Yukon projected by Messrs. McKenzie & Mann, who failed to proceed on account of opposition on the part of the Senate of Canada to the concessions offered by the Dominion Government. This has not been revived.

The Vancouver, Northern & Yukon Railway was projected in 1800, to start from Burrard Inlet and proceed to the northern boundary of the Province by way of Squamish Valley, Pemberton Meadows, Quesnel and Hazelton. A subsequent incorporation, the Kamloops & Atlin, was projected to start from Kamloops Lake and proceeding to the plateau of the Bonaparte River follow the route of the Cariboo wagon road to Quesnel and thence north to Hazelton. A concession of Graham Island was asked for the construction of a railway from Skidegate Harbour northward to the coal deposits, a distance of about forty miles.

The session of 1903 was fertile in railway legislation. In addition to those which have been previously referred to the following are among the charters obtained :

The B. C. Northern & McKenzie Valley Railway, from the mouth of Naas River by way of Naas and Skeena Rivers and Dease Lake to the northern boundary of the Province, and from Dease Lake to Glenora; also from some point on the route to Atlin City;

The Flathead Valley Railway, from a point on the International Boundary to Elko;

Kootenay, Cariboo and Pacific Railway, from Golden through the Canoe River Valley via Tete Jeune Cache, Giscome Portage, Nechaco and Skeena Rivers to Port Simpson;

Morrissey, Fernie & Michel Railway, from Fernie by way of the mouth of Morrissey Creek along Flathead River to the International Boundary;

Nicola, Kamloops & Similkameen Coal & Railway Company, proposing to construct a railway from the western extremity of Nicola Lake to Spence's Bridge;

The Pacific Northern & Eastern Railway, from Hazelton to Teslin Lake, and from Hazelton via the Skeena and through the Omineca and Peace River district to the Pine River Pass.

These incorporations indicate better than anything else the prospective lines of development—the opening up of the northern country as a result of the filling up of the Northwest Territory, and the construction of another transcontinental line having a terminus at or near Port Simpson; the development of the coal and oil fields of Southeastern Kootenay; the exploitation of the coal and mineral deposits of the Nicola and Similkameen countries; the development of the northern and interior parts of Vancouver Island; and the evident desire to reach the gold fields of Cariboo, so long denied railway communication.

RAILWAYS IN BRITISH COLUMBIA.

C. P. R. Main Line and Branches within the Province—

(OWNED).

Laggan to Vancouver	524.8	
New Westminster branch	8.2	
Mission branch to Huntingdon	10.0	
Vancouver to Coal Harbour	1.2	
Arrow Lake, Revelstoke to Arrow Head	27.7	
Vancouver to Steveston	17.2	
Lardo to Gerrard	33.6	
		722.7

(LEASED).

Line	Miles		
Columbia and Kootenay—			
Castlegar Junction to Rossland	30.7		
Rossland to Le Roi	1.3		
Trail and Smelter Junction	2.0		
Robson to Midway	99.6		
Mining spurs	23.5		
		171.1	
Columbia and Kootenay—			
Nelson and Robson	27.7		
Spur to mouth Kootenay River	0.8		
Slocan Junction to Slocan City	32 0		
		60.5	
Shuswap and Okanagan—			
Sicamous and Okanagan Landing	50.8	50.8	
Nakusp and Slocan—			
Nakusp to Three Forks	36.3		
Three Forks to Sandon	4.2		
		40.5	
B. C. Southern—			
Crow's Nest to Kootenay Landing	202.20		
Cranbrook to Kimberley	19.1		
Nelson to Proctor	20.4		
		241.70	
			1,187.3
Esquimalt and Nanaimo—			
Victoria to Wellington	78.0		78.0
Great Northern—			
Kaslo and Slocan	33.03		
Nelson and Fort Sheppard	54.70		
New Westminster Southern	24.10		
Red Mountain	9.53		
Victoria and Sidney	16.26		
Bedlington and Nelson	15.20		
*Vancouver & New Westminster	12.0		
*V. V. & E., Columbia River to Grand Forks	16.0		
			180.82
Crow's Nest Southern (Fernie to International boundary)		50.0	
B. C. Yukon (in B. C. territory)		30.0	
Logging Lines (Chemainus)		20.0	
Kettle River Valley Railway (Carson to Granby smelter)		8.0	
Lenora and Mt. Sicker Railway		12.0	
			130.00
Electric Tram Lines—			
B. C. Electric Tram (Victoria) }			
" " " (Vancouver and New Westminster) }	48.3		
Nelson Electric Railway	3.0		
			51.30
			1,627.42

* Under construction.

CAPITAL, DEBT AND COST.

	Line Completed miles.	Authorized Capital.	Bonded Debt.		Dominion Governm't Aid.	Provincial Aid.	Municipal Aid.	Paid up Capital.	Floating Debt.	Total Cost of Railway
			Authorized	Issued.						
B. C. Southern	202.20	$4,000,000	† $30,000	....	(1)	(2)	....	$6,512,892	$6,340,692	$6,340,692
Columbia and Kootenay	60.50	1,000,000	† 24,333⅓	$1,270,500	$ 88,000	(3)	....	1,391,300	....	1,290,689
Columbia and Western	157.90	1,000,000	5,691,000	5,691,000	(4)	(5)	....	6,691,000	....	5,929,139
Esquimalt and Nanaimo	78.00	3,000,000	....	....	750,000	(6)	....	3,250,000	....	3,132,112
Kaslo & Slocan	33.03	1,000,000	954,000	750,000	....	(7)	....	1,812,919	62,919	961,994
Lenora Mount Sicker	6.25	....	....	....	....	....	....	57,699	....	57,699
Nakusp & Slocan	36.30	300,000	925,000	947,074	117,760	(8)	....	1,064,834	....	* 665,250
Nelson and Fort Sheppard	54.70	1,500,000	1,500,000	1,408,000	....	(9)	....	2,908,000	....	2,670,413
New Westminster Southern	24.10	592,000	....	....	....	....	....	592,000	....	590,746
Red Mountain	9.53	190,600	238,250	217,000	....	....	....	407,600	....	409,227
Shuswap and Okanagan	50.80	750,000	1,250,000	1,250,000	163,200	(10)	....	2,052,723	....	* 1,250,000
Victoria & Sidney	16.26	500,000	300,000	300,000	....	(11)	(12)	410,500	160,422	435,585
Bedlington and Nelson	15.20	1,000,000	† 30,000	720,000	....	....	....	1,720,000	....	491,580

* Exclusive of rolling stock. † Per mile.

(1) Received $11,000 per mile from the Dominion under certain conditions and (2) 20,000 acres per mile from the Provincial Government.

(3) A land grant of 200,000 acres from the Provincial Government.

(4) No Dominion Government aid and (5) a Land Grant of 10,240 acres for narrow guage and 20,000 acres per mile from the Provincial Government.

(6) A land grant of 1,900,000 acres, with rights to coal and baser minerals.

(7) A land grant of 10,240 acres per mile.

(9) A land grant of 10,240 acres per mile.

(8) Guarantee of principal and interest by the Province under an arrangement whereby the Dominion Government subsidy was turned over to the Province as well as a certain percentage of gross traffic receipts of the railway.

(10) Guarantee of interest by the Provincial Government, the Dominion Government subsidy being turned into the Provincial Treasury with an arrangement as to traffic receipts.

(11) and (12) Guarantee of two per cent. interest on $300,000 by Provincial Government and Municipality of Victoria, each.

GAME OF BRITISH COLUMBIA

IT is difficult, in brief compass, to write about the game of British Columbia. The animals and birds which are hunted for sport are numerous and widely distributed over a vast extent of country presenting many opportunities of, as well as many obstacles to, success. The big game, such as grizzly bear, mountain sheep, caribou, are only found in the mountain fastnesses or the more inaccessible parts of the Province, and, therefore, their pursuit is not to be undertaken lightly. As, however, the difficulties and dangers incident to this life form the principal zest for true sport, British Columbia as a country is, and ought to be, a very attractive field for sportsmen. In a bulletin—No. 17—recently published by the Bureau of Provincial Information, is a check list of the more familiar birds and mammals. This was prepared by Mr. John Fannin, Curator of the Provincial Museum, than who no one is better qualified to deal with the subject. As this list, which is available for all seeking such information, gives the habitat of the game animals, it is unnecessary to more than refer to some of the phases of sport in British Columbia.

Frequent inquiries are made by persons in Great Britain and elsewhere, who are looking to this country as a field in which to shoot and fish; and there are many disappointments upon the part of such persons upon arrival in regard to the conditions which exist. Many of the big game sportsmen who come to the Province are extravagantly outfitted, and to many others the supposed cost acts as a deterrent.

In regard to big game — grizzly, caribou, and mountain sheep — it may be well to quote a letter written to a gentleman in quest of such information.

"First, as to the cost of outfitting, $500 a month, which will include a cook, a guide, and five ponies, will take any person very comfortably. Complete outfits can be obtained here, and much cheaper and better than at home, and all that are really necessary to obtain are rifles and blankets. It is a great mistake to buy expensive outfits in England, and in writing to your friends you should advise them on this point. Guides vary from $2.50 to $3.50 per day and can be obtained on the ground. Manson, of Lillooet, a half-breed son of an old Hudson's Bay Company officer, is the best guide in the country, and consequently the most expensive. He lives at Ashcroft. Indian guides can be had for $2.50 a day. Hunting parties can be outfitted at Lillooet or Hope. I would advise Manson because he knows every corner and nook of the country and is thoroughly reliable and well informed on every phase of big game sport. However, in order to obtain his services it will be necessary to give him ample notice as he is constantly in demand.

"Now then, as to the game itself, for mountain sheep, perhaps the most attractive game of British Columbia, the best places are the Bridge River country in Lillooet District, French Bark Creek, Chilcotin, and Ashnola in the Similkameen country. The last named place was the most famous for big horn in the country, but is now pretty well shot out. October and November are the best months for sheep.

"Mountain goats are found anywhere on the mountains of the Coast from the 49th parallel as far north as you can go. They inhabit the most inaccessible mountains and are not regarded as much sport as they are stupid animals and easily bagged when reached. The mountain goat can be hunted at any time in season.

"The wapiti (American Elk) are found only in the centre of Vancouver Island, where they are fairly plentiful.

"The nearest place for the caribou is in the Okanagan District. They are plentiful throughout Kootenay, in the Cariboo District and away north in the Omineca, Cassiar and Peace River Districts, where they are exceedingly plentiful. The caribou are shot principally in September and October.

"The best place for grizzly is in the Bridge River country, and they are found throughout Kootenay, in the Hope Mountains and all up the Coast Range into Alaska. May and June are the months for shooting grizzly. Black and brown bear are found everywhere in the country.

"The common kind of deer are plentiful everywhere."

The charges of good guides, who are absolutely necessary, are as a rule $2.50 and 50 cents for horses per day. Where special arrangements are made in regard to a cook, the consideration would be about $1.50 a day. In a word, the requirements depend very largely upon a man's tastes, but $500 a month is an ample allowance for two men, and it can be done very comfortably for $300. Of course, men like Manson of Lillooet and McDougall of Vernon are more expensive, but in the opinion of sportsmen who know the country they are the best obtainable and well worth the money. The following notes from Mr. W. F. Burton, from whom the information in this chapter is largely obtained, will give practically all that is necessary to be known on the subject:

For mountain sheep (ovis montana), mule deer, grizzly and mountain goat, Chilcotin and Bridge River countries are specially recommended. In respect to mountain sheep, larger heads, but less plentiful, are to be found in the Rocky Mountains, Golden being the best starting place.

In respect to other varieties of sheep (ovis fannini, stonei and dalli) moose and caribou, the Atlin country is recommended.

On Vancouver Island, wapiti (elk), black bear, black tailed deer, wolf and panther are plentiful.

Caribou, mule deer, grizzly, brown and black bear and mountain goat are to be found in the Okanagan and Kettle River country, for which Vernon is the principal starting point. Here is a very wide extent of country to be exploited.

In Cassiar there are mostly cariboo, grizzly, brown and black bear. In the far north, if the hunter had the time and would risk the expense, moose and caribou in great numbers would reward him.

In the northern interior, beaver are very plentiful, particularly in the Ootsa Lake country; very few foxes are to be found except in the extreme north land; otter are very plentiful on the Island and are found scattered on the Mainland; lynx are distributed all over the Mainland, also the wolverine. Panther are quite numerous on the Island of Vancouver. They are to be found also in the southern interior and are hunted with dogs.

In respect to feathered game and fishes it is still more difficult to specify without going into lengthy details, as they are very widely distributed.

Pheasants, which have been imported, are now very plentiful in the southern end of Vancouver Island, and on the Lower Mainland. All kinds of grouse are also plentiful in the same localities. Blue grouse are very abundant everywhere.

Snipe are found principally on Lulu Island, and this district for that particular sport is hard to beat. A good average day's shooting will give thirty brace to the man for a day, but larger bags can be had. There are also plover to be found here in the spring, and the duck shooting is excellent. Wild fowl, such as geese and ducks, are to be found in great abundance over the whole Coast, in the proper season, but particularly on the bays and inlets of Vancouver Island. Sooke Harbour on the south, and Quatsino on the north, are perhaps the most favourable localities.

Attempts have been made to give a list of lakes and streams in the Province recommended for fishing, but this is quite hopeless, as it is difficult to discriminate. As in everything else there are favourite localities, but in respect to trout nearly every part of the Province has its attractions. The best known resorts, however, on the Island are Shawnigan Lake and Cowichan River and Lake; on the Mainland the Coquitlam and Brunette Rivers, streams in Lillooet, the Shuswap and Okanagan Lakes, and the Kootenay River.

In chapter on "Fisheries" will be found reference to game fish and trout.

Salmon in British Columbia, though not ready to rise to the fly, are considered good sport during the season. Spring salmon and steelheads are caught throughout the year. Cohoes and sockeyes during the runs in the latter part of August and September and during the early part of October, according to the run, afford good sport. They may be trolled for in nearly all the waters of the Coast. The best salmon fishing in British Columbia, and possibly in the world, is to be found in Campbell River, on Vancouver Island. Fish have been caught here with rod and line, weighing over 70 pounds, while the average is about 50 pounds.

VITAL STATISTICS.

No provision has yet been made for the systematic and thorough compilation of vital statistics in this Province. The record of births, deaths and marriages is contained in the following, taken from the official reports of registration; but up until recent years registration was very imperfect, and it cannot be regarded as accurate for the whole period covered.

Year	Births	Deaths	Marriages	Year	Births	Deaths	Marriages
1872	[4 mos] 50	[4 mos] 37	[4 mos] 15	1888	462	527	342
1873	164	112	88	1889	572	552	431
1874	174	83	78	1890	641	555	431
1875	181	113	96	1891	922	750	655
1876	236	130	141	1892	1,165	757	655
1877	193	98	95	1893	1,241	827	640
1878	226	104	122	1894	1,378	836	595
1879	223	134	145	1895	1,252	735	621
1880	263	170	94	1896	1,641	1,020	636
1881	314	249	148	1897	1,331	1,013	629
1882	293	280	146	1898	2,038	1,340	965
1883	283	328	169	1899	1,755	1,415	872
1884	263	377	227	1900	1,774	1,494	1,004
1885	320	323	193	1901	2,146	1,488	1,150
1886	335	307	212	1902	1,977	1,655	1,148
1887	362	439	262				

GAME LAWS ABRIDGED.

Species of Birds, Animals, etc.	Unlawful to shoot or destroy during close season as shown below (dates both inclusive).	Unlawful to buy, sell or expose for sale, show or advertisement.	Unlawful to Kill or Take.
Beaver	1st April to 1st November		
Birds living on noxious insects	At any time	At any time	
Bittern	1st March to 31st August	At any time	
Blackbird (English)	At any time	At any time	
Caribou	1st January to 31st August	Before October 1st	More than five in one season.
Caribou (cow or calf)	At any time	At any time	
Chaffinch	At any time	At any time	
Deer (fawn under 12 months)	At any time	At any time	
Deer (buck)	15th December to 31st August	Before September 1st	More than ten in one season, or hunt with dogs, or kill for hides alone.
Deer (doe)	15th December to 31st August	At any time	
Duck (of all kinds)	1st March to 31st August	During close season	More than two hundred and fifty in one season.
Elk, Wapiti (bull)	1st January to 31st August	At any time	More than two in one season.
Elk, Wapiti (cow)	At any time	At any time	
Elk, Wapiti, calf under two years	At any time	At any time	
Grouse of all kinds (including Prairie Chicken)	1st January to 31st August	At any time, except Blue Grouse which may be sold dur'g season.	
Gull	At any time	At any time	
Hare	1st January to 31st August	Before October 1st	
Heron	1st March to 31st August	During close season	
Land Otter	1st April to 1st November		
Linnet	At any time	At any time	
Marten	1st April to 1st November		
Meadow Lark	1st March to 31st August	At any time	
Moose (bull)	1st January to 31st August	Before October 1st	More than two in one season.
Moose (cow, and calf under twelve mos)	At any time	At any time	
Mountain Goat	15th December to 31st August	Before October 1st	More than five in one season.
Mountain Sheep (ram)	15th December to 31st August	Before October 1st	More than three in one season.
Mountain Sheep (ewe or lamb)	At any time	At any time	
Partridge (English)	At any time	At any time	
Pheasant (cock)	At any time	At any time	
Pheasant (hen)	At any time	At any time	
Plover	1st March to 31st August	During close season	
Quail (of all kinds)	At any time	At any time	
Robin	Farmers only may shoot in gardens bet. June 1 & Sep. 1	At any time	
Skylark	At any time	At any time	
Thrush	At any time	At any time	
Eggs of protected birds	At any time	At any time	To take or destroy at any time.

VICTOR AND VANQUISHED.

MOUNTAIN GOATS IN THEIR NATIVE HABITAT.

LABOUR AND WAGES.

SINCE the publication of the Year Book in 1897, there has been a very considerable expansion in the influence and extent of labour unionism in this Province. In fact, from there being a comparatively few labour organizations in the larger Coast cities, embracing only a limited number of avocations, the whole of the inhabited part of the Province is organized and nearly every avocation is included. Prior to 1897 there had been organized 36 labour unions of all kinds. There are now, or was at the end of July, 1903, 187. The later organizations include fishermen, barbers, hotel and restaurant employees, musicians, laundry workers, cabmen, general labourers and the like. Agriculture is practically the only industry to which unionism does not extend. The Labor Gazette, June, 1902, officially published at Ottawa, gives a table showing the years in which the organizations were formed and the number in each year as follows (Only one organization is prior to 1884—under the head of "Metal, Engineering and Ship Building"—in 1860):

	84	85	86	87	88	89	1890	91	92	93	94	95	96	97	98	99	1900	01	02	Tot'l No. in Gr'p in Province
Building	..	..	..	..	1	1	3	..	..	..	..	..	..	2	2	4	5	2	2	22
Metal, engineering and ship building	..	1	..	..	..	..	1	1	..	..	..	..	1		1	3	4	3	1	18*
Woodworking and furnishing	..	..	..	..	..	..	..	..	..	..	..	..	..	..	..	..	2	1	..	3
Printing	1	..	..	..	1	..	..	..	..	..	..	..	1	1	2	3		1	..	10
Clothing	..	..	..	..	1	..	..	..	..	..	..	..	1	1	1	..	1	1	..	6
Food preparations	..	..	..	..	..	..	..	..	..	..	..	..	..	..	..	1	....	..	1	2
Tobacco	..	..	..	..	..	..	..	..	1	..	1	..	..	1	..	..	....	2	..	5
Mining and quarrying	..	..	..	..	..	1	1	..	..	..	..	1	..	..	1	11	2	4	..	21
Transport	..	..	1	2	2	..	2	..	1	1	..	1	..	..	2	3	1	9	1	26
Fishing	..	..	..	..	..	..	..	..	..	..	..	..	..	..	..	1	1	1	5	8
Employees of public authorities ..	..	..	..	..	..	..	..	..	..	..	..	..	..	..	..	..	....	3	2	5
Brewery workers	..	..	..	..	..	..	..	..	..	..	..	..	..	..	..	..	....	1	..	1
Hotel and restaurant employes	..	..	..	..	..	..	..	..	..	..	..	..	..	..	..	..	3	1	..	4
Barbers	..	..	..	..	..	..	..	..	..	..	..	..	..	..	1	1	1	2	..	5
Laundry workers	..	..	..	..	..	..	..	..	..	..	..	..	..	..	..	..	1	..	1	4
Clerks	..	..	..	..	..	..	..	..	..	..	..	..	..	..	..	1	....	2	1	4
Musicians	..	..	..	..	..	..	..	..	..	..	..	..	..	..	..	..	....	2	..	2
General labour ..	..	..	..	..	..	..	..	..	..	..	..	..	..	..	..	..	1	4	1	6
Total number organizations ...	1	1	1	2	5	2	7	1	2	1	1	2	3	6	10	28	22	39	14	150

In a subsequent issue, July, 1903, the list is detailed by localities and, increased to 216, showing very rapid growth. It is as follows:

* Includes one in 1860.

LABOUR ORGANIZATION IN BRITISH COLUMBIA.

Locality.	Class of Organization.	Number of Organizations in Class.	Total Number of Organizations in Locality.
Ashcroft	Transport	1	1
Camp McKinley	Mining	1	1
Cumberland	Mining	1	1
Cranbrook	Woodworking	1	
	Transport	4	5
Eburne	Fishing	1	1
Eholt	Woodworking	1	
	Transport	1	2
Extension	Mining	1	1
Fernie	Trades and Labour Council	1	
	District Union, W. F. of M., No. 7	1	
	Building	1	
	Mining	1	4
Golden	Transport	1	1
Greenwood	Trades and Labour Council	1	
	Building	1	
	Printing	1	
	Clothing	1	
	Mining	1	
	Hotel and restaurant employees	1	
	Clerks	1	7
Grand Forks	General labour	1	1
Kamloops	Tobacco	1	
	Mining	1	
	Transport	5	7
Kaslo	Mining	1	1
Kimberley	Mining	1	1
Ladysmith	Mining	1	1
Maywood	Transport	1	1
Michel	Mining	1	1
Mission City	Transport	1	1
Morissey	Mining	1	1
Moyie	Mining	1	1
Nanaimo	Trades and Labour Council	1	
	Metal	1	
	Printing	1	
	Clothing	1	
	Mining	1	
	Transport	1	
	General labour	1	7
Nelson	Trades and Labour Council	1	
	Building	1	
	Metal	1	
	Woodworking	1	
	Printing	1	
	Clothing	1	
	Tobacco	1	
	Mining	1	
	Transport	2	
	Hotel and restaurant employees	1	
	Barbers	1	
	Laundry workers	1	
	Clerks	1	
	Musicians	1	
	General labour	2	17
New Denver	Mining	1	1
New Westminster	Trades and Labour Council	1	
	Metal	1	
	Printing	1	
	Tobacco	1	
	Fishing	1	
	Transport	1	
	General labour	1	7

Locality.	Class of Organization.	Number of Organizations in Class.	Total Number of Organizations in Locality.
Phoenix	Trades and Labour Council	1	
	Building	1	
	Mining	1	
	Hotel and restaurant employees	1	
	Barbers	1	
	Clerks	1	
	General labor	1	7
Revelstoke	Trades and Labour Council	1	
	Metal	1	
	Transport	3	
	General labour	1	6
Roger's Pass	Transport	1	1
Rosebury	Transport	1	1
Rossland	Building	2	
	Printing	1	
	Mining	1	
	Barbers	1	5
Sandon	Mining	1	1
Shuswap	Transport	1	1
Silverton	Mining	1	1
Slocan City	Mining	1	1
South Wellington	Mining	1	1
Texada	Mining	1	1
Trail	Woodworking	1	1
Vancouver	Trades and Labour Council	1	
	Building Trades Council	1	
	Allied Printing Trades Council	1	
	District Association W. F. of M.	1	
	Building	9	
	Metal	11	
	Woodworking	4	
	Printing	3	
	Clothing	1	
	Food preparation	1	
	Tobacco	1	
	Transport	7	
	Employees of public authorities	3	
	Hotel and restaurant employees	1	
	Barbers	1	
	Laundry Workers	1	
	Clerks	1	
	Musicians	1	
	General labour	2	51
Victoria	Trades and Labour Council	1	
	Building Trades Council	1	
	Building	5	
	Metal	9	
	Printing	2	
	Leather	1	
	Clothing	2	
	Food preparation	1	
	Tobacco	2	
	Transport	5	
	Employees of public authorities	1	
	Clerks	1	
	Barbers	1	
	Musicians	1	
	General labour	1	34
Whitewater	Mining	1	1
Yale	Transport	1	1
Ymir	Mining	1	1
	Total for British Columbia	187	187

During and since 1899 strikes have been frequent. The whole mining industry of the Interior was affected. The difficulty largely arose out of the coming into operation of the eight hour law. At least feeling between employers and employees was greatly embittered on that account. Happily the principle became generally recognized and settlements were effected in all the mining camps. During the present year very serious strikes occurred, which promised to become general; but they were all fortunately compromised and there are not now any labour troubles existing.

In regard to wages paid, hours per week, etc., it would occupy a great deal of space to give them in detail as in every locality there are local conditions which cause them to vary. The scale is governed in each district by local organizations. It has been deemed sufficient to give the lowest and highest wage, which will indicate the variations according to locality. It must not be understood, however, that there is steady employment at the wages given. In many instances the schedule will only apply for six or eight or ten months. As a rule, too, supply is equal to demand, except perhaps in the logging camps. The following is the schedule referred to :

IN THE TRADES.

	Wages per hour.		Wages per week.		Average hours per week.		Rate of overtime.	
Millwrights	.30c	to 35c	$16 50	to $19 80	55	to 60	1¼	to 1½
Carvers	.30	35	16 50	19 00	55		1¼	
Cabinet Makers	.27½	35	15 00	16 50	55	60	1¼	1½
Polishers and finishers	.27½	30	15 10	16 50	55		1¼	1½
Bench-hands	.25	35	16 50	17 00	54	60	1¼	
Turners	.35	32½	16 50	21 00	52	60	1¼	1½
Stair builders	.30	35	16 25	19 25	52	60	1¼	1½
Door-makers	.20	30	11 00	21 00	52	58	1¼	1½
Sash and blind-makers	.20	30	11 00	21 00	52	60	1¼	1½
Frame-makers	.20	30	11 00	15 00	52	60	1¼	1½
Bench-hands' helpers	.10	25	6 00	15 00	55	58	1¼	
Machine hands	.24	30	17 00	19 00	52	60	1¼	1½
Shaper hands	.25	35	13 00	18 00	52	60	1¼	1½
Sticker hands	.25	35	13 00	18 00	52	60	1¼	1½
Band-saw hands	.25	30	13 00	21 00	52	58	1¼	1½
Jig-saw hands	.25	35	13 00	16 50	52	60	1¼	1½
Circular-saw hands	.20	30	11 00	24 00	52	60	1¼	1½
Matcher hands	.15½	35	9 00	16 50	52	60	1¼	1½
Planer hands	.15½	35	9 00	16 00	52	60	1¼	1½
Labourers	.10	20	6 00	12 00	55	60	1¼	
Blacksmiths	.25	40	16 50	19 50	55	60	1¼	1½
Blacksmiths' helpers	.20	30	11 00	18 00	55	60	1¼	1½
Body and gear builders	.25	30	14 00	18 50	55	60		
Wheelwrights	.25	30	14 00	18 00	55	60		
General painters, stripers and varnishers	.25	33 1-3	14 00	18 50	54	56		
Steam-fitters	.30	40	18 00	24 00	48	50	1½	2
Plumbers	.30	50	16 00	30 00	48	60	1½	2
Gas-fitters	.30	44	16 00	24 00	48	55½	1½	2
Plasterers	.30	75	24 00	36 00	48	54	1½	
Painters	.28	39	15 00	21 00	48	54	1½	
Glaziers	.25	44½	15 00	21 00	48	60	1½	
Tinsmiths	.25	40	16 00	24 00	54	60	1½	2
Ordinary labourers	.20	30	11 00	18 00	53	60	1¼	2
Stone drillers	.25	40	13 00	19 50	48	60	1½	
Stone cutters	.30	62½	22 00	30 00	48	54	1½	
Quarrymen	.25	40	13 00	19 50	48	60	1½	
Metal roofers	.30	40	18 00	24 00	54	60	1½	

	Wages per hour.		Wages per week.		Average hours per week.		Rate of overtime.	
Metal roofer helpers	...20c	to 25c	$10 00 to	$13 50	54 to		1½ to	
Slate roofer helpers	22	30½	13 50	15 00	49	54	1½	
Slate roofers	33	55	18 00	27 00	49	54	1½	
Derrick men	25	33 1-3	13 00	18 00	54	60	1½	
Electricians	30	40	16 00	25 00	54	60	1½	
Galvanized iron workers	.30	4)	16 00	21 00	54	55½	1½	2
Lathers	25	30	16 50	18 00	50	54	1½	
Steel workers	35		20 00		55		1½	
Coppersmiths	 30	40	16 00	20 00	54		1½	
Excavators	20	27½	11 00	15 00	48	60	1¼	1½
Felt and gravel roofers	..25	44½	13 00	21 75	49	55½	1½	
Felt and gravel roofers' helpers	20	25	12 00		49	54	1½	
Powder men	25	35	13 00	18 00	54	60	1½	
Teamsters (2 horses and waggon)	..........27½	70	15 00	42 00	54	60	1½	
Teamsters (1 horse and cart)	20	40	12 00	24 00	54	60	1¼	1½
Carpenters	............$3 to $3.50 per day..........				54		1¼	1½
Shinglers	...............$2.70 to $3 per day.........				54		1¼	1½

FARMING AND MINING.

Farm labour is becoming to be rather a serious problem in the agricultural communities, more especially on account of the Chinese per capitation tax being increased to $500. Chinese were mainly employed throughout the Province for farm labour. They received from $10 to $20 a month. Last year a considerable number of white farm labourers were employed and are paid from $20 to $30 a month with board. A large demand exists for skilled milkers, who are paid as high as $40 a month and board.

The current wages paid in and about the metalliferous mines are as follows :—

Miners ....receive from $3 00 to $3 50 per day (12 to 14 shillings)
Helpers ....receive from 2 00 to 2 50 per day (8 to 10 shillings)
Labourers ....receive from 2 00 to 2 50 per day (8 to 10 shillings)
Blacksmiths & mechanics receive from 3 00 to 5 00 per day (12 to 20 shillings)

NUMBER OF HANDS EMPLOYED, DAILY WAGES PAID, &c. (1902) IN COAL MINES.

Character of Labour.	Underground.		Above Ground.		Totals.	
	No. Emply'd.	Average Daily Wage.	No. Emply'd.	Average Daily Wage.	No. Emply'd.	Average Daily Wage.
Supervision and Clerical Assistance	63	$4 30	48	$4 85	111	$4 57
Whites—Miners	1,625	4 30	....	....	1,625	4 30
Miners' Helpers	494	2 40	....	......	494	2 40
Labourers	569	2 73	206	2 34	775	2 53
Mechanics and Skilled Labour..	47	2 81	199	3 10	246	2 95
Boys	133	1 42	23	1 15	156	1 28
Japanese	38	1 37	46	1 12	84	1 24
Chinese	132	1 37	388	1 21	520	1 29
Indians	.....	....	....	....	... ...	....
Totals	3,101	....	910	....	4,011	

EMPLOYEES AND SALARIES, PACIFIC DIVISION, C. P. R.

Class.	Number on June 30th, 1903.	Total Number of Days Worked.	Total Yearly Compensation.	Average Daily Compensation.
Officers (not general)	18	6,124	$ 32,569.70	$5.32
General Office Clerks	104	32,929	55,105.15	1.67
Station Agents	58	19,859	52,676.14	2.65
Other Stationmen	259	80,398	145,106.20	1.80
Enginemen	126	38,431	174,065.59	4.53
Firemen	135	37,601	101,752.01	2.70
Conductors	83	26,380	104,033.82	3.94
Other Trainmen	174	51,992	132,612.52	2.55
Section Foremen	153	49,461	113,425.76	2.29
Other Trackmen	633	54,530	220,918.32	1.44
Switchmen, Flagmen and Watchmen	44	15,834	37,376.35	2.36
Telegraph Operators and Despatchers	65	20,727	55,309.54	2.66
Employees—Floating Equipment	210	63,000	135,546.34	2.15
All other Employees and Laborers	1,212	239,893	494,256.06	2.06
Total	3,274	837,159	$1,854,753.50	

NOTE.—This return to cover operating expenses only.

DETAILS OF ALL OTHER EMPLOYEES AND LABORERS.

Class.	No.	No. of Days.	Yearly Compensation.	Average Comp'n.
Bridge Inspectors	3	1,095	$ 3,385.00	3.00
Road Masters	5	1,823	7,495.25	4.11
Masons	8	141	429.95	3.05
Extra Foremen	17	3,065	8,454.08	2.75
Extra Laborers	344	53,679	72,641.77	1.35
Private Car Porters	2	506	754.00	1.50
Carpenters in shops	52	15,401.3	39,985.60	2.60
Foremen in shops	17	5,619.3	17,797.34	3.17
Road Foremen	3	993	4,384.03	4.43
Laborers in shops	41	8,203.3	11,746.35	1.43
Master Mechanic	1	375	2,204.03	5.88
Pumpers and Repairers	10	3,273.3	5,673.86	1.74
Machinists	29	5,613.6	16,008.16	2.85
Other Shopmen	663	135,726.8	294,349.97	2.16
Storekeepers	3	1,109	3,300.96	2.98
Store Foremen	1	346	814.11	2.35
Storemen	13	2,924	4,931.60	1.69
Total	1,212	239,893	$494,256.06	

PRINTING AND PRESSWORK.

Wages in the printing trade vary somewhat according to locality. For machine composition the standard is 50 cents per hour on morning papers, and from 40 to 45 cents per hour for evening papers and book work; by the week on morning papers, $22.50 to $27 and from $20 to $24 for evening papers and other work. Time and a half is usually allowed for overtime per hour, 48 hours being the standard weekly time.

For hand composition wages are 50 cents per 1,000 ems on morning papers and 40 to 45 cents on evening papers and for book work; 50 to 60 cents per hour is paid on morning papers, and 31½ to 60 cents on evening and weekly papers and for book and job work. The high rate is unusual, however, and is only paid at Nelson. The weekly wage on morning papers is $21 to $22.50, and from $18 to $21 on evening papers and for other work. The usual time and a half is allowed for overtime. The hours per week vary from 42 to 54—53 and 54 being the average.

The foregoing are union wages. In towns not organized the wages are from $12 to $18 per week.

Pressmen's wages are from $3 to $3.50 per day, $17 to $21 per week, with 48 to 54 hours per week. Pressmen's assistants receive $2.50 per day and upwards, from $12 to $18 per week; apprentices from $4 to $15 per week.

*OTHER OCCUPATIONS.

Altogether there were in 1900 about 1,800 whites, 240 Chinese and 452 Japanese employed in the lumbering industry in British Columbia. With regard to wages, a foreman earn from $30 to $140 a month and board, and a Japanese labourer from 90 cents to $1.25 a day and board. Board is estimated to cost 35 cents a day. Unskilled white labour is paid from $1.50 to $2 a day, semi-skilled from $2 to $2.50 and skilled from $2.50 to $3.50, or as high as $4.50 or $5 a day.

In the same year there were 445 whites, 183 Chinese and 364 Japanese engaged in the shingle mills of the Province. The ordinary sawyer earns $2.75 a day and $3.50 if exceptionally efficient. Cord-wood cutting is done through the agency of Chinese contractors who employ the men at about $1.20 a day.

The process of salmon canning is almost exclusively done by contract, the agreement being made with boss Chinamen, who hire their own help in their own way. Certain Chinamen have become experts in the business and earn from $35 to $45 a month, being furnished generally with an advance of from $30 to $40 at the opening of the season. The contractor also supplies the provisions of his men, and it is on this that he counts on making the chief item of his profit. White men make from $40 to $100 a month, including board, which is commonly estimated at $12 a month. The value of a plant of a canner runs from $10,000 to $15,000, when capable of producing from 1,500 to 2,000 cases a day.

White girls as domestic servants can get employment in British Columbia at from $15 to $20 a month, and are very scarce. In Victoria, Vancouver, New Westminster, Nanaimo, Kamloops and Rossland Chinese domestic servants earn wages varying from $10 to $30 a month in private families and from $25 to $45 in hotels.

The laundry business is principally carried on by Chinese, there being steam laundries in but one or two of the cities. The average paid to Chinamen is from $8 to $18 a month and bord.

In merchant tailoring women and girls work at an average wage of $6 per week and men at $12 per week, high-class workmen being paid at the rate of $18 per week. There is a number of Chinese and Japanese merchant tailors. The Chinese pay from $25 to $40 a month to men, who live at from $7 to $8 per month.

* The particulars following, as contained in the Labour Gazette were gleaned from the report of the Royal Commission appointed to enquire into Chinese and Japanese labour in this Province.

In the wholesale manufacture of clothing, chiefly centred in the City of Victoria, Chinese have largely displaced white labour, although a few white women and girls find employment. From $2.25 to $6 per dozen is paid for making trousers, the work as a rule being done by contract in all lines. The boot and shoe factory in Victoria employed 16 Chinamen at from $1 to $1.35 a day and four white men from $3 to $4 a day.

The rate of wages paid to the cigarmakers of the International Union, which prevails in British Columbia, ranges from $11 to $19 per thousand, or from $1.10 to $1.90 a hundred. Some Chinese are employed at from 50 cents to $1 per hundred cigars.

In brickmaking Chinese are largely employed. They are paid from $9 to $10 per week, a Chinese labourer earning $2.50 a day. A moulder's work is 8,000 bricks a day.

Lime burning is largely done by Chinese, receiving $1 to $1.25 a day, white men receiving $45 to $50 per month.

In fruit canning, not largely developed as yet, men receive from $50 to $60 per month, women and girls 75 cents to $1 a day, boys $25 to $35 a month, and Japanese $1 a day.

In sugar-refining, in which skilled labour is mainly employed, the lowest wage paid is 20 cents per hour.

THE GOVERNMENT SCALE.

The wages paid by the Provincial Government vary somewhat, according to the district; but, speaking generally, labourers employed on public works receive from $2 to $2.50, and foremen from $3 to $3.50 per day. There is a clause in all contracts for public works that contractors must pay the rate of wage in the district current at the date of signing the contract.

OTHER EMPLOYMENTS.

In regard to a large class of unorganized employees, such as clerks, bookkeepers, stenographers, typewriters, etc., there is no general statement that would accurately define their remuneration. Experience, length of service and skill determine in a great measure the salaries which are paid. Clerks receive from $40 to $75 per month, typewriters and stenographers from $25 to $60 per month; bookkeepers and accountants receive from $60 to $125 per month. Positions of special responsibility in all these avocations command special remuneration. As a rule in all sedentary occupations of this character the supply exceeds the demand. Teachers receive salaries varying from $50 a month to $100. In the cases of the principals of the larger public schools and in high schools the salaries range higher according to position and special qualifications.

AN EXPERIMENT IN CO-OPERATION.

The only experiment in co-operation or profit-sharing which has so far been made in British Columbia is the system introduced by the British Columbia Electric Company in connection with the company's business in Vancouver and Victoria. After the ordinary shareholders have received a four per cent. dividend, the balance of the profits is divided on the following basis: Two-thirds to the shareholders and one-third to the employees. Every employee who has worked regularly for the company during the twelve months ending June 30th each year will participate in the division and the proportion of the profits will be divided equally among them. Mr. Buntzen, General Manager and Controller, is quite enthusiastic as to the general results of this policy. Recently the first dividend was declared and the employees received $25 each for their share of the profits during the year ending June 30, 1903. The Manager states: "We have about 200 regular employees. Our men have an organization of their own which the management has recognized from the start. So far no difficulties have arisen which could not be adjusted by a quiet talk, without loss of dignity to either side, and without any break in our friendly relations."

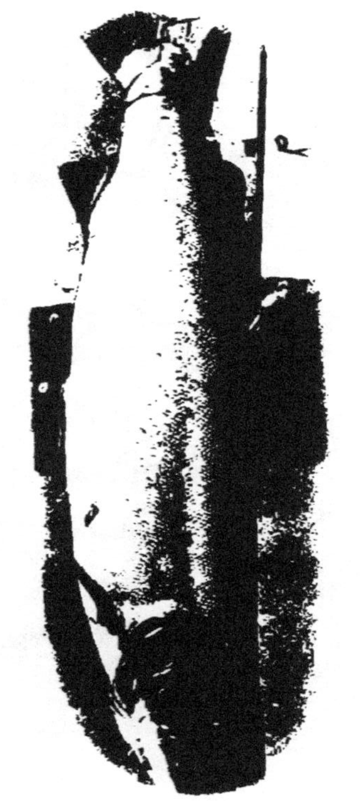

AN 11-lb. OKANAGAN TROUT.

A WINGED TROPHY (Red-Headed Duck).

A WINTER DAY'S FISHING ON OKANAGAN LAKE.

A COWICHAN RIVER CATCH.

CONDITIONS IN KOOTENAY.

The correspondent of the Labour Gazette of Ottawa, Roland A. Laird, Rossland, speaking of the industrial development of the Kootenay districts with special reference to the labour conditions, has this to say in the December number:

"The Kootenays have witnessed serious misunderstandings between employers and employed, as might be expected in a district where great industries were being established with an expedition that is probably only paralleled in the experience of the West. Each of these collisions has been followed by an understanding which ensured peace for a considerable length of time, and it would seem as if the danger of serious interruption to industrial progress from this source had about passed away. There is a desire for good feeling manifested on all sides, and this is a happy augury of continued freedom from dissension. A strong factor in maintaining this desirable state of affairs is the notable tendency to recognize and reward true merit and zeal, which is so characteristic of conditions in the Kootenays."

BOARD.

Perhaps in nothing affecting labour is there such a variation as in the matter of board. It varies according to locality and also according to quality. Private board ranges from $20 a month, which is the very cheapest, to $40 in first-class boarding houses. As to hotel and restaurant fare, that is, of course, very difficult to indicate. It ranges in price from $25 to $60 a month, or from $1 to $4.50 a day.

POLITICAL INFORMATION.

GOVERNORS OF VANCOUVER ISLAND.

Name.	From.	To.
Richard Blanshard	1849	Nov., 1851
Sir James Douglas, K.C.B	Nov., 1851	Mar., 1864
Arthur Edward Kennedy	Oct., 1864	Union, 1866

GOVERNORS OF BRITISH COLUMBIA.

Name.	From.	To.
Sir James Douglas	Sept., 1858	Apr., 1864
Frederick Seymour	Apr., 1864	June, 1869
Anthony Musgrave, C.M.G	Aug., 1869	July, 1871

LIEUTENANT-GOVERNORS SINCE CONFEDERATION.

Name.	From.	To.
Sir J. W. Trutch, C.M.G	July 5, 1871	July, 1876
A. N. Richards	June 27, 1876	July, 1881
C. F. Cornwall	June 21, 1881	Feb., 1887
Hugh Nelson	Feb. 8, 1887	July, 1892
Edgar Dewdney	Nov. 1, 1892	Nov., 1897
T. R. McInnes	Nov. 18, 1897	June, 1900
Sir Henri Joly de Lotbinière	June 21, 1900	

CHIEF JUSTICES OF V. I. AND B. C.

Name.	From.	To.
Hon. David Cameron	Dec. 2, 1853	Oct. 11, 1865
" Mr. Justice Needham	Oct. 11, 1865	Mar. 29, 1870
* " Matthew Baillie-Begbie	Sept. 2, 1858	June 11, 1894
" Theodore Davie	Feb. 23, 1895	Mar. 7, 1898
" Angus John McColl	Oct. 13, 1896	Jan. 16, 1902
" Gordon Hunter	Mar. 4, 1902	

* Knighted Nov. 26th, 1874.

LIST OF SPEAKERS.

Name.	From.	To.
Hon. J. S. Helmcken	1856	1871
" James Trimble	1872	1878
" F. W. Williams	1878	1882
" J. A. Mara	1883	1886
" C. E. Pooley	1887	1889
" D. W. Higgins (1)	1890	1898
" J. P. Booth	1898	1898
" Thos. Forster	1899	1900
" J. P. Booth (2)	1900	1902
" C. E. Pooley	1902	1903

(1) Resigned 4th March, 1898. (2) Died March, 1902.

THE SUPREME COURT.

The Supreme Court of British Columbia is composed of a Chief Justice and four Puisne Judges. Prior to the passing of the Act 42 Vict., (B.C.) Chap. 20, (1878) the Court was composed of a Chief Justice and two Puisne Judges. The Court was originally called "The Supreme Court of Civil Justice of British Columbia," and was constituted by proclamation having the force of law, issued by the Governor of the Colony of British Columbia, on the 8th of June, 1859. The following is a list of Judges appointed from the outset:

1870—March 11. The Hon. Henry Pering Pellew Crease, first Puisne Judge. Received Knighthood January 1st, 1896. Retired January 20th, 1896. (1).

1872—July 3. The Hon. John Hamilton Gray, Puisne Judge. Died June 5th, 1889.

1880—Nov. 26. The Hon. John Foster McCreight, Puisne Judge. Retired Nov. 17th, 1897.

1880—Nov. 26. The Hon. Alexander Rocke Robertson, Puisne Judge. Died Dec. 1st, 1881.

1882—May 23. The Hon. George Anthony Walkem, Puisne Judge.

1889—Aug. 14. The Hon. Montague William Tyrwhitt Drake, Puisne Judge.

1895—Feb. 23. The Hon. Theodore Davie, Chief Justice, succeeding Sir Matthew Baillie-Begbie. Died March 7th, 1898.

1896—Oct. 13. The Hon. Angus John McColl, Puisne Judge. August 23rd, 1898, appointed Chief Justice, succeeding the Hon. Theodore Davie. Died Jan. 16th, 1902.

1897—Dec. 18. The Hon. Paulus Æmilius Irving, Puisne Judge.

1898—Sept. 12. The Hon. Archer Martin, Puisne Judge. (2).

1902—March 4. Hon. Gordon Hunter, Chief Justice, succeeding the Hon. Angus John McColl.

(1). Mr. Justice Crease was appointed Deputy Judge in Admiralty of the Exchequer Court of Canada for the Admiralty District of British Columbia, 27th November, 1893. He was succeeded by Hon. Angus McColl.

(2). Hon. Archer Martin was appointed Local Judge in Admiralty in the room and stead of the Hon. Angus McColl, deceased, March 4th, 1902.

THE COUNTY COURTS.

By "The County Court Act, 1883," passed by the Legislative Assembly of the Province of British Columbia, which came into force on the 20th February, 1884, the following County Courts, which are Courts of Record, were established, namely :

The County Court of Victoria;
The County Court of New Westminster;
The County Court of Yale;
The County Court of Cariboo;
The County Court of Kootenay;
The County Court of Nanaimo.

An additional County Court, called the "County Court of Vancouver," was established by the Act 56 Vict. (B.C.) Chap. 10, which, as respects this Court, came into force on the 1st December, 1893.

Any County Court Judge may act as Judge in any other district than that assigned him for causes such as death, illness or unavoidable absence, or at the request of the Judge of that other district; the fact of his doing so with the cause to be reported in writing to the Provincial Secretary.

The several Judges of the Supreme Court may sit and dispose of any business in any County Court of the Province

After the union of the Colonies of British Columbia and Vancouver Island the procedure of the County Courts in all parts of British Columbia was amended and assimilated by the "County Court Ordinances, 1867," and the Governor of the Colony empowered to appoint any Stipendiary Magistrates or Justices of the Peace to be County Court Judges. This provision of the ordinances was repealed, and the Governor-General of Canada. Subsequently the commissions held by the then County Court Judges were revoked and the Courts were presided over by a Judge of the Supreme Court until County Court Judges were again appointed under the provisions of "The County Courts Act, 1883."

Following is a list of County Court Judges who have been appointed in British Columbia :

Name.	Place.	From.	To.
Augustus F. Pemberton	Victoria	23rd Sept., 1867	14th Jan., 1881
Edward H. Sanders	Lillooet and Clinton	18th Sept., 1867	14th Jan., 1881
Warner R. Spalding	Nanaimo and Comox	28th Sept., 1867	14th Jan., 1881
Henry M. Ball	Cariboo	18th Sept., 1867	14th Jan., 1881
Peter O'Reilly	Yale	18th Sept., 1867	14th Jan., 1881
Arthur T. Bushby	New Westminster		18th May, 1875
Eli Harrison (1)	Cariboo	25th April, 1884	2nd Aug., 1889
William N. Bole	New Westminster	19th Sept., 1889	
Clement F. Cornwall	Cariboo	18th Sept., 1889	
Eli Harrison	Nanaimo	3rd Aug., 1889	
William Ward Spinks	Yale	19th Sept., 1889	
John Forin	Kootenay	1896	
Alexander Henderson	Vancouver	6th June, 1901	
Andrew Leamy	Kootenay	13th June, 1901	
Andrew Leamy	Yale	31st Oct., 1901	

(1) Judge Harrison transferred to the County Court of Nanaimo, 3rd August, 1889.

ADMINISTRATIONS AND MEMBERS OF THE EXECUTIVE COUNCIL SINCE 20th JULY, 1871.

NAMES.	PORTFOLIO.	DATE.		CAUSE OF REMOVAL.
		From	To	
Hon. J. F. McCreight, Q.C.	Premier and Attorney-General	— Dec., 1871	23 Dec., 1872	Ministry resigned.
" A. R. Robertson, Q.C.	Provincial Secretary	— Jan., 1872	23 Dec., 1872	" "
" Henry Holbrook	Lands and Works President of Council	— Nov., 1871 15 Jan., 1872	15 Jan., 1872 20 Dec., 1872	" "
" G. A. Walkem, Q.C.	Lands and Works	12 Jan., 1872	20 Dec., 1872	" "
" Amor DeCosmos	Premier and President of Council	23 Dec., 1872	11 Feb., 1874	Resigned.
" G. A. Walkem, Q C.	Attorney-General Premier	23 Dec., 1872 11 Feb., 1874	27 Jan., 1876	Ministry resigned.
" Robert Beaven	Lands and Works	23 Dec., 1872	27 Jan., 1876	" "
" John Ashe, M.D.	Provincial Secretary	23 Dec., 1872	27 Jan., 1876	" "
" W. J. Armstrong	Without office Finance and Agriculture	23 Dec., 1872 28 Feb., 1873	28 Feb., 1873 27 Jan., 1876	" "
" Hon. A. C. Elliott	Premier, Attorney-General and Provincial Secretary	1 Feb., 1876	25 June, 1878	" " " "
" F. G. Vernon	Lands and Works	1 Feb, 1876	25 June, 1878	" "
" T. B. Humphreys	Finance and Agriculture	1 Feb., 1876	1 Feb., 1876	" "
" E. Brown	President of Council	1 Feb., 1876	11 Sept., 1876	Resigned.
" Wm. Smithe	Finance and Agriculture	10 Aug., 1876	— June, 1876	"
" A. E. B. Davie	Provincia lSecretary	15 May, 1877	— Aug., 1877	"
" G. A. Walkem	Premier, Attorney-General, Lands and Works, and President of Council	26 June, 1878	13 June, 1882	Appointed Judge.
" T. B. Humphreys	Provincial Secretary and Minister of Mines	26 June, 1878	13 June, 1882	Resigned.
" Robert Beaven	Finance	26 June, 1878	13 June, 1882	"

Name	Office	From	To	Remarks
Hon. Robert Beaven	Premier, Lands and Works, Finance, Agriculture and President of Council	13 June, 1882	30 Jan., 1883	Ministry resigned.
" T. B. Humphreys	Provincial Secretary and Minister of Mines	13 June, 1882	23 Aug., 1882	Resigned.
" J. R. Hett	Attorney-General	13 June, 1882	30 Jan., 1883	Ministry resigned.
" W. J. Armstrong	Provincial Secretary	23 Aug., 1882	30 Jan., 1883	" "
" Wm. Smithe	Premier, Lands and Works	29 Jan., 1883	29 Mar., 1887	Deceased.
" A. E. B. Davie, Q.C.	Attorney-General and Premier (April, 1887)	29 Jan., 1883	— Aug., 1889	Deceased.
" John Robson	Provincial Secretary, Minister of Finance and Agriculture.	29 Jan., 1883	— July, ——	
" M. W. T. Drake, Q.C.	President of Council	29 Jan., 1883	8 Dec., 1884	Resigned.
" Simeon Duck	Finance and Agriculture	21 Mar., 1885	15 Oct., 1886	"
" John Robson	Minister of Finance and Agriculture	16 Oct., 1886	7 Aug., 1887	
" F. G. Vernon	Chief Commissioner Lands and Works	1 April, 1887		
" Robert Dunsmuir	President of Council	8 Aug., 1887	....	Deceased.
" J. H. Turner	Finance and Agriculture	8 Aug., 1887		
" John Robson	Premier, Provincial Secretary and Minister of Mines	3 Aug., 1889	— June, 1892	Deceased.
" F. G. Vernon	Chief Commissioner Lands and Works	3 Aug., 1889	— June, 1892	Ministry dissolved.
" J. H. Turner	Finance aad Agriculture	3 Aug., 1889	— June, 1892	" "
" Theo. Davie, Q.C.	Attorney-General	3 Aug., 1889	— June, 1892	" "
" C. E. Pooley, Q.C.	President of Council	3 Aug., 1889	— June, 1892	" "
" Theo. Davie, Q.C.	Premier, Attorney-General and Provincial Secretary	2 July, 1892	4 Mar., 1895	Resigned.
" F. G. Vernon	Chief Commissioner Lands and Works	2 July, 1892	4 Mar., 1895	"
" J. H. Turner	Finance and Agriculture	2 July, 1892	4 Mar., 1895	"
" James Baker	Education and Immigration, Provincial Secretary	28 May, 1892 7 Sept., 1892	4 Mar., 1895 4 Mar., 1895	"
" C. E. Pooley, Q.C.	President of Council	2 July, 1892	4 Mar., 1895	
" J. H. Turner	Premier, Finance and Agriculture	4 Mar., 1895	8 Aug.. 1898	Ministry dismissed.
" C. E. Pooley, Q.C.	President of Council	4 Mar., 1895	8 Aug., 1898	" "
" James Baker	Provincial Secretary, Minister of Mines, Minister of Education and Immigration	4 Mar., 1895	8 Aug., 1898	" "
" G. B. Martin	Chief Commissioner Lands and Works	4 Mar., 1895	8 Aug., 1898	" "
" D. M. Eberts, Q.C.	Attorney-General	4 Mar., 1895	8 Aug., 1898	" "

The Turner Ministry was dismissed on August 8th, 1898, as the result of the elections, the Lieutenant-Governor claiming that it had lost his confidence and had not a majority of the Members-elect in support.

The Semlin Ministry succeeded August 12th, 1898, constituted as follows:

C. A. Semlin, Premier and Minister of Public Works and Agriculture.
Joseph Martin, Attorney-General and Acting Minister of Education.
F. Carter-Cotton, Finance Minister.
J. Fred Hume, Provincial Secretary and Minister of Mines.
R. McKechnie, President of the Executive Council without portfolio.

On March 10th, 1899, changes were made in the distribution of portfolios. Mr. Semlin retired from the Chief Commissionership of Lands and Works and undertook the Provincial Secretaryship, Mr. Hume resigning that but continuing to be Minister of Mines, while Mr. Carter-Cotton became Chief Commissioner of Lands and Works in addition to his office as Minister of Finance and Agriculture. Mr. Martin continued to hold the Attorney-Generalship and Dr. McKechnie the Presidency of the Council.

On July 27th at the request of the Premier, Mr. Martin resigned, and was succeeded August 7th, 1899, by Mr. Alex. Henderson. On February 27th, 1900, the Lieutenant-Governor dismissed the Ministry and called on Mr. Joseph Martin to form a Government. The Martin Ministry was composed of:

Hon. Joseph Martin, Premier and Attorney-General.
Hon. C. S. Ryder, Minister of Finance.
Hon. Smith Curtis, Minister of Mines.
Hon. J. Stuart Yates, Chief Commissioner of Lands and Works.
Hon. George W. Beebe, Provincial Secretary.

In April, 1900, Mr. Ryder retired and Mr. J. C. Brown became Minister of Finance. Mr. Martin appealed to the country and in consequence of the election resigned office June 14th, 1900. Mr. Dunsmuir was called on to form a Cabinet. Another result of the elections was the dismissal of the Lieutenant-Governor, Hon. T. R. McInnes, from office, June 21st, 1900.

Hon. James Dunsmuir was called on to form a Ministry in which he succeeded June 15th, 1900, his Cabinet being as follows:

Hon. James Dunsmuir, Premier and President of the Council.
Hon. D. McE. Eberts, Attorney-General.
Hon. J. H. Turner, Minister of Finance and Agriculture.
Hon. Richard McBride, Minister of Mines.
Hon. W. C. Wells, Chief Commissioner of Lands and Works.
Hon. J. D. Prentice, Provincial Secretary and Minister of Education.

The Premier and Messrs. Eberts and Turner were sworn in June 15th, but Messrs. Wells McBride and Prentice not until June 21st. Mr. Turner resigned September 3rd, 1901, to accept the position of Agent-General in London. Mr. Prentice became Finance Minister and Mr. J. C. Brown, M. P. P., was sworn in September 3rd, 1901, as Provincial Secretary. Mr. McBride thereupon resigned from the Cabinet in consequence of the calling in of Mr. Brown. On going back for election Mr. Brown was defeated and resigned his portfolio. Mr. McBride's place was filled by the appointment of the Hon. E. G. Prior February 26th, 1902.

Mr. Dunsmuir resigned November 21st, 1902, and Col. The Hon. E. G. Prior was called on to form a Government.

Col. The Hon. E. G. Prior, Minister of Mines, succeeded as Premier November 21st, 1902, and formed the following Administration:

Hon. Edward G. Prior, Premier and Minister of Mines.
Hon. D. McE. Eberts, Attorney-General.
Hon. J. D. Prentice, Minister of Finance and Agriculture.
Hon. Denis Murphy, Provincial Secretary.
Hon. W. C. Wells, Chief Commissioner of Lands and Works.
Hon. W. W. B. McInnes, President of the Council.

Messrs. Wells and Murphy were appointed November 22nd, and Messrs. Eberts and McInnes November 25th. Mr. Murphy relinquished office within a few days and Mr. McInnes was appointed Provincial Secretary and Minister in charge of Education December 1st, 1902, having been President of the Council for one week. On May 26th, 1903, it was announced that Premier Prior had requested the resignation of Mr. Eberts and Mr. Wells. On May 27th Mr. McInnes resigned in order, he explained, to facilitate an appeal to the country on party lines.

On June 1st the Lieutenant-Governor dismissed the Prior Ministry and called on the Hon. Richard McBride to form a Government, which he succeeded in doing as follows, dating from June 1st, 1903:

Hon. Richard McBride, Premier and Chief Commissioner of Lands and Works.
Hon. A. E. McPhillips, Attorney-General.
Hon. R. G. Tatlow, Minister of Finance and Agriculture.
Hon. Charles Wilson, President of the Council.
Hon. Robert F. Green, Minister of Mines.
Hon. A. S. Goodeve, Provincial Secretary.

Hons. A. E. McPhillips and A. S. Goodeve were both defeated and subsequently resigned.

On November 5th, the Ministry was reconstructed as follows:

Hon. R. McBride, Premier, Minister of Mines and Provincial Secretary.
Hon. R. G. Tatlow, Minister of Finance and Agriculture.
Hon. Chas. Wilson, Attorney-General.
Hon. R. F. Green, Chief Commissioner of Lands and Works.
Hon. F. J. Fulton, President of the Council.

ALIENS.

Aliens in British Columbia have the same rights in regard to the ownership of lands and real estate of every description as natural born British subjects. This was first granted by proclamation of His Excellency, James Douglas, in 1859, and has been continued in subsequent legislation. An alien, however, in order to become a pre-emptor of Crown lands must declare his intention to become a British subject, and must be a naturalized British subject before receiving a Crown grant of the same. A residence of three years in the Province is necessary for the purpose of naturalization.

QUALIFICATIONS OF ELECTORS.

The franchise in British Columbia is practically manhood suffrage. At elections for members of the Legislature of the Province every male of the full age of twenty-one years entitled to the privilege of a natural born British subject, having resided in the Province for twelve months and in the electoral district in which he claims to vote for one month immediately previous to sending in a claim to vote, shall be entitled to vote at any election. Indians, Chinese and Japanese, however, are debarred. In each electoral district there are one or more collectors of votes whose duty it is to revise the list of voters, and persons desiring to enter as a voter must make application on and according to printed forms prescribed for that purpose.

BRITISH COLUMBIA LEGISLATURE.

Table Shewing the Dates of Opening and Prorogation of the Several Sessions, and of the Dissolutions of the Legislature.

	Session.	Opening.	Prorogation.	Dissolution.
First	1	Feb. 16, 1872....	April 11, 1872....	
	2	Dec. 17, 1872....	Feb. 21, 1873....	
	3	Dec. 18, 1873....	Mar. 2, 1874....	
	4	Mar. 1, 1875....	April 22, 1875....	Aug. 30, 1875
Second	1	Jan. 10, 1876....	May 19, 1876....	
	2	Feb. 21, 1877....	April 18, 1877....	
	3	Feb. 7, 1878....	April 10, 1878....	April 12, 1878
Third	1	July 29, 1878....	Sept. 2, 1878....	
	2	Jan. 29, 1879....	April 29, 1879....	
	3	April 5, 1880....	May 8, 1880....	
	4	Jan. 24, 1881....	Mar. 25, 1881....	
	5	Feb. 23, 1882....	April 21, 1882...	June 13, 1882
Fourth	1	Jan. 25, 1883....	May 12, 1883....	
	2	Dec. 3, 1883....	Feb. 18, 1884....	
	3	Jan. 12, 1885....	Mar. 9, 1885....	
	4	Jan. 25, 1886....	April 6, 1886....	June 3, 1886
Fifth	1	Jan. 24, 1887....	April 7, 1887....	
	2	Jan. 27, 1888....	April 28, 1888....	
	3	Jan. 31, 1889....	April 6, 1889....	
	4	Jan. 23, 1890....	April 26, 1890....	May 10, 1890
Sixth	1	Jan. 15, 1891 ...	April 20, 1891....	
	2	Jan. 28, 1892 ...	April 23, 1892...	
	3	Jan. 26, 1893....	April 12, 1893....	
	4	Jan. 18, 1894....	April 11, 1894....	June 5, 1894
Seventh	1	Nov. 12, 1895....	Feb. 21, 1895....	
	2	Jan. 23, 1896....	April 17, 1896....	
	3	Feb. 8, 1897....	May 8, 1897....	
	4	Feb. 10, 1898....	May 20, 1898...	June 7, 1898
Eighth	1	Jan. 5, 1899....	Feb. 27, 1899....	
	2	Jan. 4, 1900....	Mar. 1, 1900....	April 10, 1900
Ninth	1	July 19, 1900....	Aug. 31, 1900....	
	2	Feb. 21, 1901....	May 11, 1901....	
	3	Feb. 20, 1902....	June 21, 1902....	
	4	April 2, 1903....	June 4, 1903....	June 16, 1903

MULE DEER AT HOME GRAZING.

A CARIBOU.

A DAY'S SPORT ON OKANAGAN LAKE.

A BIG-HORN TROPHY.

LIEUTENANT-GOVERNOR:
THE HON. SIR HENRI GUSTAVE JOLY DE LOTBINIERE, K. C. M. G.
Private Secretary: Robert B. Powell.

EXECUTIVE COUNCIL:

President of the Council ....Hon. F. J. Fulton
Premier, Minister of Mines and Provincial Secretary ....Hon. R. McBride
Minister of Finance and Agriculture.... .... Hon. R. G. Tatlow
Attorney-General ....Hon. Chas. Wilson
Chief Commissioner of Lands and Works........... ... . Hon. Robert F. Green

OFFICERS OF THE HOUSE:

Clerk of the Legislative Assembly. ....Thornton Fell, Victoria
Law Clerk...W. Fisher, Victoria
Sergeant-at-Arms........... ....D. O'Hara, Ashcroft
King's Printer........................... ....Lt.-Col. R. Wolfenden, Victoria
Librarian of the Legislative Assembly......................E. O. S. Scholefield, Victoria

DEPARTMENTAL OFFICERS:

Attorney-General..............................Hon. A. E. McPhillips, K. C., Victoria
Deputy Attorney-General ....H. A. Maclean, Victoria
Secretary Provincial Board of Health..................... ....C. J. Fagan, M. D., Victoria
Deputy Commissioner of Fisheries..... ....J. P. Babcock, Victoria
Superintendent Provincial Police.................................F. S. Hussey, Victoria
Superintendent Juvenile Reformatory.......... .... J. M. Mutter, Victoria
Minister of Mines..... ....Hon. R. F. Green, Kaslo
Deputy Minister of Mines........... ....R. F. Tolmie, Victoria
Provincial Mineralogist.....................................W. F. Robertson, Victoria
Provincial Assayer...H. Carmichael, Victoria
Inspector of Coal Mines..A. Dick, Cranbrook
" " ....T. Morgan, Nanaimo
" " ....J. McGregor, Nelson
Minister of Finance..................................Hon. R. G. Tatlow, Vancouver
Deputy Minister of Finance.......................................J. McB. Smith, Victoria
Auditor-General................... ....J. A. Anderson, Victoria
Inspector of All Offices...W. J. Goepel, Nelson
Inspector of Revenue and Surveyor of Taxes................. ....J. B. McKilligan, Victoria
Provincial Assessor..T. B. Hall, Victoria
Chief Commissioner of Lands and Works.... ....Hon. R. McBride, New Westminster
Deputy Commissioner of Lands and Works............. ... .W. S. Gore, Victoria
Public Works Engineer............... ....F. C. Gamble, Victoria
Provincial Timber Inspector..................................R. J. Skinner, Vancouver
Chief Inspector of Boilers....................... .... J. W. Peck, New Westminster
Provincial Secretary.....................................Hon. A. S. Goodeve, Rossland
Deputy Provincial Secretary..... ....A. Campbell Reddie, Victoria
Medical Superintendent Hospital for the Insane............Dr. Manchester, New Westminster
Superintendent Provincial Home.............................H. McLean, Kamloops
Curator Provincial Museum...John Fannin, Victoria
Secretary Bureau Information and Immigration........... ....R. E. Gosnell, Victoria
Minister of Agriculture........................... ......Hon. R. G. Tatlow, Vancouver

Deputy Minister of Agriculture	J. R. Anderson, Victoria
Commissioner of Freight Rates	R. M. Palmer, Victoria
Inspector of Fruit Pests	Thos. Cunningham, Vancouver
Inspector of Animals	J. Gibbins, Vancouver
Veterinary Inspector	S. F. Tolmie, Victoria
Minister of Education	
Superintendent of Education	Alex. Robinson, Victoria
Principal Normal School	Wm. Burns, Vancouver
Inspector of Schools	D. Wilson, Nelson
"	S. B. Netherby, Victoria
"	A. C. Stewart, Vancouver
"	J. S. Gordon, Vernon

SUPREME COURT REGISTRARS.

Victoria	B. H. T. Drake
New Westminster	J. J. Cambridge
Nanaimo	H. Stanton
Vancouver	A. E. Beck
Kamloops	G. C. Tunstall
Nelson	E. T .H. Simpkins
Atlin	E. M. N. Woods
Barkerville	John Bowron
Clinton	F. Soues
Vernon	L. Norris
Kaslo	A. Lucas
Golden	C. E. Hamilton
Grand Forks	S. R. Almond
Greenwood	W. G. McMynn
Fort Steele	J. F. Armstrong
Revelstoke	F. Fraser
Rossland	F. Schofield

COUNTY COURT REGISTRARS.

Victoria	Harvey Coombe
Vancouver	A. E. Beck
Nanaimo	H. Stanton
Kamloops	G. C. Tunstall
Nelson	E. T. H. Simpkins
Barkerville	J. McKen
Duncan	J. Maitland-Dougall
Yale	Wm. Dodd
Ashcroft	J. W. Burr
Nicola	George Murray
Cumberland	J. Baird
Chilliwack	G. W. Chadsey
Fairview	C. A. R. Lambly
Princeton	H. Hunter
Greenwood	W. G. McMynn
Vernon	H. F. Wilmot
Revelstoke	F. Fraser
Golden	F. C. Lang
Rossland	R. R. Townsend
Fort Steele	J. F. Armstrong
Grand Forks	S. R. Almond
Atlin	E. M. N. Woods
New Denver	A. McInnes
Alberni	A. L. Smith
Wilmer	E. J. Scovil
Kaslo	A. Lucas
Trout Lake	F. C. Campbell
Ladysmith	G. Thomson
Fernie	L. R. Forbes

LAND REGISTRARS.

Victoria	S. Y. Wootton
Vancouver	J. L. G. Abbott
New Westminster	C. S. Keith
Kamloops	W. H. Edmonds
Nelson	H. F. McLeod

PROVINCIAL GAOLERS.

Victoria	R. F. John
New Westminster	W. C. Armstrong
Nelson	R. E. Lemon
Vernon	A. G. Fuller
Kamloops	J. R. Vicars
Nanaimo	W. Stewart

GOVERNMENT AGENTS.

District.	Government Agent.	Address.
Cowichan	J. Maitland-Dougall	Duncan.
Alberni	A. L. Smith	Alberni.
Comox	John Baird	Cumberland.
Nanaimo	M. Bray	Nanaimo.
Newcastle	Geo. Thomson	Ladysmith.
New Westminster	D. Robson	New Westminster.
East Kootenay (Northern)	J. E. Griffith	Golden.
East Kootenay (Southern)	J. F. Armstrong	Fort Steele.
West Kootenay—		
Slocan	E. E. Chipman	Kaslo.
Nelson	R. A. Renwick	Nelson.
Revelstoke	Fred Fraser	Revelstoke.
Rossland	John Kirkup	Rossland.
Cariboo—		
Barkerville	John Bowron	Barkerville.
Quesnel Forks	W. Stephenson	Quesnel Forks.
Omineca	F. W. Valleau	Manson Creek.
Cassiar—		
Telegraph Creek	James Porter	Telegraph Creek.
Atlin	J. A. Fraser	Atlin.
Port Simpson	J. Flewin	Port Simpson.
Kamloops	G. C. Tunstall	Kamloops.
Yale—		
Ashcroft	J. W. Burr	Ashcroft.
Vernon	L. Norris	Vernon.
Osoyoos	C. A. R. Lambly	Fairview.
Clinton	F. Soues	Clinton.
Kettle River	W. G. McMynn	Greenwood.
Similkameen	H. Hunter	Princeton.

MEMBERS OF THE PRESENT LEGISLATURE.

(Elected 3rd October, 1903).

Name.	Constituency.	P. O. Address.
Bowser, W. J.	Vancouver	Vancouver.
Brown, John Robert	Greenwood	Greenwood.
Cameron, William F.	Victoria	Victoria.
Clifford, C. W. D.	Skeena	Victoria.
Cotton, F. Carter	Richmond	Vancouver.
Davidson, W.	Slocan	Sandon.
Drury, R. L.	Victoria	Victoria.
Ellison, Price	Okanagan	Vernon.
Evans, John N.	Cowichan	Duncan.
Fraser, George A.	Grand Forks	Grand Forks.
Fulton, Frederick John	Kamloops	Kamloops.
Garden, James F.	Vancouver	Vancouver.
Gifford, Thomas	New Westminster	New Westminster.
Grant, R.	Comox	Cumberland.
Green, Hon. R. F.	Kaslo	Kaslo.
Hall, Richard	Victoria	Victoria.
Hawthornthwaite, James H.	Nanaimo	Nanaimo.
Henderson, Stuart	Yale	Ashcroft.
Houston, John	Nelson	Nelson.
Jones, Harry	Cariboo	Stanley.
King, Dr. J. H.	Cranbrook	Cranbrook.
McBride, Hon. Richard	Dewdney	New Westminster.
McDonald, Archibald	Lillooet	Lillooet.
Macdonald, J. A.	Rossland	Rossland.
Macgowan, A. H. B.	Vancouver	Vancouver.
McInnes, W. W. B.	Alberni	Nanaimo.
McNiven, J. D.	Victoria	Victoria.
Murphy, James	Cariboo	Alexandria.
Munro, Chas. W.	Chilliwack	Chilliwack.
Oliver, John	Delta	Delta.
Pooley, Charles E.	Esquimalt	Victoria.
Paterson, T. W.	Islands	Victoria.
Ross, W. R.	Fernie	Fernie.
Shatford, L. W.	Similkameen	Fairview.
Tanner, Harry	Saanich	Saanich.
Tatlow, Hon. R. G.	Vancouver	Vancouver.
Taylor, Thos.	Revelstoke	Revelstoke.
Wells, W. C.	Columbia	Palliser.
Williams, P.	Newcastle	Nanaimo.
Wilson, Hon. Charles	Vancouver	Vancouver.
Wright, Harry	Ymir	Nelson.
Young, Dr. H. E.	Atlin	Atlin.

ELECTION RETURNS.

1900	Votes polled	Voters on list	1898	Votes polled	Voters on list
Alberni—					
*A. W. Neill	108	307	George A. Huff	...	227
Redford	57		*A. W. Neill	...	
J. B. Thomson	33				
Cariboo—					
*Joseph Hunter	302	804	*J. C. Kinchant	195	712
*S. A. Rogers	289		S. A. Rogers	172	
Jones	201		*Hans Helgesen	218	
J. C. Kinchant	177		Joseph Hunter	173	
Cassiar—					
*C. W. D. Clifford	318	1,011	*C. W. D. Clifford	148	336
*J. Stables	277		*J. Irving	123	
J. Irving	244		McTavish	45	
Godfrey	108				
Chilliwack—					
*C. W. Munro	267	840	*C. W. Munro	201	811
S. Ashwell	251		J. H. Turner	246	
Cowichan—					
*C. H. Dickie	224	570	William Herd	...	503
Ford	107		*W. R. Robertson	...	
Comox—					
*L. A. Mounce	338	1,018	*James Dunsmuir	297	717
McPhee	279		M. J. Allen	162	
Delta—					
*J. Oliver	324	1,357	Hy. D. Benson	221	1,245
Berry	215		*Thomas Forster	331	
T. Forster	173				
Dewdney—					
*R. McBride	338	1,117	*R. McBride	239	906
C. Whetham	285		C. Whetham	216	
Esquimalt—					
*C. E. Pooley	230	698	1W. F. Bullen	208	714
*W. H. Hayward	272		D. R. Harris	58	
D. W. Higgins	111		*D. W. Higgins	206	
D. Fraser	75		*C. E. Pooley	213	
Bizanston	50				
Kootenay—Northeast—					
*W. C. Wells	246	740	2W. G. Neilson	169	622
Armstrong	111		W. C. Wells	148	
Burnett	78				
Kootenay—Southeast—					
*E. C. Smith	428	1,612	William Baillie	144	436
J. Fernie	383		*James Baker	159	
Costigan	171				
Kootenay West—Nelson—					
*J. Houston	747	2,520	A. S. Farwell	310	941
Fletcher	508		3*J. Fred Hume	325	
Hall	293				
Kootenay—Revelstoke—					
*Thomas Taylor	513	1,661	*J. M. Kellie	371	1,212
McRae	368		William White	205	
Kootenay—Rossland—					
*Smith Curtis	1,323	3,919	*James M. Martin	569	1,399
C. H. Mackintosh	1,287		John McKane	389	
Kootenay—Slocan—					
*R. F. Green	639	2,060	*R. F. Green	525	1,505
J. Keen	373		John McKane	389	
Kane	170				
Lillooet East—					
*J. D. Prentice	164	314	*J. D. Prentice	125	342
Graham	43		D. A. Stoddart	106	

1900	Votes polled	Voters on list	1898	Votes polled	Voters on list
Lillooet West—					
*A. W. Smith	134	354	*A. W. Smith	...	286
Skinner	80		E. S. Peters	...	
Lochore	7				
Nanaimo City—					
*5Ralph Smith	763	1,344	A. McGregor	170	1,365
J. S. Yates	86		*R. E. McKechnie	678	
Nanaimo North—					
*W. W. B. McInnes	238	826	*John Bryden	249	768
John Bryden	195		W. J. G. Hillier	153	
Dixon	73				
Nanaimo South—					
*James Dunsmuir	249	580	*Ralph Smith	193	321
Radcliffe	225		W. W. Walkem	53	
New Westminster City—					
*6J. C. Brown	628	1,564	J. C. Brown	534	1,799
Reid	540		*A. Henderson	555	
Richmond—					
*Thomas Kidd	222	1,291	*Thomas Kidd	357	1,135
Rowan	204		J. McQueen	173	
Wilkinson	133				
Vancouver—					
4*J. F. Garden	1,787	7,940	W. J. Bowser	879	5,954
*Joseph Martin	1,737		John T. Carroll	954	
*R. G. Tatlow	1,645		*J. F. Garden	1,157	
*H. B. Gilmour	1,465		*Joseph Martin	1,651	
C. Wilson	1,457		W. S. McDonald	735	
R. Macpherson	1,435		*Robert Macpherson	1,795	
J. McQueen	1,391		*C. E. Tisdall	1,798	
W. H. Wood	1,344				
Joseph Dixon	853				
F. Carter-Cotton	802				
F. Williams	716				
W. MacClain	683				
Victoria City—					
*H. D. Helmcken	1,688	4,346	Robert Beaven	906	5,557
*Richard Hall	1,597		A. L. Belyea	949	
7*J. H. Turner	1,552		F. B. Gregory	1,149	
*A. E. McPhillips	1,449		*Richard Hall	1,274	
Joseph Martin	1,352		*H. D. Helmcken	1,484	
J. G. Brown	1,259		*A. E. McPhillips	1,229	
J. S. Yates	1,233		A. Stewart	1,065	
J. L. Beckwith	1,154		*J. H. Turner	1,352	
Victoria North—					
8*J. P. Booth	123	423	*J. P. Booth	144	415
White	117		T. W. Paterson	120	
Robertson	41				
Victoria South—					
*D. M. Eberts	259	730	*D. M. Eberts	236	793
Sangster	208		J. S. Yates	210	
Yale East—					
*Price Ellison	619	1,738	*Price Ellison	...	1,404
J. W. Snodgrass	351		A. Graham	...	
Raymer	45				
Yale North—					
*F. J. Fulton	504	1,451	*F. J. Deane	427	1,314
F. J. Deane	388		G. B. Martin	423	
A. J. Palmer	84				
Yale West—					
*Denis Murphy	352	824	John J. McKay	88	593
G. W. Beebe	149		*C. A. Semlin	203	

*Those with a star were elected.

1On a recount D. W. Higgins was seated, instead of W. F. Bullen.

2Mr. Neilson died before taking his seat in the House, and in the bye-election Mr. Wells was elected.

3Mr. Hume was appointed Minister of Mines, and upon returning for re-election was re-elected by acclamation, but owing to technical irregularity subsequently resigned and the seat was contested by A. S. Farwell, but unsuccessfully.

4Mr. Garden resigned his seat to contest the Burrard division in the Conservative interest for the House of Commons, but being defeated ran again, being opposed by R. Macpherson, and was elected.

5Mr. Smith resigned his seat to contest the Dominion election for the Nanaimo Riding, and was succeeded by Mr. J. H. Hawthornthwaite.

6Upon Mr. Brown accepting the office of Provincial Secretary, he was opposed by Mr. Thomas Gifford, and was defeated.

7Mr. Turner in September, 1901, resigned his seat to accept the position of Agent-General in London, Eng., and was succeeded by Col. Prior, who was appointed Minister of Mines. He was elected over Mr. E. V. Bodwell by the following vote, Prior 1,539, Bodwell 1,484.

8Deceased.

There were three bye-elections after the formation of the Prior Administration, as follows:

North Nanaimo, 15th December, 1902, W. W. B. McInnes, appointed Provincial Secretary, being elected over his opponent Parker Williams by 263 to 155.

North Victoria, rendered vacant by the death of Speaker Booth, December 23, 1902, T. W. Patterson being elected over his opponent Robertson by 196 to 153.

West Riding Yale, rendered vacant by resignation of Mr. Dennis Murphy, appointed Provincial Secretary, 26th February, 1903, Mr. C. A. Semlin being elected over his opponent, Dr. Sansom by 282 to 170.

LIQUOR LICENSES.

The following is the number of liquor licenses of all kinds (not including restaurant licenses) issued in the Province in licensing districts and in municipalities for the year 1903. The revenue arising out of licenses in the Provincial districts for 1901 was about $50,000, and in the urban municipality $110,418.53.

Licensing District.	Hotel.	Whole-sale.
Ainsworth	7	
Alberni	4	
Ashcroft	9	
Atlin	19	
Barkerville	11	1
Boundary Creek	24	
Chilliwack	1	
Comox	14	
Cowichan	7	
Dewdney	3	
Esquimalt	15	
Fort Steele	44	3
Golden	9	1
Lillooet, East	10	
Lillooet, West	3	
Nanaimo, North	7	
Nanaimo, South	16	3
Nelson	24	
Nicola	8	
150 Mile House	3	
Richmond	5	
Revelstoke	34	
Slocan	12	
Soda Creek	4	
Victoria, North	4	
Victoria, South	5	
Windermere	5	
Yale, North	8	
Yale, Northeast	7	
Yale, Southeast	16	
Yale, West	4	

MUNICIPALITIES.

	Hotel	Saloon	Shop	Whole'le
N. West.	13	2	..	1
Sandon	5	5		
Trail	9	..	..	1
Kaslo	1	5	1	1
Phœnix	14			
Greenwood	17		..	2
Kamloops	7		1	1
Nanaimo	22		..	5
Slocan	8		..	1
Rossland	15	11	1	1
Vernon	4	..	..	1
Cumberland	4	..	..	4
Vancouver	47	12	10	7
Victoria	35	39	5	18
Revelstoke	8	..	..	1
Grand Forks	7	9	2	
Nelson	15	6	..	2

PROVINCIAL GENERAL ELECTION RETURNS, 1903.

Electoral Districts and Polling Places.	No. voters on List.	No. ballots cast.	Con.	Lib.	Lab.	Soc.	Votes rejected.	Ballots spoiled.	
ALBERNI—	546	420	....	....	....	....	..	11	
Alberni	....	....	31	79	....	....	..	..	McInnes, W. W. B. (Lib.)
Banfield Creek	....	....	8	13	....	....	..	..	Hickey, R. J.
Ucluelet	....	....	3	10	....	....	..	..	
Clayuquot	....	....	5	19	....	....	..	..	
Kyoquot	....	....	2	17	....	....	..	..	
Quatsino	....	....	2	26	....	....	..	..	
Cape Scott	....	....	....	10	....	....	..	..	
Texada Island	....	....	3	58	....	....	..	..	
Wellington	....	....	21	55	....	....	..	..	
Lasqueti Island	....	....	....	7	....	....	..	..	
Nanoose	....	....	6	7	....	....	..	..	
Englishman's River	....	....	21	19	....	....	..	..	
	....	....	102	320	....	....	..	..	
ATLIN—	561	438	....	....	....	....	..	12	
Atlin	....	....	84	66	....	....	..	..	Young, H. E. (Con.)
Discovery	....	....	91	83	....	....	..	..	Kirkland, J.
Surprise Lake	....	....	28	29	....	....	..	..	
McKee Creek	....	....	12	13	....	....	..	..	
Wells	....	....	5	....	....	....	..	..	
Bennett	....	....	3	2	....	....	..	..	
Telegraph Creek	....	....	12	9	....	....	..	..	
	....	....	236	202	....	....	..	..	
CARIBOO—	541	450	A. R.	M. J.	....	....	..	..	
Richfield	....	....	46 55	55 56	....	....	..	..	Adams, William (Con.)
Stanley	....	....	26 29	38 39	....	....	..	..	Rogers, S. A. (Con.)
Quesnel	....	....	33 33	34 31	....	....	..	..	Murphy, James (Lib.)
Alexandria	....	....	8 5	12 9	....	....	..	..	Jones, Harry (Lib.)
Soda Creek	....	....	12 7	11 6	....	....	..	..	
150-Mile House	....	....	12 8	35 26	....	....	..	..	
Quesnel Forks	....	....	12 8	17 9	....	....	..	..	
Horsefly	....	....	14 3	13 11	....	....	..	..	
Keithley Creek	....	....	8 10	9 11	....	....	..	..	
Riskie Creek	....	....	12 12	6 6	....	....	..	..	
Hanceville	....	....	7 7	1 1	....	....	..	..	
Alexis Creek	....	....	7 4	3 3	....	....	..	..	
Chimney Creek	....	....	11 7	13 10	....	....	..	..	
	....	....	411 379	501 439	....	....	..	..	

CHILLIWACK—	745	597						17	
Cheam			30	47					Atkinson, J. L. (Con.)
Chilliwack			108	158					Munro, C. W. (Lib.)
Sumas			23	9					
Upper Sumas			17	17					
Abbotsford			33	30					
Peardonville			2	5					
Yale Road			8	5					
Mt. Lehman			2	9					
Wade's Landing			8	5					
Lehman's Landing			23	40					
Riverside			13	5					
			267	330					
COLUMBIA—	619								Wells, W. C. (elected by accl.)
COMOX—	981	702					24		
Cumberland			115	103					Grant, R. (Con.)
Courtenay			56	96					Young, F. McB. (Lib.)
Union Bay			32	9					
Denman Island			5	11					
Hornby Island			3	2					
Valdez Island			20	5					
Roy			2	5					
Cortes Island			6	2					
Shoal Bay			19	32					
Lund			15	2					
Read Island			28	7					
Rock Bay			32	22					
Alert Bay			12	2					
Bear River			13	7					
Granite Bay			3	25					
			361	317					
COWICHAN—	591	440						16	
Cobble Hill			20	5					Skinner, E. M. (Con.)
Cowichan Station			16	19					Evans, John N. (Lib.)
Duncan			87	87					
Somenos			18	14					
Mt. Sicker			27	33					
Cowichan Lake			8	11					
Chemainus			18	33					
Crofton			21	23					
			215	225					

PROVINCIAL GENERAL ELECTION RETURNS, 1903—*Continued.*

Electoral Districts and Polling Places.	No. voters on List.	No. ballots cast.	Con.	Lib.	Lab.	Soc.	Votes rejected.	Ballots spoiled.	
CRANBROOK—	1254	935	....	....	....	....	..	..	
Ryan	....	....	14	7	....	....	..	..	Caven, Thos. (Con.)
Moyie	....	....	51	27	....	....	..	..	King, J. H. (Lib.)
Rhoda	....	....	4	28	....	....	..	..	
Fort Steele	....	....	53	38	....	....	..	..	
Wasa	....	....	4	6	....	....	..	..	
Wardner	....	....	23	29	....	....	..	..	
Marysville	....	....	30	44	....	....	..	..	
North Star Mine	....	....	15	7	....	....	..	..	
Perry Creek	....	....	20	4	....	....	..	..	
Cranbrook	....	....	221	310	....	....	..	..	
	....	....	435	500	....	....	..	..	
DELTA—	963	756	....	....	....	....	..	24	
Westham Island	....	....	12	8	....	....	..	..	Ladner, Wm. (Con.)
Ladner	....	....	54	107	....	....	..	..	Oliver, John (Lib.)
East Delta	....	....	13	31	....	....	..	..	
Mud Bay	....	....	24	27	....	....	..	..	
Hall's Prairie	....	....	12	19	....	....	..	..	
Cloverdale	....	....	18	20	....	....	..	..	
South Westminster	....	....	46	62	....	....	..	.	
Tynehead	....	....	33	18	....	....	..	..	
Langley Prairie	....	....	20	51	....	....	..	..	
Langley	....	....	42	60	....	....	..	.	
Kensington	....	....	5	6	....	....	..	..	
Otter Hall	....	....	21	29	....	....	..	..	
	....	....	309	447	....	....	..	..	
DEWDNEY—	796	646	....	....	....	....		15	
Millside	....	....	17	9	....	....		..	McBride, Hon. R. (Con.)
Port Moody	....	....	53	9	....	....		..	Forrester, W. W. (Lib.)
Coquitlam	....	....	31	27	....	....		..	
Lake Beautiful	....	....	10	1	....	....		..	
Coquitlam Lake	....	....	2	14	....	....		..	
Port Hammond	....	....	34	25	....	....		..	
Port Haney	....	....	60	18	....	....		..	
Whonnock	....	....	21	5	....	....		..	
Ruskin	....	....	13	9	....	....		..	
Silverdale	....	....	7	7	....	....		..	

Mission City	....	....	94	29	....	....	..	..	
Hatzic	....	....	5	5	....	....	..	..	
Hatzic Prairie	....	....	12	4	....	....	..	..	
Dewdney	....	....	8	8	....	....	..	..	
Nicomen Island	....	....	10	17	....	....	..	..	
North Nicomen	....	....	12	6	....	....	..	..	
Harrison River	....	....	21	11	....	....	..	..	
Agassiz	....	....	7	7	....	....	..	..	
Harrison Hot Springs	....	....	8	8	....	....	..	..	
Port Douglas	....	....	2	0	....	....	..	..	
	....	....	427	219	....	....	..	..	
ESQUIMALT	553	451	....	....	....	....	..	..	
Esquimalt	....	....	117	114	....	....	..	..	Pooley, C. E. (Con.)
Colwood	....	....	35	29	....	....	..	..	Jardine, John (Lib.)
Metchosin	....	....	36	26	....	....	..	..	
West Sooke	....	....	18	10	....	....	..	..	
Otter Point	....	....	7	7	....	....	..	..	
Port Renfrew	....	....	14	19	....	....	..	..	
Shawnigan Lake	....	....	8	4	....	....	..	..	
East Sooke	....	....	4	3	....	....	..	..	
	....	....	239	212	....	....	..		
FERNIE—	1135	896	....	....	....	....	50	..	
Fernie	....	....	181	150	....	81	..	..	Ross, W. R. (Con.)
Michel	....	....	19	36	....	57	..	..	Smith, E. C. (Lib.)
Crow's Nest	....	....	....	8	....	4	..	..	McPherson, J. (Socialist)
The Loop	....	....	3	4	....	....	..	..	
Coal Creek Mines	....	....	14	10	....	44	..	..	
Morrissey	....	....	20	11	....	....	..	..	
Morrissey Mines	....	....	27	12	....	5	..	..	
Elko	....	....	6	17	....	1	..	..	
Jaffray	....	....	15	8	....	12	..	..	
Phillips	....	....	5	3	....	1	..	..	
Elkmouth	....	....	6	5	....	10	..	..	
Morrissey Mines (town)	....	....	17	31	....	3	..	..	
Sparwood	....	....	3	6	....	3	..	..	
	....	....	316	309	....	221	..	..	

PROVINCIAL GENERAL ELECTION RETURNS, 1903—*Continued.*

Electoral Districts and Polling Places.	No. voters on List.	No. ballots cast.	Con.	Lib.	Lab.	Soc.	Votes rejected.	Ballots spoiled.	
GRAND FORKS—	958	776							
Grand Forks			228	117		55			Fraser, Geo. A. (Con.)
Phoenix			73	31		160			Clements, W. H. P. (Lib.)
Cascade			18	17		15			Riordan J (Soc.)
Bannock			17	3					
Carson			12	5		2			
			346	173		232			
GREENWOOD—	771	666					18		
Greenwood			95	104		132			Spankie, J. E. (Con.)
Midway			12	39		4			Brown, J. R. (Lib.)
Boundary Falls			15	37		43			Mills, E. (Soc.)
Eholt			33	20		16			
Deadwood			15	18		14			
Denoro			6	4		17			
Rock Creek			5	16		3			
			181	238		229			
ISLANDS—	413	375							
North Saanich			36	67					Bullock H. W. (Con.)
Gabriola Island			9	30					Paterson, T. W. (Lib.)
Pender Island			9	16					
Salt Spring Island			41	35					
Fulford Harbour			24	30					
Mayne Island			21	22					
Galino Island			6	14					
Thetis Island			8	7					
			154	221					
KAMLOOPS—	1241	1011						25	
Savona			18	22					Fulton, F. J. (Con.)
Kamloops			279	233					Deane, F. J. (Lib.)
W. side North Thompson Riv.			9	5					
E. side North Thompson Riv.			22	15					
Louis Creek			8	11					
Ducks			32	22					
Shuswap			15	13					
Grand Prairie			20	17					

Tappen Siding	....	....	4	5	....	....	..	..	
Kualt	....	....	11	20	....	....	..	..	
Notch Hill	....	....	9	32	....	....	..	..	
Sicamous	....	....	17	14	....	....	..	..	
Salmon Arm	....	....	24	36	....	....	..	..	
Griffin Lake	....	....	4	2	....	....	..	..	
Malakwa	....	....	3	8	....	....	..	..	
Quilchena	....	....	17	13	....	....	..	..	
Douglas Lake	....	....	13	6	....	....	..	..	
Glenemma	....	....	5	9	....	....	..	..	
Stump Lake	....	....	7	12	....	....	..	..	
	....	....	517	494	....	....	..	..	
KASLO—	832	722	....	....	....	....	..	..	
Kaslo	....	....	134	135	....	28	..	..	Green, Hon. R. F. (Con.)
Ainsworth	....	....	17	16	....	1	..	..	Retallack, John L. (Lib.)
Pilot Bay	....	....	5	11	....	....	..	..	Shannon, S. (Soc.)
Whitewater	....	....	9	12	....	17	..	..	
Lardo	....	....	6	7	....	1	..	..	
Howser	....	....	7	4	....	2	..	..	
Poplar Creek	....	....	17	13	4	....	..	..	
Gerrard	....	....	4	2	....	1	..	..	
Trout Lake	....	....	35	37	....	17	..	..	
Ferguson, Silver Cup Mines	....	....	58	14	....	93	..	..	
	....	....	292	251	....	164	..	..	
LILLOOET—	370	....	....	....	....	....		..	A. McDonald (by acclamation),
NANAIMO—	1196	1105	....	....		....		6	Quennell, E. (Con.)
	....	....	....	....		....		..	Sheppard, H. (Lib.)
	....	....	325	294		486			Hawthornthwaite, J. H. (Soc.)
NELSON—	973	798	424	357					Houston, John (Con.)
									Taylor, S. S. (Lib.)
NEWCASTLE—	845	730	....	....	....	....	..	..	
Ladysmith	....	....	181	171	....	207	..	..	Bryden, A. (Con.)
Northfield	....	....	9	16	....	46	..	..	Murray, D. W. (Lib.)
South Wellington	....	....	9	4	....	19	..	..	Williams, P. (Soc.)
South Cedar	....	....	18	23	....	16	..	..	
	....	....	217	214	....	288	..	..	
NEW WESTMINSTER—	1601	1357	....	....	....	....	..		Gifford, Thos. (Con.)
New Westminster	....	....	772	575	....	....	..		Keary, W. H. (Lib.)

PROVINCIAL GENERAL ELECTION RETURNS, 1903—*Continued.*

Electoral Districts and Polling Places.	No. voters on List.	No. ballots cast.	Con.	Lib.	Lab.	Soc.	Votes rejected.	Ballots spoiled.	
OKANAGAN—	1506	1277	....	....	....	....	..	..	
Penticton	....	....	9	12	....	....	..	..	Ellison, Price (Con.)
Summerland	....	....	27	12	....	....	..	..	Sterling, W. J. (Lib.)
Peachland	....	....	43	10	....	....	..	..	
Westbank	....	....	12	7	....	....	..	..	
Killiney	....	....	4	2	....	....	..	..	
Kelowna	....	....	39	85	....	....	..	..	
Benvoulin	....	....	55	35	....	....	..	..	
Commonage	....	....	10	10	....	....	..	..	
Vernon	....	....	246	139	....	....	..	..	
Lumby	....	....	51	24	....	....	..	..	
Mabel Lake	....	....	15	12	....	....	..	..	
Cherry Creek	....	....	9	6	....	....	..	..	
Monashee	....	....	16	4	....	....	..	..	
Okanagan	....	....	10	3	....	....	..	..	
Armstrong	....	....	102	101	....	....	..	..	
Enderby	....	....	32	52	....	....	..	..	
Mara	....	....	16	16	....	....	..	..	
Deep Creek	....	....	4	1	....	....	..	..	
Hullcar	....	....	7	7	....	....	..	..	
Canoe Camp	....	....	14	10	....	....	..	..	
Silver Creek	....	....	2	1	....	....	..	..	
Salmon River Bridge	....	....	2	3	....	....	..	..	
	....	....	725	552	....	....	..	..	
REVELSTOKE—	1085		....	....	....	....	..		
Hyatts Camp	....		2	2	....	....	..		Taylor, Thos. (Con.)
McCullough Creek	....		3	12	....	....	..		Kellie, J. M. (Lib.)
Downie Creek	....		1	5	....	2	..		Bennett, J. W. (Soc.)
Rocky Point	....		8	7	....	3	..		
Clanwilliam	....		2	2	....	1	..		
Revelstoke	....		185	123	....	108	..		
Albert Canyon	....		1	4	....	....	..		
Illecillewaet	....		6	11	....	3	..		
Glacier	....		6	8	....	11	..		
Arrowhead	....		16	43	....	12	..		
Wigwam	....		3	....	....	1	..		
Camp No. Four	....		3	7	....	8	..		
Halcyon	....		1	....	..	..	..		

St. Leon	....	....	6	6	....	....	..	..	
Beaton	....	....	20	3	....	2	..	..	
Comaplix	....	....	8	29	....	4	..	..	
Camborne	....	....	40	38	....	24	..	..	
Adam's Ranch	....	....	16	4	....	1	..	..	
Goldfields	....	....	8	4	....	3	..	..	
Big Eddy Mill	....	....	7	6	....	3	..	..	
Smith Creek, Big Bend	....	....	....	2	....	....	..	..	
	....	....	342	316	....	186	..	..	
RICHMOND—	1131	810	....	....	....	....	..	30	
Steveston	....	....	79	30	....	....	..	..	Cotton, F. C. (Con.)
Eburne	....	....	76	90	....	....	..	..	Brown, J. C. (Lib.)
South Vancouver	....	....	46	21	....	....	..	..	
Burnaby	....	....	75	51	....	....	..	..	
Moodyville	....	....	7	10	....	....	..	..	
Hastings	....	....	7	1	....	....	..	..	
Howe Sound	....	....	29	14	....	....	..	..	
Squamish	....	....	10	10	....	....	..	..	
Pemberton	....	....	8	....	....	....	..	..	
North Vancouver	....	....	47	30	....	....	..	..	
Barnet	....	....	18	13	....	....	..	..	
Cedar Cottage	....	....	58	50	....	....	..	..	
	....	....	400	320	....	....	..	..	
ROSSLAND—	....	779	....	....			8	5	Goodeve, Hon. A. S. (Con.)
Rossland	....	....	343	436			..	..	Macdonald, J. A. (Lib.)
SAANICH—	582	476	....	....	....	....	..	..	
Sannichton	....	....	46	60	....	....	..	..	Eberts, D. M. (Con.)
Royal Oak	....	....	34	38	....	....	..	..	Tanner, H. (Lib.)
Boleskine Road	....	....	35	44	....	....	..	..	
Cedar Hill Road	....	....	67	54	....	....	..	..	
The Willows	....	....	34	64	....	....	..	..	
	....	....	216	260	....	....	..	..	

PROVINCIAL GENERAL ELECTION RETURNS, 1903—*Continued.*

Electoral Districts and Polling Places.	No. voters on List.	No. ballots cast.	Con.	Lib.	Lab.	Soc.	Votes rejected.	Ballots spoiled.	
SIMILKAMEEN—	616	511	....	....	....	....	6	3	
Beaverdell	....	....	14	4	....	....	..	..	Shatford, L. W. (Con.)
Westbridge	....	....	8	10	....	....	..	..	McLean, W. A. (Lib.)
Rock Creek	....	....	13	19	....	....	..	..	
Sidley Mountain	....	....	13	20	....	....	..	..	
Camp McKinney	....	....	27	19	....	....	..	..	
Okanagan Falls	....	....	12	10	....	....	..	..	
Fairview	....	....	31	24	....	....	..	..	
Camp Fairview	....	....	16	7	....	....	..	..	
White Lake	....	....	20	11	....	....	..	..	
Olalla	....	....	17	13	....	....	..	..	
Keremeos	....	....	20	11	....	....	..	..	
Hedley	....	....	44	40	....	....	..	..	
Nickle Plate Mine	....	....	5	11	....	....	..	..	
Princeton	....	....	43	19	....	....	..	..	
Granite Creek	....	....	7	1	....	....	..	..	
Tulameen, Otter Flat	....	....	9	5	....	....	..	..	
	....	....	299	214	....	....	..	..	
SKEENA—	531	352	....	....	....	....	..	9	
Port Essington	....	....	51	72	....	....	..	..	Clifford, C. W. D. (Con.)
Port Simpson	....	....	20	7	....	....	..	..	Hermann, P. (Lib.)
Inverness	....	....	2	2	....	....	..	..	
Metlakahtla	....	....	6	6	....	....	..	..	
Naas River	....	....	14	3	....	....	..	..	
Skidegate	....	....	3	3	....	....	..	..	
Lorne Creek	....	....	8	6	....	....	..	..	
Hazelton	....	....	23	7	....	....	..	..	
Surf Inlet	....	....	4	11	....	....	..	..	
Namu	....	....	9	....	....	....	..	..	
River's Inlet	....	....	13	3	....	....	..	..	
Bella Coola	....	....	37	26	....	....	..	..	
Kitimaat	....	....	6	5	....	....	..	..	
Port Nelson	....	....	1	4	....	....	..	..	
	....	....	197	155	....	....	..	..	
SLOCAN—	813	647	....	....	....	....	..	25	
Winlaw	....	....	15	14	....	....	..	..	Hunter, W. (Con.)
Slocan	....	....	79	88	....	....	..	..	Davidson, W. (Lib.)

Enterprise Landing	....	....	5	23	....	....	..	..	
Silverton	....	....	23	24	....	....	..	..	
New Denver	....	....	51	37	....	....	..	..	
Roseberry	....	....	12	6	....	....	..	..	
Three Forks	....	....	12	16	....	....	..	..	
McGuigan	....	....	3	24	....	....	..	..	
Sandon	....	....	40	96	....	....	..	..	
Nakusp	....	....	38	24	....	....	..	..	
Burton	....	....	8	6	....	....	..	..	
Deer Park	....	....	3	....	....	....	..	..	
	....	....	289	358	....	....	..	..	
VANCOUVER CITY—	7378	5700	....	....	....	....	..	..	
	....	....	2303	....	....	....	..	..	Bowser, W. J. (Con.)
	....	....	2510	....	....	....	..	..	Garden, J. F. (Con.)
	....	....	2301	....	....	....	..	..	Macgowan, A. H. B. (Con.)
	....	....	2655	....	....	....	..	..	Tatlow, Hon. R. G. (Con.)
	....	....	2403	....	....	....	..	..	Wilson, Hon. Chas. (Con.)
	....	....	....	1416	....	....	..	..	Baxter, T. S. (Lib.)
	....	....	....	1465	....	....	..	..	Brydone-Jack, W. D. (Lib.)
	....	....	....	1547	....	....	..	..	Martin, Jos. (Lib.)
	....	....	....	915	....	....	..	..	Monck, Clarence (Lib.)
	....	....	....	1197	....	....	..	..	Turnbull, J. D. (Lib.)
	....	....	....	....	....	285	..	..	Griffiths, Wm. (Soc.)
	....	....	....	....	....	1333	..	..	Mortimer, J. C. (Soc.)
	....	....	....	....	1166	....	..	..	McLaren, John (Lab.)
	....	....	....	....	1248	....	..	..	Perry, Albert G. (Lab.)
	....	....	....	....	958	....	..	..	Stebbings, A. R. (Lab.)
	....	....	....	....	1355	....	..	..	Williams, Francis (Lab.)
	....	....	12172	6540	4727	1618	..	..	
VICTORIA—	4496	3653	....	....	....	....	..	..	
	....	....	1401	....	....	....	..	..	Hayward, C. (Con.)
	....	....	1339	....	....	....	..	..	Helmcken, H. D. (Con.)
	....	....	1232	....	....	....	..	..	Hunter, Jos. (Con.)
	....	....	1301	....	....	....	..	..	McPhillips, Hon. A. E. (Con.)
	....	....	....	1863	....	....	..	..	Cameron, W. G. (Lib.)
	....	....	....	1844	....	....	..	..	Drury, R. L. (Lib.)
	....	....	....	1661	....	....	..	..	McNiven, J. D. (Lib.)
	....	....	....	1555	....	....	..	..	Hall, R. (Lib.)
	....	....	....	....	....	699	..	..	Waters, J. C. (Soc.)
	....	....	5273	6919	....	699	..	..	

PROVINCIAL GENERAL ELECTION RETURNS, 1903—*Continued.*

Electoral Districts and Polling Places.	No. voters on List.	No. ballots cast.	Con.	Lib.	Lab.	Soc.	Votes rejected.	Ballots spoiled.	
YALE—	644	510	....	....	....	....	..	..	
Ashcroft	....	....	44	82	....	....	..	..	McManamon, T. G. (Con.)
Agassiz	....	....	36	31	....	....	..	..	Henderson, Stuart (Lab.)
Mammet Lake	....	....	....	10	....	....	..	..	
Keefer's	....	....	6	3	....	....	..	..	
Spuzzum	....	....	5	6	....	....	..	..	
Aspen Grove	....	....	2	12	....	....	..	..	
Otter Valley	....	....	5	3	....	....	..	..	
22-Mile House	....	....	5	1	....	....	..	..	
Yale	....	....	6	10	....	....	..	..	
Lower Nicola	....	....	2	18	....	....	..	..	
Lytton	....	....	28	29	....	....	..	..	
Hope	....	....	20	11	....	....	..	..	
Camp No. 16	....	....	7	9	....	....	..	..	
Coutlee	....	....	4	22	....	....	..	..	
Nicola Lake	....	....	6	35	....	....	..	..	
North Bend	....	....	10	8	....	....	..	..	
Spence's Bridge	....	....	15	19	....	....	..	..	
	....	....	201	300	....	....	..	..	
YMIR—	1064	863	....	....	....	....	35	3	
Trail (including switch)	....	....	113	84	....	....	..	..	Wright, H. (Con.)
Castlegar	....	....	8	9	....	....	..	..	Parr, A. (Lib.)
Fire Valley	....	....	15	7	....	....	..	..	
Slocan Junction	....	....	17	2	....	....	..	..	
Granite School House	....	....	13	6	....	....	..	..	
Athabasca-Venus Mine	....	....	15	5	....	....	..	..	
Silver King Mine	....	....	2	9	....	....	..	..	
Fairview	....	....	85	47	....	....	..	..	
Willow Creek	....	....	13	3	....	....	..	..	
Procter	....	....	14	1	....	....	..	..	
Sirdar	....	....	16	8	....	....	..	..	
Creston	....	....	23	19	....	....	..	..	
Kitchener	....	....	5	5	....	....	..	..	
Hall Siding	....	....	3	1	....	....	..	..	
Ymir	....	....	49	47	....	....	..	..	
Ymir Mill	....	....	42	33	....	....	..	..	
Salmo	....	....	27	22	....	....	..	..	
Erie	....	....	7	6	....	....	..	..	
Waneta	....	....	10	8	....	....	..	..	
Porto Rico	....	....	8	7	....	....	..	..	
Arlington Mine	....	....	2	11	....	....	..	..	
	....	....	483	323	....	....	..	..	

.E. | Houghton | ewdney. | ewdney. | ewdney. rnard. :wdney.) rnard. | ara. | ara. | RARD.) | Iaxwell. | Iaxwell. IcPherson. | ras succeeded

ANALYSIS OF ELECTION RETURNS.

The election returns in these pages were printed without being fully completed. The totals are :—

* Number of voters on list in Province, 1903	39,296
" ballots actually cast	32,293
" votes cast for Conservative candidates	28,295
" " Liberal candidates	23,801
" " Labour "	5,085
" " Socialist "	4,123
" ballots rejected	141
" " spoilt	201
" votes polled, 1900	47,204
" voters on the list, 1900	43,979
" votes polled, 1898	31,048
" voters on the list, 1898	34,334
" votes polled for candidates, 1903	61,304

* It will be observed that the number of votes cast largely exceeds the number of voters on the lists. This is accounted for by the fact that in some Electoral Districts there were more than one candidate to be elected, as in Vancouver and Victoria, and, consequently, each elector had as many votes as there were candidates to be elected.

In Lillooet and Columbia Districts, in which candidates were elected by acclamation, the whole number of votes in the list is credited to the respective candidates.

The number of votes registered in the Rossland District is 965.

By mistake, the vote cast for the Labour candidate in Slocan is credited to the Liberals in the table of election returns.

n.)

ELECTORAL DISTR
POLLING PLA

YALE—
Ashcroft ....
Agassiz ....
Mammet Lake ..
Keefer's ....
Spuzzum ....
Aspen Grove ....
Otter Valley ....
22-Mile House ..
Yale ....
Lower Nicola ...
Lytton ....
Hope ....
Camp No. 16 ...
Coutlee ....
Nicola Lake ....
North Bend ....
Spence's Bridge .

YMIR—
Trail (including sw
Castlegar ....
Fire Valley .....
Slocan Junction .
Granite School Ho
Athabasca-Venus
Silver King Mine
Fairview ....
Willow Creek ...
Procter ....
Sirdar ....
Creston ....
Kitchener ......
Hall Siding .....
Ymir ....
Ymir Mill ....
Salmo ....
Erie ....
Waneta ....
Porto Rico ......
Arlington Mine ...

BRITISH COLUMBIA REPRESENTATIVES IN HOUSE OF COMMONS.

Members Elected House of Commons.	Cariboo.	New Westminster.	Vancouver.	Victoria.	Yale.
1st Parliament, 1871-72.	J. Spencer Thompson.	Hugh Nelson........	Robert Wallace.......	Hon. Henry Nathan.. Hon. Amor DeCosmos	Chas. F. Houghton
2nd Parliament, 1872-74.	J. Spencer Thompson.	a Hugh Nelson........	Hon. Sir Francis Hincks	Hon. Henry Nathan.. Hon. Amor DeCosmos	Edgar Dewdney.
3rd Parliament, 1874-78.	J. Spencer Thompson.	James Cunningham...	Hon. Arthur Bunster..	Hon. Amor DeCosmos Francis James Roscoe.	Edgar Dewdney.
4th Parliament, 1878-82.	b J. Spencer Thompson. James Reid.......... (vice Thompson.)	a T. R. McInnes...... J. A. R. Homer ..... (vice McInnes.)	Hon. Arthur Bunster..	Sir John Macdonald.. Hon. Amor DeCosmos	Edgar Dewdney. F. J. Barnard. (vice Dewdney.)
5th Parliament, 1882-86.	James Reid	J. A. R. Homer......	D. W. Gordon........	E. C. Baker......... Noah Shakespeare....	F. J. Barnard.
6th Parliament, 1886-91.	a James Reid .... F. S. Barnard .... (vice Reid.)	b Donald Chisholm .... G. E. Corbould...... (vice Chisholm.)	D. W. Gordon........	e Noah Shakespeare.... Col. Hon. E. G. Prior. (vice Shakespeare.) d E. C. Baker......... Thos. Earle .... (vice Baker.)	J. A. Mara.
7th Parliament, 1891-96.	F. S. Barnard .... (YALE-CARIBOO.)	G. E. Corbould	b D. W. Gordon....... A. Haslam .... (vice Gordon.)	Lt.-Col. E. G. Prior.. Thos. Earle	J. A. Mara. (BURRARD.)
8th Parliam't, 1896-1900	Hewitt Bostock	Aulay Morrison......	W. W. B. McInnes ...	Col. Hon. E. G. Prior Thos. Earle	G. R. Maxwell.
9th Parliament, 1900....	W. H. Galliher......	Aulay Morrison......	Ralph Smith	f Col. Hon. E. G. Prior Thos. Earle .... Geo. E. Riley	g G. R. Maxwell. R. G. McPherson.

a Appointed Senator. b Died. c Appointed Indian Commissioner. d Resigned. e Appointed Postmaster. f Resigned in 1901 and was succeeded by George E. Riley. g Died in 1902 and was succeeded by R. G. McPherson.

DOMINION ELECTIONS IN BRITISH COLUMBIA, 1896.

	Burrard.	New Westm'r.	Vancouver.	Victoria.	Yale and Cariboo.
*George Maxwell	1,512	....	....	....	....
G. H. Cowan	1,214	....	....	....	....
W. J. Bowser	420	....	....	....	....
*Aulay Morrison	....	1,758	....	....	....
R. McBride	....	1,460	....	....	....
*W. W. B. McInnes	....	....	1,020	....	....
A. Haslam	....	....	823	....	....
James Haggart	....	....	647	....	....
*Hon. E. G. Prior	....	....	....	1,647	....
*Thomas Earle	....	....	....	1,551	....
Wm. Templeman	....	....	....	1,452	....
Dr. Milne	....	....	....	1,355	....
*Hewitt Bostock	....	....	....	....	1,824
J. A. Mara	....	....	....	....	1,479
Number of valid votes polled	3,146	3,218	2,490	6,005	3,303

DOMINION ELECTIONS IN BRITISH COLUMBIA, 1900.

	Burrard.	New Westm'r.	Vancouver.	Victoria.	Yale and Cariboo.
*George R. Maxwell	2,716	....	....	....	....
James F. Garden	2,089	....	....	....	....
Hon. E. Dewdney	....	1,627	....	....	....
*Aulay Morrison	....	1,772	....	....	....
*Ralph Smith	....	....	1,256	....	....
Clive Phillips-Wolley	....	....	868	....	....
William Sloan	....	....	832	....	....
*Hon E. G. Prior	....	....	....	1,872	....
*Thomas Earle	....	....	....	1,775	....
R. L. Drury	....	....	....	1,657	....
George Riley	....	....	....	1,640	....
*W. A. Galliher	....	....	....	....	3,112
C. Foley	....	....	....	....	2,652
John McKane	....	....	....	....	2,583
Number of valid votes polled	4,805	3,999	2,956	6,944	8,347
Rejected votes	36	9	26	33	43
Spoiled	33	21	16	37	84

ected.

NEWSPAPERS OF THE PROVINCE.

Name of Paper.	Editor or Manager.	Kind.	Price per annum.	Place of Publication.	When estb'd
Armstrong Advertiser...	E. V. Chambers......	Weekly.....	$ 2 00	Armstrong	1901
Atlin Claim............	A. C. Hirschfield	"	5 00	Atlin	1898
B. C. Mining Exchange..	Sheldon Williams....	Monthly....	1 00	Vancouver	1898
B. C. Mining Journal...	F. C. Reynolds......	Weekly.....	2 00	Ashcroft	1895
B. C. Mining Record ...	H. Mortimer Lamb ..	Monthly....	2 00	Victoria	1895
Boundary Creek Times..	Duncan Ross........	Weekly.....	2 00	Greenwood....	1896
Chilliwack Progress	W. T. Jackman......	"	1 50	Chilliwack ...	1891
Colonist (Daily)........	A. G. Sargison	Morning....	10 00	Victoria ...	1858
"	"	Semi-weekly	1 50	"	1896
Columbian (Daily)......	J. D. Taylor	Evening	8 00	New Westm'r..	1886
"	"	Weekly.....	1 00	"	1862
Camborne Miner	....	"	2 00	Camborne	1901
Cumberland News	W. B. Anderson	"	2 00	Cumberland...	1891
Cranbrook Herald......	F. E. Simpson.......	"	2 00	Cranbrook	1899
Dispatch (fom'y Advance)	C. M. Crouse........	"	2 00	Midway	1894
Delta Times	G. R. Mauley	"	1 00	Ladner.......	1903
Evening Sun....	G. A. Evans	Semi-weekly	2 00	Grand Forks..	1901
Fernie Free Press	H. G. Watson.	Weekly.....	2 00	Fernie.......	1898
Golden Star	....	"	1 50	Golden	1902
Grand F'ks News-Gazette	L. E. Tutt..........	"	2 00	Grand Forks..	1896
Grand Forks Miner.....	G. E. McCarter	"	2 00	"	1896
Herald................	H. Aitken	Daily	5 00	Nanaimo......	1899
Independent...........	Geo. Bartley	Weekly.....	1 00	Vancouver	1899
Inland Sentinel	F. J. Deane	"	2 00	Kamloops.....	1880
International	Brown & Penrose	"	2 00	Wardner......	1897
Kootenaian............	Kootenaian Pub. Co..	"	2 00	Kaslo	1896
Kootenay Mail.........	A. E. Haggen	"	2 00	Revelstoke....	1897
Kamloops Standard.....	F. E. Young	"	2 00	Kamloops	1897
Ladysmith Recorder....	A. C. Thompson.....	"	1 00	Ladysmith ...	1903
Lardeau Eagle	E. G. Woodward	"	2 00	Ferguson	1899
Ledger	Ledger Pt'g & Pub. Co	Daily.......	3 00	Vancouver	1903
Ledge	R. T. Lowery	Weekly.....	2 00	New Denver ..	1893
Mt. Pleasant Advocate.	Mrs. R. Whitney.....	"	1 00	Vancouver	1899
News....	F. J. Deane	Daily	5 00	Nelson	1902
Nanaimo Free Press	Norris Bros	"	8 00	Nanaimo	1874
" " " ...	"	Semi-weekly	1 50	"	1874
News-Advertiser	F. C. Cotton	Daily	8 00	Vancouver	1886
"	"	Weekly	2 00	"	1886
Nelson Economist	D. M. Carley........	"	2 00	Nelson	1897
Outcrop.......	W. P. Evans........	"	2 00	Wilmer.. ...	1900
Prospector............	....	"	1 00	Lillooet	1898
Phoenix Pioneer........	W. B. Wilcox........	"	2 00	Phoenix	1899
Paystreak	E. C. Bissell	"	2 00	Sandon	1896
Prospector	A. B. Grace.........	"	1 50	Fort Steele....	1895
Revelstoke Herald	A. Johnson	Semi-weekly	2 00	Revelstoke....	1897
Rossland Miner	C. E. Race..........	Daily	6 25	Rossland	1896
Rossland Weekly Miner.	"	....	2 00	"	1895
Saturday World...... .	J. H. Fletcher.......	Weekly.....	2 00	"	1899
Sandon Standard.......	Joseph G. Potter.....	"	2 00	Sandon	1903
Similkameen Star......	A. E. Howse........	"	2 00	Princeton	1900
Slocan Drill	C. E. Smitheringale..	"	2 00	Slocan	1899
Trail Creek News......	Esling & Anderson...	"	2 00	Trail	1895
Tribune	J. Houston..........	"	2 00	Nelson	1892
Trout Lake Topic......	....	"	2 00	Trout Lake City	1899
Vernon News..........	J. A. McKelvie......	"	2 00	Vernon	1891
Victoria Daily Times....	John Nelson.........	Evening	10 00	Victoria	1884
Victoria Times	"	Semi-weekly	1 50	"	1896
Vancouver Daily Province	W. C. Nichol........	Daily.......	....	Vancouver	1898
Western Clarion........	R. P. Pettipiece.	Weekly.....	0 50	" ...	1903
World	C. H. Gibbons	Daily	8 00	"	1888
"	"	Semi-weekly	1 50	"	1888
Ymir Mirror	C. Dell Smith	Weekly.....	1 00	Ymir	1900

REGISTERED MORTGAGES.

Return of Mortgages on Realty made by the Registrars of the Land Registry Offices for the year ending 31st December, 1901.

	Victoria	Vancouver	Kamloops	Nelson	New Westminster	Total.
Mortgages on Realty remaining undischarged Jan. 1st, 1901—						
Number incorporated companies	841	2,157	522	665	1,303	5,488
Amount	$2,616,747	$6,438,770	$1,224,711	$968,479	$5,016,399	$16,265,106
Number private loans	2,321	2,025	556	389	1,870	7,161
Amount	$5,101,952	$8,374,755	$2,192,210	$746,346	$3,917,703	$20,332,966
Mortgages Registered during year ending Dec. 31st, 1901—						
Number incorporated companies	68	271	117	235	86	777
Amount	$103,218	$508,305	$440,843	$311,752	$269,776	$1,633,894
Number private loans	358	304	199	189	119	1,169
Amount	$1,027,727	$547,780	$1,289,635	$689,515	$142,658	$3,697,315
Mortgages Discharged during year ending Dec. 31st, 1901—						
Number incorporated companies	129	146	10	82	74	441
Amount	$374,996	$259,695	$24,147	$106,709	$138,576	$904,123
Number private loans	327	154	23	83	83	670
Amount	$924,699	$201,350	$19,120	$69,802	$110,180	$1,325,151

Total number loans by incorporated companies	6,706	
" " private loans	9,000	
		15,706
Total amount loaned by incorporated companies	$18,808,123	
" " " private parties	25,355,432	
		$44,163,555
Total number of loans in 1897		10,005
" amount " "		$32,261,914

FAILURE STATISTICS—Canada and B. C. Compared.

	Total Commercial			Manufacturing		Trading		Other Commerc'l.	
	No.	Assets	Liabilities	No.	Liabilities	No.	Liabilities	No.	Liabilities
1897									
British Columbia	66	$ 549,585	$ 504,487	13	$ 132,450	51	$ 369,037	2	$ 3,000
Canada	1,809	10,574,529	14,157,498	459	3,659,135	1,315	9,931,806	35	566,557
1898									
British Columbia	59	560,247	543,795	10	290,118	47	253,177	2	500 00
Canada	1,300	7,692,094	9,821,323	303	2,229,083	964	7,412,240	33	18o,000
1899									
British Columbia	65	387,610	363,200	17	73,468	47	288,732	1	1,000
Canada	1,287	7,674,673	10,658,675	318	4,594,153	950	5,953,138	19	111,384
1900									
British Columbia	115	897,080	975,368	12	267,600	103	707,768	......	....
Canada	1,355	8,202,898	11,613,208	308	3,201,665	1,010	7,252,340	37	1,159,203
1901									
British Columbia	88	1,270,945	1,267,750	6	45,500	79	1,195,210	3	27,040
Canada	1,341	7,686,823	10,811,671	289	3,595,095	1,029	6,845,329	23	371,247
1902									
British Columbia	101	1,275,600	1,582,550	10	136,300	90	1,444,250	1	2,000
Canada	1,101	7,772,418	10,934,777	209	4,247,723	874	6,221,017	18	466,037

HOSPITAL STATISTICS, (1902).

(SIX MONTHS).

	Remaining in Hospital 1st July, 1902.	Admitted.	Discharged.		Died.	Average No. admitted per month.		Average No. paying per month.	Average No. free per month.	Average days treatme't per month.	Remaining in Hospital 31st Jan., 1903.
			Cured.	Incurable		Male.	Female.				
Atlin	2	75	78	..	1	14	4	3	13	162	..
Barkerville	..	13	8	..	1	3	..	2	1	57	3
Bella Bella	4	36	28	9	3	5	3	4	4	70	2
Chemainus	5	55	54	1	2	12	3	6	8	195	4
Cranbrook	15	179	143	20	8	38	8	26	18	542	23
Cumberland	6	23	19	2	2	8	1	5	5	186	6
Fort Steele	..	12	11	2	..	2	1	2	..	42	1
Golden	1	55	37	3	3	10	2	4	8	122	7
Grand Forks	4	19	17	.	2	5	2	3	6	93	..
Greenwood	7	39	35	..	6	10	2	10	2	168	4
Kamloops	8	92	51	31	6	20	6	56	85	287	7
Nanaimo	23	195	180	..	12	42	19	17	23	747	27
Nelson	16	66	62	4	3	16	6	15	6	325	10
New Westminster	17	134	118	2	5	28	11	30	9	660	24
Phoenix	4	33	33	..	..	7	1	7	2	81	1
Port Simpson	8	27	26	1	3	7	3	3	7	281	5
Revelstoke	..	74	51	12	4	13	4	14	5	151	7
Rossland	11	74	70	.	10	19	2	18	3	279	5
Sandon	2	26	23	1	1	5	..	5	..	42	1
Vancouver	41	374	318	16	32	85	22	74	33	1398	46
Vernon	6	59	56	1	1	10	8	12	3	207	6
Victoria	35	451	349	55	37	80	35	61	55	1414	45
Ymir	6	135	134	..	..	30	..	30	1	289	6

Up until the year 1902, there was no regular system of apportioning Government aid to Hospitals. During the Session of 1902, legislation was introduced dealing comprehensively with the subject, intituled "An Act to Govern Public Aid to Hospitals." Under this Act no aid is given to any Hospital except such as has been approved by the Lieutenant-Governor in Council. For the purpose of appropriation, Hospitals are divided into seven classes, according to the number of days treatment in a year, payment being arranged on a sliding scale: the first, in which the total number of days treatment in a year is over 365, and not less than 500; and the last, in which the total number of days treatment in a year exceeds 20,000.

Hospitals are open to inspection by a Government official, and all by-laws made by directors or managers are approved by the Lieutenant-Governor in Council. The Act in question came into force on the 1st of July, 1902, and the foregoing returns only include the six months ending December 31st, 1902.

PROVINCIAL DEVELOPMENT.

	1881.	1891.	1901.
Capital invested	$2,952,835	$ 7,246,662	$22,901,892
Amount yearly wages	929,213	3,586,897	4,332,445
*Value articles produced	2,926,784	11,999,928	19,447,778

*The figures for 1901 only include establishments employing five hands or over, and, therefore, do not form an exact basis of comparison.

The increase in development of British Columbia is shown by the following:

	1881. (census.)	1891. (census.)	1901.
Number of miners	2,792	4,591	9,500
Number of fishermen	1,850	3,798	18,500
Number of farmers	2,381	5,874	7,500
Number of houses	6,992	16,775	34,000
Population	49,459	98,173	177,272

	1871.	1881.	1891.	1901.
Provincial Revenue—	$ 102,000 00	$ [illegible]97,035 06	$ 1,038,237 95	$ 1,605,920 00
Exports—	$1,912,907 00	$2,255,753 00	$ 6,199,280 00	$21,645,000 00
Imports—	$1,790,352 00	$2,489,246 00	$ 5,477,411 00	$11,137,436 00
	$3,702,459 00	$4,744,999 00	$11,676,691 00	$32,782,436 00
Revenue Post Office—	$ 14,705 00	$ 22,519 00	$ 103,875 00	$ 2[illegible]0,000 00
Revenue, Customs—	$ 353,865 00	$ 601,000 00	$ 1,344,[illegible]56 00	$ 2,364 000 00
By Province to Dominion—	$ 376,318 00	$ [illegible]95,330 00	$ 1,862,145 00	$ 3,391,180 00

	1874. Tons.	1881. Tons.	1891. Tons.	1901. Tons.
Coal Mined—	81,000	228,000	1,029,097	1,692,000

	1871.	1881.		
Gold produced	$1,799,440	$1,046,737	$ 429,811	$ 5,318,603
Total mineral produced	....	....	3,521,102	20,086,780

Mileage railways 1,627.42

	(1888.)		
Timber output	80,500,000 ft.	118,617,000 ft.	274,000,000 ft.

	1881.		
Value fisheries	$1,500,000	$3,000,000	$7,943,000
Salmon cases	177,300	314,179	1,236,156
Postal revenue	$ 22,500	107,000	250,000

ROADS AND TRAILS.

The following table gives the approximate mileage of all roads and trails in the several electoral ridings throughout the Province, built and maintained by the Province of British Columbia up to the year 1900:

District	Roads	Trails
South Victoria	117.75	....
North Victoria	46.75	12.50
Esquimalt	178.10	16.90
Cowichan	142.25	21.50
Alberni	82	65
Nanaimo City	20	....
South Nanaimo	167.50	56.50
North Nanaimo	157	....
Comox	82 25	12
Westminster	282.12	124.40
Yale—North Riding	723	144
Yale—West Riding	601	12
Yale—East Riding	664	258
Lillooet—West Riding	181.25	155
Lillooet—East Riding	302.50	5
Cariboo	721	757
West Kootenay—Revelstoke Riding	106.50	513
West Kootenay—Slocan Riding	109.37	355.25
West Kootenay—Nelson Riding	97	290.50
West Kootenay—Rossland Riding	164.40	124
East Kootenay—North Riding	178.50	565
East Kootenay—South Riding	440	385
Cassiar	51.25	542
Grand Totals	5,615.49	4,414.55

Since the above statement was compiled by the Department of Public Works no further information has been prepared in detail by districts. Approximately, however, the number of miles of new roads is about 200, and the number of miles of trail 100.

POST OFFICE.

	Gross Postal Revenue.	Amount Orders issued.	Amount Orders paid.	Savings Bank Deposits.	Withdrawn
1902	$259,831	$2,383,670	$1,445,227	$ 372,004	$ 371,908
1901	249,460	1,951,200	1,175,898	*397,081	343,581
1900	237,356	1,864,091	895,764	368,041	344,822
1899	242,235	1,033,144	754,330	390,870	304,020
1898	247,282	1,396,605	705,768	392,923	299,807
1897	204,219	1,142,974	606,240	408,822	298,326
1896	156,883	1,053,339	545,925	336,851	231,008
1892	127,328	1,089,791	487,170	278,891	439,844
1888	67,183	656,507	334,461	496,129	980,234
1884	34,244	604,301	364,064	1,516,704	1,306,739
1880	17,886	171,108	100,032	906,277	891,510
1876	15,507	10,416	11,294	919,609	881,523
1872	8,809	21,283	....	717,564	672,380

*Including interest.

LOANS, BRITISH COLUMBIA, TO 30TH JUNE, 1903.

Year.	Amount Issued.	Amount Redeemed.	Amount Payable.	Rate of Interest.	When Redeemable.
1877	$ 727,500	$264,810	$ 462,090	6 per cent.	July 1, 1907
1887	996,190	614,980	381,210	4½ per cent.	July 1, 1917
1891*.........	2,139,141	....	2,139,141	3 per cent.	July 1, 1941
1893*.........	599,945	....	599,945	3 per cent.	July 1, 1941
1895*.........	2,037,000	....	2,037,000	3 per cent.	July 1, 1941
1899*.........	1,649,000	....	1,649,000	3 per cent.	July 1, 1941
1902*.........	3,496,850	....	3,496,850	3 per cent.	July 1, 1941
1897*.........	100,000	50,000	80,000	3½ per cent.	July 1, 1907

*Issue of inscribed stock.

The following have been guaranteed in aid of railways:

1890—Interest of the Shuswap & Okanagan Railway Company's bonds, 4 per cent. per annum on $1,249,763..........................$49,980 52

1892—Interest of the Victoria & Sidney Railway Company's bonds, 2 per cent. per annum on $300,000.................................. 6,000 00

1893—Principal and interest of the Nakusp & Slocan Railway Company's bonds, interest at 4 per cent. per annum on $647,072............ 25,882 88

All of the above are terminable in 25 years.

Against the guarantee to the Shuswap & Okanagan and Nakusp & Slocan Railways, the Province receives 40 per cent. of the gross earnings, under agreement with the C. P. R. Co., which company is operating both lines.

In aid of dyking and drainage, the Dkying Acts guarantee the payment by the Government of the principal on $671,000 of debentures redeemable in 1937, with interest at 3½ per cent. per annum. As security to the Government, the lands of the six dyking districts are liable for the payment, by a special dyking rate, levied annually.

Net public debt of the Province, being balance of liabilities over assets at 30th June, 1903..$8,539,632
Net revenue, 1903 2,044,630
Net expenditure, 1903 3,393,182

IMPORTS, 1903.

Statement showing IMPORTS into the Province of British Columbia by Ports for the Fiscal Year 1903.

	Dutiable.	Free.	Total.
Grand Forks	$ 212,895	$ 232,467	$ 445,362
Kaslo	40,029	7,313	47,342
Nanaimo	231,466	98,540	330,006
Nelson	433,083	310,758	743,841
New Westminster	403,033	304,290	707,323
Rossland	232,831	73,213	306,044
Vancouver	4,019,178	1,476,498	5,495,676
Victoria	2,490,124	515,350	3,005,474
Total........................	$8,122,639	$3,018,429	$11,141,068

STATEMENT BY CLASSES, SHOWING THE VALUE OF GOODS EXPORTED FROM EACH PORT IN THE PROVINCE OF BRITISH COLUMBIA DURING THE FISCAL YEAR 1903.

	The Mine.	The Fisheries.	The Forest.	Animal Products.	Agricultu'l Products.	Manufactures.	Miscellaneous Articles.	Coin and Bullion.	Total.
	$	$	$	$	$	$	$	$	$
Grand Forks	913	....	56	2,341	....	5,157	....	....	8,467
Kaslo	32,648	....	81	3,475	....	1,250	....	....	37,454
Nanaimo	2,882,092	....	394,233	....	....	24,935	....	....	3,301,260
Nelson	1,261,638	6	2,459	5,356	21	134,086	....	2,000	1,405,566
New Westminster	543,546	1,816,905	95,288	24,886	954	59,454	3,353	38,786	2,583,165
Rossland	2,871,486	36	684	865	10	27,203	....	....	2,900,284
Vancouver	1,742,880	202,131	495,706	209,063	632,890	722,994	27,549	175	4,033,388
Victoria	105,228	699,042	13,404	162,604	5,869	257,577	81,131	10,417	1,335,312
	9,440,431	2,718,119	1,001,951	408,590	639,744	1,232,656	112,033	51,372	15,604,896

IMPORTS. BRITISH COLUMBIA. EXPORTS.

By 4-year periods. Ending—	For home consumption. Dutiable.	Free.	Total.	Duty collected.	Value.
June 30, 1872	$1,603,361	$ 166,707	$ 1,767,068	$342,400 48	$ 1,858,050
June 30, 1876	2,237,069	707,906	2,944,978	488,384 52	2,714,082
June 30, 1880	1,614,165	122,451	1,736,616	450,175 43	2,584,001
June 30, 1884	3,337,642	702,693	4,040,335	884,076 21	3,075,177
June 30, 1888	2,674,941	729,266	3,401,207	861,465 14	3,858,618
June 30, 1892	4,306,921	1,831,069	6,137,970	1,412,878 27	6,275,774
June 30, 1896	3,963,050	1,593,894	5,496,944	1,306,738 56	10,289,908
June 30, 1900	7,815,925	2,516,894	10,322,819	2,354,779 06	17,851,812
June 30, 1901	8,311,650	2,825,788	10,805,794	2,358,842 64	21,648,191
June 30, 1902	7,946,110	2,445,146	10,391,256	2,354,404 78	18,385,335

TONNAGE SEA-GOING VESSELS.

Statement showing the number and tonnage of sea-going vessels which arrived at and departed from British Columbia ports during the fiscal year 1903.

	Arrived.		Departed.	
	No.	Tons.	No.	Tons.
Chemainus	83	35,836	71	42,317
Comox	112	115,841	112	115,841
Nanaimo	120	134,009	177	149,020
Ladysmith	161	132,373	195	137,056
New Westminster	149	15,520	177	17,312
Douglas	43	1,081	40	772
Vancouver	787	565,960	811	555,396
Victoria	1,271	1,053,384	1,232	1,002,894
Port Simpson	12	4,098	12	4,098
Stickeen	10	2,777	10	2,777

VESSELS IN COASTING TRADE

Statement showing the number and tonnage of vessels engaged in the Coasting Trade which arrived at and departed from British Columbia ports during the fiscal year 1903:

	Arrived.		Departed.	
	No.	Tons.	No.	Tons.
Comox	674	148,534	678	150,103
Chemainus	127	7,874	142	8,804
Kaslo	719	192,224	718	192,059
Nanaimo	1,503	350,214	1,521	352,242
Nelson	5,125	1,699,831	5,125	1,699,831
New Westminster	1,098	172,933	1,117	172,242
Douglas	4	136	5	270
Vancouver	3,583	850,154	3,740	768,629
Victoria	1,956	633,483	1,985	681,998
Ladysmith	491	67,433	478	67,378
Port Simpson	28	746	28	746
Nakusp	1,010	397,854	1,010	397,854
Rykerts	10	2,034	10	2,034

CLEARING HOUSE RETURNS.

	Victoria.	Vancouver
1900	$32,295,337	$46,161,432
1901	30,801,369	46,738,805
1902	28,580,754	54,223,969

INLAND REVENUE COLLECTIONS.

1902-3.	Island.	Mainland.
Spirits	$119,721 30	$156,526 35
Malt	23,576 56	31,989 48
Manufactured Tobacco	29,469 57	59,391 50
Cigars	10,208 04	22,461 72
Raw Leaf Tobacco	3,714 42	81,229 79
Licenses	1,465 00	3,030 00
Methylated Spirits	139 40	313 65
Other Receipts	338 13	3,193 20
Fines and Seizures	.....	178 66
	$188,632 42	$285,314 35

	Island.	Mainland.
1903	188,632	285,314
1902	191,049	277,206
1901	192,010	290,056
1900	184,011	324,370
1899	220,095	293,010
1898	192,970	229,017
1897	155,702	172,055
1896	106,555	127,870
1892	148,782	89,184
1888	87,819	
1880	38,016	
1870	14,943	

DOMINION GOVERNMENT OFFICIALS.

J. S. Clute	New Westminster	Inspector of Customs.
A. R. Milne, C.M.G	Victoria	Collector of Customs.
J. M. Bowell	Vancouver	" "
A. Munn	New Westminster	" "
B. R. McDonald	Rossland	" "
George Johnstone	Nelson	" "
B. H. Smith	Nanaimo	" "
R. R. Gilpin	Grand Forks	" "
E. H. Fletcher	Victoria	P. O. Inspector, V. I.
W. H. Dorman	Vancouver	P. O. Inspector, Mainland.
Jos. H. McLaughlin	Vancouver	Asst. Receiver-General.
Wm. Gill	Vancouver	Inspector Inland Revenue.
Richard Jones	Victoria	Collector Inland Rev., V. I.
J. E. Miller	Vancouver	" " " Mainland.
Hugh Findley	Victoria	Inspector Weights and Measures.
E. Baynes-Reed	Victoria	Supt. Meteorological Office.
Wm. Henderson	Victoria	Supt. Public Works Office.
Geo. C. Keefer	New Westminster	Resident Engineer Public Works.
John McKenzie	New Westminster	Agent Dominion Lands.
E. A. Nash	Kamloops	" " "
James Gaudin	Victoria	Agent Marine and Fisheries Dept.
C. B. Sword	New Westminster	Inspector of Fisheries.
J. C. Whyte	New Westminster	Warden, Penitentiary.
James Leamy	New Westminster	Inspector of Timber.
A. W. Vowell	Victoria	Supt. Indian Affairs.
Lt.-Col. J. G. Holmes	Victoria	D. O. C. Militia.

TABLE OF CONTENTS.

	Page
Title Page.	
Introduction	3
Physical Characteristics	5-49
Geology of British Columbia	7-9
Rivers and Lakes	10-11
Political Divisions	11-16
A Coast Trip	16-25
Climate	25-47
Agriculture	49-128
Upper Mainland	52-71
Lower Mainland	71-80
Vancouver Island and Adjacent Islands	80-90
General Conditions	91-99
Fruit-growing in Okanagan	99-100
Poultry-raising in B.C.	101-102
Hog-raising	102
Sheep-raising	102
Cattle-raising	103
Dairying	103-106
Fruit-growing	106-108
General Farming	108-109
Dominion Census Returns	109-114
Land Returns	115-117
Prices, Current Market, Etc.	116-120
Laws Affecting Agriculture	122-128
Natural History Society of B.C.	128
Mining in British Columbia	129-212
Mining Statistics	137-139
Coal and Coke Production	139-140
Placer and Hydraulic Mining	141-142
Mining by Districts	142-186
Coal Mining	186-190
Iron Ores in B.C.	190-198
Coal and Coke Supply	199-204
Synopsis of Mining Laws	204-208
Gold Commissioners and Mining Recorders	209-211
The Fisheries	213-236
Forest Wealth	237-256
Legislation Affecting Manufacture of Pulp	248-249
Timber Statistics	250-256
Timber on Dominion Lands	268
Educational	257-269
Provincial Health Laws	268
Taxation and Aassessment	270-272
Municipal	273-289
Our Indians	290-292
Towns and Cities	293-312
Census of British Columbia	313-318
Railway Enterprise	318-324
Game of British Columbia	324-328
Labour and Wages	329-337
Political Information	337-371
Trade and Navigation Statistics	371-375

LIST OF ILLUSTRATIONS.

	Page
Frontispiece: Parliament Buildings, Victoria.	
Olympian Range from Victoria	8
Oak Bay, showing Mount Baker	8
Siwash Rock, Burrard Inlet	16
Scene in Stanley Park, Vancouver	16
Esquimalt Harbour	17
Shipping in Vancouver Harbour	17
View from Bamfield Creek (Cable Station)	24
Alberni Canal	24
An Alberni Pastoral Scene	25
Haying on Vancouver Island	25
Nicola River	32
Rapids, Kicking Horse River	40
Hon. J. D. Prentice	47
Sunset on Harrison Lake	48
Exhibition Buildings, New Westminster	56
Exhibition Buildings, Victoria	56
City Market, New Westminster	57
Flour Mill, Enderby	57
Round-up of Cattle, Nicola	64
Rounding-up Cattle, Kamloops	65
Branding of Cattle, Kamloops	65
Thoroughbred Stock, Ladner	72
Harvesting Scene, Delta	73
A Westminster District Farm-house	75
Harvesting, Vernon	80
Peeps into Vancouver Island Interior	96
Bonnington Falls, Kootenay River	97
Powell Lake Falls	97
Reflection on Okanagan Lake	104
Powell River Falls	104
Okanagan Lake	105
Str. "Aberdeen" on Okanagan Lake	105
Yale	112
Kaslo	112
Junction Woss and Kla-anch Rivers	113
Foot of Woss Lake, Vancouver Isl.	113
Van Anda Smelter	120
B.C. Copper Co.'s Smelter	121
Boundary Falls Smelter	121
Atlin	128
Freighting into Cariboo	128
Fort St. James	128
Fort McLeod	128
Atlin Gold Diggings	129
Atlin Views	129

Page
Tyee Smelter, Ladysmith 136
Crofton Smelter 136
Coke Works at Comox.......... 137
Hall Smelter, Nelson 137
Views in Atlin, 1901.......... 144
Two views of social life in Atlin... 144
Thibert Creek Mining 145
Canyon Creek, Kettle River 145
Lytton, Looking South 152
Lillooet 152
Kamloops 153
Princeton 153
Skeena River 160
Glenora 161
Telegraph Creek 161
Tulameen Valley 168
Ptarmigan 169
Marble Canyon 169
Peace River, below Canyon 176
Mount Selwyn, Peace River 177
Lake Louise, Rocky Mountains ... 184
View of Interior Vancouver Island. 184
Estero Basin, Frederick Arm 185
Stikine Glacier 200
Nootka 200
Nimkish River 201
Chief Maquinna 208
Mt. Burgess, Emerald Lake 208
Salmon Fleet on Fraser 209
Thompson River 209
Hon. R. F. Green 212
Fishing Fleet Mouth of Fraser.... 216
Indians Fishing 224
An Oolachan Catch 224
Trap Fishing 225
Scow-load of Salmon 225
Hon. A. E. McPhillips 236
Hastings Saw Mill 240
Cutting Down Big Trees.......... 248
Forest Undergrowth 249
Luxuriant Growth Devil's Club... 249
Hon. Richard McBride 250
Pioneer Steamer Beaver 256
Schools and Churches, Victoria.... 257
Hauling Logs 264
Harrison Saw Mill 265

Page
Brunette Saw Mill 265
Churches, Vancouver 272
Public Schools, Vancouver........ 272
Public School, Kettle River....... 273
Public School, Nanaimo 273
All Hallows School, Yale 273
Public School, Rossland 273
Penitentiary, New Westminster.... 280
Asylum for Insane 280
Indians Spearing Fish 281
Indians Working Gold 281
New Westminster, 1864 288
New Westminster of To-day...... 288
Bridal Veil Falls, Kamloops...... 289
Stave River Falls 289
Kicking Horse River 289
Yale Creek Falls 289
Chief John and His Son.......... 296
A Chilliwack Chief 296
Tal-Tan Indians (Full dress)..... 297
Kanaka Creek Falls 304
Boulder Creek Falls 304
Peace River 305
Fort St. John 305
Skeena River 305
An Ideal Trout Stream 312
A Prospecting Expedition 312
Lake Louise, Rocky Mountains ... 313
A Great Glacier 313
Manson, Big Game Hunter and Guide 320
A Grizzly Asleep 320
Bruin Taking a Nap 321
Elk Hunters, Vancouver Island.... 321
Victor and Vanquished 328
Mountain Goats "In Place" 329
Fish and Game 336
Days' Fishing 337
A Caribou 344
Mule Deer at Home 344
A Big Horn Trophy 345
Day's Sport, Okanagan 345
His Honour Lieutenant-Governor Sir Henri Joly de Lotbiniere, K. C. M. G. 375
First Conservative Administration. 376

INDEX.

A

Page
Abattoirs 103
A. Rhombifolia.... 242
Aberdeen, Lord 56
Abbottsford 73
Abies Grandis 241
Academies 262, 263
Acreage, Municipal 278
Active Pass 19, 218
Active Gold Mining Company..... 162
Adams Lake 11
Adams Lake Series 130, 168
Adams Lake Valley 60
Adams River 21

Page
Adams River Railway Company.. 321
Addenda, Towns 310
Administrations, Since Confederation 340, 341.
Agassiz......20, 30, 31, 32, 36, 38, 40, 41, 42, 43, 46, 77, 78, 109, 116, 125, 293.
Agent Dominion Lands 127
Ages of People 315
Agriculture 28, 29, 119, 49-126
Agricultural Acts 100
Agricultural Associations..119, 122, 277
Agricultural Credit Societies Act.. 124
Agricultural Census Returns...109, 113

Page
Agricultural Department 122
Agricultural Implements 111
Agricultural Lands......16, 23, 56, 57
60, 61, 68, 69, 70, 75, 175.
Agriculture, Laws Affecting....... 122
Agriculture, Minister of 47
Agricultural Statistics 110
Aid to Railways 324
Ainsworth Mining Division...... 130,
132, 158, 159, 181.
Alamo Mine 131
Alaska..10, 15, 17, 24, 25, 175, 224, 326
Alaska Salmon Pack.........233, 234
Alberni......16, 17, 18, 37, 39, 40, 41,
42, 43, 48, 84, 88, 89, 116, 169, 172,
192, 210, 293.
Alberni Canal...16, 17, 18, 89, 170, 172
Alberni Farmers' Institute 120
Alder......21, 52, 62, 64, 73, 74, 76, 78,
79, 80, 82, 83, 85, 88, 90, 242.
Aldergrove 73
Aldermen, Qualifications, Etc., of. 273
Alert Bay..26, 86, 87, 188, 228, 229, 310
Alexandria.............14, 65, 66, 173
Alfalfa 50, 63, 96
Alkali Lake 65, 66, 67
Alkali Lake, Dog Creek, Big Bar
and Empire Valley........... 115
Allison 293
Alma Fraction 152
Almonds 13, 94
Alnus Rubra 242
Alpine Trias 8
Alsike 61, 72, 88
"American Boy" Mine........158, 160
Analysis, Coal......165, 168, 200, 201,
203, 204.
Analysis, Iron......191, 192, 193, 197,
198. 199.
Anchovy 223
Anderson Lake 215
Animals and Cattle Acts......... 124
Animal Pests 96
Animal Products 111, 114
Anneville 183
Annual Pack of Salmon 233
Anoplopoma Fimbria 223
Anthracite Coal....8, 173, 187, 188, 190
Antimony 136
Antler Creek 141
Antoine Mine 131, 159, 160
Anvil Island 78
Apiculture 95
Apples......48, 52, 53, 54, 55, 56, 57,
58, 59, 60, 62, 64, 66, 67, 69, 70,
72, 73, 74, 75, 76, 77, 80, 81, 82, 85,
86, 88, 89, 90, 94, 100, 106, 107,
110, 112, 118.
Apricots..........54, 55, 57, 60, 64, 82
Arable Land 91, 96, 166
Arbutus 83, 88, 242
Arctic Current 25
Arctic Slope Hydraulic Mining Co. 184
Archaean Rocks 8
Areas 110, 115
Area British Columbia 109, 313
Areas, Comparative 11
Areas Cultivated Lands 115
Areas Districts 12
Page
Area Farm Lands............... 112
Area Lakes 11
Areas 110-113
Argenta 293
Argolytes 8, 9
Arlington Mine 158, 160, 162
Armstrong.....56, 57, 93, 106, 108, 294
Armstrong Creamery 104
Arrow Creek 194, 195
Arrowhead 182
Arrow Lakes......11, 12, 26, 70, 181,
200, 201.
Arsenic 136
Arsenopyrite 134, 135, 182
Asbestos 137, 190
Ashcroft......13, 14, 63, 65, 74, 115,
183, 294.
Ashnola 325
Aspen Grove 62, 183, 202
Aspen Poplar 241
Assay Office—Provincial Gov't.... 199
Assessment and Taxation.........270,
272, 275, 278.
Assessment Work 205, 206, 207
Assets, Municipal....284, 285, 286, 287
Atlin...15, 142, 175, 178, 209, 294, 326
Atlin Lake 11, 175, 176, 177
Atlin Lake Mining Company...... 177
Atlin Mining Company 177
Atlin Mountains 176
Atlinto River 175
Australian Trade 248
Australian Wool 50, 102

B

Babcock, J. P., Report of......... 217
Babine Lake 8, 11, 23
Babine River 10, 187
Back Narrows 20
Bacon 97
Bait, Fish 224, 225
Baker Mountain 165
Balsam 61, 83, 88, 89, 90
Balsam Fir 78, 231
Banff 186
Banfield 310
Banks Island 175
Banksian Pine 175
Bar Diggings 206
Barkerville......14, 28, 29, 30, 32, 36,
38, 39, 42, 43, 166, 167.
Barkley Sound......16, 17, 18, 191, 192
Barley......49, 53, 62, 63, 64, 65, 67,
72, 86, 87, 93, 108, 110, 113.
Barnston Island 73
Barrier River 60
Bartlett Pears 106
Bass 224
Basking Shark 83, 225
Beans 60, 64, 110, 113
Bears 58, 326
Bearberry 243
Bear Creek 178
Bearwood 88
Beaver 20, 178, 326
Beaver Creek 84, 88
Beaver Creek Station, C.P.R..... 179
Beaver Cove 21

Page
Beaverdell 294
Beaver Foot Creek 178
Beaver Mouth 180
Beaver Point 89
Bedlington & Nelson Railway......318, 321, 323, 324.
Beecher Bay 17, 218
Beef............61, 86, 88, 92, 96, 118
Beef Cattle 61
Bees..........64, 84, 88, 95, 111, 113
Bee-keeping 84, 95
Beets 65
Behring Straits 23
Bella Bella Indians 23
Bella Coola......23, 36, 38, 42, 43, 78, 79, 175, 228, 229, 310.
Bella Coola Farmers' Institute.... 120
Ben D'or 180
Bench Lands 54, 56
Bennison 179
Bennett 175, 294
Bentinck Arm 23, 79
Berries 24
Betula Papyrifera 242
Bickley Bay 21
Big Bar 65, 66, 67
Big Bend............10, 70, 178, 180
Big Copper 157
Binns Creek 167
Birch......21, 57, 61, 62, 63, 74, 78, 242
Birch Creek 177
Births 327
Birthplace of People 314
Bismuth 136, 158, 179
Bismuthinite 134
Bituminous Coal....8, 60, 187, 189, 200
Black Bear 58
Blackberries 48, 107
Black Cod 223
Black Jack Creek 183
Black Pine 65, 73, 239
Black Prince Mine 160
Black Sands 172
Black Spruce 73
Black-tailed Deer 326
Blackwater 14
Blairmore 200, 202, 203
Blinkinsop Bay 21
Blueback Salmon 214
Bluebird Mine 161
Blue Birds 48
Bloaters 224
Blue Canyon 177
Blue Grouse 326
Blue Jays 98
Blue Joint 72
Blue Water Country 178
Board, Cost of 357
Boat Harbour 90
Bob White Quail 90
Bog Ore 191
Bonanza Mine 146
Bonaparte 65
Bonaparte River 13
Bond Holder Mine 160
Boot and Shoe Factory Labour.... 336
Boot Jack Lake 166
Boot Jack Mine 185
Boston, The, Mine 18
Boston, The 18
Bornite 182, 183
Boulder Creek 177, 178
Boundary Bay 71
Boundary Creek 52
Boundary District......13, 52, 53, 55, 98, 128, 135, 148, 151, 156, 201, 210.
Boundary Falls 154, 148, 149, 157
Boundary Mining Co. 151
Boundary Ores 134
Bowen Island 78, 219
Bow River 5, 8
Bowman's Creamery, Sumas...... 106
Boyd Creek 181, 182
Brandon & Golden Crown Mining Company 155
Brandon Mine 163
Breeds of Cattle 104
Breeding Stock Act 124
Brenton Crossing 84
Brick 53, 138, 190, 336
Brickyards 24, 75
Bridge Creek 65, 115
Bridge River Country.....180, 325, 326
British American Copper Co., Ltd. 145
British Columbia Cattle Co. 61
British Columbia Chartered Co. 149, 154
B.C. Copper Company....149, 151, 154
British Columbia Exploration Syn. 174
B.C. Fraction 154
B.C. Fruit Growers' Association.. 120
B.C. Mills & Timber & Trading Co. 251
B.C. Mine 149, 156
B.C. Northern & McKenzie Valley Railway 322
B.C. Southern Ry........202, 323, 324
British Columbia Syndicate 152
British Born 314
British Pacific Railway 79
British Yukon Railway.......318, 323
Britannia Mine 174
Brockton Point 20
Bromus Inermis 103
Brooklyn Mine 150, 155, 156
Broughton Archipelago 21
Broughton Straits 21
Brown's River 173
Browning Harbour 90
Brunette River 327
Buckthorn 243
Buckwheat 113
Bugaboo Creek 179, 198, 199
Buffalo 68
Building Stone 138, 190
Buildings, Values 114
Bulkley Valley.....10, 91, 185, 187, 319
Bullar Creek 181
Bullion 310
Bull Pine 61, 63, 68, 88, 241
Bull River 137, 165
Bunch Grass.......26, 27, 52, 54, 63, 67, 68, 93, 103.
Bureau of Provincial Information.. 99
Burnaby 14, 75
Burnaby and South Vancouver.... 116
Burrard Farmers' Institute 120
Burrard Inlet...........7, 20, 78, 174
Bush Fire Act 125
Butter......54, 69, 73, 74, 77, 85, 104, 105, 106, 111, 114, 117, 118.
Bute Inlet 14, 15, 20, 78, 79

Page
Butts Claim 167
By-Laws, Municipal 274, 275

C

Cabbage 47, 118
Cabinets Since Confederation ..340, 341
Cache Creek 63, 168
Cactus 63
C. F. & T. Company............ 89
California Salmon Pack.......... 235
Camborne 182, 310
Cameron District 83
Camp Anthracite 187
Campbell Creek 59, 60
Campbell River 20, 85, 327
Camp Creek 180
Camp McKinney....148, 149, 157, 295
Camp Robertson 187, 188
Camp Wilson 187
Canada Western Co. 66
Canadian Geological Survey.......134, 176, 191.
Canadian Northern Railway....20, 199, 200, 201, 321.
Canadian Pacific Railway......10, 13, 14, 20, 23, 24, 46, 59, 61, 62, 65, 66, 68, 69, 74, 75, 76, 78, 79, 107, 128, 130, 152, 166, 178, 180, 183, 185, 186, 191, 199, 200, 201, 321, 322.
C. P. R. Branches 318, 322, 323
C. P. R. Lands 128
Canadian Smelting Works 129
Canadian Yukon Railway 321
Canal Flat 68
Candle Fish 223
Canmore Mines 200
Canned Vegetables 108
Cannel Coal 187, 189
Canneries, Salmon.......103, 227, 228, 229, 233, 235.
Canning Factories 107
Canning Salmon 221
Canoe Birch 242
Canoe Pass 71
Canoe River 168
Canoe River Valley 91, 319
Canterbury 310
Canyon Creek 179
Cape Beale 17
Cape Caution 21, 22
Cape Cook 19
Cape Fox 25
Capella Mine 158
Cape Scott......19, 37, 39, 42, 43, 86, 87, 310.
Cape Scott & Comox Railway..... 321
Capital of Railways 324
Capital Invested Fisheries........ 232
Capital Invested in Timber....... 245
Carbonate Landing 179
Carbonate Mountain 179
Cariboo......10, 12, 14, 15, 27, 58, 65, 67, 91, 139, 141, 158, 166, 167, 175, 186, 191, 194, 209, 322, 326.
Cariboo Consolidated, Ltd. 166, 167
Cariboo Crossing 295
Cariboo Exploration Co 167
Cariboo Gold Fields, Ltd. 167

Page
Cariboo-McKinney Mining & Milling Company 149, 157
Cariboo Mountains 5
Cariboo Waggon Road..13, 65, 66, 166
Caribou 325, 326
Caribou Creek 179
Carmanah...7, 17, 36, 38, 40, 41, 42, 43
Carnes Creek 70
Carolina Channel 18
Carrots 54, 65, 81, 118
Cascade 145, 146, 295
Cascade Mountains 20, 22
Cascade Power Company 153
Cassiar......10, 12, 15, 139, 141, 175, 209, 326.
Castle Mountain 8, 85
Cattle......58, 59, 60, 61, 64, 65, 67, 69, 73, 76, 79, 80, 83, 85, 86, 87, 88, 89, 92, 96, 97, 103, 109, 111, 114, 124, 270.
Caulfield 37, 39, 42, 43
Cauliflower 47
Cayuse 50
Cayuse Creek 180
Cedar.......19, 21, 22, 23, 24, 53, 61, 68, 71, 73, 74, 76, 79, 82, 85, 86, 87, 88, 89, 90, 95, 237, 238.
Cedar District 83, 84
Cement 190
Census Returns, Agricultural .....109, 112, 113, 114.
Census of British Columbia...313, 318
Census Returns, Indians 292
Central Farmers' Institute 123, 269
Central Nicola 61
Central Park 310
Centre Star Mine....143, 145, 146, 147
Certificate of Improvement 126
Champion Creek 160
Channel, Carolina 18
Charcoal 197, 239
Charleston 159
Chatham Point 21
Chatham Straits 24
Cheam Mountain 78
Cheese 74, 77, 117
Cheese Factory 123
Cheese and Butter Associations... 124
Chemainus 82, 83, 191, 197, 295
Chemainus River 82
Chemainus Saw Mill 252, 254
Cherries......48, 54, 55, 57, 62, 64, 67, 69, 70, 73, 76, 81, 84, 93, 107, 110, 112, 118.
Cherry Bluff 191
Cherry Creek 13, 59, 88
Cherry Creek Copper King Mines.. 169
Chickens 94, 101, 113, 114, 118
Chieftain Creek 168
Chief Justices of British Columbia. 338
Chilco Lake 11
Chilcotin.........23, 27, 37, 39, 42, 43, 48, 66, 67, 91, 115, 325, 326.
Chilcotin River 10, 67
Chilliwack......14, 36, 38, 42, 43, 71, 74, 77, 101, 102, 104, 106, 107, 116, 125, 295.
Chilliwack Agricultural Association 119
Chilliwack Farmers' Institute 120
Chimney Creek 65

Page
China Creek 170, 172
China Hat Village 23, 228, 229
Chinese Labour......54, 56, 58, 61, 62, 74, 81, 83, 86, 108, 162, 221, 333, 335, 336.
Chinese, Number of 317, 318
Chinook Salmon 48, 215, 235
Chopped Feed 117
Christina Lake ....52, 148.
Christie Passage 22
Church of England 24
Cigarmaking 95, 336
Cinnabar Mines 137, 168
Cities, Coast 116
Cities, Population of 316
Clams 225, 232
Clay 53, 57, 192
Clayoquot.......18, 37, 39, 41, 43, 48, 88, 89, 116, 169, 310.
Clayoquot Sound 18
Clearing 92, 98
Clearing House Returns 373
Clerks, Municipal 289
Climate......25, 29, 30, 31, 33, 34, 35, 36, 37, 38, 39, 40, 41, 42, 44, 45, 51, 52, 54, 55, 69, 79, 86, 87, 89, 104, 107, 176, 182, 184.
Clinton 65, 115, 295
Clo-oose 17
Clovers......54, 55, 56, 58, 59, 61, 63, 65, 72, 73, 74, 80, 83, 85, 87, 89, 90, 96, 108, 113.
Coal....8, 15, 19, 20, 21, 54, 60, 83, 133, 138, 139, 164, 165, 168, 172, 173, 183, 185, 186, 187, 188, 189, 190, 198, 199, 200, 201, 202, 203, 204, 208, 337.
Coal Creek 164, 165, 189
Coast Cities 116
Coast, The 54, 101, 104, 130, 173
Coast-Kootenay Railway 320
Coast Range....6, 9, 22, 25, 27, 46, 52, 326.
Cobalt 133
Cobble Hill 311
Cockles 225
Cod...................213, 223, 224, 232
Codlin Moth 94
Cohoe Salmon .....214, 215, 221, 233, 235, 327.
Coke......133, 136, 138, 139, 140, 164, 183, 188, 202, 204, 271.
Coldstream Ranch ......37, 39, 42, 43, 56, 108.
Cold Storage..............96, 103, 222
Collieries 173
Colony of Norwegians 23
Columbia & Kootenay Railway....145, 146, 323, 324.
Columbia & Kootenay Valley 162
Columbia Mining Company....177, 178
Columbia Lake 68
Columbia River ......5, 10, 12, 67, 69, 133, 141, 142, 143, 148, 178, 179, 180, 181.
Columbia & Western Railway.....128, 134, 148, 152, 154, 155, 157, 320, 323, 324.
Columbia River Valley....26, 28, 70, 91
Colwood 80

Page
Comaplix 295
Comiaken 82
Commonage 56, 57
Commons, House of, B.C. Representatives in 346
Comox......8, 11, 15, 16, 84, 85, 89, 116, 169, 173, 190.
Comox Agricultural Assos....119, 120
Comox Creamery 104
Comstock Mine 172
Condensed Milk 104, 106
Conditions of Labour 143
Coniferae........ 52, 95, 235, 240, 241
Conqueror Group 198
Consolidated Spruce Creek Placers, Ltd. 178
Contagious Diseases Act 125
Cook, Captain 19
Co-operative Creameries 55
Co-operative Mill 56
Co-operation 51, 123, 336
Copper......16, 18, 84, 132, 133, 136, 137, 138, 139, 144, 155, 169, 171, 172, 174, 175, 178, 179, 182, 185, 198.
Copper Camp 135
Copper Canyon 170
Copper Creek 157, 179
Copper Island 172, 192, 197
Copper King 168
Copper Mountain 182, 202
Copper Ore 134, 135, 202
Coquitlam......14, 37, 39, 42, 43, 75, 115, 125.
Cordilleran Region 9, 95
Cormorant Island 21
Corn..........48, 79, 85, 108, 110, 113
Cornell Mine 173
Cortez Island............20, 22, 86, 87
Cottonwood......56, 61, 62, 64, 70, 73, 74, 79, 80, 242.
Council of Public Instruction 258
Councils, Municipal 273
County Courts, Constitution of.... 339
Courtenay 106, 311
Cowichan.......16, 82, 83, 97, 116, 119
Cowichan Agricultural Association. 119
Cowichan Creamery...82, 104, 105, 106
Cowichan Farmers' Institute 120
Cowichan Lake....82, 83, 170, 171, 327
Cowichan River 82, 327
Cows.............58, 61, 62, 85, 111
Coyotes...........50, 54, 56, 97, 98, 102
Crab Apple..75, 83, 85, 88, 89, 225, 243
Cracroft Island 21
Craigellachie 58, 115
Cranberries 51
Cranberry District 83, 173
Cranbrook..12, 26, 37, 39, 42, 43, 68, 69
Cranbrook to Kimberley, Railway.. 321
Creameries......55, 82, 83, 85, 93, 104, 105, 106, 111, 123.
"Creek" Claims 205
Creek Diggings 206
Creighton Valley 56
Creston 295
Cretaceous Rocks 8, 9
Crofton 136, 171, 296
Chromium 198

Page
Crops.......49, 60, 63, 64, 65, 66, 68, 69, 79, 80, 82, 85, 88, 89, 94, 96, 110, 111.
Crown Grants 126 204
Crown Lands 126, 127
Crown Silver 153
Crows 98
Crow's Nest Pass........12, 133, 162, 196, 199, 202.
Crow's Nest Pass Coal Company..139, 162, 163, 164, 186, 189, 202, 321.
Crow's Nest Pass Railway......12, 69, 128, 163, 195, 200.
Crow's Nest Smelter 12
Crow's Nest Southern Railway.321, 323
Cucumber 64
Cultus Cod 224
Cumberland........37, 39, 42, 43, 173
Cumberland Mine 131
Currants...........24, 56, 82, 83, 118
Current Prices, New Westminster Market 118
Curriculum, High and Public Schools 259, 262
Curing Fish 226
Customs Revenue 337
Customs Statistics 372-373
Cypress 24, 238
Cyanide Plant 183

D

Daffodil Mine 163
Dairying......28, 50, 55, 57, 59, 60, 65, 66, 67, 68, 69, 72, 73, 75, 76, 77, 80, 81, 83, 84, 85, 87, 88, 89, 90, 93, 97, 103, 104, 108.
Dairymen's Association 97, 119, 120
Dairymen's Association Act 124
Daisy Fraction 154
Danish Colony 19, 86
Dardanelles Mine 131, 158, 159
David Claim 198
Davie, Hon. Theodore 268
Dawson 46, 47
Dawson, Dr. G. M......7, 8, 13, 187, 188, 189, 193, 194.
Dayton 157
Deadwood Camp........148, 149, 151, 153, 156, 296.
Dean Channel 228, 229
Dease Lake 15, 190
Deaths 327
Debentures, Municipal 274
Debt, Municipal 278-288
Debt, Provincial 371
Debt, Railways 324
Deciduous Trees 240, 241, 242
Deep Water Fisheries 87
Deer...........21, 58, 68, 87, 90, 326
Delta 14, 71, 72, 116
Denman Island 20, 85
Denoro Mines 154, 156, 311
Departmental Officials 345
Deriphine Group 162
Desolation Sound 20
Dewdney..........14, 75, 76, 77, 116
Dewdney Trail 143
Discovery (town) 296
Discovery Claim 207
Discovery Island 220
Discovery Pass 20, 205
Dissolution of Legislative Assembly, Dates of 344
District of B.C. 313
Divorced Population 314
Dixon Creek Valley 60
Dixon Entrance 25
Dog Creek....66, 67, 73, 83, 88, 89, 90
Dog Fish 225
Dog Salmon 214, 216, 221
Dogwood 243
Dominion Copper Co. 149, 154
Dominion Geological Survey...130, 186
Dominion Government Lands..128, 268
Dominion Government Officials 374
Donald 178
Don Julio 151
Douglas Channel 23
Douglas, David Botanist 237
Douglas District 83, 173
Douglas Fir......19, 21, 54, 57, 63, 68, 70, 71, 73, 78, 83, 85, 90, 237, 238.
Douglas Lake Cattle Co. 61
Douglas Portage 66
Downie Creek 70, 180
Drag Nets 217
Dragon Creek Co. 167
Drainage.......26, 51, 82, 83, 84, 85, 87, 90, 92, 98, 125.
Drany & Shotbolt 23
Dredging...........167, 169, 207, 208
Drift Nets 219
Dry Belt 25, 51, 52, 94
Dry Diggings 206
Dry Ore Belt 160
Ducks........22, 58, 113, 114, 118, 327
Ducks (town) 59, 115
Duffin, Mr. 17
Duncan..37, 39, 42, 43, 83, 87, 106, 296
Duncan River 181
Duncan's United Mines 161
Dunsmuir, R. & Sons 84
Dyking.....14, 51, 68, 71, 72, 75, 76, 87, 88, 89, 98, 125.

E

Eagle River 58
Earthquake 48
East Delta 71
Eastern Fish Combine 222
East Kootenay....10, 12, 26, 46, 68, 91, 132, 137, 139, 162, 163, 198, 202.
Eddystone Lighthouse 17
Eden Bank Creamery 104, 106
Educational Facilities 77, 257, 267
Eelgrass 224
Effingham, Port of 18
Eggs......50, 70, 75, 77, 80, 83, 84, 86, 88, 90, 97, 101, 111, 114, 117, 118.
Eholt..................154, 156, 296
Eight-hour Law 143
Eight-Mile Creek 332
Elk 19, 21, 68
Elko 12, 296
Elk River 164, 165, 189
Election Returns 249, 352, 362
Elections Acts, Municipal 273
Emma Mine 149, 150, 154, 185

Page
Empire Development Co. 169
Empire Valley 66, 67
Enderby......37, 39, 40, 41, 42, 43, 56, 58, 59, 93, 108, 206.
Engelmann's Spruce 239
Englishman's River 83, 84
Enterprise Mine..........131, 158, 160
Erie Mine 160, 162, 311
Erie Group 182
Esquimalt......16, 27, 80, 81, 116, 297
Esquimalt & Nanaimo Railway....16, 82, 83, 85, 318, 320, 323, 324.
Esperanza Bay 19
Estevan 18
Estelle Mine 162
Euclataw Narrows 20
Eva Mine 182
Evaporated Vegetables 108
Evening Star Mine 145
Everett Smelter 162
Everett & Spokane Mining Co.... 150
Evermann Sockeye 215
Examiners, Board of 257
Exchange 160
Executive Council, Members of.... 345
Exemption Act 127
Exemptions 271, 278
Expenditure, Education 263, 265
Expenditure, Municipal ..280, 283, 288
Experimental Farm, Dominion .....31, 46, 78.
Exports 373
Extension 83, 311
Extension Mines 83, 173

F

Fairplay Fraction 152
Fairview 183, 297
Fall Salmon 216, 220
Families, Number of, B.C.....313, 317
Fannin, John 325
Fantail Route 176
Farming...52, 60, 75, 91, 108, 112, 114
Farmers' Institutes, Etc......120, 122, 123, 269.
Farmers, Number of 337
Farm Labour 53, 333
Female Population 313
Fences Act 125
Ferguson 297
Fernie..12, 69, 133, 140, 164, 203, 311
Fern Mine 161
Field 178, 297
Field Crops 110, 111
Fifteen-Mile Creek 179, 182
Findlay Creek 162
Findlay River 184
Findlay Valley 165
Fir......53, 56, 61, 62, 63, 64, 74, 76, 79, 80, 82, 85, 86, 87, 88, 89, 96, 241.
Fire Clay 190
Fire Valley 56
Fish and Fishing......16, 55, 62, 68, 71, 76, 79, 86, 87, 89, 90, 175, 184 213, 236, 326, 327.
Fish Companies 226
Fish Creek Camp 70, 181
Fish River 181
"Fisher Maiden" Mine 159
Fishing Resorts 226
Fishermen, Statistics of.......214, 337
Fish Oil 232
Fitzhugh Sound 22
Flathead Valley Railway 322
Flax 51, 109, 110, 113
Fleming, Sandford 67
Flockmasters' Association 97, 120
Florence Mine 158
Florentia Island 18
Flores Island 18
Flounder 222, 224
Flour 53, 61, 117
Flour Mills 56, 57, 67, 108
Forage 54, 113
Foreign Shipments, Lumber 251
Forestry..93, 95, 98, 110, 112, 238, 256
Fort Constantine 47
Fort Graham 311
Fort McLeod 14, 163, 311
Fort McLaughlin 23
Fort Rupert 21, 22, 86
Fort St. George 311
Fort St. James 14, 311
Fort St. John 14
Fort Simpson 24
Fort Steele ......12, 68, 69, 115, 162, 163, 210, 297, 311.
Fort Stuart 14
Forty Thieves Claim 180
Forty-Third Mining & Milling Co. 184
Forward Inlet 19
Four Ace Group 185
Foxes 326
Fraser Canyon 25
Fraser River......6, 8, 10, 14, 20, 23, 27, 52, 63, 65, 66, 67, 71, 72, 73, 75, 76, 77, 78, 103, 141, 142, 173, 180, 183, 188, 194, 215, 217, 219, 220, 223.
Fraser River Canneries 227, 229
Fraser River Valley....14, 46, 91, 102, 108.
Fraser's Lake 311
Free Goods, Canadian Customs... 118
Free Miners 204, 205, 207
Free Schools 262
Freight Rates 63, 136, 185
French Creek......20, 30, 32, 36, 38, 40, 41, 42, 43, 84, 180.
Friday Creek 182
Frock 78, 79
Frosts........41, 46, 48, 52, 54, 57, 58
Fruit.......13, 24, 28, 52, 53, 54, 55, 56, 57, 58, 59, 60, 61, 63, 64, 69, 70, 71, 72, 75, 77, 79, 81, 82, 83, 85, 86, 89, 91, 92, 93, 94, 95, 96, 100, 106, 107, 110, 111, 112, 117.
Fruit Canning Factory 123, 336
Fruit Growers' Association of British Columbia 122, 123
Fry, Distribution of 231
Fuca, Straits of 219
Fuel..............130, 196, 199, 201
"Full House" Mine 163
Fungus Diseases 49, 107
Fur Sealing 232

G

Page
Gabriola Island 83, 84
Gadidae 224
Gadus 224
Galena......67, 68, 70, 129, 132, 134, 135, 159, 160, 163, 178, 179, 181, 311.
Galiano Channel 22
Galiano Island 22
Gambier Island 78, 89
Game......21, 55, 58, 62, 69, 73, 74, 76, 79, 81, 84, 87, 88, 89, 325, 328.
Game Fish 225
Game Laws 327
Gang Ranch 66
Gardens .... .87, 110
Gardner Inlet 23
Gardom, R. 43
Garry Point......29, 30, 37, 39, 40, 41
Gaspard Creek 66
Geese......22, 48, 58, 77, 87, 113, 114
Geleorhainus Galeus 225
Geographical Position 248
Geological Formation.......7, 130, 137, 142, 157, 159, 161, 162, 164, 169, 170, 176, 178, 187.
Georgia Glacier 7
Georgia, Straits of......16, 17, 19, 20, 22, 219.
Germansen Creek 183, 184
Gerrard 297
Giant Arbor Vitae 238
Giant Mine, the 145, 146
Gillis Bay 197
Gill Nets 217, 219
Glacier Creek 181
Glacier House 297
Glaciers 23, 25, 95
Glen Iron Mine......168, 169, 190, 193
Glenora 10
Glue 103
Goat, Mountain 326
Goat River 163, 195
Goat River Canyon 194
Gold........16, 19, 20, 74, 84, 133, 134 135, 136, 137, 138, 139, 141, 144, 148, 155, 160, 162, 166, 167, 168, 169, 170, 171, 172, 173, 175, 177, 179, 182, 184, 185, 198, 206.
Gold Commissioners ..206, 207, 208, 209
Gold Dredge 169
Gold Drop Mine 150, 155, 156
Golden......67, 68, 115, 162, 178, 179, 208, 326.
Golden Chariot Mine 145
Golden Crown Mine......149, 150, 155
Golden District 178, 210
Golden Eagle Mine 172
Gold Mountains...........5, 9, 12, 56
Goldstream Lake.......37, 39, 40, 41, 42, 43, 48.
Golden Monarch Mining & Milling Company 161
Goldstream and Britannia 174
Golden Slipper Claim 173
Goldstream 70, 80, 170
Goletas Channel 19
Good Luck Mine 163
Gooseberries........24, 82, 83, 84, 118
Page
Gordon River 17, 172, 197, 198
Government Buildings 128
Government Lands......53, 58, 61, 67, 76, 88, 89, 90.
Governors B.C. 126
Government Scale of Wages...... 336
Graham Reach 23
Graham Island 7, 187
Grains......49, 59, 61, 62, 67, 69, 75, 80, 82, 84, 85, 108, 113.
Granby Co.'s Mines 150
Granby Consolidated Mining, Smelting & Power Co. 149, 150
Granby Smelter 169
Grand Forks......52, 53, 151, 156, 208
Grand Forks & Kettle River Ry.. 321
Grand Prairie 59
Grand Trunk Pacific Railway.319, 320
Granite Creek.....53, 62, 172, 182, 311
Grapes......13, 46, 53, 54, 57, 63, 64, 73, 94, 107, 112.
Graphite 170
Grasses......53, 54, 56, 58, 59, 60, 61, 68, 72, 74, 75, 78, 80, 83, 87, 89, 90, 93, 96, 97, 98, 104.
Gray Eagle Mine 150
Gray Eagle Mining Co. 149
Grayling 175
Grazing Lands 87, 91, 166
Great Central Lake 89
Great Lake Trout 326
Great Northern Railway......130, 133, 183, 321, 323.
Great Western Mine 145
Grenville Channel 23
Green Hills River 202
Green, Hon. R. F., Portrait of.... 212
Greenwood......148, 153, 154, 155, 156, 157, 298.
Grey's Harbour Salmon Pack..... 234
Gribbel Island 23, 175
Grizzly Bear 58, 325
Ground Hog Basin 180
Grouse 48, 58, 87, 90, 326
Grouse Creek 167
Guano, Fish 224
Guichon Creamery 104, 106
Guides, Hunting 325, 326
Gulf of Georgia..13, 16, 20, 71, 84, 192
Gulls 22
Gulf Side 71
Gulf Stream 25
Gypsum 190

H

Haddington Island 21, 86
Halcyon Hot Springs 209
Halibut...........87, 89, 213, 222, 232
Hall Creek 161
Hall Mines 132, 160
Hall's Landing 70
Hampton 159, 160
Hanceville 311
Haney 76
Happy Valley 80
Hardie Cinnabar Mine 169
Hardwoods 243
Hardy Bay 169

Page
Hardhack 74
Hardwicke 86
Hardwick Island 20, 21
Hardy Bay to Rupert Arm, Railway 321
Haro Straits 81, 218, 219
Harper's Camp 290
Harriot Harbour 192
Harrison Hot Springs 78, 290
Harrison Lake 11, 66, 78
Harrison River 10, 78
Hartford Junction 155
Hartley Bay 23
Hartney 158
Haslam Creek 84
Hasting Saw Mill 251, 254
Hatcheries 201, 217
Hatzic Prairie 77, 125
Hay......48, 53, 55, 57, 58, 59, 60, 62, 63, 65, 69, 72, 73, 74, 77, 79, 81, 82, 84, 92, 96 108, 110, 113, 117, 118
Hazelton...........10, 15, 23, 183, 311
Hazlemere.....36, 38, 40, 41, 42, 43, 48
Health Laws, Provincial 268
Hector Mine 178
Hedley City.............182. 183, 209
Hematite......76. 78. 83. 85, 86, 87, 88, 89, 90, 137, 165, 194.
Hemlock......19, 21, 23, 24, 61, 71, 73, 74, 237, 240, 247.
Henry Creek 182
Hens 113, 114
Hernando Island 20. 22, 86
Herring 224, 232
Hesquoit 18
Hewitt Mine 158
Highland District 80, 81
High Schools 257, 266
Hilda Mine 154
Hill Barr 141
Hippoglossus Vulgarus 222
Hocsall 185
Hog-raising 59, 76, 86, 102
Holdings, Land 61
Homalko River 79
Homestake Creek 168, 169
Homestead Act 125. 127
Homesteads, Taxation of 271
Homesteaders, Timber 268
Honey 84, 88, 114
Hope.........13, 53, 71, 116, 183, 311
Hope Mountain..........182. 201. 326
Hornby Island..............20, 85, 86
Hops.....51, 56, 75, 79, 81, 95, 109, 113
Horned Cattle......54, 69, 73, 111, 113
Horsefly 166
Horses......50, 56, 58, 60, 61, 62. 65, 67, 68, 69. 70, 72, 74, 75, 80, 81, 86, 96. 111, 113, 114.
Horticulture 82, 94
Horticulture. Board of 123
Horticultural Society of British Columbia 122
Hospitals 277
Hospital Statistics, Table of....... 368
Household Effects, Taxation on.... 271
Houses, Number of B.C. .313, 317, 337
House of Commons, B.C. Representatives in 363
Howe Mine 174
Howe Sound.......20, 78, 79, 174, 219
Hydraulic Mining.......141. 142. 162, 165, 166, 167, 169, 172, 177, 178.
Hydraulic Leases 204, 207
Hydraulic Mining Co. 167
Hudson's Bay Co.......14. 22, 23, 24, 69, 287.
Hudson's Hope 186
Humming Birds 48
Humpback Salmon........214, 216, 221
Hunting 232, 325, 328
Huntingdon 311
Hydralagus Colliaei 225
Hypomesus Pretiosus 223

I

Icebergs 25
Idaho Mine 150
"Ida May" Mine 180
Illecillewaet 312
Immigrants to B.C. 316
Imports .... ~~307~~ 373
Improved Farms....58, 61, 62, 67, 68, 69, 70, 73, 74, 76, 80, 81, 83, 86, 89, 90, 91, 110.
Improvements, Municipal Taxation 278
Income Tax 270, 272
Incorporated Cities, Statistics re....273 280, 289.
Indian Corn.............54, 55, 60, 81
Indian Labour......54, 56, 58, 61, 62, 70, 81, 83, 333.
Indian Reserve 78
Indians......17, 18, 20, 21, 22, 23, 24, 54, 56, 58, 61, 62, 70, 81, 83, 213, 214, 215, 221. 263, 267, 290, 292, 317, 318.
Industrial Schools 24
Industries, Statistics of 329, 337
Ingenica River 184
Inland Agricultural Associat on.... 119
Inland Revenue Collections 374
Insect Pests 93, 98, 107
Inspector of Fisheries 221, 232
Insurance Companies, Taxation of. 271
International Basin 179
Introduction 2
Inverness 312
Iola Smelter 160
Iphigenia 17
Iron Mask Mine 145, 168
Iron......16, 20, 84, 135, 137, 168, 169, 173, 174, 181, 185, 190, 191, 192, 193, 194. 195, 197, 198.
Irondale 173, 191, 197
"Iron Horse" 160
Iron Range 194, 195
Irrigation........51, 52, 54, 55, 56, 57, 59, 60, 61, 62, 63, 65, 67, 68, 69, 70, 80. 91, 94, 96, 98, 108.
Island Railway 321
Islands, The....16, 21, 52, 89, 97, 107, 108, 116.
Islands Agricultural Associations..119, 120.
Island Range 6
Italian Bees 88
"Ivanhoe" Mine 158. 160
I. X. L. Mine 145, 185

J

Page
Jack Pine 61
Jackspruce 175
James Island 81
Jam-making 108
Japan Current 25
Japanese............214, 216, 221, 317
Japanese Labour.........56, 61, 62, 74, 81, 83, 86, 333, 335.
Jerseys 104
Jervis Inlet 15, 20, 174
Jewell Mine 149
Jewitt, Armourer 19
"Jim Crow" Mine 158
Johnston Straits.......20, 21, 218, 219
Joly de Lotbiniere, The Hon. Sir Henri G. 345
Jordon Meadows 80
Josie Mine 143, 144
Juan de Fuca Straits..........27, 220
Jubilee Mountais 178
Judges, List of 338
Juneau 25
Juniper 64, 242

K

Kaleanza River 186
Kamloops......10, 13, 14, 20, 29, 30, 32, 36, 38, 39, 40, 41, 42, 43, 51, 54, 59, 60, 61, 63, 96, 108, 115, 128, 168, 169, 191, 193, 210, 290.
Kamloops Agricultural Assos..119, 120
Kamloops Lake 10, 63, 226
Kammutseena River 21
Kaslo....12, 37, 39, 42, 43, 70, 71, 300
Kaslo & Slocan Railway......130, 318, 323, 324.
Keithley Creek 166, 167, 312
Kelowna......55, 56, 95, 100, 106, 300
Kelp 224
Kendrick, Capt. 18
Kennedy Lake Camp 172
Kennedy River 89
Kennerley's Sound 215
Kent 14, 75, 78
Kent Agricultural Assos......119, 120
Keremeos.........53, 54, 115, 183, 300
Kettle Creek 181
Kettle River.......52, 54, 98, 189, 201
Kettle River, North Fork..52, 200, 202
Kettle River Country.....13, 106, 115, 148, 326.
Kettle River Valley Railway...... 323
Key City Mine 170, 171
Kicking Horse Pass 199
Kicking Horse River 5, 68
Kildare Creek 183
Kildella River 192
Killarney 56, 70
Kimberley 12, 69, 163, 301, 312
Kincolith 312
Kindergarten Schools 263
Kingcombe Inlet 15
King Mining Co..........150, 154, 156
"King Solomon" Mine 157
Kispyox River 10, 185
Kispyox Valley 91, 319
Kitchener 137, 194, 195, 196, 301
Kitimaat 15, 23
Kitimaat & Northern Railway.... 321
Kitloop Indians 23
Kitloop Inlet 23
Kitsilas Canyon 15
Kitsilas Mountain 185, 186
Klem-too 23
Klondike 46, 50, 175
Klootchmen 221
Knight's Inlet 15, 191
Knob Hill..........148, 149, 150, 151
Koksilah River 82
Kootenay........12, 13, 26, 55, 57, 98, 127, 139, 140, 326, 337.
Kootenay Central Railway 321
Kootenay Lakes......8, 10, 11, 12, 26, 70, 71, 129, 158, 159, 160, 163, 181, 226.
Kootenay Landing 312
Kootenay River......10, 12, 68, 69, 70, 71, 160, 162, 163, 194, 327.
Kootenay Valleys Company.....68, 69
Kuper Island 36, 38, 42, 43, 48, 82
Kuskanook 312
Kyuquot Bay 19

L

Labour......53, 54, 56, 58, 59, 61, 62, 64, 65, 66, 67, 68, 69, 70, 72, 73, 74, 75, 76, 78, 79, 80, 81, 83, 84, 86, 89, 90, 98, 103, 108, 109, 111, 143, 163, 329, 337.
Labour, Unions 329, 337
Lac la Hache 65
Lacoore 157
Ladner........36, 38, 42, 43, 71, 104, 106, 301.
Ladysmith........83, 84, 136, 169, 172, 173, 301.
Ladysmith Smelter 172
La Forme Group 180
Laggan 312
Lake District 81, 116
Lakes 10, 11
Laketon 312
Lama Passage 23
Lambs 86, 90
Lanark Mine 160
Land Grants to Railways 324
Lands......52, 53, 54, 55, 56, 57, 58, 61, 62, 67, 68, 69, 70, 72, 73, 74, 75, 76, 77, 79, 80, 81, 83, 110, 111, 112, 126, 127.
Land Acts 125, 126, 127
Lands, C. P. R. 128
Land Clauses Consolidation Act... 125
Land Clearing 98
Lands, Pre-emption of 126, 127
Land Returns 115, 116, 121
Lands, Schedule of 112
Land Values 8, 111, 114
Langley.....14, 71, 72, 73, 74, 116, 312
Langley Agricultural Associations 119, 120
Larch 57, 241
Lard 117
Lardeau 181, 301
Larks 48
"Last Chance" Mine......158, 159, 160

Page
Lasqueti Island 88, 84
Lavina Mine 158
Laws Affecting Agriculture....122, 125
Laws, Mining 204
Lead......131, 132, 137, 138, 139, 159, 164, 179.
Leech River 141, 169, 170
Legislative Assembly, Members of..348, 350.
Legislature since Confederation.... 344
Lenora Mine 170, 171
Lenora & Mt. Sicker Railway.....318, 321, 323, 324.
Le Roi Mines......133, 143, 144, 145, 146, 154.
Lesser Dog Creek 67
Lexington Creek 181, 182
Lexington Mountain 182
Liard River.............6, 10, 14, 15
Libraries, Travelling 260
Licenses, Liquor, Statistics of..... 351
Licenses, Timber 268
Lieutenant-Governors Since Confederation 337
Lignite Coal 8, 180
Lightning Creek 141
Lillooet.....12, 13, 14, 65, 66, 91, 115, 139, 141, 180, 217, 301, 325, 327.
Lillooet River 10
Lime......6, 8, 20, 53, 130, 135, 190, 193, 198.
Liquor Licenses 276
Liquor Licenses, Statistics of...... 351
Little Sheep Creek 142
Live Stock 49, 113
Loans, Provincial 371
Lode Mining 137, 178
Lodge Pole Creek 203
Log Cabin 176
Logging 21, 72, 82, 238
London Hill Mine 159
Long Lake 57
Lorne Mine 180
Lost Creek Mine 183, 184
Louis Creek 60
Lowe Inlet 23, 228
Lower Arrow Lake 56, 70
Lower Columbia 26
Lower Kootenay River 10
Lower Mainland......52, 71, 97, 106, 107, 108, 116.
Lower Nicola 61, 62
Lower Thompson River Valley... 63
Lowhee Creek 167
Lucerne 63
Lulu Islands 116, 326
Lumbering....14, 16, 77, 194, 243, 256
Lumby 301
Lummi Island 219
Lynx 326
Lytton 10, 63, 66, 115

Mc

McCullough Creek 180
McDougal Creek 181
McDougall, Guide 181, 326
McEwen's 67
McGill University 262
McGuigan 158, 312
McGuigan Basin 160
McKee Creek 176, 177, 178
Mackenzie Mountain 182
Mackenzie Basin 47
Mackenzie River 11
Mackenzie & Mann Railway...... 321
McMurdo Creek 179
McRae Creek 181

M

Mable Lake 56
Mable Lake Valley 58
Mabon Group 160
Mackerel 220
Macoun, Prof. ... .237, 245
Magnetite.......37, 109, 171, 172, 191 192, 197, 198.
Magnetic Iron 169
Mainland, The......15, 20, 21, 22, 27, 46, 49, 50, 91, 101, 136, 173, 188, 191, 192.
Mainland, Lower 52, 71, 97
Malahat Mountain 171
Malaspina Straits 79
Malcolm Island 21
Male Population 313
Manganese 191, 193
Mangolds 81
Manson Creek 183, 184
Manson, Guide 325, 326
Manson Town 312
Manual Training Schools 263
Maple......48, 64, 78, 79, 80, 82, 83, 85, 88, 89, 90, 95, 241, 242.
Maple Bay Mine 170
"Maple Leaf" 156
Maple Ridge 14, 75, 76, 116
Maple Sugar and Syrup 112
Maquinna, King 18
Mara 57, 93
Marble 8, 20, 21, 190
Marble Bay Mine 173
Marble Canyon 66
Marble Creek Valley 87
Markets......49, 50, 52, 53, 61, 63, 67, 69, 70, 71, 73, 74, 75, 78, 81, 82, 84, 88, 89, 90, 92, 101, 107, 108, 109, 116, 196, 197, 204, 244, 247.
Market for Coal 204
Market for Iron 196, 197
Markets for Paper and Pulp...... 247
Market for Timber 244
"Marion" Mine 158
Marriages 327
Married Population 314
Marten Creek 164
Mary Island 20
Marysville 301
Massett.......37, 39, 40, 41, 42, 43, 48
Matsqui......14, 36, 38, 40, 41, 42, 43, 71, 73, 74, 116, 120, 125.
Matsqui Prairie 30, 32
Maverick Mine 163
Mayors, Qualifications, Etc., of.... 273
Meadow Land 54, 75
Meares, Capt. 17, 18
Meares Island 18
Meat Packing 103
Mechanics' Institutes 277

Page
Melons 3, 64, 107
Members of the Legislative Assembly 348
Menhinick 181, 182
Menzies Bay 20
Mercury 159
Metallic Iron 192, 193, 199
Metchosin 80, 116
Metchosin Farmers' Institute..... 120
Meteorological..25, 27, 29, 30, 31, 33, 43
Meteorological Tables.......33, 34, 35, 36, 37, 38, 39, 40, 41, 42, 44, 45.
Metlakahtla 24, 312
Methodists 17, 24
Michel..........12, 164, 165, 189, 302
Mica 168, 190
Midway......13, 29, 30, 32, 36, 38, 40, 41, 42, 43, 54, 134, 302, 320.
Midway & Vernon Railway 320
Milch Cows....59, 73, 80, 88, 111, 113
Mill Bank Sound 23
Milling 49, 54, 94
Millstream Valley 84
Mineral Act 205, 207
Mineral Claims..205, 206, 208, 270, 271
Miners, Number of 337
Mines and Mining......70, 89, 92, 129, 134, 135, 136, 137, 138, 139, 141, 143, 144, 148, 158, 162, 163, 173, 209, 210, 333.
Mining Divisions 209, 210
Mining Laws, Synopsis of 204
Mining Recorders 208, 209, 210
Minister of Mines 212
Ministries Since Confederation.340, 343
Mission........14, 75, 76, 106, 116, 302
Mission Junction 76
Mission Schools 263
Mixed Farming.....51, 60, 90, 93, 103
Molly Gibson Mine 150
Molybdenite 154, 173
Monk Creek 163
Monitor Mine...131, 158, 159, 260, 172
Montana Gold Mining Co. 161
Monte Christo Mine 145
Montezuma Mine 150, 155
Montgomery Claim 167
Montreal & Boston Copper Co.....149, 153, 154, 156.
Montreal-Boundary Creek Mining Company 153
Moodyville Saw Mill 254
Moose 18, 326
Morehead Lake 166
Morning Star Mine 160
Morrison Mines, Limited 156
Morrissey 12, 165, 203, 302
Morrissey Creek 164, 189
Morrissey, Fernie and Michel Ry.. 322
Morrissey Siding 164
Mortgages Registered, Return of... 366
Mt. Brenton 170, 171
Mountain Alder 242
"Mountain Chief" Mine 158
Mountain District 83
Mountain Goat 58, 68, 326
Mountain Larch 241
Mt. Selwyn 183
Mountain Sheep 58, 68, 325, 326
Mt. Lehman 73
Page
Mt. Murchison 5
Mount Sicker.......136, 170, 171, 302
Mountain View Mine 156
Mother Lode Mine...148, 149, 151, 152
Moyie................12, 69, 163, 302
Mud Bay 71, 72
Mule Deer 326
Municipal Aid, Railways 324
Municipal Acts 273, 277
Municipalities, List of 289
Municipal Statistics 278, 289
Museum, Provincial 128, 325
Mosquito Pass and Point 218
Mutton 50, 86, 90, 118
Mutual Credit Associations....109, 123
Myrtle Creek 160

N

Naas District 319
Naas Harbour....37, 39, 40, 41, 42, 43
Naas River...........10, 24, 175, 225
Nakusp 302
Nakusp & Slocan Railway.130, 323, 324
Namu Harbour...........23, 228, 229
Nanaimo......8, 16, 20, 31, 37, 39, 40, 41, 42, 43, 71, 74, 79, 82, 83, 84, 88, 90, 116, 169, 173, 302.
Nanaimo District 210
Nanaimo Mining Division 173
Nanaimo, North 83
Nanaimo River 84, 173
Nanaimo, South 83
Nanoose Bay 83, 84
Narrow Gauge Railway 144
Natal 204
Nationalities of People 314
Native Copper 135
Native Silver 160
Natural History Society of British Columbia 128
Nechaco Valley and River......8, 14, 91, 183, 319.
Nectarines 82, 94
Neepawa Mine 158
Nelson......12, 36, 38, 40, 41. 42, 43, 70, 71, 85, 129, 132, 136, 137, 160, 161, 191, 120, 302.
Nelson, N. C. 43
Nelson River 14
Nelson & Fort Sheppard Railway..318, 323, 324.
Nelson Smelter 161, 169
Nesparti Bay 19
Nettie L. Mine 181
Nets, Salmon 219
New Caledonia 23, 237
New Denver 12, 303
New England Fish Co. 222
New Fairview Corporation....... 183
New Metlakahtla 24, 25
Newspapers of the Province, List of 365
New Vancouver Coal Co. 84
New Westminster......10, 30, 32, 36, 38, 39, 40, 41, 42, 43. 71, 73, 74, 75, 76, 77, 90, 104, 105, 125, 127, 128, 303.
New Westminster Creamery Co. .. 100
New Westminster & Southern Railway 318, 323, 324

Page
Nickle ... 133
Nickle Plate Mine...55, 145, 182
Nicola District, Lake and River...8, 9, 10, 12, 13, 29, 30, 36, 38, 40, 41, 42, 43, 53, 54, 61, 62, 63, 115, 168, 182, 183, 189, 201, 202, 322.
Nicola, Kamloops & Similkameen Coal & Railway Co. ... 322
Nicomekl ... 72
Nicomen ... 75
Nicomen Island ... 76
Night Hawk ... 158
Nimkish Lake, River and Valley.. 21, 215.
Nimrod Syndicate ... 178
Nitinat Lake ... 17
No. 1 Mine ...144, 149
No. 7 ...149, 150
Noble Five Mine ...158, 159
Nootka ...18, 101
North Arm Burrard Inlet ... 174
North Bend ...115, 312
Northern Part Vancouver Island and Adjacent Islands ... 86
Northfield ... 312
Normal School ...257, 262
Northern Interior ... 186
Northern Spy ...100, 106
North Fork of Kettle River.52, 53, 148
North Kootenay Pass ...200, 203
North Nanaimo ...83, 85
North Nicomen...29, 30, 32, 36, 38, 40, 41, 42, 43, 48.
North Pender Island ... 90
North Saanich ...16, 81, 110
North Side of Fraser River... 75
Northport Smelter ...144, 161
North and South Thompson River Valleys ... 91
North Star Mine ...162, 165
North Surrey ... 72
North Thompson River...10, 13, 59, 60, 61, 168.
North Vancouver ...14, 312
Notre Dame Mine ... 163
Norwegians ...23, 86
Norwegian Colony ... 79
Notch Hill ...58, 59
Novelty Fraction ... 154
Noxious Weeds ... 98
Noxious Weeds Prevention Act... 125
Number of Fruit Trees in B.C.... 112
Nurseries ... 110
Nursery Stock ... 111
Nut Pine ... 65

O

Oak...8, 80, 81, 83, 85, 240
Oats...53, 55, 58, 59, 60, 61, 62, 63, 64, 65, 67, 68, 69, 72, 73, 74, 76, 77, 79, 80, 81, 82, 86, 87, 88, 89, 93, 108, 110, 113, 117, 118.
Observatory Inlet ... 15
Offal ... 221
Officials, Departmental ...345, 347
Officials, Dominion ... 374
O. Gorbuscha ...214, 216, 221
Oil, Fish ...225, 232
Okanagan Creamery Association.. 106
Okanagan...12, 13, 49, 51, 56, 57, 58, 91, 93, 95, 96, 99, 108, 109, 320
"O. K." Mines...163, 168, 169
Okanagan Falls ... 312
Okanagan Landing ... 183
Okanagan Lake...11, 55, 56, 57, 58, 201, 226, 327.
Okanagan Mission...37, 39, 42, 43, 48, 55, 115.
Okanagan River ...103, 182
Okanagan Valley..28, 93, 115, 148, 320
O. Keta ...216, 221
O. Kisutch ...214, 216, 221
Ollalla ...182, 312
Old Ironsides ...149, 151
Omineca...10, 14, 23, 141, 183, 186, 209, 326.
Omineca River ...15, 184
One Hundred and Fifty Mile House.14, 16, 66, 312.
One Mile Creek ... 182
Oneesh (little red fish) ... 215
O. Nerka ...217, 221
Onions...54, 66, 90, 117, 118
Onward Creek ... 167
Oolachan, The ...222, 223
Ootsa Lake Country ...91, 310, 326
Opening of Legislative Assembly, Dates of ... 344
Ophiodan Elongatus ... 224
Oro Denoro ... 156
Orcas Island ... 219
Oregon Coast Salmon Pack... 235
Oregon Pine ...237, 238
Organizations, Labour ... 328
Oriental Trade ... 248
Origin of Population ...314, 317
Ormonde Claim ... 185
Osbourne Bay ... 171
Oslinca River ... 10
Osoyoos ...54, 115
Osmerus Thaleichthys ... 223
Otter ... 320
Otter Creek ... 53
Otter Point ... 218
Otter Tail ... 178
O. Tschawytscha ...214, 215, 221
Ou-Ou-Kinsh Bay ... 19
Output of Mines...137, 138, 139, 141, 144, 146, 148, 158.
Ovis Dalli, Fannini, Montana, Stonei ... 326
Owls ... 98
Owikana Lake ... 11
Oyster Bay ...83, 84, 116, 173
Oyster-Criterion Group ... 182
Oyster District ... 83
Oyster Harbour ... 136

P

Pacific...19, 22, 25, 51
Pacific Coast Salmon Pack...232, 233, 234.
Pacific Division C.P.R. Employees. 334
Pacific Northern & Eastern Ry... 322
Pack of Salmon...231, 232, 233, 234
Palliser ... 178
Panther...21, 58, 97, 98, 326
Paper and Pulp Industry...245, 249

Page
Paradise Group 162
Park Commissioners 277
Parksville 84
Parliament Buildings 86
Parsnip River 183, 184
Parsnips 54
Passenger and Freight Earnings... 318
Pastoral Land 91, 98
Pasturage 68, 93
Pavillion 66, 115
Paystreak Mine 158
Payne Mine 131, 158, 160
Peace River and District.......5, 8, 9, 10, 14, 15, 183, 186, 319, 326.
Peaches......13, 46, 52, 54, 55, 57, 63, 64, 70, 73, 82, 94, 107, 110, 112, 118.
Peachland 55, 304
Peardonville 73
Pears........52, 54, 57, 58, 59, 60, 70, 72, 73, 75, 76, 81, 84, 86, 88, 90, 94, 106, 107, 110, 112, 118.
Peas ......59, 62, 76, 80, 82, 86, 89, 110, 113.
Pedder Bay 80
Pemberton Meadows 66
Pender Island 90
Pendugwig Creek Company 177
Penticton 304
Personal Property, Assessment of. 272
Personal Property Tax 270
Peter Mine 165
Petroleum 165, 190, 208
Phesants 90, 152, 326
Phillips Arm 16
Phoenix 148, 154, 150, 304
Phoenix-Viking 160
Physical Characteristics 5
Picea Engelmanni 239
Picea Sitchensis 240
Pig Lead 129
Pig Iron........173, 191, 192, 196, 198
Pigs 97
Pilot Bay..........37, 39, 42, 43, 304
Pine........53, 54, 56, 63, 70, 241, 242
Pine, Black 62, 65, 239
Pine, Bull 63
Pine City 176
Pine Creek...........142, 175, 177, 178
Pine Falls 177
Pine Grass 65, 68
Pine River 186
Pine River Pass 319
Pine, Western White 239
Pinks (Salmon Pack) 235
Pinto Mine 159
Pinus Banksiana 239
Pinus Contorta 242
Pinus Monticola 239
Pinus Murrayana 239
Pinus Ponderosa 57, 241
Pirus Rivalaris 243
Pitt Lake 173
Pitt Island 23
Pitt Meadows 75, 125
Pitt River 10, 173
Placer Mines......138, 141, 162, 165, 169, 170, 172, 177, 182, 189, 205, 206, 208.
Plant Diseases 93, 97
Plateau, Interior 52

Page
Platinum 137, 175, 182, 190
Pleuronectes Vetulus 224
Pleuronectidae 222
Plover 327
Plumbago 190
Plumper's Pass 218
Plums......52, 54, 55, 56, 57, 58, 59, 60, 62, 67, 70, 72, 73, 76, 81, 84, 86, 88, 90, 93, 107, 110, 112, 118.
Point Atkinson 219
Point Breakers 18
Point Claim 167
Point Gray 20, 219
Point Holmes 20
Point Roberts 20, 219
Police 276
Police Commissioners 276
Police Magistrates 276
Political Divisions 111
Polly Lake 166
Pool Creek 181
Poorman Mine 161
Poplar...8, 57, 61, 62, 63, 90, 175, 242
Population......71, 86, 88, 90, 91, 175, 313, 318, 337.
Population, Municipal 279
Populus Tremuloides 241
Populus Trichocarpa 242
Porcupine Mine 159
Porcupine Group 162
Port Bobs....37, 39, 40, 41, 42, 43, 48
Port Colville 69
Port Cox 18
Port Douglas 66
Port Effingham 18
Port Essington......24, 37, 39, 42, 43, 48, 223.
Port Haney 75
Port Hartney 21
Port Kells 73, 312
Port McNeill 21, 86, 188
Port Moody 304
Port Neville 21
Port Renfrew 17, 88, 89
Port San Juan 17, 218, 220
Port Simpson....32, 36, 38, 40, 42, 43, 304, 319.
Port Simpson, Southeastern Kootenay 322
Pothook Mine 168
Potatoes......24, 47, 48, 53, 55, 57, 58, 59, 60, 61, 62, 64, 66, 67, 68, 69, 71, 72, 73, 74, 76, 79, 82, 84, 86, 87, 88, 90, 110, 113, 117, 118.
Poultry......28, 58, 60, 61, 64, 66, 68, 70, 73, 75, 77, 80, 81, 83, 84, 86, 88, 90, 110, 111, 114, 117.
Prairie Chicken 58
Prairie Mountain 179
Precious Stone Diggings 206
Precious Minerals 206
Pre-emptions, Taxation of 270
Pre-emption of Lands.........126, 127
Prevost Island 89
Prices Current at New Westminster Market 117, 118
Prices, Produce......53, 55, 56, 58, 59, 60, 61, 62, 64, 65, 67, 69, 72, 73, 74, 76, 79, 81, 82, 83, 89, 90, 116, 101, 116, 117.

Page

Price of Land....51, 53, 58, 83, 92, 99
Princeton........32, 37, 39, 42, 43, 48, 53, 54, 55, 61, 183, 201, 304.
Princess Royal Island 23, 175
Produce, Prices of (see Prices, Produce).
Prospecting Coal and Petroleum... 208
Petroleum 208
Protection Island 173
Prorogation of Legislative Assembly, Dates of 344
Providence Mining Company...... 149
Provincial Aid Railways 324
Provincial Assessment, Table of... 272
Provincial Dairymen's Association. 124
Provincial Library 269
Provincial Museum 128, 325
Prunes......52, 56, 57, 59, 73, 76, 84, 90, 106.
Pseudo Tsuga Douglasii 237
Ptarmagan Group 185
Public Schools 88, 257
Public Works Loan Act.......... 321
Public Works, Municipal 275
Puget Sound....191, 192, 217, 219, 221
Puget Sound Iron Company...191, 197
Puget Sound Pack, Salmon 234
Pulp Companies 247
Pulp, Legislation Concerning..247, 248
Pulp Wood 241, 245, 249
Purcell Mountains 162
Purse Nets 217, 220
Python Creek 168, 169

Q

Quadacha River 184
Quadra 18
Qualicum 83, 84
Qualifications, Municipal 274
Quamichan Lake 82
Quatsino 16, 19, 86
Quarries 53
Quarrying 136
Qualo Salmon 221
Quartz 159
Quartz Mining 167, 170
Quatsino Sound......169, 172, 188, 327
Queen Mine 162
Queen Bess Mine 158
Queen Charlotte Coal Mining Co.. 187
Queen Charlotte Islands....6, 8, 9, 15, 187, 191, 192, 213, 223, 239.
Queen Charlotte Islands Railway.. 322
Queen Charlotte Sound....21, 22, 222, 223, 225.
Queen of the Hills Mine 163
Quercus Garryana 240
Quesnel 166, 183, 305
Quesnel Forks 166, 305
Quesnel Lake 11, 167
Quesnel Mouth 10
Quesnel River 14, 15, 166, 167
Quilchena 61
Quinnat Salmon 214, 215, 219

R

Race Island 17
Race Passage 17
Race Rock 80, 218, 220
Railways, Etc. ......16, 28, 54, 61, 89, 92, 127, 130, 133, 134, 143, 161, 250, 260, 271, 318, 324.
Railways, Mileage 322, 323
Rains and Raintall......26, 30, 37, 39, 41, 44, 46, 48, 103.
Rambler Mine 156, 159
"Rambler-Cariboo," Mine 159, 160
Ranges, Cattle 93, 103
Raspberries......24, 56, 60, 77, 82, 83, 84, 87, 107, 108, 118.
Ratepayers, Number, Municipal... 279
Ratfish 225
Rawhide Mine 150, 155, 156
Real Property, Assessment of..270, 272
Receipts, Municipal......280, 281, 288
Reclamation Farm 36, 38
Reco Mine 131, 158, 160
Red Cedar 78, 83, 87, 238
Red Clover 48, 79, 88
Red Cod 224
Red Fish, The Little............ 215
Red Fox 159
Red Mountain 143
Red Mountain Railway.......144, 318, 321, 323, 324.
Redistribution Act 13, 94
Redonda 86
Red Pine 54
Reeves, Municipal 274
Refinery at Trail 129
Refining Ores 144
Regulations, Fishery..217, 219, 220 221
Religions of the People........202, 315
Renfrew District 198
Renfrew, Port 17
Revelstoke.....12, 70, 37, 39, 180, 191, 210, 305.
Revenue, Provincial 337
Revenue Tax 271
Revision, Court of 275
Rhubarb 48, 118
Richmond 14, 75, 119, 120
Richard III. Mine 170, 171
Rivers and Lakes 10
Rivers Canal 22
Rivers Inlet......22, 29, 30, 32, 38, 40, 41, 42, 43, 191, 192, 312.
Roads 88
Roads and Trails, Mileage of...... 370
Robbie Burns Basin 179
Robins 48, 98
Robson 134, 305
Roche Harbour 218
Rock Creek 53, 54, 158, 305
Rocky Mountains....5, 8, 9, 10, 12, 25, 26, 46, 53, 54, 67, 69, 162, 166, 178, 184, 200, 326.
Rocky Point 80
Roots......53, 55, 58, 59, 61, 65, 69, 72, 73, 74, 75, 78, 79, 81, 83, 84, 86, 87, 93, 110, 113, 117.
Rosario Strait 218, 219, 220
Roseberry Group 180
Rossland........12, 70, 129, 132, 133, 142, 144, 154, 210, 305.
Rossland Great Western Mine.145, 146
Rossland Mines 132, 162
Rowan Mine 163

Page
Royal Oak........37, 39, 40, 41, 42, 43
Ruby Creek 78, 181, 182
Ruby Mine 157
Rural Municipalities, Statistics.286, 287
Ruth Mine 131, 159, 160
Rye..............54, 55, 56, 110, 113

S

Saanich............7, 16, 81, 82, 169
Sable Creek 181
Sage Brush 63
Sahtlam 82
Salaries................258, 333, 334
Salmo Gairdneri 226
Salmo Kamloops 226
Salmo Salar 214
Salmon.....115, 231, 223, 225, 226, 232
Salmon Arm.......56, 58, 59, 119, 306
Salmon Canneries......16, 21, 22, 23, 24, 71, 76, 80, 87, 227, 228, 229, 235, 335.
Salmonidae 213, 223
Salmon Pack...221, 229, 230, 231, 232
Salmon River and Valley....21, 57, 59, 183.
Saltery 22
Salted Salmon 222
Salt Spring Island 16, 89, 116
Sandon.....12, 130, 132, 158, 160, 306
Sanfoin 61, 63, 65
Sasquash 188
San Josef Valley 19
San Juan........17, 169, 172, 198, 199
San Juan de Fuca Strait 218
San Juan Island 19, 218
San Juan Valley 17
Sardines 223
Sardis 102, 104, 106
Sarita River 192, 197
Saturna Island...37, 39, 42, 43, 89, 218
Savona 59, 62, 63, 169
Sawmills......21, 22, 23, 24, 56, 78, 82, 243, 245.
Schools........71, 78, 88, 257, 267, 277
School Boards 258
School Property 265
Schools, Indian 267
Scotia Bay 176
Scott Creek 181, 182
Sealing 223, 232, 235
Seaton Lake 13, 215, 217
Sechart Group 172, 192, 197
Second Relief Mine 162
Selkirks..5, 6, 8, 12, 25, 26, 67, 162, 178
Selwyn, Dr. 162, 186
Semiahmoo Bay 72
Sequoia 8
Serpentine River 8, 72
Settlers 51, 52
Settlers' Effects 119
Seventy Mile House 65
Seymour Creek 173
Seymour Narrows 7, 15, 19, 20, 27
Shad 225
Shark, Tope 225
Shawnigan Lake.....82, 171, 306, 327
Sherringham Point 218
Shingles and Shingle Mills.....78, 244, 250, 252, 254, 335.

Page
Sheep Creek 200
Sheep and Sheep-raising....49, 50, 54, 56, 58, 59, 61, 64, 67, 68, 69, 70, 73, 74, 75, 77, 80, 83, 89, 90, 97, 102, 111, 113, 114, 270.
Shipping 372-3
Shooting 325, 328
Shuswap 58, 59, 115
Shuswap Lake......10, 11, 27, 56, 57, 58, 59, 226, 327.
Shuswap & Okanagan Railway.....13, 55, 58, 323, 324.
Sicamous.......13, 56, 58, 59, 183, 306
Sidley 53
Sidney 81, 89, 306
Sidney Inlet 18
Sidney Island 218
Silver........16, 84, 131, 132, 133, 134, 135, 136, 137, 138, 139, 144, 155, 160, 163, 164, 168, 169.
Silver Creek 181, 182, 184
"Silver Cup" Mine 181
"Silver Glance" Mine 158, 160
Silver King Mine 160
Silver Lead Ores........129, 132, 144, 158, 159, 162, 178.
Silver Salmon 214, 216
Silverton 306
Similkameen.....13, 53, 54, 62, 91, 94, 106, 182, 103, 191, 199, 201, 202, 320, 322, 325.
Similkameen River 41, 182, 190
Single Population 314
Sitka Spruce 240, 247
Sixteen-Mile Creek 182
Skeena...............15, 24, 185, 209
Skeena River......6, 8, 10, 15, 23, 24, 175, 183, 185, 186, 187, 229.
Skidegate Inlet...........8, 187, 188
Skil 223
Skirt Mountain 170
Slate............16, 20, 130, 159, 170
Slate Creek 183, 184
Slocan......12, 129, 130, 131, 158, 160, 163, 210, 307.
"Slocan Boy" Mine 158
Slocan Junction 307
Slocan Lake 11, 130, 160
Slocan River 160
Slocan Star Mine 131, 158
Slough Creek, Ltd. 167
Small Fruits.......54, 57, 58, 59, 60, 62, 64, 65, 66, 67, 68, 69, 73, 75, 76, 81, 83, 87, 89, 90, 93, 106, 107, 110, 112.
Small Holdings 84, 96, 109
Smelters and Smelting....55, 132, 133, 134, 136, 144, 147, 154, 171, 191, 199, 201.
Smelts 223
Smith Creek 180
Smith's Camp 157
Smith's Inlet 22, 228, 229
Snipe 326
Snow and Snowfall.....38, 40, 41, 42, 48, 52, 54, 58, 78, 184.
Snowshoe Mine......149, 150, 152, 159
Snowshoe Creek 166
Snowshoe Mountain 167
Snuggery Cove 17

Page
Societe Miniere de la Columbia Brittanique 177, 178
Sockeye Salmon ....214, 215, 217, 218, 221, 229, 234, 327.
Soda Creek......10, 14, 15, 65, 60, 67, 115, 307.
Soft Maple 73, 74, 89
Soho 159
Soil......51, 52, 53, 54, 55, 57, 59, 60, 61, 62, 64, 65, 66, 67, 69, 70, 71, 73, 74, 76, 81, 82, 84, 85, 86, 87, 88, 89, 90, 93, 94, 95, 107, 108.
Solander Island 19
Soles 224
Somas River 18
Somenos 82
Sooke.....7, 80, 85, 116, 188, 191, 192, 193, 327.
Sooke Mountains 170
Sooke River 169, 170
Southgate 79
Southfield 173
South Nanaimo 83
South Saanich 81, 116
South Thompson River 10, 13
South Vancouver 14, 75
Spallumcheen........56, 59, 108, 115, 120, 178.
Spallumcheen Landing 179
Spallumcheen River 56, 57, 59
Spawning, Salmon 215, 217
Speakers of Legislative Assembly.. 338
"Spectator" Group 159, 160
Spence's Bridge......13, 27, 54, 61, 62, 63, 64, 183, 201, 307.
Spike Dog Fish 225
Spitzee Mine 145, 146
Spokane Northern Railway....143. 157
Sport......19, 64, 67, 68, 69, 77, 81, 84
Spring Salmon......214, 215, 219, 221, 229, 234, 237.
Sproat Lake 18, 88
Spruce......19, 21, 22, 23, 24, 61, 62, 65, 70, 71, 78, 79, 85, 87, 88, 90, 237, 239, 240, 247.
Spruce Creek 177
Spruce Tree Creek 179
Squalus Acanthias 225
Stamp Harbour 18
Standard Basin 180
Standard Cannery 23
Standard Mine 149, 150, 162
Stark's Crossing 83
Stations, Meteorological 43
Steamboat Communication....28, 84, 87
Steam Fuel........188, 199, 200, 201, 202, 204.
Steel 137, 198
Steelheads 226, 327
Stemwinder Mine....150, 155, 163, 183
Sterling Creek 182
Steveston 307
Stikine River 6, 10, 15, 175
Stipendiary Magistrates 276
Stock-raising........50, 54, 60 ,62, 96, 108, 111, 114.
Strait of Georgia....7, 17, 19, 20, 22, 46, 173.
Strawberries.....24, 52, 54, 56, 60, 77, 81, 82, 83, 84, 86, 90, 107, 108, 118.
Page
Strikes, Labour 331
St. Eugene Mine 162, 163
Straits of Fuca 7, 19
Strength of B. C. Timber, Table of 253
Stuart Lake...11, 37, 39, 40, 41, 42, 43
Stuart River 183
Stump Lake 61
Stupart, R. F., Article on Climate.45, 47
Sturgeon 223, 225
Subsidies, Railways 320, 324
Sugar Lake 56
"Sullivan" Mine 162, 163
Sulphur....135, 159, 191, 193, 197, 198
Sumas 71, 74, 116
Sumas Dyking Works 125
Sumas Lake 74
Summer Frosts 26, 54
Summit Camp 154, 156
Summit City 307
Sunflower Mine 151
Sunset Mine 140, 153, 158, 159, 182
Supreme Court, Constitution of.... 338
Surprise Lake 177
Surrey....14, 71, 72, 73, 116, 119, 120, 125.
Swamps 85
Swine.......58, 60, 62, 66, 67, 68, 70, 72, 73, 75, 83, 86, 88, 90 111, 113, 114.

T

Tacla Lake 11
Tagish Indians 175
Tagish Lake 11, 175
Tailoring, Merchant, Labor 335
Taku Arm 176, 177
Taku City 176
Taku Inlet 175
Taku Mountain 186
Tamarack..........53, 68, 71, 160
Tappen Siding 58, 59 115
Taxes, Arrears of 275
Taxation and Assessment, Chapter on 270-272
Taxation of Mines 208
Taxation, Municipal..274, 275, 278, 279
Taxus Brevifolia 242
Taylor Arm and Road.... 89
Teachers' Institutes 258
Teachers, Public School.......258, 267
Telegraph Creek 10, 307
Telegraph Passage 23
Telephonic Communication 61
Telkwa River 185
Temperature, Tables, Etc........26, 29 31, 33, 34, 35, 37, 39, 41, 46, 47, 176
Templar Channel 18
Ten Broeck Mine 151
Ten-Mile Creek 183
Teslin Lake 11
Teslin Mining Division.... 175
Tete Jeune Cache 190
Texada Island ....20, 22, 83, 84, 136, 137, 173, 191, 193, 197.
Thaleichthy Pacificus 223
Thetis Island 82
Thistle Co. 167
Thompson River.....10, 59, 63, 64, 163, 141, 142, 168, 169, 189, 190, 217, 226

Page
Thompson's Landing 70
Thompson River Valley.....59, 94, 106, 107, 108.
Thompson, Sailmaker 19
Thoroughbred Stock 97
Three Forks..........12, 130, 158, 307
Thurlow 86
Thuya Excelsa 238
Thuya Gigantea 238
Tiles 53, 190
Timber......16, 20, 21, 23, 24, 52, 53, 54, 55, 56, 57, 59, 61, 62, 63, 64, 65, 66, 68, 69, 71, 72, 73, 74, 76, 78, 79, 80, 81, 82, 83, 85, 86, 87, 88, 89, 90, 175, 182, 237, 256, 268.
Timothy......53, 54, 56, 58, 59, 61, 65, 69, 72, 73, 79, 80, 84, 88.
Tip Top Mine 150
Titanium 197, 198
Title page ....
Toad Mountain 160
Tobacco........46, 51, 55, 95, 110, 113
Tobacco Plains......29, 30, 32, 36, 38, 40, 41, 42, 43, 48, 68, 69.
Toba Inlet 15, 20
Tocheica River 184
Tofino Inlet 197
Tom Creek 183
Tomatoes.13, 48, 54, 63, 64, 94, 107, 118
Tom Creek 184
Tongas Islands 25
"Tonquin," The 18
Tookwa Claim 169
Tope Shark 225
Torquart Harbour 18
Towns and Cities in B.C...293-312, 316
Toy's Bar 184
Trades and Labour Organizations.. 329, 330, 331.
Trade Dollar Mine 158
Trade and Navigation Returns.....
Trades, Wages in..............329-337
Traffic, Railways 218
Trail....12, 133, 142, 143, 144, 156, 307
Trail Creek District 142
Trails in B.C., Mileage of........ 370
Trail Smelter 129, 146, 161, 169
Tranquille 59, 169
Transportation 58, 201
Traps, Fish 219, 220
Travelling Libraries 269
Trees, Fruit 112
Trennant 71
Triangle Fraction 150
Triune Mine 181
Trolling 327
Trout.......175, 215, 225, 226, 232, 327
Trout Creek 55, 182
Trout Lake...11, 55, 70, 137, 181, 182, 308.
Truckee Mine 154
Trustees, Schools 257
Tsimnaws River 186
Tsimpsean Peninsula 24
Tuberculosis 125
Tulameen 54, 190
Tunnel Mine 173
Turkeys 77, 113, 114
Turnips 81, 118
Turtle Mountain 204
Page
Twenty-Mile Creek 182, 202
Tyee Copper Co. 136, 170, 171, 215

U

Ucluelet 18, 88
Ungava 11
Union 173
Union Bay 173
Union Coal Mines 85
Union Colliery Co. of B.C., Ltd.... 173
Union Iron Works 191, 197
Union Jack Mine 162
Unimproved Land 73, 110
United States 51, 53, 102
U.S. Boundary 74
Universities, Affiliation with 262
Upper Arrow Lake 181
Upper Columbia Valley......26, 67, 68
Upper Country 50, 56, 115, 116
Upper Fraser 226
Upper Fraser, Valley of the....... 66
Upper Kootenay River 162
Upper Sumas 74, 104
Upper Mainland 52
Upper Nicola 51
Urban Municipalities 284, 285
Urban Municipalities, Expenditure 280, 283
Urban Municipalities, Liabilities of 284, 285
Urban Municipalities, Receipts of 280, 281
Urban Population 317
Urquhart, A. 106

V

V. & M. Mines 160
Valdez Island......20, 22, 86, 116, 219
Van Anda Mines 173, 197
Vancouver......14, 19, 20, 29, 32, 37, 39, 40, 41, 42, 43, 46, 71, 73, 74, 75, 76, 77, 78, 79, 87, 90, 101, 173, 199, 308.
Vancouver, Captain..........18, 22, 23
Vancouver Island......6, 7, 8, 9, 12, 15, 16, 17, 19, 20, 21, 22, 27, 46, 50, 51, 55, 80, 82, 83, 87, 97, 101, 102, 106, 107, 116, 129, 136, 137, 141, 169, 170, 173, 188, 190, 191, 197, 198, 213, 215, 218, 220, 243, 322, 327, 376.
Vancouver & Lulu Island R.R..... 321
Vancouver & New Westminster R.R. 323
Vancouver Island Collieries 186
Vancouver Northern & Yukon R.R. 321
Van Horne, Sir W. 106
Vargas Island 18
Vashti Mine 154
Vegetables.......53, 57, 59, 63, 65, 72, 74, 79, 81, 86, 87, 91, 93, 94, 96, 108, 110, 111, 184.
Vegetation 25, 26, 27
Velvet Mine 145, 146
Vermillion Creek 189
Vernon..13, 55, 56, 57, 70, 108, 210, 309

Page

Victoria.......8, 16, 17, 19, 27, 29, 30, 31, 32, 36, 39, 40, 41, 42, 43, 71, 74, 79, 81, 82, 83, 88, 89, 101, 106, 116, 128, 150, 151, 199, 309.
Victoria & Sydney Railway....16, 318, 323, 324.
Victoria & Seymour Narrows Railway Co. 321
Victoria Creamery 104, 106
Victoria District 80, 81, 210
Victoria Lumber & Manufacturing Company 252
Victoria Mining Division..169, 172, 192
V. V. & E. Railway.......320, 321, 323
Village Island 18
Vine Maple 73, 89, 242
Vineyards 110
Vital Creek 183, 184
Vital Statistics 327

W

Wages 58, 300-337
Waggon Roads 130
Wakefield Mine 158
Walker Group 192
Wapiti 326
War Eagle Mine 143, 144, 145
Ward Horsefly 167
Wards, Municipal 274
Washington Mine 131
Washington, West Coast Salmon Pack 235
Water..............55, 56, 61, 95, 103
Water Clauses Consolidation Act 118, 125
Water for Agricultural Purposes... 118
Watermelons 13, 94
Water Power 87, 182 246
Water Rates 96
Waverley Hydraulic 167
Webster's Corners 75
Wellington.........20, 83, 84, 173, 309
Wellington Collieries Company 173
Wenatchee 183
West Coast............46, 88, 137, 229
Western Condensed Milk, Canning, Coffee & Creamery Co....105, 106
Western Fuel Company 173
Western Hemlock 240
Western Larch 241
Western Union Telegraph Co...23, 185
Western White Fir 241
Western White Oak 240
Western White Pine 239
Western Yellow Pine 241
West Fork Country 320
Westham Island 71
West Kootenay ......12, 30, 46, 69, 70, 115, 130, 139, 202.
Westminster District........12, 13, 14, 51, 91, 243.
West Redonda Island 192
West Vancouver Commercial Co... 188
Whale, The 22
Wheat.....53, 57, 58, 59, 60, 61, 62, 63, 64, 65, 66, 67, 68, 69, 72, 73, 74, 79, 80, 81, 82, 94, 106, 108, 110, 113, 118.

Page

Wharnock 75, 76
Whelks 225
White Bear 146
White Clover 48
White Fir 73
White Fish 175
White Grouse, Mountain 195
White Labour 61, 62, 333
White Lake 53
White Leghorns 101
White Pass & Yukon Railway..... 176
White Pine 71, 83, 88, 89
Whites, Number of 317, 318
White Valley 56, 70
Whitewater.........158, 159, 160, 310
Whitewater Mine 131
Wiccaninish 18
Widowed Population 314
Wigam River 202
Wilcox Mine 161
Wild Fowl 327
Wild Horse Creek 141, 162
Wild Horses 54, 98
Wild Land Tax 270, 272, 278
Wild Meadow Land 96
Williams Creek 141, 167
Williams Lake 65, 115
Willow......61, 62, 64, 65, 73, 74, 79, 83, 90, 95.
Willow Creek 176, 177
Willow Creek Hydraulic Company. 177
Windermere.......67, 68, 115, 162, 310
Winnipeg 150
Winnipeg Mine 149, 155
Winter Harbour 19
Winthrop Claim 167
Wolves 58, 97, 98, 326
Wood Block Pavement 244
Woodchuck Mine 180
Wool...50, 59, 73, 81, 88, 102, 111, 114
Woollen Mill 24, 50, 90, 97
Wolverine 326
Wormwood 63
Wreck Bay 18
Wright Creek 177
Wyandottes 101
Wyatt Island 86

Y

Yakoun River 187, 188
Yale......10, 12, 13, 14, 46, 52, 74, 75, 130, 141, 310.
Yellow Cedar 83, 89, 237, 238
Yellow Head Pass....20, 199, 200, 319
Yellow Pine 62, 63, 64
Yew 73, 83, 88, 89, 242
Ymir 160, 161
Ymir Mine 161
Yorke Mine 157
Yukon 11, 46, 47
Yukon River 15, 175

Z

Zinc 131, 159, 160
Zinc Blend 181
Zinc Smelters 159
Zymoetz River 10

www.ingramcontent.com/pod-product-compliance
Lightning Source LLC
Chambersburg PA
CBHW022116300426
44117CB00007B/729

* 9 7 8 3 3 3 7 1 8 6 3 1 9 *